The Politics of American

The Politics of American Democracy

THIRD EDITION

Democracy

Marian D. Irish   Professor,

Department of Government,   The Florida State University

James W. Prothro   Professor of Political Science

Research Professor,   Institute for Research in Social Science,

The University of North Carolina   *Prentice-Hall, Inc.*

Englewood Cliffs, N. J.

PRENTICE-HALL INTERNATIONAL, INC., *London*
PRENTICE-HALL OF AUSTRALIA, PTY., LTD., *Sydney*
PRENTICE-HALL OF CANADA, LTD., *Toronto*
PRENTICE-HALL OF INDIA PVT. LTD., *New Delhi*
PRENTICE-HALL OF JAPAN, INC., *Tokyo*

68542-C

Preface

Each time we set out to revise our treatment of the American political system, we are startled to discover how much revision is needed. We like to think that this stems not so much from inadequacies in the previous edition as from progress in political science as a discipline. New and far-reaching political events—such as the reapportionment decisions that reached their climax in 1964—require analysis, of course, but this aspect of a revision is much less challenging than the changes called for by new findings and interpretations that help us better to understand political events of the past, present, and future.

In this third edition, we have again attempted to apply the latest research findings and theoretical developments to an understanding of how American democracy works and why it works as it does. We have not been able to supply final answers to these questions. Indeed, the chief educational value for the authors in revising a text is the necessary confrontation with both the tentative and the cumulative nature of our knowledge of politics. The fourth edition of this text should be better than the third; if we have taken proper advantage of developments in the discipline, this edition should be better than the second.

Our primary purpose has been to write a reasonably short book realistically portraying the way American government works. Where we fall short of this objective, the failure can be attributed to the shortcomings of the authors or of the discipline of political science—not to any feeling that undergraduates are incapable of understanding the best that the discipline has to offer. Indeed, the original motivation to write this book came from the conviction that the most advanced propositions on American politics can be made not merely comprehensible but also challenging and exciting to undergraduates. We have therefore kept both our colleagues and our students in mind throughout the preparation of this book. In the many areas where the authors themselves have engaged in no original research, we necessarily turn to our colleagues for data, explanations, and unanswered questions. We have thus attempted to write *from* a professional viewpoint. But we have attempted to write *for* undergraduate students—to give them a sense of the excitement, the basic processes, and the unanswered questions that characterize American politics.

We have avoided the idea that theory and practice can be separated. Instead, we have taken the view that "facts" have little meaning except as a route to explanatory generalizations, and that theory is of little value unless it explains actual practice. We emphasize analysis more than mere description, and current politics more than historical background. Thus fact and theory, past and present, are inextricably intertwined. Although an effort to explain the workings of the political system abjures the encyclopedic or journalistic approach, it necessarily introduces those descriptive details the student needs in order to understand the system. Facts are essential for understanding, but we have attempted to present them only for that purpose—*i.e.*, not as isolated bits of information to be learned for their own sake but as the basis of explanation or of doubt.

We have organized this edition more explicitly around the concept (or "model") of politics as a system of activities. This emphasis is expressed in a number of changes that will, we hope, lend greater clarity to the operation of the political system, the interdependence of its parts, and the linkages between the system and the environment. In the first chapter we explain what it means to look at American politics as a system and the basic functions of the system for American society.

To underscore the fact that any system of activities responds to its environment, Part I considers the cultural, ideological, constitutional, and federal context of American national government. Part II is concerned with inputs, the demands, supports, and apathy which are injected into the system through political opinions, political parties, pressure groups, public relations, and the electoral system. Part III focuses on the activities of authoritative decision-making which represent the core of the governmental process. In Part IV, we consider outputs, the rewards and deprivations that come with every decision. In analyzing these substantive activities, we focus throughout on the functions they perform and the structures through which they are carried out.

The most radical change produced by this organization is the shift of material on civil rights and liberties from the early chapters of the book to the last part on policy outputs. We hope this change will enable students more easily to view civil rights as an output of the political system, not as a set of immutable principles existing outside politics. We retain the conviction that a series of chapters summarizing current policies on agriculture, business, labor, welfare, and so on, are unnecessary to an understanding of political processes and functions. In order to explore the rewards and deprivations which stem from the policy outputs of the system, Part IV includes chapters on civil rights and liberties, general welfare and common defense, and foreign policy and national security. The last two of these chapters are new to this edition; we feel that they strengthen the book by recognizing explicitly that the American political system is shaped in no small measure by its interactions with other systems around the world. Beginning with the American cultural context, we end with an outward look at the worldwide context of our politics.

The analysis includes coverage of the 1964 presidential election, the Civil Rights Act, the "war on poverty," the new approach to cooperative federalism, and—perhaps most important—the court decisions on legislative reapportionment and individual rights. These events indicate that we are in a period of such rapid political change that the current facts presented in this book will soon be outdated. We hope that the basic approach will be helpful to students in appraising the new circumstances they will confront as citizens. The bibliographical essay at the end of the book offers the student a guide to new materials and different approaches to the study of contemporary American politics.

We have received valuable help from many people in the preparation of this book. A principal source of encouragement has been the students who have read earlier editions, not only our own students at the Florida State University and the University of North Carolina, but also those at institutions other than our own who have gone to the trouble of writing to us. If we have succeeded in stimulating new undergraduates in this book, much of the thanks must go to two astute editors, James J. Murray III and Wilbur E. Mangas, of Prentice-Hall. Among our colleagues, particular assistance in this revision has been given by James D. Barber of Yale University, Robert E. Craig of the University of North Carolina, Malcolm E. Jewell of the University of Kentucky, Ned V. Joy of San Diego State College, William S. Livingston of the University of Texas, Lewis C. Mainzer of the University of Massachusetts, William C. Mitchell of the University of Oregon, John H. Schaar of the University of California at Berkeley, and Peter Woll of the University of California at Los Angeles. We owe a special debt to Elke Frank at The Florida State University for her counsel in preparation of the manuscript and assistance in editing the proof. Finally, we express our appreciation for the unflagging interest and assistance of Mary Prothro, who has seen us through all three editions.

As we have tried to suggest above, some of the inadequacies of this book may be attributed to the nature of political science as a growing discipline. Readers who discover factual errors or faulty interpretations, however, are invited to call them to the attention of those who are individually and jointly responsible—the authors.

MDI   JWP

Tallahassee, Florida
Chapel Hill, North Carolina
February, 1965

Contents

The International Environment of American Foreign Policy. The Domestic Environment of American Foreign Policy. The Inputs of Foreign Policy: Demands and Supports. Decision-Makers and Their Decisions in Foreign Policy.

The Context of American Politics

PART ONE

CHAPTER ONE

The Cultural

Context

On January 20, 1965, in Washington, D.C., a wildly

enthusiastic crowd of Democrats and a goodly number of polite

Republicans witnessed the inauguration of Lyndon B. Johnson

as the thirty-sixth President of the United States. Exhilaration in

victory and sobriety in defeat are equally important elements of

democratic politics. Both reflect the fact that politics involves a struggle over the highest stakes—the authority to make and carry out policies that are binding on the entire society.

In view of the magnitude of the stakes in "the game of politics," many people are surprised to learn that about a third of our adult citizens fail to participate, even as kibitzers. But 70 to 75 million Americans are involved in politics, either as participants or as spectators, and they have the satisfaction of knowing that the apathetic minority will be governed, like it or not, by policies they have no direct part in shaping.

Active support for particular candidates and policies, like active demands on the government, is not universal, even in a democratic political system. But the authoritative policies which are the output of the system apply to everybody in the society. The game of politics therefore qualifies even better than baseball as *the* American pastime. You can refrain, with equal disdain, from rooting for the New York Mets, the Los Angeles Dodgers, the Democrats, or the Republicans. You can decline to palpitate when Mickey Mantle hits a home run or Everett Dirksen delivers a metaphor. You can refuse to follow the standings of the major league clubs or of major bills in Congress. And, if you create a superb shell of indifference, you might even ignore the World Series and the presidential election. But this is where the similarity stops: you may go farther and refuse to become a part of the consequences of organized baseball, declining to drink Falstaff beer or to shave with a Gillette razor, for example, but you cannot refuse to become a part of the consequences of organized politics. Many Americans are fully aware of the impact of government only when they receive a message of "greetings" which tells them to report for military service; others are reminded only on April 15, when they submit their income tax returns. But even these people realize, if only vaguely, that the size of the armed forces and the amount of their taxes are products of politics.

Politics cannot be understood in a vacuum. And yet, if we are to give it the keen scrutiny that its importance demands, we must somehow manage to isolate the political from the other processes of society. We must go even farther, for this is a book on government, and an added level of abstraction is called for if we are to focus on governmental as distinguished from church, business, or fraternity politics. The first task of this chapter, then, is to pin down what we mean by this book's title, *The Politics of American Democracy*. In narrowing our focus to governmental politics, we are doing pretty much what the novelist does when he concentrates on one central character. He does not forget the hero's family and friends altogether. He brings them into the story, however, only when he thinks they impinge on the hero's life in some meaningful way.

Now political scientists may not resemble novelists in many respects, but they do have this one thing in common: they both concentrate deliberately on one part of a mixed-up whole. If political scientists were denied this privilege, they would simply have to go out of business. But in reading political science—or a novel, for that matter—never forget that the author is consciously *abstracting*. The novelist never forgets that his hero, like Tennyson's Ulysses, is "a part of all that he has met"; and the political scientist never forgets—or at least he *should* never forget—that politics influences and is influenced by every other phase of American life, from business ethics to child-rearing practices.

Political Activities As a Political System

"Politics," "power," and "government" are terms that all of us use in everyday conversation. We also talk, from time to time, about business, religion, sex, and sports, and everyone recognizes that the subject is being changed when a shift is made from one of these topics to another. To be sure, they are not always distinguishable—golf is usually a sport for the great majority of those Americans who over-run the suburban courses of the nation on pleasant summer week-ends, but it may become a business activity when an amateur uses it to sell insurance or an Arnold Palmer or a Jack Nicklaus pursues it for a livelihood. Without expecting to draw a firm line between politics and other activities, we can identify those activities that are peculiarly political in nature, and we can specify the circumstances under which a normally non-political act becomes political.

Politics, Power, and Government

The atmosphere surrounding a victorious candidate is heady with excitement. To some extent the excitement is the same as that infecting a college football team that has just defeated its traditional rival. Everybody likes to win, especially against a familiar foe. But the exaltation of victorious politicians goes beyond satisfaction in winning for its own sake—they have also gained *power*. Although power is a central concern of politics, it cannot be handed to the winning candidate in a neatly wrapped bundle. What he gains is a status or position in which he is expected—and legally authorized—to exercise power in various relations with others. The extent of his actual power will depend on the skill with which he manages his official position.[1]

Power is not something that can be grasped, then, in the physical sense that a monkey can grasp a coconut. Power is not a tangible *thing* like a coconut that can be thrown from a tree to the ground or from one person to another. Rather, it is a *relationship*. It can no more exist without someone to respond to the claims of the powerful than it could without someone to assert such claims.[2] A relation of power exists whenever one individual or group is subordinate to another with respect to some form of activity. A person, accordingly, enjoys power whenever he can influence the behavior of others to conform with his own intentions. Under this definition of power, it is not only possible but altogether common for Jones to have power over Smith with respect to one kind of activity and for Smith to have power over Jones with respect to a different kind of activity. One

---

[1] See Richard Neustadt, *Presidential Power* (New York: John Wiley and Sons, Inc., 1960).

[2] See H. D. Lasswell, *Power and Personality* (New York: W. W. Norton and Company, Inc., 1948), p. 10; and H. H. Gerth and C. W. Mills (tr. and ed.), *From Max Weber: Essays in Sociology* (New York: Oxford University Press, 1946), p. 180.

of the authors of this book, for example, recently challenged one of his students to a tennis match. The disparity in abilities was so great (the student having failed to mention that he had been captain of the tennis team at another university) that the "match" was transformed into a series of tutorial sessions. On the tennis court, the power relationships between student and professor were the reverse of what they were in the classroom. Each exercised power over the other—influenced his behavior in accord with the power-wielder's intentions—in one form of activity, and each responded to the other's power in another form of activity.

Although each of the individuals in a group might conceivably have equal power to make a certain set of decisions, this situation seldom occurs. Ordinarily, some have more authority than others. This is where *politics* comes in. In its broadest sense, politics may be defined as the pursuit and exercise of power. The distinctive power relations we have in mind when we speak of politics are those in which some people fix policies or rules of behavior that others are obligated to follow. And this means that politics is indistinguishable from government.[3] The late V. O. Key, one of our most distinguished political scientists, equated politics with the "workings of governments generally, their impact on the governed, their manner of operation, the means by which governors attain and retain authority." [4] This point of view is quite different from the assumption of occasional luncheon-club speakers that politics is something evil and somehow quite distinct from government. On examination, however, "politics" as used on such occasions frequently appears to refer to the acquisition or exercise of power for ends disapproved by the speaker; "governance," "statesmanship" and other sonorous terms he reserves for the acquisition or exercise of power for ends he approves. Stripping away his personal values, he is talking about the same kinds of activities in both cases. A recent study of *The Politics of the Developing Areas* [5] represents an opposite extreme from that of the luncheon-club speaker; it uses "politics" interchangeably with the broad term "political system." We shall similarly talk of "American politics" or "the American political system" as synonymous with "American government."

Let's see if we can pin down exactly what we mean when we use these key terms. In its broadest sense, *government* is the process by which rules of behavior are set up and enforced to realize group interests and specify individual rights. But for our purposes this definition is obviously too broad, since it takes in such institutions as the family, business corporation, labor union, church, and college

---

[3] Our reference to "government" here should not be taken to imply that the term has some real meaning that all right-thinking people can discover. Like all words, "government" is merely a term invented by human beings to help them communicate; we use it here to mean government as the term is generally defined. Unless we specifically stipulate a definition (as we shall, immediately below, for government), we shall attempt to use all words in their generally accepted (or lexical) meanings throughout this book.

[4] *Politics, Parties, and Pressure Groups* (New York: Thomas Y. Crowell Company, 1958), 4th ed., p. 4.

[5] Gabriel A. Almond and James S. Coleman (eds.), *The Politics of the Developing Areas* (Princeton: Princeton University Press, 1960), pp. 5–9.

fraternity, as well as the formal government. When fraternity members tell plebes how to behave, they are exercising governing power in the broad sense. But fraternity rules and regulations are certainly not what we have in mind when we speak of "the government." We are not directly concerned with the internal politics of such private groups; they will come into our analysis only insofar as they affect the broader political system of which all Americans are a part. So we shall have to narrow the definition down to the process by which rules or laws are made that apply to society as a whole.

Our definition of formal or *public* government, then, might read like this: Government consists of the structures and processes through which rules or policies are *authoritatively* determined for society as a whole.[6] These rules may be directed toward realizing such contradictory goals as continuing peace or military victory, widespread prosperity or class privilege, popular freedom or strict conformity. But whatever its substantive goals, public government differs from private governing agencies in that it can legitimately rely on physical compulsion, which means that its rules are *authoritatively* prescribed. Furthermore, only the policies of the government apply to *society as a whole*. If a man loses faith in the creed of his church, its power to excommunicate him no longer operates as a punishment; but if he loses faith in the policies of his government, its power to put him in jail remains very much in force.

If you are in the habit of thinking about government as nothing more than official agencies and the legal decisions they make, you may need to re-read the definition above. We are using the term in a more comprehensive sense, to include all the interactions that influence public policy or its enforcement. We stress "politics" and "the political system" as synonymous with "government" because it is easier to think of these substitute terms as referring to more than formal institutions and legal codes. Our analysis will include not only official agencies like Congress, but also the political aspects of informal structures like political parties, the media of communication, and social classes. We shall be greatly concerned with laws as formal policies, but we shall also be concerned with unofficial norms that govern our behavior. If the norms of an area deny Negroes access to public facilities, these denials—and the threat of coercion that supports them—are actually part of our political system. The political system includes all the activities that shape public policy and that determine how it is enforced.

The Political System

We have focused thus far on the *political* aspect of the concept "political system." What are the implications of viewing American politics as a *system?* To begin with, just what is a system? The notion of "system" is common to all of us; we talk easily about such things as the electrical system of a house or the fraternity

---

6 See David Easton, *The Political System: An Inquiry into the State of Political Science* (New York: Alfred A. Knopf, 1953), especially Chapter 5, for a discussion that supplies much of the orientation of this section. See also Harold D. Lasswell and Abraham Kaplan, *Power and Society: A Framework for Political Inquiry* (New Haven: Yale University Press, 1950).

system in a college and have at least a vague notion of what a system entails. Social scientists are sometimes equally vague, but the concept of a "political system" is sufficiently important to warrant as careful attention to the noun as to the adjective.

An eminent political theorist, Carl J. Friedrich, recently offered this definition of a system. "When several parts that are distinct and different from each other compose a whole, bearing a defined functional relation to each other which establishes a mutual dependence of these parts upon each other so that the destruction of one entails the destruction of the whole, then such a constellation shall be called a system." [7] This definition is broad enough to apply to any sort of active system—a solar system, the human body, an economic system, or, of course, a political system.[8] Like any system of activity, the American political system will have certain basic attributes simply by virtue of the fact that it *is* a system.

Let us examine the meaning of system more closely. First, a system has identifiable parts or elements—units of which it is composed. The elements of a political system are political actions, all those activities that bear on the formation and enforcement of authoritative policies. These activities tend to structure themselves in political roles and political groups. In the United States, the political structure is highly visible and differentiated. We have an elaborate system of courts, for example, to settle disputes in the application of public policy to particular individuals. In more primitive cultures, these activities may not be so highly differentiated or visible, but they exist nonetheless. Political structure appears to be a universal attribute of human societies, despite considerable variations in the nature of the structures.[9]

Second, a system constitutes an identifiable whole, which means that it has recognizable boundaries and that the different activities of the system are to some degree integrated or coordinated. The way a system works is in part determined by the environment in which it operates; that environment includes many other systems of activity that affect the political system but from which it must be distinguished if it is to be examined in full detail. We have already seen that politics can be abstracted from other activities by asking if they directly affect public policy. Thus, when a church endorses a given code of behavior, it is normally engaged in religious activity. But if the endorsement calls for legislation to prohibit the sale of contraceptives or of alcoholic beverages, it has entered directly into the political system. In addition to recognizable boundaries to the political system, the idea of an identifiable whole also implies some measure of cooperation among the different units of the system. Even though they may be performing

---

[7] *Man and His Government: An Empirical Theory of Politics* (New York: McGraw-Hill Book Company, Inc., 1963), p. 25.

[8] It would not include such usages as "a mountain system," since the definition we are using implies activity by the system rather than merely the combination of things or parts into a complex whole.

[9] See Gabriel A. Almond, "A Functional Approach to Comparative Politics," in Almond and Coleman (eds.), *The Politics of the Developing Areas*, pp. 10–11.

different kinds of activities, one element of a system cannot operate in complete disregard of the activities of other elements without disrupting or destroying the system. The American system of law (a subset of activities and doctrines within the total political system) was seriously threatened, for example, when Governor George Wallace of Alabama "stood in the doorway" of the University of Alabama to prevent the entrance of two Negro students whose admission had been ordered by a federal court. Had he not capitulated, the American political system would have been threatened with destruction or drastic modification.

Third, the constituent units of a system are interdependent, so that each part affects and is affected by all the other parts. Although some differentiation or division of labor exists in all systems, the performance of each part is to some extent a function of the performance of the other parts. Friedrich's statement that the destruction of one part of a system entails the destruction of the whole seems to go too far.[10] Systems tend to persist and to adapt to changes both in the outside environment and within the system itself. If the planet Venus were destroyed, for example, all other parts of the solar system would be affected, but the system itself would persist in a modified form. The American political system might similarly survive the loss of the United States Senate. The loss of the entire Congress, however, would probably lead to the creation of an entirely different political system. The interdependence of all elements within a system does not mean, then, that all elements play equally vital roles. The functional importance of the component parts of the American political system will accordingly be a recurrent concern in this book.

What are the other consequences of viewing American politics as a system of activity? Some of the more important are recapitulated in Figure 1-1, which diagrams the preliminary features of a political system.

To begin with, the area in white, which represents a political system, indicates that political life is separable, at least analytically, from other activities and systems. Second, in viewing politics as a system, we are forced to recognize that "the operation of no one part can be fully understood without reference to the way in which the whole itself operates." [11] The entire political system is therefore presented as linked together in a pattern of interrelated activities. Third, the operation of the whole political system (and therefore of its parts) can be understood only in terms of the environment in which it operates. The shaded area around the political system suggests that it is a part of a broader culture by which it is influenced, and which it in turn influences. Fourth, the lack of a neat

---

[10] Professor Friedrich is aware of this: despite the unqualified nature of the statement of mutual dependence in his definition, he distinguishes immediately thereafter between constitutive elements, which are necessary to survival of the system, and supplementary elements, which may play important roles but which could be lost without the destruction of the entire system.

[11] David Easton, "An Approach to the Analysis of Political Systems," *World Politics*, IX (April, 1957), p. 383. See also his book, *The Political System*. Although our diagram of a political system departs radically from that offered by Professor Easton in *World Politics*, this entire discussion has benefited greatly from his work.

geometric shape for the political system, and the breaks in its boundaries, means that—although identifiable—the area of society occupied by the system varies with circumstances and the activities of other systems. During World War II, for example, the economic system of the United States was almost wholly absorbed by the political system, with the government deciding on such things as price levels and what goods should be produced. In peacetime, too, America's political and economic systems overlap, but the economy is not so completely dominated by the government as it is in war.

In addition to these general characteristics, the diagram is designed to suggest the substance of basic processes of government. As a system of activities, American government—or any government, for that matter—is made up of an interrelated set of activities, all bearing on the authoritative determination and implementation of policies. This broad function is what we mean by governance, or the act of governing. But to say that the function of the political system is to govern is almost a truism, and it is at best such a general statement that it offers few clues on how to analyze American politics. The diagram attempts to break up this all-encompassing function into different stages of political activity. (In the next section, we shall add more specific functions to the diagram.)

At the core of the governmental process are the *activities of authoritative decision-making*, which are performed by identifiable political agencies or structures. These are represented by the circle at the center of the political system. In a tribe ruled largely through customs, with a few elders who interpret their meaning, these official decision-making activities may not be highly structured or even easily discovered. African specialists report that early British requests to "take me to your leader" sometimes produced bizarre results in areas where the leadership structure was not only loosely defined but was also described by different words. In the United States, on the other hand, the highest levels of political leadership are occupied by full-time politicians with distinctive titles, office buildings, seals of office, and all the other paraphernalia of authority. The President is a constant focus of public attention, whether he is lifting a dog by its ears or using dozens of pens to sign a statute. Both houses of Congress, the Supreme Court, and—to a lesser extent—the vast bureaucracy under the President are also visibly engaged in the decision-making activities by which we are governed.

Figure 1-1

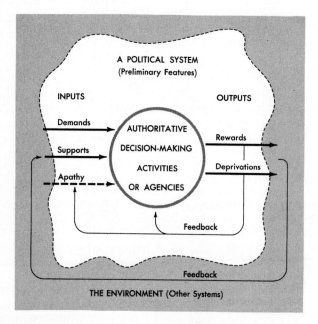

The neat circle which represents these decision-making activities should not suggest an undifferentiated or a perfectly harmonious set of activities. The diagram vastly oversimplifies the complex realities in order to draw attention to the principal features of the system. The decision-making circle could be broken up and represented as a number of subsets, each connected with all the others by crisscrossing arrows representing inputs and outputs. Whatever their internal relationships, however, all these agencies are engaged in authoritative decision-making.

We use the term *inputs* to refer to those activities which keep the system going. The most obvious forms of inputs are demands on the decision-makers—a "March on Washington" demanding congressional enactment of a civil rights act, a flood of letters to the President urging him to veto a statute, a lawsuit challenging the constitutionality of a local ordinance regulating picketing, an application from a college professor seeking National Science Foundation funds to support a research project. These and countless other demands of citizens on a democratic government are often generated outside the political system. A drought in Texas or an earthquake in Alaska will dramatically demonstrate how non-political events create conditions that are translated into political demands. More gradual changes in the environment, such as the change from a rural to an urban way of life, produce less dramatic but more enduring demands on government, from regulation of the food and drug industry (begun in 1908) to the creation of a Department of Urban Affairs (not yet achieved). But political demands may also be generated *within* the political system, for example, when the President urges Congress to pass a particular bill.[12] To recognize this pattern of influence, the diagram includes an arrow to represent impacts on inputs from within the political system as well as from the non-political environment.

The input of *supports* in the political system includes attitudes and behavior supporting the political system at every level: the political community, the structure of government, the current administration exercising the power of government, and particular government policies. Children in the United States learn to support "America the Beautiful" and the American constitutional system so early that support for these basic levels of the system is largely taken for granted. But the fact that, like sanitary drinking water, we take them for granted does not lessen their importance. The turmoil in some of the new African nations, where support for the very idea of a political community is weak, demonstrates the importance of support at this level for any political system. And the stability of the French system has suffered, despite strong support for the idea of France as a

---

12 Professor Easton uses the term "withinputs" to refer to this generation of influences on inputs by the political system itself. Such an awkward term appears necessary because his diagram of a political system includes only what we have labeled "authoritative decision-making activities or agencies." Inputs therefore appear to be outside the political system in his model. (See the article cited earlier in *World Politics.*) If the political system is more broadly conceived as including inputs, decision-making, and outputs as analytically separable parts of the same system, then one part of the system can easily be understood to affect other parts.

political community, because of weaker support for the established structure of government. A drop-off in support in the United States occurs only when we reach the level of the current administration controlling the government. And even there, Republicans *accept* and *pledge to support* (though not to prefer) a Democratic administration until the next election. Democrats, of course, return the compliment when the Republicans win. Support for particular policies is not nearly so widespread, although most Americans at least accept official decisions as legitimate. But the input of supports for policies goes beyond acceptance of their legitimacy; in the United States, it usually includes widespread belief in their effectiveness and desirability. Once established, an originally controversial program is not easily changed, as indicated by the mixture of amusement and shock that greeted Senator Barry Goldwater's suggestion that the Tennessee Valley Authority—once widely denounced as socialistic—should be sold to private corporations.

Many political scientists would probably say that the third input identified in our diagram—*apathy*—should not be included. How can apathy enter into and influence the decision-making activities of government? It certainly operates in more indirect fashion than the demand and support inputs, and we recognize this by using a broken line to indicate its linkage to decision-making activities. Nevertheless, widespread apathy may be almost as important as active demands on government in shaping public policy. In the most thorough study ever made of the attitudes and behavior of the American voter, a research team at the University of Michigan found woeful ignorance on the most prominent issues in American politics. On sixteen "burning" issues of the day, the average proportion of citizens who had an opinion, some notion of what the government was doing, and some feeling about the differences in party policy, was a rousing 28 per cent! [13] A majority of American citizens would thus have great difficulty in making demands or offering support in connection with most public policies. Ignorance does not necessarily mean apathy, of course, as is demonstrated by the fact that a majority of American adults—almost two-thirds—have voted in recent presidential elections. But a sizeable proportion of the citizenry—at least a fifth and probably a third—is both ignorant of and indifferent to politics. This apathy is not the same as support, although it implies at least acquiescence in basic governmental arrangements. For particular policies, it is entirely neutral, which means that the freedom of decision-makers to act without concern for public reactions increases as the proportion of apathetic citizens increases. In an indirect fashion, then, the degree of apathy in a political system has important consequences for the way it performs.

Since we view the political system as a set of activities related to authoritative decision-making, the *outputs* of the system are, by definition, decisions or public policies. The substance of these policy outputs may be identified, as in our

---

[13] Angus Campbell *et al.*, *The American Voter* (New York: John Wiley and Sons, Inc., 1960), p. 182. These findings are based on most generous application of the criteria: if an individual said he knew the position of the government on an issue, for example, he was counted as informed even though he misperceived the actual policy of the government.

diagram, as *rewards* and *deprivations*. These outputs represent the translation of demands, supports, and apathy by the decision-making agencies into rules or policies that maintain order—and, therefore, the survival and adaptation of the system to changing circumstances. The consequences of inputs show up primarily in the way the political system operates, the consequences of outputs in the impact of its operation on the environment. The adoption of a national income tax early in the twentieth century, for example, has profoundly affected America's economic and social systems. The arrow representing the rewards and deprivations of public policy therefore moves into the general environment, but it also circles directly back to early stages within the political system itself. When the Supreme Court interprets an act of Congress—and most dramatically, on the rare occasions when it rules a congressional enactment unconstitutional—the content of the decision has a direct effect on the Congress no less than on the non-political environment. Just as we suggested that inputs affecting decision-makers may be generated by the decision-making agencies themselves, so may the decision outputs directly affect decision-making agencies and the inputs to which they respond.[14]

Throughout this book, we shall conceive of government decisions as bestowing rewards and imposing deprivations. When an irate citizen seeks an injunction to prevent his neighbor from practicing the trombone at 2:00 A.M., the court's decision will quite evidently please one of the parties and displease the other. If the judge grants the injunction, the trombone player will lose his freedom to exercise his talents at times of his own choosing; if the plaintiff's petition is denied, he loses not only the case but undisturbed sleep. The rewards to the winner, whatever the decision, are equally obvious. But what if the judge refuses, for some reason, to render a decision? Even then, a decision has been reached, so far as the citizens are concerned, in favor of music and against sleep.

The fact that the failure of government to act does involve a decision (which will be viewed as a deprivation by some and as a reward by others) is obvious when we are talking about a lawsuit. But many people are not so quick to see that the same reasoning applies to the refusal of *any* government agency to decide a question put to it. Under the rules of the United States Senate, for example, a minority of members (33 per cent plus 1) may prevent a majority from bringing a proposal to a vote. One of the justifications for this practice is to say that important decisions should not be made by a bare majority of 50 per cent plus 1. If a larger majority is required, genuine support approaching consensus will fix public policy. Whether the requirement of an extraordinary majority is wise or foolish, this particular argument ignores the fact that *a refusal to act does involve a decision*—a decision to continue the status quo, which is perceived as rewarding by some but not by others. If a minority can block action, it has at least a negative control over policy. Prolonged Senate consideration of the Civil Rights Act in 1964 seemed so unfair to many Americans that they could

---

[14] This pattern of influence is not included in Easton's model, since his "political system" includes only what we call "authoritative decision-making activities or agencies." Adopting his terminology with regard to inputs, however, this output linkage would be called "withoutputs."

probably accept our interpretation of the nature of negative decision-making without difficulty. But many of the same people would stoutly defend the requirement that three-fourths of the states must approve a constitutional amendment, on the ground that such a momentous change should be made only if approved by an overwhelming majority. Again, the argument ignores the fact that refusal to act is a decision that carries rewards and deprivations. If 37 states ratified an amendment and 13 states rejected it, the 13 would determine policy.

We have talked thus far about rewards *and* deprivations as the substance of policy decisions, as if every decision included both. Can a decision carry *only* rewards *or* deprivations? Political scientists are divided on this question, some maintaining that no outputs of government are neutral, while others argue that governments may act to the benefit of all. Our position throughout this book will be that political decision-making is never neutral, and that the outputs of the political system always involve differential effects. Notice that we speak of "differential effects" rather than of rewards and punishments. This is to take account of the fact that some decisions of government involve no direct deprivations. Some unknown person in the Post Office Department must decide, for example, on the colors that will be used for a particular stamp. Most of us are wholly indifferent to such routine decisions. Even so, philatelists may be quite interested, and some will be pleased while others are disappointed by the choice. No one suffers a serious loss from this sort of decision, but within the general atmosphere of indifference those who are affected will react differently. The less consequential a decision is, the closer it may appear to approach neutrality. The greater its consequences for the citizenry, however, the more obvious are the rewards and deprivations that it entails.

The concept of *feedback* in our diagram of a political system simply gives explicit recognition to points we have already made—the interdependence of the political system with the other systems of society. Governmental decisions represent not only the adaptation of the system to its environment but also the efforts of the system to modify that environment.

Functions of the Political System

In adapting to and modifying the environment, every political system performs certain basic functions in order to survive as a system. Up to this point, we have talked about the basic elements of politics without much concern for the functions which make a given set of activities recognizable as a political system. We have already mentioned that the underlying function of politics is the authoritative determination of policy for society as a whole and that activities can be identified as political insofar as they bear on this process. The general concept of functions has thus already been put to use. But we have talked about the basic elements of politics without concern for their specific functions. Nor have we explained what we mean by "functions." Like so many English words, this one is used with a variety of meanings. We refer to a college dance or a cocktail party, for example, as a "social function." But when we talk of the functions of government, we certainly do not have public gatherings of this sort in mind.

Another usage, and one that is harder to distinguish from our concern for governmental functions, identifies motives or purposes with functions. From this point of view, the function of an act of Congress could be determined by finding out what Congress intended to accomplish when it passed the act. But, from the point of view of political science, the *function* of a law—or of any activity or structure—is not necessarily the same as its *purpose;* the function of anything is understood more clearly in terms of its *effect.* In other words, we may undertake an activity with a firm purpose in mind, only to find that the ultimate effect or outcome of the activity is quite different from what we had expected. Thus our *purpose* in going to college may simply be to get a college degree or to kill time between leaving preparatory school and entering the family business. Contrariwise, the effect—that is, the *function*—of going to college may be the stimulation of a permanent intellectual curiosity or the development of new career plans. To get at the real function of college for an individual, we ask— "What would his life have been like without such an experience?" To clarify the primary functions of government we may ask the same question—"What would our lives be like without government?"

In the broadest sense, then, functions refer to the effects or consequences of an activity. Biological and social scientists have developed a more specific meaning, which regards functions as the consequences of activities that promote the survival of the acting system. The awkward term "dysfunctions" refers to consequences that tend to disrupt or destroy the system. As a leading sociologist puts it: "*Functions* are those observed consequences which make for the adaptation or adjustment of a given system; and *dysfunctions*, those observed consequences which lessen the adaptation or adjustment of the system." [15] The basic output functions of the political system are fairly obvious. Clearly, the system must furnish some general rules or policies to maintain order and to satisfy demands on the system. In addition to deciding on rules or policies, the system must carry them out, applying them in actual practice. Also, it must settle disputes among citizens, as in the case already mentioned of the nocturnal trombone player and his neighbor.

Figure 1-2 represents a more complete diagram of a political system than Figure 1-1, with these and other basic functions added to the elements of the system. The three functions we have mentioned—rule-making, application of rules, and settlement of disputes—are outputs or consequences of decision-making activity. They are easy for Americans to grasp, because each tends to be centered in a highly visible political agency—the Congress, the President and the bureaucracy he heads, the Supreme Court and lower courts. Whatever the form of government, however, these three output functions will somehow be performed. In adding these functions to our diagram of a political system, we are simply recognizing another dimension of the system's outputs. The decisions of a political

---

[15] Robert K. Merton, *Social Theory and Social Structure,* (Glencoe, Illinois: The Free Press, 1949), p. 50. Merton also differentiates manifest functions—consequences that accord with the declared purpose of an activity—from latent functions—the unintended consequences of an activity.

system will thus be viewed as carrying the substance of rewards and deprivations, and as performing the functions of rule-making, application of rules, and settlement of disputes. Other dimensions of output might also be identified—for example, the kinds of goals toward which policy is aimed. The diagram should therefore be regarded as a representation of only some of the key features of a political system, not as a complete model.

The function of *political socialization* is presented at the base of the political system, and as between outputs and inputs. This is because the process of political socialization supports the entire system, and also because the process is in some respects an output of the system and in other respects an input. (All aspects of the system are interrelated, but political socialization is so much a part of both inputs and outputs that it cannot be identified with one to the neglect of the other.)

A simple view of political socialization is to call it "the process of induction into the political culture." [16] But this definition implies that the individual who is "socialized" politically already exists as a social (and therefore political)) creature, and that he is brought into the political system by the addition of appropriate political attitudes to those he already has. In a more basic sense, however, the

---

[16] Gabriel A. Almond, "A Functional Approach to Comparative Politics," in Almond and Coleman (eds.), *The Politics of the Developing Areas*, p. 27. Although Almond recognizes that political socialization is an activity through which the political system perpetuates itself, he still treats it as an input function.

Figure 1-2

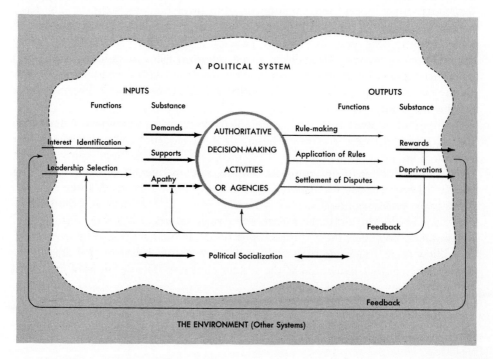

appropriate attitudes and behavior patterns *make* a human being. Children who have existed in a condition of extreme isolation may be *homo sapiens* in a physical sense but they do not become human beings in a social sense—their only resemblance to human beings is physical. Such an isolated individual can be socialized through careful and expert guidance but only if his isolation is ended at a fairly early age.[17] The process of socialization thus creates human beings; political socialization, as a part of this general process, creates citizens or subjects—human beings who share in some degree the political community's way of acting and thinking about politics.

From this point of view, political socialization is an output function of the political system. Political systems tend to perpetuate their values and practices, and they do this by developing new members who share those values and follow those practices. In all political systems, children are somehow indoctrinated in the political processes and beliefs of their society. In Plato's *Republic*, political socialization can easily be recognized as an output function because children were to be brought up by an official agency of government rather than by their parents. In actual political systems, the process is considerably more informal. Children learn largely from observation and imitation in informal contacts with others, but somehow they pick up the normal way of doing things (including political things). The process begins in the family, is continued in contacts with playmates, and—in more highly developed countries—is furthered by formal schooling, television programs, and other contacts with the world far beyond the family. The acquisition of specifically political attitudes begins fantastically early,[18] but it continues into adulthood, with individuals adding new and perhaps contradictory attitudes through job contacts, marriage, and other experiences. Except for the public schools, these socializing agencies are not part of the official structure of government. But even the family is acting as a part of the political system when it imparts political knowledge and attitudes.

Although political socialization is thus an output of every political system, it can also be viewed as part of the input activities of the system. The kinds of demands and supports that enter the system, the general level of apathy, and the aspects of the system toward which citizens are indifferent—all these are heavily influenced by the processes of political socialization. Almost all American children grow up with the idea that American government is democratic and that democracy is the best system of government. Within this general set of facts and values, however, they may learn quite different things. A child whose parents never directly discuss politics will probably be a different sort of citizen from another whose parents insist that all politicians are crooked, and from a third child whose parents begin to pin campaign buttons on him during his infancy.

Two other broad functions are necessary for a political system: *identification*

---

[17] Kingsley Davis, "Final Note on a Case of Extreme Isolation," *American Journal of Sociology*, LII (March, 1947), pp. 432–437. Professor Davis estimates that the maximum age to which a person could remain isolated and still retain the capacity for socialization is 10 to 15 years.

[18] Herbert Hyman, *Political Socialization* (Glencoe, Illinois: The Free Press, 1959).

of interests in the population and *selection of leaders* or official decision-makers. These are more exclusively input functions than is political socialization.

Somehow, every political system must identify the basic interests that unite and divide its citizens.[19] This function is performed in quite different ways and by quite different kinds of political structures from one country to another. In the United States, a congressman's difficulty in identifying the needs and desires of his constituents stems in part from the fact that their interests are expressed so freely. He gets a steady flow of mail from individual constituents, he hears from scores of pressure groups in and out of his district, he receives advice from local and national party organizations, and he reads about his duty in the newspapers. The massive census program carried out every ten years by the government itself may be viewed as an additional way of identifying the interests to which government must respond. In a dictatorship, the flow of communication from individuals and groups to the decision-makers may not be so free. Nevertheless, the government must somehow identify the conditions in society on which it must act.

The second input function—selection of leaders—is equally universal. The process is exceedingly simple in some societies. For example, the eldest male heir of a particular family may be designated to hold the highest office. In such a system, leadership positions are ascribed rather than achieved through successful competition. In modern democracies, millions of people, not just one, are eligible for the highest office. The informal norms of the system usually reduce the active prospects for top positions to a mere handful, but those who reach this select position have usually survived a lengthy series of tests. More people are elected to more offices in the United States than in any other democracy, and lower-level positions are frequently available to almost anybody who will take them. The political structures that perform the central tasks in American leadership selection are, of course, the political parties; but pressure groups, official agencies of government, the media of communication, and the voting public all play important parts, too.

---

[19] Our discussion of functions has benefited greatly from Gabriel A. Almond, "A Functional Approach to Comparative Politics," in Almond and Coleman (eds.), *The Politics of the Developing Areas*, pp. 3–64. It differs in four respects. He includes "political recruitment" as a specialized form of political socialization; we use instead the broader concept "leadership selection." He regards political socialization as an input function; we think it cannot be properly understood without recognizing its importance as an output function. We omit one of his input functions, "political communication," because communication is inherent in both the substance and the functions of all political activities. Moreover, communication is as much a part of output activities as it is of input activities. Finally, he talks of "interest articulation" and "interest aggregation" as two separate functions. Since some combination of interests has occurred in virtually every expression of interests, and since aggregated interests are articulated, this does not appear a meaningful distinction. Hence, we use the broader concept, "interest identification." Even interests that are not articulated may have important effects for policy. The Soviet Union, for example, goes to considerable expense and trouble to gain information on the unarticulated interests of citizens. See Alex Inkeles, *Public Opinion in Soviet Russia* (Cambridge: Harvard University Press, 1950).

The view that American politics comprises a system of activities governs the organization of this book. Since any system of activities responds to the environment in which it operates, we begin with a consideration of the context within which American politics operates. The second part of the book is specifically concerned with the entry of demands, supports, and apathy into the system. Third, we shall focus on decision-making as the central activity of the system. Finally, we consider the outputs of rewards and deprivations that come with every decision. In analyzing these substantive activities, we shall also focus on the functions they perform and the structures through which they are carried out.

Politics As a Cultural Heritage

The political behavior of Americans springs in part from their culture. We can predict a good deal about a baby's future values and behavior if we know the culture into which he is born. In a Miss America contest, we can safely forecast that American judges will not award first prize to the young lady with the most elaborate tattoos, the most elongated lips, or the most elegantly deformed feet. Although each of these attributes is essential to true "beauty" among some people, Americans choose to value different abnormalities, such as spectacularly large bosoms in combination with unusually small waists.

If beauty, which appears at first glance to be an inherent and universally recognizable quality, is subject to such extreme variations, political values must also be molded by culture. If we know that a person has been brought up as an American, we can predict how he will normally react to certain political situations. We can say, for example, that he will probably not support a man who claims an office to which he has not been elected. And if he is an elected official himself, he will relinquish his office whenever he is defeated in a popular election. True enough, you may say. But what do these obvious generalizations have to do with the details of American political behavior? They simply suggest that we ought to look at the relationship of culture to politics in a more systematic way than we usually do.

Where do our national peculiarities—which seem so "natural" and "right" to us—come from? By *culture* we mean the habitual modes of thought and behavior characteristic of a given society—"a *way* of thinking, feeling, believing." [20] In other words, the culture of any society is its social heredity, the man-made part of the environment, the ideas and habits that are acquired by all normal people in the

---

[20] Clyde Kluckhohn, *Mirror for Man: The Relation of Anthropology to Modern Life* (New York: McGraw-Hill Book Company, Inc., 1949), p. 23.

process of growing up—or of being "socialized"—in that society.[21] This means that culture includes political behavior no less than courtship practices and funeral customs. It means that politics is not isolated from other activities, even though we may study it separately. In a study focused exclusively on American government, this is an important point to bear in mind. It will help us to be more objective in our appraisal of political behavior, and will keep us from the pitfall of provincialism.

John Dewey, a noted American philosopher of this century, once suggested that the customs of the society in which an individual grows up may be compared with the total vocabulary of his native language, and that his own influence on that society may be compared with the number of words that his immediate family picks up from his baby talk. On the basis of her long study of different cultural patterns, anthropologist Ruth Benedict concluded that this is no exaggeration. "The life history of the individual," she said, "is first and foremost an accommodation to the patterns and standards traditionally handed down in his community." [22] Thus our political expectations, aspirations, and activities arise in large measure from the simple fact that most of us have been reared as members of the American society.

Journalist Walter Lippmann painfully discovered the meaning of this truth for politics. After an early career in which he had vainly tried to convince Americans of the need for reforms, he concluded that we do not approach politics with an open mind: "For the most part we do not first see, and then define, we define first and then see. In the great blooming, buzzing confusion of the outer world we pick out what our culture has already defined for us, and we tend to perceive that which we have picked out in the form stereotyped for us by our culture." [23]

Opinions are not built in a neutral fashion, then, on the basis of systematic observation. Indeed, we have attitudes toward many things we may never observe, from British socialized medicine to French sex life. And we acquire attitudes toward countless other things, from college professors to communists, long before we observe the actual object of the opinion. Having picked up the attitude unencumbered by experience, we tend later to notice particularly those events that support our preconception. If college professors are expected to be absent-minded, we perceive any absent-minded act by a professor as typically professorial, while we perceive similar acts by doctors or lawyers as personal idiosyncrasies. When we have strong feelings about a subject, like communism, for example, we find it hard to accept any facts that may be contrary to those feelings. Our culture not only shapes our *opinions* but it also helps determine which *facts* we will notice and how we will interpret them.

---

[21] Robin M. Williams, Jr., *American Society: A Sociological Interpretation* (New York: Alfred A. Knopf, 1960), 2nd ed., pp. 22–25; and Ralph Linton, *The Study of Man* (New York: D. Appleton-Century Co., 1935), p. 288.

[22] Ruth Benedict, *Patterns of Culture* (New York: Mentor Books, 1934), p. 2.

[23] Walter Lippmann, *Public Opinion* (New York: The Macmillan Company, 1922), p. 81.

Students of politics have to be on guard against the danger of mistaking values for facts. They must also attempt the more difficult task of holding opinions, even those that were received ready-made from their culture, with enough flexibility to permit the recognition of contradictory evidence. The truly curious person is like a scientist in that he welcomes facts that challenge his opinions. But most people rarely question the ideas with which they grow up.

In learning to speak, some Americans pick up the habit of using such words as "mick," "wop," "Polack," "frog," or "nigger" in referring to the Irish, Italians, Poles, French, or Negroes. In doing so, they are not simply acquiring a neutral term for referring to an ethnic group, for these very words carry with them certain "natural" attitudes toward these groups in particular and toward human beings in general. For example, just from knowing that a person uses such terms, we would probably be safe in predicting that he would oppose such political measures as strong civil-rights legislation. And he could also be identified as a potential follower of any demagogue who appealed to race prejudice. Our choice of terms often carries with it a built-in political meaning.

The "American Character" in Politics

The political system of every country is thus molded by its cultural setting. This influence is especially obvious to the traveler, for to him the politics of a new country appears fresh and foreign rather than inevitable and natural. The American "national character" has been analyzed by an endless series of foreign commentators, and some of them—Alexis de Tocqueville, for example, an early nineteenth-century French visitor [24]—have given us precious insight into our national peculiarities. More recently, social scientists have tried to identify a systematic pattern of cultural traits so widely shared that they offer a general picture of how the "ideal" or normal American will approach politics. Hopefully, the contemporary student relies much more on a general theory of human behavior and less on sheer intuition than a journalist or a traveler like Tocqueville, but almost all students of American character have come to similar conclusions. [25]

Popular writers like Vance Packard occasionally wring best-selling books out of the discovery that American character has drastically changed; in the case of Packard, because we have suddenly become "status seekers." [26] The discovery in such cases generally represents not a change in American values so much as the recent perception (and exploitation) of long-standing values by the writer. Americans have been described as status seekers since the early nineteenth century. Tocqueville himself, in describing the destruction of aristocracy by

---

[24] See his classic, *Democracy in America* (New York: Vintage Books, 1954), I, II, first published in 1835.

[25] For a review of the literature on national character, see Alex Inkeles and Daniel J. Levinson, "National Character: The Study of Modal Personality and Sociocultural Systems," in Gardner Lindzey (ed.), *Handbook of Social Psychology* (Cambridge: Addison-Wesley, 1954), II, pp. 977–1020.

[26] Vance Packard, *The Status Seekers* (New York: Pocket Books, Inc., 1961). (Originally published in 1959 by David McKay Company, Inc.)

American democracy, says, "They have swept away the privileges of some of their fellow creatures which stood in their way, but they have opened the door to universal competition." [27] In a penetrating work on American social character, an influential sociologist, David Riesman, submitted in 1953 that Americans have abandoned reliance on fixed, personal standards ("inner-direction") for a radar-like response to whatever standards appear in vogue with their associates ("other-direction").[28] But virtually the same language was used by Harriet Martineau, an English liberal visitor to the America of 1830: "[Americans] may travel over the world, and find no society but their own which will submit to the restraint of perpetual caution, and reference to the opinions of other." [29] The chief point made by these reassessments of American social character may be that Americans are self-critical, with constructive intentions but without a deep grounding in American history.

The image of radical change in social character is based on the assumption that material conditions determine social values. From this point of view, the shift of American society from a predominantly rural and individualistic way of life to a predominantly urban and bureaucratic pattern must necessarily entail a radical change in values. Much can be said for the Marxist view that material conditions determine values. But the values of a society also appear to influence the way it responds to materialistic changes. Thus Max Weber, a renowned German sociologist, argued that the "Protestant ethic," with its emphasis on individual responsibility and achievement, was a prerequisite for the development of a capitalistic economic system.[30] This is, of course, directly opposite to the Marxist view that values are mere "super structure" shaped by material forces. Basic social values are highly stable; they help to shape the way we respond to technological change rather than being merely responsive to such change.

The basic value that appears to have shaped American social character from the outset is the *aggressive assertion of equality in social relations*. We began with the bold declaration that "all men are created equal" rather than with an aristocratic order inherited from the feudal caste system.[31] Despite the conspicuous exception of slavery (which Jefferson denounced in the original draft of the Declaration of Independence), this emphasis on equality is probably the unique feature of American society. Urbanization, industrialization, and political democracy are characteristics we share with others; the deeply ingrained and insistent stress on equality, however, has been peculiarly American. Thus

---

[27] *Democracy in America*, II, p. 146.

[28] *The Lonely Crowd* (New York: Doubleday Anchor, 1953).

[29] Harriet Martineau, *Society in America* (New York: Sanders and Otlay, 1837), III, p. 14. Quoted in S. M. Lipset, "A Changing American Character?" in S. M. Lipset and L. Lowenthal (eds.), *Culture and Social Character* (New York: The Free Press of Glencoe, Inc., 1961), p. 143.

[30] Max Weber, *The Protestant Ethic and the Spirit of Capitalism*, trans. by Talcott Parsons (London: George Allen & Unwin, Ltd., 1930). First published in German, 1922–1923.

[31] For an interpretation of American political thought that emphasizes the continuity of this value and the importance of this beginning, see Louis Hartz, *The Liberal Tradition in America* (New York: Harcourt, Brace and Company, 1955).

Baedeker's handbook for the European visitor to the United States late in the nineteenth century warned that he "should, from the outset, reconcile himself to the absence of deference, or servility, on the part of those he considers his social inferiors." [32]

America's stress on equality leads to three other basic social characteristics that have also long been noted by foreign visitors: *competition* or *individual achievement, status uncertainty*, and *conformity*. At first glance, some of these attributes may appear incompatible, but on examination each may be seen to lead to the other. Democratic egalitarianism, as Tocqueville saw, leads to intense competition and stress on achievement. If one's "station in life" is not fixed by a rigid class system, he must establish it himself. And in America we tend to measure achievement primarily in terms of money. With hereditary rank eliminated, cash value becomes the most obvious measure of status. As one anthropologist puts it, "Money comes closer with us than with any other people to being the universal standard of value." [33] Ask an average American, "What is Tom Smith worth?" and you are likely to get an answer in terms of dollars rather than class position, religious standing, military rank, knowledge, or political or social contributions.

The fact that Americans must achieve whatever rank they claim, rather than assuming it as a birthright, leads to uncertainty about their status. Because of its unique rate of immigration and its social and geographical mobility, America is in some respects a nation of *parvenus*. [34] Early foreign observers of American society insisted that our emphasis on equality and opportunity actually led to greater consciousness of status than was found among the aristocracies of Europe. After all, people are unsure about positions they have newly acquired. On a national level, this uncertainty can still be seen in celebrations of "I Am an American Day." Somehow, it is difficult to imagine Frenchmen or Japanese setting aside a day to proclaim their nationality—they *know* that they are French or Japanese.

At the individual and group level, status uncertainty has expressed itself in such things as an addiction to titles, "exclusive" resorts, and fraternities and sororities. Commenting on these efforts to create badges of superiority, D. W. Brogan, a British political scientist, explains, "It is only an apparent contradiction in terms to assert that the fundamental democratic and egalitarian character of American life is demonstrated by the ingenuity and persistence shown in inventing marks of difference and symbols of superiority. In a truly class-conscious and caste-dominated society, the marks of difference are universally recognized even if resented. In America, they must be stressed, or they might easily be forgotten. . . ." [35] The conspicuous display of wealth is, of course, the most simple and direct way of advertising one's status. Texas, as the new frontier of the new

---

[32] Quoted in Lipset, "A Changing American Character?" in Lipset and Lowenthal (eds.), *Culture and Social Character*, p. 143.

[33] Kluckhohn, *Mirror for Man*, p. 241.

[34] Gabriel A. Almond, *The American People and Foreign Policy* (New York: Harcourt, Brace and Company, 1950), p. 63.

[35] D. W. Brogan, *U.S.A.: An Outline of the Country, Its People and Institutions* (London: Oxford University Press, 1941), p. 116.

rich, is noted for the most vulgar current display of sudden riches—without his Neiman-Marcus wardrobe, the oil millionaire might be indistinguishable from the farmer he was yesterday.

Status uncertainty leads to conformity. Whereas Europeans have found security in following the standards of earlier generations, Americans tend to feel insecure unless they are "up-to-date" in clothing, slang, furniture, and child-rearing practices. Some anxiety inevitably attends such a form of conformity, for what is "up-to-date" changes from day to day. The person insensitive to cues or without enough money to replace his wardrobe with each shift in fashion is in constant danger of being left behind. As our earlier quotation from Harriet Martineau reveals, the American's extreme sensitivity to the opinions of others was discussed more than a hundred years before David Riesman coined the term "other-directed personality."

How do these "American character" traits show up in political attitudes and behavior? In a sense, this whole book is an extended answer to this question, but the impact of each basic characteristic deserves at least one illustration here at the outset.

In attempting to link national character to specifically political attitudes, we need to recognize that, as Professor V. O. Key said in an early draft of *Public Opinion and American Democracy*, the hazardous task of delineating national character requires "heroic guesswork." Kindly man that he was, he changed the phrase in galley proofs to read "educated intuition." [36] Whether they are based on heroic guesswork or educated intuition, our statements on American character do not represent firmly established propositions. We do have firm data on recent political attitudes, thanks largely to the research of the University of Michigan Survey Research Center and to Professor Key's synthesizing book based on that research. If we find widely shared political ideas that might be said to stem from the apparent traits of American character, we can be more confident that the traits have been correctly identified.[37]

First, a vast majority of Americans are suspicious of power, regardless of who exercises it. This is precisely the attitude that would be predicted from the proposition that Americans are peculiarly and aggressively committed to equality. American opinion surveys consistently find large majorities who feel that the bosses, labor unions, or business corporations have "too much power." [38] Moreover, the people who believe that "big business" should not have too much say in the way government is run have the same belief about labor unions. The suspicion is not just of a particular group; it applies to any accumulation of power that appears to threaten our basic equality. Moreover, if no threat to equality is clearly present,

---

[36] V. O. Key, Jr., *Public Opinion and American Democracy* (New York: Alfred A. Knopf, 1961), p. 42.

[37] The discovery of political attitudes logically deducible from traits of national character does not, of course, demonstrate a causal connection. But it does lend additional credence to traits that have been identified on the basis of different evidence.

[38] Key, *Public Opinion and American Democracy*, p. 44. Unless otherwise noted, other references to political attitudes in this section come from the same source, pp. 41–50.

we can always invent one. Many a candidate for public office has directed his campaign against some invisible "power elite" that threatens the public.

Second, the American value of individual achievement appears to be reflected in a number of political attitudes. The problems that concern Americans are overwhelmingly personal, not political, and most people are optimistic about their personal prospects. Moreover, the American parent thinks his children have a good chance to be better off than he is. This tendency of Americans to rely on themselves rather than on government seems to be a facet of their general optimism rather than an indication of anti-governmental convictions. The typical attitudes are simply *non*governmental. When asked if they think the government ought to engage in a particular program, such as medical care for the aged, most Americans will agree. But the issue is not at the center of their interests, which leaves officials considerable discretion and permits small groups who are actively interested to play a role that far outweighs their numbers.

The status uncertainty of Americans can be seen in the high degree of ethnocentrism that marks their political attitudes. This is so conspicuous that it is the first trait of American "political character" noted by Professor Key: ". . . the American characteristically manifests an uncommonly high degree of loyalty and satisfaction with things American—an attitude that, on occasion, approaches smugness and, at times, extreme intolerance of matters regarded as un-American." [39] Proponents of any new measure must be able to demonstrate that it is not an alien practice before it can receive serious consideration. Thus policies that have become commonplace in most other democracies may be long delayed here precisely because they were developed elsewhere. A cataclysmic economic depression was required before we could join other democracies, for example, in providing social security for our citizens.

The social trait of conformity expresses itself most obviously in a disposition to abide by the majority will. As Key says, acceptance of an unwanted decision may stem simply from "resignation to the fact that the majority has more spears and dissent is futile." [40] But the quality of acceptance of majority decisions in the United States seems to go beyond mere resignation. Indeed, immediately after an election, about 10 per cent more voters claim to have supported the winner than actually voted for him on election day! People like a winner, some so much that they cannot face the fact that they did not contribute to his victory. Once a new administration has had a chance to stabilize itself, bare-knuckled opposition reappears. But even opposing politicians tend to rally 'round the winner long enough to give him a brief "honeymoon" during which consensus seems to prevail.

The existence of a national "political character" can be demonstrated on the basis of attitudes shared by a large majority of the population. And the content of these attitudes is consistent with what would be expected from the somewhat more speculative propositions about the national "social character." In brief,

[39] *Ibid.*, p. 42.
[40] *Ibid.*, p. 48.

American politics is distinctively American, and must be understood in its cultural setting.

The Physical Environment As a Political Setting

Does this mean that all Americans respond to politics in exactly the same way? Not at all. True, the pervasive influence of culture does tend to smooth out individual differences, but concealed beneath what we have been calling the "American character" are all kinds of variations. The newly arrived foreigner thinks all Americans look and act alike, but the longer he observes us the more he comes to see our differences. If we are to appreciate the true impact of culture on politics, we must look closely at the geographic, demographic, class, economic, and historical roots of these differences.

From the very dawn of civilization, government leaders have had to take into account the facts of geography—the distribution of natural resources, the effect of a nation's size and location on its military strength, the pattern of natural trade routes. And yet nowadays many of us give little thought to the influence of geography, forgetting that the American political tradition is in large part a product of the physical setting in which it developed. Although federalism (with its distribution of powers between the national and state governments) exists only as a possibility in a small land like Switzerland, in a vast country like the United States it is almost a necessity.

The Natural Environment and the American Tradition

Three geographic factors have contributed mightily to shaping the American political tradition: the country's isolation from Europe, the vastness of its territory, and the richness of its natural resources.[41] Among other things, isolation from Europe meant the absence of a feudal tradition with its concept of fixed status. Consequently, Americans took equality and freedom for granted almost from the outset, whereas in Europe the fight for equality consumed the political energies and dominated the ambitions of the "lower classes" for centuries. The vast land always stretching on beyond the frontier gave a new vitality to the principles of equality and freedom for individual achievement to every generation of Americans up to the twentieth century. The availability of cheap or free land served as a psychological "safety valve" and as a form of cheap economic relief for those who were denied equal opportunity in the settled regions of the East. Our rich treasure of natural resources, combined with political freedom, meant that Americans could turn to commerce and industry while their European contemporaries were still struggling to win basic rights from oppressive governments.

One of our most eminent historians, the late Carl Becker, concluded that America's social equality and political freedom were casual and lavish gifts bestowed by nature rather than hard-won privileges earned through battle or

---

[41] See Carl L. Becker, *Freedom and Responsibility in the American Way of Life* (New York: Vintage Books, 1955), p. 12.

careful reasoning.[42] Receiving so many advantages with such relative ease, Americans have tended to pursue a politics of self-congratulation. Even the Puritans came to assume that God was the special servant of the American people rather than vice versa. Today we easily forget how much we owe to the abundance of our natural resources and the lucky accident that we spanned the continent just when technological developments made it possible to weld the land into a political and economic unit. We tend to give ourselves all the credit; Reinhold Niebuhr, a contemporary theologian, ironically notes that on Thanksgiving Day we "have congratulated God on the virtues and ideals of the American people, which have so well merited the blessings of prosperity we enjoy." [43]

This spirit of complacency promotes our characteristic ethnocentrism, the feeling that all things American are superior. This feeling helps explain our failure to take advantage of successful experiments with new policies elsewhere. By definition, they are non-American; ethnocentrism translates non-American into un-American. Our self-satisfaction also throws light on the prejudice and discrimination to which every generation of immigrants has been exposed. In international politics our pride sometimes leads to an emotional rather than a rational appraisal of events; assuming that America is omnipotent, we find it hard to adjust foreign policy to the unpleasant fact that some things are beyond our easy control. When the communists won power in China after World War II, for example, many Americans assumed that someone in their own government must have been responsible. And we were shocked in 1961 when an ill-organized invasion failed to overthrow the Castro regime in Cuba. We disliked the Castro dictatorship, so we assumed that it could not last, just as we had assumed in 1917 that the Communist regime in Russia could not survive.

The kindness of geography has been a mixed blessing in American politics. To be sure, it helped to give us great prosperity, but it also led us to accept our good fortune without thinking how to sustain it. It permitted a foreign policy of isolationism for over a century, and left us ill prepared for both the responsibilities of world leadership and the realities of world politics.

The Natural Environment and Political Differences

Li'l Abner has more in common with a New Yorker than with a Samoan. And yet even within the United States there are important regional variations in the food people eat, the language they speak—and in the way they behave politically. For example, anti-Catholic attitudes seem to be more common among southerners than among other Americans. President Kennedy was estimated to have suffered a 17 per cent loss of votes in the South in the 1960 presidential election simply because he was a Catholic; in the rest of the nation, he picked up a 1½ per cent advantage because of his religion.[44] Opinions on many political problems vary in

---

[42] *Ibid.*, p. 21.

[43] *The Irony of American History* (New York: Charles Scribner's Sons, 1952), pp. 52–53.

[44] Philip E. Converse *et al.*, "Stability and Change in 1960: A Reinstating Election," *American Political Science Review*, LV (June, 1961), pp. 269–280.

this way from one region to another. During the 1950's, when excitement about alleged communist control of American businesses, labor unions, government offices, military commands, and churches was at a peak, people were questioned on their willingness to grant certain rights to socialists, atheists, communists, and persons accused of communism. The largest proportion of relatively tolerant people was found in the West, and the smallest proportion in the South.[45] Even when the comparison is between westerners and southerners with the same amount of education, or living in the same kind of community (urban or rural), the regional differences are still significant.

These regional contrasts are remarkably endurable, but they should not mislead us into adopting the notion of geographic determinism. People who move from one section of the country to another tend to keep the political attitudes of the region where they grew up rather than picking up the viewpoint of their new environment. And when the newcomers are the dominant group in the locality, they can maintain their political distinctiveness for generations. A place

---

[45] Samuel A. Stouffer, *Communism, Conformity, and Civil Liberties* (Garden City, N.Y.: Doubleday & Company, Inc., 1955), pp. 129–130.

Drawing by Ed Fisher; © 1961 The New Yorker Magazine, Inc.

"Well, *Ah* do *hope you won't go back North with the impression that those moderates speak for* all *us Southerners.*"

like Edwards County in southeastern Illinois, which was settled in 1818 by relatively well-off, well-educated, anti-slavery colonists from England, remains more Republican to this day than the surrounding counties that were originally settled by pro-slavery southerners. Since Edwards County has the same geographic characteristics as the surrounding counties, its political distinctiveness suggests that political habits are an autonomous force rather than a simple reflection of the natural environment.[46]

The combination of regional contrasts and local variations within regions lends great variety to American politics. The candidate for Congress in Seattle, for example, will campaign quite differently from the candidate in a South Carolina farming community. The former will normally be less critical of nonconformists, less hesitant to adopt a position that might be denounced as "unAmerican," and more inclined to support proposals for the admission of more immigrants into the United States.

The People at the Base of American Politics

We can say two things about the American people: there are more and more of them, and they are all immigrants or the descendants of immigrants. Both characteristics have many important political implications.

More People with New Characteristics

The 1960 census was a record of dramatic change, and changes in the population always have political repercussions. Between 1900 and 1950, the population of the United States doubled, and in the single decade between 1950 and 1960 it increased 18.5 per cent, to reach a new high of 179,323,175. This rapid rate of growth has meant a greater drain on natural resources that were once exploited with abandon. Conservation programs have become more than just pious notions to be forgotten in the competitive drive for profit. With every leap in population, the efforts of lumber and cattle interests to exploit the public domain, the fate of the offshore oil lands, programs of soil conservation and reforestation, all become matters of increasingly urgent public concern.

As they have grown in numbers, the American people have also shifted about the country. During the first half of the century, the population of the West grew at a rate of 499 per cent; the population of New England grew at a rate of only 67 per cent. The old westward movement has shifted to become a movement toward the relatively underdeveloped periphery of the country. The five states with the greatest rates of growth between 1950 and 1960 were Florida (78.7 per cent), Nevada (78.2), Alaska (75.8), Arizona (73.7), and California (48.5). In contrast

---

[46] V. O. Key, Jr., *American State Politics: An Introduction* (New York: Alfred A. Knopf, 1956), p. 225. Also see V. O. Key, Jr., and Frank Munger, "Social Determinism and Electoral Decisions: The Case of Indiana," in Eugene Burdick and Arthur J. Brodbeck (eds.), *American Voting Behavior* (Glencoe, Illinois: The Free Press, 1959), pp. 281–299.

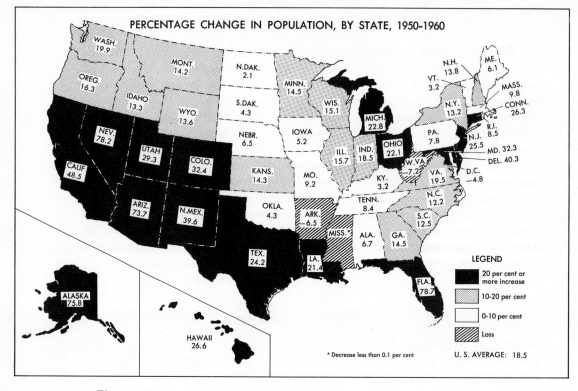

PERCENTAGE CHANGE IN POPULATION, BY STATE, 1950-1960

LEGEND

- 20 per cent or more increase
- 10-20 per cent
- 0-10 per cent
- Loss

* Decrease less than 0.1 per cent   U. S. AVERAGE: 18.5

Figure 1-3

Map from Bureau of the Census, United States Department of
Commerce, *1960 Census of Population: Advance Reports, Final
Population Counts*, p. 6.

to their phenomenal growth, only one New England state (Connecticut) had an
increase greater than the national average (see map). Even if we ignore percentages
and talk in terms of actual numbers of additional people, New York just beat
out Texas for third place, while California and Florida were first and second. In
the future, the old areas of the East can expect to exercise less influence over
such crucial political contests as that for the presidency. California and Texas
are already supplying more and more national leaders to the major political
parties.

This high rate of mobility makes some of the current arguments about
"states' rights" seem rather anachronistic. An early Virginia congressman's boast
that "My patriotism begins to wane as I leave the borders of Virginia" may have
sounded meaningful in 1800, but it would make little sense to the mobile Americans
of today. About 40 per cent of all native "white" Americans move from one
state to another after growing up, and southern Negroes have been moving out
of the South in a steady stream.[47] Between 1950 and 1960, the Census Bureau
recorded the greatest migration for a single decade in American history—the

---

[47] Campbell *et al.*, *The American Voter*, p. 442.

movement of nearly 1½ million Negroes from the South to other areas of the country. Of the 36 million Americans who change their residence every year, about 11 million move to a different county, and half of these cross state lines. Americans who have lived in several states tend to keep the attitudes with which they grew up. Regardless of where they were reared, most Americans think of "the government" as the government in Washington, not the government of a county in which they may have resided for a few short months. And on election day they show where their primary political interest lies: the largest number of voters turn out for national elections, with state elections ranking second and local elections third in stimulating voter interest.

What about separate groups within this restless, shifting population? The percentage of the population 65 years old and over increased from 4 per cent in 1900 to 9 per cent in 1960. Despite the great increase in the number of old people, the median age of the population actually decreased in the last decade, for the first time in American history. How can the median age drop when the aged portion of the population is increasing? The answer can be seen in crowded maternity wards and schoolrooms: the proportion of the population under 18 was increasing even faster than the very old group, to account for 36 per cent of the total population in 1960. Women began to outnumber men in the United States for the first time in 1950 (with 100 women to every 99 men) and their majority had increased by 1960 (to a 100–97 ratio). The number of married people has continued to increase, from 53.9 per cent of all Americans 14 years old or over in 1900 to 67.4 per cent in 1960. Finally, the rate of growth of the Negro population (25.4 per cent) exceeded that of the white population (17.5 per cent) during the decade, as did the rate of growth of all other "non-white" groups.

What effects do these changes have on government? The increasing number of very old and very young people means that a larger portion of the population is not engaged in productive work and must be supported by the smaller percentage that is actively employed. The elderly now require national programs of pensions and public assistance, and such programs have become a fixed part of the government's responsibilities. The high birth rate of the last two decades has already produced tremendous strains in our educational system. Since financing the public schools is beyond the capacity of local governments in many parts of the country, the federal government will have to play an increasingly important role. The greater number of women in the population will almost certainly accelerate their movement into what were once "men's jobs" in industry and government. Contrary to popular impression, the urban environment continues to produce earlier marriages than were common in the old rural environment; this means that persistent demands will be heard for the construction of new homes, either in public housing projects or with government financing. And the increase in the nonwhite ethnic groups will bring increasing insistence on additional government guarantees of civil rights. Both political parties agree on the need for more federal activity to solve these and other problems, but they do not agree on how much aid and for what needs.

The most radical changes in American life have sprung from the shift of the population from farms to cities. In the first fifty years of this century, the ratio of urban to rural dwellers was almost exactly reversed, from 40/60 in 1900 to 64/36 in 1950.[48] The 1960 census reported an urban majority of 70 per cent, but with a shift from central cities to their surrounding suburbs. If cities were, as Jefferson thought, "sores on the body politic," this sudden concentration of Americans in urban and suburban areas would have imperiled the health of the democracy. Fortunately, however, the modern city-dweller is no less responsible a citizen than his country cousin. Indeed, he is generally both better educated and better informed on current political problems. The regional differences in toleration of unpopular political ideas that we mentioned above are matched by equal differences between urban and rural residents: in every section fewer rural people than city-dwellers are tolerant of nonconformists, even when the comparison is between groups with the same amount of schooling. We are not sure just what makes small-town and farm communities more intolerant of divergent opinions, in violation of the democratic tradition. But here is one suggestion: "In the anonymity of city life it is much easier for deviant behavior to flourish than in the goldfish bowl of a small community. In the large community there are sometimes so many goldfish that nobody bothers to look at them. In the small town a lone exotic specimen can be viewed with careful, critical, and occasionally devastating attention." [49]

Urban tolerance may, of course, be a greater blessing for the maverick than for the typical citizen. Although the city has been the breeding ground for most of the great achievements of mankind, it has also displayed many of the worst aspects of human behavior. Rural and smalltown life may suggest tight-lipped disapproval of those who neglect church or PTA functions, or—in extreme cases —it may bring to mind the posse or the lynch mob. But many Americans have recently been shocked at the emergence of an opposite extreme in the cities: for several dozen citizens to witness a public act of murder without intervening or even calling the police goes beyond mere tolerance; it reaches the point of extreme indifference to the fate of one's fellows. Acts of brutality and callousness are no doubt less likely to become known when they occur in a rural area. Nevertheless, many people have felt that the excitement of life in the city is not worth the loss of freedom safely to stroll through the park at night. The movement of the American population to urban areas has accordingly shifted from central cities to the suburbs.

America's change from a predominantly rural to an overwhelmingly urban way of life has countless consequences for government. One of the most pervasive is the fact that the new urban majority is still represented by only a minority of legislators. The political districts from which state and national legislators are elected have simply not been adjusted to correspond to the new distribution of voters. This urban underrepresentation is acute at the state level, where over two-

---

[48] References, here and elsewhere, to the urban-rural division of the population rely on the findings of the Bureau of the Census, in which places are defined as "urban" if they contain over 2,500 persons and "rural" if they contain less than 2,500 persons.

[49] Stouffer, *Communism, Conformity, and Civil Liberties*, p. 130.

thirds of the people (the urban dwellers) hold less than one-third of the legislative seats. Urban voters indignantly demand fair representation, but their efforts run aground on a basic law of politics—those who exercise a form of power do not voluntarily surrender that power to people with different interests. And the very people who are asked to turn over control of the state legislature to urban representatives are legislators from rural constituencies. Over a decade ago, one political scientist was so impressed by the futility of urban efforts that he asked, "Is there any way except revolution by which the urban residents . . . may secure their constitutional right to equal representation in the state legislature? If there is another remedy, it has not yet been discovered." [50]

The political system does adjust to its environment, however; exactly a decade after this dire conclusion, the urban majority took significant strides toward equal representation without shedding a single drop of blood. The crucial change in the environment was revealed in the 1960 census: by that year, urban residents made up a majority of the population in 39 states. Urbanites therefore have particular access to governors, presidents, and United States senators, all of whom are elected on a statewide basis rather than by smaller districts. And all citizens have legal access to federal judges, who are appointed by the President with Senate approval. Tocqueville said in 1835, "Scarcely any political question arises in the United States that is not resolved sooner or later into a judicial question." In 1962, the United States Supreme Court recognized the validity of the urban resident's claim to a constitutional right of an equal voice with his rural cousin in choosing state legislators.[51] The decision had an immediate impact. By 1964, 42 states had taken some action on the apportionment of seats in state legislatures—court decisions in 24 states required reapportionment or threatened redistricting by the courts unless the state legislatures acted, and 24 states adopted redistricting plans of some kind.[52] In 1964, the Supreme Court further held that districts for *both* houses of state legislatures must be "substantially equal." [53] This decision rendered invalid all so-called "little federal" plans—in which representation was based on population in one house and on geography in the other house— even if the plan had been adopted through a popular referendum. The Supreme Court also applied the standard of "one man, one vote" to congressional districts in a landmark decision that ruled Georgia's congressional districts for the United

---

[50] George A. Graham, *Morality in American Politics* (New York: Random House, 1952), p. 102.

[51] *Baker* v. *Carr*, 369 U.S. 186 (1962). Four out of seven justices participating in a 1946 case on malapportionment of congressional districts said the issue was justiciable (appropriate for decision by the Court), but one member of the majority voted with the three-man minority against Court action because he felt the period of time for corrective action before the next election was too short. *Colegrove* v. *Green*, 328 U.S. 548 (1946).

[52] Alaska, Arizona, Arkansas, Hawaii, Minnesota, South Carolina, and South Dakota were the only states in which there was no major reapportionment activity, and most of these had redistricted their legislative seats shortly before the decision.

[53] *Reynolds* v. *Sims*, 377 U.S. 533 (1964). The decision found existing schemes of representation in 6 states unconstitutional, and suits on the same ground were pending in almost 40 more states.

States House of Representatives unconstitutional.[54] Four days after this decision was rendered, the Georgia legislature—including a Senate that had been redistricted under the 1962 decision—adopted a new districting plan for congressional elections. The urban citizen is coming into his own.

The American As Immigrant

President Franklin Roosevelt once alienated the Daughters of the American Revolution by greeting them as "My fellow immigrants. . . ." He was, of course, chiding those Americans who feel superior to more recent arrivals. The "melting-pot" character of the American population does seem to be a source of strength rather than weakness. John Gunther reported in *Inside U.S.A.* that both Arkansas and Mississippi proudly claim to have the highest percentage of native-born population in the country.[55] The 1960 census reveals, however, that both of these states are among the three that *lost* population in the last decade. The alleged advantages of homogeneity seem to be ignored by Americans when they decide where to live.

However varied the languages, religions, and political ideas they brought to the United States, all Americans (except the Indians) are alike in one respect— they are immigrants or the descendants of immigrants. And the political habits of Americans have naturally been influenced by their common immigrant backgrounds.

According to Margaret Mead, all Americans exhibit the "third-generation" trait of rejecting the father as a model of authority.[56] Whatever success the father may have had in becoming "Americanized," he is still marked by the "old country," or—if he is not in fact second-generation—he at least follows some of the old and therefore outmoded ways. The desire to "belong" is so powerful that each generation is encouraged by the fathers themselves to "go further," to achieve more, to be somehow different. For a son to follow in his father's footsteps generally produces as great a sense of failure in the father as in the son. In this tendency to reject the father as a model, Miss Mead finds a basic source of the American's disrespect for authority.

Although this interpretation is a prime example of the "educated intuition" about which Professor Key spoke, it may help to explain Americans' deep-seated distrust of power. For a fuller explanation, however, we must remember that America's political history has been marked by a similar rejection of authority. The American Revolution has been interpreted as a rejection of authority *per se*, rather than as a rebellion against English rule alone. And the weakness of the state governments that were set up in the new nation suggests that the newly independent American was almost as distrustful of his own government as he was of the king's. The governors elected under the first state constitutions were so

---

[54] *Wesberry* v. *Sanders*, 376 U.S. 1 (1964).

[55] *Inside U.S.A.* (New York: Harper & Brothers, 1947), pp. 658–659.

[56] *And Keep Your Powder Dry: An Anthropologist Looks at America* (New York: William Morrow & Company, 1942).

strait-jacketed that one might almost think they were still being appointed by the mother country.[57]

When an immigrant child is sent to the neighborhood school to be "Americanized" along with native-born children, he learns that the revolution against England was a highly praiseworthy act. He reads in his elementary-school texts that the English were black-hearted villains and the colonists shining heroes.

In effect, then, the child is taught that the rejection of both family and political authority is sanctioned by adults. The very idea of authority becomes repugnant to him, and to reject it becomes a laudable—a peculiarly "American" —action. We must not go too far with this interpretation today, when many Americans seem to be looking on government and authority with less and less disfavor.[58] But it highlights an underlying aspect of political socialization that has by no means disappeared.

The American's desire to belong reflects an insecurity about his status as a "real American"—an insecurity that gives rise to the peculiar practice we have noted of condemning activities because they are un-American. Swedes, Lebanese, and Australians denounce practices that they think unwise, but the notion of an un-Swedish, un-Lebanese, or un-Australian activity is not common political currency. Yet Americans who are only shortly removed from immigrant status (whether in fact or in their fears) are insecure enough to feel that they must protest their Americanism more loudly than others. Ironically, they are joined by some of the "old" Americans who feel that their status is threatened by the rise to acceptance and influence of more recent arrivals.

In the competition to "prove" that one is a "true American," the easiest route may lie in demonstrating that one is *more* American than others. This impulse quickly leads to direct accusations that others are *un*-American, with all the attendant dangers of bigotry and the excitement of ferreting out heretics. Unfortunately, the insecure attain their greatest sense of Americanism through impugning the loyalty of those who appear beyond reproach: to be more American than one's next-door neighbor may be gratifying, but to be more American than a national leader is a glorious achievement. In the era after World War II, when Senator Joseph McCarthy (R-Wisconsin) was leading the self-proclaimed super-patriots, the Secretary of State was a favorite target. More recently, the John Birch movement has satisfied those who feel the more grandiose need to suspect (and therefore feel superior to) the President himself—with both Republican and Democratic presidents as targets of attack.[59]

---

[57] See Geoffrey Gorer, *The American People: A Study in National Character* (New York: W. W. Norton and Company, Inc., 1948).

[58] Attitudes toward strong leadership and expanding government programs are not unfavorable, even though a generalized suspicion of authority may remain. See Campbell, *et al.*, *The American Voter*, especially Chapters 8 and 9; and H. McClosky, *et al.*, "Issue Conflict and Consensus among Party Leaders and Followers," *American Political Science Review*, LIV (June, 1960), pp. 406–427.

[59] See Nelson W. Polsby, "Towards an Explanation of McCarthyism," *Political Studies*, VIII (October, 1960), pp. 250–271; and George Barrett, "Close-up of the Birchers' 'Founder,'" *The New York Times Magazine*, May 14, 1961, pp. 13ff.

Class Structure As a Political Force

Although the American people share a common culture, they are by no means a homogeneous group. We have already found, for example, that political attitudes vary according to region and urban or rural residence. Do they also vary according to social class? Or can we say that Americans are free from class-consciousness —that their only differences are purely individual ones within a single predominant class? The American emphasis on social equality leads to some embarrassment even in admitting the possibility of class differences. But the emphasis on achievement and uncertainty about status suggest that class differences may actually be quite pronounced. Questions of this sort have preoccupied every serious student of politics. Aristotle was just as convinced that a large middle class was essential to stable government as Karl Marx was that class conflict would persist until communism produced a completely classless society.

America's first politicians disagreed about the role of class in politics, but in a fashion that would seem most peculiar today—the conservatives talked about class hostility while the liberals stressed class harmony. In the early years of the Republic—when the vote was limited by property and tax-paying qualifications— conservative leaders of the Federalist and Whig parties (men like Alexander Hamilton and Daniel Webster) stoutly emphasized the inherent antagonism between classes, while Jeffersonian and Jacksonian Democrats denied that class conflict was inevitable. Thus an arch-conservative Federalist, Chancellor Kent, argued in New York's Constitutional Convention of 1821 that "the tendency of universal suffrage is to jeopardize the rights of property," while an unknown liberal opponent replied, "Let us not, sir, disgrace ourselves in the eyes of the world, by expressing such degrading opinions of our fellow citizens." [60] When a majority of adult males won the vote in the 1820's and 1830's, conservative leaders began to use less insulting terms to describe them, while liberal leaders borrowed discarded conservative arguments about class differences.

Why the switch in arguments? If we recognize that politics is the pursuit of power, the change of positions is easy to understand. Before the Jacksonian Democrats had extended the right to vote, conservatives could hope to keep the suffrage restricted by alarming worthy citizens with the threat of lower-class hostility. In order to win the vote for their poorer supporters, on the other hand, the liberals had to argue that Americans were not separated by basic class differences. With suffrage extended, however, the desire of each group to win elections produced a different emphasis: conservatives wooed the new and poorer voters by maintaining that all Americans were really "one big happy (and classless) family"; liberals sought their votes by insisting that the interests of the "rich, well-born, and able" were opposed to those of the "common man."

[60] From debates in the New York Constitutional Convention of 1821, as quoted in Alpheus Thomas Mason, *Free Government in the Making: Readings in American Political Thought* (New York: Oxford University Press, 1949), pp. 400–405.

Class Differences in Political Participation at the Popular Level

Americans like to think that class differences are less acute in the United States than in Europe; indeed, some even insist that the idea of "classes" is alien to our way of life. Nor has there been a lack of evidence to support this point of view. George Gallup has reported, for example, that 88 per cent of our population say they are middle class whereas only 6 per cent identify themselves with the upper or lower classes. A *Fortune* magazine survey found that 79 per cent of the people identify themselves with the middle class. These findings do suggest that "class-consciousness" is of no real importance to American politics, that disagreements arise from individual rather than class differences.

But more rigorous research on class-awareness, and on the relationship of class to political behavior, tells quite a different story. The overwhelming middle-class identification reported in such surveys as those cited above appears to have come from a desire on the part of workers to avoid the term "lower class" when the choices were arbitrarily limited to upper, middle, or lower class. Whatever their actual positions in society, Americans seem hesitant to claim that they are "upper class," and loath to say that they are "lower class." A growing body of research in the last two decades has demonstrated that, when the more common term "working class" is added to the list of choices, a majority of Americans describe themselves as working class rather than middle class.[61] In 1964, for example (as Table 1-1 indicates), 56 per cent of the American electorate claimed

TABLE 1-1   *Subjective Class Identification of Adult Americans (1964)*

		PERCENTAGE SAYING
Middle class		39
Aware of social class [a]	23	
Unaware of social class [a]	16	
Working class		56
Aware of social class [a]	37	
Unaware of social class [a]	19	
Upper class		1
Reject idea of class		2
Don't know; not ascertained		2
Total ($N = 1,571$)		100.0

[a] Respondents were asked if they ever thought of themselves as belonging to the middle class or to the working class. The 60 per cent who said "yes" are labeled as "aware of social class"; the 35 per cent who said "no," but subsequently chose a class when asked to do so, are labeled as "unaware of social class."

Source: The 1964 presidential election survey conducted by the University of Michigan's Survey Research Center. It is based on a cross-sectional sample chosen by strict probability methods from all adult citizens living in private households in the United States. The authors are grateful to Aage Clausen, Study Director, for the special tabulation used for this table.

[61] So few people claim upper- or lower-class identification that some researchers have dropped these terms from their list of choices. See Richard Centers, *The Psychology of Social Classes* (Princeton: Princeton University Press, 1949); Joseph A. Kahl, *The American Class Structure* (New York: Rinehart and Company, Inc., 1957); and Campbell *et al.*, *The American Voter*.

working-class status, while 39 per cent said they were middle class. Rather than a homogenized middle-class America, then, the evidence reveals a population divided into a working-class majority and a middle-class minority.

How meaningful is this class-identification in political behavior? First, it has a direct impact on the basic question of who takes part in politics and who doesn't. Political activity may take many forms. Seeking information about public affairs through newspapers or TV, voting, attending campaign rallies, talking with others about elections and trying to influence their votes, giving money to a party or candidate, and becoming a candidate for public office are among the most common. Only a tiny minority ever seek public office, but we like to think that practically all citizens get involved in the mass forms of political participation. Political involvement is not scattered evenly throughout the population, however; *a greater proportion of middle-class than of working-class people are active in every form of political participation.* (For figures on participation in 1964 see Table 1-2.)

TABLE 1-2   *Political Participation in 1964 According to Class Identification*

FORM OF PARTICIPATION CLAIMED BY RESPONDENT	MIDDLE CLASS $N = 549$	WORKING CLASS $N = 788$
Voting [a]	86%	72%
Talking to others about voting for a party or candidate	40%	24%
Giving money, buying tickets, etc., to help the campaign of a party or candidate	16%	4%
Attending political meetings, rallies, etc.	14%	5%
Working for a party or candidate	8%	3%
Belonging to a political club or organization	5%	3%

[a] For an explanation of the larger proportions reporting voting than the proportion of people who actually voted (60.6 per cent), see Campbell *et al., The American Voter,* pp. 93–96.

Source: Data furnished by the University of Michigan's Survey Research Center. (See Table 1-1 for information on the sample.) Entries are proportions in each class who reported participation of the type indicated.

In Chapter 5, we shall try to explain why some people vote and why others don't. As for the class factor, we may briefly note here that working-class people, when compared with the middle class, have less control over their own time, are more absorbed in the task of meeting their immediate family needs, feel less effective and self-confident in public affairs, and have less information on how governmental policies affect them.[62] Our concern here is not, however, to account for class differences in participation; it is simply to demonstrate that class is a general factor in American politics, influencing every form of participation. Whether we assign Americans to classes according to their own choices or ac-

---

[62] For a more complete list of factors decreasing participation by lower-status people, see Robert E. Lane, *Political Life: Why People Get Involved in Politics* (Glencoe, Illinois: The Free Press, 1959), Chapter 16.

cording to some objective criterion (like income or education), the results remain basically the same: lower-status groups observe, discuss, and take part in politics less than do higher-status groups.

Class Differences in Chances for Political Leadership

Although class differences show up clearly in mass forms of political participation, perhaps a look at the impact of class in a second area will tell a different story. Does our population enjoy equal opportunities to assume political leadership? Is the log-cabin-to-White-House motif, so prominent in American folklore, an accurate reflection of the facts of political life? Or does class status tend to open the door for some and slam it to others? The fact that political participation is less common for lower-status groups does not necessarily mean that these groups contribute less than their share of top leaders; the smaller proportion of the working class who participate might be enough motivated to rise to the top.

The evidence indicates, however, that class differences are even more acute in chances for political leadership than in mass participation. Donald R. Matthews, in a systematic study of *The Social Background of Political Decision-Makers*,[63] demonstrates that class distinctions in American society apply to political leadership as well as to other areas of behavior. Certainly the United States has no caste-like élite with a monopoly over all high offices; but those of higher class origin do fill a disproportionately large number of political offices, while those from the lower strata fill relatively few.

Examining the occupations of the fathers of American officeholders (see Table 1-3), Matthews concludes: ". . . American political decision-makers . . .

TABLE 1-3 *Occupational Class of Fathers of American Political Decision-Makers*

OCCUPATIONAL CLASS OF FATHER	PRESIDENT, VICE-PRES., CABINET 1789–1934	HIGH-LEVEL CIVIL SERVANT 1940	U.S. SENATORS, 81ST CONGRESS 1949–51	U.S. REP., 77TH CONGRESS 1941–43	LABOR FORCE 1890 [b]
Professional	38%	28%	22%	31%	5%
Proprietors & officials	20	30	33	31	6
Farmers	38	29	40	29	26
Low-salaried workers	[a]	3	1	0	5
Wage-earners	4	10	3	9	36
Servants	0	0	0	0	7
Farm laborers	0	0	0	0	15
Unknown, unclassified	0	0	1	0	0
	100%	100%	100%	100%	100%
	(N = 311)	(N = 180)	(N = 109)	(N = 186)	

[a] Less than 1%.
[b] Subject to substantial error because of incomplete data.
Source: Matthews, *The Social Background of Political Decision-Makers*, p. 23.

[63] *The Social Background of Political Decision-Makers* (New York: Doubleday & Company, Inc., 1954).

are, with very few exceptions, sons of professional men, proprietors and officials, and farmers. A very small minority were the sons of wage earners, low-salaried workers, farm laborers or servants. When this fact is compared with the occupational distribution of the labor force in 1890 (about the median time of birth of all these groups except the first), the narrow base from which political decision-makers appear to be recruited is clear." [64]

Judged in terms of fathers' occupations, the impact of class on chances of political leadership is clear: 22 per cent of the population get 0.0 per cent of the offices considered, while 5 per cent of the population at the other extreme get an average of 30 per cent of the offices. Similar analyses in terms of race, ethnic origins, religion, education, and occupation lend further support to this point. In each case the group with higher social status enjoys a disproportionately large share of offices (in comparison with its proportion of the total population), while groups with lower status tend to be virtually excluded from office. The advantage lies, for each of these classifications, with: whites over Negroes; native-born over foreign-born, and immigrants from northwestern and central Europe and Canada over those from eastern and southern Europe and Asia; [65] Protestants (especially Congregational, Presbyterian, Episcopalian, and Unitarian) over Catholics and Jews; the highly educated over citizens at large; and lawyers over everyone else. [66]

The explanation of this upper- and upper-middle class domination of important political offices lies not in any "ruling-class" plot but in certain evident features of American society. First, only those at the upper level of the social scale are likely to enjoy the money, experience, and contacts required for active political life. Second, some occupations possess a greater degree of what social scientists call "role dispensability." Whereas the doctor or architect would find his professional competence impaired if he became preoccupied with politics, political activity is actually an advantage in the profession of the law; hence the lawyer's dominance in public office. Third, opportunities for rising to positions offering status, money, and leisure are highly unequal, with those who start nearer the top having a great advantage. Finally, as members of a stratified society with recognized symbols of success, even those citizens at the lower levels tend to prefer people of established "worth" as their representatives. [67]

In emphasizing unequal class opportunities, we must not forget that leaders of upper-class background sometimes become strong champions of the under-privileged. A group or class need not be *literally* represented in public office in

---

[64] *Ibid.*, pp. 23–24.

[65] In many areas it is a definite advantage to be a first- or second-generation American of a dominant ethnic group, but this generalization still holds for the country at large and especially for higher offices.

[66] See Matthews, *The Social Background of Political Decision-Makers*, pp. 24–32. John R. Schmidhauser has more recently reported similar findings on the social backgrounds of justices of the Supreme Court. See his *The Supreme Court* (New York: Holt, Rinehart and Winston, 1960), p. 32.

[67] Three of these four points may be found in Matthews, *The Social Background of Political Decision-Makers*, p. 32.

order to have access to and influence on the decision-making process. A given group may well find its most effective spokesman in an individual from a quite different class. But in terms of extent of personal participation, the class structure does serve to "freeze out" a sizeable portion of the total population.

Economic Influences on Politics

Discerning Americans have long realized that there is an intimate relationship between economics and politics. " 'Tis . . . certain that *property* in fact generally *confers* power, tho' the possessor of it may not have much more wit than a mole or a musquash," wrote James Otis almost two centuries ago.[68] James Madison, the "father" of our Constitution, put it this way: ". . . The most common and durable source of factions has been the various and unequal distribution of property. Those who hold and those who are without property have ever formed distinct interests in society. . . . *The regulation of these various and interfering interests forms the principal task of modern legislation. . . .*" [69]

The historian Charles A. Beard made this same point a century and a quarter later, in his controversial book, *An Economic Interpretation of the Constitution of the United States.*[70] Although Beard elaborated on Madison's thesis in explaining the ratification of the Constitution, he was condemned by the press for "insulting" the Founding Fathers! This ironic turn of events supports the assertion that, "In popular American mythology there has been a tendency to assume that economics and property relationships are areas of human interest and activity quite distinct, and properly so, from the political and governmental spheres. The fact that the myth has had little if any relation to historic conditions even in the United States has not shaken the faith of many that such an artificial line may be drawn." [71]

The Idea of Economics As Independent of Politics

What had happened in the 125 years between the publication of Madison's argument in *The Federalist* and Beard's restatement of the same position in his *Economic Interpretation?* What had encouraged the popular delusion that the Professor mistreated the memory of the Founding Father when he developed the same thesis—that economics conditions politics?

In the first place, America had turned to an exaltation of material values that was to make its way of life known as "Our Business Civilization." [72] Pre-

---

[68] James Otis, *The Rights of the British Colonies* (Columbia, Mo.: University of Missouri Studies, 1929), IV, p. 51.

[69] Alexander Hamilton, John Jay, and James Madison, *The Federalist* (New York: Random House, 1937), Modern Library Edition, p. 56.

[70] *An Economic Interpretation of the Constitution of the United States* (New York: The Macmillan Company, 1913).

[71] Richard C. Snyder and H. Hubert Wilson, *Roots of Political Behavior: Introduction to Government and Politics* (New York: American Book Company, 1949), p. 315.

[72] See, for example, James Truslow Adams, *Our Business Civilization* (New York: Boni, 1930).

occupied with the rugged job of civilizing a new continent, Americans had little time for intellectual or artistic pursuits. Since the most immediate problems were physical and tangible, the person who could accumulate things came to enjoy more respect than the person who could manipulate ideas. Clyde Kluckhohn underscores the American identification of worth with wealth in the comment, " 'Success' is measured by two automobiles—not by two mistresses as in some cultures." [73] The point was more bluntly made in the official organ of the Chamber of Commerce: "A man is worth the wages he can earn." [74] This exaltation of the material received something close to official sanction in 1893 when a justice of the United States Supreme Court explained human motivations in this fashion:

> The man who writes books, paints pictures, moulds statues, builds houses, pleads causes, preaches sermons, or heals the sick, does it for the money there is in it; and if, in so doing, he acquires a reputation as an author, painter, sculptor, architect, jurist, or physician, it is only an incident to his success as a money-getter. The motive which prompted Angelo to plan the dome of St. Peter, or paint the frescoes of the Sistine Chapel was essentially the same as that which induces a common laborer to lay brick or dig sewers. [75]

The Justice, in his exclusive emphasis on economics, might appear to have outdone both Madison and Beard, and to have rivaled Karl Marx. But notice that he meant to bestow unstinted praise on economic motivation, rather than to complain about the influence of economics on politics.

The idea that economics can be separated from politics was encouraged, in the second place, by the American's traditional distrust of authority. The first struggle against arbitrary power was directed at the British government, not at some powerful economic or social class. Developed during the revolutionary struggle to throw off British rule, the belief that government is a threat to freedom continued to flourish in nineteenth-century America. Although Americans today do not single out government as a particular target of suspicion, their generalized fear of authority seems to have taken a particularly anti-governmental form at least up to the twentieth century.

"Government is a necessary evil"—"That government is best which governs least"—these ideas were virtually beyond challenge to nineteenth-century Americans. To be sure, the people who recited such maxims were actually using the government to promote a variety of economic interests. The government was furnishing homesteads to settlers, subsidizing shipping interests, maintaining tariffs to protect American manufacturers from foreign competition, and building roads and canals to benefit western settlers. And yet the colonial distrust of government persisted—government was worthy of promoting economic interests but it could not be trusted to regulate them. Indeed, our natural resources were

---

[73] *Mirror for Man,* pp. 242–243.

[74] Eden Phillpotts, "A Reply to Socialism," *Nation's Business,* 17 (January, 1929), p. 26.

[75] Henry B. Brown, "The Distribution of Property," *Reports of American Bar Association* (Philadelphia: Dando Printing and Publishing Company, 1893), XVI, pp. 226–227.

so great and opportunities so widespread that voters had little reason to consider the government as a force for controlling the economy.

Once the frontier had disappeared and "big business" had begun to dominate the economy, however, farmers and workers started to demand that the government regulate business interests. Government interference in the economy—in the form of subsidies, land grants, and tariff benefits—had long been accepted as "the American system," but regulation was something new. Business interests suddenly began to complain that it was un-American for the government to tamper with the economy! And the anti-governmental bias of most Americans was so deep that they were blind to the inconsistency. Government controls over the economy were achieved later in the United States than in any other democracy.

Several nineteenth-century assumptions about economic behavior and institutions furnished a third support for the belief that economics could be separated from politics. Like the American's materialism and his distrust of government, these assumptions led to the idea that economics was an independent domain with which government had no proper concern.

First was the assumption that most people owned *private property*, and that ownership carried with it control over and responsibility for the management of that property. Second, *wealth* was thought of primarily in terms of such tangibles as wheat, buildings, shops, land, and ships. Third, *private enterprise* suggested an individual or a small group of partners actively engaged in directing a business they owned. Fourth, *individual initiative* was believed to enjoy wide latitude, with daring, ingenuity, and nonconformity reaping rich rewards. Fifth, the *profit motive* was conceived as the mainspring of progress, in view of man's innate desire for material acquisition. Sixth, *free competition* was thought to assure that the interests of consumers, laborers, and other businessmen could not be ignored without economic loss. Finally, permeating all these assumptions was the belief in a *natural economic order* in which the price mechanism guaranteed a just distribution of economic rewards.[76]

The reluctance with which these assumptions have been sloughed off (and the nostalgic stubbornness with which they are still invoked by some) can be explained by the fact that they worked so well for so long. Particularly suited to a young and growing nation rich in resources and on the threshold of the industrial revolution, they helped promote tremendous technological advancement, the spanning of a continent, and the development of a material standard of living that is the envy of the world. These assumptions were never held with complete seriousness or consistency, of course, but they were widely enough accepted to give business a relatively free hand in extending the nation and building its economic facilities. As Reinhold Niebuhr insists, we undoubtedly give our economic system and ourselves too much credit for America's economic progress; our prog-

---

[76] This series of assumptions is drawn primarily from Adolph A. Berle and Gardiner C. Means, *The Modern Corporation and Private Property* (New York: The Macmillan Company, 1932).

ress can be largely explained in terms of a fortuitous combination of undeveloped resources with the advent of the industrial revolution.

The Twentieth-Century American Economy

We have already seen that America's commitment to *laissez-faire* had never been quite genuine. The Constitution itself was at least in part an economic document, providing general protection for property, insuring the rights of creditors, and preserving the binding force of contracts. In 1789, the first session of the First Congress of the United States violated free competition by establishing tariffs and providing subsidies for shipping interests. Later, the disposal of the free land of the West served as a vast public relief program. In fact, government promotion of economic interests has marked our entire political history. *Laissez-faire* and free enterprise have been enthusiastically displayed whenever government regulation was mentioned, but they were hidden away when the question of government aid came up.

With the closing of the frontier and the development of a corporate economy, more serious defects showed themselves in the old assumptions. The severe depression of the 1930's convinced many thoughtful Americans that economics could not be separated from politics. Adolph A. Berle and Gardiner C. Means, in their study of *The Modern Corporation and Private Property*, pointed out in 1932 that the classical economic theory dating from Adam Smith's eighteenth-century writings was not applicable to the realities of the twentieth century.

Private property is no longer widely owned, and it plays a less influential role in our economy than it did a century ago. Small plants, privately owned and managed, still exist, but they produce only a small part of our industrial output. The important property now is not really private; it is found in the business corporation's great *instruments of production*. These are quite unlike the old blacksmith's hammer and anvil—they are huge machines and complicated plants too costly to be owned by a single person. Thousands of stockholders legally "own" these industrial plants, but most stockholders never see "their" plant and would have no idea of how to manage it. The property is actually controlled by a corps of non-owning managers, not by a private owner. Similarly, *wealth* has taken on new meanings. It refers more often to *intangible rights* to income from corporate stocks and bonds than to such tangible things as buildings, land, or ships.

The *private enterprise*, then, has been replaced by the *corporate enterprise* as America's dominant economic unit. And a modern corporation hardly resembles a private shop. In the small private enterprise, the same person is typically owner, worker, and manager; in the corporation, some people (stockholders) are owners, others are workers, and still others are managers. The corporation is a device, then, for combining the money, labor, and managerial skills of many people under unified direction. Without the unified efforts of all these people, we could not enjoy such intricate products as airplanes and television sets. Such unified efforts, however, cannot be achieved without sacrificing *individual initiative* in the interest of *conformity*; careful coordination geared to the assembly line cannot tolerate wide personal deviation from the prescribed routine. The rugged individualist of frontier days has been replaced by the "organization man" who can follow orders and cooperate with fellow members of the "team."

The *profit motive* that classical economists thought of as underlying all economic activity has also been drastically modified. The profits of a modern corporation go to the stockholders, not to those who actually direct the work of the enterprise. Since the top directors do not receive the profits, they must be motivated by the desire for other rewards, such as large *salaries*, generous *bonuses*, extravagant *expense accounts*, and the *prestige* that comes from exercising *power* over other people. Formerly, it was assumed that the drive of many concerns competing for profit would produce *free competition*, which in turn would keep prices down to a "natural" level at which only the most efficient individuals could prosper. But today most sectors of the economy—such as automobiles, steel, and oil—are dominated by a few large concerns, which compete for sales through advertising wars rather than through price wars. These industrial giants *fix prices by administrative decision* rather than leaving them to be fixed by the uncertainties of consumer demand. And, as the Senate Subcommittee on Antitrust and Monopoly revealed in 1961, the giants sometimes get together and *fix prices by collusion.*

Finally, the underlying assumption of a *natural economic order* has come to sound increasingly anachronistic in the twentieth century. Anthropologists were demonstrating in the 1920's that what seems "natural" at one time or in one place may seem quite "unnatural" at another time or in another place. The anthropologists' term for describing these variations in values from one society to another—*cultural relativity*—is now an accepted part of the vocabulary of most literate Americans. And the concept of cultural relativity does not fit well with the idea that a single economic order is "natural" (and therefore "right") for all men at all times. In particular, how could *laissez-faire*—leaving nature alone—be justified in view of the fact that most human progress has been made by *controlling the forces of nature?* "Unnatural" levees prevent annual floods, and careful interference with nature breeds grain and roses in lieu of weeds. In brief, the laws of men are sometimes preferred to the laws of nature.

What are the basic characteristics of the new industrial order that has undermined the nineteenth-century assumptions? At the beginning of World War II, Merle Fainsod and Lincoln Gordon, careful students of this problem, described the high points of our economy in terms of seven key features:

1. Considerable unevenness in the distribution of income.

2. Dominance of industry by large-scale enterprise.

3. Considerable concentration of control over economic activity, particularly in certain areas.

4. A consequent decline of competition in many areas.

5. The organization of hitherto little-organized groups—such as labor—for effective economic action.

6. Signs of increasing maturity, such as a decline in the rate of economic growth.

7. An increasingly important, positive role on the part of government.[77]

Most of these pre-World War II characteristics still apply to our economy. The dominance of industry by large-scale enterprise, for example, continued in the postwar period. In 1954, as in 1935, the 200 largest manufacturing companies accounted for 37 per cent of the total value of the product of all such firms.[78] Control over such a tremendous portion of the economy carries with it the power to make decisions that affect every citizen in the nation.

The first feature stressed by Fainsod and Gordon—unevenness in the distribution of income—was de-emphasized throughout the 1950's and into the 1960's. In America's dual stress on equality and achievement, equality tends to be emphasized during some periods and achievement during others. During the '50's and early '60's, our focus was decidedly on conditions associated with achievement. The general assumption was that America had solved the problem of extreme economic inequality and needed to turn to the problems of general affluence.

In 1952, an eminent commentator wrote about *The Big Change*, "the democratization of our economic system" since early in the century when poverty was a problem.[79] A year later, a former New Deal Director of the Tennessee Valley Authority, once damned for allegedly socialistic proclivities, submitted that "today one finds the physical benefits of our society distributed widely, to almost everyone, with scant regard to status, class, or origin of the individual.[80] In 1958, John Kenneth Galbraith, a prominent Harvard economist, analyzed our problems as those of *The Affluent Society*.[81]

Most of these points were not invalid; they simply focused on what has admittedly been an impressive achievement and on the problems that it has brought. In 1963, however, Michael Harrington shifted the focus in a popular and influential book, *The Other America*—the America of "internal exiles," people living in a land of luxury but trapped themselves in a cycle of poverty.[82] Because the truly poor live off the beaten track—along rutted roads around Pennsylvania mining towns, in city tenements only glimpsed from the trains or the freeways that

---

[77] *Government and the American Economy* (New York: W. W. Norton and Company, 1948), pp. 16–20. Insofar as differences in the form of presentation permit, this list is a direct quotation. The third edition of this book (1959) discusses changes since World War II.

[78] These figures are from the Report of the Subcommittee on Antitrust and Monopoly, *Concentration in American Industry*, 85th Cong., 1st Sess., 1957, p. 11; and a report of the Federal Trade Commission, *Changes in Concentration in Manufacturing, 1935 to 1947 and 1950* (Washington, D.C.: Government Printing Office, 1954), p. 115. See also Robert J. Lampman, *The Share of Top Wealth-Holders in National Wealth, 1922–56* (Princeton: Princeton University Press, 1962).

[79] Frederick Lewis Allen, *The Big Change* (New York: Harper & Brothers, 1952), p. ix.

[80] David Lilienthal, *Big Business: A New Era* (New York: Harper & Brothers, 1953), pp. 95ff.

[81] John Kenneth Galbraith, *The Affluent Society* (Boston: Houghton Mifflin Company, 1958).

[82] Michael Harrington, *The Other America* (Baltimore: Penguin Books, 1964). Originally published in 1963 by The Macmillan Company.

lead to suburbia—the other America is less visible than ever before. But such people as the poor farmers, the unskilled workers, and the minority groups who suffer from a combination of slum dwellings, poor schools, and restricted opportunities do not share in the general prosperity. Harrington's shocking conclusion was that America's poor include, at a minimum, some 32,000,000 people and that the figure probably approaches 50,000,000. To say that these people are better off than the average citizen of Hong Kong or than the medieval upper class is not, Harrington submits, relevant to their needs. "The American poor are not poor in Hong Kong or in the sixteenth century; they are poor here and now, in the United States. They are dispossessed in terms of what the rest of the nation enjoys. . . . They live on the fringe, the margin. They watch the movies and read the magazines of affluent America, and these tell them that they are internal exiles." [83]

Many Americans, accustomed to hearing about our high standard of living, find it hard to believe that 20 to 25 per cent of their fellow citizens share none of the prosperity of which we boast. For one thing, the cheapest foods are fattening, so when we do see the poor they do not look emaciated. Then again, most of us are unaware that, partly because of our poverty and partly because of our lack of general medical assistance programs, our infant mortality rate is higher than that of ten other countries.[84] Unpleasant statistics of this sort seldom receive much attention. And for those statistically minded, figures on family income look better every year, even for our poorer citizens.

The dollar income of almost all Americans has been going up, partly as a result of general increases in prosperity and partly as a result of gradual inflation, which means that a dollar today buys much less than it did during earlier periods. The extent to which inequalities have been reduced can therefore be approached better by finding out what proportion of the nation's total personal income a group receives than by examining its dollar income.

If we divide America's families and unattached individuals into ten groups, from the poorest to the richest, and look at their shares of the national income, the persistence of extreme inequality is startling. Table 1-4 shows that the share of the poorest tenth in 1910 was only 3.4 per cent of the national personal income. By 1959, this low proportion had *dropped* to a depressing 1.1 per cent! Indeed, if we total the portion of the national income received by half the population in the five lowest groups, we find a decrease from 26.8 to 22.7 per cent of the nation's personal income. At the other extreme, the best rewarded tenth of the population enjoyed 33.9 per cent of the income in 1910 and 28.9 per cent 50 years later. The extreme inequalities of which Fainsod and Gordon spoke show no signs of disappearing.

The income tax is supposed to reduce these inequalities, but its effect is less than one would gather from the pained protests of those in the upper tax brackets. Those with the highest incomes enjoy advice from the best tax experts, and

---

[83] *Ibid.,* p. 190.

[84] See Gabriel Kolko, *Wealth and Power in America* (New York: Frederick A. Praeger, Publisher, 1964), p. ix. Except for the Preface, this is a second printing with 1962 as the original publication date.

TABLE 1-4 *Percentage of National Personal Income, Before Taxes, Received by Each Income-Tenth* [a]

	HIGHEST TENTH	2ND	3RD	4TH	5TH	6TH	7TH	8TH	9TH	LOWEST TENTH
1910	33.9	12.3	10.2	8.8	8.0	7.0	6.0	5.5	4.9	3.4
1918	34.5	12.9	9.6	8.7	7.7	7.2	6.9	5.7	4.4	2.4
1921	38.2	12.8	10.5	8.9	7.4	6.5	5.9	4.6	3.2	2.0
1929	39.0	12.3	9.8	9.0	7.9	6.5	5.5	4.6	3.6	1.8
1934	33.6	13.1	11.0	9.4	8.2	7.3	6.2	5.3	3.8	2.1
1937	34.4	14.1	11.7	10.1	8.5	7.2	6.0	4.4	2.6	1.0
1941	34.0	16.0	12.0	10.0	9.0	7.0	5.0	4.0	2.0	1.0
1945	29.0	16.0	13.0	11.0	9.0	7.0	6.0	5.0	3.0	1.0
1946	32.0	15.0	12.0	10.0	9.0	7.0	6.0	5.0	3.0	1.0
1947	33.5	14.8	11.7	9.9	8.5	7.1	5.8	4.4	3.1	1.2
1948	30.9	14.7	11.9	10.1	8.8	7.5	6.3	5.0	3.3	1.4
1949	29.8	15.5	12.5	10.6	9.1	7.7	6.2	4.7	3.1	0.8
1950	28.7	15.4	12.7	10.8	9.3	7.8	6.3	4.9	3.2	0.9
1951	30.9	15.0	12.3	10.6	8.9	7.6	6.3	4.7	2.9	0.8
1952	29.5	15.3	12.4	10.6	9.1	7.7	6.4	4.9	3.1	1.0
1953	31.4	14.8	11.9	10.3	8.9	7.6	6.2	4.7	3.0	1.2
1954	29.3	15.3	12.4	10.7	9.1	7.7	6.4	4.8	3.1	1.2
1955	29.7	15.7	12.7	10.8	9.1	7.7	6.1	4.5	2.7	1.0
1956	30.6	15.3	12.3	10.5	9.0	7.6	6.1	4.5	2.8	1.3
1957	29.4	15.5	12.7	10.8	9.2	7.7	6.1	4.5	2.9	1.3
1958	27.1	16.3	13.2	11.0	9.4	7.8	6.2	4.6	3.1	1.3
1959	28.9	15.8	12.7	10.7	9.2	7.8	6.3	4.6	2.9	1.1

[a] In terms of "recipients" for 1910–1937 and "spending units" for 1941–1959.

Source: Gabriel Kolko, *Wealth and Power in America: An Analysis of Social Class and Income Distribution* (New York: Frederick A. Praeger, Publisher, 1962), p. 14.

Congress has provided countless loopholes through which they can earn their fees. Before the 1964 revision of the income tax, for example, the theoretical maximum tax was 91 per cent. But the average tax of individuals earning over a million dollars a year was 42 per cent.[85] As a move to "combat poverty," the theoretical maximum tax was reduced to 70 per cent in 1964. Aside from tax loopholes, the most affluent Americans also enjoy benefits from corporate hunting lodges, yachts, safaris to Africa, "business" trips to Paris, and expense accounts, none of which counts as "income." Finally, 9 to 14 per cent of the nation's personal income is not reported on income-tax returns, and most of the oversight comes from those with the highest incomes. Since the salaried worker has all of his income tax withdrawn before he receives his pay check, the inequality in American incomes is not greatly decreased by our system of taxation.[86]

Although the share of the national income received by the poor has not

[85] Kolko, *Wealth and Power in America*, p. viii.

[86] Indeed, since most state and local taxes are regressive (taking a greater percentage of income from the poor than the rich), the percentage of income paid in all taxes does not vary as much as expected from one income level to another. Those who receive less than $2,000 a year pay about 21 per cent of their income in taxes, compared with 22

increased, their purchasing power has. Moreover, they are the chief beneficiaries of expanded government services, such as public parks and hot lunches in the schools, that are—like the corporate expenditures enjoyed by the wealthy—ignored in most studies of personal income. The poor may be as deprived as ever in comparison with their fellow citizens, but their absolute standard of living has improved. The United States Department of Health, Education, and Welfare (HEW) reported in 1964 that the number of families with incomes below $3,000 (measured in terms of the 1962 value of the dollar) had decreased from 32 per cent in 1947 to 20 per cent in 1962.[87] Recognizing that perfect agreement on the dividing line between poverty (inability to satisfy basic and irreducible needs) and a minimum standard of subsistence is impossible, HEW conservatively estimated the number of impoverished Americans at 35,000,000, one-fifth of the population.

Back in the depression years of the 1930's, President Franklin Roosevelt called for a New Deal because of the shameful fact that one-third of our nation was "ill-fed, ill-housed, and ill-clothed." After more than a generation of prosperity, we have reduced this proportion by a little more than ten percentage points, but the absolute number of people enduring poverty has hardly decreased at all. In 1964, President Lyndon Johnson's call for a War on Poverty shifted America's attention from the problems of achievement back to the needs of equality.[88] But the proposal was for a limited war, calling for expenditures of only $970 million, 1 per cent of the national budget. That the program sounded radical to many people, in and out of Congress, attests to the continued importance of our nineteenth-century economic assumptions, bias against government interference, and materialism. After all, we happily spend over $10 *billion* a year on advertising, spending the nation's resources to create new desires often for bizarre products.

Although any corporation that did not enlarge its budget and its outstanding stock (that is, its debt) would be regarded as a poor risk, President Johnson had to juggle figures to make his new program appear *not* to enlarge the national budget. Rather than regarding an expanding budget and debt as a sign of strength, as we do for business corporations, we view such signs of activity by government with suspicion. So long as we view production for the satisfaction of private wants as the all-important goal of our economy and look on public services as a necessary evil, this contrast will continue. We will continue to regard the manufacture of school toilet seats as an increase in our wealth and education itself as a burden. We will manufacture more and bigger automobiles, and waste precious hours looking for space to park them.

Why do we emphasize private production for even the most dubious needs

---

per cent for those with $10,000–15,000 incomes and 34 per cent for those with over $15,000. The data in the footnote and in the preceding paragraph are from Kolko, *Wealth and Power in America*, p. 37 and *passim*.

[87] *Health, Education, and Welfare Indicators*, February, 1964, p. ix.

[88] *The War on Poverty: The Economic Opportunity Act of 1964*, a compilation of materials relevant to S. 2642 prepared for the Select Subcommittee on Poverty of the Committee on Labor and Public Welfare, United States Senate, 88th Congress, 2nd Session (Washington, D.C.: U.S. Government Printing Office, 1964).

and neglect public services of the most pressing sort? The answer is, at least in part, that we continue to think of economics as a private sphere that operates best without government interference. "To suggest that we canvass our public wants to see where happiness can be improved by more and better [government] services has a sharply radical tone . . . ," Professor Galbraith submits. "By contrast the man who devises a nostrum for a nonexistent need and then successfully promotes both remains one of nature's noblemen." [89] Galbraith's underlying theme is that our real problem is not *how much* but *what* we should produce, and for *whose benefit*.[90] If the decision about what should be produced were made deliberately, he says it would almost inevitably involve increased control by the government over economics.

Despite our long-standing prejudice to the contrary, politics and economics have in fact grown ever more interdependent, and the process has been hastened by a relatively recent phenomenon that can be described as a "balance of bigness." The political response to "big business" has been the development of "big government," and both have stimulated the emergence of "big labor" as another powerful "countervailing" force. Indeed, in our "mixed" economy of today, government and economics have become virtually inseparable. We are not socialistic in any doctrinaire sense, as the existence of private control of key instruments of production like the railway and steel industries attests. But neither are we capitalistic or *laissez-faire* in any doctrinaire sense, as our publicly owned and operated schools, highways, post offices, and power plants attest. Even such apparently private enterprises as railroads and power companies are subject to a variety of government regulations. In short, much of our industry—and our economy as a whole—stands between the extremes of *laissez-faire* and socialism.

Although it is the way we conduct our politics that primarily distinguishes American democracy from other systems of government, our politics itself is a part of the more general pattern of human interactions that we call "the American way of life." Beginning with the American culture at the most general level, we have suggested how culture and the related factors of the natural environment, population, class structure, and economics affect government. With this broad cultural picture in mind, we shall turn now to the context of ideas that shapes our government.

---

[89] *The Affluent Society*, p. 269.

[90] On the latter, see his article, "Let Us Begin: An Invitation to Action on Poverty," *Harper's*, March, 1964, pp. 16–26.

CHAPTER TWO

The Context of Ideas

Democracy is more than a way of governing; it is also an idea. And ideas are the key to understanding human behavior. The carpenter who helps build a house, the clerk who sells shoes, the lawyer who defends the property rights of his client—all may be convinced that they are dealing more directly with "reality" than the student of ideas. But the way we produce, distribute, protect, and evaluate material objects stems from those elusive human attributes variously called opinions, myths, stereotypes, prejudices, convictions, or principles. American politics, like any other facet of our behavior, may be understood only within the context of the ideas that shape our lives.

Men have interests of the sort that we mentioned in the preceding chapter, but they also have beliefs and ideas *about* those interests. Intangible though they are, beliefs exert the most powerful control over behavior. During disputes over concrete economic interests, businessmen and labor spokesmen sometimes show a dedication to "principle" that cannot be shaken even by the threat of financial loss. Voluntary sacrifices in time of war demonstrate the force of national beliefs and ideas on countless citizens, from the Boy Scout who collects scrap iron to the soldier who volunteers for combat duty.

In the United States the general pattern of ideas that pervades politics—and against which we judge politicians—is found in democratic political theory. Public opinion surveys have shown that an overwhelming majority of Americans regard democracy as the only proper form of government. And apparently this conviction is just as strong at the official level, as anyone who has ever been exposed to Fourth of July oratory can testify.

Democratic Political Theory

Just what do we mean when we claim to be democratic? There is no simple, ready-made answer. The model state of communism or fascism is relatively easy to define, but the ideals of democracy are much more elusive.

Democracy is more ambiguous than ideologies with a fixed creed. Indeed, the whole notion of democracy revolves around the belief that each generation can fix its own goals. A contemporary political scientist, employing formal logic to produce a "rational justification" of the superiority of democracy to other forms of government, proposes this as the ultimate "must" of democracy: "Do not block the possibility of *change* with respect to social goals." [1] Despite the emphasis on change in democratic beliefs, political philosophers have identified several ideals as implicit in any democratic society.

Like the traits of "national character," these ideals are based in large measure on "educated intuition." Philosophers, more library-oriented than anthropologists, can perhaps claim the advantage in terms of formal education. Anthropologists, through field trips not experienced by philosophers, may claim the advantage of richer intuitive insights. For the most part, neither can claim that his propositions are supported by systematic empirical observation. Nevertheless, political philosophers offer helpful commentaries on the ideals logically implied by a democratic way of life just as anthropologists furnish us helpful clues on national character.

---

[1] Thomas L. Thorson, *The Logic of Democracy* (New York: Holt, Rinehart and Winston, 1962), p. 139. Emphasis added.

Any political philosophy is built on a few guiding beliefs or assumptions about the nature of man, the nature of society, and the nature of politics. Half a dozen beliefs of this sort characterize classical democratic theory. The democratic view of the nature of man is based on the principles of *equality* and *humanitarianism;* the democratic view of the nature of society is based on the principles of *individualism* and *progress;* the democratic view of the nature of politics is based on the principles of *majority rule* and *minority rights.* Democratic theory leans on these beliefs—equality, humanitarianism, individualism, progress, majority rule, minority rights—and from them gains its enduring appeal.

10 Q

The Democratic View of Man

The most fundamental belief of democratic theory—that which distinguishes it from all other political creeds—is the concept of *equality*. Critics of democracy like to sneer that any obstetrician can explode the myth that "all men are created equal," since it is obvious that they come in a great variety of sizes, shapes, and colors, and with a great range of endowments. But this is an attack on a straw man. Even Thomas Jefferson, the patron saint of America's equalitarian tradition, recognized that people are unequal in talent and virtue no less than in appearance. What Jefferson and other equalitarians insist on is that differences in prestige and position should not be determined before birth, that they should reflect unequal talents rather than unequal opportunities, personal ability rather than artificial advantage.

People are not so alike as so many identical twins, but neither are they so different that they must be classified into different species. Since potential ability may turn up anywhere, in the slum as well as in the mansion, democratic theory disapproves of inherited privileges. Hereditary leadership in politics or business is as senseless as a hereditary professorship in political science. Simply by virtue of their common humanity, all men share equally an intrinsic moral worth. They ought, therefore, to have equal opportunity to develop their own personalities according to their inclinations and their abilities.

The democratic view of human nature adds the concept of *humanitarianism* to the belief in equality. Despite his capacity for evil, man is viewed as somewhat closer to the angels than to unreasoning animals. Although this idea has led some enthusiasts to believe in human perfectibility, realistic democratic theory makes the more modest claim that man's capacity for good outweighs his potential for evil. Conflict arises wherever men live together, but so does cooperation. And since cooperation is necessary even in waging conflict, it appears to be more basic to human nature. Controversy and competition lend zest to life, but it is man's cooperative efforts that make social life possible.

Both *laissez-faire* and Marxian materialists picture man as a helpless pawn of economic forces—forces that he may understand but cannot direct. Democratic theory, however, insists that man is capable of pursuing humane values. Trying to control his own destiny, but tinged even in the attempt with concern for the welfare of others, man has demonstrated an inextinguishable desire to grope for a broader good than pure self-interest. The willingness of the Soviet government to starve millions of peasants in order to establish collectivized agriculture seems incomprehensible to the democrat. Even if the objective itself were desirable, he feels that nothing could justify such a deliberate forfeiture of human life. Democracy will not choose human suffering in the "long-run" interest of any abstract system; its humanitarian bent simply will not permit the sanctity of human life to be forgotten.

The Democratic Concept of Society

Extended from man to society, the principles of equality and humanitarianism take the form of *individualism* and *progress*. The democrat evaluates the processes, institutions, and power structure of society according to the effect they have on the individual. Regarding society as nothing more than interrelationships among individuals, democratic thought rejects the idea of any "national interest" separate from the needs of the citizens. The democrat thinks it absurd to sacrifice the welfare of the citizen for that of the "fatherland"; for him the fatherland exists only to promote the welfare of its citizens and to secure their "rights" as individuals.

Similarly, democratic theory puts a higher value on the individual than on any segment of society. It recognizes that the military, the church, the academic, and the business communities all make important contributions to society, but it gives none of them pre-eminent status. A former head of General Motors turned Secretary of Defense touched off an uproar early in the Eisenhower Administration when he was quoted as having innocently remarked that "What's good for General Motors is good for the country." [2] The resulting excitement stemmed, not from disrespect for General Motors, but from the conviction that the general welfare *begins* with the welfare of the individuals who constitute the society. Other values are important, of course, but they are secondary to individual freedom. Whether the argument is for "freedom of enterprise" or "freedom from economic royalists," "academic freedom" or "freedom from propaganda," democratic theory judges the argument by what it means for the individual as a free agent.

Democratic thought is dedicated to the irrepressible ideal of progress. Indeed, the ideals we have already mentioned virtually demand the inclusion of progress in the democratic creed, for most governments throughout history have violated the democratic ideals of equality, humanitarianism, and individualism. A democrat living under an undemocratic regime must either believe in progress or else abandon his other political beliefs. Although we need no longer agree with Rousseau that "man is born free but everywhere in chains," anyone who is committed to the ideals of equality and humanitarianism can always find ways to improve the lot of the individual.

---

[2] This remark was attributed to Charles Wilson during hearings before the Senate Armed Services Committee on his nomination to the office of Secretary of Defense. The record shows that, in response to a question about whether he could make a decision "extremely adverse to the company, in the interests of the United States Government," he actually said: "Yes, sir; I could. I cannot conceive of one because for years I thought what was good for our country was good for General Motors, and vice versa. The difference did not exist." See *Hearings* before the Committee on Armed Services, United States Senate, 83rd Cong., 1st Sess., January 15, 1953, p. 26.

Social conditions undergo constant change, and it is the task of democracy to translate this change into progress. At the very heart of democracy is the continuing attempt to direct rather than to thwart change. New forms of privilege and new threats to the individual constantly crop up to replace the old, making it impossible for democracy to be permanently satisfied with any set of policies or of governmental agencies. The progress exalted by democratic theory consequently takes two forms. First, there is the constant attempt to bring society closer and closer to the basic values of democracy. Second, there is the constant attempt to improve policies and institutions so that the gains that have already been won will not be lost in a changing world.

The Democratic Theory of Government

What happens when we apply this rather abstract democratic theory to actual government? The central principles of government based on democratic theory are majority rule and minority rights. Taken together, these principles constitute the briefest possible definition of democracy. The simple phrase "majority rule and minority rights" can only hint at the complex attitudes and habits that undergird democracy. When the implications of these principles are spelled out, however, they appear as satisfactory as any other capsule phrase for summarizing the basic beliefs about democratic government.

If we genuinely accept the principles of equality and individualism in our appraisal of man and society, we must inevitably embrace the idea of *majoritarianism* in the conduct of government. If men are basically equal, and if each has an inherent moral worth by virtue of his humanity, no individual or group can have a monopoly on truth. From this viewpoint, the only way we can approach truth is through the free flow of ideas, through the process of give-and-take by which a wide variety of special "truths" are compromised. This means that each individual must enjoy the freedom to work out and contribute his own version of truth. And, since self-development requires self-government, the democratic theory in government is firmly based on the concept of popular consent or majority rule.

The ambiguity of democratic theory stems largely from an apparent conflict between *majority rule* and the equally basic principle of *minority rights*.[3] In its extreme form, majoritarianism holds that the majority view is always right; in less extreme form, that it must always be followed, right or wrong. But democracy holds some freedoms to be "unalienable rights," beyond the reach even of majority preference. Since absolute truth has been revealed to no one, the majority is quite capable of making mistakes. And the individual who finds himself temporarily in a minority does not automatically renounce his own beliefs to adopt the majority opinion. There is no need for him to submerge his individuality in the majority. Those who voted for Stevenson in 1956 did not suddenly decide that Eisenhower was after all the better candidate, nor did the Goldwater supporters

---

[3] For a strong majoritarian statement, see Henry Steele Commager, *Majority Rule and Minority Rights* (Gloucester, Mass.: Peter Smith, 1943). For a strong defense of minority rights, see Walter Lippmann, *Essays in the Public Philosophy* (Boston: Little, Brown and Company, 1955).

of 1964 switch their preference to Johnson as soon as the election returns were in. They accepted the outcome, however, as if the majority had been correct and as if they had been in error. At the same time, they reserved the right to insist that the majority was dead wrong and to work actively against the policies of the new government.

The majority-minority relationship in a free election is, when you stop to think about it, a wondrous thing. But, as described, it does not pose the potential conflict between majority rule and minority rights in its most difficult form. Minority acceptance of the majority's victory could reflect realistic acceptance of the fact that one is out-numbered and that defiance would be suppressed. For the winners, who exercise the power of government, to respect the rights of the losers requires self-restraint rather than simply a sense of being restrained. What if the majority denies the right of the minority to oppose the new government, or even to enjoy other basic freedoms such as the right to a fair trial? Does democratic theory choose majority rule or minority rights?

Absolute majoritarianism says the majority decision must be followed. If today's majority declares opposition unconstitutional, democracy will be extinguished. Such risks are among the costs of democracy; putting its faith in majority rule, democracy must accept the possibility of mistaken judgments without cringing. At worst, says absolute majoritarianism, the people may destroy democracy by endorsing a dictatorship that eventually eliminates majority rule no less than minority rights. But majority preference cannot be denied; one can only hope that self-restraint and self-education will come to the majority through a realization that it has erred.

Much can be said for this argument, but democratic theory has generally emphasized the principle of minority rights as a restraint essential to majority rule itself. The Declaration of Independence may have placed somewhat more emphasis on majority rule and the Constitution may have been somewhat more concerned with minority rights, but both principles are clearly present in both documents. The general theory underlying this interpretation is that no individual or group can have absolute power. Not even the majority is competent to speak perfectly or permanently for all. If such competence were granted, at the cost of minority rights, majority rule itself could not survive. For majority rule to exist as a *continuing* principle, today's minority must have a chance to become tomorrow's majority. Majoritarianism thus implies the corollary principle of minority rights.

What Is Democratic Government?

Democracy As One Way of Governing

If the "man in the street" were asked to define the different systems of government, he would probably find it very difficult to engage in such abstractions. A few who are well-read and articulate might reply that democracy is government by the many, that aristocracy or oligarchy is government by the few, and that monarchy or dictatorship is government by one. Actually, this definition is neither clear nor true. But it has been offered since Aristotle's day, and it consequently enjoys so much prestige that it occasionally crops up even among contemporary political scientists. In fact, simply because it is physically impossible to bring them all together, "the many" can never participate directly in the process of governing. The Greek city-state would not qualify as a democracy on this count, since only a minority were citizens; and even the famous New England town-meeting of colonial times appears to have been controlled by interested minorities, such as Sam Adams' Caucus Club. The full-time task of governing is always allocated to a relatively few specialists.

At the other extreme, no one person can govern by himself, because it is physically impossible for him to make all the important decisions that must be made. Hitler and Stalin may have enjoyed much more power than any other single individual, but neither was able to govern entirely by himself. Even in the most totalitarian nation, there is always a small core of the party faithful who share in the burdens of government.

Government, then, is always by the few. To identify different forms of government by the proportion of citizens who take part in governing is therefore not feasible. The effort is as pointless as trying to identify a bird as a pigeon, eagle, or robin by asking whether it has one, two, or four wings— all birds have two wings and all governments are conducted by a small minority of the citizens. We may accordingly discard the idea that democracy is government by the many and that dictatorship or monarchy is government by one.

If all governments are by the few, we must find some grounds other than the number of rulers for distinguishing between different political systems. The most important feature that varies from one government to another is the *relationship* between the governing few and the governed many. Where a responsible relationship exists, we may say that democracy exists, regardless of the structure of government, the content of policy, or the number or quality of the rulers. Where the relationship is irresponsible, the government is an oligarchy or—in more contemporary terms—a dictatorship.

Democracy is singularly lacking in dogmas; it is without absolutes. There is no democratic theorist, comparable to Karl Marx for the communists, to whom we can turn for the "correct" attitude on every problem. Indeed, to identify democracy with a single formula would be to reject its very essence. Notice that we have come right back to the two basic principles of the democratic theory of government. These principles refer to a *method* of governing—or, more precisely, to a method of deciding who shall govern—rather than to a complete, fixed creed. This means that we can identify democracy by two essential features: (1) *majority rule*, which exists so long as the public at large is free to choose the men who make public policies, and (2) *minority rights*, which exist so long as those in the minority may openly attempt to win majority support for different leaders and policies without a loss of the individual rights enjoyed by the majority. Notice that democratic theory puts only one restriction on majority rule. It forbids that anyone be denied individual freedoms because he opposes the majority, either as an individual or as part of a concerted effort to persuade a majority to join the opposition.

Actually, of course, no government meets these two standards in an absolute sense. No democracy insures the perfect and continuous response of rulers to majority opinion; and no democracy tolerates freedom of dissent to the extent of permitting dissenters to overthrow the government by force or violence. Conversely, even the most totalitarian regime covets the support of the majority and may even permit some freedom for dissenters. Neither democracy nor dictatorship, in other words, reaches the logical extremity of its principles in terms of actual practice.

And yet we can use these two features—majority rule and minority rights—as criteria for identifying some governments as democratic and others as dictatorial. If we were allowed to ask only two questions in trying to identify any government as democratic or dictatorial, we would first ask: Are its rulers chosen by the votes of a majority? A country in which elections are hard fought between opposing parties, neither of which is certain of victory, insures enough government responsibility to the voters to be meaningfully called a democracy. On the other hand, a country where the voters can only approve the official slate, with no chance to choose between candidates, provides nothing more than false majority rule; it must be called dictatorial. Second, we would ask: Do the losers —the minority—enjoy the same basic rights in relation to government as the majority, including the freedom to make demands on the government and to advocate the selection of new leaders in the next election? If minorities are free to agitate, organize, and propagandize for the peaceful overthrow of the ruling party without fear of punishment, they are "free" in the democratic sense. But if dissenting minorities are punished for demonstrating their opposition to the ruling party, they are "unfree" in the democratic sense.[4]

Basic Institutions of Democratic Government

When our discussion shifted from democratic theory to democratic government, you may have noticed that we began to mention some of the institutions (such as political parties and elections) through which the theory expresses itself in concrete situations. This is because democratic government depends on certain peculiar institutions, some official and some unofficial. For free communication of ideas, we rely on such agencies as the press, pressure groups, and the schools. The very first article in the American Bill of Rights guarantees freedom of speech, freedom of press, and freedom of association. As Justice William Douglas has pointed out, "Full and free discussion has indeed been the first article of our faith. We have founded our political system on it."[5] When the institutions by which public opinion is formed and expressed begin to lose their vigor, democracy itself is in danger. If majorities and minorities are to discover the areas in which they agree and the areas in which they conflict, and if they are to influence

---

[4] For a penetrating analysis of the meaning of freedom, see Felix E. Oppenheim, *Dimensions of Freedom: An Analysis* (New York: St. Martin's Press, 1961).

[5] Dissenting opinion in *Dennis* v. *U.S.*, 341 U.S. 494 (1951).

the course of government accordingly, they must be free to give and take in the "market place of ideas."

Political parties are the unofficial institutions, and a free election system is the official institution, that are most essential for majority rule on a continuing basis. Political parties enable interested citizens to join forces in their attempt to win control of government and to get what they want out of politics. The party system is thus one of the principal structures through which a democratic polity performs the key input functions necessary to any political system— identification of basic interests in society and leadership selection. Equally crucial to the democratic performance of these functions is a system of popular elections. Elections permit the combination of interests that make up a political party to compete peaceably with any opposing party for control of the government's decision-making apparatus. Democracy counts ballots instead of bullets. The citizens of a democracy can express their support for or dissent from government policies and personnel through political parties and elections rather than through conspiracies and assassinations.

Since the precise form taken by these institutions varies widely from time to time and from place to place, we cannot say that they must exist in some "ideal" form in order for a government to be regarded as democratic. After all, the perfect democracy is just as unattainable as the perfect dictatorship. Even imperfect and erratic responses to majority opinion indicate that democratic processes are at work, though perhaps at a crude, immature level. But to say that democratic institutions vary widely in form does not mean that we have no way of evaluating them. Specifically, we can evaluate any political institution in terms of how good a job it does in promoting *majority control* on a *continuing* basis—that is, with respect for the right of today's minority to become tomorrow's majority. Within this frame of reference, we can say, for example, that pure one-party politics is *un*democratic, because it fails to keep rulers accountable to changing public opinion. And even if party leaders are chosen by popular vote, we can say that a one-party system is *less* democratic than a two-party system; since competition in one-party politics is merely between personalities, group responsibility for the conduct of government is lacking.

Perhaps American educators are not completely free in the pursuit of truth, perhaps freedom of the press is diluted for newspaper readers by the decline in the number of competing newspapers, perhaps some pressure groups have a disproportionately loud voice in public affairs while others are scarcely heard. Still, in spite of their imperfections, our schools, press, and pressure groups enjoy enough freedom to place the United States in the democratic camp. The search for truth does go on, information about public affairs is widely disseminated, and every group can present its viewpoint. There is room for improvement, of course, but these institutions operate far differently here from the way they operate under totalitarian governments. On rare occasions, Russian schools, newspapers, or special group spokesmen are permitted to deviate from the opinions of the dominant group, but it is always on sufferance, always about incidentals rather than fundamentals, and always at some risk to life and freedom.

The loose organization and lack of discipline in American political parties leave legislators free to vote against their party's platform without fear of being punished by party leaders. We might conclude that American parties are less democratic than the more united and disciplined British parties, because unified parties can better carry out their pledges to the national majority who put them in office. But even our loosely organized parties give us a measure of majority control that makes our system so different in degree as to be different in kind from that of Franco Spain, with its one-party rule.

The important point is this: Just because we judge one form of an institution to be *more* democratic than another, the rejected form does not automatically become *un*democratic. Somewhere along the line between universal suffrage and a complete absence of popular elections, for example, democracy is lost; but it does not make sense to suppose that there is an *exact point* at which democracy ceases to exist.

Remember that throughout most of American history only a minority has enjoyed the right to vote. And yet we think of the United States as having been democratic from the very start. Clearly, we do not regard voting qualifications based on age, sex, and literacy as necessarily out of keeping with democracy. But we *do* regard qualifications based on religion, race, or property ownership as undemocratic. In other words, it is the *function* of the restriction that determines whether or not the restriction itself is compatible with democratic principles.

When a large group of citizens is denied the right to vote only because their interests are in conflict with those of the ruling group, we have a denial of democracy. The exclusion of slaves from voting in this country, for example, was clearly undemocratic, for it denied the right of suffrage to an entire racial and economic group. If we grant that the United States was democratic before the Civil War, it can only be because the excluded group was relatively small in number. The denial of the vote to women, on the other hand, was less a denial of democracy as such, because women constituted a less homogeneous class or set of interests and their needs were not totally unrepresented in our government.

At one extreme in political theory is the model of the perfectly democratic government, with rulers clearly responsible to majority opinion and with all citizens completely free to express every viewpoint. At the other extreme is the model of the perfectly dictatorial government, with rulers utterly unresponsive to public opinion and with citizens who have no opportunity to dissent. All actual governments fall somewhere between these extremes.

Since rulers must suppress opposition if they hope either to ignore or to control majority opinion, the criteria of majority rule and minority rights are closely related—irresponsible rulers and suppression go together just as responsible rulers and freedom of dissent go together. But the close relationship is not perfect. Figure 2-1 suggests the degree to which a few major powers may be said to meet these two criteria. (The diagram should not be accepted as a precise location of nations in terms of democracy or dictatorship; it is presented simply to suggest *how* our criteria may be applied.) Although France may be as tolerant of dissenting opinions as the United States, her chaotic multi-party politics is more likely to obscure responsibility, even under a charismatic leader like de

Gaulle. Notice that the government of the United States lies well within the gravitational field of *both* majoritarianism *and* freedom. As the diagram suggests, we are probably not so close to the democratic ideals as England (with her more highly developed party responsibility and her ingrained toleration of even the most hated opinions), but we are probably closer than France, and we have an entirely different kind of government from Spain, Communist China, and Russia.

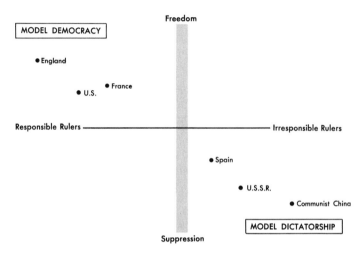

Figure 2-1   Location of selected major powers in terms of majority control and minority rights.

The American Creed and Its Detractors

So far in this chapter, we have been concerned with democracy in general rather than with American politics in particular. In talking about democracy, Americans naturally tend to have their own country in mind. We need to remember, however, that democracy is neither exclusively nor peculiarly American. Our general discussion of the concept should apply to Australia or Sweden or India as well as to the United States. With this perspective, we are ready to ask: How does American political thought fit into the general pattern of democratic beliefs?

The Declaration of Independence: The Conscience of America

On the surface, America gives an impression of extreme contrasts—religious, ethnic, class, and regional. Beneath this surface, however, in which individuals and groups seem to be struggling for conflicting ends, the astute observer detects a remarkably homogeneous and stable political faith. Gunnar Myrdal, the Swedish economist who made a classic study of the Negro in America, concluded that the American Creed is unique both in its clarity and in its acceptance by the people:

When the American Creed is once detected, the cacophony becomes a melody. The further observation then becomes apparent; that America, compared to every other country in Western civilization, large or small, has the *most explicitly expressed* system of general ideals in reference to human interrelations. This body of ideals is more widely understood and appreciated than similar ideals are anywhere else. The American Creed is not merely—as in some other countries—the implicit background of the nation's political and judicial order as it functions. To be sure, the political creed of America is not very satisfactorily effectuated in actual social life. But as principles which *ought* to rule, the Creed has been made conscious to everyone in American society.[6]

Almost every one of us has experienced what Myrdal is talking about here. Recently, a college student was arguing that the generally accepted norms cited by Myrdal do not really exist in America. In making his case, he referred to an injustice he had observed in a student Honor Court meeting—specifically, a denial of the concept of equality for all before the law. But in pointing out this injustice, he was in fact applying the American Creed itself as a norm, and he was perfectly confident that the people he was talking to would automatically accept it as a norm. Admittedly, we depart from our standards on occasion, in national politics no less than in campus politics, but the point is that we *do* have a recognized and semi-official norm by which to identify our departures.

Myrdal says that "America is continuously struggling for its soul." And that "soul" is embodied in the Declaration of Independence. Sometimes it seems that crass material forces are dominating American life, but somehow the high ideals of the American Creed as developed by Thomas Jefferson and the other leaders of the Revolution have always reasserted themselves. "Call it a dream or call it vision," wrote John Dewey, "it has been interwoven in a tradition that has had an immense effect upon American life."[7]

When the British tried to tighten their control over the American colonies, the first protests came from conservative men and were based on points of law. The colonial gentry, who found the British taxes and trade restrictions extremely inconvenient, voiced their opposition in humble petitions to His Sacred Majesty begging for recognition of their property rights as Englishmen. The conservative gentry made opposition to England respectable, but their arguments were too limited to satisfy revolutionary firebrands like Sam Adams, Patrick Henry, and Tom Paine. The radical agitators turned resistance into something less genteel, and began to organize the people to give it its most impolite expression—open rebellion. Tom Paine destroyed the last vestige of politeness and gentility when he called the king a "miserable worm" whom it was a sacrilege to address as "His Sacred Majesty," and announced that the House of Lords was no better than a gang of robbers with titles for aliases.

It is probably fair to say that the colonists lost the debate over the points of

---

[6] *An American Dilemma: The Negro Problem and Modern Democracy* (New York: Harper & Brothers, 1944), p. 3. The McGraw-Hill Book Company brought out a two-volume paperback edition in 1964.

[7] *Freedom and Culture* (New York: G. P. Putnam's Sons, 1939), p. 55.

law. They had long admitted their subordination to the mother country and had begun to protest only when the British regulations proved uncomfortably burdensome. But the more radical leaders who were shaping the American Creed put their argument in a way that simply could not be countered. Scorning legalistic quibblings over the *privileges of Englishmen* under the *British Constitution*, they demanded the *rights of men* under the *law of nature*. This position proved particularly embarrassing to English leaders because it was very close to the theory with which John Locke had justified Parliament's assumption of supremacy after the Glorious Revolution. If Parliament's own power was legitimate, how could the colonists be denied their own natural right to self-government? If no such natural right existed, was not the power of Parliament itself illegitimate?

In 1776, the Continental Congress, out of a "decent respect to the opinions of mankind," appointed a committee to explain America's act of "separation" from England. It fell to Thomas Jefferson to prepare the declaration of the revolutionists' position. "Neither aiming at originality of principles or sentiments, nor yet copied from any particular and previous writing," as Jefferson explained later, "it was intended to be an expression of the American mind." The tremendous appeal the Declaration has had for all mankind demonstrates how well Jefferson succeeded in stating the revolutionists' principles. A simple rephrasing of its central proposition suggests how different its impact would have been had not the radical argument replaced the conservative: "We hold this truth to be self-evident, that it is a right of British subjects not to be taxed except by their own consent." [8]

The enduring appeal of the Declaration of Independence as the foundation of the American Creed springs from these propositions: (1) There is a *higher law*, found in the "laws of nature and of nature's God," that embodies certain self-evident truths against which institutions and practices may be judged. (2) Society must recognize that "*all men are created equal*," with the right to make their own decisions, to have an equal opportunity to develop their talents, and to enoy equality both under the law and in the chance to influence the law. (3) All men have "*certain unalienable Rights*," including those of "Life, Liberty and the pursuit of Happiness," by virtue of their common humanity and equality under God. This list of rights was not made exhaustive, to insure that as situations changed new rights could be asserted. But the recognition of the moral worth of every life, and the freedom to use that life as one sees fit, was specifically included. (4) *Government is an instrument of the people*, to be used by them for the twofold purpose of protection and service, or, in the words of the Declaration, of "Safety and Happiness." As a tool "to secure these rights," government is not an object of veneration or an end in itself. (5) "*Consent of the governed*" is the only legitimate basis of power; this proposition implies the *right of revolution*—"That whenever any Form of Government becomes destructive of these ends, it is the Right of the People to alter or to abolish it, and to institute new Government. . . ." (6)

---

[8] This rephrasing comes from the definitive study of the Declaration: Carl Becker, *The Declaration of Independence: A Study in the History of Political Ideas* (New York: Alfred A. Knopf, 1951).

Democracy cannot be identified with any fixed principles or forms of government; instead, democracy consists of a *method* of governing by popular consent. All people should be free to organize their government as they see fit, "laying its foundation on such principles and organizing its powers in such form, as to them shall seem most likely to effect their Safety and Happiness." (7) *Popular government is practical and stable,* despite its continuing dependence on popular consent. ". . . All experience hath shown, that mankind are more disposed to suffer, while evils are sufferable, than to right themselves by abolishing the forms to which they are accustomed." (8) When government becomes irresponsible, citizens have more than a right to rebel—"it is their *duty to throw off such Government.*" The prospects of popular government depend on the capacity of the people to accept burdensome duties.

These are the high standards with which the American nation began— standards which, as we shall see in the next chapter, were to influence the Constitution and inspire the Bill of Rights. True, we have repeatedly fallen short of realizing them, but the very existence of the creed has made us conscious of and dissatisfied with our shortcomings. Vernon L. Parrington, the great interpreter of American ideas, had this to say about the influence of the Declaration of Independence:

> The humanitarian idealism of the Declaration has always echoed as a battle-cry in the hearts of those who dream of an America dedicated to democratic ends. It cannot be long ignored or repudiated, for sooner or later it returns to plague the council of practical politics. It is constantly breaking out in fresh revolt. . . . Without its freshening influence our political history would have been much more sordid and materialistic.[9]

The eight central propositions that we have just set forth appear in the writings of John Locke as well as in our own Declaration of Independence—a reminder of our indebtedness to the entire Western civilization of which America is only a part. Our ideals are the general ideals of democracy, and no nation has a monopoly on them. "The American Creed is older and wider than America itself." [10]

Agreement on the Idea of Democracy

In analyzing the ideas of the Declaration of Independence, we were talking about America's more or less official creed. Now we are ready to ask if the ordinary citizen champions this creed as much as students of our heritage seem to think he does. In a democracy, there cannot be too great a gap between the official creed and the beliefs of the people at large, but the two are not necessarily identical.

One of the most impressive facts about Americans is that they are almost unanimous in their commitment to the concept of democracy. And yet opinion

---

[9] Vernon L. Parrington, *Main Currents in American Thought* (New York: Harcourt, Brace and Company, 1930), III, p. 285.
[10] Myrdal, *An American Dilemma*, p. 25.

surveys show that the public is startlingly ignorant about even the most important political issues of the day.

Several years after the United Nations was created, and after it had held several well-publicized meetings in the United States, one out of every four Americans admitted that they either had never heard of the U.N. or had no idea what its purpose was. In presidential elections, about half the people may be unable to name the vice-presidential nominees of either party. The University of Michigan's Survey Research Center reports that only about a fourth of the eligible voters can be said to have the minimum information necessary for their votes to be informed on important public issues. By "minimum information," we mean that this one-fourth meets three simple conditions: They have opinions on important issues; they think they know what the government is doing about the issues; and they think they know what the party differences on the issues are.[11] In April of 1961, 63 per cent of the people admitted they had never heard of the well-publicized John Birch Society; and of those who had heard of it, a number said that this extremist right-wing and anti-communist organization was "too radical" or was "dominated by communists."

On the basis of consistent findings of this sort, students of public opinion have come to the conclusion that at least 20 per cent of the American public is completely ignorant on almost any given subject (and the figure is usually closer to 40 per cent). But when we check the results of surveys designed to find out what Americans think about democracy, we find that an overwhelming majority of them endorses democracy as the most desirable form of government. Moreover, *four out of five Americans can give a meaningful definition of the concept "democracy."* The public at large is not at home with abstractions. And yet 80 per cent choose to define democracy in terms of its two essentials, popular rule and freedom—both of which are highly abstract concepts. Americans are unmistakably committed to democracy, at least in general terms.

As soon as we begin to probe beyond the concept of democracy, however, the picture becomes less reassuring. When asked to identify the Bill of Rights—the constitutional amendments that formally guarantee our basic freedoms—Americans do very poorly. In one recent survey, 31 per cent of the adult population said they had never heard of the Bill of Rights, an additional 36 per cent said they had heard of it but were unable to identify it, and another 12 per cent identified it incorrectly. Only 21 per cent could identify it correctly. Still, even this seeming ignorance is less alarming than it appears at first glance. What is important to democracy is not the "Bill of Rights" label but the ideas behind the label. If Americans are genuinely dedicated to popular freedoms, it matters very little whether or not they know that these freedoms are enumerated on a piece of paper. Democracy draws its vigor from living ideas, not from legal principles.

---

[11] Angus Campbell *et al.*, *The American Voter* (New York: John Wiley & Sons, Inc., 1960), pp. 171–183. The "informed" percentage would have been further reduced had incorrect perceptions of government activities or of party stands been taken into account.

More disquieting are the inconsistent attitudes that Americans show toward the specific problems of democracy. Although nearly everyone endorses the principle of free speech, a majority would deny socialists and atheists the right to speak in their own communities. About 57 per cent of the general electorate agree with the statement, "Freedom does not give anyone the right to teach foreign ideas in our schools." Americans are nearly unanimous in endorsing the idea of a free press, but they divide evenly on this proposition: "A book that contains wrong political views cannot be a good book and does not deserve to be published." [12]

Even here, however, the situation may not be so alarming as it appears. The problem is not that Americans consciously reject democracy, but rather that they fail to see the connection between *different values*. As one student of the "American mind" has perceived, most Americans tend to place equal stress on a whole battery of values, not recognizing that values must be arranged in some sort of hierarchy if the most fundamental ones are really to operate.[13] When an American is asked a question about atheists or socialists, he tends to give an anti-socialist or anti-atheist answer, not stopping to think that it may also be anti-democratic. When the inconsistency of his response is called to his attention, however, he usually modifies it in favor of the more basic values of democracy. Hostile as he may be to communists, he is reluctant to deny anyone his civil liberties.

Community leaders tend, moreover, to reply in a far more tolerant or democratic way to questions about unpopular groups. Accordingly, they may be expected to lead others in recognizing that an attack on the freedoms of an unpopular minority is an attack on democratic values. This higher level of tolerance is shown by the leaders of the most conservative groups as well as by the leaders of the most liberal groups in America.[14] The implication is clear: The American creed is so liberal in itself that even our conservatives work to preserve what is essentially a liberal heritage. Unlike the citizens of European democracies, almost all Americans are committed to the concept of liberal democracy. So strongly are they committed, in fact, that they label the infinitesimal minorities of "right" and "left" who openly reject democracy as the "lunatic fringe."

What Is the Public Ideology?

The fact that almost all Americans claim to believe in democracy, coupled with the nation's early and stirring expression of democratic sentiments in the Declara-

---

[12] Herbert McClosky, "Consensus and Ideology in American Politics," *American Political Science Review*, LVIII (June, 1964), p. 367. Earlier references to public opinions are from the American Institute of Public Opinion (Gallup Poll) and Herbert H. Hyman and Paul B. Sheatsley, "The Current Status of American Public Opinion," in Daniel Katz *et al.* (eds.), *Public Opinion and Propaganda* (New York: The Dryden Press, 1954), pp. 33–48.

[13] Henry Steele Commager, *The American Mind* (New Haven: Yale University Press, 1950), p. 39.

[14] Samuel A. Stouffer, *Communism, Conformity, and Civil Liberties* (Garden City, N.Y.: Doubleday & Company, Inc., 1955), pp. 26–48. McClosky, "Consensus and Ideology in American Politics."

tion of Independence and the Bill of Rights, has led many observers to conclude that consensus on both abstract and specific principles unites virtually every citizen of the United States. But can we assume that liking democracy means accepting the specific principles it implies?

The average American's commitment to democracy is most impressive, to be sure, but his inconsistent attitudes suggest that the nature of the commitment requires further examination before we can talk about a democratic ideology at the popular level. For many citizens, the commitment to democracy actually appears to go no further than an acceptance of the democratic ideal in the most general terms. Consensus—agreement by majorities approaching 100 per cent— exists on the abstract idea of majority rule and minority rights but on little beyond that. Continuing majority rule logically requires, for example, the right of any group peaceably to increase its influence through the ballot. But recent research has found no consensus even on such a statement as the following: "A professional organization like the AMA (American Medical Association) has the right to try to increase the influence of doctors by getting them to vote as a bloc in elections." Researchers have failed to find consensus on a whole series of such statements, all similarly derived from the principles of majority rule and minority rights.[15] They have accordingly been forced to conclude not only that consensus disappears when democratic principles are put in concrete terms, but also that citizens are closer to complete discord (a 50–50 split) than to perfect consensus (a 100–0 split) on many such questions.

What, then, is the average voter's ideology? It includes a belief in democracy and the abstract principles by which it is defined. But, contrary to the assumption of some political theorists, that's about as far as any conscious consensus seems to go. The bulk of the citizenry fails to carry the notion of democracy through to a consistent democratic creed, principally because most citizens lack the inclination, the information, or the intellectual skills needed to entertain *any* coherent ideology. When we think about the real people behind that abstract term "the public," rather than about the logical expectations of theorists, the lack of popular ideology is not surprising. Americans are distinctively non-theoretical in their approach to public problems. Continuing investigations of political attitudes by the Survey Research Center demonstrate that most citizens respond to (or ignore) each new issue on its merits, not in terms of any well-defined system of ideas—whether generally democratic, or specifically liberal or conservative. If a political ideology means a close-woven structure of attitudes that expresses a person's basic values and determines his stand on particular issues, less than three per cent of the population can be said to have a genuine ideology.[16]

With such vague acceptance, how does the American Creed work as well as it does? The difficulties posed by this question help explain why so many people have assumed that consensus on fundamentals must exist. Widespread

---

[15] James W. Prothro and Charles M. Grigg, "Fundamental Principles of Democracy: Bases of Agreement and Disagreement," *Journal of Politics,* XXII (May, 1960), pp. 276–294.

[16] Campbell *et al., The American Voter,* especially Chapters 8–10.

acceptance of certain specific rights (such as the right of a professional organization to act as a political bloc) seems logically necessary if one accepts the abstract principles of majority rule and minority rights. And we tend to assume that what people *should* (logically) believe is what they *do* (in fact) believe. But real human beings, certainly pragmatic Americans, somehow fail to follow the neat logical patterns of the political philosopher.

The late V. O. Key, Jr., systematically pursued the ghost of consensus on fundamentals and discovered that it haunts the learned observer rather than members of the general public, most of whom couldn't care less about such a rarefied subject as ideology.[17] Examining the actual distribution of opinions on a wide variety of subjects, Key discovered consensus where conventional doctrine calls for disagreement and disagreement where the doctrine calls for consensus. First, very high agreement, or consensus, prevails on some concrete questions of public policy, such as support for public education or for social welfare benefits to the aged. But this is not the kind of agreement called for by the doctrine of consensus on the fundamentals. Second, a little data and a lot of heroic guesswork suggest that consensus exists on some general attitudes of the sort we described as part of the "American character" in Chapter 1, but these attitudes are not directly political. Third, except for the highly general commitment to democracy mentioned above, no consensus can be found on the basic principles of democracy.

Professor Key's analysis suggests that the democratic system works without consensus but *as if* consensus prevailed. One explanation for this oddity is that consistent democratic values and habits are more prevalent among the politically active minority. However much they may disagree on issues, political activists seem to serve as the carriers of the democratic creed, learning through actual experience to recognize the problems of others, to compromise differences rather than insisting on total acceptance of their own particular principles, and to appreciate the relation of specific actions or issues to broader democratic principles. But leaders imbued with democratic values are not enough. A second reason why the system can work as if we had a conscious public ideology is found in the continuing interaction between leaders and the mass of the population: the expectations and opinions of the general public are, if not highly systematic, at least compatible with democratic procedures. A complete democratic ideology is not necessary throughout the population so long as public acceptance is given to the ways in which political power is won and exercised—that is, so long as agreement exists on the general idea of democracy. The key word here is *acceptance:* "Apathy can play a constructive role if it leads those who reject the techniques called for by the democratic creed to inactivity or to acceptance of decisions they themselves would not have made." [18]

---

[17] V. O. Key, Jr., *Public Opinion and American Democracy* (New York: Alfred A. Knopf, 1961), Chapter 2.

[18] James W. Prothro and Charles M. Grigg, "Societal Coordination by the Educated Minority," *Political Research: Organization and Design* (now *American Behavioral Scientist*), III (January, 1960), p. 8.

Discussions of democracy tend to overlook the functional nature of apathy for the system. No one is surprised to hear that what people *say* they *believe* and what they *actually do* are not necessarily the same. We usually assume that verbal positions represent a higher level—a more "democratic" stance—than non-verbal behavior. But something close to the opposite may also be true: Many people express undemocratic principles in response to questioning but are too apathetic to act on their undemocratic opinions in concrete situations. And in most cases, fortunately for the democratic system, those with the most undemocratic principles are also those who are least likely to act. A sizable number (42.0 per cent) of the voters in a southern city recently said, for example, that "a Negro should not be allowed to run for mayor of this city," but a few months before the survey was taken a Negro actually did conduct an active campaign for that office without any efforts being made by the "white" people to obstruct his candidacy.

In this case, the behavior was more democratic than the verbal expressions. If the leadership elements—the carriers of the creed—had encouraged undemocratic action, it might have materialized (as it did in the murder of civil rights workers who attempted to encourage Negro voter registration in Mississippi). But, in fact, people with basically undemocratic opinions either abstained from acting or acted in a perfectly democratic fashion. "The successful working of the system is not deliberately aimed at by those who work it," John Plamenatz says, "but is the result of their behaving as they do." [19] Continuance of the American Creed seems to depend, then, on having leaders in all walks of life (from the local PTA to Congress) who are dedicated to a coherent democratic ideology. But it also depends on having followers who are dedicated to the general idea of democracy and who either (1) recognize the implications of the creed once some opinion leader points out the connection between a specific issue and the basic ideals of democracy, or (2) accept the creed in practice without thinking about the principles their behavior implies, or (3) entertain notions inconsistent with the basic creed but are too few or too apathetic to carry out their undemocratic beliefs.

Threats to Democracy

Democracy may be threatened by two quite different kinds of danger: first, the provincial tendency to narrow the meaning of democracy to the institutional patterns of a particular time and place, and second, the deliberate attempt of totalitarians to replace democracy with some other form of government. We shall speak of the totalitarian threat in the next section. Here we shall focus on the provincial threat, which, because it is less obvious and sometimes unintended, is the more insidious.

---

[19] "Cultural Prerequisites to a Successfully Functioning Democracy," *American Political Science Review*, L (March, 1956), p. 123.

Provincialism As a Threat to Democratic Values

Surveys reveal that 88 out of every hundred Americans consider the United States a democracy; only 60 per cent regard Great Britain as a democracy, and even fewer believe that France is democratic.[20] These findings demonstrate the tendency of Americans to identify democracy—which is a *method* of governing that may follow a variety of forms and principles—with one particular form and one particular set of principles. Chances are that a good many English and French citizens would say that the United States is not a democracy, just because it is neither England nor France. The *existence* of this tendency, however, does not make it *rationally defensible*. You may remember that you once regarded your high school as the best in the land. But you hardly went so far as to insist that it was the *only* real high school in the country and that all the others were reformatories!

Thomas Jefferson once argued that men are willing to put up for a long time with the worst possible arrangement simply because it is familiar to them. They are even more inclined to find all virtue in a situation that is satisfactory as well as familiar. This feeling might be laudable enough if it were not carried to extremes, and if it were not so suspiciously confined to the most uninformed citizens. In its extreme form, it constitutes a serious threat to democracy. It leads men to insist on conformity of ideas. If this insistence became widespread, only the ideas of the dominant majority would survive. In other words, it would kill democracy. Since democracy, unlike totalitarianism, does not make government synonymous with society, even the most loyal citizen must have the freedom to criticize government when he feels that criticism is needed.

Only the misguided patriot insists that democracy is limited to a single set of institutions and principles. Change is the one unchangeable feature of human life and, again, such an insistence dooms democracy. The Constitution has been changed twenty-four times by formal amendment and countless times by interpretation and usage, and our economic and social life has undergone constant transformation over the years. How can we say that now, at this moment of this day, all change must cease?

Many of us assume, without reflection, that such prized American achievements as a written constitution, separation of powers, checks and balances, judicial review, federalism, and private enterprise are essential to the very existence of democracy. We shall look closely at these features of our government in later chapters, but here we shall just make two observations about how they are related to democracy.

First, none of these institutions is functionally necessary to a political system with majority rule and minority rights—the two requisites of democracy. They all bear some relation to both these requisites, but none of them is perfectly identified with either. In other words, they are *supplementary* rather than *primary* institutions—in the sense that primary institutions are those essential to the

---

[20] Hyman and Sheatsley, in Katz *et al.* (eds.), *Public Opinion and Propaganda*, p. 41.

existence of democracy itself, whereas supplementary institutions derive their importance merely from their relation to primary institutions. To be more specific: We cannot enjoy majority rule or minority rights unless we are free to organize political parties, compete in elections, and have access to a free press (these are primary institutions, without which the functions of leadership selection and

Drawing by Mahood; © 1960 The New Yorker Magazine, Inc.

"They certainly don't look like Commies to me."

interest identification could not be performed in response to changing public opinion). But we can very well have both majority rule and minority rights without separation of powers or federalism (these are merely supplementary institutions, which may be functional or not for a democratic system, depending on circumstances of time and place).

In the second place, any well-traveled or well-read person knows that democracies *do* exist without many of the features that are characteristic of our American government. Although these other democracies may seem less attractive to us than our own, we must recognize that they can be responsible to their own majorities without becoming completely "Americanized." We may believe that federalism and checks and balances are more suitable to our country than a unitary government with integrated powers, but we cannot say that *all* governments must have these particular features before they can be regarded as democracies.

An institution is essential to democracy *only if* its absence means that we can no longer have majority rule on a continuing basis. A member of the British Labour Party once insisted, in a debate with an American businessman, that private enterprise leaves vast amounts of power in the hands of men who do not have to account to the public for their use of that power. And, since democracy requires that those vested with power be responsible to the people, he argued, private enterprise is undemocratic by definition. The point he missed was that Americans have simply not chosen to nationalize their key industries, even though they are perfectly free to do so (by constitutional means) should they ever change their minds.

The American businessman, in turn, argued that the British had automatically relinquished democracy when they gave the socialists control of the government in the 1945 election. Since democracy means liberty and since private enterprise is a form of liberty, he insisted, any socialist government is undemocratic by definition. The American was blind to the same point that had escaped his opponent. The British, who had freely chosen to nationalize certain key industries, were equally free to return them to private control should they ever change their minds.

This debate could never be won, since neither of the spokesmen could prove that either private enterprise or socialism is *directly related* to majority rule and individual liberty. The doctrinaire socialist might have argued—as some do—that economic power in irresponsible hands leads inevitably to such complete domination of the newspaper, radio, television, and school systems that elections degenerate into a meaningless ritual in which the "big business" candidate always wins. The facts, however, seem to belie this argument. In six out of eight national elections in the United States from 1936 through 1964, "big business" was on the side of the *loser*. Similarly, the doctrinaire advocate of private enterprise might have insisted—as some do—that socialism's combining of economic and political authority gives government officers such tremendous power that a dictatorship becomes inevitable, with the scrapping of free elections. Here, too, the facts seem to belie the argument. After five years of socialist rule, the British voters returned the Conservative Party to power in an election as free as any ever held, and they went back to the Labour Party in 1964.

Naturally, in the United States we hear more extreme arguments in favor of private enterprise than in favor of socialism. During a recent election campaign, a city was trying to decide whether it should retain its municipally managed power plant or sell its existing facilities to a private utility company. The company ran the following advertisement in the local press: "He who fights for private business fights for democracy and for freedom. If that war should be lost to us we cannot have the consolation that the struggle was a matter of little moment, for private business, political democracy and Christian religion all go down together." As it turned out, the citizens of the city voted in favor of municipal management, but no disruption of business activities, church services, or scheduled elections was ever reported. Although the utility company never recanted, democracy seems to survive despite the "inroads of socialism."

Totalitarian Attacks on Democratic Ideas

So far, we have been speaking about the corrosive effect of the false friends of democracy. Now we shall turn to the frontal attacks of the avowed enemies of democracy. Here we meet the anti-democratic position in its baldest form. Throughout Western history the champions of oligarchy—whether in the guise of monarchy, theocracy, militarism, fascism, or communism—have consistently denied the democratic assumptions about man, society, and government. They have viewed human nature through the lenses of "élitism" or materialism rather than through the lenses of equality and humanitarianism. They have understood society—and they still do—in terms of the needs of the "fatherland," an élite class, or the single "true" party, rather than in terms of the needs of the individual. They replace progress with stability and order as the goals of society. In government, they supplant majority rule with the dominance of a superior and irresponsible minority; they substitute conformity for freedom.

The most powerful contemporary form of dictatorship is communism, and the communist rejection of democracy illustrates the nature of totalitarian attacks on democratic ideas. Communist rulers in the Soviet Union, the People's Republic of China, and eastern Europe have re-interpreted Karl Marx's theories to a point where he might scarcely recognize them; but these are the communists with whom we are concerned, because they are the ones with power. As the word "totalitarian" suggests, theirs is a form of dictatorship in which an irresponsible minority tries to absorb the total power of society and to command unquestioning obedience. Thus communism, in all its varying forms, flatly rejects the two essentials of democratic government.

The communists discard the notion of majority rule as a "bourgeois" sop to the masses, and they look on man as a helpless pawn buffeted about by economic forces beyond both his understanding and control. So misguided that he votes against his own best interests, man is clearly not competent to govern himself. Despite the communists' use of such slogans as "Workers of the world unite—you have nothing to lose but your chains," communist practice is based on the idea of an élite. The superior few who are able to understand and take advantage of economic determinism become, of course, the leaders of the communist movement. Only through these leaders—who always constitute the "vanguard of the proletariat"—can the majority be led to perceive what is best for them.

What happens when the communists succeed in gaining power? Considerable variation exists from one communist nation to another, as is indicated by the differences among such countries as the Soviet Union, the People's Republic of Communist China, Yugoslavia, and Poland. Each nation tends to interpret communism in terms of its own political culture. Nevertheless, communists have much in common in all countries. Convinced that they possess final and absolute truth, they leave little room for freedom to dissent—the freedom that is basic to democracy. Once a man has come face to face with perfect truth, why should he tolerate error? The suppression of dissent that appears so offensive to us becomes a lofty duty to the zealot. A British official once tried to point out to the Russian people how much they suffered from the lack of freedom of the press. *Pravda*, the official organ of the Communist Party, replied that Russians enjoy perfect freedom of the press: They are free to express and hear all ideas except the lies perpetrated by "enemies of the people." With the official press publishing the truth every day, who would possibly complain about the absence of lies *except* an enemy of the people?

But why, if communism is so evidently bent on destroying man's hope of governing himself, has it had such a wide appeal? Actually, it has had less appeal among people who have experienced democracy than we often give it credit for. Remember that the communists have never been voted into power by the majority of any free electorate. They have always seized control as a minority movement and then imposed their beliefs on the population as a whole. By means of incessant propaganda and coercion, they may have "engineered" consent *after* they acquired power, but they have never honored the democratic arrangement in which power *follows* majority consent.

The communist practice of seizing power without waiting for a majority vote in a free election is enough, in itself, to damn communism to most people in Western democracies. But this characteristic has little effect on the attitudes of people who have never experienced self-government, and they make up a vast majority of the world's population. The present generation seems to be engaged in a "participation explosion" which is injecting mass opinions—often violently—into the decision-making processes of governments all over the world. People in established democracies are tempted to interpret this as meaning that other people clamor for democracy as we know it. But the form that mass participation will take is in real doubt. The aspects of Western culture that are most easily diffused are its industrial technology and rational bureaucracy. These have obvious payoffs that are desperately needed in underdeveloped areas. They are found in the Soviet Union, however, no less than in the United States or Britain. Political modernization can clearly be achieved without the element we would most like to share— our democratic political culture. The abstract ideals of democracy have wide appeal, but the attitudes and practices that undergird those ideals are not easily transmitted to people who have not grown up with them. Two students of mass attitudes and political culture warn us, "What must be learned about democracy is a matter of attitude and feeling, and this is harder to learn." [21] In the rush for national independence and modernization, the "participant subject" mode of participation is, they warn, as likely as that of the "influential citizen."

Imagine a country, like so many in Asia, Africa, and Latin America, where no government has ever been chosen by the people. A new group, called the communists, organizes enough mass support, with help from trained Russians or Chinese, to seize control of the government. The lack of a majority vote in a free election would hardly be noticed if the country had never known a free election. This coup might appear different from all the previous ones only in its greater efficiency, its somewhat larger base of popular support, and in its claim to represent a true people's democracy. Such an excitingly new kind of dictatorship might look like genuine democracy to an habitually oppressed people. And the demonstrated scientific achievements of the U.S.S.R., or the increased military might and claims of progress by China, would certainly lend a glamorous appeal and stir the ambitions of people in the new "democracy."

The unpleasant fact is, then, that communism does have great appeal for millions of people, especially among the relatively undeveloped areas of Africa, Asia, and Latin America. Americans themselves occasionally feel that Russia is "doing the better job of winning people around the world to its point of view." [22] The response to communism is greatest in countries marked by mass illiteracy and poverty, where the oppressed peasants are willing to agree that they "have nothing to lose but their chains." Familiar with misery and squalor, but strangers to democracy, these people are ill equipped to analyze communist slogans about a blissful "people's democracy" in which all needs are perfectly met. Whereas fascism represents a comparatively naked evil to believers in democracy, communism is clothed in a humanitarian disguise that makes it that much more dangerous. Quick to exploit any weakness that will serve their ends, communist leaders promise dignity, economic security, and national independence to people who are desperately in need of all three and who are unaware that communism would crush any chance they might have to secure them.

In most democracies, on the other hand, as Mr. Justice Douglas has pointed out, the communists are "miserable merchants of unwanted ideas." Since democratic means have proved themselves able to reduce the evils that Karl Marx perceived in early industrialism, Marxist ideology appears as a set of outmoded slogans, and communist practice as a brutal assault on human dignity and freedom. Even in the democracies, however, there are minorities—ranging from the infinitesimal in the United States and Britain to the sizeable in Italy and France— who do embrace communism. This support is most likely to exist, as in the "colonial" areas, where severe grievances stand unresolved.

---

[21] Gabriel A. Almond and Sidney Verba, *The Civic Culture: Political Attitudes and Democracy in Five Nations* (Princeton: Princeton University Press, 1963), p. 5.

[22] American Institute of Public Opinion (Gallup Poll), *Public Opinion News Service,* February 3, 1961.

Of the millions of people who vote for the Communist Party in France and Italy, only a small minority are actually party members. These protest voters, as compared with the electorate in general, come disproportionately from male workers in lower income and educational categories. These are not people who reject the ideals of the system so much as they are people who reject the system because of its failure—in their experience—to realize professed ideals. The average communist voter is more often reformist than revolutionary; he recognizes shortcomings in the Communist Party, but it still gives him a way of expressing his dissatisfaction with the failures of the established system. Most communist voters are caught, then, in a politics of despair, voting against the system they see as responsible for their bleak lives without really wanting a communist regime. A large-scale study of communist voters in France and Italy ends with this quotation from a French tool- and die-maker, who robustly expresses the alienation of most communist voters from *any* available ideology:

> Hell, I have to work under any system. I got my family to think of. The kids need shoes and the wife needs a coat. Where the hell do you think I can get the money? What the workers want is a good standard of living and more opportunities for themselves and their kids.
>
> I don't care if the workers get a good standard of living under capitalism or socialism. It doesn't make any difference to me. I don't want a revolution; I just want change. It's none of my business what workers do in other countries. They don't concern themselves about me; why the hell should I concern myself about them? Let them fight their own battles, and I'll fight mine.
>
> But nothing I say is going to make any difference.
>
> All I want is to enjoy myself in this life. For all I know it may be the only one I have. When you're dead, maybe you've had it. Hell, I don't know. All I want is to have a good life, that's all. Is that too much? [23]

But what motivates some people who do not suffer any apparent deprivations to submerge themselves, even at great risk, in the Communist Party? For these the chief appeal of communism seems to lie in the very feature that makes it so repugnant to democrats—its guarantee of an authoritative answer to every problem. Apparently not everyone desires freedom and self-government, for freedom involves responsibilities as well as privileges. And the burdens of self-responsibility are more taxing than the perverted kind of freedom that comes with a surrender of independence. When a man gives up his freedom of choice, he at least gains freedom from the difficult responsibility of making his own independent decisions.

Erich Fromm has analyzed this tendency in his brilliant book *Escape from Freedom*.[24] In a complex, urban, industrial society the individual finds himself surrounded by the "bigness" of impersonal forces that challenge his understanding

[23] Hadley Cantril, *The Politics of Despair* (New York: Basic Books, Inc., 1958), pp. 211–212.

[24] *Escape from Freedom* (New York: Farrar & Rinehart, Inc., 1941). Also see David Riesman, *The Lonely Crowd* (New Haven: Yale University Press, 1950); and T. W. Adorno *et al.*, *The Authoritarian Personality* (New York: Harper & Brothers, 1950). Gabriel Almond's *The Appeals of Communism* (Princeton: Princeton University Press, 1954) is a systematic analysis of why people join and quit the Communist Party.

and belittle his powers of control. Caught up in feelings of insecurity, impotence, and loneliness, he may, if he is not made of sturdy stuff, join the search for subjugation rather than face the uncertainties of self-responsibility. The Communist Party holds out the promise of belonging to a world-wide movement in which one is told what to think and do, and in which the painful doubts of democracy are replaced by the absolutes of an authoritarian creed. In a democracy, the individual must be able to live with ambiguity. But the authoritarian personality—whether he responds to the appeal of communism or to some other type of authoritarianism —cannot bear the burdens of uncertainty.

A Reaffirmation of the Democratic Faith

Since democracy as an ideal is older than democracy as a practice, a number of unrealistic assumptions were worked into the ideal along with the enduring truths. Early theorists of democracy, unacquainted with the everyday operation of popular government and eager to stir people into radical change, overstated their case. Today's theorists, enjoying the advantage of having lived with democracy, are in a position to discard these unrealistic assumptions. Unencumbered by false assumptions, democracy is in a better position to resist the efforts of its false friends and recognized enemies.

Discarding Unnecessary Assumptions

One of the assumptions that was designed to heighten democracy's appeal but that really made it look foolishly unrealistic might be called *the image of the rational political man*.[25] First cousin to the "economic man" of classical economic theory, this creature was presumed to be heavy with virtues—an intense interest in politics, tireless activity in gathering accurate information on which to base political decisions, keen logic and rationality in reaching conclusions, and an unwavering eagerness to register his views at the polls. This glowing picture was useful in arguing for a more broadly based government, but it has proved a woefully inaccurate description of real citizens in real democracies. The average American is only mildly interested in politics. The little information he has he picks up from sources that agree with his preconceived convictions or prejudices. And when it comes to voting, only a little over half of the eligible voters appear at the polls.

The image of the rational political man is unnecessary to democratic theory. Democracy does not really require that all citizens be perfectly rational and keenly interested in politics. In the first place, non-voters are generally among the most uninterested and uninformed citizens—those who are least qualified to vote. In a sense, these people are automatically disqualified from participation in

---

25 In the following discussion we are indebted to Carl J. Friedrich, *The New Image of the Common Man* (Boston: The Beacon Press, 1950); and Bernard R. Berelson, Paul F. Lazarsfeld, and William N. McPhee, *Voting: A Study of Opinion Formation in a Presidential Campaign* (Chicago: The University of Chicago Press, 1954), pp. 305–323.

politics. We set up no barriers of race, sex, religion, or wealth, but we do require that the adult citizen be sufficiently motivated to register and vote. From this point of view, get-out-the-vote campaigns are pernicious if they induce uninterested citizens to vote. Only if they generate genuine interest in the important issues of the day do they produce properly qualified voters at the polls.

A second reason why democracy does not require a nation of rational political men stems from the specialization and division of labor through which modern society operates: a high level of political power and knowledge are required in only a relatively few specialists. We do not expect all citizens to know how to make shoes, and we need not expect them all to know how to make public policy. Some commentators are horrified at how few Americans show any interest in public policy or can even name such important officials as the Secretary of Defense. But would the ability to name the Secretary of Defense make a person more capable of deciding what our defense policy should be? And even if the average citizen did become convinced that he knew what our policy should be, would he not be foolish to believe that he as an individual could get his idea adopted? [26] What actually happens is that various organized groups with expert representatives exert a real and informed influence on policy. Most Americans are members of such groups and, responding in a realistic way to the specialization that marks twentieth-century America, they usually leave it to their spokesmen to represent their interests. The minority who take time to write letters to their congressmen supplement this organized representation. But only through organized representation can most people influence policy and at the same time take care of their routine daily commitments.

A third reason why democracy does not require that all citizens be rational political men is that democracy depends on different kinds of political participation. Too many good citizens could actually be bad for the system. If we were all highly motivated in politics and stubbornly committed to well-conceived principles, for example, the flexibility of our system would be lost and our politics might reach permanent stalemate. True, democracy requires reasonable men who reasonably disagree; but it may also benefit from less reasonable men who are only occasionally interested. The less highly motivated citizens vote less regularly and change their party affiliation more often. But what would our politics be like without this kind of behavior? With all adults voting in every election and firmly dedicated to their principles, we would be divided into solid, permanently opposed voting blocs. Elections could be called off, except to record the preferences of the young men and women who had just reached voting age. Successful democracy needs *both* stability *and* change, and these are qualities that are not supported by the same individuals. The requirements of the system call for variety among the citizens who comprise it.

Three other assumptions that have needlessly encumbered democracy are

---

[26] For an application of this line of reasoning to foreign policy, see Gabriel A. Almond, *The American People and Foreign Policy* (New York: Harcourt, Brace and Company, 1950), pp. 226–241.

more or less implicit in the image of the rational political man. Perhaps most closely related is the assumption of *extreme individualism*—that any "common man" is competent to play any political role. As Andrew Jackson put it in his first message to Congress in 1829, "The duties of all public officers are, or at least admit of being made, so plain and simple that men of intelligence may readily qualify themselves for their performance. . . ." In practice, Americans abandoned this assumption long ago. For example, we have designed rigorous civil service examinations that only a small minority can hope to pass. But some defenders of democracy still feel obliged to talk as if the common man as an individual were capable of performing any political task. All that the democratic faith really requires, however, is a more modest assumption that *the people in a collective sense* are capable of giving general direction to public policy.

A second assumption that is related to the romanticized picture of the political man is that "*the voice of the people is the voice of God.*" In countering the royal claim to rule by divine right, early crusaders for democracy made equally extravagant boasts about the citizenry at large. But experience has made it clear that voting returns have no mystical quality that renders the majority verdict unerringly wise. Nor does democracy need such a belief. It need only assume that over the long run the majority shows relatively greater wisdom than any minority. Remember that the self-appointed "wise men" of history actually resemble Adolf Hitler more than they do Plato's "philosopher king." With this in mind, the fallible majority seems preferable to the fallible élite.

Finally, there is the assumption that the "common man" can make *correct decisions on technical matters* requiring expert judgment or rare taste. This claim is both unnecessary to a belief in democracy and indefensible as a logical proposition. Voters in America are not called upon to decide whether the TVA should have a new generator or what is the best way to build space vehicles. Although they would be incapable of solving such problems intelligently, they are able to judge broader questions related to the specific problems. Arguments about public versus private power or the state of our space program do enter election campaigns. And this is all that democracy requires. The judgment of the voters need be called for only on *general questions of public policy*. Once the policy has been decided, the details are turned over to qualified experts responsible to elected political leaders.

Democracy As a Practical System

Agreeing that men are not perfectly rational creatures, defenders of democracy sometimes go a step further and agree that instability and inefficiency are the price that democracy must pay for popular freedom. But the record of history suggests that democracy is actually more stable and efficient than the dictatorships that curb freedom in the name of stability and efficiency. The two oldest and most stable governments among the major powers are those of Britain and the United States. On the other hand, Hitler's Third Reich, which boasted that it would endure for a thousand years because it had escaped the uncertainties and confusions of democracy, lasted scarcely a dozen.

How is it that the system which exalts freedom over order actually enjoys increased order with its greater freedom? Apparently the political arrangement that endures is the one that makes room for conflicting aims and that turns mistaken judgments to advantage. A dictatorship looks efficient only because it shoves its inconsistencies and errors beneath the surface. To wash one's dirty linen in public may be an admission that mud has been thrown, but it is also an indication that the mud has been discovered and washed away. Studies conducted in Germany and Japan after World War II reveal that gross miscalculations were made simply because people were afraid to admit their own mistakes or criticize the mistakes of their superiors. Undetected or concealed from those in top positions, errors tended to multiply themselves and breed miscalculations. Democrats and Republicans alike tend to decry the "key-hole" columnists who pry into the conduct of public officials. But these men do call attention to even the relatively trivial malpractice—and often they get it corrected. All human beings make mistakes; democracy benefits from mistakes by discovering and correcting them.

If democracy has these advantages, why has it not become the universal form of government? Although democracy seems best adapted to the needs of free men, the people of many cultures do not even desire it. Certain conditions seem to be necessary before the desire for democracy arises: (1) a relatively high level of literacy, (2) some measure of economic security, and (3) an acceptance of the dignity of human life. The first two conditions seem to be necessary for the last. An illiterate and poverty-stricken people can hardly develop the ideals, the power, and the organizational skills necessary for the achievement of responsible government.

While literacy and economic security are *necessary*, they are not always *sufficient* to produce a recognition of human dignity. And without wide respect for man's worth, democracy does not develop. With advanced methods of propaganda and coercion, a modern dictatorship may continue to violate human dignity and to forestall democracy long after the population has achieved literacy and decent standards of living. In Russia, for example, the newly literate peasantry read only ideas approved by the Communist Party, and their economic security is tied to political conformity. Consequently, they may never develop the idea of democracy in the Western sense. It is difficult to imagine the citizens of Moscow manning the barricades against a government armed with the instruments of mechanized warfare. Yet there may be some who will try, as testified by the magnificent, though tragic, Hungarian revolt in the fall of 1956.

Another reason that may help to explain why democracy has not been embraced by all the people of the world is that it has no "set" creed to sell. Democracy is rooted in *patterns of behavior* rather than in *consensus on principles*. Suppose you were to ask a banker waiting for a haircut in an American barbershop if he and the lawyer, carpenter, mechanic, and college professor sitting with him were "equal." Chances are he would answer with a flat "no," or else ask you to clarify the question. But when the barber asks "Who's next?" each of the men would automatically look at the others to decide who had arrived first, and would then wait his turn. In other words, even though they may have no well-defined or rationalized principle of equality, they all *behave* as if they consciously endorsed the principle.[27] And it is this customary behavior rather than overt agreement on well-defined principles that characterizes democracy. Habitual behavior of this sort is not easily destroyed—that is why democracy is much sturdier than its enemies realize. Unfortunately, however, habitual behavior is not easily or quickly created either—that is why it proved impossible to set up a series of democracies by writing democratic constitutions for European countries after World War I.

Ultimately, democracy rests on the simple idea that every person has an equal right to make his own choices, to say what he likes, to be heard. And if everyone has an equal right to be heard, the only practical way of deciding on public policy is by majority vote. There is only one alternative to majority control: if rulers are not held responsible to the majority, they will be responsible to a minority. But minorities are made up of imperfect human beings, too, and their imperfections are magnified by irresponsible power. As Thomas Jefferson put it, "Sometimes it is said that man cannot be trusted with the government of himself. Can he, then, be trusted with the government of others? Or have we found angels in the forms of kings to govern him? Let history answer this question."

---

[27] See Friedrich, *The New Image of the Common Man.*

CHAPTER THREE

The Constitutional Background

If we were to trace all the historical forces

that have helped shape the American political system, we should

go back to the very beginnings of Western civilization. But our

purpose here is to make *contemporary* politics in the United

States more understandable; therefore we shall start with more

recent experiences than those of the Greek *polis*.

The United States was born in revolution against British colonialism. This is the primary fact of our national existence. In today's world the United States is a great power. Its political stability, economic prosperity, technological proficiency, and military capability make it the foremost nation. How did this happen?

In this second half of the twentieth century more than a billion people in Asia, Africa, and Latin America have resorted to revolution against colonialism. Eager to dissolve their traditional societies, most of them are determined to achieve the modern way of life. Approximately a third of the members of the United Nations are new nations that obtained their political independence after World War II. Nearly all of them can be described as economically underdeveloped and not yet politically viable. No doubt the success of the American Revolution of 1776—measured by the power position of the United States today—has been one basis for the "revolution of rising expectations" among these newly independent countries. On the other hand, nearly a billion people under communist regimes are testing a very different model of modernization through revolution. The Soviet Union is no mean rival: its rapid industrialization and almost fantastic economic growth within one generation after revolution, its vast military might, its extraordinary advances in missiles and rocketry, its technical and scientific achievements, all add up to an impressive demonstration of how to modernize a backward people in record time.

In this chapter, we shall look at the beginnings of the American government as a problem in "nation-building." How did the United States, breaking ties with the mother country, create and develop its own national system? To what extent does the early American experience offer guidelines to the newly developing nations today?

The First Steps Toward Constitutional Government

The First State Constitutions

In July, 1776, the Second Continental Congress declared to the world that the American colonies "are and of right ought to be free and independent states." Even before this Declaration of Independence, seven of the colonies had established independent governments, and by 1777 all the states had adopted new constitutions except Massachusetts, which adopted hers in 1780. Benjamin Fletcher Wright, one of the keenest students of American constitutional history, reminds us that this "great feat of constitution-making was unprecedented and remains unparalleled in the history of modern constitutionalism."[1]

A constitution need not be written. A constitution is a fundamental set of political practices, not a historic piece of paper. A textbook on British government cannot conveniently include in its appendix a concise copy of the British

---

[1] Benjamin Fletcher Wright, *Consensus and Continuity, 1776–1787* (Boston: Boston University Press, 1958), p. 8.

constitution, because it has never been written out as a single document. But this does not mean that the British people do not live under a constitutional government. Indeed, many of the great landmarks in the development of British constitutional government, such as Magna Carta (1215), the Petition of Right (1628), and the Bill of Rights (1689), are also part and parcel of the American constitutional background. Because the American colonies had long been governed by written charters, however, the American states quite naturally chose to launch their new governments with formal written documents. Most of the states framed entirely new constitutions, but some, such as Connecticut and Rhode Island, simply made minor changes and converted their old charters into new constitutions.

A constitution need not be ratified by the whole people. In fact, most of the early state constitutions were established through ordinary legislative procedures. But the Massachusetts Constitution of 1780 came to be regarded as a "model constitution" because it was written by a convention elected especially for that purpose, and because the document itself was submitted to the people for final ratification. Thus it appears as a more concrete expression of the eighteenth-century notion of a "social compact," an agreement setting up a government by the people themselves.

A constitution expresses the fundamental political philosophy of the people. It outlines the basic structure and the major functions of the government. And, in a general way, it describes the relations between individual citizens and their government. We would therefore expect to find that the revolutionary leaders expressed much the same democratic philosophy in these early state constitutions as they did in the Declaration of Independence.

The framers of the first state constitutions, like the authors of the Declaration of Independence, borrowed most of their ideas from seventeenth- and eighteenth-century English and French political philosophers. The Americans were deeply impressed with the doctrine of "popular sovereignty," the idea that all political power is derived from the people and that every government must have the consent of the governed. The Declaration of Independence was signed "in the Name and by Authority of the good People of these Colonies." The Massachusetts Constitution explicitly stated that "The People in this commonwealth have the sole and exclusive right of governing themselves as a free, sovereign, and independent state."

All the new state constitutions were republican. They recognized the principle of popular representation, and they provided for government by officials who were accountable to the public and who held office for a fixed term or for "good behavior." Popular sovereignty did not, however, mean majority participation in the government. The Revolution did not democratize suffrage in the states. Arthur Bromage, an authority on state government, says of this period that "Popular sovereignty was more nearly property sovereignty." [2] Those who

---

[2] Arthur W. Bromage, *State Government and Administration in the United States* (New York: Harper & Brothers, 1936), p. 25.

could vote and hold office were those who owned property and paid taxes.

The new constitutions made no clean break with the past. The idea of "natural rights" or "unalienable rights" that was expressed in the Declaration of Independence is rooted deep in our English history. And a bill of rights was attached to nearly all the state constitutions, thus forming "a link in the long chain of institutional development running back through the English Bill of Rights and Petition of Right to Magna Carta."[3] The Revolutionary leaders did not regard these bills of rights as conferring any new rights, but merely as protecting those rights already possessed by Englishmen and therefore by Americans from "time immemorial." The Virginia Bill of Rights states the general principle:

> All men are by nature equally free and independent, and have certain inherent rights of which, when they enter in a state of society, they cannot, by any compact, deprive or divest their posterity, namely the enjoyment of life and liberty, with the means of acquiring and possessing property, and pursuing and obtaining happiness and safety.

These bills of rights, for all their sweeping generalizations about "popular sovereignty" and "natural rights," were not mere abstractions; they reached down to the practical level of "civil rights" and gave very real protection to the liberties of the individual. They included such fundamental rights as freedom of speech, freedom of press, freedom of religion, and freedom of assembly. Just as the Declaration of Independence spelled out the grievances of the colonists against the British king, so these early constitutions specified the civil rights of the people: speedy and public trial, trial by jury, protection against unreasonable search and seizure, protection against self-incrimination, and all the other guarantees of fair procedure that Americans still cherish as their heritage of constitutional rights.

The Revolutionary leaders were more concerned with the principles of freedom than they were with the structure of government. But they were taken with the idea of separation of powers, which many of them had read about in the popular writings of the French political philosopher, "the celebrated Montesquieu." Six of the new state constitutions expressly proclaimed "separation of powers" as a principle of popular government. The Virginia Constitution of 1776, for example, declared, "The legislative, executive, and judicial departments should be separate and distinct so that neither exercises the powers properly belonging to the others." And yet, in practice, the new governments leaned heavily in the direction of legislative supremacy. In some of the states the governor was appointed by the legislature, and in most of the states the judges were also appointed by the legislatures.

All the new constitutions set up various combinations of checks and balances to restrain executive power. The American Revolution was ostensibly fought against the British king, but the king was a symbol thousands of miles away. Con-

---

[3] William S. Carpenter and Paul T. Stafford, *State and Local Government in the United States* (New York: F. S. Crofts & Co., 1936), p. 8.

sequently, the Revolution turned against the royal governors and the king's judges within the colonies. This animus was reflected in the first state constitutions. As Bromage puts it, every one of the new state governments at the outset established "an impotent governor and an all but omnipotent legislature." [4] Within a year after the Declaration of Independence, however, the New York Constitution provided for the popular election of the governor, a pattern followed by Massachusetts in 1780, and by all the states in a few years.

The Articles of Confederation: "A Firm League of Friendship"

While the states were setting up their new constitutions, Congress was attempting to draft a constitution for the government as a whole. In July, 1775, Benjamin Franklin had presented to Congress a design for "Perpetual Union" and, immediately following the Declaration of Independence, Congress appointed a committee to consider the Franklin proposals. This committee quickly made its report to Congress in the form of *Articles of Confederation.* Congress debated the report for more than a year, however, before it finally agreed on a draft, which it submitted to the state legislatures with the stipulation that the Articles should not go into effect until every state had approved them. Maryland was the last state to ratify, in 1781, and so legally the Articles did not go into effect until that year. Thus between 1776 and 1781 the United States as a single nation had no constitutional government; there existed only thirteen separate and independent state governments.

The Articles of Confederation proclaimed "a firm league of friendship" in which each state was explicitly protected in its "sovereignty, freedom, and independence, and every power, jurisdiction, and right, which is not by this confederation expressly delegated to the United States, in Congress assembled." Throughout history, most confederations and federations have developed as fighting organizations. And this one was no exception. The states joined together "for their common defense" in a mutual security pact, "binding themselves to assist each other, against all force offered to, or attacks made upon them." [5] The Articles accordingly represented a compact of states and not a government "of the people, by the people, for the people." The United States under the Articles was more comparable to an international organization than to a national state.

Under the Articles, Congress was the center of the governmental organization. But Congress merely represented the states; like the United Nations today, it could not make laws directly governing the people of the member states. Delegates to Congress were chosen by the legislature of each state, and no state was represented by less than two or more than seven members; no matter how many delegates a state had, it enjoyed only one vote in Congress. The Articles made

---

[4] *State Government and Administration in the United States,* p. 24.

[5] For varying accounts of the United States under the Articles, see John Fiske, *The Critical Period of American History, 1783–1789* (Boston: Houghton Mifflin Co., 1916); Merril Jensen, *The New Nation: A History of the United States During the Confederation, 1781–1789* (New York: Alfred A. Knopf, 1950); A. C. McLaughlin, *The Confederation and the Constitution* (New York: Harper & Brothers, 1905).

no provision for an executive, though a "committee of the states," consisting of one member of Congress from each state, managed the general affairs of the government when the whole Congress was not assembled. This committee appointed one of its members to act as president for one year at a time; a man who had served as president was not immediately re-eligible for the office. The Articles established no national judiciary, but Congress did act as a sort of Supreme Court for disputes between states "concerning boundary, jurisdiction, or any other cause whatever."

The Articles assigned numerous important responsibilities to Congress. Actually, the Articles did little more than transfer to the government of the United States those functions that had belonged to the British crown in the colonial government. Congress was given "the sole and exclusive right and power of determining on peace and war," of sending and receiving ambassadors, of entering into treaties and alliances, and in general of making the rules for the conduct of war (something that was of immediate and common concern). Congress also had "the sole and exclusive right and power" to regulate the value of coin, to fix the standard of weights and measures throughout the United States, to regulate trade with the Indians and to manage Indian affairs, to establish and regulate post offices, to appoint all officers of the navy and to commission all other officers in the service of the United States, to make all rules for the regulation of the land and naval forces, and to direct their operations. Certainly, the national government was entrusted with a good many political functions.

Critics have emphasized that the loose organization of government under the Articles encouraged the states to take off in different directions rather than work closely together for the general good. The text of the Articles suggests, however, that its framers meant to establish a constitutional union and not merely to affirm the friendship of the member states. The people of each state were guaranteed the freedom to travel to and return from any other state, and the citizens of each state were entitled to the "privileges and immunities" of citizens in all the states, including all privileges of trade and commerce. The Articles provided that fugitives from justice could be extradited from one state to any other. And each state was required to give "full faith and credit" to the records, acts, and judicial proceedings of the courts and magistrates of every other state.

Moreover, the states, in ratifying the Articles, agreed to accept certain limitations on their sovereignty. Without the consent of Congress no state could enter into any "conference, agreement, alliance, or treaty with any king, prince or state," engage in diplomatic relations with foreign governments, or enter into any interstate compact or agreement. No state could levy any imposts or duties that might interfere with treaties made by the United States. Without the consent of Congress no state could engage in war unless it was actually invaded or threatened with imminent danger. No state could maintain a navy, but every state was expected to keep up a well-regulated militia and enough armament to defend itself.

Basic Problems in Nation-Building: 1776–1787

Winning the war of independence, writing a constitution, and setting up a new political structure—these are the usual preliminaries to nation-building. But much more fundamental problems are involved in order to establish justice, insure domestic tranquility. . . . The people must first be prepared to recognize and accept the authority of the new government. Every revolutionary government experiences this crisis of legitimacy. The people have joined in the revolution and they feel an identity of purpose in fighting together for a common cause. But when the shooting is over they may fall into difficulties as they discard one set of beliefs and attempt to substitute a new hierarchy of values. It is one thing for the revolutionary leaders to capitalize on dissent, to encourage iconoclasm and incite to violence. It is quite different and much more difficult to return to constructive efforts and to work for consensus among dissident groups.

The American Revolution of 1776 had been not only a war against parliament and king in London, but also a series of local uprisings against unpopular tax collectors and county judges. Once quickened among the citizenry, the spirit of revolution does not immediately abate when the war is won. A decade after the Declaration of Independence, many Americans throughout all the states were still in arms against political authority; debtors were released from jails, records were destroyed, mob violence prevented courts from sitting. Many of the wealthy, upper-class Tories who would normally have served to temper revolutionary extremism had been exiled. A transfer of power had to be effected not simply on paper but in the minds of the people. Former leaders of the Revolution, alarmed by the persistent tendency of the general citizenry to resist any form of government, moved into the official positions which Tory leaders had vacated and set about restoring the public order and protecting private rights.

Lucian Pye, analyzing the problems of nation-building in modern Asia, conceives the process of political development as involving a series of crises: *identity, integration, penetration, participation, distribution*.[6] The American experience after the Revolution can be illuminated within this modern conceptual framework. The comparative approach, although it spans centuries and continents, might give us a clearer understanding not only of what happened in the United States in the critical years 1783 to 1790 (and years after) but also of what is now occurring within most of the new nations in the modern world. This is not to say that the conditions of nation-building were the same for Americans in the eighteenth century as they are for Asians and Africans in the twentieth century; disparities of input and output are obvious but the basic similarities make the analogy meaningful.[7]

---

[6] "Transitional Asia and the Dynamics of Nation Building," in Marian D. Irish (ed.), *World Pressures on American Foreign Policy* (Englewood Cliffs, N.J.: Prentice-Hall, Inc., 1964), pp. 154–172.

[7] Seymour Martin Lipset views the United States in historical and comparative perspective in *The First New Nation* (New York: Basic Books, Inc., 1963). See also

The Articles of Confederation, which established "a firm league of friendship" among the thirteen states, could hardly be regarded as forming a new nation. Rather the emphasis remained on the sovereignty and equality of the separate states. Congress was not to legislate on any matter unless it had the consent of nine of the thirteen states; and no alteration could be made in the Articles unless it was unanimously accepted by Congress and then confirmed by the legislature of every state. But unanimity grew increasingly uncommon when the Revolution came to a close and the states no longer faced a common foe.

The fundamental weakness of government under the Articles, however, was not merely a matter of political structure. By emphasizing the sovereignty and equality of the separate states, the new government could not draw strength from a popular sense of *national identity*. Since the national government under the Articles did not directly govern the people, the average citizen felt little political loyalty to the United States. His first allegiance was still to his own state. For the United States to become a single nation, the people in all of the states would have to develop enough political cohesion to think of themselves primarily as Americans rather than as Virginians or Pennsylvanians.

The crisis of *integration* (in terms of the Pye model) involves the relationship of the political system to the social structure. This is essentially a problem of communication—the task of bridging the gap between political leaders and divergent factions among the people. With no mass media of communication, the problem was serious in the eighteenth century. An intercolonial postal system had been established in 1753, with Benjamin Franklin of Pennsylvania and William Hunter of Virginia as Joint Deputy Postmasters General for North America. Regular mail routes were maintained under the Articles, but bad roads and poor connections slowed up the service. A letter mailed from New York might reach Philadelphia the next day, but it took at least six days for mail from Boston to Philadelphia, three to four weeks from Philadelphia to Lexington, Kentucky, or to Savannah, Georgia.

Difficult as communications were between the people of different states, the process of integration had begun before the Revolution. The colonial patriots kept in touch with one another on political matters through the Committees of Correspondence established in 1764. The First Continental Congress, which met in Philadelphia in 1774, set a pattern of centralized, coordinated intercolonial action. The Second Continental Congress in 1775 assumed the functions of a national legislature, designated George Washington as Commander of a unified Continental Army, created a navy and marine corps, issued paper currency to help finance the Revolution, and entered into diplomatic relations with France and other European governments. It is also important to mention the promotion of intercolonial trade, the intercolonial circulation of newspapers and pamphlets, and the intercolonial meetings of religious groups—Baptists, Friends, Methodists,

---

Richard L. Merritt's essay, "Nation Building in America: The Colonial Years" in Karl W. Deutsch and William J. Foltz (eds.), *Nation-Building* (New York: Atherton Press, 1963), pp. 56–83.

and others and the revivals such as the Great Awakening, which cut across colonial boundaries. It would probably be stretching the facts too far to claim that the colonists had developed what Walter Lippmann describes as a "public philosophy." [8] Nevertheless, all this intercolonial exchange—of ideas, things, and persons—did build up a sense of community that encompassed all thirteen colonies. And this common political socialization established a national foundation for the United States of America.

The third major crisis in nation-building—the crisis of *penetration*—involves the ability of the national government to reach into the local communities and to carry out public policies in the national interest. Under the Articles, the United States almost foundered because the central government could not take direct action in the states and local communities and hence was virtually impotent in economic affairs. True, Congress had exclusive power over coinage, but the states were free to issue great quantities of paper money in an attempt to appease the increasing number of debtors. The resultant monetary confusion aggravated the business depression that followed the Revolution. Congress was unable to regulate interstate commerce, which rapidly developed into an economic "cold war" among the states. Moreover, it had to depend on contributions from the states to cover all expenses for the common defense and the general welfare. The contribution of each state was based on the value of the land, buildings, and improvements in that state. The central government could not levy taxes; only the legislatures of the states had that power. Actually, the flow of funds into the national treasury depended on the good will and good faith of the individual states; and as time passed, the states showed themselves less and less inclined to meet their obligations to the central government. Congress could borrow money on the credit of the United States but, since it had no means of its own to raise revenue, its credit became increasingly shaky. During the last years of the Articles, the United States was unable even to meet the interest due on its foreign and domestic debt.

The crisis of *participation* is closely related to the crisis of identity, but it goes beyond psychological identification since it is concerned with drawing the general citizenry into the national political process. Under the Articles of Confederation the citizens in the several states did not vote directly for any representatives in the national government. The members of Congress, chosen by the state legislatures, were under no pressure to respond to popular mandate. Since Congress had no power to levy taxes on the individual citizens, or to pass other laws affecting them directly, the people as a whole did not feel personally involved in the nation's affairs. If the national government were to succeed, it would have to establish a more direct and functional relationship with the many interest groups and various factions that comprised the dynamic community.

The final crisis in nation-building is that of *distribution*, the problem of decid-

---

[8] Walter Lippmann, *Essays in The Public Philosophy* (Boston: Little, Brown and Co., 1954).

ing who gets what under the new system. Rising expectations are a part of every revolution, in any century, among all peoples. The criterion of success for the new government, from the viewpoint of those who helped create it, is the pay-off. The American Revolution had strong ideological motivations. It was a fight to secure "certain unalienable rights," but it was also an economic war, a struggle to toss off the yoke of colonialism and to promote American commercial and business interests. In fact, the greatest dissatisfaction with the Articles seems to have come from the merchants, planters, and businessmen who thought that the national government should be more actively concerned with the economic development of the country.

The first moves to amend the Articles reflected the demands of economic groups who equated their rising expectations with a stronger national economy. Twice under the Articles amendments were proposed to permit Congress to levy duties on imports. In 1781, a proposal to levy a 5 per cent duty on enumerated imports was defeated by the single veto of Rhode Island. Two years later a similar amendment proposed duties on sugar, molasses, tea, coffee, pepper, and other commodities; all proceeds were to be used to pay the public debt. This one was defeated by the veto of New York. Moreover, although Congress could regulate foreign commerce, it had no power over commerce among the states. In an attempt to exclude the commerce of their neighbors, many states had set up tariff barriers and tonnage duties. Economic rivalry among the states reached such a pitch of tension and frustration that the states themselves began to demand a stronger national government.

In 1785, delegates from Virginia and Maryland met in Alexandria, Virginia, to work out an agreement on problems of navigation and commerce on the Potomac River and Chesapeake Bay. Because that conference was unsuccessful, the Virginia legislature called a general economic conference to meet in Annapolis, Maryland, in September, 1786. The Annapolis Conference in its turn was also a failure, for only twelve delegates appeared to represent five states whose interests were predominantly commercial: New York, New Jersey, Pennsylvania, Delaware, and Virginia. It took only a few days for the delegates to draft their *Report* under the leadership of Alexander Hamilton from New York. Observing that the situation of the United States under the Articles had become "delicate and critical," the *Report* recommended that all the states appoint commissioners to meet at Philadelphia on the second Monday in the following May (1787) "to devise such further provisions as shall appear to them necessary to render the Constitution of the Federal government adequate to the exigencies of the Union."

Immediately after the Annapolis Conference several of the states began to name delegates to the meeting in May. In February, 1787, Congress itself finally endorsed the movement for a convention, resolving that it was "expedient" for a convention to meet "for the sole and express purpose of revising the Articles of Confederation and reporting to Congress and the several legislatures such alterations and provisions therein as shall when agreed to in Congress and confirmed by the states render the federal constitution adequate to the exigencies of Government and the preservation of the Union." All the states except Rhode Island eventually responded by appointing delegates to the Constitutional Convention to meet in Philadelphia in May, 1787.

The Constitutional Convention at Philadelphia

Seventy-four delegates were appointed to the Philadelphia Convention. Nineteen of them never appeared, and of the fifty-five who attended only thirty-nine signed the final document which became the Constitution. On May 14, 1787, the day fixed for the opening session, only Virginia and Pennsylvania were represented. Bad weather conditions and impassable roads made travel exceedingly difficult, especially for the men from the New England states. But gradually the delegates began to arrive, and a quorum of nine states was obtained on May 29. The Georgia delegates arrived two days later; the Maryland delegates, though close by, did not show up until June 2. The New Hampshire delegates, among the first appointed, were the last to arrive, some time in July. Rhode Island appointed no delegates and boycotted the whole proceeding. The New England representation was never large, and only six men stayed on hand to sign the Constitution. The southern delegations were the largest in attendance and the most influential in debate; fourteen southern delegates gave their support to the very end.

Gentlemen of Principle and Property

Roger Sherman of Connecticut and Robert Morris of Pennsylvania were the only men who put their names to all three of the great documents of the period: the Declaration of Independence, the Articles of Confederation, and the Philadelphia Constitution. Only eight of those who had signed the Declaration of Independence were appointed as commissioners to the Convention of 1787. Four of them were from Pennsylvania—Benjamin Franklin, Robert Morris, George Clymer, and James Wilson; and all four signed the Constitution. Elbridge Gerry of Massachusetts, who had signed both the Declaration of Independence and the Articles of Confederation, took an active part in the Convention but would not give his approval to the outcome. George Reed of Delaware signed both the Declaration and the Constitution. George Wythe of Virginia, who had signed the Declaration of Independence, was called home by the death of his wife during the Convention; though he was not present at the signing, he later expressed his approval of the proposed Constitution. Clearly, however, a considerable turnover had occurred among the decision-makers in the eleven years since 1776.

Few of the popular leaders who had been the most active agitators during the Revolution appeared in Philadelphia. They were suspicious that any central government would serve the aristocracy just as the English government had, and their suspicions were strengthened as they noted that those most critical of the Articles were also inclined to be most skeptical of democracy. They scorned "aristocratic plots" and were confident that they could block any attempt to transfer power to the gentry simply by controlling a single state legislature.

Understandably, they made little effort to seek nomination as delegates, or even to accept the opportunity when it fell their way. Patrick Henry summed up the attitude of the Revolutionary firebrands when he announced that he "smelt a rat" and refused to attend the Convention. Had he realized that a completely new constitution was to be pushed through, he might have changed his mind.

Most of the nationalist leaders in modern nation-building are relatively young men whose professional ambitions and personal fortunes are tied to the central government. For the most part, they belong to the elite class, the well-born and able, ideological innovators, social and economic promoters.

Not too surprisingly, the Founding Fathers of "the first new nation" fit neatly into this pattern. The average age of the men at the Philadelphia Convention was forty. Many of those whose voices were strongest during the debates were in their thirties: Alexander Hamilton 33, James Madison 37, Gouverneur Morris 38, Elbridge Gerry 37, Edmund Randolph 32, Charles Pinckney 24, William Paterson 34. Benjamin Franklin, the most venerable member of the group, was 82. George Washington, who was unanimously elected as presiding officer, was 52. Others who proved conspicuous in debate were somewhat older than the average: Roger Sherman 60, James Wilson 45, George Mason 60. The term "Founding Fathers" conjures up images of old grey-beards. In fact, however, our American Founding Fathers were like most new nation-builders—relatively young men—and more important, they were zealous young men fired with ideas and ideals.

That the work of the Founding Fathers has survived the test of time may be attributed to their preoccupation with the fundamental principles of government. Practical men of affairs, they made every effort to combine scholarship with statesmanship. With a respect for philosophical learning that seems almost inordinate in our technical age, they examined the texts of political writers from the earliest days of history. Aristotle, Plutarch, Cicero, Locke, Montesquieu, Vattell—these were familiar names in their discourse. They studied history and analyzed the comparative forms of government: the Athenian democracy, the Roman republic, the Hanseatic League, the Belgian and Dutch confederacies, the Germanic Empire, the British and French kingdoms, and the Swiss cantons.

This conscious joining together of scholarship and statesmanship in the Convention of 1787 resulted in a political design that did far more than merely meet the exigencies of the new Republic. The Framing Fathers deliberately developed a public philosophy based on certain concepts concerning the nature of man, the nature of society, and the nature of government. That this public philosophy happened to bolster their self-interest and personal predilections does not detract from the intrinsic merit of the Constitution which they made the "supreme law of the land." The "gentlemen at Philadelphia" were not only "rich and well-born"; they were also exceptionally "able." Combining their own practical experience in government with the insights of the ancient and contemporary political philosophers, they developed basic rules for political behavior that still apply amazingly well to vastly changed circumstances.

General Washington expressed the consensus of his colleagues when he wrote to General Lafayette, his old ally of Revolutionary years, that what the Convention hoped for was "a government of respectability under which life, liberty, and property will be secured to us." In the term often used by the Framing Fathers themselves, they were "gentlemen of principle and property." That they did, indeed, have principles is no less important than that they had property. It is not surprising, however, that none of the principles they established was in conflict with the property they were convened to protect. To suggest that their view of the general interest was conditioned by their private interests is simply to recognize that the Founding Fathers were normal human beings.[9]

In the course of debate, the gentlemen passed many remarks that have frequently been cited as evidence that they were less concerned with securing the blessings of liberty than with protecting the rights of private property and the sanctity of contracts. Gouverneur Morris of Pennsylvania, arguing that wealth as well as numbers should be represented in Congress, declared that property was the main object of society: "If property then is the main object of government, certainly it ought to be one measure of the influence due to those who are to be affected by the government." John Rutledge of South Carolina said that these were his sentiments too: "Property is certainly the principal object of society." On the other hand, as Madison's notes on the Convention indicate, James Wilson, counsel for extremely wealthy interests in Pennsylvania, ". . . could not agree that property was the sole or primary object of government and society. The cultivation and improvement of the human mind was the most noble object. With respect to this object, as well as to other personal rights, numbers were surely the natural and precise measure of representation."

Charles Beard, in his *Economic Interpretation of the Constitution*, analyzed the personnel of the Constitutional Convention in terms of their economic interests and professional pursuits. He found that a majority of the members were lawyers by profession; that not one represented the small farming or mechanic class; that the overwhelming majority held government bonds which they were eager to protect; that many were land speculators anxious for a strong government which would insure their interests; that many were wealthy merchants who hoped to advance their commercial interests; that many were slaveholders who wanted their property rights specifically guaranteed.

Beard's thesis was shocking and provocative when it was first published in 1913. He charged that the Constitution was based "upon the concept that the fundamental private rights of property are anterior to government and morally beyond the reach of popular majorities"; that it was "an economic document drawn with superb skill by men whose property interests were immediately at stake"; and that "as such it appealed directly and unerringly to identical interests

---

[9] For varying accounts of the personnel and proceedings at the Philadelphia Convention, see Max Farrand, *The Framing of the Constitution* (New Haven: Yale University Press, 1913); Fred Rodell, *Fifty Five Men* (New York: The Telegraph Press, 1936); Carl C. Van Doren, *The Great Rehearsal* (New York: The Viking Press, 1948); Broadus Mitchell and Louise Mitchell, *A Biography of the Constitution of the United States* (New York: Oxford University Press, 1964).

in the country at large." [10] In time, these pioneering generalizations from Beard's carefully collected data have become part of the conventional wisdom in the literature of American government. No single modern study has been so influential in the interpretation of the Constitution of 1787.

Not all historians and political scientists, however, have been willing to accept all of Beard's economic interpretation. In *The Making of the Constitution*, Charles Warren, a long-time student of our constitutional background, makes a careful analysis of the daily debates at Philadelphia. On the basis of what was said and how the voting went at the Convention, Warren disagrees with Beard's view that property interests of the members shaped the main outlines of the Constitution. [11]

More recent critics of the economic interpretation, pursuing Beard's own methodology, have arrived at different conclusions. Forrest McDonald, after gathering much new data, especially from the state ratifying conventions, declares that "it is impossible to justify Beard's interpretation." [12] He finds that the delegates in the Convention "behaved as anything but a consolidated group." Furthermore, Beard's thesis that the contest over ratification was between large personal property interests on the one hand and small farming and debtor interests on the other "is entirely incompatible with the facts." Examining the voting records in each of the state conventions, McDonald observes no grounds for Beard's claim that the holding of public securities was a significant factor in ratification. Economic interests were certainly important, though they were not so simply and clearly aligned as Beard claims; the conflicts were too numerous and complicated to assign any single motivating economic force either for or against the Constitution.

If you want to use your own judgment in this controversy, you should first examine Max Farrand's *Records of the Federal Convention* (three large volumes) and find out for yourself what the various members had to say about the role of property in government, the basis of representation, qualifications for franchise, individual liberties, and property rights. [13] You will notice that some of the most articulate and colorful delegates in debate were frequently outvoted. Three of those most conspicuous in the proceedings refused to sign. Be sure to take a hard look at the final text of the Constitution. However heated the debates, the cold decision is what counts.

---

[10] Charles Beard, *An Economic Interpretation of the Constitution of the United States* (New York: The Macmillan Company, 1913).

[11] Charles Warren, *The Making of the Constitution* (Boston: Little, Brown and Company, 1937).

[12] Forrest McDonald, *We the People* (Chicago: The University of Chicago Press, 1958), p. 350 and p. 357. For still another attack on the Beard thesis, see Robert E. Brown, *Charles Beard and the Constitution* (Princeton: Princeton University Press, 1956).

[13] Max Farrand, *The Records of the Federal Convention of 1787* (New Haven: Yale University Press, 1911), 3 vols. Unless otherwise noted, the many quotations in this chapter from the debates in Philadelphia are taken from these records.

Personalities at the Convention

George Mason of Virginia, who was later to denounce his colleagues in the fight against ratification, wrote to his son that he was pleased to find in the Convention "many men of fine republican principles . . . many gentlemen of the most respectable abilities . . . of the purest intentions." James Madison wrote one of his friends that he was impressed with the good company: "in several instances the most respectable characters in the United States and in general . . . the best contribution of talents the states could make for the occasion." William Pierce of Georgia, on whose contemporary notes we depend for characterizations of the individual members, said that he was gratified to sit in "the wisest council in the world."

Many of the Convention delegates were gentlemen of learning; about half of them were college graduates from such schools as Princeton, Yale, Harvard, Columbia, Pennsylvania, William and Mary. In his "character sketches," William Pierce called special attention to their educational qualifications: Dr. Samuel Johnson of Connecticut, "one of the first classics in America"; Colonel Hamilton of New York, "reputed to be a finished scholar . . . he enquires into every part of his subject with the searchings of phylosophy"; William Paterson of New Jersey, "a Classic, a Lawyer, and an Orator"; Captain Dayton, also of New Jersey, "possesses a good education and some reading"; James Wilson of Pennsylvania, "He is well acquainted with Man, and understands all the passions that influence him. Government seems to have been his peculiar Study, all the political institutions of the World he knows in detail and can trace the causes and effects of every revolution from the earliest stages of the Greecian commonwealth down to the present time"; John Dickinson of Delaware, "a Scholar, and said to be a Man of very extensive information"; George Wythe of Virginia, "the famous professor of Law at the University of William and Mary. . . . From his close attention to the study of general learning he has acquired a compleat knowledge of the dead languages and all the sciences. . . No Man it is said understands the history of Government better than Mr. Wythe . . ."; James Madison of Virginia "blends together the profound politician, with the Scholar"; Governor Randolph of Virginia, "a young Gentleman in whom unite all the accomplishments of the Scholar, and the States-man"; Charles Coteworth Pinckney, "a Gentleman of Family and fortune" from South Carolina, "has received the advantage of a liberal education and possesses a very extensive degree of legal knowledge"; Abraham Baldwin of Georgia, "having laid the foundation of a compleat classical education at Harvard College, he pursues every study with ease." And so down the roster; of only a few could Pierce say, "But little education."

Gentlemen of property, men of learning, nearly all of them were also practical politicians: members of Congress, governors of states, members of state legislatures, businessmen with political interests. It was bread and butter and gravy for them to design a government that would please the majority of the electorate. If in our day it seems that they spoke too frankly about the rights of property and the tendency toward a natural aristocracy, we should keep in mind that in their day the exercise of suffrage and the holding of office were generally restricted by property qualifications. Moreover, the average citizen was then a small farmer and ownership in land was widespread among the people, so that property qualifications were not so restrictive then as they would be today.

In the debates on representation, Charles Pinckney of South Carolina went into a long discourse on class structure in the country; he found three classes, the professional men, the commercial men, and the landed gentry; the latter, the most numerous, "are and ought ever to be the governing spring in the system." But he concluded objectively that, however distinct they are in their pursuits, the three classes should be considered "individually equal in the political scale," since "after all there is one, but one great and equal body of citizens composing the inhabitants of this Country among whom there are no distinctions of rank, and very few or none of fortune."

The proceedings of the Constitutional Convention were intended to be kept secret. A secretary, Major Jackson, was appointed to keep a record of all the motions and the votes the delegates cast on them. In order to encourage a spirit of accommodation, the record of voting was kept by states rather than by members; this made it possible for delegates to change their minds during the course of debate without filling the records with apparent inconsistencies. Rules were set up forbidding members to make copies of the resolution; after the Convention was over, however, it appeared that several gentlemen had spent the evenings transcribing their notes on the daily debates. But during the Convention they saw to it that neither the general public nor even close friends and relatives were informed on the nature of the discussions under way in the old State House in Philadelphia.

This was probably the most practical way to proceed with the business; once men are forced to defend their positions in public, any compromise tends to appear as a retreat from principle. "Open covenants openly arrived at" makes a better slogan than it does a bylaw. If, in the early weeks of the Convention, the press had been allowed to report the debates, it seems most unlikely that the members would have been able to continue their deliberations until they had reached final agreement. Even as it was, the early differences of opinion threatened the success of the Convention.

The Randolph and Paterson Plans

The Convention first tackled the problem of national identity, redesigning the central government so that it would have a more direct and functional relationship to the people in the states. Edmund Randolph from Virginia opened the session on May 29 by presenting fifteen resolutions. First, Randolph proposed a strong consolidated union which, he candidly confessed, was intended to be stronger than any federal government. He would establish a national legislature with two branches: the first branch to be elected by the people of the several states; the second branch to be chosen by the first from a list of persons nominated by the state legislatures. Representation of the states in both houses would be determined by their population or the amount of taxes they paid. This national legislature would retain all the functions that Congress performed under the Confederation and would also be empowered to "legislate in all cases in which the separate states are incompetent or in which the harmony of the United States may be interrupted by the exercise of individual legislation." In addition, the national legislature would have the authority to nullify any law passed by the states that it felt contravened the Constitution, and to call out the full force of the Union against any state that failed to meet its obligations under the Constitution.

The Randolph Plan proposed a modified parliamentary form of government. The national legislature was to choose the national executive for a fixed term. It would also choose the members of the national judiciary, who would hold office during "good behavior." The executive and the judiciary would compose a "council of revision," with the power to veto all laws, national or state, that it judged to be contrary to the intent of the Constitution. Obviously the doctrine of separation of powers—that is, the independence of the executive, legislative, and judicial branches—had not as yet made much impression on the thinking of Governor Randolph, or of James Madison (who probably had more to do with shaping the plan than the young Governor who had the honor of presenting it).

For several weeks the delegates at Philadelphia debated the Randolph Plan. Naturally it was favored by the large states and attacked by the small. Under the Articles, all states, whether large or small, enjoyed equal representation in Congress. Under the Randolph Plan, the more populous states and the wealthiest states would have the preponderance of representation in both houses.

On June 15, William Paterson of New Jersey brought in a combination of counterproposals that had been worked up by delegates from Connecticut, New York, New Jersey, and Delaware. Whereas the Randolph Plan had scrapped the Articles in order to set up a strong national government, the Paterson Plan would strengthen but preserve the existing Confederation. The Paterson Plan would add to the powers of the present Congress the authority to regulate commerce among the states, to raise revenue by tariff, and to obtain financial contributions from the states in proportion to the number of citizens. It would also give Congress the power to choose an executive who would serve a fixed term and be ineligible for a second term. It would establish a judiciary, the judges to be appointed by the executive and to serve during good behavior. The "king-pin clause," later to appear in the Constitution, appears first in the Paterson Plan. This clause made the acts of Congress passed under the Articles and all treaties ratified under the authority of the United States "the supreme law of the respective states and of their citizens anything in the respective laws of the individual states to the contrary notwithstanding."

With the Randolph Plan and the Paterson Plan the Convention was faced with two alternatives: on the one hand to construct a new and strong consolidated union; on the other, to continue a fairly loose association of states—a confederation. Both plans were republican at the national level and at the state level. Under the Randolph Plan, Congress was composed of two houses, with a state's representation determined by its population or the amount of taxes it paid to the national government. Under the Paterson Plan, the Congress would remain unicameral, the state legislatures would choose the representatives, and the states would be represented equally. The Randolph Plan would give Congress plenary power to legislate in all matters of national concern affecting the general welfare. The Paterson Plan would give Congress only enumerated powers. Actually, however, both plans were calculated to strengthen the national government. They differed in terms of the degree to which it would be strengthened.

Representation

The Paterson Plan for a unicameral Congress with equal representation of the states sparked the great debate over whether the United States should become a national union or remain a confederation of states. Colonel George Mason of Virginia declared that "notwithstanding his solicitude to establish a national government, he never would agree to abolish the state governments or render them absolutely insignificant." Luther Martin of Maryland agreed with Colonel Mason on the importance of the state governments: "He would support them at the expense of the general government which was instituted for the purpose of that support."

James Wilson of Pennsylvania advocated the Randolph Plan; he did not think "state governments and state sovereignties to be so much the idol of the People that they are averse to receive a national government." Alexander Hamilton was the most outspoken in denouncing the idea of a mere confederation. He felt that "great economy might be obtained by substituting a general government" for the state governments, though he admitted he would not shock public opinion by pressing for such a drastic measure. James Madison reviewed the history of ancient and modern confederations and found in all of them "the same tendency of the parts to encroach on the authority of the whole"; he begged the smaller states to drop their "pertinacious adherence" to the Paterson Plan.

The text of the Constitution bespeaks for the "great compromise" that was finally worked out between the large and small states. The "more perfect union" is neither a consolidated national government nor a confederation of sovereign states. In the Congress of the United States there are two houses: the House of Representatives represents the people of the states and representation is proportioned to their number; the Senate represents the states as equal political units, with two senators from each state. And the Constitution provides that equal representation in the Senate cannot be abridged even by constitutional amendment.

For purposes of proportioning representation in the House, it was agreed that "the people" would include the free inhabitants and three-fifths of the slaves in each state. (It was also part of the deal to include three-fifths of the slaves in the apportionment of "direct taxes.") There is no moral or logical defense for this compromise. It is simply a formula upon which the free and the slave states were willing to agree. Northerners generally thought that the number of free inhabitants was the proper basis of representation; the northern states had the proponderance of free inhabitants. Southerners generally thought that wealth, particularly wealth invested in slaves, should be counted in apportioning representation; the southern states had the preponderance of slaves. Elbridge Gerry of Massachusetts brutally asked, "Why then should the blacks, who were property in the South, be in the rule of representation more than the cattle and horses of the North?" Gouverneur Morris of Pennsylvania pointed out that if the Negroes were counted for purposes of representation, the people of Pennsylvania would revolt at the idea of being put on a footing with slaves. William Davie of North Carolina announced that it was high time for him to speak out: if the eastern states meant to exclude slaves from representation, "the business was at an end."

The Electorate

The Convention attempted to meet the problems of popular participation and of penetration first by providing for direct representation in the House of Representatives and then by giving Congress the power to levy and collect taxes from all the people. The individual with a pocketbook interest in his government (whose leaders he helps to choose) is not so likely to be indifferent to how that government operates. When it came to determining the basis of representation and taxation, everyone agreed that all the free inhabitants should be counted. But disagreement sprang up over what the qualifications of the electorate should be. Only a few of the delegates were willing to trust all the people with the vote. John Dickinson of Delaware urged that the right of suffrage be limited to the freeholders—that is, to the property-holders—of the country; he felt that such a limitation was a "necessary defense against the dangerous influence of those multitudes without property and without principle, with which our country like all others will in time abound." James Madison of Virginia was inclined to agree with Dickinson, for he too feared the time when "the great majority of the people will not only be without landed, but any other sort, of property." Such people were bound to become "the tools of opulence and ambition." The good Dr. Franklin objected, reminding the Convention that "our common people" had displayed much virtue and public spirit during the Revolution; he would not disfranchise them for their pains.

The delegates failed to reach a compromise on this matter of voting qualifications and simply returned the problem to the states. To this day, the Constitution makes no guarantee of the right to national suffrage; whoever has the qualifications to vote for the most numerous house of his state legislature may also vote for United States senators, representatives, and presidential electors.

Many delegates to the Constitutional Convention showed little feeling for democracy in the modern sense. In protesting against the popular election of legislators, Elbridge Gerry of Massachusetts declared, "The evils we experience flow from the excess of democracy." No doubt Shays' Rebellion in Massachusetts on the eve of the Convention had pointed up the gentleman's fear of "the levilling spirit." On the other hand, James Wilson of Pennsylvania argued that the legislators in the lower house be chosen by popular election, because "he was for raising the federal pyramid to a considerable altitude, and for that reason wished to give it as broad a base as possible." When the work of the Convention was finally done, the delegates had indeed raised the federal pyramid to a considerable height above the general citizenry. "The people" were given a direct part only in the election of the House of Representatives. The Senate was to be chosen indirectly through the state legislatures. The President was to be selected by electoral colleges in the states. The judges were to be appointed for good behavior by the President, with the confirmation of the Senate.

Some of the Framers yearned to move even farther from popular control and establish an aristocracy. In the debates on the bicameral legislature, Gouverneur Morris of Pennsylvania argued almost plaintively, "The second branch ought to be composed of men of great and established property—*an aristocracy* . . . such an aristocratic body will keep down the turbulence of democracy." As the debates went on, however, it became increasingly evident that Gouverneur Morris' claim for aristocracy was intended to give greater weight in the government to the eastern commercial interests. "He thought the rule of representation ought to be so fixed as to secure to the Atlantic States a prevalence in the National Councils." He was opposed to any rule of representation based on mere numbers, for this would give too much power to the western people: "They will ruin the Atlantic interests. The Back members are always most averse to the best measures." But he was also opposed to counting slave property in apportioning representation, for this would give the southern states too much power.

The class-consciousness of Gouverneur Morris and his supporters must have seemed shallow and pretentious even to their contemporaries. As Louis Hartz points out in *The Liberal Tradition in America*, would-be aristocrats have always been frustrated in American politics because of "the absence of an aristocracy to fight, the absence of an aristocracy to ally with, and the absence of a mob to denounce." [14] Certainly, in 1787, the gentlemen who debated the Constitution could not look to any *ancien régime* outside the Convention to put up a fight for special privileges. And certainly no angry mobs ever besieged the State House in Philadelphia to force the Framers to form a democratic government.

The Framers designed the careful separation of powers and the complicated system of checks and balances to protect the country against both "the excesses of democracy" and "the mischief of aristocracy." The great majority of them claimed, whether they believed it or not, that this new country comprised "one great and equal body of citizens." Indeed, members who spoke out boldly for "kingly power" and "natural aristocracy" usually ended up by apologizing for any remarks they may have made that were susceptible to misinterpretation. The Framers were not democratic in the sense that they were ready to offer political power to the masses. Yet they were firmly republican in their principles, and they were determined to establish a strong representative government for the whole country.

The Executive and the Courts

The Philadelphia Convention was particularly concerned with the problem of legitimate leadership. A revolutionary government which has come to power by

---

[14] Louis Hartz, *The Liberal Tradition in America* (New York: Harcourt, Brace and Company, 1955), p. 96.

overthrowing traditional authority inevitably finds it difficult to secure an effective substitute for the rejected authority. Seymour Lipset, a prominent political sociologist, points out the extraordinary role played by General Washington, who presided over the Constitutional Convention. Lipset suggests that the charismatic leadership of George Washington—"first in war, first in peace, first in the hearts of his countrymen"—bridged the critical years between the revolution against the British king and the constitutional establishment of a strong President.[15] Fortuitously, the Commander in Chief of the Revolution, who was also slated to be the first President of the new republic, was committed to the idea of constitutional government.

Almost all members of the Convention agreed that the new government must be republican—that is, non-monarchical—in form. Some may have felt privately that the British monarchy was the best model, for, after all, this was the age of monarchy. Only a few years had passed since all the delegates had been pleased to describe themselves as "His Majesty's most faithful subjects." The grievances against the British king spelled out in the Declaration of Independence, however, had made a deep impression on the popular mind. The people were bound to repudiate any plan for a hereditary ruler.

The Randolph Plan provided for a national executive to be chosen by the national legislature. Gouverneur Morris of Pennsylvania was opposed to this scheme, for he thought it would tend to make the President a mere creature of the legislature; he preferred election at large by the freeholders of the country. But Mr. Pinckney of South Carolina objected to election by the people on the practical grounds that the most populous states could join in support of one candidate and manage to carry every election. Colonel Mason of Virginia felt it would be "as unnatural to refer the choice of a proper character for chief magistrate to the people, as it would, to refer a trial of colours to a blind man." Not until nearly the end of the Convention was a compromise effected: the President and Vice-President were to be selected by electoral colleges appointed by the states in whatever manner their legislatures might direct. James Wilson of Pennsylvania insisted that this device favored aristocracy, for it meant that the people would have no more than an indirect part in the election. Most of the other members were better pleased with it, though probably none of them was completely satisfied.

Randolph had initially proposed that the President's term of office run for seven years. Dr. McClurg of Virginia moved that the President be permitted to serve during "good behavior"; Gouverneur Morris of Pennsylvania seconded the motion, announcing that he was indifferent to how the executive was chosen so long as good behavior determined tenure. Colonel Mason thought that to base tenure on good behavior was but a step away from hereditary monarchy. The final compromise was to make the President's term four years, with indefinite re-eligibility.

The question of the judiciary provoked comparatively little discussion at the

---

[15] *The First New Nation*, p. 18.

Convention. There was no disagreement on the need for a supreme national court; the establishment of inferior courts was left to the discretion of Congress. The Convention was not persuaded to accept the Randolph proposal for a "council of revision" in which the executive shared with the judges the power to declare national and state laws "unconstitutional." Elbridge Gerry of Massachusetts objected to the idea of "making statesmen of the judges; and setting them up as the guardians of the rights of the people; he relied for his part on the representatives of the people as the guardians of their rights and interests." James Madison argued that, since experience showed the powerful tendency of the legislature "to absorb all power into its vortex," it was necessary to give "every defensive authority to the other departments that was consistent with republican principles."

Some years later, Chief Justice Marshall, in the case of *Marbury* v. *Madison* (1803), claimed for the courts the right to review the constitutionality of congressional legislation.[16] The Convention itself bestowed no such power on the judiciary. It voted against the council of revision and voted for giving the executive a qualified veto over legislation. The power Marshall asserted was that of reviewing the laws in terms of their *constitutionality*; what the Convention had voted against was the power of reviewing the laws in terms of *policy*.

Delegation and Distribution of Powers and Functions

Much has been written to show that the Constitution was essentially an economic instrument for the protection of property and the promotion of commerce. In proof of this interpretation there are several specific provisions dealing with the public debt, taxation, commerce, sound money, bankruptcy and obligations of contract, weights and measures, patents and copyrights, post offices and post roads. Professor William Crosskey, of the University of Chicago Law School, has produced two volumes, *Politics and the Constitution*, in which he carefully investigates eighteenth-century word-usage. He maintains that the Framing Fathers intended, when they said Congress should have the power "to regulate Commerce . . . among the several states," to include the internal business activity of the entire country. Crosskey's research bears out his thesis—despite a long line of Supreme Court opinions to the contrary—that it was the deliberate intent of the Framers to give Congress total authority over commerce without regard to state lines.[17] The recorded debates of the Convention shed little light on this question.

Actually, the debate in the Convention focused on foreign rather than domestic commerce. The southern states, whose economy depended on agricultural exports, feared that the northern states might succeed in levying taxes on exports to the disadvantage of the South. Colonel Mason of Virginia stated the problem clearly: "A majority when interested will oppress the minority." If the interest of the eight northern states was different from that of the five southern states, the southern states had good reason to be suspicious. Pierce

---

[16] *Marbury* v. *Madison*, 1 Cranch 137 (1803).

[17] William Crosskey, *Politics and the Constitution* (Chicago: The University of Chicago Press, 1953), 2 vols.

Butler of South Carolina strenuously opposed giving the national government power to tax exports as "unjust and alarming to the staple states." The upshot was that an explicit limitation on Congress was put into the Constitution: "no tax or duty shall be laid on articles exported from any state." Northern business interests were pleased, however, by a provision that granted Congress the power to tax *imports*, for they felt that this would enable them to throw up a tariff wall behind which new manufacturers could prosper.

Perhaps what disturbed the southern delegates most was the possibility that, if the national government were granted power over foreign commerce, the northern states might try to prohibit the slave trade. Mr. Pinckney of South Carolina vehemently attacked every proposal for extending the power of Congress in this matter; his state was "expressly and watchfully" opposed to any "meddling with the importation of negroes." Colonel Mason of Virginia, attributing "this infernal traffic" to the "avarice of British merchants" and to the "lust of gain" of "some of our Eastern brethren," believed it "essential in every point of view that the general government should have the power to prevent the increase of slavery." Virginia already had more than enough slaves, and its delegates could afford to be more moral than those of South Carolina and Georgia, which still had a pressing need for cheap labor. John Rutledge of South Carolina warned the Convention that the people of South Carolina and Georgia would never be such fools as to give up so important an interest. The final decision was an attempted compromise between morality and economics: Congress was not to prohibit the slave trade before 1808 but could levy a head tax of ten dollars on all slaves imported into the states until that time.

The delegates to the Convention spent more time debating problems of governmental structure than questions of governmental functions: the relation of the states to the Union and to one another; the separation of powers—executive, legislative, and judicial—and the check and balance of these powers. The Constitution's treatment of the enumerated powers of Congress and the functions of the national government seems incomplete, oddly deficient. Many special powers were suggested during the course of debate, such as the authority of Congress to create corporations, but apparently they were struck out in order to make the document politically palatable. If serious objection was raised to any provision, strategy dictated that it be omitted—and the argument postponed to future congresses—in the interest of promoting agreement on the general plan of the Constitution.

The most complete and detailed powers to be retained in the Constitution were those dealing with war, for the imminent danger of foreign aggression induced the delegates to give ample authority to the central government as a fighting organization. The Constitution grants the national government almost absolute authority in time of war. Even the writ of habeas corpus may be suspended when the country is threatened by insurrection or invasion. The only concession the Convention made to the widespread yearning for peace—in 1787 the people were tired of war and its chaotic aftermath—is the clause that forbids Congress to make any appropriation for the army for a longer term than two years.

The Fight for Ratification

The work of the Constitutional Convention came to an end on September 17, 1787. Dr. Franklin rose to urge all "for our own sakes and for the sake of posterity" to act "heartily and unanimously" in recommending the Constitution. Three members, though they confessed that they were "painfully embarrassed," declined to sign the document—Governor Randolph, Colonel Mason, and Mr. Gerry. Thirty-nine delegates, representing twelve states, did affix their names.

Three members of the Convention, James Madison of Virginia and Rufus King and Nathaniel Gorham of Massachusetts, were also members of Congress, and they immediately carried the document to New York City, where Congress was in session. On September 28, 1787, without making any recommendation of its own, Congress submitted the proposed Constitution to the states.

Ratification Procedure

The problem of ratification had presented the Convention itself with a rather delicate problem. In writing a new constitution, the delegates had clearly exceeded their authority—which was simply to propose amendments to the Articles of Confederation. Since the members of both Congress and the state legislatures were sworn to the "perpetual union" under the Confederation, they could hardly vote to scrap the Articles. Even before the Convention had met, James Madison had written to Thomas Jefferson that he felt it expedient "to lay the foundation of the new system in such a ratification by the people themselves as will render it clearly paramount to their legislative authority."

In the Convention itself, some of the members demurred at departing from the amending procedure outlined in the Articles, which demanded the unanimous consent of the state legislatures. The continued absence of Rhode Island from the Convention, however, made unanimity obviously out of the question. Moreover, as Madison pointed out, since the powers that the Constitution granted to the general government had been taken mainly from the state legislatures, the legislatures might decide to reject the document. To refer the document to conventions in the states, elected for the express purpose of considering the new Constitution, seemed a feasible solution. And so the Convention decided that the Constitution would be "ordained and established" when nine state conventions had ratified it.

Conventions called by the state legislatures in Delaware, Pennsylvania, New Jersey, and Georgia swiftly and unanimously adopted the new Constitution. In other states, the debates were more prolonged and in some instances the voting was very close. It is not easy for us now, looking back over the years, to analyze the climate of public opinion during the fight for ratification. Although suffrage restrictions barred a majority of the free citizens from voting for the delegates to the conventions, it does not follow that the common people were inarticulate or without influence. Gentlemen of property and education spoke out in every state to champion the people's rights. Propaganda for and against ratification took many forms: pamphlets, editorials, letters to the editor, caricatures, handbills, and platform lectures.

The Struggle for Support

Probably the most important single contribution to the literature of American political theory was *The Federalist*, which first appeared as a series of letters in the press explaining and defending the Constitution to the people of New York. The three authors, Alexander Hamilton, John Jay, and James Madison, writing under the name of *Publius*, were careful not to reject the popular doctrines of natural rights, individual freedom, and popular participation. But their arguments skillfully wrought the case for a strong national government, limitations on the powers of the states, and "stability in government." Madison wrote to his father that *The Federalist* was "the best commentary on the principles of government which was ever written." [18] It was also most effective propaganda in the program to explain and justify the proposed Constitution.

The Federalist certainly had an influence on the New York convention. Later, when the letters were collected in book form, they were effectively used in the Virginia campaign as well. They made a particularly strong impression on John Marshall, who was fighting for ratification in the Virginia convention; not many years later, as Chief Justice of the Supreme Court, Marshall referred frequently to *The Federalist* in citing the intentions of the Framing Fathers. We must bear in mind, however, that *The Federalist* was not an impartial exposition of the original Constitution, for it was first published as a piece of electioneering. We must also remember that during the campaign for ratification a great deal was said and written in opposition to the proposed Constitution. But, because most of this material never found its way into book form, and because it championed the losing side, it has disappeared while *The Federalist* has lived on.

As counter-propaganda to *The Federalist*, for example, *Agrippa* (James Winthrop) wrote in the *Massachussets Gazette*, "The question before the people is whether they will have a limited government or an absolute one. . . . It is the opinion of the ablest writers on this subject that no extensive empire can be governed upon republican principles and that such a government will degenerate to a despotism unless it be made up of a confederacy of smaller states each having the full powers of internal regulation." And *Cato* (Governor Clinton) warned the people of New York to beware "the proferred constitution of Caesar" which denies the doctrine of separation of powers and gives authority to the President that is too vast and important for any one man without limited tenure. *Sidney* (Robert Yates) argued in the *New York Journal* that the new Constitution would "destroy the rights and liberties of the people." [19]

---

[18] Many editions of *The Federalist* are available, including: Max Beloff (ed.) (New York: The Macmillan Company, 1950); Henry Steele Commager (ed.) (New York: Appleton-Century-Crofts, Inc., 1949); Edward Mead Earle (ed.) (New York: Modern Library, 1937).

[19] The primary source for the fight over ratification is Jonathan Elliot, *The Debates in the Several State Conventions and the Adoption of the Federal Consitution* (Philadelphia: J. B. Lippincott Co., 1888).

The opponents of the proposed Constitution hammered away at its most conspicuous weakness: the absence of any Bill of Rights. This omission seemed especially glaring because eight of the new state constitutions contained a separate Bill of Rights, and three guaranteed fundamental liberties within the main text. And yet, until the very end of the Philadelphia Convention, no one had mentioned the idea of a Bill of Rights. Even after it had been suggested, none of the members showed much interest. Later, James Wilson explained to the Pennsylvania ratifying convention that a "Bill of Rights is neither essential nor a necessary instrument in framing a system since liberty may exist and be as well secured without it." Charles C. Pinckney told the South Carolina convention that the Framers had hesitated to enumerate specific rights lest it be later construed that the government could take away any rights that were not enumerated; but he also candidly admitted that a Bill of Rights generally begins with a declaration that all men are born free and equal, and the Philadelphia Convention felt it could make no such statement since "a large part of our property consists in men who are actually born slaves."

The arguments of the Framers, however logical, were not convincing. The Framers had thought that the principle of separation of powers combined with an ingenious system of checks and balances and the enumeration of specific powers to the central government were sufficient safeguards against tyranny. But the majority of the citizens believed they were entitled to a Bill of Rights and that no just government "should refuse or rest on inference." The New York, Massachusetts, and Virginia conventions agreed to ratify the new Constitution only after receiving the solemn promise of its advocates that it would immediately be amended to include a Bill of Rights as part of the supreme law of the land.

The fight over ratification was in part a sectional one: the eastern seaboard and the tidewater south were generally in favor; the western people were inclined to be suspicious and doubtful. Economic lines were rather roughly drawn: merchants and bankers, slaveholders and persons of property were more often in favor of ratification than were the small farmers, shopkeepers, mechanics, and debtors. But the contending groups were not solid blocs: there were both advocates and opponents of the proposed Constitution in all the states, in every community, among all classes. The important fact is that a majority of the conventions in nine states were finally persuaded to approve.

The Constitution was adopted by a process as democratic as any available at that time. Certainly the process of ratification was more democratic than the procedures by which either the Declaration of Independence or the Articles of Confederation had been adopted.[20] Some historians make much of the fact that probably not more than 3 per cent of the male population actually participated in the election of delegates to the ratifying conventions. Actually, many more persons could have voted but did not bother to exercise their right to do so. Granted that the right to vote was limited by property qualifications and other

[20] Alfred H. Kelly and Winfred A. Harbison, *The American Constitution* (New York: W. W. Norton and Company, Inc., rev., 1955), p. 161.

requirements; still the problem of non-voting, then as now, seems to have been due in large measure to the lack of organization and the disinterest and apathy of the less educated and less prosperous citizens.

On September 17, 1788, Congress resolved to put the new Constitution into effect. The first Wednesday in January, 1789, was fixed for choosing the presidential electors; the first Wednesday in March for the opening session of the first Congress under the Constitution. On April 30, 1789, George Washington was inaugurated as the first President of the United States.

"Intentions of the Framers"

Students of American government have examined and re-examined the "intentions" of the Framing Fathers.[21] We must remember, however, that the historical record itself is not absolutely dependable.

At the end of the Convention, the secretary was instructed to turn over his notes and the official *Journal* to the presiding chairman. In 1796, President Washington deposited this material with the State Department, observing at the time that the notes had been imperfectly kept, some pages of the *Journal* were loose, other papers were missing, and the whole was in disorder. In 1819, following the instructions of Congress, Secretary of State John Quincy Adams worked over the official notes and the *Journal* of the Convention to prepare them for publication. Adams wrote letters to James Madison and Charles Pinckney to check their records and recollections of what had happened. Meantime, the autobiographies and memoirs of the Founding Fathers were beginning to appear in print, and they offered many variations on "the Philadelphia story." Even as early as the first administration, men who had participated either in the framing of the Constitution or in its ratification were voicing conflicting interpretations. The authors of *The Federalist*—Jay, Hamilton, and Madison—soon parted company in the political battles that boiled up in the early years of the Republic.

Revolutionary or Reactionary

Compared with the Declaration of Independence, which only a decade before had boldly proclaimed to all mankind the doctrine of revolution, the Constitution of 1787 seems almost reactionary. But judgments of this kind—"revolutionary" or "reactionary," "liberal" or "conservative"—depend largely on the frame of reference. In the age of monarchy, the Framers established in the New World a republican, representative government on a scale hitherto unventured at any time, in any place. True, some were apprehensive of popular government, but their view of human nature made them distrustful of all men in office. Their major concern was to prevent despotism and to check tyranny, by one man, by a few people, or by the masses.

---

21 See William Anderson, "The Intention of the Framers," *American Political Science Review,* XLIX (June, 1955), pp. 340–352.

Separation of powers combined with checks and balances may seem to us a deliberate barricade against majority rule, but the "enlightened patrons of liberty" in the eighteenth century believed otherwise. All the state constitutions, including those written at the peak of revolutionary fervor, embodied this fundamental principle. The Massachusetts Constitution, adopted in 1780 by statewide referendum, spells it out most clearly because the Massachusetts voters had rejected an earlier draft that did not provide adequate checks and balances. Federalists and Antifederalists were agreed on the principle of separation of powers—Adams and Jefferson both vigorously defended it. Within the Convention of 1787, all the members seem to have taken the principle for granted; only Franklin and Hamilton showed opposition, and these two were poles apart in their perspective on popular government. Madison, in *The Federalist*, refers to separation of powers as "this essential precaution in favor of liberty" and as "the sacred maxim of free government."

Whether we consider the Constitutional Convention more conservative than the Second Continental Congress depends in part on which documents we have in mind. If we compare the Articles of Confederation with the Constitution, we note a considerable progress in notions of democratic government between 1776 and 1787. Under the Articles, the people had no feeling of participation in the central government; members of the unicameral Congress were chosen in the state legislatures. The Constitution of 1787 gave the people direct representation in Congress in proportion to their numbers in each state, a novel feature in the history of federalism. Although the executive was not to be popularly elected, Madison explains in *The Federalist* that "it was desirable that the sense of the people should operate in the choice of the person to whom so important a trust was to be confided." If we accept Madison's explanation, the electoral college was not undemocratic in conception; on the contrary, it was designed to give the people in the states a more active role in determining the leadership of the national government. As to the appointment of the federal judges, that was simply following prevailing practice in the states. The idea of electing judges as part of democracy is a nineteenth-century innovation.[22]

That the Framers were concerned with individual liberties is evidenced by specific provisions in the original text protecting the individual against being held for a crime without cause (writ of habeas corpus); punished for an act that was not illegal when it was performed (ex post facto law); singled out for punishment by an act of Congress (bill of attainder); or convicted of treason except for offenses and by procedures spelled out in the Constitution. True, the Constitution did not grant national suffrage, but neither did it impose suffrage restrictions as some members had urged. The Convention did prohibit religious tests for any office or public trust under the United States, though such tests were common in the state governments. It seems fair to conclude that the omission of a more complete Bill of Rights was a tactical error, not a sinister decision. Significantly,

---

[22] For a discerning study of democratic ideology in 1776–1787, see Wright, *Consensus and Continuity,* "Was the Constitution Reactionary?", pp. 40–60.

James Madison, who had been most conspicuous in the Convention, took the lead in the First Congress to secure a Bill of Rights.

The Articles were never submitted to the people; they went into effect when all the state legislatures approved them. In contrast, the Constitution was approved in state conventions popularly elected on the single issue of ratification. Actually, these elections to the state conventions constituted the only national referendum in our political experience until the voters of 1933 elected conventions to ratify the Twenty-first Amendment. The Articles could not be amended except by unanimous consent of all the state legislatures. Certainly the Constitution was much more liberal in its provision for changes in the original script.

From the vantage point of the present day, the Constitution of 1787 seems undemocratic in many respects: separation of powers, checks and balances, indirect election of the President, indirect election of the Senators, appointment of judges for life tenure contingent on good behavior, the presidential veto, and judicial review. But within the context of the times, the very idea of writing a constitution, with the consent of the whole people, guaranteeing a republican form of government in every state, providing for the direct election of representatives in the national government, and limiting the powers both of the national government and of the states was indeed most remarkable. Whether strengthening the national government was more or less democratic in tendency is an argument that rages yet today. But over the years, the greatest concern for civil liberties and human rights has been manifested in the national government rather than in the states or local communities.

The Framers: Contentions about Their Intentions

Repeated incidents demonstrated that the Framers themselves could not agree on what "intentions" they had expressed in the Constitutional Convention. In 1793, President Washington went to the Supreme Court for advice on questions of international law arising out of the French Revolution. John Jay, who was then Chief Justice, informed the erstwhile Chairman of the Convention that the Framers had not intended the judiciary to furnish advisory opinions to the executive. In 1796, Alexander Hamilton and James Madison took opposite sides in the constitutional debate over the treaty negotiated by their former collaborator, John Jay. The House precipitated the issue by refusing Washington's request for appropriations to implement the treaty. Alexander Hamilton and Chief Justice Ellsworth, both of whom had helped shape the decisions at Philadelphia, advised President Washington (who had himself presided over the Convention!) that the House was under a constitutional obligation to appropriate funds to carry out the treaty. James Madison, "Father of the Constitution," disagreed, insisting that the Constitution did not make the House a rubber-stamp for international commitments made by the executive. And so the arguments continued, with the meaning of the Constitution following the party battles of the period.

James Madison, who had kept voluminous notes at the Convention, apparently went back over his papers from time to time, making additions and alterations. Without impugning his integrity, it does seem that his memory over the years may have been somewhat influenced by the partisan politics in which he played so energetic a part. Madison's *Notes on the Convention* were not published until 1840, a few years after his death. Since they are the most detailed record we have of the proceedings, they have come to be regarded as also the most authentic. And yet we might do well to recall Madison's own warning following the publication of the official *Journal:*

> As a guide in expounding and applying the provisions of the Convention, the debates and incidental decisions of the Convention can have no authoritative character. However desirable it be that they should be preserved as a gratification to the laudable curiosity felt by every people to trace the origin and progress of their political institutions, and as a source perhaps on the science of government, the legitimate meaning of the Instrument must be derived from the text itself; or if a key is to be sought elsewhere, it must be not in the opinions or intentions of the Body which planned and proposed the Constitution, but in the sense attached to it by the people in their respective State Conventions when it received all the authority which it possesses.

Madison's advice holds good today; constitutional law begins with the living text of the Constitution, not with the proceedings of the Convention that were kept secret at the time and that remain relatively unknown to this very day.

New "Intentions" and New "Framers"

When the Constitution was written, the Founding Fathers were moved to "awe and apprehension" over the magnitude of their task. A gigantic task it was: designing a federal union for thirteen distinct and independent states, setting up a republican government for nearly four million people, ruling a "vast territory" outlined by fifteen hundred miles of coastline and stretching westward from the Atlantic all the way to the Mississippi. They could not possibly have imagined that this instrument of government they fashioned would be operating more than one hundred and seventy-five years later, on more than one hundred and ninety million people, in fifty states, from Florida to Alaska, from Maine to Hawaii.

In 1787, the mere size of the country appalled the Framing Fathers; a republican government had never before been tried on so grand a scale. Yet today it takes less time for California's congressmen to reach the national capital by plane than it did for the New York delegates to travel by stagecoach to the Philadelphia Convention. In 1787, Philadelphia, then the second largest city in the states, had a population under 30,000; New York, which had been the capital under the Articles, had a population of about 40,000. Today the population of New York City alone is approximately three times the total population of the country as reported in the first census of 1790. More than 90 per cent of the population were living on farms and plantations when George Washington was inaugurated as first President; today less than 15 per cent of the people are engaged in farming. "The butcher, the baker, the candlestick maker" typify the village business that was known to the Framing Fathers, a very different world from the nationwide economy of Armour, National Biscuit, and Westinghouse. When the delegates returned to their homes after the Convention had adjourned, traveling by horseback, stagecoach, and sailboat, they could have had no idea of the mass communications and rapid transportation of the future—American Telephone and Telegraph, Columbia Broadcasting System, General Motors, General Dynamics.

In the time of the Framing Fathers, there were only a few hundred corporations in the entire country, mainly in banking and transportation. Individual proprietorship was the prevailing pattern of business in "commerce among the states." As the delegates stopped along the way at the taverns and the blacksmith shops, they could not have conceived of what has since become the American Way: United States Steel, Alcoa, Firestone, Metropolitan Life, Borden, Woolworth, the corporate form, absentee multiple ownership, mass production, professional management, collective bargaining.

We cannot regard the Constitution merely as a monument to the memory of the Founding Fathers. A constitution, as "the supreme law of the land," must be "a live, growing organism which never stands still for a single day." [23] If it is to be the organic law of the people, and not merely a holy relic, the Constitution must grow and change with the country, for it reflects as much as it determines the political relations among the people.

The American Constitution is now the oldest written constitution in the world. The constitutional histories of France and America span nearly the same period of time; but while we have been able to keep our Constitution in relatively good working order, the French have tried out and discarded fourteen different constitutions. That the work of the Framing Fathers has stood the test of time so well may in part be attributed to their own doubts and dissatisfactions. None of them wholly approved the Constitution they finally proposed. All hoped and anticipated that suitable changes would be made later on. That is why they made sure that the new Constitution would be far more flexible than the old Articles of Confederation. They incorporated four methods of amendment into the Constitution, and allowed only two exceptions to them: slave trade could not be prohibited before 1808, and no state could be deprived of its equal suffrage in the Senate without the consent of the state itself. Otherwise they left the way open for posterity to do what it pleased. Since 1787, Americans have chosen to use this freedom to modify the primary text twenty-four times.

The Constitutional Amendments

When the final draft of the Constitution was read to the Convention in 1787, Benjamin Franklin expressed the general sentiments of those who signed it:

---

[23] See William B. Munro, *The Governments of Europe* (New York: The Macmillan Company, 1938), p. 18. "The Constitution of the United States includes not only the original document of eighty-one sentences which were so laboriously put together at Philadelphia in 1787, but the vast mass of statutes, judicial decisions, precedents, and usages which have grown up around it. It is a live, growing organism which never stands still for a single day, and it never can stand still so long as Congress sits and the Supreme Court hands down decisions."

> I doubt whether any other Convention we can obtain may be able to make a better Constitution. For when you assemble a number of men to have the advantage of their joint wisdom, you inevitably assemble with those men, all their prejudices, their passions, their errors of opinion, their local interests, and their selfish views.

Franklin was willing to sign, not because he thought the Convention had designed a perfect instrument of government, but because the members had done the best they could under the circumstances. Probably no one who signed was entirely satisfied. It was for this very reason that they had provided for a flexible constitution, one that could be changed fairly easily.

The Framing Fathers provided two methods for proposing, and two for ratifying, amendments to the Constitution. An amendment may be proposed either by a two-thirds vote in both houses of Congress or by a national convention called by Congress at the request of the legislatures of two-thirds of the states. Despite the belief of Jefferson and other early leaders that every generation should call a national convention for general constitutional revision, the method of proposing amendments through a national convention has never been used. In practice, then, we see that every procedure authorized by the *official* Constitution is not necessarily a part of our *real* "constitution" in the sense of our customary political practices.

An amendment may be ratified either by the legislatures in three-fourths of the states or by special conventions in three-fourths of the states. All the amendments except one (the Twenty-first) have been adopted by the state legislatures. Here we see that both procedures authorized by the Constitution have been made part of our actual practices.

In *The Federalist*, Alexander Hamilton commented on the zeal of those who would amend the Constitution even before it was established. Twelve amendments were added in the first fifteen years of the Republic. Obviously the Founding Fathers themselves were willing, even eager, to make changes in the original document. Professor William Munro in his study of *The Makers of the Unwritten Constitution* remarks, ". . . it would be difficult to find, at any stage in American history, a group of men more benevolently inclined toward amendments than were the Fathers themselves." [24] Indeed, subsequent generations have added only twelve amendments to the twelve that were adopted before 1804. All told, although some 5,000 amendments have been introduced in Congress only twenty-nine of these have been submitted to the states and only twenty-four have been ratified by the required three-fourths of the states.

The Constitution puts only two restrictions on amendments. One of these —the one that relates to the slave trade—has long been obsolete. The second is still in force, for no state may be deprived of its equal suffrage in the Senate. Otherwise, there seems to be no restriction on the content or substance of amendments. For example, many people protested the Eighteenth Amendment, which gave

---

[24] W. B. Munro, *The Makers of the Unwritten Constitution* (New York: The Macmillan Company, 1930), p. 5.

Congress the power to prohibit the sale or consumption of intoxicating liquors. They argued that the states alone could regulate the morals of the people and that the amendment therefore invaded the reserved rights of the states. Some citizens of Maryland similarly questioned the validity of the Nineteenth Amendment, which extended suffrage to women. They claimed that "so great an addition to the electorate, if made without the state's consent, destroys its autonomy as a political body." But the United States Supreme Court, refusing to consider any arguments on validity of subject matter, upheld both amendments.[25]

Congress specifies whether ratification shall be by state legislatures or by state conventions. A state is not free to substitute any other mode of ratification; when Ohio submitted the Eighteenth Amendment to the direct vote of the people, the United States Supreme Court held that the Ohio legislature had no authority to delegate its constitutional obligations.[26] Congress may also fix a time limit on ratification; it called for ratification within seven years for the Eighteenth, Twentieth, Twenty-first, and Twenty-second Amendments. Congress proposed a child-labor amendment in 1924 without any time limit for ratification. Thirteen years later, the Kansas legislature ratified it despite the argument that the amendment had "lost its vitality" because of the long lapse of time. Both the Supreme Court of Kansas and the U.S. Supreme Court upheld the belated Kansas ratification. If Congress does not choose to fix "a reasonable time" for ratification, then the states are free to approve at any later date.[27]

Individual Rights

The most conspicuous weakness of the original Constitution was the deliberate omission of a Bill of Rights. The fight for ratification pivoted on this point in both the New York and the Virginia conventions. They were finally persuaded to approve the Constitution, but only with the understanding that it would be immediately amended to include the traditional guarantees of private rights and personal liberties. Consequently, one of the first things Congress did in its first session was to propose twelve amendments in the form of a Bill of Rights. Three-fourths of the states forthwith ratified ten of these proposals, and they at once became an integral part of the Constitution.

They include the free exercise of religion, freedom of speech and press, rights of assembly and petition (Amendment I); the right of the people to keep and bear arms (II); protection against quartering of soldiers in private homes (III); protection against "unreasonable searches and seizures" of persons, houses, papers, and effects (IV); procedures protecting the rights of persons accused of crime, and guarantees of "due process of law" with respect to life, liberty, and property (V); further rights of the accused, including trial by jury and the right to counsel (VI); provisions for trial by jury in civil cases (VII); prohibition of excessive bail or fines or cruel and unusual punishments (VIII); the reserved rights of the people beyond those enumerated (IX); the reserved powers of the states (X).

---

[25] *Leser* v. *Garnett*, 258 U.S. 130 (1922); *United States* v. *Sprague*, 282 U.S. 71 (1931).
[26] *Hawke* v. *Smith*, 253 U.S. 221 (1920).
[27] *Coleman* v. *Miller*, 307 U.S. 433 (1939).

The first eight amendments spell out individual rights and liberties, but the Ninth Amendment clearly states that this enumeration must not be regarded as complete and exclusive. One of the amendments proposed in Congress—the one that James Madison, its sponsor, declared to be "the most valuable of the whole list"—was rejected by the Senate. It read as follows: "The equal rights of conscience, the freedom of speech or of the press, and the right of trial by jury in criminal cases shall not be infringed by any state." The first nine amendments were regarded as restrictions on the national government—"Congress shall make no law. . . ." This rejected one would have placed restrictions on the states. But the state legislatures were not yet willing to accept such specific restrictions from the outside on their state power, though the state constitutions included similar provisions.[28]

The Framers of the Constitution of 1787 *created* a new government, "a more perfect union." Accordingly, their main concern was, on the one hand, to establish the basic pattern of the central government and to give it specified powers and, on the other hand, to restrict the states in certain areas where national authority seemed necessary and proper. The addition of the Bill of Rights was in essence Part II of the Constitution. Part I, the Constitution of 1787, establishes the new government; Part II, the Bill of Rights, puts restraints on the government, particularly in its relations with individual persons.

Ironically, in view of the furor over the Framers' omission of the Bill of Rights, American civil rights were hardly at issue until after the Civil War. As Ray Forrester, Dean of the Law School at Tulane University, points out, "before the Civil War not one great case is to be found in the Supreme Court under the First Amendment—the amendment which many regard as the keystone of our society as well as of our Constitution." [29] But constitutional conflicts may be settled by agencies of government other than the Supreme Court. For example, a serious problem relating to the First Amendment was posed by the Sedition Act of 1798. This was the Act that called forth the Virginia and Kentucky Resolutions, in which Madison and Jefferson challenged the whole doctrine of national supremacy. In the election of 1800, the Jeffersonian Republicans attributed the abridgment of individual rights to the deterioration of states' rights and won a great victory at the polls. In the short period that the Sedition Act was on the federal statute books, some 70 persons, mostly vociferous Republican editors, were jailed and fined. But before any of them had time to get their cases appealed to the Supreme Court, the Jefferson Administration moved to free all who had been jailed, returned all the fines collected under the Act, and suffered the Act itself to expire without mourning. Not until 1940, with the passage of the Smith

---

[28] For an authoritative analysis and interpretation of the Constitution of 1787 and its amendments, see *The Constitution of the United States of America*, prepared by the Legislative Reference Service, Library of Congress, Edward S. Corwin (ed.) (Washington, D.C.: Government Printing Office, 1953). Easier reading and briefer in comments is Edward S. Corwin and Jack Peltason, *Understanding the Constitution*, rev. ed. (New York: The Dryden Press, 1958).

[29] Ray Forrester, *Constitutional Law* (St. Paul, Minn.: West Publishing Co., 1959), p. 533.

Act, did the federal government in peace time again attempt to legislate against "sedition."

In the period before the Civil War, the most important decision of the Supreme Court affecting basic federal relations in the area of civil rights was *Barron* v. *Baltimore* (1833). In this early case, Chief Justice John Marshall interpreted the Bill of Rights as referring only to the national government. Barron, a citizen of Baltimore, thought he had been deprived of this property without just compensation when the city had destroyed the usefulness of his wharf while grading the streets. Barron brought suit for damages in federal court. The Supreme Court held that the suit was improper in a federal court since the Fifth Amendment restrained only the general government and was not applicable to the states or their local governments.[30]

After the Civil War, however, the Thirteenth and Fourteenth Amendments extended federal guarantees of civil rights into the states themselves. The Thirteenth forbids slavery or involuntary servitude any place in the United States. The Fourteenth, an extremely complicated amendment, has been the subject of seemingly endless litigation in the courts. It defines United States citizenship in accordance with the English principle of *jus soli*—place of birth. "All persons born or naturalized in the United States, and subject to the jurisdiction thereof, are citizens of the United States and of the state wherein they reside." The Framing Fathers had deliberately omitted any such definition of citizenship, no doubt because they had so recently been subjects of His British Majesty. The Fourteenth Amendment also forbids the states to abridge "the privileges or immunities of citizens of the United States," but the Amendment does not set forth in detail just what these privileges and immunities are. Finally, the Amendment prohibits the states from depriving "any person of life, liberty, or property without due process of law," and from denying to "any person within its jurisdiction the equal protection of the laws."

National Power and States' Rights

The debates between the proponents of strong nationalism and the advocates of states' rights were sometimes sharp at the Philadelphia Convention, but they became even sharper during the fight for ratification. To allay any fear that the national government might use the new Constitution to absorb the states, the Tenth Amendment provides that, "The powers not delegated to the United States by the Constitution, nor prohibited by it to the states, are reserved to the states respectively, or to the people."

What did the Tenth Amendment actually add to the Constitution? Supporters of national power and advocates of states' rights have always answered this question differently. The answer in terms of government practice, however, has generally favored national power. And the evidence indicates that the framers of the Amendment themselves merely intended to reaffirm the principle of federalism implicit in the original text of the Constitution—that the national

---

[30] *Barron* v. *Baltimore*, 7 Pet. 243 (1833).

government has delegated powers and the states have reserved powers. When the Amendment was drafted in 1789, Congress voted down an attempt to insert the word *expressly* before the word delegated. Apparently, then, the framers did not mean to limit national power only to those powers expressly delegated.

A new undeveloped nation, emerging from colonialism, is bound to pressure its government for economic assistance. The first new nation was no exception. As Lipset points out, Washington's Administration, especially the Treasury Department under Alexander Hamilton, was much concerned to promote industry and manufacturing through a national tariff under the commerce power. Although the Constitution gives Congress no express power over banking, the First Congress (the same Congress that sponsored the Tenth Amendment) established a national bank to carry on the financial business of the national government. True, the Federalists were in control of the Congress that established the first Bank of the United States and they were exponents of strong central power. Years later, when the Antifederalists were in control of Congress, they in turn set up the second Bank of the United States even though they were exponents of states' rights. Finally, Chief Justice John Marshall, in the famous case of *McCulloch* v. *Maryland* (1819), upheld the right of Congress to create a national bank as an "implied power." [31] Under this doctrine, Congress may employ whatever powers are "convenient and useful" in carrying out any powers delegated to the national government. And what is "convenient and useful" changes with the times.

The Eleventh Amendment was adopted in 1798 as a special concession to the sensibilities of the Antifederalists and states'-rights partisans of the early period. It protects the states against being sued in federal courts by citizens of other states. In 1793, the Supreme Court had permitted a private citizen, named Chisholm, to sue the State of Georgia. Article III of the Constitution had extended the judicial power of the national government to controversies "between a state and citizens of another state. . . ." This was probably no more than a stylistic error; it is doubtful that the Convention contemplated such presumption and effrontery as appeared in the person of Chisholm! Indeed during the debates over ratification in 1787, when the Antifederalists pointed out that under the judicial article an individual could hale a state into a federal court, the Federalists replied that of course no "sovereign state" would ever be sued without its consent. When Chisholm dared to sue the "sovereign state" of Georgia, all the states were so indignant that Congress moved with "vehement speed" to prevent subsequent affronts to the dignity of states. [32] More than the dignity of a sovereign state was probably at issue, however. When the Eleventh Amendment was proposed, many states were in financial difficulties and had defaulted on their debts. The states could therefore use the new amendment not only in defense of theoretical sovereignty but also in a more practical way to forestall suits by individual creditors.

We conclude that the Framers of the Tenth and Eleventh Amendments

---

[31] *McCulloch* v. *Maryland*, 4 Wheat. 316 (1819).
[32] *Chisholm* v. *Georgia*, 2 Dall. 419 (1793).

made no great alteration in the principles of federalism laid down in the original document. The national government has powers expressly granted and it also has any implied powers that are "necessary and proper" in carrying out its delegated powers. The states have reserved powers—all powers that are not granted explicitly or implicitly to the national government and that are not denied to the states. The states are also entitled to respect in the federal union and cannot be sued by individuals in the federal courts.

Democratizing the Constitution

The problem of popular participation has been a continuing crisis in American politics. Since 1787, eight Amendments to the Constitution have very considerably broadened the political basis of the national government.

The Twelfth Amendment (1804) provides that the electoral colleges must cast separate ballots for President and Vice-President. In itself, this change may not seem very significant. But it does show how the Constitution must be kept abreast of changing conditions—in this case, the emergence of a national party system, something the original Framers had not anticipated.

In the presidential election of 1800, Thomas Jefferson and Aaron Burr both ran as candidates of the Republican Party. When the members of the electoral colleges cast their votes, each Republican elector voted for both men. As a result, Jefferson and Burr tied for first place. The Framers had intended that the candidate with the *highest* number of votes (providing it added up to a majority) would become President; if there was a tie, or if no one received a majority, the decision would go to the House of Representatives. The candidate with the *second highest* number of votes would become Vice-President; if there was a tie, the decision would go to the Senate. In 1800, Jefferson was actually the Republican Party's candidate for President and Burr was the party's candidate for Vice-President. But the House, in which the Federalists still held a majority, almost prevented the popular choice from taking office; it took thirty-six ballots in the House to give the presidency to Jefferson. In order to prevent this sort of thing from happening again, the Twelfth Amendment was adopted before the next election came around.

Although the Twelfth Amendment made only a slight change in procedure, its adoption was necessary because of a development of fundamental importance—the rise of political parties as agencies "democratizing" the choice of the President. National party conventions now nominate candidates for President and Vice-President. The people themselves now vote for the members of the electoral colleges, and in each state these electors are morally pledged, if not legally bound, to cast their votes for the candidates named by their respective party conventions. The electoral colleges thus become an automatic voting machine in which the electors simply record, state by state, the peoples' choice of party candidates. Although the electoral college system is still far from accurate in recording popular preferences, political parties have succeeded in turning it into a basically democratic device for majority rule.

We must mention here, however, that the Twelfth Amendment itself has generated certain changes. As its opponents predicted, for instance, it has tended to minimize the role of the Vice-President. The first two Vice-Presidents of the United States, who were elected before the Amendment was passed, were men of such stature that they later moved on to the presidency in their own right. Following the passage of the Amendment, only one Vice-President, Martin Van Buren, became President without succeeding to the office through the death of the elected President.

The Fifteenth (1870), Nineteenth (1920), Twenty-third (1960) and Twenty-fourth (1964) Amendments have promoted universal suffrage, the very thing that many of the Framing Fathers feared the most. The Fifteenth, adopted after the Civil War, forbids any restriction of suffrage on the basis of race, color, or previous condition of servitude. The Nineteenth, ratified after World War I, forbids any restriction of suffrage on the basis of sex. And yet, even with these amendments, the Constitution does not give Negroes and women the right to vote. To this day, the federal Constitution grants no rights of suffrage. The states themselves still decide on qualifications for voting, and these qualifications vary considerably from one state to another. All that the Fifteenth and Nineteenth Amendments say is that no state may deprive any person of the right to vote because of race, color, or sex.

The Twenty-third Amendment allows citizens of the District of Columbia to participate in the election of the President and Vice-President. The District of Columbia is now entitled to the number of presidential electors assigned the least populous state (three). The electors meet in the District and cast their ballots for President and Vice-President in the same manner that presidential electors perform their duties in each of the states. As originally introduced, the Amendment also gave the District a non-voting delegate in the House of Representatives, but to expedite ratification this provision was dropped before the Amendment went to the states. Some opposition came from race-conscious southerners who noted that a majority of the population of the District is Negro. Some Republicans were also wary that this move might put three more votes into the Democratic column of presidential electors, since the Negro vote is overwhelmingly Democratic. But national sentiment in favor of a vote for all Americans produced ratification in the record time of 286 days; repeal of the Prohibition Amendment took 288 days!

The Twenty-fourth Amendment provides that the right of citizens of the United States to vote in any primary or other election for President or Vice-President, for electors for President or Vice-President, or for Senator or Representative in Congress, shall not be denied or abridged by the United States or any state for failure to pay any poll tax or other tax. Actually this Amendment affected but five southern states which still retained a poll tax as a prerequisite for voting. The poll tax had long since lost whatever effectiveness it may have had, when first adopted, as a means of disfranchising southern Negroes and poor whites,[33] so the Amendment may be regarded as a "cleaning-up" operation in

---

[33] V. O. Key, Jr., *Southern Politics* (New York: Alfred A. Knopf, 1949); Frederic A. Ogden, *The Poll Tax in the South* (University, Alabama: University of Alabama Press, 1958).

affirming the national principle of universal suffrage. It was not expected to produce basic changes in the peculiar political order of the South. Indeed, any state which insists on placing a price tag on the vote is free under the Amendment to retain the poll tax as a requirement for voting in elections of local and state officials.

The Seventeenth Amendment (1913) provides for the popular election of senators. Originally the Constitution stipulated that senators be chosen by the state legislatures. Too often this meant in actual practice that party machines or special interest groups in the states dictated the choice of senators. Even when no corruption or malpractice was charged, the people could still complain that too many of the senators were wealthy men tied more closely to the business community than to their state as a whole. During the first decade of this century, progressives and "muckrakers" were insistent that "the cure for the evils of democracy is more democracy," and they stirred widespread demand for direct election of senators by the people. The proposed change was blocked for a long time in the Senate itself but finally, with the ratification of the Seventeenth Amendment in 1913, the popular election of senators was achieved.

The Twentieth Amendment (1933) fixes the twentieth of January as the beginning of the terms of the President and Vice-President, and the third of January as the beginning of the terms of congressmen. This is known as the "Lame Duck Amendment." Prior to its passage, congressmen who were defeated in the November elections continued to sit (like lame ducks) in the December session following their defeat, while the new congressmen usually could not take their seats until thirteen months after they had been elected. Before the adoption of the Twentieth Amendment, the President and Vice-President elected in November did not take office until the following March.

The Twenty-second Amendment (1951) revises the judgment of the original Framers, who felt that the President should be permitted to run for office as many times as he wanted. President Washington set a precedent for his successors by retiring after two terms. The election of Franklin D. Roosevelt to four terms outraged many persons (though he received a majority of the popular vote in each election). Early in the Truman Administration, the Twenty-second Amendment was proposed in Congress and was speeded through the required number of state legislatures without much debate or publicity. Under its provisions no person may be elected to the office of President more than twice; and no person who has acted as President for more than two years may stand for more than one election. The incumbent was specifically excluded, so that President Truman, after having served out the remainder of President Roosevelt's fourth term, and after having been elected for one term on his own, could have chosen to run for another term. He did not so choose. This restriction on the number of terms a President can serve may actually decrease rather than enhance democratic control. In the first place, it denies future majorities the chance to continue a successful President in office, a freedom of choice that might be critically important in a time of crisis. For this reason, former President Eisenhower urged repeal of the restrictive Amendment. Another probable effect is a decline in presidential leadership during second terms. The degree to which Eisenhower's influence in national politics decreased during his second term is difficult to assess since his concept of presidential leadership was one of restraint from the outset. In general, however, other office holders are less likely to pay attention to an incumbent who has no chance of heading the next party ticket.

Economic and Social Changes

Two Amendments—the Sixteenth and Eighteenth—were directed toward what Pye calls the crisis of penetration.

In 1894, Congress levied a 2 per cent tax on incomes over $4,000. The next year the Supreme Court declared the law invalid on the ground that a tax on income from real estate was a "direct tax" and that the Constitution required direct taxes to be apportioned among the states according to their population.[34] This decision was finally reversed by the Sixteenth Amendment, despite vociferous outcries from the "rich and few" against what they regarded as "socialism."

The Sixteenth Amendment (1913), authorizes Congress "to lay and collect taxes on incomes, *from whatever source derived*, without apportionment among the several States, and without regard to any census or enumeration." It has had a revolutionary impact on the American economy. Not only did it shift the burden of financing the government toward those who were most able to pay; it also brought about a gradual redistribution of national wealth under the taxing power. Most local and state taxes remain regressive, taking larger proportions of the incomes of the poor than of the rich. But the principle of progressive taxation developed under the Sixteenth Amendment redresses the balance in favor of those with lower incomes. Moreover, the great revenue brought in through the income tax has permitted a vast expansion of public services, on which poorer citizens are especially dependent. The Sixteenth Amendment is probably the most important change that has so far been made in the text of the original Constitution.

The Eighteenth Amendment (1919) was an extraordinary attempt to change the character of American society. Its passage through Congress as a war measure in 1917 and its subsequent ratification in three-fourths of the state legislatures make an outstanding case study in pressure politics. The Anti-Saloon League, organized in 1893 to wage war against "Demon Rum," pressed first for temperance legislation in the states. Early in the twentieth century, the League marshalled its forces for nationwide prohibition. By 1917, the League had become one of the most powerful pressure groups in the country, strong enough to persuade two-thirds of Congress and three-fourths of the state legislatures to vote the whole country "dry."

The Eighteenth Amendment prohibited the manufacture, sale, or transportation of intoxicating liquors within the United States, and their import into and export from the United States, for beverage purposes. This attempt to incorporate the moral code of one part of the public into the organic law of the nation failed, for many people simply would not recognize the code as binding. Boot-

---

[34] *Pollock* v. *Farmers' Loan and Trust Co.,* 157 U.S. 429 (1895).

legging and gangsterism flourished throughout the country. Violation of prohibition under the Eighteenth Amendment was so general and widespread that a dangerous disrespect sprang up for the "supreme law of the land."

One of the earliest and most popular acts of the New Deal was its proposal to end "the noble experiment" by repealing the Eighteenth Amendment. The Twenty-first Amendment (1933) specifically repeals the Eighteenth Amendment. It does, however, give some constitutional aid and comfort to those who are set on keeping their own states "dry," for it forbids the transportation or importation of intoxicating liquor into any state in violation of that state's laws.

The Continuing Constitution

The Framers of the original constitutional document were scarcely democratic in the modern sense; they were not too concerned about pleasing the current majority. Their great task was to write a constitution that would serve as "the supreme law of the land" not only for themselves but their posterity. They had to decide what principles of government were so basic and fundamental to the whole people that they ought to be placed above and beyond ordinary political action. This is the real meaning of constitutionalism—the idea that even if a proposed change is attuned to popular opinion, it may not have the force of law if it is not in pursuance of the Constitution.

When, however, we try to ascertain "the plain meaning of the Constitution," we must go beyond the text of 1787. The Framers include not only the members of the Philadelphia Convention but the many thousands of congressmen, state legislators, and members of state conventions who have been involved since 1787 in the introduction and ratification of the Amendments which are now an integral part of the formal written Constitution.

In brief summary, the Framing Fathers (all of them over the years) have designed: (1) a *federal* government with powers divided and functions shared by the national government and the states; (2) a *national* government supreme in all external affairs and in certain enumerated domestic matters; (3) a *republican* government—national and state—in which the people choose their principal policy-makers, executive and legislative; (4) a *democratic* government in which the citizens enjoy universal suffrage, participate in periodic elections, and directly influence the public policies; (5) a *limited* government in which specific prohibitions are placed on both the national and state government; a government in which fundamental *individual rights* are guaranteed even against *majority rule*; (6) a *representative* government with the people of each state directly represented in proportion to their numbers in the House of Representatives and approximately in the same proportion in the presidential electoral colleges; (7) a *presidential* government with independent tenure and *separation of powers* (but also *checks and balances*) as between the executive and legislative branches.

In this chapter, we have looked on the constitutional design as significant input for the American government in action. Constitutional lawyers like to remind us that the Constitution is designed to serve the *status quo*. In order to change an existing situation by law, the instigator must surmount a series of constitutional hurdles. He must obtain approval of his proposal by a majority in both houses of Congress. He must then win the approval of the President or run the risk of a veto which could not be overridden without the consent of a two-thirds majority in both houses. Even so, a proposal enacted into law may still be declared null and void by the courts. All these blocks in the normal legislative process seem to contradict one of the principles that we have described as essential to democracy—majority control.

But the Constitution is a conservative instrument only in a procedural sense. It was never intended to be a rigid strait jacket embracing a single economic or social philosophy. The Constitution can be amended in any part, with no limitations on substantive modification. Thus the Framers recognized ultimate freedom of dissent, leaving the way open for future generations to alter the Constitution as they might see fit.

The Constitution is not merely an historical document; it is rooted in the experience of the nation. The Constitution retains its vitality and validity because it is both input and output in the continuing political process. All policy-making in American government is perforce conditioned by the constitutional prescription. But in the same process all policy-making makes an impression on the Constitution. Congressional and presidential interpretations have considerably expanded the original intentions. Judicial review has given new and different meanings to the ancient words and phrases. Unofficial practices and long accepted usages have made substantial additions and alterations. We shall, then, re-examine the contemporary Constitution in the concluding section of this book as an output of the political process.

CHAPTER FOUR

The Context
of Federalism

When Alexis de Tocqueville visited

America in the 1830's, he considered the Constitution of the

United States to be "the most perfect federal constitution that

ever existed." He felt, after an extended look at America and

its institutions, that the United States combined the advantages of

both large and small states—"happy and free as a small people, and glorious and strong as a great nation." [1] K. C. Wheare, a contemporary British political scientist, regards the American Constitution as the prototype of "what federal government is" today.[2] Students from abroad apparently perceive more clearly what we ourselves see but dimly. Certainly no principle of American government has been more controversial in these (or this) United States.

Concepts of Federalism

Most Americans would find it difficult to explain what federalism means. Even many politicians have only the vaguest idea what federalism really implies. Americans generally tend to think of federalism as whatever it is that America has; and our political ethnocentrism is such that whatever we have must be the best. But many other countries, such as the Soviet Union, Canada, Australia, the Federal Republic of Germany, Mexico, and Brazil, also are federal political entities. Their common political structure leaves room for significant differences among them. The Soviet Union is a dictatorship, for example, whereas Australia is a democracy; the United States has a two-party system of government, whereas Mexico has a one-party system. They can all claim to have a federal form of government, however, because in each the powers of government are divided, on a constitutional basis, between a general or national government and regional units or states; and both the national government and the states have authority to act in ways which directly affect the people. A definition in terms of structure is relatively simple; but when we try to describe how a federal system actually operates—in terms of policies and programs and activities that affect the daily lives of the people—the problem becomes much more complex.

The major function of federalism is not so much structural and institutional as it is political, economic, social, and cultural. A federal system of government is designed to accommodate and protect territorial diversity in a nation without weakening the basic unity that makes it a distinctive political system. Every society is more or less pluralistic, with variations in race, nationality, language, religion, and class. No nation is wholly unified; even a totalitarian or highly centralized government recognizes various groups and makes allowances for differences in local government. When significant differences develop along geographic lines, however, each territorial unit tends to demand political arrangements that will preserve its peculiar interest and values.

---

[1] Every student of American government should examine Alexis de Tocqueville's *Democracy in America*. Originally published in 1835, it still is most discerning in its observations on American political character. It is now available in an inexpensive paperback edition edited by Phillips Bradley (New York: Vintage Books, 1954), 2 vols.

[2] K. C. Wheare, *Federal Government*. This classic, first issued under the auspices of the Royal Institute of International Affairs in 1946, is now available in its 4th edition as a Galaxy Book, paperback (New York: Oxford University Press, 1964).

"The Union Is Older Than the States"

The American colonists considered themselves "one people" when they dissolved their political bonds with the mother country. Most of them—or their forbears—had come to this country from the British Isles; they spoke the same language and brought with them a common law and similar political ideas. Tocqueville thought that the American people had been able to create a federal union because in all the states they had arrived at the same stage of development. (Desirable and successful as Tocqueville found federalism in the United States, he thought it would be unsuited to Europe, where even the smallest country showed greater cultural diversity than there was in all America.)

As we indicated in Chapter 3, even before the Declaration of Independence, the intercolonial network of communication and numerous cultural and economic ties had developed an awareness of community, if not yet of nationality. Other forces also were at work. Continuing clashes with the imperial government fostered the idea of political unity. And even before the Revolution, plans of union for defense, security, and economic advantages, such as the one Benjamin Franklin presented to the Albany Congress as early as 1754, were being considered. Committees of Correspondence, by functioning as intergovernmental agencies in the decade before the final break with the British government, helped institutionalize political ties among the colonies. The First Continental Congress, meeting in Philadelphia in 1774 to coordinate colonial opposition to the so-called Intolerable Acts, established a network of subsidiary political bodies which provided an over-all, albeit modest, system of union. The Second Continental Congress, which proclaimed "these United Colonies are, and of right ought to be free and independent states," at the same time proposed the Articles of Confederation, which brought the thirteen new states into "a perpetual union."

It may be pushing the point too far to say (with President Lincoln) that "the Union is older than the States." Actually, the original states were founded at different times, by different kinds of settlers, and for different purposes. When the American colonists decided to absolve themselves from all allegiance to the British Crown, they were not yet fully prepared for the consequent switch in roles—from his majesty's subjects to citizens of the United States. They preferred to keep their individual political identities as Pennsylvanians, or Virginians, or South Carolinians. A similar psychological lag exists among many people in the emerging nations today. As colonists they were enthusiastically engaged in the common cause of revolution, but when independence was achieved they were not yet sufficiently integrated as citizens to establish a unitary government. The American solution was the Articles of Confederation, which set forth a "firm league of friendship" and a legal framework for interstate relations. But even before the first decade of independence had passed, the American people, or their leaders, were ready to revise their first constitution and "to form a more perfect union." This acceleration in national development we can probably attribute to the common process of political socialization which was already well under way in the American colonies long before the Declaration of Independence.

Although federalism is a basic principle in the American system of government, the Framing Fathers offered no official definition of the term. In fact, neither the word *federation* nor *federal* appears in the text of the Constitution. The Preamble does no more than declare the intent of the people "to form a more perfect union." To most of the delegates at the Philadelphia Convention in 1787 this meant setting up a stronger national government than had existed under the Articles of Confederation. Even so, the champions of the small states managed to defeat those parts of the Virginia Plan that would have created a "consolidated" national government. The intensity of state pride and the extent of state rivalries ruled out any real prospect of a unitary national state. But the Framing Fathers of 1787 were experienced politicians determined to work out a *practical* design of government which could accommodate the *diverse* as well as the *uniform* needs of the American people. Thus they made three significant decisions: to preserve the states; to create a strong national government; and to form a union that would embrace both the states and the national government in a *new* constitutional framework.

Perhaps we are lucky that the Framing Fathers did not precisely define "federalism." If they had, we would have been required to invent a different term for the system of government they helped create—because they used the term "federal" as the adjectival form of "confederation." In the terminology of their day, they were striving to replace the purely federal structure of the Confederation with a new (and un-named) structure that would blend federal features with the consolidated features of a national government. As James Madison put it, "the *federal* form . . . regards the Union as a *Confederacy* of sovereign states," whereas "a *national* government . . . regards the Union as a *consolidation* of states." In the thirty-ninth number in a series of essays that was later (and ironically) to be called *The Federalist* papers, he carefully explained that the proposed Constitution was neither federal nor national in nature, but was a mixture of the two. This new combination of ingredients, lying between the state sovereignty of confederacy and the unitary government of consolidation, is what *we* call federalism.

But the features of the Constitution, by any name, are equally suitable for explaining the three basic decisions mentioned above. Madison pointed out in *The Federalist* (No. 39) how the Constitution mixes the features of confederation and consolidation in five of its basic features—the process of adopting the Constitution, the sources from which ordinary powers of government are drawn, the operation of these powers, the extent of national power, and the method of amending the Constitution. (1) The Constitution is ratified by the people, "not as individuals composing one entire nation" but as separate majorities in all "the distinct and independent States." In terms of its adoption, then, the Constitution is *confederative* (Madison said "federal"), not national. (2) In terms of the sources of government power, the House of Representatives (chosen by the people, and represented in the same proportion and by the same principle as they are in the states) is national; the Senate (with equal representation for each state) is confederative, and the President (chosen by a complex mixture of popular and state action) blends national and confederative sources of power. Over-all, the sources of power are clearly *mixed*. (3) As to the operation of the government, national power operates directly on individual citizens, whereas the central government in a confederation can act only on the independent states that make it up. In this respect, the Constitution is *national*. (4) National power "extends to certain enumerated objects only," and it is supreme in those areas, but the states retain a "residuary and inviolable sovereignty over all other objects." Even while trying to refute charges of consolidation by Antifederalists, Madison could not quite bring himself to use the word "confederation" in describing the extent of national power under the proposed constitution, but he did claim that, in respect to its power, "the proposed government *cannot be deemed a national* one." (5) The amending process is not wholly national: amendments are approved by extraordinary majorities in separate states, not by a simple majority of the people in a consolidated Union. But neither is it wholly confederative: a state can be bound by an amendment without its consent if three-fourths of all the states approve. The amending power, like the over-all powers of government under the Constitution, was thus a *mixture of confederation and consolidation*.

If we follow Madison's analysis—beginning with the thesis, a league of states, and confronting it with the antithesis, a unitary national state—then the resulting synthesis, "this mixed Constitution," actually offers us a novel political structure and a new concept of federalism. The American federal union was the first of its kind, but it has subsequently served as a working model for nearly every federal union in the modern world.

Federalism and Nation-Building

The members of the Constitutional Convention are not our only "Framing Fathers." Two-dozen amendments have become an integral part of the Constitution, and their authors, too, must be counted among the framers. The framers of the Bill of Rights or the civil rights amendments, for example, went considerably beyond and altered the intentions of the original Framers. The income tax amendment in effect provided for a redistribution of wealth by permitting the national government to provide increased services on which the poor are particularly dependent. As the organic law of the nation, no less than as a legal document, the Constitution must reflect the massive changes in American society as well as the impact of momentous events in the world since 1787.

Unquestionably, the concept of federalism became more and more diluted as the nation expanded beyond the first union of the thirteen states. The early settlers came to Connecticut, or to Virginia, or to Georgia; but millions of immigrants who came to the new world in the nineteenth century knew only of "America." The belief in "manifest destiny," the westward movement of settlement from the Atlantic seaboard to the Pacific, fostered a spirit of nationalism. Frontiersmen were not nearly so interested in the legal or theoretical aspects of federalism as they were in its utility. Federalism meant cooperation and joint enterprise between the national government and the states, partnership rather than rivalry in building a prosperous nation. The new states in the Union, with none of the traditional separatism of the original states, looked to the national capital for all kinds of federal aid.

Daniel Elazar's recent study of intergovernmental relations in the United States in the nineteenth-century,[3] based on very careful sifting of data and documents in national and state archives, demonstrates that virtually all governmental activities since the early days of the Republic have been cooperative endeavors shared by national and state agencies. The theory of "dual federalism" with clear demarcation of powers and responsibilities between the national government and the state governments does not seem to have been borne out in practice at any time in American history. Indeed, the beginning of cooperative federalism antedates the Constitution; the Northwest Ordinances of 1785 and 1787, pledging the national government to grant a section of land in each township of the Territory for the support of common schools, established the precedent of national-state collaboration in public education.

Probably the most crucial problem in building a new nation, especially a democratic one, is the improvement of communication and transportation facilities. The Framing Fathers had recognized this need by giving Congress power to establish post offices and post roads. Congressional power to develop a nation-wide system of communication was the subject of many heated debates in the early years. It was critically important for the new nation to maintain close ties—political, economic, and cultural—between the people in the original states and the ever increasing number of settlers moving westward. Strict constructionists, who narrowly interpreted the powers of the national government under the Constitution, succeeded in blocking an American system of internal improvements planned and financed by the national government. Nevertheless, the exigencies of nation-building on a continental basis generated a variety of cooperative intergovernmental programs. Ironically, John C. Calhoun, best known for his passionate espousal of states' rights in the slavery issue, was one of the leading architects of cooperative federalism in the broad field of internal improvements.

For those brought up to believe that the national government has only recently carried its activities into the local communities, Elazar's account of *The American Partnership* provides an entirely different basis for understanding the federal system of government. Intergovernmental cooperation in the nineteenth century included a multitude of internal improvements projects (roads, canals, railroads, harbors, public buildings, river improvements, mineral production and extraction, agricultural development); a variety of land-grant programs (the development of common schools in the states carved out of the Northwest Territory, the establishment of colleges of agriculture and mechanical arts in every state and

[3] Daniel J. Elazar. *The American Partnership*. (Chicago: The University of Chicago Press, 1962.) This section relies heavily on Elazar's fresh approach to federalism. *A Nation of States* edited by Robert A. Goldwin (Chicago: Rand McNally & Co. 1961) includes a variety of viewpoints, including essays by Morton Grodzins, Russell Kirk, James Kilpatrick, *et al.*

territory); and land grants, cash grants, materials grants, and services for all kinds of purposes in the states (railroad construction, irrigation of desert lands, drainage of swamp lands, soldier homes, agricultural experiment stations, welfare institutions).

So far we have tried to emphasize the functional nature of federalism in terms of its unifying aspects. Remembering that an institution or activity can be called "functional" if it has consequences that tend to promote the survival of the system without major disruption, we can certainly say that some aspects of federalism are highly functional for the American polity. It would be highly unrealistic, however, to deny or ignore the dysfunctional aspects of federalism—divisive and separatist tendencies as well as unifying effects have characterized American federalism. Reverberations of the great debates of the nineteenth century—between the promoters of national power and the supporters of states' rights over slavery and other issues—still rankle in the minds of many Americans. To some of us, the doctrines of dual federalism, division of powers and separation of functions, nullification and secession, may be little more than verbal images, but once they were potent enough to tear the country asunder and to provoke four years of civil war. The current battles over congressional legislation and judicial decisions in the area of civil rights dramatically attest to the persistence of disunity in the American Union. Despite past crises and current strains, however, the continuous pattern of formal and informal intergovernmental activities that constitutes American federalism has promoted unity no less than diversity.

The initial motivation for American federalism—thirteen unlike states—continues as a tradition among the present fifty states. But the trend toward nationalism in most aspects of American life vitiates some of the old arguments for political decentralization. Urbanization, industrialization, and especially rapid and convenient means of transportation have made Americans the most mobile people in history. Since World War II, one-fifth of the American people have changed their places of residence every year. He is a rare person today who lives his whole life in the community in which he was born and reared. The media of mass communication, radio and TV, play up national affairs so that the average citizen is much more aware of what goes on in Washington or in communities across the country than he is of the run-of-the-mill news in his home town. National systems of social security and veterans' benefits encourage citizens in every state to look to Washington for extension of the general welfare. We talk about "national interests," "national purposes," "national goals" even in areas long regarded as local concerns, such as health, housing, education, farm prices, labor standards, and civil rights.

William G. Carleton, a shrewd commentator on the American political scene, points out that "all parts of America are becoming more alike, but more alike in their diversity." [4] In early years, America's diversity was more geographical

---

[4] William G. Carleton, "Centralization and the Open Society," *Political Science Quarterly*, LXXXV (June, 1960), p. 259.

and state-oriented; actually, modern American society is much more pluralistic than it was in the relatively simple economy of the eighteenth century. But similar differences appear in each community; our divisions have become horizontal rather than vertical. Hence the distribution of powers between the national government and the states, based on the political and cultural individuality that characterized the original states, appears unrealistic and out of date when applied to the current problems of twentieth-century pluralistic America.

A national constitutional convention, called today to reconsider fundamental principles of American government, would probably make substantial modifications in the distribution of powers between the national government and the states. But it would, no doubt, retain the federal system, which is still highly functional. For all the talk about uniformity and conformity in American life, the United States remains a panorama of many different regions with marked variations in diet, dialect, cultural patterns, degrees of urbanization and industrialization, and political backgrounds.

The states are convenient means by which to multiply the choices of the American people on issues where national uniformity is not imperative, or may not be desirable. An alternative is especially important when the majority of the people in a given region dissent from national views. The states may offer a delay or break action by the national government. On the other hand, as Lord Bryce observed many years ago, "Federalism enables a people to try experiments in legislation and administration which could not be safely tried in a large centralized country." [5] Thus the states may serve as laboratories for new policies and progressive legislation which the country as a whole might not be ready to accept.

The Constitutional Pattern of Federalism

The 1964 presidential campaign frequently focused on the issues of federalism, not only in the volatile and emotion-packed area of civil rights but throughout the whole range of governmental activities from foreign policy and national defense to economic well-being and social security. Thus the constitutional pattern of federalism shapes much contemporary policy. In this chapter we shall first examine the original distribution of national and state powers according to the Constitution of 1787, together with the subsequent formal amendments, and then take a look at some of the political patterns of federalism that have actually evolved out of the more pragmatic unwritten constitution, the tradition and practices of shared intergovernmental functions.

The States in the Union

The decision to retain the states in the union determines the basic character of federal or intergovernmental relations in the United States. In a sense, there is

---

[5] James Bryce, *The American Commonwealth* (New York: The Macmillan Company, 1914), new ed., I, p. 353.

almost no national government in the United States. Congress, the President, the courts, the whole national administration reflect strong state interests.

The Senate represents the states directly and equally, with two senators from each state always standing guard over the state's rights. The House of Representatives represents the people of the several states; the representative's constituency is not the nation as a whole but the people in his own district who have elected him to promote their particular interests. The boundaries of each congressional district are still determined by the respective state legislatures. Congress so far has not been moved to set up guide lines for districting despite the pressure of recent judicial decisions.[6]

When James Madison was discussing the general problem of federalism in *The Federalist* (No. 46), he pointed out that "beyond doubt the first and most natural attachment of the people will be to the governments of their respective states." The years have borne out his prediction that "a local spirit" will usually prevail among the members of Congress. Thus the first concern of every congressman seems to be how to get as much as he can out of the nation for his own state —appropriations for hydroelectric projects, flood control, disaster relief, military installations, post offices, airports, veterans' hospitals, improvement of rivers and harbors. Moreover, this representation of the states, or the people of the states, in both houses of Congress has tended to prevent national action; too often Congress takes the easy way out of controversy by passing the buck to the states. For example, even though Congress has the power to tax and to spend for the general welfare, it has often found it more politic to turn tax money over to the states through such devices as grants-in-aid and tax credits.

The Constitution requires that senators and representatives be inhabitants of the states they represent. It is the custom, though it is not required by the Constitution, that each representative be a legal resident of the district he represents. Residence requirements of this sort make it impossible for Americans to elect a truly national legislature—like the British Parliament. Members of the House of Commons are chosen from local constituencies, but British voters are far more willing than Americans to support a non-resident candidate so long as he represents their point of view on national issues. The British Parliament has traditionally been a council of the wise and great men of the realm. As Edmund Burke remarked in an address to his Bristol constituents in 1774: "Parliament is a deliberative assembly of one nation, with one interest, that of the whole; where, not local purposes, not local prejudices, ought to guide, but the general good resulting from the general reason of the whole." Under the American system, however, we simply assume that every state and every congressional district can recruit favorite sons who are capable of serving as outstanding statesmen for the nation at large. Or, granting that our local representatives will not take a national view, we assume that the national interest will emerge from adding together all the local interests that are represented. Not that the quality of the British Parliament

---

[6] Especially *Wesberry* v. *Sanders*, 376 U.S. 1 (1964).

is necessarily superior to that of the American Congress. Rather, the focus of the two tends to be different: the British M.P. does not ignore the interests of his constituency, but he puts national interests first; the American senator or representative does not deliberately act against national interests, yet he puts the interests of his state and those of his constituency first.

Although the American President represents a more national viewpoint than Congress, the Constitution makes his office, too, a creature of the states. Technically, the President is elected not by the people of the United States, but by an electoral college system in which each state has as many electors as it has representatives and senators in Congress. Each state legislature may decide how the state's presidential electors are to be chosen; today, all of them are chosen in state-wide elections, although other procedures have been followed in the past. Congress has designated the first Tuesday after the first Monday in November of every fourth year as the time for choosing presidential electors. Actually, the major parties meet in conventions months before to nominate their candidates for President and Vice-President. But the state is the basic unit in the political conventions as well; each state sends about twice as many delegates as it has representatives in Congress.

In presidential elections, the voter must vote for the whole slate of presidential electors offered by one of the parties; he may not split his vote. In effect, then, the voter must choose between the parties, which means that the presidential elections directly express the people's choice in each state. And yet, since popular votes are translated into electoral college votes at the *state* level, the electoral colleges operate in such a way that the popular choice in the nation as a whole may not be elected.

In 1964, Lyndon Johnson amassed the largest popular vote in American history and won 486 votes out of 538 in the electoral college. But in one state, Alabama, President Johnson's name was not even on the ballot. The voters could choose between electors pledged to Goldwater (68.4 per cent did) and a slate of unpledged electors.

Actually, the presidential electors never come together in one place to cast their votes; they merely go to their respective state capitols and register their votes on the first Monday after the second Wednesday in December. The electors of the winning party are obliged, both by custom and by state laws, to cast *all* the votes of their state for their party's candidates, regardless of how the popular vote has split.

On the sixth of January, the President of the United States Senate, in the presence of the Senate and the House, announces the electoral votes from each state. A majority of electoral votes is required to elect either the President or Vice-President. If no presidential candidate succeeds in winning a majority of the electoral votes, the House of Representatives, voting by states, chooses from among the top three. If no vice-presidential candidate succeeds in winning a majority of the electoral votes, the Senate chooses between the top two. Only two Presidents have been chosen by the House. We shall go no further at this point in analyzing the procedures by which the President and Vice-President are elected.[7] Suffice it to say that the Constitution gives the state a basic position in the election machinery of the nation.

The national legislature and the national executive reflect strong state and local interests and influence; the same can be said of the national judiciary. The Constitution requires that the President nominate and appoint justices of the Supreme Court, and all other officers of the federal courts, with the advice and consent of the Senate. "Senatorial courtesy" further requires that the President clear all nominations in advance with the senators (or party officials) of the state in which his nominees legally reside. The Senate Committee on the Judiciary, which has first crack at all presidential nominations of federal judges, is most solicitous in checking with the senators from the states concerned. Nearly all appointments to the district courts actually originate with the President's party organization within the judicial district concerned. In recent years, the Supreme Court has tended to pass the buck back to the district courts for implementing its decisions in cases involving desegregation of the public schools—or reapportionment of the state legislatures or congressional districts. Stereotypes of a federal judiciary pitting its alien (i.e. national) views against the customs of the local community are obviously much distorted. Federal judges (and U. S. marshals too) are almost always local people who have reached their official status in the national government via state and local politics. How else could they have been appointed under the prevailing rule of party patronage?

The states are also powerful political units in national administration. Again, according to the custom of senatorial courtesy, the President is expected to consult the Senator of his own party from a state before he makes patronage appointments within the state—postmasters, federal attorneys, commissioners, marshals, public health officers. Before making an appointment of this sort, the President must clear with the senators and representatives of the state concerned. If the senator or representative is not of the President's party, the President is expected to clear appointments through party officials in the state. Senatorial courtesy also enters into the appointments of purely national officers, such as members of the Cabinet, ambassadors, heads of executive agencies, and foreign service officers. Finally, appointments to the civil service in Washington follow a quota system, roughly proportionate to the population of each state. This rule is not strictly followed in practice, but even its existence is a concession to the continuing influence of "the indestructible states."

"Equal Footing with the Original States"

When the Constitution was written, the Framers anticipated that new states would shortly be admitted to the Union, but they left the conditions of admission entirely to the discretion of Congress. It is now a firm doctrine of constitutional law that all states, new and old, enjoy equal rights and hold identical powers in the Union. In 1787, however, the Founding Fathers were not ready to accept such a doctrine;

---

[7] We shall discuss elections more fully in Chapter 8.

by a vote of nine to two, the Convention actually voted down a proposal that would have guaranteed equality for new states. The delegates from eastern states had no intention of admitting the western territories on an equal footing, but Congress decided differently. Each of the first two states to be admitted—Vermont and Kentucky—came in "as a new and entire member of the United States of America." When Tennessee was admitted in 1796, it was "on an equal footing with the original states in all respects whatsoever." The precedent became so well established that in 1911 a unanimous Supreme Court could declare, "The constitutional equality of the state is essential to the harmonious operation of the scheme upon which the Republic was organized." [8]

The Constitution does not specify the procedure to be followed for the admission of new states. It does prohibit Congress from creating a new state within the jurisdiction of an established state, and from joining two or more old states together to form a new state, without the consent of the state legislatures concerned. Ordinarily, when a substantial number of persons within a territory desire statehood, they petition Congress to pass an "enabling act." If Congress is favorable to the request, it will by legislation "enable" the people of the territory to elect a constitutional convention. The territorial convention then meets and frames a constitution, which it presents to Congress for approval. If Congress finds the proposed constitution acceptable, it passes a joint resolution recognizing the territory as a new member of the Union and seats the elected senators and representatives of the new state. Although the procedure seems simple enough, the process by which a territory actually wins statehood is always complicated by political, social, economic, and even personal issues. There is no way by which the people of a territory, however well organized and ready for statehood they are, can force Congress to pass an enabling act or to approve its proposed constitution.

When the Territory of Arizona became a state in 1912, *The New York Times* commented, "Perhaps Alaska may be a state within half a century but we need not worry about a place for that star yet awhile." The Territory of Alaska began asking for statehood in 1916, and after 1933 Alaskan statehood bills were introduced in every successive Congress. Alaska did not gain its long-coveted admission to the Union, however, until 1958—just four years short of the half-century delay predicted by *The New York Times*. Approximately one year later, also after many unsuccessful efforts, Hawaii achieved statehood in the Union.

---

[8] *Coyle* v. *Smith*, 221 U.S. 559 (1911). The congressional enabling act for the admission of Oklahoma had provided that the capital of the new state should be at Guthrie and that it should not be moved from there before 1913. In 1910, the Oklahoma legislature moved the capital to Oklahoma City. The Court held that Oklahoma was as free as any other state to locate its capital wherever the people wanted it. Congress may put restrictions into the enabling act but these cannot be enforced when the territory becomes a state if they are not generally found in all the states.

Obligations of the National Government to the States

The Constitution specifies that the states shall have certain rights and privileges in the Union. It is the obligation of the national government to insure these rights: (1) the United States shall guarantee to every state in the Union a republican form of government; (2) it shall provide equal representation for all the states in the Senate and representation proportioned to population in the House; (3) it shall protect each of them against invasion or domestic violence.

The guarantee of a republican form of government has never really been put to a test. When two opposing factions claimed to be the legitimate government of Rhode Island in the 1840's, the Supreme Court held that Congress has the power to decide which is the legitimate—the "republican"—government in a state.[9] When Congress admits the senators and representatives of a state, it thereby recognizes the authority of the government they represent.

For many years, the Supreme Court steadfastly refused to consider "political questions," but more recently the justices have appeared willing, even eager, to jump into what Mr. Justice Frankfurter aptly called "the political thicket." Long before Congress was ready to enact civil rights legislation to insure constitutional voting rights, the Supreme Court recognized the national interest in suffrage and elections in the several states. Declaring that "the United States is a constitutional democracy," the Court has consistently maintained the right of all qualified citizens to vote in state as well as in national elections, in party primaries as well as in general elections, without discrimination. The Court holds that citizens not only have the right to cast their ballots but also to have them counted and that the national government has the power to enforce these rights.[10]

The Supreme Court has now taken on the much more complicated problem of legislative malapportionment in the states. Pointing out that "legislators represent people, not trees or acres," the Court held in 1964 that "as a basic constitutional standard, the Equal Protection Clause requires that the seats in both houses of a bicameral state legislature must be apportioned on a population basis." [11] The Court has rejected the "so-called Federal analogy" as precedent for

---

[9] *Luther* v. *Borden*, 7 How. 1 (1849).

[10] See Chapter 13 for an extended discussion of voting rights protected by federal authority. The quotation here is from Justice Reed's opinion, delivered for the Court, in *Smith* v. *Allwright*, 321 U.S. 649 (1944); this case in effect outlawed "white primaries" in the southern states.

[11] The quotation is from Chief Justice Earl Warren's opinion in *Reynolds* v. *Sims* 377 U.S. 533 (1964). The Chief Justice delivered the main constitutional opinion for the Court. Three justices dissented vigorously and at length—Clark, Stewart, and Harlan.

In *Colegrove* v. *Green*, 328 U.S. 549 (1946), the Supreme Court had considered malapportionment the kind of "political question" which it would not accept for judgment. Thus it refused to hear a case from Illinois involving malapportionment in congressional districting. In *Baker* v. *Carr*, 369 U.S. (1867), involving an attack on the apportionment of seats in the Tennessee legislature, the Court held (in 1962) that legislative apportionment is a justiciable issue, and if violations of constitutional rights

state legislative apportionments. As the Court views it, the equal representation of states in the U. S. Senate was an historical compromise on the part of the original thirteen states which surrendered some of their sovereignty, and delegated some of their powers (but not all), to the national government when they entered the federal union. But the political subdivisions of the states—counties, cities or whatever—never were sovereign; they have, in fact, always been subordinate entities within the state.

No doubt these recent political opinions embodied in judicial decisions are a far cry from what the members of the Constitutional Convention meant when they wrote into the original document, "The United States shall guarantee to every state in this union a republican form of government." The Court reminds us, however, that significant changes have occurred in American society since the eighteenth century. The nation, once primarily rural in character, has become predominantly urban. Representation schemes once considered fair and equitable have become archaic and outdated. We must keep in mind that the authors of the Fourteenth Amendment also acted as Framing Fathers. When they wrote into the Constitution that no state should deny equal protection of the laws to any person, they added new dimensions to the "original intentions" of 1787. It remains to be seen what impact these federal judicial opinions will have on state practices and state institutions long sanctioned and preserved by vested political interests.

No serious *legal* problem has arisen since the Reconstruction era in connection with the national government's obligation to grant the states equal representation in the Senate. The *political* problems inherent in the principle of equal representation of states as disparate in population as Alaska and New York (in 1960 the population range was 226,167 to 16,782,304 and the differentials in interests were even more significant) cannot be met, however, except by constitutional amendment. Any such suggestion is purely academic because the Constitution itself provides that "no State, without its consent, shall be deprived of its equal suffrage in the Senate."

The principle of representation according to population in the House of Representatives presents many problems. Article I of the Constitution gives at least one seat to every state, but if the population of the least populous state becomes the unit for representation, then the number of representatives from all the states would turn the House into an oversized body. Congress has by law fixed the size of the House at 435 members and provides for automatic apportionment of the 435 seats among the 50 states by a complicated mathematical formula, after each decennial census. As Justice Harlan observed, however, it is "whimsical" to assert that "the principle of equal representation in the House of equal numbers of people" is built into Article I.[12] In 1960, the population of an average congres-

---

are involved, a judicial remedy is available. *Baker* v. *Carr*, along with *Brown* v. *the Board of Education*, 347 U.S. 497 (1954) (holding that segregation in the public schools is unconstitutional), and many civil rights cases involving discrimination in public accommodations, have revolutionized national-state-individual relationships in the federal system; since the revolution is still in progress, we cannot appraise the final outcome.

[12] *Wesberry* v. *Sanders*, 376 U.S. 1 (1964). See also Chapter 9.

From *What's Got Your Back Up?* Copyright © 1961 by Bill Mauldin. Reprinted with the permission of Harper & Row, Publishers.

Stars fell on Alabama.

sional district was 410,481; Alaska, Nevada and Wyoming were each guaranteed at least one representative although their respective populations were 226,167; 286,278; and 330,066.

In 1964, the Supreme Court ruled that the size of congressional districts within each state must be equalized according to numbers of people.[13] The majority of the justices thought that this was in line with "the principle solemnly embodied in the Great Compromise" of 1787. Justice Harlan, who dissented in the case, claimed that the Court had misinterpreted the historical context and disregarded the realities of political life by focusing exclusively on numbers and by not taking into consideration such other factors as the area and shape of the district and the party affiliations of people within the district. He also charged the Court with substituting its own judgment for that of Congress, since Congress had repeatedly refused after 1929 to renew its one-time requirement that congressional districts be equal in population. Nevertheless, the majority opinion was a decision, a decision that called for action promptly on the part of the state legislatures. Redistricting would have to take place even though it meant upsetting a great many political applecarts. But no amout of redistricting is likely to bring a final solution to the problems of representation which are inherent in any democratic government, and especially so in a federal government.

In return for national protection in case of invasion or insurrection, every state in the union must give up the privilege of maintaining arms. No state, without the consent of Congress, may keep troops or ships of war in time of peace or engage in war unless it is actually invaded. The Constitution provides that the national government will protect any state against domestic violence whenever the legislature or the executive of the state asks for it. On several occasions, however, the national government has intervened without waiting for an invitation. Lincoln called for the national militia to put down insurrection in the southern states. In 1894, despite the protest of Governor Altgeld, President Cleveland sent

---

[13] *Ibid.*

federal troops into Illinois, ostensibly to protect the United States mails, actually to break up a railroad strike. A dramatic use of this power occurred in 1957 when President Eisenhower ordered federal troops to Little Rock, Arkansas, to enforce a desegregation decree of the federal district court in Arkansas, despite vigorous opposition of the state's governor. In less dramatic fashion, President Kennedy sent U.S. Marshals into Alabama in 1961 to protect "Freedom Riders" who were interstate bus passengers; and in 1964, President Johnson ordered several hundred U.S. sailors to assist in the search for missing civil rights workers in Mississippi. Apparently, whether the state approves or not, the national government will send federal forces into any state whenever it is necessary to avert national danger or serious industrial strife, to protect the constitutional rights of citizens, or simply to enforce federal laws.

"The Indestructible Union"

Before 1861, lively arguments were waged over whether a state has a constitutional right to secede from the Union. This is the one constitutional debate that Americans have settled by civil war. As the Supreme Court said in 1869, "The Constitution in all its provisions looks to an indestructible union, composed of indestructible states." [14] No state can break its constitutional bonds, for the Union is perpetual and indissoluble.

As a less extreme argument, advocates of states' rights have long advanced the doctrines of nullification and interposition. The nullification idea is that a state government can nullify an act of Congress and render the act inapplicable within the state simply by declaring it unconstitutional; the interposition idea is that a state government can achieve the same result by interposing its authority between an unconstitutional act and the people of the state.

As early as 1798, resolutions passed by the Virginia and Kentucky legislatures questioned the constitutionality of the Alien and Sedition Acts passed by Congress. In support of these resolutions, Thomas Jefferson, leader of the Antifederalist Party, declared that "where powers are assumed which have not been delegated, a *nullification* of the act is the rightful remedy." James Madison, who had drawn up the Virginia Resolutions, and who only a few years earlier had been the "father of the Constitution," asserted that the states could and should *"interpose"* their authority against "palpable and alarming infractions of the Constitution." The New England states, meeting in the Hartford Convention in 1814 to protest against a national embargo on foreign shipping, also claimed the right of the states to interpose their authority to protect the liberties of the people.

The outstanding advocate of nullification was John C. Calhoun, whose *South Carolina Exposition* (1828) was a carefully reasoned attempt to justify the idea of state nullification of federal laws. But when South Carolina declared the Tariff of 1832 "null, void and no law," President Andrew Jackson responded firmly, "I

---

[14] *Texas* v. *White*, 7 Wall. 700 (1869).

consider the power to annul a law of the United States, assumed by one of the states, incompatible with the existence of the Union." Nevertheless, the doctrines of nullification and interposition continued to be heard, especially on the issue of slavery. On the eve of the Civil War, the legislature of Wisconsin affirmed its obligation to interpose the sovereignty of the state between the federal fugitive slave laws and the constitutional rights of the people. But federal officers continued to enforce the law despite local hostility.

The right to interpose state sovereignty and to nullify federal laws that go beyond constitutional limits has thus been claimed at one time or another by states in every section of the country. The most recent and vigorous claims have come from the southern states since the 1954 desegregation decisions of the United States Supreme Court. But notice that in earlier cases the states were protesting against *acts of Congress*. The 1956 version of interposition claimed that "the Supreme Court has no constitutional authority to adjudicate disputes between a sovereign state and the federal government." [15]

Brown v. *Board of Education* (1954 and 1955) [16]—the desegregation decision of the Supreme Court—prompted a hundred congressmen from eleven southern states in March 1956 to present "A Declaration of Constitutional Principles." In the nature of a manifesto, this document excoriates the Court—"the naked judicial power"—"the clear abuse of judicial power"—"the unwarranted decision" which is "in derogation of the authority of Congress" and which "encroaches upon the reserved rights of the states and the people." It commends "the motives of those states which have declared the intention to resist forced integration by any lawful means." With Alabama and Virginia in the lead, most of the southern legislatures proceeded to draft their own declarations of "interposition." None went so far as to declare the Supreme Court decision null and void, but all were intent on circumventing it.

In the fall of 1960, in response to a federal court order, the New Orleans School Board announced its plan to begin desegregation in the New Orleans public schools. Five Negro girls, of first-grade age, were to be admitted to formerly all-white schools. This plan so excited the Louisiana Legislature that, in extraordinary session, it passed 27 measures including an Interposition Act designed to prevent integration in the state's public schools. That the Legislature represented the

---

[15] The quotation is from a speech of Dean Clarence Manion, formerly of Notre Dame University, one of the leading exponents of interposition. Excerpts appear in the *Congressional Quarterly*, April 27, 1956, p. 466.

[16] *Brown* v. *Board of Education*, 347 U.S. 483 (1954). The different basis of this decision from earlier ones is probably more apparent than real; the words of the Constitution are not self-interpreting. For years the Court has openly interpreted various provisions in the light of social and economic facts. Even the decision that first interpreted the "equal protection" clause to permit state-enforced segregation was based on sociological considerations about the difficulty of changing human nature by law. The difference appears to be that in the more recent case the sociological reasoning of the justices was buttressed by scholarly authorities rather than simply taken for granted. However shocking this may be to some lawyers, most social scientists regard it as a gratifying improvement. See Mr. Justice Brown's opinion in *Plessy* v. *Ferguson*, 163 U.S. 537 (1896).

more vocal public opinion in New Orleans was evidenced by nation-wide TV coverage of angry mobs besieging the schoolhouses to which the Negro children were admitted under armed guard. Nevertheless, the Federal District Court stood firm: "The conclusion is clear that interposition is not a constitutional doctrine. If taken seriously, it is illegal defiance of constitutional authority." The Court held unconstitutional the whole package of laws enacted by the Louisiana Legislature with respect to school integration. The U.S. Supreme Court, by refusing to rehear the case, upheld the ruling of the District Court. It found that Louisiana's claim of the right to interpose its authority in the field of education was "without substance." [17]

We could point out that the argument of states' rights has usually been rather specious, that the constitutional doctrines of nullification and interposition have generally been designed to cover up other issues. Certainly in the current controversy, the political concern of the southern states is deeply rooted in the social and economic institutions of the region. On the other hand, we must also admit that whether the nation as a whole can impose a fundamentally different pattern of behavior upon the South is in the final analysis a question that goes beyond constitutional law.

"A More Perfect Union"

"The better to secure and perpetuate mutual friendship and intercourse among the people of the different states in this Union," the Articles of Confederation provided that: (1) *full faith and credit* be given in each of the states to the records, acts, and judicial proceedings of every other state; (2) the citizens of each of the states be given the *privileges and immunities* of citizens in the several states; (3) *extradition* of fugitives from justice be obtained on demand of one governor to another; (4) *interstate compacts* be made with the consent of Congress. The Constitution of 1787 incorporates all four provisions with virtually no change in wording.

Full Faith and Credit. The Constitution provides that "Full Faith and Credit shall be given in each state to the public Acts, Records and judicial Proceedings of every other State." Because Americans move about the country more and more freely, this provision has become increasingly important. Those who go out of their state to get married; those who seek a divorce outside their own state; those who try to evade alimony or child support by moving out of the state whose court decreed the financial settlement; the beneficiaries of an estate who are not residents of the state in which the will was probated; and the out-of-state owner of a car involved in a traffic accident—all these instances, and many more, come under the coverage of the Constitution.

The intent of the full faith and credit clause is clear; it is to protect the everyday legal rights of the citizen as he moves from one state to another. It is also intended to prevent a person from evading his legal obligations simply by skipping out of state. But, in practice, one of the most acute problems in interstate

---

[17] *Bush* v. *Orleans School Board*, 364 U.S. 500 (1960).

relations today is the failure of the states to meet their obligations under the full faith and credit clause. This is particularly true in cases of divorce and alimony. For example, a couple may be legally married in one state but their marriage may not be recognized in another state.[18]

Privileges and Immunities of Citizens. The Constitution reads: "The Citizens of each State shall be entitled to all Privileges and Immunities of Citizens in the several States." The meaning of this clause has never been entirely clear even to constitutional lawyers. It stems from the common citizenship which the colonists enjoyed when all were subjects of the British monarch. The Framers of the Constitution included the "privileges and immunities" clause in order to continue this concept of common citizenship. In general, what it means is that no state may discriminate against citizens from another state in favor of its own.[19]

There is no dependable rule for determining the privileges and immunities of citizens in the several states. They seem to include rights to police protection, to sue in court, to acquire and hold property, to move in or out of a state, to reside in any state, and to earn a living without discriminatory restrictions. The citizen does not take with him all the privileges and immunities of his home state, however, when he enters another state; nor does the out-of-state citizen immediately acquire all the privileges and immunities of legal residents in a state. For example, a state may charge tuition to out-of-state students who enter its public schools; it may require a doctor or lawyer moving in from another state to meet its own standards for professional practice; it may require a period of residence in the state as a prerequisite for holding a state job; or it may restrict political privileges, such as voting, to citizens who have resided in the state for a certain number of years.

Extradition. The Constitution provides for the "interstate rendition" or "extradition" of fugitives from justice. The obligation and the procedure are clearly stated: "A Person charged in any State with Treason, Felony, or other Crime, who shall flee from Justice, and be found in another State, shall on Demand of the executive Authority of the State from which he fled, be delivered up, to be removed to the State having Jurisdiction of the Crime." But there is no way to enforce the obligation. The duty to surrender fugitives is a moral one; the Supreme Court concedes that it has no power to compel the governor of a state to fulfill his constitutional obligation. Ordinarily, of course, since no state wants to harbor the criminals of another state, in a sense the provision is self-enforcing.

---

[18] Since divorce is so common, it is at least entitled to a small footnote. The status of "out-of-domicile" divorces is sharply controverted under the full faith and credit clause. Because divorce proceedings are difficult and unpleasant in some states, the unhappily married in these states are tempted to seek divorce in other states where residence requirements are short and divorce laws are lenient. Such out-of-domicile divorces, however, are frequently questionable in the light of Supreme Court decisions. In *Williams* v. *North Carolina*, 317 U.S. 287 (1942) and 325 U.S. 226 (1945), the unfortunate Mr. Williams, a resident of North Carolina, who went off to Nevada to get a divorce and remarry, and who then returned to North Carolina with his second spouse, was convicted for "bigamous cohabitation" under North Carolina law.

[19] Further interpretation has excluded corporations from protection under the clause, though this has been more than made up by their full coverage as "persons" under "due process of law."

Occasionally, however, governors have felt morally impelled to refuse extradition. Northern governors have sometimes been reluctant to return Negroes to southern states. When one northern governor declared that he had not the heart to return a fugitive to the "chain gang" of a particular southern state, the southern governor replied that he in turn was ready to deliver all the criminals in his state to the peculiar hospitality of the northern governor. Some years ago, the Governor of Florida refused to extradite a husband and wife wanted in Massachusetts on a charge of "kidnapping." As residents of Massachusetts, this couple had adopted a baby. Subsequently, Massachusetts claimed the adoption was a faulty one because the baby's natural mother was Roman Catholic and the adopting parents were Jewish (Massachusetts requires the adopting parents to be of the same religion as the child's natural mother). Rather than surrender their adopted daughter, the couple fled with her to Miami. The Governor of Florida decided that his moral obligation to keep the child with her adopted parents outweighed his moral obligation under the Constitution to "deliver up" the "fugitives" to Massachusetts.

Because extradition is such a cumbersome and uncertain process, Congress has simplified the problem of dealing with criminals who flee across state lines by making it a federal offense for a person to move from one state to another in order to avoid prosecution or imprisonment.

Interstate Compacts. The Constitution provides that "No State shall, without the Consent of Congress . . . enter into any Agreement or Compact with another State." In practice, this provision has been rephrased to read: "with the consent of Congress the several states may enter into compacts or agreements with each other." In our federal government we recognize that some problems are too big for a single state to tackle, yet too limited to warrant the attention of the national government. For such problems, which involve more than one state but do not concern the whole country, the interstate compact appears to be a reasonable approach.[20]

In years gone by, most interstate compacts were nothing more than agreements on boundary lines. More recently, however, the interstate compact has been used as a regulatory device to meet social and economic problems shared by several states. For example, several interstate agreements deal with the conservation of natural resources; here the efforts of one state would be fruitless without the cooperation of other states. Thus interstate agreements are used to protect the salmon resources of the Columbia River, and migratory fisheries of the Atlantic states. Similar agreements govern the amount of petroleum produced in different states and establish interstate flood control along the Connecticut River. New compacts are now appearing, especially in the welfare field: they

---

[20] The Council of State Governments has dealt with the subject of interstate compacts in numerous publications. For legal aspects, see Vincent V. Thursby, *Interstate Cooperation: A Study of the Interstate Compact* (Washington: Public Affairs Press, 1953); for a consideration of administrative problems see, Richard H. Leach and Redding S. Sugg, Jr., *The Administration of Interstate Compacts* (Baton Rouge, La.: Louisiana State University Press, 1959).

provide for interstate cooperation in such problems as parole supervision, control of juvenile delinquency, and care of mentally ill patients.

Interstate compacts have often been used by adjoining states to improve navigation and transportation. In 1921, New York, New Jersey, and the United States joined in compact to erect the Port of New York Authority. This Authority is the planning and administrative agency for the whole Port of New York. A new development in compact activities is now appearing in the metropolitan areas of mass transportation. A recent amendment to the 1921 Port of New York compact authorizes the interstate Authority to take over and operate an electric rapid transit system between New Jersey and Manhattan terminals. Interstate agreements have also been worked out for such objectives as public utility regulation, civil defense, and highway safety.

"The consent of Congress," express or implied, has been readily obtained for more than a hundred interstate compacts. Only once has Congress reacted unfavorably toward a proposed interstate agreement. In 1947, the Conference of Southern Governors called on Congress to authorize a regional agreement for the improvement of professional and higher education in the southern states. In 1948, the Conference agreed to set up a Board of Control for Southern Regional Education. This board was to plan a regional program for higher education to be supported by tax money from the southern states. With such a program, the Conference hoped to improve educational facilities in the South for both whites and Negroes, but it also expected the plan to fit the traditional southern pattern of segregation. Congressional debates on the southern compact centered on the segregation issue. Eventually the Senate killed the compact by referring it back to the Judiciary Committee.

Having been denied the consent of Congress, the southern states decided that their compact did not have to receive congressional approval after all. They argued that the consent of Congress is necessary only when a compact infringes on national power; since education is "reserved" to the states, congressional sanction was really not necessary. Thus they went ahead with their compact and with their plans to develop graduate and professional schools on a regional basis. Since 1949, thousands of southern students, white and Negro, have taken advantage of the regional scholarships offered by the Board of Control, especially in the fields of dentistry and medicine. The Southern Regional Compact continues in force, its constitutionality as yet unchallenged in the courts.[21] And it has served as model and impetus for similar compacts in the New England region and also among the western states.

The Delaware River Basin Compact represents a new departure in intergovernmental relations. Its Commission, organized in 1961, comprises a representative from each of the member states (Delaware, New Jersey, New York, and Pennsylvania) appointed by the governors of the respective states, and also a

---

[21] See Redding S. Sugg, Jr., and George H. Jones, *The Southern Regional Education Board: Ten Years of Regional Cooperation in Higher Education* (Baton Rouge, La.: Louisiana State University Press, 1960) for an account and an appraisal of the Compact in operation.

representative of the United States government appointed by the President. The first chairman of the Commission was Stewart Udall, Secretary of the Interior. This is the first interstate compact to which the national government is a signatory and a party. As an experiment in national-regional administration, it bears watching. Activities of the Commission include the planning and construction of flood prevention and water supply facilities and other water resource needs.

Interstate Disputes. In 1787, at the time the Constitution was drafted, ten of the thirteen states were involved in serious disputes over boundaries, lands, and river rights. Under the Articles of Confederation, Congress had had the authority to hear such interstate disputes. The Convention shifted the authority over to the courts. The Constitution gives the Supreme Court power to settle *all* cases involving two or more states, but the Court itself has refused to hear what it considers "non-justiciable" disputes—that is, disputes that cannot be settled by some rule of law. In recent years, the states have brought an increasing number of suits to the Supreme Court—not only over boundary rights but also over such matters as water rights, disposal of sewage and garbage, and diversion of water resources.

The problem of enforcement is one reason why the Supreme Court is so choosy in the kind of interstate disputes it will hear. How can the Court compel a state to accept its judgment? The problem is illustrated in a long drawn-out conflict between Virginia and West Virginia. At the time West Virginia seceded from Virginia (when Virginia seceded from the Union), West Virginia agreed to assume its just proportion of the public debt. When West Virginia later refused to meet this debt obligation, Virginia finally commenced suit in the Supreme Court in 1906. The Supreme Court decided against West Virginia in 1915, but West Virginia ignored the decision. In 1917, Virginia again asked the Supreme Court for a judicial order that would compel the West Virginia legislature to levy a tax to pay its debt to Virginia. While the Court was stalling on this proposition, West Virginia accepted the Court's earlier judgment and finally paid its debt to Virginia.[22] But if West Virginia had not given in, how could nine justices of the Supreme Court have made the West Virginia legislators act against their will?

The Supreme Court's obligation to decide controversies among states is an essential feature of American federalism. Our system could endure, as Justice Oliver Wendell Holmes observed, without the Court's power to declare an act of Congress void. The British courts, for example, do not have the power to invalidate acts of Parliament. But it is hard to conceive of a federal union—in which the Constitution is the supreme law of the land—without judicial authority to settle controversies between states and between citizens of the different states. Moreover, Justice Holmes thought the Union would be imperiled if the Supreme Court could not pass judgment on the constitutionality of state laws. Without this ultimate national authority, we might be beset by constant bickering among the states and be completely confused by fifty different interpretations of constitutional law. Nevertheless, the Supreme Court has become the whipping boy of many states'

---

[22] The various litigations of *Virginia* v. *West Virginia* before the Supreme Court cover twelve years, 1906 to 1918.

rights extremists who feel that the Court's jurisdiction over state laws should be sharply restricted by congressional legislation or even by constitutional amendment.

Enumerated Powers and Implied Powers

We could work out a very neat pattern showing how powers are distributed between the national government and the states: (1) Certain powers are assigned to the national government and belong to it exclusively—the conduct of foreign affairs, for example, or the control of currency. (2) Certain powers are assigned to the national government but are also held concurrently by the states—taxation or regulation of commerce. (3) Certain powers are specifically denied to the national government—for example, Congress may not tax exports or give preference to the ports of one state over those of another. (4) Certain powers are specifically denied to the states—for example, no state may enter into any treaty, alliance, or confederation, or lay any imposts or duties on imports or exports. (5) All other powers are reserved to the states or to the people—those powers that are neither delegated to the national government nor denied to the states.

This neat pattern of federalism looks fine on paper. But in actual practice, lawyers and politicians have almost as much difficulty in drawing a sharp line between national power and states' rights as churchmen and laymen do when they try to separate what belongs to God from what belongs to Caesar. Those who stress national power point to Article VI, Section 2, sometimes called "the national supremacy clause." They regard this article as the keystone in the arch of American federalism, because it explicitly states that the Constitution and the laws and treaties of the United States shall be the supreme law of the land. Proponents of states' rights point to the Tenth Amendment, which provides that "The powers not delegated to the United States by the Constitution, nor prohibited by it to the States, are reserved to the States respectively, or to the people." What the Tenth Amendment actually added to the original intentions of 1787 is not at all clear.[23] When the Amendment was drafted in 1789, Congress voted down an attempt to insert the word *expressly* before the word *delegated*. Nevertheless to this day, the advocates of states' rights continue to claim that the national government is limited to powers expressly delegated to it!

The Articles of Confederation plainly held that each state retained "every power, jurisdiction, and right" not *expressly* delegated to the United States. The Constitutional Convention was well aware of this wording; so was the First Congress, which rejected similar wording for the Tenth Amendment. In the landmark case of *McCulloch* v. *Maryland*,[24] Chief Justice Marshall declared that the Framers, both of the Constitution of 1787 and of the Amendment in 1789, had experienced

---

[23] For a brief and scholarly essay see Walter Bern's "The Meaning of the Tenth Amendment," in Goldwin (ed.), *A Nation of States*. For an opposing viewpoint, see "The Case for 'States' Rights'" by James Jackson Kilpatrick in the same collection of essays. Walter Berns is a professor of political science at Cornell University; James Kilpatrick is editor of the Richmond *News Leader*.

[24] 4 Wheaton 316 (1819).

"such embarrassments" from this restrictive wording that they "probably omitted it to avoid those embarrassments." But for those not satisfied with Marshall's interpretation alone, the constructive actions of the Congress may be more convincing.

When Congress in 1791 chartered the Bank of the United States, the action was bitterly criticized before and after the passage of the act. Indeed the establishment of the Bank was one of the major party issues during the first decades of the federal union. Alexander Hamilton, who proposed the Bank, felt it was a "necessary and proper" exercise of power delegated to the national government. As Secretary of the Treasury, he planned to make the Bank sole depository for the government funds. Also, since the Treasury minted only gold and silver coins, he counted on the Bank to issue notes that could be used as currency in business transactions. Jefferson and his friends, who opposed the establishment of the Bank, maintained that Congress should not act beyond its expressly assigned powers. Behind their opposition on legal grounds, however, was the fear that a Bank of the United States—in which the national government had a proprietary interest— would offer too formidable competition to the state banks. Moreover, they looked on a central banking system as a device to give the merchants and financiers more influence and greater stakes in the national government. Nevertheless, Congress voted to approve the charter and its constitutionality was never attacked in the courts.

A Second Bank of the United States was chartered by Congress for another 20 years in 1816, again amid sharp controversy between the advocates of states' rights and the supporters of national power. The Second Bank was initially sponsored by the Democrats to help the national government manage some of the financial problems that beset the country after the War of 1812. Later the Bank was attacked by the Jacksonian Democrats, ostensibly on constitutional grounds, actually on a variety of counts: that the Bank was a political machine for the Federalists; that it represented the commercial interests of the eastern seaboard as against the western farmers; that its stock was largely held by British and other foreign investors; that its inefficient and corrupt management contributed to the failure of many local banks in the postwar depression. The Second Bank became such an object of popular mistrust that a number of states passed laws restricting its activities.

In *McCulloch* v. *Maryland*, the Supreme Court considered the question whether a state could by law restrict the activities of a federal instrumentality. Before answering the question, the Court first determined that Congress had the power to incorporate the Bank even though the Constitution does not specifically mention banking as one of the enumerated powers. The Court pointed out that the enumeration of powers in Article I, Section 8, ends with a blanket clause giving the Congress power "to make all laws which shall be necessary and proper for carrying into execution the foregoing powers, and all other powers vested by this Constitution in the government of the United States, or in any department or officer thereof." This clause is placed with the powers of Congress, not among the limitations, and it purports to grant additional power, not to restrict those already granted. As Marshall construed the meaning of "necessary and proper," Congress was given discretion to choose whatever means it deemed convenient, useful, or essential to perform its legislative functions. Since Congress chose to establish a Bank to facilitate the fiscal operations of the national government, the Bank must be regarded as a federal instrumentality.

The same constitutional interpretation that upheld the establishment of the Bank of the United States has also given judicial sanction to subsequent acts of Congress extending the national controls over banking—the National Banking System inaugurated in 1863, the Federal Reserve System established in 1913, and the Federal Deposit Insurance Corporation in 1933. Indeed, the doctrine of implied powers which develops out of this early case becomes the crucial doctrine which justifies expansion of national instrumentalities and activities to meet the increasing and changing needs of the American people.

McCulloch v. *Maryland* also established a second doctrine, almost as important in setting the functional pattern of federalism—the immunity of national government activities from state controls. Maryland had attempted to restrict the Bank by placing a heavy tax on its activity within the state. The Court held that the tax was unconstitutional. The Chief Justice argued that the power to create implies a power to preserve. Since the national government had the power to create the Bank, it logically follows that the national government had also the power to preserve the Bank. Marshall then argued that the power to tax involves the power to destroy; again it follows logically that, if a state has the power to tax, it would also have the power to destroy a federal instrumentality. As Marshall saw it, the people of the United States created a national government and made its laws supreme. The states have no power, *by taxation or otherwise*,[25] to impede or in any manner control the operations of the national government that are undertaken either under the powers specifically enumerated or under those which can be reasonably implied. Thus the Maryland law was declared null and void by the Court.

The opinion of Chief Justice Marshall in *McCulloch* v. *Maryland* is generally conceded to be one of the great state papers in exposition of American federalism. Keep in mind, however, that it was the policy of Congress in creating the First Bank, and then the Second Bank, which actually set the federal pattern of implied powers. The Court did no more than give judicial affirmation to congressional policy. The decision of the Supreme Court was not delivered until 1819, but Congress chartered the First Bank of the United States in 1791. Constitutional interpretations over the years have been similarly used to justify a great many changes in the actual functioning of American federalism. Policy-making at any time, however, represents a continuous intermeshing of legislative, executive, and judicial decisions, in the national government and in the states.

---

[25] The decision with respect to tax immunities in the federal system has been reduced to constitutional history by subsequent legislative policies. In numerous cases, the Court has since upheld extension of the national taxing power over many kinds of state activities, and vice versa. In answer to Marshall's dictum, the "power to tax involves the power to destroy," Justice Holmes once retorted, "but not while this court sits."

Political Patterns of Federalism

A discussion of federalism entirely in terms of constitutional law sounds almost superficial and is certainly incomplete. The "indestructible states" within the "indestructible union," all on an "equal footing" with one another, each claiming "sovereign rights" and "reserved powers"—these are fine abstractions but reflect the stereotyped vocabulary of endless and fruitless debates. A functional approach to federalism offers a more realistic account of intergovernmental relations as they have developed in actual practice within the constitutional framework. As we turn our attention to specific governmental policies (i.e., courses of political action) it is obvious that changes in environment since the eighteenth century—physical, technological, economic, cultural, intellectual, and political—have had a tremendous impact on American federalism.

Cooperative Federalism

The relationship between the national government and the states may be viewed from various perspectives. The most familiar one is to regard the federal structure as a three-level hierarchy—the local communities at the base, the state governments at the intermediary level, and the national government at the apex. Another model focuses on the national government as the central government, remote from the people who live in the states and local communities, some at great physical (and cultural) distance from the national capital. If we accept either of these models of federal government, we are led to believe that the state or local governments are "closer" to the people than the national government. If, however, without referring to either of these models (which are in effect abstractions to control your thinking) you take a fresh look at American federalism in action, you will observe that many agencies of the national government are at work in your local community. As a matter of fact, most activities of the national government are administered locally, and about 90 per cent of the federal civilian employees live and work outside of the District of Columbia. Certainly the national government is "close" to the people, whether we think of "closeness" in terms of physical proximity, communications, or direct controls and primary services. Consult your telephone directory and see how many *local* phone numbers are listed under "United States Government": the Post Office, the Department of Justice, the Department of Agriculture, the Veterans' Administration, the Treasury Department, Health, Education, and Welfare, and others.

That the Framing Fathers well understood the operational as well as the structural side of federalism, even in 1787, is implicit in the numerous constitutional provisions for cooperative and concurrent action by the national government and the states.[26] Some years ago, Morton Grodzins, director of the Federalism Work-

---

[26] Daniel Elazar tabulates seventeen constitutional provisions for "sharing." See *The American Partnership*, p. 309.

shop at the University of Chicago, was asked to examine "The Federal System" for the President's Commission on National Goals. Through his study, he found that American federalism has never been a system of separated governmental activities. At all times in our history, the national government and the states have shared activities, powers, and responsibilities. Grodzins maintained that this is a first principle and a continuing practice in American federalism.[27]

To illustrate the practice of cooperative federalism, Grodzins offers us a job description of a health officer, a "Sanitarian" of a rural county.

> The sanitarian is appointed by the state under merit standards established by the federal government. His base salary comes jointly from state and federal funds, the county provides him with an office and office amenities and pays a portion of his expenses, and the largest city in the county also contributes to his salary and office by virtue of his appointment as a city plumbing inspector. It is impossible from moment to moment to tell under which governmental hat the sanitarian operates. His work of inspecting the purity of food is carried out under federal standards; but he is enforcing state laws when inspecting commodities that have been in interstate commerce; and somewhat perversely he also acts under state authority when inspecting milk coming into the county from producing areas across the state border. He is a federal officer when impounding impure drugs shipped from a neighboring state; a federal-state officer when enforcing standards of industrial hygiene; a state-local officer when inspecting the city's water supply; and (to complete the circle) a local officer when insisting that the city butchers adopt more hygienic methods of handling their garbage. But he cannot and does not think of himself as acting in these separate capacities. All business in the county that concerns public health and sanitation he considers his business. Paid largely from federal funds, he does not find it strange to attend meetings of the city council to give expert advice on matters ranging from rotten apples to rabies control. He is even deputized as a member of both the city and county police forces.[28]

Here, in this one job description, we see how federalism operates through much intermeshing of national, state, and local government activities.

The Commission on Intergovernmental Relations, created by Congress at the request of President Eisenhower, points up the complexity of federalism in the mid-twentieth century.[29] The Committee examined the major fields in which both the national government and the states were active: agriculture, civil aviation, civil defense, education, employment security, highways, housing and urban renewal, natural disaster relief, natural resources and conservation, public health, vocational rehabilitation, and welfare. Not one of these fields is even mentioned in the Constitution of 1787, although today all of them are of vital national concern. The

---

[27] The President's Commission on National Goals, *Goals for Americans.* © 1960 by The American Assembly, Columbia University, N.Y. By permission of Prentice-Hall, Inc., publisher. Morton Grodzins, Chapter 12, "The Federal System," p. 268.

[28] *Ibid.,* pp. 265–266.

[29] The Commission was created by statute in 1953. Its first chairman, Clarence Manion, was shortly succeeded by Myer Kestnbaum, of Illinois, who directed the work of the task forces. The Commission was thereafter known as the Kestnbaum Commission. It made its official *Report to the President,* with supporting documents, June, 1955.

Commission pointed out that broad interpretations of constitutional law have given the national government almost unlimited power. Faced with the practical problem of allocating responsibilities, the Commission found that the crucial question is not which government has the constitutional right but rather which government can perform most effectively in meeting the needs of the people.

Because the Commission did not evolve a national policy or prepare any blueprint for the improvement of intergovernmental relations, President Eisenhower next persuaded the Governors' Conference to establish a Federal-State Joint Action Committee. The hope was that this Committee would make some specific recommendations for unwinding the complicated pattern of modern federalism—that is, for returning to the states as many activities as they were willing and able to handle without federal interference or assistance.

The Federal-State Joint Action Committee labored diligently over its assignment to "decentralize" the federal government.[30] It finally came up with several recommendations—that the states assume full financial support for some of the older programs in vocational education such as practical nurse training and the training program for the fisheries trade; that the states manage and finance their own problems of sewerage and water pollution. But even these modest recommendations came to grief in the political arena when the interest groups affected converged on Washington. State departments of education, educational interest groups, the nurses' associations, and the fishing industry all sent representatives to oppose any cuts in federal aid for vocational education. The U.S. Conference of Mayors, the American Municipal Association, and various sportsmen's associations also sent their spokesmen to ask for more, not less, federal aid for local waste disposal, which they testified was a grave national problem. And so Congress was persuaded not to cut back these particular programs in health, education, and welfare.

When it comes to concrete proposals to curtail specific activities of the national government, proponents of such steps are usually defeated by local demands on Washington for continuing and increasing federal aid. In fact, cooperative federalism correlates with the pattern of political power in America today. The alliance between conservative rural representatives and powerful economic interests in many states resists regulatory governmental activities and also produces economy-oriented budgets which do not adequately meet public needs. Because state governments, especially rural-dominated legislatures, have failed to respond to the urgent demands of urban and industrialized communities, the people of the cities, a majority of the population in most states, have felt frustrated and in their frustration have turned to the national government for help. U.S. senators serve state-wide constituencies; U.S. representatives come from

---

[30] The Federal-State Joint Action Committee was organized at the Governors' Conference at Williamsburg in 1957. It made its first *Report to the President* in 1958 and President Eisenhower immediately requested Congress to follow through with appropriate legislation, but Congress was persuaded not to take action. Later the Governors' Conference voted to continue the Committee but did not extend its approval to the Committee's specific proposals for the transfer of program responsibilities.

congressional districts much more populous than the units of representation for state legislators; and, of course, the President represents a nation-wide electorate. Hence the national government may be much more accessible to city people who cannot get what they want in their own states because of under-representation. If in the near future, however, state legislatures are elected on the principle of equal representation of people—as the Supreme Court has decreed—it is conceivable that the patterns of power will quickly change within the states. Perhaps some functions now performed by the national government may then be returned to the states.

Often the arguments for or against activities of the national government are really arguments for or against governmental activities in general. Actually it is difficult to single out programs of the national government in which state and local governments do not participate. Even in matters of national defense, the state and local governments play a considerable part. The national guard is composed of state militia units which remain under command of their respective governors until called into emergency service by the United States; training must meet the national standards and, in return, the national government pays most of the costs. The Selective Service is responsible for implementing the Universal Military Training and Service Act, but actual administration is largely left to the state headquarters and the local draft boards. And quite obviously, the location of military bases throughout the country reflects local community pressures as well as strategic considerations; the payroll of a military base is a bonanza for any Main Street.

In the area of law enforcement, state and local police officers have access to the fingerprint files, reporting service, and other facilities of the Federal Bureau of Investigation, including special courses in the FBI's famous National Academy for training in modern police methods. Immediately following the passage of the Civil Rights Act of 1964, the new Director of Community Relations personally conferred with state and local officials, especially in the southern states, to plan for the implementation of the controversial legislation through "voluntary compliance." This is the usual pattern of intergovernmental relations—personal conferences, joint planning, continuous consultation, interchange of facilities, awareness of common enterprise in the public interest. Whatever the field of intergovernmental activity, professional interests and professional standards are likely to be more important at the program level than legal verbalisms and political platitudes. The U.S. geologist works professionally with the state geologist on the problems of conserving water resources. Inspectors from the Food and Drug Administration meet their counterparts in the state departments of agriculture. Rangers in the U.S. Forest Service cooperate with state forest rangers to preserve our forests. These examples of official collaboration and cooperation can be multiplied until they cover the whole range of intergovernmental activities.

The most friendly personal relations alone do not make a partnership. In a truly federal system, shared activities mean shared finances. Earlier in this chapter, we gave some account of the development of grants-in-aid from the national government to the states—land grants, service grants, and cash grants. Most important in modern federalism are the cash grants. The grant-in-aid has become an essential tool of modern federalism, a device not only to alleviate the wide disparities in financial resources among the states but also to promote minimum national standards for the general welfare of the people in all the states. The national government systematically supplements state finances with cash grants for specified programs in areas of national concern. Thus in some sixty grant programs, shared activities and responsibilities are underwritten by the national government.

The first major grant-in-aid program was established in 1862 for state agricultural experiment stations. Forest fire protection was added in 1911, agricultural extension in 1914, the federal highway system in 1916, vocational education in 1917, public health in 1918, vocational rehabilitation services in 1920, and maternal and child health services in 1921. In 1930, total grants by the national government to the states amounted to somewhat over $100 million.

Then came the depression and a tremendous increase in federal programs under the impetus of the New Deal: employment service and school lunches in 1933; unemployment compensation, public assistance, services for crippled children and child welfare in 1935. Notice, however, that, while grants-in-aid made their greatest initial gains during economic depression and under a Democratic administration, they continued to grow during war and post-war prosperity and under a Republican administration. Since World War II, only the Eighty-second Congress, engrossed in the Korean War and "McCarthyism," failed to add new grant-in-aid programs to the now lengthy list. Grants-in-aid to state and local governments in the eight years of the Eisenhower Administration more than doubled. And the Kennedy-Johnson Administrations added still more programs. Nearly two-thirds of all our grant programs, including such important ones as those for urban renewal, education, aid to federally impacted areas (areas overcrowded by such federal facilities as military establishments), national defense education, hospital and medical facilities, sewage facilities, public works acceleration, and urban mass transportation, were established after World War II.[31]

Figures on governmental expenditures are always impressive, even awesome, in total amounts. Because the methods of reporting vary from one governmental unit to another and from one year to the next, tables and charts on public finance are never too reliable. Nevertheless, the distribution of fiscal resources is so crucial to cooperative federalism that we must scrutinize the basic facts and figures.

All governmental expenditures—national, state, and local—have skyrocketed since the Great Depression in 1932 (Table 4-1). In thinking about these ever-

---

[31] The facts and figures in this section are taken from the *Report* of the Advisory Commission on Intergovernmental Relations, "The Role of Equalization in Federal Grants," January, 1964.

TABLE 4-1   *General Governmental Expenditures (in millions of dollars)*

YEAR	TOTAL FEDERAL, STATE, LOCAL	FEDERAL	STATE	LOCAL
1932	$ 12,437	$ 4,266	$ 2,568	$ 5,609
1936	16,758	9,165	3,144	4,449
1940	20,417	10,061	4,545	5,811
1946	79,707	66,534	6,162	7,011
1952	99,847	71,568	13,330	14,948
1956	115,796	75,991	18,379	21,426
1962	174,417	112,217	29,200	33,000

Source: Facts and Figures on Government Finance, Tax Foundation, Inc., 12th ed., 1962–1963 (Prentice-Hall, Inc.: Englewood Cliffs, N. J., 1963).

increasing expenditures, however, we should keep in mind that the population of the United States also is expanding rapidly. In 1930, the census counted about 123 million persons in the United States; in 1960, about 180 million persons. In recent years the population has been growing at the rate of approximately 3 million persons a year. "Population explosion" is one explanation for increasing governmental expenditures.

Table 4-1 indicates that the increase in federal expenditures during the past thirty years has been overwhelming. But if we do not include expenditures for national defense and external activities, then federal expenditures do not appear so much out of line with the normal increases attributable to the growing population. Moreover, changes in the value of the dollar account for much of this apparent increase. Table 4-2 shows federal general expenditures for civil functions only, exclusive of national defense, international affairs and finance, space technology, veterans' benefits, and services and interest on debt.

TABLE 4-2   *Federal General Expenditures for Civil Activities (in millions of dollars)*

1932	$ 1,878
1936	5,686
1940	7,035
1946	8,340
1952	12,001
1956	16,854
1962	29,817

Source: Advisory Commission on Intergovernmental Relations, *Report,* "The Role of Equalization in Federal Grants," January, 1964, Table I, p. 14.

Even more significant, perhaps, is the changing pattern of living. Industrialization and urbanization have many implications in terms of essential governmental services (education, health, sanitation, hospitals, recreation, welfare, streets, utilities). And, of course, rising standards of living call for new and more governmental expenditures; what was good enough for the fathers is not enough for the sons and daughters. We expect a cloverleaf at the crossroads; a nuclear reactor as well as a stadium and modern dormitories for the state university; a golf course, a little league baseball diamond, and a civic auditorium for the townspeople, as well as paved streets and parking facilities; soil conservation experts for the farmer and home demonstration agents for the farmer's wife.

Governmental expenditures keep getting bigger and bigger. But the Sixteenth Amendment has given the federal government an effective device—through the progressive income taxes—for tapping the national fiscal resources. These resources have increased enormously in terms of the gross national product. (The gross national product—GNP—is the total market value of all final goods and services produced in the nation's economy within a given period of time.) Table 4-3 shows the relation of federal, state, and local expenditures to the gross

TABLE 4-3 *Government Expenditures and Gross National Product (in millions of dollars)*

| | | | AS A PERCENTAGE OF GNP [a] | | |
YEAR	GNP	TOTAL FEDERAL, STATE, AND LOCAL [a]	TOTAL	FEDERAL	STATE & LOCAL
1932	$ 58,466	$ 10,607	18.1	5.5	12.7
1936	82,743	15,882	19.2	10.3	8.9
1942	159,133	64,032	40.2	35.3	5.0
1946	210,663	47,004	22.3	17.6	4.7
1952	346,999	94,425	27.2	20.6	6.6
1956	419,180	107,559	25.7	17.1	8.5
1961	518,725	156,293	30.1	19.7	10.4

[a] Total figures here include expenditures for national defense, international relations, and so on. The percentages also are based on the all-inclusive expenditures.

Source: Facts and Figures, Table 12, p. 27.

national product. Except in the midst of World War II, the total governmental expenditures are less than a third of the GNP. These figures obviously belie the cries of "socialism."

But here we are mainly concerned with the distributive aspects of federal financing. Table 4-4 shows the trend of grants-in-aid to the states since the 1930's,

TABLE 4-4 *Federal Aid to State and Local Governments (in millions of dollars)*

| | | FEDERAL AID AS A PERCENTAGE OF STATE & LOCAL REVENUE | FEDERAL AID AS A PERCENTAGE OF FEDERAL GENERAL EXPENDITURE | | FEDERAL AID AS PERCENTAGE OF GNP |
YEAR	TOTAL FEDERAL AID		TOTAL	CIVIL	
1932	232	3	6	12	0.4
1936	948	11	10	17	1.1
1940	945	10	10	14	0.9
1946	855	7	1	10	0.4
1952	2566	10	4	21	0.7
1956	3335	10	5	20	0.8
1962	7857	14	8	26	1.4

Source: Advisory Commission on Intergovernmental Relations, *Report,* "The Role of Equalization in Federal Grants," January, 1964.

in amounts and in percentages. Notice that the amounts seem to zoom but that the percentages after 1932 are fairly stable. The percentages of the total federal expenditures that go to the states is modest indeed, and the percentages in terms of GNP reduce the whole grant-in-aid system to chickenfeed.

When we examine the grant-in-aid system in greater detail (Who gets what?) a realistic picture of cooperative federalism begins to emerge out of all the facts and figures. To begin, there is considerable variation in federal contributions to state and local revenues. In early grant programs, the states were usually expected to match the federal grants dollar for dollar. More recently, equalizing features have been introduced—allocation formulas calculated to grant federal aid on the basis of program need or financial need. Actually, "equalization" of federal grants may mean a number of different things: equal grants to all the states; or equal grants per unit of need; or grants designed to bring about more equal program levels in the different states. The problem is highly complicated by the fact that the states are unequal or unlike in various ways. The states not only have unequal capacities to finance but quite different inclinations toward supporting public programs fostered by the federal government. And it is the very essence of federalism to tolerate interstate differences—even in the face of a "strong national interest."

The federal government redistributes its nationally collected tax monies to the states via some sixty grant-in-aid programs. No state has to accept a federal grant—not all the states avail themselves of every grant offered—but once a grant is offered, the pressure to accept is usually too great for a single state to resist. The most numerous federal aid programs are in the fields of education, health, hospitals, and natural resources. But in dollar amounts, highways and public welfare account for nearly three-fourths of current grant distributions. Table 4-5 shows the distribution of federal funds to the states by activities in 1962. Federal aid for roads is nothing new in American history; but the numerous grants for health, education, and welfare reflect a profound change in the public philosophy.

TABLE 4-5 *Federal Grants-in-Aid by Activities*

NUMBER OF PROGRAMS	ACTIVITIES	1962 EXPENDITURE (MILLIONS)	PERCENTAGE DISTRIBUTION
1	Highways	2,743	39.1
7	Public welfare	2,448	34.9
14	Education	622	8.9
1	Employment security	439	6.2
3	Housing and urban renewal	309	4.4
9	Natural resources	165	2.4
14	Health and hospitals	152	2.2
1	Air transportation	57	0.8
10	All other	79	1.1
60		7,014	100.0

Source: Advisory Commission on Intergovernmental Relations, *Report,* "The Role of Equalization in Federal Grants," 1964, p. 28.

The assumption of national responsibility for the less fortunate persons in our society was effected by the New Deal of the 1930's.

The national government gives grants-in-aid to the states only if the states are willing to meet conditions specified by Congress. The national agencies that administer the funds require the states to submit their plans for advance approval.

As a matter of fact, many of the "conditions" that are attached to the grants are determined by personal consultation and professional collaboration between the federal and state agencies concerned. In some programs, the conditions are but one-shot affairs; that is to say, when the program is established, the state may have to agree to do something in particular (set up a governmental agency, provide a merit system for personnel involved) but otherwise there are few continuing conditions to meet except appropriating the matching funds. For some programs, however, federal agencies view the state programs in operation, inspect the work that is done with federal aid, and audit the accounts of the "cooperating" state agencies. State officials naturally are inclined to resent excessive federal "meddling" in state affairs.

No doubt federal grants-in-aid stimulate the states to provide services they might not otherwise undertake. No doubt, also, a state legislature is sometimes stimulated by the promise of federal money to undertake programs that the tax-payers of the state cannot afford. Legally, of course, the states are quite free to reject grants-in-aid; strictly speaking, grants-in-aid involve no coercion. State legislators find it extremely difficult, however, to explain to their constituents why their state should be denied what appears to be a generous piece of the national pie. Thus the same state legislature that berates the national government for in-vading states' rights in one field will do everything it can to qualify for federal grants-in-aid in half a dozen other fields.

Reactions to federal grants-in-aid are both pro and con. All agree that the states have been able to provide many necessary and desirable services that they could not have afforded without federal aid. Those who oppose "nationalization" are most frequently those who in principle are equally opposed to "welfare government" at any level. Others are genuinely apprehensive that the states will be tempted to surrender all their sovereign rights in the Union "just for a handful of silver." Most of the "conditions" attached to grants-in-aid with respect to personnel policies and fiscal practices have actually improved standards of admin-istration in the state agencies. Rapport between the federal agencies and pro-fessional workers in the state service is usually high. Nevertheless, many people tend to equate "big government" and "centralization" with "socialism" and "regimentation." Still others have a kind of nostalgia for "plain and simple government," a sort of moral resistance to "subsidies, doles and paternalism." The best test of what the people want, however, seems to be what they reach out and take. And every state in the Union has reached out for federal grants-in-aid and has generally taken as much as it can get out of the federal treasury.

Inputs of the Political System: Demands, Supports, and Apathy

PART TWO

Political Opinions and Voting Behavior

American candidates *run* for public office, British candidates *stand* for their positions, Soviet leaders who are named to the communist slate are *approved* without opposition, and the Shah of Iran is *born* to office. These considerable and slight variations in political systems can be understood only within the context of different cultures.

But if we are to go beyond a mere catalog of cultural traits, we must look at more specific elements of the political culture itself. In Part 1 we therefore moved from the broad cultural context to the ideas, the legal basis, and the formal structure of the American political system. We are now ready to look at the elements of the political process in action.

What do people want from their government? How much public support do the practices, policies, and leaders of government enjoy? And to what extent are citizens simply indifferent to their government? These questions get to the substance of what we have called the "input" activities of the political system. And they suggest that public opinions—or, more specifically, political opinions—are the ultimate foundation on which all governments, democratic or dictatorial, ultimately rest.

The importance of public opinion is more obvious in democracies, of course, for many of their institutions depend on public preference. But all political systems must somehow perform the basic function of identifying the interests of the public. Even the most absolute dictator is aware that public opinion sets limits that he can violate only at his own peril. The elaborate pretensions that Machiavelli recommended to *The Prince* in the interest of maintaining public support are almost as complicated as the processes of a genuine democracy. And when the rulers of the Soviet Union were forced to modify their campaign against religion, they painfully discovered that Machiavelli's warnings still apply in the twentieth century. Although the anti-religious laws did not lead to actual rebellion, they proved so difficult to enforce and so destructive of morale that they were relaxed. Today the Soviet government goes to great trouble and expense to keep its knowledge of public opinion up to date—a knowledge that the elected officials of a democracy acquire almost automatically.[1] The shrewd dictator never forgets that revolution and chaos are the price that must be paid for a complete disregard of public sentiment.

The Meaning of Public Opinion for Politics

Before we can investigate *political opinions* in American democracy, we must first understand the meaning of the parent term, "public opinion." Although we are primarily concerned with political opinions, we must remember that they are just one aspect of public opinion.

In popular usage, "public opinion" is a vague and ambiguous concept. When a congressman says that "public opinion" demands that a certain bill be passed, exactly what does he mean? And how does he know? He probably does not mean all the people of the United States, since Americans have never agreed unanimously on anything. Does he mean a majority of the *people* of the United States, or only a majority of the *citizens*? If he means citizens, does he mean a

---

[1] See Alex Inkeles, *Public Opinion in Soviet Russia* (Cambridge: Harvard University Press, 1950).

majority of citizens who are eligible to vote, or of citizens who actually do vote? Perhaps he is referring to the voters of his own state or district, or to the voters who belong to his own political party. Or he may mean something even narrower than that. He may have in mind a majority of those who voted for him, or of those who contributed to his campaign, or of those key friends and supporters whom he regards as trustworthy. How the congressman has gone about ascertaining what his "public" thinks of the bill is an even greater mystery.

What Is Public Opinion?

This sort of imprecision is not surprising in popular discussions, but it has no place in a serious investigation. The social scientist differs from the layman in that he tries to stipulate exactly what he is talking about—what "public" he is concerned with and what he means by "opinion." [2] So we shall begin by considering what public opinion is before we ask how it is formed and expressed.

Even leading students of the subject do not agree completely on the precise meaning of public opinion—in the sense, for example, in which chemists agree on the meaning of H_2O. Nor should we, perhaps, expect complete agreement on such a complex concept. Fortunately, however, researchers have assembled a wealth of information by using definitions couched in terms of specific problems. So long as we make clear what we are investigating—what kind of public and what sort of opinions—we can evaluate our findings without confusion. Like the researchers, we need not wait for unanimous agreement on a general definition.

For our purposes here, we shall define public opinion as the *expression of attitudes on a social issue*. Notice that this definition includes three parts. First, unless an attitude is *expressed*, it is neither public nor opinion, since attitudes are internal predispositions that cannot be directly observed and opinions are the expressions of those predispositions. We say that a milquetoast employee has no opinions in the presence of his boss even though we assume that he does have attitudes of some kind. Attitudes must somehow be communicated to others— that is, they must be expressed—to become part of public opinion. Suppose that three-fifths of the people in a country harbor secret attitudes disapproving of their rulers, but that they fail for some reason to express their disapproval in talking with friends, in behavior at political meetings, in voting, in responses to interviewers, or in any other way. Such attitudes would not be part of public opinion, although they would constitute a highly important potential or latent public opinion. Unexpressed opinions have an influence in government but only because public officials must make guesses as to what opinions a given course of action would bring into play.[3]

---

[2] See any standard text on public opinion for a discussion of this concept. The discussion here probably follows most closely that of Leonard W. Doob, *Public Opinion and Propaganda* (New York: Henry Holt and Company, 1948), pp. 33–43. Also see Daniel Katz *et al.*, (eds.), *Public Opinion and Propaganda: A Book of Readings* (New York: The Dryden Press, 1954), pp. 49–84; and Bernard Berelson and Gary A. Steiner, *Human Behavior: An Inventory of Scientific Findings* (New York: Harcourt, Brace and World, Inc., 1964), pp. 557–558.

[3] M. Brewster Smith, Jerome S. Bruner, and Robert W. White refer to the individual

Second, public opinion requires an *issue* of some kind. To say that John Jones has an opinion tells us practically nothing, except that he is not a vegetable. For the statement to be meaningful, we need to know the object of his opinion (Democrats, dry martinis, federal aid to education, etc.), and whether his attitude is pro or con. Because of their pro or con characteristic, opinions always deal with some object or issue that can evoke favorable or unfavorable responses. Some accepted practices, such as the monogamous family in the United States, rarely present a public issue, so that public opinion about it is normally latent. But when such a practice is challenged—that is, when an issue is presented— attitudes are quickly translated into public opinion.

Third, public opinion deals with *social* rather than purely private questions. A hypochondriac's operation, however enthusiastically he expresses opinions about it, is not a social issue. It becomes a social issue, and an object of public opinion, only if others are stimulated to form opinions on the subject. Public opinion refers, then, to the opinions of an aggregation of individuals rather than to those of a single person. Despite our tendency to assume that the only *real* social issues are those *we* know are important, public opinions exist on a tremendous range of questions—from whether Roger Maris really broke Babe Ruth's home run record to problems of world peace. Any question on which people have favorable or unfavorable attitudes can, in other words, become an object of public opinion.

We started with a deliberately broad definition of public opinion as a reminder that every question of public concern is not necessarily political.[4] Some sort of public opinion is undeniably created and expressed by every change in the weather. But these opinions become political only as they acquire relevance for government—if they deal with the need for more municipal snow-plows, for example. If we use "public opinion" to mean the expression of attitudes on a social issue, then *political opinion* refers somewhat more narrowly to the expression of attitudes on a political issue. The issue may be presented by any politically relevant object of opinions, such as candidates, parties, or policies.

Not only must we guard against the temptation to claim that all public opinion must deal with our favorite kind of *issues*, but we must also be careful not to assume that the particular people we are interested in make up the entire *public*. Unqualified references to opinions of *the* public are frequently mis-

---

as "holding" an opinion to describe the predisposition we call an "attitude"; they say he "expresses" an opinion in the same way that we do. See *Opinions and Personality* (New York: John Wiley & Sons, Inc., 1956), p. 40. Either usage seems satisfactory; we use different terms to make certain that the distinction between unobserved attitudes and announced opinions is clear.

[4] From our point of view, V. O. Key's definition of public opinion as "those opinions held by private persons which governments find it prudent to heed" is too narrow. It is also subject to the charge of employing one of the terms defined in the definition. V. O. Key, Jr., *Public Opinion and American Democracy* (New York: Alfred A. Knopf, 1961), p. 14. Despite this difference in definition, we have relied heavily on Key in this chapter, and we highly recommend his book to the student who wishes to examine public opinion in detail. The narrow definition reflects Professor Key's specific concern for returning the study of public opinion to a governmental setting. Our chapter's concern is similarly with political opinion.

leading. Statements about "the public" scarcely ever mean literally everyone in the country; the person making the statement is usually thinking of a more restricted group. Some people, for example, confuse the opinions of newspaper publishers with the opinions of the population as a whole, and others assume that only rational and well-informed people have opinions.[5] Most of us are guilty of assuming that our own contacts are *the* public, but election results occasionally bring us sharply back to reality. Once the voting lever has been pulled or the ballot marked, the opinion is registered—no matter what the profession, the rational prowess, or the social contacts of the person who has expressed it.

The General Role of Public Opinion in American Politics

But even in a democracy all opinions do not have equal weight. On election day itself, when we most nearly approach a situation in which every individual is assured an equal role, some opinions are still more influential than others. In the first place, those who have no attitude toward the issues or the candidates, or hold only weak attitudes, may not vote at all. In addition, in all segments of the population informal opinion-leaders influence the attitudes of their associates.[6] Finally, formal opinion leaders hold key positions in the mass media of communication, the government, and the political parties, and they influence both the informal opinion-leaders and the public at large. Once the votes have been cast, they are all equal,[7] but whether they *will* be cast and for *whom* they are cast depend on influences in which every citizen's role is by no means equal.

What role do the opinions of the general public play in democracy? We can better answer this question at the end of this chapter. At the outset, however, we can say that the average citizen plays little part in initiating or directing day-to-day policies. Recent research has amply borne out arguments Walter Lippmann offered thirty years ago.[8] The average citizen has little interest in public affairs, and he expends his energy on the daily round of life—eating, working, family talk, looking at the comics (today, TV), sex, sleeping. Not knowing what the government is doing about public problems, he has no basis for opinions on most policies of his government. Even if he had an interest in politics, he would have great difficulty getting accurate information; since the events of politics unfold at a great distance, he cannot observe them directly, and the press offers a partial and distorted picture. Finally, assuming that he were somehow to get the needed information, he would find that, as a member of the unorganized general public,

---

[5] See, for example, A. Lawrence Lowell, *Public Opinion and Popular Government* (New York: Longmans' Green and Company, 1926), pp. 16–27. First published in 1913.

[6] See Paul F. Lazarsfeld, Bernard Berelson, and Hazel Gaudet, *The People's Choice* (New York: Columbia University Press, 1948), 2nd ed., pp. 49–51, 150–158; and Elihu Katz and Paul F. Lazarsfeld, *Personal Influence* (Glencoe, Illinois: The Free Press, 1955).

[7] The vote of a city dweller has long been unequal to that of a rural citizen in the sense that urban dwellers have been under-represented, but each vote within a given electoral district has equal weight. Moreover, as we saw in Chapters 1 and 4, recent Supreme Court decisions have applied the "one man-one vote" principle to require that the more extreme of these inequalities be eliminated.

[8] *Public Opinion* (New York: Harcourt, Brace and Company, 1922); and *The Phantom Public* (New York: Harcourt, Brace and Company, 1925).

he could not take any effective initiative in translating his opinions into policy.

All of this is no doubt true; indeed, Professor Key suspects that it has been doubted only "in the autointoxication of political oratory directed to the average man." [9] But it does not mean that mass opinion plays a negligible role in government; it simply means that the role of public opinion is less simple and direct than old-fashioned oratory suggests. In assessing the policy influence of public opinion, we need to distinguish between two kinds of decision-making—day-to-day decisions on the specifics of policy, and relatively enduring decisions on the broad direction of policy. In the first sphere of decision-making, unorganized public opinion plays little direct role. The authors of *The American Voter* put it this way: "Of course, those involved in policy formation do exercise intensive 'public' pressures for and against particular policy alternatives. But these emanate almost entirely from limited, special publics, often speaking through organizations, and not from the electorate as a whole." Decision-makers try to anticipate possible reactions of the general public to their policies, but "the fact that the details of these policies will be very largely unknown to the general electorate" [10] gives the government official considerable discretion.

When we turn to the broad goals of public policy, however, we find that general public opinion is considerably more effective. And this is the only policy area where democratic theory really requires a controlling role for public opinion (see Chapter 2). To begin with, the general bounds of public policy are set by latent public attitudes. Some matters, such as government control of the press or nationalization of industry, are ruled out as possible policies in the United States by underlying public attitudes. In addition to this negative influence, mass political opinions play a more positive role through the election system. The broad goals of public policy are set on election day. Although the typical election carries no clear mandate for a particular set of policies, it at least empowers the winners to act as if they had a mandate. To revive our awareness of the importance of the ballot box, we need only compare the public services received by Negroes in communities where they vote with those in communities where they do not vote. Once the vote has been won, the "payoffs" expected from larger numbers of voters may be exaggerated.[11] But in areas where *no* Negroes are allowed to vote, as in some Mississippi counties, their helplessness in relation to government reminds us of the importance of the franchise. Imagine living as a Negro in such a locality and you can picture what the relation of general political opinions to public policy would be without elections.

Since many people do not vote, we must recognize, when we refer to the "function of public opinion" in American politics, that the politically functioning public is only a portion of the total population. The basic political functions of public opinion in America are to choose our political leaders and to com-

---

[9] *Public Opinion*, p. 5.

[10] Angus Campbell *et al.*, *The American Voter* (New York: John Wiley & Sons, Inc., 1960), p. 544.

[11] See William R. Keech, *The Negro Vote as a Political Resource* (unpublished Ph.D. dissertation, University of Wisconsin, 1965).

municate public interests to official decision-makers. These functions are, of course, officially sanctioned in the Constitution, and their free performance is precisely what makes our politics democratic. An indispensable agency for the exercise of these functions is the political party, through which a majority of the population is given an opportunity to capture control of the government and to express its opinions as official policies. In practice, an actual majority of the total adult population never unites solidly in support of any policy or candidate, so the word "opportunity" must be stressed in viewing parties as vehicles of majority opinion. Political parties remain indispensable, however, because they at least bring more opinions to bear on politics than does any other group.

In fact, those who argue for stronger parties delight in pointing to the alternative institutions that offer to mediate between citizens and their government. Take pressure groups, for example. The most continuous, importunate, and effective expressions of opinions that impinge on government officials come from these groups. Although their spokesmen assert that their supporters are as numerous as they are enthusiastic, they never claim to represent a majority. Organized minorities are as characteristic of democracy as political parties are, but if pressure groups are stronger than parties, a smaller public will be influential in policy-making. Although freedom for the expression of minority opinions is essential in a democracy, control by a majority of the participating citizens is an even more essential feature. This problem is so crucial that the next two chapters will be devoted to an examination of the competing and overlapping roles of political parties and pressure groups in the political process.

How should political opinions—from those expressed by the majority party down to those urged by the smallest interest group—be weighed by the official decision-makers? Should congressmen, as the framers of general policies, mirror public opinion, or should they lead it? And should they pay more attention to nationwide or to local sentiment? These are questions to which different answers have been offered. The answers of American congressmen, for example, tend to be different from the answers of their British counterparts. In the United States, minority opinions have relatively greater weight in decision-making; in Britain, majority opinions are favored. In the United States, greater emphasis is placed on local opinions; in Britain, on national opinions.

These alternative answers are clearly related to the size of a country and to the number of different interests it comprises. They are also related to the formal organization of the government, as our discussion of the Constitution and of federalism indicated. The same questions will arise in our consideration of political parties, pressure groups, elections, and Congress. At this point they call to mind the importance and the complexity of the role of public opinion in a democracy.

How Political Opinions Are Formed: Secondary Forces

The founder of psychiatry, Sigmund Freud, initially concluded that the human organism had only one basic need, variously called sex, libido, love, and Eros. (As he became older, and presumably more exhausted with these thoughts, Freud added the opposing urge to die.) Subsequent students have pointed out that, although it is impossible to overstate the importance of sex for understanding human behavior, Freud achieved the impossible. Freud's attempt to explain the rich variety of human life in terms of a single innate need has profoundly affected contemporary man's outlook, but no single-factor explanation can satisfactorily account for the complexities of human behavior. Later psychologists went to an opposite extreme, spelling out such an exhaustive list of instincts that their work is equally difficult to apply in political science. (And it suffers from the additional difficulty of including human tendencies that appear to be culturally induced rather than innate.) As a result, most political scientists today take the human organism as a "given" and examine political behavior and opinions as products of environment and of personality (the given organism as modified by environment).

James C. Davies has recently returned human nature—in the sense of innate needs of the organism—to the study of political behavior. Modifying the work of contemporary psychologists,[12] he examines four categories of basic needs:

1. physical (water, food, sex, freedom from bodily harm);
2. social (love, affection, belongingness);
3. self-esteem (subjective equality; identity apart from groups);
4. self-actualization (activities enjoyed for their inherent satisfaction in the pursuit of happiness).

These needs are basic in the sense that they are pursued for their own sake and by all individuals, regardless of their varying social experiences. Moreover, Davies proposes that these needs fall into a hierarchy, so that physical needs will take priority over social needs, social needs over self-esteem, and self-esteem over self-actualization.

Despite the importance of innate needs, Davies believes that no particular political opinion can be organic or innate. Political opinions may reflect universal tendencies but the particular forms that they take can be better explained by personality and environment. For our purposes, Davies' work is important primarily in pointing out that no public opinion is possible until basic needs of the organism have been met. As the great British playwright, George Bernard Shaw, once said, "Man does not philosophize on an empty stomach."

Few writers or readers of college texts have ever experienced prolonged and severe deprivation. Hence, when we hear that most people in most countries are ill-fed, ill-clothed, and ill-housed, we wonder why they don't do something about it—put in a new government that will encourage industrialization, institute land reform—in some hope of improving their lot. This is no doubt about the reaction

---

[12] Primarily A. H. Maslow, "A Theory of Human Motivation," *Psychological Review*, L (July, 1943), pp. 370–396. For Davies' own provocative analysis, see *Human Nature in Politics: The Dynamics of Political Behavior* (New York: John Wiley and Sons, Inc., 1963).

that would occur if properly nourished people with well-established social ties, a sense of self-esteem, and experience in self-expression were threatened by such conditions. But people who have long existed on the edge of starvation are apolitical; their main concern is the immediate problem of survival, not broad political questions. Indeed, only an unrelated collection of people in a common territory, not a general public, exists under such conditions.

Political opinions are rooted in the basic needs of human nature, and they cannot exist unless the more basic of those needs are reasonably satisfied. But they are most directly influenced by the actual events that create political issues, by the media of communication through which these issues are presented and ex-plained to the citizen, and by the political leaders and parties that offer to cope with the issues. More immediately, however, the frame of reference within which we react to political issues is molded by the people with whom we associate day by day. We might say that the stance we assume toward the problems of the day depends on our particular combination of social and professional roles in the community, what earlier generations would have called our "station in life."

Beneath these proximate influences lies a whole set of secondary factors that help determine our basic outlook on politics—the culture in which we live, our family background, and our class, residential, and ethnic identifications. Since most of these underlying factors have already been discussed as part of the cultural context of politics, here we shall simply review their role in determining political opinions.

The Family Heritage

The first opinion-shaping agency the individual meets—first in influence as well as in time—is his family. The citizen inherits his political preferences just as he inherits his church preference, for both are part of a general attitudinal struc-ture that dictates what he "naturally" thinks. School children have been found to be uniformly warm and positive in their attitudes toward their political com-munities.[13] Although we could hardly have imagined that they would have rejected their own nation in favor of Castro's Cuba or some other alien (un-experienced) political environment, we might have expected them to be childishly indifferent about the matter. But American satisfaction—at its extreme, ethno-centricism—comes early.

Many college students, who set a high value on rationality and independence of mind, resent the implication that their political opinions have been acquired in such an apparently irrelevant, almost thoughtless, fashion. But the fact that the process begins with the individual's first awareness of the world around him, and is so nearly automatic, so little marked by critical scrutiny, is precisely what makes it so effective. Ideas that are as natural as breathing are built into the personality so intimately that they stand beyond question. The biological function of the American family is to propagate the species in a physical sense, but its social

---

[13] David Easton and Robert D. Hess, "The Child's Political World," *Midwest Journal of Political Science*, VI (August, 1962), pp. 236–237.

function is to propagate *Americans* rather than just human beings—that is, to transmit the general norms of the American culture appropriately modified by a particular subculture. It is this function that perpetuates national and sectional variations in opinion.

Moreover, when we look more closely, this automatic acquisition of ideas within the family is more logical than it might seem. Only an extreme deviant would reject the one nation he has known. In terms of more specific loyalties within the national community, the fledgling citizen is a member of the same ethnic group as his parents, and he tends to be identified with the same religion and social class. Consequently, the attitudes that are appropriate to his parents as members of these groups will be no less appropriate for him. Because the Democratic Party has, for the last generation, been regarded as the champion of ethnic "out-groups" like the Negroes and the immigrants from Slavic countries, children of these groups have the same reasons to vote Democratic as their parents have. Despite Republican appeals to such groups, the Democrats continue to win a higher percentage of support from minority groups than from the population as a whole. By the same token, if members of the professional and managerial class find Republican policies more in keeping with their needs than Democratic policies, they and their children will have the same reasons for supporting the Republican Party.

Family influence on political opinions does not merely operate indirectly, through the transmission of religious, ethnic, and class identifications. At a remarkably early age, children pick up direct political cues from their parents and express similar attitudes on a wide range of political issues. But the strongest and most persistent influence is on party identification. Issues may be too complicated for children to understand, but even the dullest child learns at an early age to tell the "good guys" from the "bad guys" on TV. In politics, when his parents agree (as most do) in their attitudes toward the parties, the child has an ordering device almost as simple as that of TV westerns—he can tell the good guys from the bad guys not by whether they are clean-shaven or unkempt but by their party labels. As a result, when children are asked how they would vote in an election, a vast majority report the same preference as their parents.[14] And this inherited party preference is maintained remarkably well in adult life: among those voters who remember both parents as supporting the same party, around 80 per cent report that their first vote was also for that party; 69 per cent of all adults say they are still for their parents' party, as compared with 13 per cent who support the other party and 17 per cent who call themselves independents.[15]

Family influence is seen not only in inherited party preference but also in "independent" attitudes. If children of active party members tend to support their parents' party, what political heritage is shown by children of people who shift

[14] Herbert Hyman, *Political Socialization* (Glencoe, Illinois: The Free Press, 1959); H. H. Remmers, "Early Socialization of Attitudes," in Eugene Burdick and A. J. Brodbeck (eds.), *American Voting Behavior* (Glencoe, Illinois: The Free Press, 1959), pp. 55–67; unpublished data in the Political Studies Laboratory, University of North Carolina.

[15] Less than 1 per cent of the offspring of parents who agree in their party choice have no identification. From data in Key, *Public Opinion*, ftnt. 2, p. 301, and Table 12.1, p. 296.

parties or who fail to vote? They, too, reflect their upbringing—such children are much more likely to identify with no party at all. Among voters whose parents were for the same party, only 17 per cent are independents; among those who do not know how their parents voted, or whose parents did not vote, 32 per cent are independents; and among voters whose parents shifted parties, 39 per cent are independents.[16]

Similarly, people reflect in their adult life the degree of interest their parents had in politics. The greater the parents' interest, the greater the children's sense of involvement and efficacy in politics. Family influence can also be spotted in attitudes on policy questions, such as international affairs or labor-management disputes, but not so clearly as on questions of party choice or political involvement. The family cues on policy are not so clear to begin with, and new issues arise that leave the adult more nearly on his own. Like our parents, we tend to have a clearer notion of our party preference than of opinions on specific issues.

If the family influence is so strong, how do we account for the minority who depart from the politics of their parents? An obvious answer would be simply to say that some children hate their parents and take joy in voting against the parental party at the first opportunity. Some psychologists have toyed with this notion but they find that, even among children who reject their parents, the act of rejection generally takes a non-political form. (Only in highly politicized families is politics important enough for the rebellious offspring to choose it as his vehicle for rebellion.) [17] So we must turn to less dramatic influences to account for the erosion of family agreement. Most people seem somehow to select marriage partners with similar political views, but when they don't, one or the other is often ripe for political conversion. Since politics is culturally defined as more masculine than feminine in the United States, the agreement is most often reached by wifely acquiescence in the husband's view.[18] Consequently, agreement between husbands and wives is even greater than agreement between parents and children.

Other forces eroding family influence include exposure to a different class environment, residence in a community in which the dominant sentiment runs counter to the parental party choice, the experience of political events that work to the advantage of the non-parental party, and contact with friends and co-workers predominantly identified with a different party.[19] Although we discuss all

---

[16] *Ibid.*, p. 296.

[17] See Henry W. Riecker, "Primary Groups and Political Party Choice," in Burdick and Brodbeck (eds.), *American Voting Behavior*, pp. 162–183; and Eleanor E. Maccoby *et al.*, "Youth and Political Change," *Public Opinion Quarterly*, XVIII (Spring, 1954), pp. 23–39.

[18] In other areas, such as home decoration, our culture expects the husband to defer to the wife. See Robert E. Lane and David O. Sears, *Public Opinion* (Englewood Cliffs, New Jersey: Prentice-Hall, Inc., 1964), p. 30.

[19] Excellent sources on these influences are Herbert McClosky and Harold F. Dahlgren, "Primary Group Influence on Party Loyalty," *American Political Science Review*, LIII (September, 1959), pp. 757–776; and Bernard R. Berelson, Paul F. Lazarsfeld, and William N. McPhee, *Voting: A Study of Opinion Formation in a Presidential Campaign* (Chicago: The University of Chicago Press, 1954).

these influences below, be sure to keep two points in mind: (1) most people live in a homogeneous political environment, so that conflict between family and other influences is the exception; (2) even when conflict is created, as by membership in a class different from that of one's parents, the family influence on political opinions never disappears completely. Professor Key's conclusion that the family functions as a conserving influence for the political system is accordingly most appropriate:

> The family is conserving in that it tends to project into the future the prevailing pattern of social and occupational status with the associated political outlooks. It is conserving in that it tends to perpetuate the prevailing system of identifications with political parties and other politically relevant groups. . . . A radical father may also have a radical son, but collectively families tend to project the existent national pattern of party loyalties and to a lesser extent the existent attitudinal pattern on policy into the future where it becomes subject to reinforcement or alteration by new forces.[20]

Class Status

Americans are not acutely class conscious. In 1960, for example, a national cross-section of the adult population was asked: "There's quite a bit of talk these days about different social classes. Most people say they belong either to the middle class or to the working class. Do you ever think of yourself as being in one of these classes?" Even with the encouraging assurance that most people say they belong to a class, only 73 per cent replied that they ever thought of themselves in class terms.[21] If something like a quarter of the voters never picture themselves as belonging to a class, we might conclude that class identification is of little consequence for political opinions in America. But a closer look suggests that such a hasty conclusion is unwarranted.

In the first place, less than 2 per cent of American adults flatly reject the idea of classes. Of the people who say they do not think of themselves as belonging to a social class, almost all are willing and able to say what class they would call themselves if they had to make a choice. In the second place, however tenuous class consciousness may seem in America, it "works" in the sense that it has significant effects on attitudes and behaviors. Indeed, we saw in the very first chapter of this book that both political participation and chances for political leadership vary markedly along class lines. Americans are not so different from other people on the question of class, then, as we sometimes like to believe. A UNESCO survey in nine countries found a pattern of class identification among other peoples surprisingly similar to that of Americans. Moreover, when the people in each country were asked if they felt that they had "anything in common" with fellow countrymen who were not members of their own class, Americans were not at all unique in their feeling of common interests across class lines. The percentage in each nation who acknowledged something in common with different classes of their fellow citizens was: Australia, 78; United

---

[20] *Public Opinion*, p. 313.
[21] From data furnished by the University of Michigan's Survey Research Center.

States, 77; Britain, 67; Norway, 64; Germany, 64; France, 63; Mexico, 56; Netherlands, 50; Italy, 50.[22]

How meaningful is this class-identification as an influence on political opinions? Granted that class is important in determining whether a person will participate in politics, does it also have an influence on the content of his opinions —that is, on the direction of his preferences? Let's look at this question in terms of opinions on two of the most important elements of politics—public issues and political parties.

Class identification has a direct impact on many political attitudes. Richard Centers, a social psychologist who carried out one of the first systematic studies of this problem a generation ago, found that people who thought of themselves as middle class were significantly more conservative than those who identified with the working class. (See Table 5-1.) The political importance of working-class radicalism as opposed to middle-class conservatism may be seen from the highly charged political nature of the attitudes Centers used to measure "conservatism-radicalism." He found that working-class people were more likely than middle-class people to believe the following: America is not truly a land of opportunity; people in the United States do not get what they deserve; we would all be better off if working people had more power and influence in government; wages and salaries would be fairer, jobs steadier, and unemployment lower if the government took over and ran our mines, factories, and industries; the government should guarantee every person a decent and steady job and standard of living; workers rather than employers are usually right in strikes and industrial disputes; employers sometimes take advantage of working people. American attitudes on the most basic political questions, then, cannot be understood without taking class differences into account.

Almost countless studies since Centers' seminal investigation in 1945 have rounded out his findings. And, whether class is determined subjectively by the choice of the individual or objectively by such criteria as occupation, income, or education, the results are much the same. Perhaps the most significant modification is the discovery that "conservatism" and "liberalism" have several dimensions, and that a person who is conservative along one dimension may be liberal along another. Academicians and journalists have tended to think of liberalism as a coherent set of beliefs that includes at least three dimensions: approval of government measures to help the underprivileged and promote equality; belief in social experimentation rather than automatic acceptance of the status quo; and tolerance toward the rights of others.

Centers' measure tapped only the first dimension of liberalism, since he dealt with issues of equality and social welfare. On questions of this kind, lower-status individuals are consistently and markedly more liberal than those of higher status. But it turns out that they are *less* liberal on both the other dimensions that were once assumed to go along with the first. On underlying attitudes toward

---

[22] William Buchanan and Hadley Cantril, *How Nations See Each Other* (Urbana: University of Illinois Press, 1953), p. 18.

Table 5-1   *Class Differences in Conservatism-Radicalism as Measured by Social Welfare Issues*

		PERCENTAGE WHO ARE:				
	N	ULTRA-CONSERV-ATIVE	CONSERV-ATIVE	INDETER-MINATE	RADICAL	ULTRA-RADICAL
Total Cross Section:						
Upper Class	29 a	42	24	17	10	7
Middle Class	467	35 b	33 b	21 b	7 b	4 b
Working Class	564	12 b	23 b	33 b	19 b	13 b
Lower Class	13 a	—	23	31	31	15
Urban:						
Middle Class	391	34 b	31 b	22 b	8 b	5 b
Working Class	435	10 b	20 b	33 b	22 b	15 b
Rural:						
Middle Class	76	41 b	38	14 b	3	4
Working Class	129	14 b	35	32 b	11	5

ᵃ These cases are obviously too few for statistical reliability, but are included here as suggestions of the general trend.

ᵇ Differences between adjacent figures marked thus in the same column are statistically significant at the 95 per cent level or better.

Source: Richard Centers, *The Psychology of Social Classes* (Princeton: Princeton University Press, 1949), p. 120. Class membership was determined by the respondent's choice of his own class affiliation.

social change, for example, Herbert McClosky has found that lower-status individuals are much more likely than upper-status people to accept the ways of the past and to resent innovation.[23] As Table 5-2 indicates, two-thirds of the people with college training are liberal in their attitudes toward change, while less than a fourth of those with only grade school training are liberal.

Table 5-2   *Status (Educational) Differences in Conservatism-Liberalism as Measured by Attitude toward Change*

	EDUCATION		
ATTITUDE	GRADE SCHOOL	HIGH SCHOOL	SOME COLLEGE
Liberal	6.2%	16.3%	30.5%
Moderately liberal	15.9	32.7	35.7
Moderately conservative	34.6	32.3	23.8
Extremely conservative	43.3	18.7	10.0
Total (*N* = 1,082)	100%	100%	100%

Source: Herbert McClosky, "Conservatism and Personality," *American Political Science Review,* LII (March, 1958), p. 35. The data are from a Minnesota survey; a fuller examination of this problem will be available in a forthcoming book by Professor McClosky.

---

[23] See citation in Table 5-2.

On our third measure of liberalism—tolerance toward the rights of others—lower-status individuals once again rank low. This dimension of liberalism was measured by willingness of respondents in a national sample to permit free speech and other civil liberties for unpopular groups like communists, alleged communists, critics of churches and religion, and champions of nationalized industry. Table 5-3 points up the extent to which tolerance toward nonconformists increases as we go up the occupational scale. Even when tolerance is measured in terms of support for the rights of ethnic minorities, such as Negroes, higher status people are markedly more tolerant than are those of lower status.[24]

Table 5-3   *Status (Occupational) Differences in Conservatism-Liberalism as Measured by Tolerance of Nonconformists*

PERCENTAGE OF MEN SCORING "MORE TOLERANT"

Professional and semiprofessional	66
Proprietors, managers, and officials	51
Clerical and sales	49
Manual workers	30
Farmers or farm workers	20

Source: Samuel A. Stouffer, *Communism, Conformity, and Civil Liberties* (New York: Doubleday & Co., 1955), p. 139; and Seymour M. Lipset, *Political Man* (Garden City, N.Y.: Doubleday & Company, Inc., 1960), p. 104.

What implications can we draw from the findings on all three dimensions of liberal and conservative opinions? The most compelling is that class, whether determined by personal feelings or by educational and occupational status, is an essential concept for understanding political differences. Perhaps even more significant, class-related opinions are not systematic enough to form the base of an ideology. On the contrary, political opinions more nearly approximate *ad hoc*, unrelated responses to each issue in terms of immediate and fairly obvious self-interest. On the bread-and-butter, social-welfare issues, the working class emerges as more liberal than the middle class. But when we move into more complex questions that involve long-run goals or the ability to relate abstract principles to specific problems, the middle class looks more liberal. This conclusion is not only called for by the findings above; it is also necessary if we are to account for additional attitudes that would otherwise be inexplicable. Take the question of whether taxes should be reduced even if it means the government must postpone things that need to be done. People with low income agree with this proposal more than people with high income! "Although this finding runs counter to political folklore," its surprising quality disappears as soon as we discard "long-standing

---

[24] See Herbert H. Hyman and Paul B. Sheatsley, "Attitudes Toward Desegregation: 1942–1963," *Scientific American*, Vol. 211 (July, 1964), pp. 16–23. In the South, however, a very high level of education is necessary before anti-Negro attitudes are basically modified. Donald R. Matthews and James W. Prothro, *Negro Political Participation in the South* (forthcoming).

assumptions about ideological structure on these matters." [25] To the sophisticated observer, it may seem inconsistent for a low-income person to favor both expanding social welfare benefits and postponing needed government activities in order to cut taxes. But the apparent inconsistency stems from the sophisticate's assumption that other people are as ideologically oriented as he is. The simple desire to improve one's economic lot, without regard to ideological niceties, renders both views consistent to the average citizen—should he bother to think of one in connection with the other.

Even with the ideological trappings eliminated, a serious qualification must be noted to round out our picture of class and attitudes on public issues: sharp class differences do not exist on all issues, nor are these differences equally strong or weak at all times. All the problems we have discussed so far do involve differences, but this should not be taken to mean that every issue produces disharmony. We would not expect to find class differences in attitudes on the weather. (Although farmers and lazy baseball players might prefer rain when carpenters and eager golfers would prefer sunshine, these are not systematic class differences.) But we might expect more difference than Table 5-4 shows on the

Table 5-4 *Status (Occupational) Differences on the Question of Restraining Big Business Influence*

	PROFESSIONAL	BUSINESS	CLERICAL	SKILLED	UNSKILLED	FARMERS
Agree [a]	53%	48%	52%	56%	42%	54%
Depends	8	8	5	6	3	5
Disagree	23	24	20	13	10	14
No opinion	16	20	23	25	45	27
	100%	100%	100%	100%	100%	100%
N	163	243	169	487	235	180

[a] "The government ought to see to it that big business corporations don't have much say about how the government is run."

Source: Key, *Public Opinion,* p. 126. The data are from the 1956 presidential election survey of the Survey Research Center, University of Michigan.

proposal that the government ought to see to it that big business corporations don't have much say about how the government is run. The general endorsement of the statement seems to reflect a feeling among all occupational groups that, while business should have a say, it should not be allowed to dominate the government. Another reason for the lack of sharp differences, and one that is often overlooked, is that the lower-status groups are much less likely to have an opinion on such difficult questions. Once again, the lack of political information and involvement on the part of the working class becomes important. Almost half the unskilled workers reported no opinion on the role of big business in 1956, a time

---

[25] Campbell *et al., The American Voter,* p. 196.

of prosperity. During a depression, these people probably would have an opinion; class differences vary from time to time as well as from issue to issue.

In the first chapter, we saw the importance of class for mass participation and chances for political leadership. We have just seen how it affects attitudes on public issues. An even more direct political consequence is the influence of class-identification on voting behavior. Members of the working class typically vote Democratic, while middle-class voters tend to favor the Republicans. Tables 5-5, 5-6, and 5-7 present the differences for three presidential elections. In every

Table 5-5   *Voting Preferences of Middle-Class and Working-Class People in 1944*

VOTING PREFERENCE	MIDDLE-CLASS RESPONDENTS $N = 415$	WORKING-CLASS RESPONDENTS $N = 472$
Democratic	49%	70%
Republican	49	29
Other, don't know, refused	2	1
Total	100%	100%

Source: Centers, *The Psychology of Social Classes,* p. 124. Class membership was by the respondent's choice of his own class affiliation. The sample included white males only; while this is unfortunate, subsequent studies indicate that the differences would not have been substantially reduced had Negroes and females been included.

Table 5-6   *Voting Preferences of Middle-Class and Working-Class People in 1952*

VOTING PREFERENCE	MIDDLE-CLASS RESPONDENTS $N = 389$	WORKING-CLASS RESPONDENTS $N = 811$
Democratic	30%	54%
Republican	69	43
Other, don't know, refused	1	3
Total	100%	100%

Source: Heinz Eulau, "Perceptions of Class and Party in Voting Behavior: 1952," *The American Political Science Review,* XLIX (June, 1955), p. 364. Class membership was determined on the basis of the respondent's occupation, income, and education.

Table 5-7   *Voting Preferences of Middle-Class and Working-Class People in 1964*

VOTING PREFERENCE	MIDDLE-CLASS VOTERS $N = 470$	WORKING-CLASS VOTERS $N = 570$
Democratic	56%	77%
Republican	43	21
Other, don't know, refused	1	2
Total	100%	100%

Source: The 1964 presidential election survey conducted by the University of Michigan's Survey Research Center. Class membership was by the respondent's choice of his own class affiliation.

case, whether the victor was a Democrat or a Republican, the Democrats fared relatively better among the working class while the Republicans did better among the middle class. Even in Franklin Roosevelt's decisive defeat of Thomas Dewey in 1944, middle-class people voted as heavily for Dewey as they did for Roosevelt; and Eisenhower's great triumph over Stevenson in 1952 still saw working-class voters preferring Stevenson.

Neither political party, faced with these facts, can afford to forget where its heaviest support comes from. Hence, while both parties urge people to "vote as you please but please vote," the Republicans make a special effort in upper-income precincts and the Democrats go all out to mobilize the lower-income districts. The Democrats have to be particularly concerned about turnout, since more of their potential supporters fail to vote. On the other hand, American class division in voting is a far cry from incipient class warfare. Each party gets substantial support from both the broad classes. Moreover, the influence of class varies considerably from one election to the next. Class-awareness seems to have been much less marked in 1960 or 1964 than in 1944 or 1948, for example. Philip Converse has demonstrated that the relation between class and attitudes dropped sharply from 1945 to 1956, as did the relation between class and voting.[26] Class-awareness is not a constant factor, then, in American politics. It is reduced by the emergence of issues that cut across class lines, such as problems of war and foreign policy, by the appeal of a magnetic personality like Eisenhower, by the injection of an issue like religion into a campaign, or by the extreme positions of a candidate like Goldwater. It presumably reaches a peak of influence during depression periods, when resentment over the uneven distribution of wealth is keenest; and attachments formed at such times may carry over into periods of prosperity. Despite its varying influence, class-identification ranks second only to party affiliation as a general clue to political attitudes and behavior.

Residence

A generation ago, sectional conflicts would probably have received major attention in a discussion of forces shaping public opinion. Considering the regional distribution of opinion in the last decade, however, Professor Key concluded that *similarities from one region to another are more characteristic than differences*.[27] The Midwest has long been viewed as a center of isolationist sentiment, for example, but World War II and subsequent events have largely obliterated the regional differences in public attitudes on broad foreign-policy questions. Most Americans accept U.S. commitment to an active internationalist role, and the dissenting minority is not much greater in the Midwest than in the rest of the country. Similarly, we tend to think of the South as peculiarly conservative on economic issues—opposing such government activities as aid for medical care, the guarantee of a job for everybody who wants to work, and electric power and

---

[26] "The Shifting Role of Class in Political Attitudes and Behavior," in Eleanor E. Maccoby *et al.* (eds.), *Readings in Social Psychology* (New York: Henry Holt and Company, 1958), 3rd ed., pp. 388–399.
[27] *Public Opinion*, Chapter 5.

housing programs. On these and similar questions, however, southerners turn out to have a range of opinions remarkably similar to other Americans. Only when these questions impinge on race relations does the position of the South appear especially distinctive.

Why, then, do we so often hear American politics described as if the people of different regions held sharply opposing views? First, the deep sectional differences that *do* exist center on policies of the gravest national and international import—racial injustice cuts to the core of the democratic creed. The increasingly effective expression of Negroes' dissatisfaction with second-class citizenship in the South, widespread sympathy with their demands among white and Negro voters outside the South, and the extreme anti-Negro sentiments and measures in many parts of the South, all these tend to identify politics with sectional differences. Second, the press exaggerates any sectionalism that shows up in other areas of politics, because journalists thrive on conflict and because sectionalism is an easy and dramatic way to describe differences. Third, our system of representation, with a single legislator representing an entire district, magnifies regional differences. We tend to think of representatives or senators as reflecting the opinions of entire districts or states rather than the opinions of some constituents who may be bitterly opposed by others in the locality. Assuming that congressmen reflect the preferences of a majority of their constituents, 51 per cent in favor of a bill in one section and 51 per cent opposed in another section would be translated into solidly opposed sectional blocs in Congress. "Small differences within the public may create marked differences in Congress. . . ." [28] Fourth, sectional differences do exist on some questions other than the rights of Negroes.

We mentioned in Chapter 1 that people in different regions vary in the degree to which they are willing to tolerate nonconformists. Why is this true? Why, for example, are people in the West more likely than people in the South to respect the freedom of speech of socialists, atheists, communists, and persons accused of communism? An easy explanation would be that the difference is not regional at all—that it disappears when we take into account such things as the lower educational level of the South. But the differences are still significant, even when the comparison is between westerners and southerners who are matched in terms of educational and other characteristics. So we must conclude that different regions develop political subcultures that are distinctive in some respects. Perhaps this results from the original sources of settlement—consider the wider variety of backgrounds represented in the West. Perhaps it also results from important events particularly affecting a region—for instance, the development of slavery as the "peculiar institution" of the South. While American opinions on most of the broad issues of politics do not show marked regional influences, then, regional distinctiveness in attitudes has certainly not disappeared entirely.

Residential differences in political opinions today are actually more clear-cut when the comparison is in terms of size of place—metropolitan center, suburb, small city, or country—than when it is in terms of regions. On international

---

[28] *Ibid.*, p. 107.

issues, the rural residents are, as expected, more isolationist. Similarly, rural residence is associated with intolerance of nonconformity. But on social-welfare measures, rural people are not the most conservative, as many would expect. The most liberal attitudes on these bread-and-butter issues are in the metropolitan centers, and the most conservative attitudes are in small cities. Higher status groups seem to dominate the politics in small cities (from 10,000 to 50,000 people) more easily than anywhere else. Competing centers of political influence, such as politically active labor unions, are rare in such cities, but they are large enough for the views of the Chamber of Commerce and the businessman's service clubs to find effective expression. Laborers are accordingly much less likely to vote Democratic if they live in a small city than if they live in a metropolitan center.[29]

Ethnic Groups

The influence of religion on political opinions in America, though it is quite apparent in some cases, is sometimes overemphasized. Systematic differences on social-welfare issues are found in the major religious groups in the United States. Despite individual and sectional variations, in the country as a whole the Congregational, Presbyterian, and Episcopalian groups rank as most conservative, and the Jewish, Catholic, and Baptist groups rank as most liberal. With the exception of the Jewish group, however, these differences appear to be based more on class status than on religion. The ranking of every one of the other major denominational groups on politico-economic questions is identical with its class-status rank, whether class is measured in terms of education, income, or occupation. Differences of opinion also occur *within* each denominational group and the differences are again related to class status. Baptists as a group are more liberal on politico-economic questions than Episcopalians, but rich, college-trained executives are equally conservative whether they are Baptists or Episcopalians. In summary, class rather than religion seems to be the decisive factor.[30]

But religious affiliation does sometimes outweigh other influences. Upper-class Jews, for example, continued to be overwhelmingly Democratic in the Eisenhower era, in contrast to other people in the same educational, economic, and occupational positions, because of special circumstances that applied to them as a group. Aware of anti-Semitism as a widespread prejudice, even upper-class Jews may have felt deprived of prestige and therefore may have been influenced by psychological pressures not unlike those that beset lower-class groups. Moreover, the Jewish creed encourages a liberal political view, and the Jews were historically identified with the Democratic Party because of the party's earlier

---

[29] See Nicholas A. Masters and Deil S. Wright, "Trends and Variations in the Two-Party Vote: The Case of Michigan," *American Political Science Review*, LII (December, 1958), pp. 1078–1090; Leon J. Epstein, "Size of Place and the Two-Party Vote," *Western Political Quarterly*, IX (March, 1956), pp. 138–150.

[30] The discussion in this paragraph is based on Wesley and Beverly Allinsmith, "Religious Affiliation and Politico-Economic Attitude: A Study of Eight Major U.S. Religious Groups," *Public Opinion Quarterly*, XII (Fall, 1948), pp. 377–389.

opposition to Nazism (with its acts of genocide against the European Jews).[31]

The situation of the Catholics is perhaps more ambiguous. Although their religion does not appear to influence their attitudes on general issues, Catholics do tend to vote Democratic more often than the population at large, even when we compare voters in similar socio-economic positions. This is one of the many regularities in political behavior that have not yet been explained. One reason may be that the immigration of the Irish, Polish, and Italians to the United States was heaviest at a time when the Democratic Party controlled most of the eastern cities where these immigrants settled. Predominantly Catholic, they developed into good Democrats at the same time they developed into good Americans. And they may have passed on their party identification to their children along with their new nationality. Party identification may itself shape behavior; it need not always depend on some other force. In this case, the descendants of these immigrants seem to be voting simply as Democrats, not as Catholics.[32]

When a religious issue is injected into politics, however, religious preference becomes highly relevant. Members of some Protestant denominations regard the consumption of alcoholic beverages as sinful, for example, and many Catholics regard the use of birth-control devices as sinful. Given a chance to vote on such questions, members of the churches concerned will tend to vote according to their religious beliefs. The important question, then, is this: how salient is religious affiliation for politics? When a candidate is criticized because of his religion, his fellow religionists will suddenly find that their church membership is highly salient and directly relevant to politics. In 1960, Catholics who had voted for Eisenhower in 1956 returned in overwhelming numbers to the support of the Democratic candidate—a Catholic under fire because of his religion. Since Nixon's Protestantism was not under fire, religion played a much smaller role for many Protestants. Even so, Protestantism was not irrelevant to political preference; Protestant Democrats who attend church most regularly were much more likely than infrequent attenders to vote against Kennedy.[33]

Racial identification and national origins appear to influence political opinions in much the same way as do religion and other ethnic characteristics. When members of any ethnic group are deprived of political rewards—or only of prestige—because of their ethnic identification, they will tend to support policies or candidates that recognize their interests. Hence the hot conflicts between Italian and Irish groups in many New England cities as the more recently arrived Italians fought for a foothold in Irish-dominated city politics. The desire for recognition in the form of public office, appointive jobs, and improved municipal services heavily influences the votes of people who are hungry for acceptance but

---

[31] See Lawrence E. Fuchs, *The Political Behavior of American Jews* (Glencoe, Illinois: The Free Press, 1956).

[32] Angus Campbell and Homer C. Cooper, *Group Differences in Attitudes and Votes: A Study of the 1954 Congressional Elections* (Ann Arbor: Survey Research Center, Institute for Social Research, University of Michigan, 1956), p. 36.

[33] Philip E. Converse *et al.*, "Stability and Change in 1960: A Reinstating Election," *American Political Science Review*, LV (June, 1961), pp. 269–280.

who have also been just plain hungry. In many industrial areas, both parties offer a "United-Nations" slate of candidates—a ticket carefully chosen to include every significant ethnic group.

Ethnic groups want to achieve both welfare and status objectives, but specific public issues occasionally pose a painful conflict between the two kinds of goals. Should Negroes support a new public housing project in an all-Negro area? This would meet the welfare need for more housing but at the expense of the status need to escape from a ghetto-style residential arrangement. Negro leaders in New York recently split on just this question, with the result that the Housing Authority took advantage of divided Negro opinions to win approval for the project.[34] In most elections, the lower-status group has a more clear-cut choice: the party or candidate most responsive to its material needs is generally also most attuned to its need for symbolic recognition. In many areas of the South, no candidate positively supports Negroes' interest; in that milieu, the only practical course is to vote for the candidate who is least *anti*-Negro. The civil rights issue is so acutely important to Negroes that they probably constitute, as a result of this one overriding consideration, the most issue-oriented ethnic group in American politics. Ironically, many Americans who deplore the lack of attention to issues also deplore this strong issue commitment as "bloc voting." But two points should be kept in mind on bloc voting: (1) no group, including southern Negroes, votes as a perfectly solid bloc; (2) bloc voting in the sense of predominant support for a given candidate is characteristic of *all* groups when the group itself is a target of rewards or deprivations. So long as ethnic groups are made such a target, they can be expected to respond in terms of their group needs. The nearly unanimous support of President Johnson by Negro Americans in 1964 was a dramatic demonstration of this point.

How Political Opinions Are Formed: Proximate Forces

The secondary forces that we have been exploring give the individual an early political slant that conditions his response to more immediate and less constant factors for the rest of his life. The basic function of family, class, residential, and ethnic influences for the political system is, then, to lend continuity to politics by perpetuating the basic distribution of political opinions.

Proximate forces do, however, play a significant role in influencing political opinions. Were this not so, dramatic shifts from one election to the next (as from 1928 to 1932, or from 1948 to 1952) would never occur. An individual's identification with family, culture, class, section, and ethnic group is far more stable than his political allegiances. Clearly, then, such secondary factors can only begin to explain the formation of political opinions. Among the forces that have a more

---

[34] See James Q. Wilson's penetrating analysis of Negro politics outside the South, *Negro Politics: The Search for Leadership* (Glencoe, Illinois: The Free Press, 1960), p. 211.

immediate impact on political opinions are the mass media of communication that give the citizen his picture of political events, the political preferences of his associates, his reactions to the key issues of the day, his response to political leaders, and his party identification.

Eighty per cent of Americans are exposed to a daily newspaper, and the 1960 census revealed that 88 per cent of American homes have one or more television sets. Newspapers, television, radio, and magazines inundate the United States every day with such a flood of output that Americans seem to have little reason for not being well informed on politics. But a closer look suggests a different conclusion. Political news is submerged in an even greater outpouring of entertainment and trivial or sensational news items. Newspapers still reflect enough of their early tradition of deep political commitment to print news rather than advertisements or comics on the front page, in marked contrast to the secondary emphasis on news on radio and TV. Even in newspapers, however, reports on sporting events contribute the largest portion of items, accounting for 11.6 per cent of the total as compared with 2.8 per cent for reports on the national government.[35] Moreover, the political events that are reported appear typically as "spot" news—that is, as brief reports of isolated events with no interpretive treatment indicating which interests stand to be hurt and which to be helped by the development. Television, which is in the tradition of the Indian medicine show and of vaudeville rather than of a crusading press, presents capsule versions of the spot news appearing in newspapers.

Should we condemn the mass media for offering such meager and superficial coverage of public affairs? Before we do, we should realize that the comics get more attention than any other category of newspaper content. And, as their chief source of political information, more people rely on TV—the most superficial source—than on any other medium. Magazines, a few of which offer serious analyses of public affairs, come in last as a source of political information.[36] Spokesmen for the mass media are quick to point out that most people don't want the political information that is available; millions of viewers would no doubt be lost if "Gunsmoke" were replaced by a public affairs program. The critics often fail to recognize that the main business of the mass media is to sell advertising rather than to inform the public. On the other hand, both the commercial sponsors and the broadcasting companies have found it good business to upgrade their public service programs. Sponsors have been more than willing to forego regular programs to take advantage of the vast audience in homes eager to watch the

---

[35] Charles E. Swanson, "What They Read in 130 Daily Newspapers," *Journalism Quarterly*, XXXII (Fall, 1955), pp. 411–421.

[36] The percentage of people reporting each medium as its primary source of information during the 1956 presidential election was—television: 49; newspapers: 24; radio: 10; magazines: 5; combinations of media: 3; didn't follow campaign, don't know, and no answer: 9. These and other specific data in this section are from the excellent collection in Key, *Public Opinion*, Chapters 14 and 15.

national political conventions in progress or to tally up election returns reported by the networks across the country. Prior to the 1960 elections, NBC and CBS actually pleaded with Congress to amend the communications laws so they could offer more "free" time to candidates of the major parties. (They could not afford to offer free and equal time to the fourteen other candidates for the presidency besides Kennedy and Nixon!) The resultant legislation permitted the now famous debates. It is estimated that upwards of 100 millions Americans heard one or more of these debates.

In addition to the pervasive criticism of superficial and inadequate news coverage, three serious complaints are frequently lodged by students of the mass media. First, competition among daily newspapers has decreased alarmingly in recent decades, at the very time when the newspaper-reading public has been rapidly increasing. During the first half of this century, the population of the twenty-five largest cities increased by 133 per cent; the number of daily newspapers in these same cities *decreased* by 44 per cent. In 1910, some 57.1 per cent of the nation's cities had competing dailies; by 1960, the figure had dropped to 4.2 per cent.[37] Since radio and television stations tend to rely on the local newspaper and the same news services it uses, the population enjoys much less freedom of the press (in the sense of having access to differing interpretations of the news) than might be supposed.

Second, the common sources of information present an increasingly standardized and commercialized combination of entertainment and news. The news presented by most newspapers, as well as by most TV and radio stations, comes straight from national news services—the Associated Press and United Press International. Syndicated columnists have replaced the crusading editors of the past. Without the tradition of a crusading past, radio and television have tended to avoid anything "controversial" because sponsors are interested in selling products rather than in stimulating critical thought. The singing commercial usually takes priority over any serious appraisal of political issues, for politics is always controversial.

Third, the attempt to avoid controversy is said to entail a consistently conservative bias. Dependent on a mass audience, the media must be careful to avoid offending any commercially significant group—and virtually everybody buys soap. If no distasteful views can be presented, and if communication is impossible without some opinions creeping in, then the media must take care to echo currently accepted opinions. In avoiding divisive issues, then, the mass media necessarily serve to sanctify the status quo.[38] When the status quo is challenged in such a newsworthy way that the mass media must discuss the challenge, they are more likely to please the manufacturer of the soap than the fellow who needs it for dirty fingernails. This does not mean that advertisers "buy" the mass media; they don't need to. Since the media of communication are big businesses,

---

[37] Raymond B. Nixon and Jean Ward, "Trends in Newspaper Ownership and Inter-Media Competition," *Journalism Quarterly*, XXXVIII (Winter, 1961), p. 5. Thirty-one per cent of the TV stations are affiliated with this declining number of newspapers.

[38] Joseph T. Klapper, *The Effects of Mass Communication* (Glencoe, Illinois: The Free Press, 1960), pp. 38–43.

too, the men who control them quite naturally share the convictions of other businessmen.[39]

All these complaints frequently lead to an image of the mass media as irresistible manipulators of public opinion. Such an image appears wildly unrealistic. In the first place, no more than 10 per cent of all adults can be called careful followers of political events. If you don't see the propaganda, it can't manipulate you. Those who are attentive tend to notice items agreeable to their own preferences and to neglect items that make them uncomfortable—that is, items that do not fit their biases. What political activist hasn't turned off the TV set when he could no longer endure listening to a hated candidate? Subtle propaganda may not register, or it may be reinterpreted to fit the frame of reference of the recipient. Finally, when the political message is unmistakable but distasteful, we begin to use it to decide how *not* to vote. A political leader dependent on lower-class votes in a one-newspaper town explained to one of the authors that he loved having the local paper against him—it insured his election!

Realistically, the mass media cannot be said to have direct control over political opinions, but they do have significant effects. Short-run effects can be great enough to make any candidate nervous about the way the press might treat last-minute charges which he will have no chance to refute. The candidate can expect his supporters to discount such charges, but he knows that undecided voters are more susceptible to propaganda because of their lack of clear preferences. Most people may lack standards by which to judge new issues or candidates, such as sudden developments in international affairs or unknown opponents in a party primary. Initial opinions on such unfamiliar events and personalities may be markedly affected by the way the press describes them. In the long run, however, party, union, lodge, church, and other sources of political cues dull the impact of newspapers and TV. The residual effects of the mass media are extremely hard to judge. With their heavy emphasis on entertainment, perhaps their chief function is to divert Americans from serious attention to politics. And, since inattention favors the status quo, the tone of the mass media may help to set the conservative limits within which American politics operates.

Primary Group Influences: Home, Friends, Co-Workers

Another proximate factor conditioning the citizen's political attitudes is his personal environment. Just as the individual's earliest view of politics comes from his parental family, so are his current opinions molded by his own immediate family, his friends, and his co-workers. Since opinions are formed and expressed through such primary groups, we cannot really understand even the effects of the mass media without considering primary group influences.

Communication does not flow in a single direct step, from media to an undifferentiated mass of individuals; as an influence on opinions, it can better be understood as a two-step flow, from media to informal opinion leaders, and

---

[39] See The Commission on Freedom of the Press, *A Free and Responsible Press* (Chicago: The University of Chicago Press, 1947), pp. 59–62.

from opinion leaders to small groups.[40] These opinion leaders—or "influentials" —are found in all sorts of groups, in all walks of life, and at every educational and social level. And, in the same group, different people may act as influentials depending on what topic is under consideration. In the family, for example, the influential on politics is normally the father; on house decoration, it is the mother; and on choice of breakfast cereals, it is the children ("Get the box with the miniature rocket-launcher in it, Mommy!"). Political influentials follow public affairs more closely and through more of the media than their associates do; hence they are able to interpret public events in the light of the group's informal norms. In the process of interpretation, they may, of course, modify or reinterpret the meaning that the mass media give to events. Since the trusted, face-to-face informant has more influence than an impersonal source, we have another explanation for the inability of the media to manipulate a mass audience. Instead of directly reaching an undifferentiated audience, the messages of the media filter through—perhaps in modified form—to myriads of small-group audiences.

The pressure to conform to group judgments is perhaps most dramatically demonstrated by the fact that people respond to group influence even in their perception of physical objects. When other members of a group unanimously maintain that the longer of two objects is really shorter, for example, people tend to reject the evidence of their own senses and to acquiesce in the group judgment.[41] If the individual thus manages to adjust his perception of purely physical objects to the norms of his group, he can easily adjust his attitudes on the much more ambiguous subject of politics. Through group experiences, individuals not only develop their definition of themselves—their social identity— but also their picture of the external world.

Most of us associate with people from similar family, class, residential, and ethnic backgrounds. As a result, we tend to find ourselves in a basically homogeneous political environment. To the extent that we do not find such homogeneity, we create it. The highest level of political agreement is found in the immediate family; about 90 per cent of husbands and wives vote, for example, in support of the same candidates. In the rare cases where political agreement is not reached in the home, the offspring will tend to be politically apathetic or independent—and ripe for political conversion if they grow up to marry someone from a politically unified family. Even our friends tend to be politically like-minded. As Table 5-8 indicates, young people more often find themselves with at least one friend of a different political persuasion. But with advancing years, one's immediate friends tend to be increasingly unified in their political outlook. From middle age on, a vast majority can comfortably report that they and their three closest friends will all vote for the same candidate. Moreover, the minority who

---

[40] See Katz and Lazarsfeld, *Personal Influence.*

[41] See S. E. Asch, "Effects of Group Pressure upon the Modification and Distortion of Judgments," in Dorwin Cartwright and Alvin Zander (eds.), *Group Dynamics* (Evanston, Ill.: Row, Peterson, 1953), pp. 151–162. This and other studies of group influence are cogently summarized in Lane and Sears, *Public Opinion,* pp. 34–39.

Table 5-8   *Age and Political Agreement of Friends*

AGE	PERCENTAGE REPORTING SAME VOTE INTENTION AS THREE BEST FRIENDS
21–25	53%
26–34	69
35–44	75
45+	77

Source: Berelson, Lazarsfeld, and McPhee, *Voting*, p. 97. Percentages include only respondents who knew the vote intention of all three friends.

cannot report such political agreement are most unstable in their own preferences.

The degree of consensus among co-workers is not quite so great as among friends, since the individual cannot ordinarily choose the people with whom he works.[42] But the more homogeneous the political environment in which a person works, the firmer his attitudes will be. Labor-union members, whose normal Democratic predilections are intensified by their union contacts, are morely likely to vote Democratic than are non-members, even when the comparison is between workers whose occupation, class, education, age, religion, and non-political attitudes are identical.

Conversely, individuals in a personal environment that is politically divided are more vulnerable to the pressures of the dominant attitudes in the larger community. In a predominantly Republican community, the Republicans win more votes than the Democrats from people whose friends and co-workers are politically divided. In the 1952 election, for example, voters of the Jewish faith who had the fewest contacts with non-Jews—housewives in Jewish neighborhoods and students in Jewish colleges—voted more heavily Democratic than did Jews as a whole; Jewish voters in predominantly Republican suburbs, on the other hand, showed greater defections to the Republicans.[43]

Political Influences: Issues, Candidates, Parties

Three additional influences—issue orientation, candidate orientation, and party identification—modify the impact of all the other proximate factors we have discussed. After a whole generation of presidential victories, the Democrats lost votes in 1952 and 1956 from almost every social group. Unless we take into account the appeal of the issues, candidates, and parties, the Eisenhower victories remain inexplicable.

How sharply a citizen perceives the chief issues of the day, and the strength of his feelings about them, affect both his inclination to vote and his voting preference. If he has an overriding interest in a single current issue, the stand of the

[42] Berelson, Lazarsfeld, and McPhee, *Voting*, p. 98.
[43] Fuchs, *The Political Behavior of American Jews.*

candidates or parties on that one question may determine his vote. Thus the position of southern Democrats on civil rights seems to have induced great numbers of Negro southerners to shift from a Democratic to a Republican vote in 1956. Similarly, Kennedy's telegram of sympathy to Martin Luther King, the highly respected Negro leader who was arrested on traffic charges in Georgia during the 1960 campaign, helped set a tone that brought Negro voters in the South back to the Democratic column. Senator Goldwater's vote against the Civil Rights Act of 1964 brought him votes from southern segregationists who were concerned with that issue alone. When an issue is not of critical importance to a voter, however, he tends to ignore his own party's disagreement with his opinion, or the opposing party's agreement with it, and proceeds to project his own opinion onto his favored candidate.[44]

Issues play a more important part in some elections than in others. In 1948, issues were the decisive factor: the popular preference for the Democratic Party's stand on domestic economic problems probably motivated the last-minute swing to Truman. In 1952 and 1956, issue orientation was outweighed for most voters by the personal appeal of "Ike" Eisenhower. And yet the very nature of the issues in any postwar period enhances the attractiveness of a great war hero. Suddenly, citizens lack the unifying exhilaration of the war effort, and are beset by the uncertainties and tensions that wars always create. So the issues of the time call for the hero of war to resolve the perplexities of peace—after World War II both Democrats and Republicans courted General Dwight D. Eisenhower as a presidential candidate. The effective issue of 1960 was John Kennedy's Catholicism: defections among Protestant Democrats reduced his victory to a razor-thin margin. In 1964, Senator Barry Goldwater's attitude toward "extremism" returned the advantage on issues to the Democrats.

Certainly candidate orientation played a predominant role between 1948 and 1952, with the entry of the nation's most popular general onto the political battlefield.[45] The resounding victory of the Republicans, achieved with the support of about 25 per cent of those who had voted Democratic in 1948, was based on the Republican candidate rather than on the party or its position on issues. A highly informative study by the University of Michigan's Survey Research Center reports that the new Republican voters of 1952 showed little enthusiasm for the Republican Party or for its stand on issues, but their preference for the Republican candidate was great enough to outweigh issue orientation and party identification.[46] The appeal of the new President was almost universal: except for the Negroes and two groups (the college-educated and the professional-managerial class) which were already heavily Republican in 1948, every economic and social group shifted in some degree to the Republican candidate. In

---

[44] Berelson, Lazarsfeld, and McPhee, *Voting*, p. 220.

[45] So great was his appeal, it appears that Eisenhower could have won as handily in 1948 as he did in 1952. See Herbert Hyman and Paul B. Sheatsley, "The Political Appeal of President Eisenhower," *Public Opinion Quarterly*, XVII (Winter, 1953–1954), p. 442.

[46] Angus Campbell, Gerald Gurin, and Warren E. Miller, *The Voter Decides* (Evanston, Illinois: Row, Peterson and Company, 1954).

the 1956 election, Eisenhower won even greater support from virtually every group, despite his party's failure to win control of either house of Congress—a fate that had befallen no party with a winning presidential candidate since 1848.

While Republicans were voting for the man in 1956, the more faithful Democrats were voting on the basis of party preference, despite the fact that they too admired Eisenhower greatly. For many people the political variable of party identification is thus a crucial factor, influencing or overshadowing opinions about both issues and candidates. Over three-fourths of the voters support the same party from one election to the next, and most have decided how they will vote even before the post-convention campaigning begins.[47] Although voters are much less "regular" than party leaders in their opinions on issues, they do tend to change their opinions during the course of an election campaign to conform with their party's position. If they differ with their party on issues they regard as particularly vital, or if they find the other candidate particularly appealing, of course, they may break away to the other party. But for some voters the attachment to party, regardless of issues or candidates, appears virtually unassailable.

To talk about party attachment simply as another political force that intervenes between secondary influences and a specific electoral decision somehow fails to do justice to the importance of party identification. Unlike reactions to the transient issues or personalities of particular campaigns, party identification, like family and class background, may be viewed also as a secondary influence that helps to shape our view of the political world in an enduring way. Remember that the process of political socialization which begins in the family is to a large degree a process of inculcating attitudes toward political parties, and that children pick up parental party preferences remarkably early. Party attitudes not only influence our votes, then, but also the way we respond to the mass media and the way we evaluate people and policies.

The staunch party adherent is sometimes chided for an allegedly blind loyalty—"You'd vote for an idiot or a crook if he ran on the Democratic (or Republican) ticket!" But the critics miss the point—the convenience of party as a clue in evaluating men and issues. If a man wins the nomination of a party, its faithful followers will decide that he must have some sterling qualities. Remember the re-evaluation of Barry Goldwater by Republicans who had denounced him before he won the Republican nomination in 1964. Formed early and generally growing more intense with age, party identification is the most important single factor both in shaping general political outlooks and in determining voting preference.

Journalists frequently describe political opinions as oscillating wildly in response to each subtle move of politicians. This probably stems partly from eagerness to find something newsworthy for each day's deadline, partly from the notion that other journalists, cab drivers, and bartenders represent the general public, and partly from ignorance of basic forces in political opinions. The underlying distribution of party preference is, in fact, remarkably stable. In the period

---

[47] Berelson, Lazarsfeld, and McPhee, *Voting*, p. 18.

from 1952 to 1964, for example, Table 5-9 shows that virtually no change in party identification occurred, despite variations in party fate at the polls during the same period. The Democrats now enjoy an impressive advantage, claiming about 60 per cent of those with some degree of party identification; and earlier surveys

Table 5-9 *Distribution of Party Identification, 1952 to 1964*

	OCT. 1952	OCT. 1954	OCT. 1956	OCT. 1958	OCT. 1960	NOV. 1962	OCT. 1964
Strong Republican	13%	13%	15%	13%	14%	12%	11%
Weak Republican	14	14	14	16	13	16	13
Independent Republican	7	6	8	4	7	6	6
Independent	5	7	9	8	8	8	8
Independent Democrat	10	9	7	7	8	8	9
Weak Democrat	25	25	23	24	25	23	25
Strong Democrat	22	22	21	23	21	23	26
Apolitical, "Don't know"	4	4	3	5	4	4	2
	100%	100%	100%	100%	100%	100%	100%
Number of Cases	1,614	1,139	1,772	1,269	3,021	1,289	1,571

Source: Survey Research Center, University of Michigan.

show that this advantage extends back to the 1930's.[48] But the Republicans' 1952 and 1956 victories, and their near victories of 1948 and 1960, demonstrate that voting does not perfectly mirror party identification. Why not?

The Democrats' dominance is reduced, in the first place, by the fact that more Democrats than Republicans have a low level of political involvement. Hence, they are less likely to vote and are more likely to cast a casual vote for the other party's candidate.[49] When these features of low involvement are taken into account, the Democratic edge is reduced from 60–40 to about 54–46 or 53–47.[50] With the Democrats' effective party identification reduced to 53–54 per cent, we can more easily see how short-term influences give the Republicans a good chance to win elections. Just *how* good a chance is a difficult question to answer. But Donald E. Stokes, a student of elections, has undertaken to find the answer. Through a careful analysis of variations in the presidential vote from 1892 through 1960, he concludes that, with the present division of party loyalties, the minority party has about three chances out of ten to get into office as a result of short-term influences.[51]

Every election has its own peculiarities, with a new blend of events, issues, and personalities, and the short-term influences are as likely to help one party as

---

[48] The Republicans presumably enjoyed a similar preponderance in the 1860–1932 era.
[49] We do not elaborate the point here; the relatively low level of involvement found in groups identifying with the Democrats is discussed in Chapter 6.
[50] Converse *et al.*, *American Political Science Review*, LV (June, 1961), p. 274.
[51] "1960 and the Problem of Deviating Elections," a paper delivered at the annual meeting of the American Political Science Association, September 6, 1961.

the other. Granted the importance and the stability of party loyalties, the minority party cannot win office unless the short-term influences run fairly strongly in its favor. The peculiarities of the 1960 election, for example, aided the Republicans, but not quite enough to put them in office. With a greater boost from short-term forces in 1964, the Democrats won by the largest margin in America's history of popular elections.

Voting—The Final Measure of Political Opinions

The Psychology of Voting

A variety of psychological mechanisms operates within the secondary and proximate influences on political opinions. The act of voting is still shrouded in mystery, but a wealth of statistical data has been assembled that throws some light on the two really crucial questions of any election day: Who will vote? How will they vote? Voting is one of the few human activities on which modern societies keep statistical records, and thousands of researchers have sifted these records in a search for patterns that might explain the psychology of voting. A group of social scientists at Columbia University has summarized both the regularities that have been found and the explanations that have been offered to account for them.[52] Their explanations are in terms of enduring characteristics of the social and economic system. Since we considered the importance of changing political and economic conditions above—in accounting for the varying importance of class in politics, for instance—we shall rely on their findings here to suggest some of the continuing factors in the psychology of voting.

To Vote or Not To Vote

On the question of *who* will vote, the Columbia study identified four general explanatory propositions. More members of a group will vote if: (1) its interests are more strongly affected by government policies; (2) it has more access to information about the relevance of government policies to its interests; (3) it is exposed to social pressures that demand voting; (4) the pressures to vote do not point in different directions, thereby creating a conflict over which way to vote. These four propositions are broken down in Table 5-10. Notice, for example, that wheat farmers are exposed to economic pressures requiring government action (1b) because of periodic declines in wheat prices and the monopolistic position of industries, such as the railroads, on which they depend. Wheat farmers find relevant policy alternatives (1e) eagerly offered by opposing parties that are bidding for their votes. The effects of government policies are directly visible to them (2a) in the level of price supports. Hence a

---

[52] Seymour M. Lipset, Paul F. Lazarsfeld, Allen H. Barton, and Juan Linz, "The Psychology of Voting: An Analysis of Political Behavior," in Gardner Lindzey (ed.), *Handbook of Social Psychology* (Cambridge: Addison-Wesley Publishing Company, Inc., 1954), II, pp. 1124–1175.

relatively high percentage of wheat farmers enter the polling booths on election day.

Table 5-10 *Explanatory Factors for Rate of Voting Turnout*

1. Social factors affecting the relevance of government policies to the individual:
   a. Dependence on government as one's employer
   b. Exposure to economic pressures requiring government action
   c. Exposure to government economic restrictions
   d. Possession of moral or religious values affected by government policies
   e. Availability of relevant policy alternatives
   f. General crisis situations
2. Social factors affecting access to information:
   a. Direct visibility of effects of government policies
   b. Occupational training and experience making for general insight
   c. Contact and communication
   d. Amount of leisure
3. Social factors relating to group pressure to vote:
   a. Underprivilege and alienation
   b. Strength of class political organization
   c. Extent of social contacts
   d. Group norms opposing voting
4. Social factors relating to cross-pressures:
   a. Conflicting interests
   b. Conflicting information
   c. Conflicting group pressures

Source: Lipset *et al.,* "The Psychology of Voting," *Handbook,* II, p. 1128.

A list of the groups that have shown varying rates of voter turnout, together with a summary of the factors that account for these variations, is offered in Table 5-11.

In the left-hand column are pairs of social characteristics that are correlated with voter turnout; the category with the higher turnout is listed first in each pairing. When we read across the table, we discover that most of these social categories are associated with more than one factor that serve to raise or lower their voting participation.

The much higher rate of voting among miners than among servants in all democracies is related, for example, to almost all the factors. First, *government policies are more obviously relevant* to miners because mining is more vulnerable to the effects of technological change and to the pressures of economic crises. Second, the relevance of government policies is more *directly visible* to miners in the form of wage, hour, and safety regulations and of frequent government intervention in labor-management relations. Third, *training and job* experience are not conducive to high voting turnout for either miners or servants. Fourth, social *contact and communication*, which encourage political awareness, are much more common among miners than servants. Virtually all the job and social contacts of a miner are with other miners because of the technical nature of mining and the isolated location of mining communities. In contrast, domestic servants

Table 5-11 *Explanatory Factors Related to Differences in Voting Turnout in Western Democracies*

SOCIAL CHARACTERISTICS	RELEVANCE OF GOVERNMENT POLICIES	DIRECT VISIBILITY	AWARENESS OF RELEVANCE DUE TO			SOCIAL PRESSURE TO VOTE	ABSENCE OF CROSS-PRESSURE	VOTING RATE
			TRAINING, JOB EXPERIENCE	CONTACT, COMMUNICATION	AMOUNT OF LEISURE			
High income	+	+	+	+	+	+	+	Higher
Low income	+	−	−	−	−	−	−	Lower
Miners	+	+	−	+	−	+	+	Higher
Servants	−	−	−	−	−	−	−	Lower
Workers in Europe	+	−	−	+	−	+	+	Higher
Workers in America	+	−	−	−	−	−	−	Lower
Government employees	+	+						Higher
Private employees	−	−						Lower
Wheat farmers	+	+						Higher
Nonmarket farmers	−							Lower
Jews	+							Higher
Non-Jews	−							Lower
Whites						+		Higher
Negroes						−		Lower
Old residents						+		Higher
Newcomers						−		Lower
Age 35–55			+	+	+	+	++	High
Over 55			−	−	−	−	−	Medium
Under 35								Low
Men						+	+	Higher
Women						−	−	Lower

Note: Plus sign indicates condition relatively more favorable to voting; minus sign, one relatively less favorable, with respect to the groups compared.
Source: Adapted from *ibid.*, p. 1135.

generally work and sometimes live in isolation from other workers and in close contact with the middle or upper class. Fifth, *leisure time* for political activity is not great in either case. Sixth, the *social pressure to vote* is much greater among miners, who, in contrast to servants, are highly unionized, a factor we have already discovered to be related to political activity. Seventh, *cross-pressures* created by conflicting upper- and lower-class values are weak among miners because of their geographic isolation, but they are strong among servants because of their daily exposure to such conflicts.

Whether a single individual has ᵗhe impulse to vote depends on many factors not included in this analysis. But we can say that the chances of his voting will be much greater if he is a member of a group for which government policies have obvious relevance; if he has the training, contacts, and leisure to become aware of this relevance; and if he is exposed to group or class pressures to vote and is free of conflicting interests, information, or group pressures.

To Vote Left or Right

On the question of *how* people will vote, observed regularities and explanations are usually expressed in terms of liberal-conservative, or left-right, preferences. As we have noted, "left" is most often defined as a tendency to advocate greater political, economic, or social equality, and "right" as a tendency to oppose greater equality and to support a more traditional and hierarchical order. A basic left-right cleavage has been found between low-income groups and high-income groups. Since low-income groups tend to support parties on the left, and high-income groups tend to support parties of the right, the general explanation is based on simple economic self-interest. Those who are in advantageous positions vote to maintain their advantages, while those who are not so well off vote to better their positions. There is considerable variation from this tendency, however; we shall attempt to account for the variation among lower-income groups.[53]

Notice that, for the rest of this section, we are taking for granted the leftist voting of low-income groups *as a whole*. Given this general tendency, we shall try to account for variations *within* the low-income groups. When we talk about some low-income groups as more leftist than others, then, do not forget that the "others" are still more leftist than high-income groups.

Since some social groups within the lower-income category regularly vote more heavily to the left than others do, some motivations other than discontent with one's economic lot must also be at work. Students of political behavior have identified the following *other needs*, the frustration of which appears to increase leftist voting by citizens with low incomes:

1. The need for *security of income*. This is quite closely related to the desire for higher income as such; however, the effect of periodic unemployment or collapse of produce prices seems to be important in itself.

---

[53] High-income groups deviate from class voting, too; for reasons of space, we confine the discussion in this section to low-income groups.

2. The need for *satisfying work*—work which provides the opportunity for self-control and self-expression, and which is free from arbitrary authority.

3. The need for *status*—for social recognition of one's value, and freedom from degrading discrimination in social relations.[54]

Failure to satisfy these other needs tends to produce a leftist political response. But some workers live under social conditions that further encourage group action. The principal *conditions* under which these other needs will lead to leftist political action are the following:

1. *Channels of communcation* are required through which the deprived group can become aware of its common problem and develop collective political action.

2. *Individualistic solutions*, as through social or geographical mobility, must be relatively unavailable, so that discontent will be channeled into collective action.

3. *Traditionalistic attitudes* and relationships which limit people's aspirations and inhibit attacks on existing social institutions must be weak.[55]

When both the *other needs* that give rise to discontent, and the *conditions* that encourage the expression of discontent, exist side by side, leftist voting seems to follow.

The left-hand column in Table 5-12 summarizes the social characteristics that are related to variations in the rate of leftist voting within the lower-income group; the attribute associated with the greater tendency to vote leftist appears first in each pair. The column headings summarize the explanations that have been offered to account for these regularities. Thus two factors help explain the more leftist voting among European than among American workers: (1) European workers have better intra-class communications because their greater class-consciousness leads them to live in a more nearly isolated world of their own, free of social contacts with higher economic groups; (2) European workers have less expectation of rising to a higher economic level because they live in "closed-class societies" which do not hold out the American promise that workers can rise to higher economic levels.

As with attempts to explain variations in the rate of voting, these explanations of leftist voting emphasize the extent to which patterns of psychological forces, rather than single factors, operate within groups of voters. Two explanations are offered, for example, as to why manual workers vote more leftist than white-collar workers. Although the manual worker may be as well or better off economically than the white-collar worker, he is aware of a lack of *prestige*. Contrary to the expectations of Karl Marx, white-collar workers tend to derive satisfaction from their association with management and from their higher prestige—satisfaction that often leads to conservative voting. Deprived of this prestige, manual workers may turn to leftist political programs. Moreover, manual workers have

---

[54] Lipset *et al.*, "The Psychology of Voting," *Handbook*, II, pp. 1137.
[55] *Ibid.*

Table 5-12 *Explanatory Factors Related to Left-Right Voting within Lower-Income Groups in Western Democracies*

SOCIAL CHARACTERISTIC	TYPES OF DEPRIVATION			FACILITATING CONDITIONS			LEFT VOTE
	INSECURITY OF INCOME	UNSATISFYING WORK	LOW PRESTIGE STATUS	GOOD INTRA-CLASS COMMUNICATIONS	LOW EXPECTATION OF MOBILITY	LACK OF TRADITIONALISM	
Workers in:							
Large plants	++	+	++	+	+	+	Higher
Small plants		−		−		−	Lower
Workers in:							
Large cities				+		+	Higher
Small towns				−		−	Lower
Workers in:							
Europe					+		Higher
United States					−		Lower
Manual workers			+	+			Higher
White-collar			−	−			Lower
Minority group			+	+			Higher
Majority group			−	−			Lower
Commercial farmers, fishermen	+		+	+	+	+	Higher
Local-market, subsistence farmers	−	−					Lower
Miners, lumbermen	+			+		+	Higher
Servants, service workers	−	+		−		−	Lower
Economically advanced areas	+					+	Higher
Backward areas	−					−	Lower
Men				+		+	Higher
Women				−		−	Lower

Note: Plus signs indicate factors favoring leftist voting in lower classes.
Source: Adapted from *ibid.*, p. 1143.

better *intra-class communications:* they tend to be in close contact only with other workers, to be aware of common problems, and to be organized for collective action. White-collar workers, on the other hand, lack organization and group-consciousness, and come in close contact with higher levels of management. Accordingly, white-collar workers are more frequently conservative.

The Functions of Political Opinions

Public opinion is not translated into public policy in the simple and direct way that early democratic theorists expected. Having looked at the formation and expression of political opinions, we are in a better position to understand why. We should also be in a better position to understand the functions of political opinions in terms of the individual and of the political system.

The Functions of Opinions in Terms of the Individual

Like other forms of behavior, expressions of political opinions reflect the current adjustment of personalities (created by past interaction of organism and environment) to their present situation and experiences. One way of viewing opinions, then, is by describing the way they express an individual's personality. Someone who is incapable of dealing in abstractions, for example, will have a limited range of opinions dealing with specific and unrelated subjects. We could describe his opinions simply as consistent with his innate capacities or as expressive of his personality. In functional terms, however, we would say that his limited range of opinions serves to reduce his environment to manageable size. This is to suggest that, just as we analyze the political system in terms of its functions for society, so we may analyze political opinions in terms of their functions both for individual personalities and for the political system.

Opinions are functional for an individual insofar as they promote his response to—or survival in—the environment without serious disruptions or disturbances. This view of opinions as mediating between the inner demands of the individual and the outer demands of the environment does imply that "functional opinions" are merely defensive adjustments to the environment. At the highest level of sophistication, such mediation involves probing and testing the environment through the rigorous methods of scientific inquiry. In such cases, the individual actively seeks evidence that might contradict his ideas and he readily modifies them in the light of changing evidence. Most people, however, arrive at their opinions more casually and modify them more reluctantly.

After a quasi-clinical study of the opinions of ten normal men, a team of Harvard psychologists identified three basic functions that opinions perform for the individual—object appraisal, social adjustment, and externalization of inner requirements.[56] These functions are served by opinions about every sort of object,

---

[56] M. Brewster Smith, Jerome S. Bruner, and Robert W. White, *Opinions and Personality* (New York: John Wiley and Sons, Inc., 1956), pp. 39–46.

from the writings of Plato to the performance of football teams, but all three may be explained in terms of opinions about politics.

By *object appraisal*, we mean that an individual's opinions serve to orient him to the world in which he lives, enabling him to categorize and to "size up" the objects and events around him. Since an opinion expresses a favorable or unfavorable predisposition toward some set of objects, it enables the individual to react without much trouble to any new object that can be classified as falling in some set about which he has an opinion. If a person has been reared a loyal Republican, for example, he has an immediate clue for evaluating candidates and proposals—the initial predisposition is favorable if they are Republican and unfavorable if they are not. Without such convenient categories for evaluating the countless stimuli that confront us, the world would appear, as Walter Lippmann once said, a great buzzing confusion. Each event simply cannot be approached with the genuine innocence and naïveté of an infant, or we would never manage to react to the countless stimuli that surround us. Accordingly, when voters must react without the convenience of differentiating party labels—as in party primaries and non-partisan elections—preferences are much more unstable and more responsive to influence by such agencies as the mass media of communication.

Social adjustment refers to the consequences of opinions for improving, disrupting, or maintaining an individual's relations with others. In the family, the child discovers early that some opinions win approval, others disapproval. And anyone who has ever been an uncertain freshman in college knows that the consequences of opinions for social adjustment do not end with departure from the home environment. Family and college associates tend to constitute "reference groups"—groups with which we feel a sense of identity or kinship and from which we derive standards for judging ourselves. But a reference group may also be quite impersonal, involving no face-to-face contact, and it may be negative as well as positive. The lonely intellectual in a small town may willingly and even eagerly incur the disrespect of his neighbors in order to enjoy the feeling that he is acting in ways that would satisfy the editors of the *Partisan Review*. In this case, his immediate neighbors constitute a negative reference group (his self-esteem is enhanced by their disapproval) and the editors of the *Partisan Review* represent a positive reference group (his self-esteem is enhanced by the feeling that he conforms to their standards).

An individual thus tends to find his social identity and his self-esteem by relating his opinions to those of others. When a person asks himself, "What am I?" he tends to answer in terms such as "a human being," or "a carpenter." When he asks himself, "What am I in politics?" he tends to answer "a Democrat" or "a Republican." The most important clue to his political identity is his party preference, and it will color his responses to all other political stimuli. When a political party is a positive reference group, it furnishes the standards to which an individual adjusts his opinions. Should he answer "What am I in politics?" with "I don't know," he has no specific political group with which to identify. The chances are that he will be a non-voter or an inconsistent (independent) voter who responds to transient factors.

By *externalizing inner requirements*, opinions may serve to reduce a sense of anxiety produced by some unresolved psychological problem of the individual. Herbert McClosky of the University of California at Berkeley has discovered, for example, that people who are personally insecure and afraid of the future tend to adopt a conservative political philosophy that extols the merits of stability, the wisdom of the past, and the dangers to society that social experimentation would bring.[57] And Robert E. Lane of Yale University found that people unable to tolerate ambiguity showed some tendency to vote for a candidate who offered simple solutions to difficult problems.[58] Such adoption of political opinions because of a feeling, often unconscious, of analogy between an issue and a personal psychological difficulty is not likely to represent a rational approach to political

---

[57] Herbert McClosky, "Conservatism and Personality," *American Political Science Review*, LII (March, 1958), pp. 27–45.

[58] Robert E. Lane, "Political Personality and Electoral Choice," *American Political Science Review*, XLIX (March, 1955), p. 181.

Drawing by Ed Fisher; © 1961 The New Yorker Magazine, Inc.

"When I joined the reform movement, I sure never thought I was joining an 'in-group.'"

ends. But it is not a tendency that is associated with one party more than another. One difficulty in attempting to understand politics through psychological analysis is that, while it may permit the prediction of certain psychological tendencies, these tendencies may take opposite political forms. Intense sibling rivalry, for example, has been cited as the source of habitual hostility and aggressiveness, but for some this condition leads to fascist tendencies and for others to communist tendencies.[59] For still others, it no doubt leads to mistrust of all politics. On rare occasions when the same political opinions serve the function of externalization for great numbers of people, a Hitler or a McCarthy era emerges.

For the individual, opinions thus help him relate to the world around him, to other people, and to himself. For our purposes, the more important functions of political opinions reside in their consequences for the political system.

The Functions of Opinions in Terms of the Political System

Basically, and in general terms, political opinions support the system and help it adapt to changing circumstances. From the point of view of the controlling regime, opinions are viewed as functional insofar as they support the personnel and policies of the regime. But what is "functional" at one level may be "dysfunctional" at another. Dissatisfactions with the scheme of American government under the Articles of Confederation were dysfunctional for that particular regime (they helped destroy it), but they seem to have been highly functional for the American political community (they strengthened it and helped it to survive changing circumstances). Only rarely do rulers recognize that opinions which support their regime may be highly dysfunctional for the political community as a whole. The cynical but penetrating remark of Louis XV, eighteenth-century King of France—"After me, the deluge!"—represents the exceptional case in which a ruler was able to recognize that the perpetuation of his regime was dysfunctional for the perpetuation of the political community.

Favorable or indifferent public opinions are not only necessary to the survival of a political system but also are necessary to its creation. Without some sense of community or of common identity among a people, they can hardly create a common political system. Active consensus on principles is too much to expect, but a common frame of reference—at least to the point where disagreements center on what is best for a recognized society—appears essential. A research team headed by Karl Deutsch at Yale reports, for example, that a necessary condition for the integration of small political units into a larger whole is "compatibility of the main values held by the politically relevant strata of all participating units." [60] Although extremist groups such as the John Birch Society and the Ku Klux Klan demonstrate that basic democratic values are not pursued by all Americans, even these groups drape their appeals in terms of the needs of the American political community. Even the American communists insist that they

---

[59] Robert E. Lane, *Political Life: Why People Get Involved in Politics* (Glencoe, Illinois: The Free Press, 1959), p. 119.

[60] Karl W. Deutsch *et al.*, *Political Community and the North Atlantic Area* (Princeton: Princeton University Press, 1957), p. 48.

are seeking the improvement of American society, not the promotion of Russian interests.

Political opinions thus create the sense of community necessary to a political system and promote the survival of the system. So far as democratic politics is concerned, another necessary function of political opinions is to create a widespread sense of the relevance of government, of its importance for and accessibility to the mass of citizens. Only when government is regarded as a potential instrument of the people does a democratic polity become possible. If most people regard the government as an alien and inaccessible creature, and if they cannot imagine it otherwise, they may constitute a political community but they are unlikely to develop a democratic political system.

The three underlying functions of political opinions that we have suggested all apply to the society as a whole and deal with conditions necessary for the emergence of political systems. What about the functions of opinions *within* the political system? These are much more difficult to discuss. In the first place, research on politcal opinions has dealt primarily with mass attitudes or with elite activities. The difficult and complex task of tracing the linkage between mass opinions and the attitudes and performance of government officials has scarcely begun.[61] Moreover, political opinions do not represent a separate institution or structure of government even though they are vitally important for every institution and function of the political system. Mass opinions are particularly important for the input functions of interest identification and leadership selection, but their importance is expressed through such structures as political parties, pressure groups, and the electoral system. When we talk about the functions of these institutions in the next three chapters, we shall accordingly be considering also the functions of political opinions.

Despite the difficulties that confront any attempt to relate political opinions to specific government actions, three functions can be roughly sketched out. First, political opinions perform a *permissive function*. Public indifference or ignorance about most public questions is so widespread that official decison-makers enjoy a wide range of discretion. The public may favor government action on many issues long before the government acts. But often this sentiment may not be strongly expressed. On the admission of Hawaii to the Union and on the right of permanent residents of the national capital to vote in presidential elections, for example, a vast majority of the public expressed approval ten to fifteen years before Congress took favorable action.[62] The people did not feel strongly on either subject, however, and the chances are that no member of Congress felt that his re-election was threatened by failure to support public opinion on these subjects.

---

[61] In his typically penetrating work on *Public Opinion and American Democracy*, Professor Key's primary objective was to analyze the "linkages" between public opinion and official actions, but the section on linkages is the weakest part of the book. Significant research in this area by Warren Miller and Donald Stokes of the University of Michigan will be considered in Chapter 8.

[62] Key, *Public Opinion*, pp. 32–33. The data on the two following functions of political opinions are also from Key, pp. 29–39.

The consequence of such a situation is to permit government officials to act as they see fit without fear of public reprisal.

Second, political opinions perform a *supportive function*, endowing existing policies and actions with a general sense of legitimacy and public approval. However intense the opposition to a measure, it tends to receive widespread support once it becomes the "law of the land." The Social Security Act of 1935, for example, was bitterly opposed by Republicans, but its provisions were approved by about 90 per cent of the voters as soon as it was enacted. This supportive function tends, of course, to stack the cards (or the votes) against those who try to change approved policy. As a candidate for President in 1964, Senator Barry Goldwater took pains to endorse an extension of the Social Security system in order to counteract the impression made by an earlier proposal that it be made voluntary. The importance of the supportive function is underscored by the occasions on which it is missing. Consider the difficulties that confronted officials who were charged with carrying out the prohibition amendment.

Third, political opinions sometimes perform a *demand function*. At all times, of course, small segments of the public stridently support particular measures. And permissive support often enables a small but intense group to block legislation about which the vast majority of the general public is relatively unconcerned. (The American Medical Association's long success in opposing general government aid for medical care is perhaps the prime recent example.) But the opinions of the general public occasionally take such clear form that officials can ignore them only at their peril. Although opinion survey data do not go back to the early 1930's, the voters of that era seem to have been in a mood that demanded some government response to the country's economic depression. More recently, the intense dissatisfaction of American Negroes with the stigma of "second-class citizenship," coupled with the supportive or permissive attitudes of most other Americans, required some kind of positive response from the government.

The permissive and supportive functions of political opinions apply to all political systems. The demand function is constitutionally supported only in democracies. In the next three chapters, we shall consider the principal institutions—political parties, pressure groups and public relations, and the electoral system—through which these functions are carried out in the United States.

CHAPTER SIX

Political

Parties

Politics is the struggle for power among groups, not among isolated individuals. Early democratic theorists assumed that individuals could exist in a "state of nature" quite apart from groups. But today this notion seems untenable, for we know that even such essential human attributes as speech cannot be developed by children who are isolated from contact with other human beings. As David Truman, a student of interest groups, puts it, "We do not, in fact, find individuals otherwise than in groups; complete isolation in space and time is so rare as to be an almost hypothetical situation." [1] Both opinions and behavior are largely shaped by group affiliations. Having identified the political attitudes and behavior patterns that differentiate various groups within the population, we now turn to groups in the purer sense of the term—that is, as aggregations marked by some degree of *interaction* or *relationship* among the members.

Among the unofficial agencies through which public opinion performs the basic input functions of selecting leaders and of communicating public interests to official decision-makers, the most important are political parties, pressure groups, and professional public relations organizations. We shall concentrate first on the political party, which is both the broadest of these three kinds of groups and the one that is most central to a democratic system.

The American Party System

In all societies that we know about, human beings are born and grow up under some kind of government. Realistically, this means that the enduring problem of politics is not that of devising a form of government and selecting people to man it. The truly enduring problem is the management of transfers of power. Instead of devising a government, human beings are presented with the problem of maintaining or changing the governments under which they live. Responses to this problem vary from apathy, to support for established rulers, to demands for a change.

The questions of who shall succeed to power, and through what processes, have been variously answered by different kinds of political systems. Hereditary monarchies solved these questions through a biological lottery, although bloodshed following or leading to the death of rulers was frequent enough to furnish gory material for Shakespeare and other writers.[2] Modern dictatorships have been equally troubled by the problem of succession when rulers have fallen into disfavor, become senile, or died. Perhaps the greatest achievement of democracy is the development of political parties as peaceable agencies for expressing public reactions to rulers and preferences as to their successors. Political parties may be viewed as democratic equivalents of groups found in all governments—those supporting the established regime and those conspiring to overthrow it.

Granted the importance of political parties for democracy, we might expect that they would be among the most respected groups in democratic America.

---

[1] David B. Truman, *The Governmental Process: Political Interests and Public Opinion* (New York: Alfred A. Knopf, 1951), p. 48.

[2] The notion of a biological lottery and much of the substance of the above paragraph are from the late V. O. Key, Jr., *Politics, Parties, and Pressure Groups* (New York: Thomas Y. Crowell Company, 1964), 5th ed., Chapter 1.

That they are *not* is one of the mysteries of politics that we cannot fully explain. One explanation of this irony is a false expectation of both the Framers and the opponents of the United States Constitution—the expectation that popular elections would give citizens direct control over government without the need for any intermediary organization. Generations of political experience, however, have convinced observers that parties are essential to the functioning of any group of people. No large group of individuals can behave as a unit until they are organized by those who are actively seeking to speak for the group and to formulate its policies. "Affairs of a group—be it a nation, a church, a union, or a chamber of commerce—do not and cannot take care of themselves; small factions of men must advance proposals and put themselves forward as willing to assume responsibility for handling the affairs of the group." [3] In democratic societies, political parties seek to exercise this leadership in quite a different way from the strong-arm tactics adopted by the rulers of non-democratic societies.

The Common Purpose of Political Parties

What is a political party? It can be distinguished from other political groups by its peculiar purpose and methods.[4] The *purpose* of a party is to win and exercise political power—specifically, to gain control of the government. It is this purpose that sets political parties apart from other institutions that struggle for political power. Pressure groups, for example, try to influence public policy, but they are concerned with *specific* policies rather than with control of the government *as a whole*. The Women's Christian Temperance Union would like to determine policy on matters relating to alcoholic beverages, but it is not interested in assuming over-all responsibility for such matters as taxation and foreign affairs. The Chamber of Commerce and the AFL-CIO have interests that are just as sober and much broader, but not even these groups press for continuous control of the entire government. If any one of these organizations were to move beyond the attempt to influence specific policies and seek to capture general control of the government, it would transform itself into a political party.

The effort to take over responsibility for the over-all conduct of the government, then, distinguishes a political party from a pressure group. And actual proximity to power distinguishes the true political party from the "minor" parties that operate on the fringes of politics. To be an authentic party, a political group must either enjoy power now or have a fair prospect of gaining power in the foreseeable future. Consequently, such organizations as the Socialist, Prohibitionist, Greenback, and Vegetarian parties, which have no real stake in the outcome of American elections, are educational movements or interest groups rather than political parties. Many state laws recognize this distinction, and require that an organization must have received a specified percentage of

---

[3] *Ibid.*, 3rd ed., p. 217.

[4] For a brief discussion of the concept of party (similar to that employed here) and for the formulation of the concept by noted authorities, see Alfred de Grazia, "Party," in J. Gould and W. L. Kolb (eds.), *A Dictionary of the Social Sciences* (New York: The Free Press of Glencoe, 1964), pp. 482–483.

the vote in the preceding election (2 per cent in California, 5 per cent in Illinois, 10 per cent in Colorado) [5] before it can be classed a "political party" with the right to appear on the official ballot.

If we try to define political parties in terms of more specific purposes, rather than simply in terms of the attempt to gain control of the government, the definition loses its generality. Perhaps the most famous concept of party is that advanced by Edmund Burke, a British statesman of the eighteenth century: "Party is a body of men united, for promoting by their joint endeavours the national interest, upon some particular principle in which they are all agreed." But what "particular principle" serves to "unite" such Democrats as Senators Harry Byrd of Virginia and Paul Douglas of Illinois, or such Republicans as Senators J. Strom Thurmond of South Carolina and Jacob Javits of New York? Their disagreement on principles is exceeded only by their lack of unity in Senate voting. Clearly, principles vary from one member to another within the same party, but *all* the members are united in their desire to win control of the government. Although the motives and objectives of the members would have to be included in a study of a single party, a definition general enough to apply to all parties must stop short with the statement that their broad objective is to acquire political power.

The Distinguishing Method of Political Parties

The method by which a political party tries to achieve this objective is based on attempts to mobilize votes. Indeed, David Truman insists that we should forget purpose altogether and define political parties exclusively in terms of this distinguishing method.[6] Non-party organizations, like public relations and pressure groups, also try to mobilize votes, but they do not themselves offer candidates who seek office under their banners. The habitual method of seeking power through ballots rather than through bullets is peculiar to democratic regimes. It may be that the party is primarily an organ for the expression of combative instincts, but it serves to sublimate those instincts and to promote a peaceable settlement of differences.

The peaceable method of parties in a democracy distinguishes them from the "parties" of totalitarian regimes like the Soviet Union and Nazi Germany. To "become a party" to something means to identify oneself with one group rather than with another—in other words, to make a *choice*. Since totalitarian regimes deny individuals this right to choose one party instead of another, they never permit parties to function.[7] For parties to operate in a meaningful way,

---

[5] See Joseph P. Harris and Leonard Rowe, *California Politics* (Stanford, California: Stanford University Press, 1959), 2nd ed., p. 31; Austin Ranney, *Illinois Politics* (New York: New York University Press, 1960), p. 18; Curtis Martin, *Colorado Politics* (Denver: Big Mountain Press, 1960), p. 35.

[6] "Whatever else it may be or may not be, the political party in the United States most commonly is a device for mobilizing votes, preferably a majority of votes." Truman, *The Governmental Process*, pp. 270–271.

[7] Sigmund Neumann, *Modern Political Parties: Approaches to Comparative Politics* (Chicago: The University of Chicago Press, 1956), p. 395. We are not saying that the

they must be tolerated by the government. Conversely, they must "tolerate" the government once they have achieved power—that is, they must not transform the government simply into an arm of the party. For a government to outlaw communist or any other parties as *vote-mobilizing* organizations is thus undemocratic. But for a government to prohibit them from pursuing political power by means *other than* peaceful vote-mobilization is certainly *not* undemocratic. Moreover, if parties are to operate, the victorious party must not transform the government into an instrument for eliminating all opposition. Although totalitarian parties may be active in a democratic system—as the communists are in France and Italy—their success would destroy the system itself, for all totalitarian parties have an implacable urge to set themselves up as the *only* "party."

Functions of Political Parties

Since freely competing political parties are unique to democracy, students of parties have suggested that almost anything essential to the maintenance of democracy must be a consequence of party activities.[8] When we described the basic political functions of public opinion (Chapter 5) as the choice of leaders and the communication of public interests to official decision-makers, we also pointed out that political parties are indispensable to the democratic achievement of these results. In the broadest terms, then, the consequences of party activity for the political system as a whole are the public choice of leaders and the open and organized expression of public interests. Political parties can therefore be said to democratize the input functions that must be performed by all viable political systems.

In addition to their contribution to the input functions common to all political systems, political parties perform more specific functions for the individual as well as the political system. At the individual level, parties are reference groups which help the citizen organize his opinions. Once he has decided

---

word "party" has a single true meaning. We do maintain that our definition better fits popular usage and makes it easier to understand actual political practices than a definition that would include the single political organization of a totalitarian system as a political party.

[8] Samuel J. Eldersveld, for example, has recently discerned seven "critical" functions of parties for democracies: "to recruit leadership, formulate policy, organize decision-making, communicate upward and downward between leaders and public, promote consensus, enforce responsibility, and thus move society toward the effective and expeditious resolution of its conflicts." *Political Parties: A Behavioral Analysis* (Chicago: Rand McNally & Company, 1964), p. 22. Frank J. Sorauf speaks of three manifest functions (electing, propagandizing, and governing) and of six latent functions of parties: "They reduce effectively the number of political options to manageable numbers, bring order and focus to the political struggle, simplify issues and frame alternatives, compromise conflicting interests, recruit political leadership, personalize and dramatize politics, stabilize political debate and allegiances, and enhance the political power of the 'insignificant' individual." *Political Parties in the American System* (Boston: Little, Brown and Company, 1964), pp. 165–166.

which party he prefers, he has a reliable cue for reacting to new issues and personalities with a minimum of effort—he need only discover where his party stands or, if he likes real economy of effort, he can support his party on the assumption that it supports the correct position. Second, party activity tends to increase voting turnout, to strengthen party loyalty, and to create more favorable attitudes toward active partisan work among those who are exposed to it. Third, exposure to party activity results in greater interest in and information about public affairs. Even among citizens who frequently watch television, those exposed to local party activity are much better informed on national affairs than those not so exposed.[9] The competition of parties for votes thus leaves citizens more politically oriented, more active, more interested in politics, and better informed about public affairs.

At the level of the political system, political parties serve many functions in addition to their basic role in leadership selection and interest identification. If you can imagine what our political life would be like without political parties, you will be able to identify these additional functions. With no political parties, the struggle for power would certainly be less open, less predictable in its outcome, more susceptible to minority manipulation, and more likely to take the form of *coups d'etat* or even of revolution. Without parties, the countless groups in society could be expected to pursue extremely different policies, and so many opposing alternatives would be available that choice would be difficult. Each election, assuming that elections continued to prove feasible, would present such an overwhelming array of individual candidates that voters could hardly know what policies or even general tendencies they were supporting. Finally, with no party program to help organize their work, official decision-makers would presumably rely much more heavily on those interest groups that were organized to promote special interests. If these speculations are valid, we have identified at least three additional functions that political parties perform for American politics.

First, parties structure the conflicts of society. Parties did not create the struggle for power; they function to control, direct, and stabilize conflict so as to permit a peaceable expression of differences.[10] In structuring social conflict, parties develop legitimate opposition to those in control of government and become the functional equivalent of revolutionary movements.[11] Second, political parties serve to moderate the differences among opposing groups, to stabilize political allegiances, and, in Lord Bryce's phrase, to "bring order out of the chaos of a multitude of voters." In order to win majority support, they must avoid taking an extremist position. Consequently, they must appeal to a

---

[9] Eldersveld, *Political Parties*, p. 542. The second and third findings are both from Eldersveld's research in the Detroit metropolitan area.

[10] Clinton Rossiter calls this the primary function of a democratic party from which all others are derived. *Parties and Politics in America* (Ithaca, New York: Cornell University Press, 1960), p. 39.

[11] As Professor V. O. Key put it, "The strivings of the outs for office become . . . a sublimation of revolutionary movements." *Politics, Parties, and Pressure Groups*, p. 204.

wider group than just their own hard core of doctrinaire and dogmatic faithful.[12] Third, political parties organize the decision-making activities of government in such a way as to give ordinary citizens a much better chance of having their interests recognized. William Chambers, in a study of the origins of American political parties, finds this the "great role" of parties and party competition: "shaping and clarifying options for popular choice or decision, and . . . giving such choices some effect in the conduct of government." [13]

In all these functions, political parties have a strong majoritarian bias that we better appreciate by considering what our politics would be like without parties. And this consideration need not be entirely speculative. In the early days of the Republic, before the emergence of the party system, future members of Jefferson's Republican Party complained about the advantages enjoyed by "the Weight of Talent, Wealth, and personal and family interest." Melancton Smith argued that the "influence" of

> . . . the well-to-do and eminent will generally enable them to succeed in elections. [Those of] conspicuous military, popular, civil, or legal talents . . . easily form associations; the poor and middling classes form them with difficulty. . . . A substantial yeoman, of sense and discernment, will hardly ever be chosen. From these remarks, it appears that the government will fall into the hands of the few and the great. This will be a government of oppression.[14]

We still hear charges that the "poor and middling classes" are too little recognized in decision-making. But they have a weight that they could not possibly have achieved without political parties.

The Two-Party System

The most important single feature of the political wars in the United States is that they are conducted within a two-party system. True, we have many so-called "minor parties." But parties are power vehicles, and political power in the United States is effectively monopolized by the Republican and Democratic parties. In 1964, for example, the minor parties failed to win a single seat in Congress, the governorship of any state, or even one of the 7,629 seats in the state legislatures. Quite clearly, ours cannot be described as a multi-party system. Nor could it be called a one-party system. The Republicans almost always win the elections in about nine states, and the Democrats in about thirteen, but both parties *share* political power in the national government and in a majority of the states.[15] Moreover, areas completely dominated by a single party are apparently

---

[12] This is more true in two-party than in multi-party systems, but even in multi-party systems the most extreme of the "class parties," the communists, lay claim to representing the true interests of society as a whole. See Neumann, *Modern Political Parties*, p. 397. Three of the functions listed here may be found, in somewhat different form, in this same source.

[13] *Political Parties in a New Nation* (New York: Oxford University Press, 1963), p. 13.

[14] Quoted in *ibid*.

[15] On the basis of elections for President, United States senator, and governor between 1914 and 1953, Austin Ranney and Willmoore Kendall have developed a threefold clas-

disappearing everywhere outside the South, and even there one-party rule is weakening.[16]

How does the two-party system compare with the single-party and multi-party systems? The single-party system is generally described as altogether incompatible with democracy, but this is not necessarily the case. In southern states, the Democratic party primary does give the voters a choice between competing personalities or factions, even though the winner of the primary is assured of victory in the official election. But competition between individuals —which inevitably means that there is no continuing group responsibility— seems a poor substitute for competition between parties. One-party politics can promote popular control of policy only through competition between factions that are well enough organized to resemble parties.[17] Since such continuing competition between recognized factions is rare in one-party areas, elections become primarily personality contests. At its best, then, the one-party system is an anomaly in a democracy.

A multi-party system, on the other hand, can claim two advantages over a two-party system: it permits more shades of opinion to be represented in the legislature, and it vests party membership with greater meaning. And yet, to most American observers, the two-party system seems to be more satisfactory, for the following reasons:

First, it guarantees that both parties will have a wide appeal to the electorate. This sometimes makes the parties so similar that any choice between

sification of state party politics in the United States: (1) *two-party states,* "in which the second party had won over 25 per cent of the elections"; (2) *modified one-party states,* "in which the second party, while winning less than 25 per cent of all elections, has won over 30 per cent of the vote in over 70 per cent of all elections and has won over 40 per cent of the vote in over 30 per cent of all elections"; and (3) *one-party states,* "in which the second party has won less than 25 per cent of all elections, and has also won over 30 per cent of the vote in less than 70 per cent of all elections and has won over 40 per cent of the vote in less than 30 per cent of elections."

The one-party states during this period were: *Republican*—Vermont; *Democratic*—Alabama, Arkansas, Florida, Georgia, Louisiana, Mississippi, South Carolina, Texas, and Virginia. The modified one-party states were: *Republican*—Iowa, Kansas, Maine, New Hampshire, North Dakota, Oregon, Pennsylvania, South Dakota; *Democratic*—Kentucky, North Carolina, Oklahoma, Tennessee. The remaining twenty-six states were two-party. "The American Party Systems," *American Political Science Review,* XLVIII (June, 1954), 477–485. Attempts to establish more refined systems of classification may be found in Robert T. Golembiewski, "A Taxonomic Approach to State Political Party Strength," *Western Political Quarterly,* XI (September, 1958), 494–513; Edward C. Cox, "The Measurement of Party Strength," *Western Political Quarterly,* XIII (December, 1960), 1022–1042; Joseph A. Schlesinger, "The Structure of Competition for Office in the American States," *Behavioral Science,* 5 (July, 1960), 197–210.

[16] On the "erosion of sectionalism," see V. O. Key, Jr., *American State Politics* (New York: Alfred A. Knopf, 1956), pp. 26–28. While competition diverges in some degree from the perfect two-party model in most states, the politics of even the pure one-party states can be understood only as an integral part of a national two-party system. See Angus Campbell *et al., The American Voter* (New York: John Wiley & Sons, Inc., 1960), p. 557.

[17] Lewis Bowman and G. R. Boynton, "Coalition as Party in a One-Party Southern Area: A Theoretical Case Analysis," *Midwest Journal of Political Science,* VIII (August, 1964), pp. 277–297.

them means little or nothing, but it also produces certain advantages. Since both parties must seek majority support in order to acquire power, they both must please substantially the same people. The fact that they resemble each other so closely, then, may simply mean that both are doing a good job of interpreting public opinion, and their similarity certainly strengthens the unifying and moderating function of parties. Because a majority coalition cannot be built on an extremist position, the age-old fear of a "tyranny of the majority" becomes unrealistic in a heterogeneous society like our own.

Drawing by B. Tobey ; © 1964 The Saturday Review.

"I've always meant to ask you, Henry—What are you, a Democrat or a Republican?"

Second, the two-party system makes for compromise *within* each party *before* the election, rather than compromise among several parties after they have taken their seats in the legislature. This means that the ultimate coalition in control of the government is chosen by the voters rather than by legislative blocs. This method of reaching compromise enhances the role of the voters in choosing their government, and it also tends to *fix responsibility* on a continuing and recognizable group. (This advantage is often said to be reduced in the United States by the failure of the winning party to maintain a high degree of unity in Congress.)

Third, by making certain that *someone* will win a majority in every elected body, the two-party system increases the chances of coherence and stability in government. The classic argument is that, under a two-party system, control of the government is fixed by the voters for the entire period between elections, rather than being subject to overthrow with every shift in alliance among a multitude of parties. The second part of the argument clearly fits the American system: with only two parties, post-election maneuvers do not determine which party will control the government. But the first part of the argument refers too neatly to "the government" to fit the American system without modification. In a federal system like ours, with separation of powers in both state and national governments, "control of the government" is considerably more complicated than in a unitary and parliamentary system like that of Britain. An election in an American locality may mean victory for non-partisan city officials, a Republican governor and state senate, a Democratic state house, a Republican President, and a Democratic Congress. In such a case, which party can be said to have control of "the government"—or, for that matter, of any level of government?

Realistically, the two-party system is less certain to produce coherence and stability in the United States than its proponents claim. Even so, control of each elective body goes to one winning party rather than to a post-election coalition. More important, the tendency is toward unified control at each level of government—the President and Congress usually represent the same party, as do most governors and state legislatures.[18] While we cannot accurately claim, then, that the voters in the American two-party system always put control of the government in the hands of one winning party, we can say that the system works in that direction. The confusion is in our separate election of many governing bodies, not in the two-party system. Just imagine how much *more* complicated our system would be with the various branches of our different levels of government each controlled by different combinations of minor parties.

A fourth advantage of the two-party system applies more clearly to the United States: it insures that the chief executive will represent a general body of opinion. Where only two parties are competing for power, the successful candidate for president or governor must inevitably represent the broad base of one of the two parties. With "energy in the executive" even more essential today than when Alexander Hamilton first argued for its necessity, this is a real advantage indeed.

Finally, recent research throws serious doubt on the claim that the multi-party system heightens citizen interest. A comparison of French and American political attitudes reveals a lower level of awareness of political parties in France than in the United States.[19] Rather than the multiplicity of parties heightening citizen interest by offering a party to fit almost anyone's tastes, as had been supposed, the multiplicity may confuse citizens and lessen their interest.

Why Two Parties?

Clearly, democracy thrives when there is more than one party. But why do some democratic countries stop at just *two?* Let's look at a few of the explanations. Some say that "the two-party system seems to correspond to the nature of things," because "political choice usually takes the form of a choice between two alternatives."[20] Thomas Jefferson, however, pointed to the nature of man, rather than to the nature of things: "The sickly, weakly, timid man fears the people and is a Tory by nature. The healthy, strong, and bold, cherishes them and is formed a Whig by nature. . . ."[21] Alexander Hamilton found the ex-

---

[18] In 1965, for example, the same party controlled the governorship and both houses of the legislature in 29 states, as compared with 19 states that had a party division. (The two remaining states, Minnesota and Nebraska, have nonpartisan legislative elections.) At the national level, from 1900 to 1966, the President and both houses of Congress were of the same party for 52 years; at least one house of Congress was of a different party for 14 years.

[19] Philip E. Converse and Georges Dupeux, "Politicization of the Electorate in France and the United States," *Public Opinion Quarterly*, XXVI (September, 1962), pp. 1–23.

[20] Maurice Duverger, *Political Parties: Their Organization and Activity in the Modern State*, trans. Barbara and Robert North (New York: John Wiley & Sons, Inc., 1955), p. 215.

[21] See Charles A. Beard, *Economic Origin of Jeffersonian Democracy* (New York: The Macmillan Company, 1936), fn. 2, pp. 420–421, for letter to Lafayette (November 4, 1823).

planation in economic factors: "All communities divide themselves into the few and the many," he argued before the Constitutional Convention. "The first are the rich and the well born, the other the mass of the people." [22] Some observers cite the historical fact that the United States divided into two parties early in its history, although this is obviously a circular line of reasoning that throws no light on the reasons behind the division. Others emphasize the lack of irreconcilable religious, racial, or class cleavages among the American people. In explaining Britain's two-party system, one observer has even suggested that the division is rooted in "the sporting instincts of the British people, which lead them to view political campaigns as a match between rival teams"!

Now these explanations may or may not be relevant to the reasons behind the two-party system. But there is one general technical factor—the officially prescribed electoral system—that is a key factor in the party system of *every* country. The *single-member district system with plurality election* correlates almost perfectly with the two-party system. The "single-member district system" means that only one representative, rather than several, is elected to a given office from any one district. "Plurality election" means that the candidate with the largest vote is elected even if he fails to win a majority, so that there is never any need for a second balloting to produce a majority vote. Since parties always direct their efforts toward winning elections, the election procedures that are prescribed by law cannot help but mold the character of party politics. A country that has a two-party system almost always uses this electoral scheme; and if it uses this electoral scheme, it will almost certainly have a two-party system. [23]

The way in which the single-member district system freezes out minor parties is fairly obvious. Only one victor is possible in each race, whether for the presidency or for the legislature. And since the minor parties have no chance at all of capturing the presidency, and very, very little chance of ever enjoying any legislative power, they quickly die out.

The influence of plurality election is also important—though it is often overlooked. In countries where a majority vote is required for victory, a second balloting between the candidates who led on the first ballot is necessary. This system encourages minor parties to offer candidates in the first election in the hope of slipping into the "run-off." (The second ballot was one of the causes of the multi-party system in France's Third Republic.) But in countries where only a simple plurality is needed for victory, minor parties are encouraged to join forces with one of the major parties, in the hope that they may become

---

[22] Max Farrand, *The Records of the Federal Convention of 1787* (New Haven: Yale University Press, 1911), p. 299.

[23] As Duverger explains, the exceptions to this rule are rare (Canada offers the only current exception) and result from special conditions. He accordingly finds the limits of this system's influence to be as follows: "It tends to the creation of a two-party system inside the individual constituency; but the parties opposed may be different in different areas of the country." Duverger, *Political Parties*, p. 223. For insight into this problem, the authors are particularly indebted to Duverger's discussion on pp. 216–228, and to E. E. Schattschneider, *Party Government* (New York: Farrar & Rinehart, Inc., 1942), Chapter V.

identified with the winner. Understandably, the major parties tend to make concessions to the minor parties in order to broaden their base of support. Where there is only one election, then, coalitions *must* be formed in advance, rather than in the interval between elections.[24]

Although these technical features of the electoral system seem particularly well adapted to two-party politics, we cannot say that the party system of a country is a direct result of its electoral system. From data on five European countries, John G. Grumm of the University of Kansas concludes that the party system shapes the electoral system rather than the other way around.[25] Without attempting to unravel cause and effect, we can say that single-member districts and plurality elections are found together with two-party systems, just as proportional representation from multi-member districts and majority elections (calling for "run-off" elections) are associated with multi-party systems.

So many factors work to shape both the electoral and the party system of a country that the question of *why* such systems are followed probably cannot be answered exactly.[26] In general terms, the cultural context is important in making our election system seem "natural" to us. Early in our history, Americans divided sharply into groups supporting and opposing adoption of the Constitution. Once that fight was settled, each side adjusted remarkably well to the Constitution's basic procedures, even though they continued to represent opposed interests. America has never been marked by the social homogeneity and consensus of one-party systems or by the social fragmentation and unbridgeable cleavages of multi-party systems.[27] After a bitterly fought election, Thomas Jefferson observed in his First Inaugural Address, "We have called by different names brethren of the same principle. We are all Republicans, we are all Federalists." With the "American Creed" so widely accepted, the differences among Americans have not been basic enough to drive many voters into splinter parties.

Finally, any pattern of behavior, once established, tends to perpetuate itself. Although this tells us little about the origins of our two-party system, it reminds us that American practices were influenced by the English background of most of our first politicians. Since their day, the *idea* of the two-party system has been consciously and consistently ingrained in the American political mind. Generations of American citizens have been taught that the two-party system is the most satisfactory system of all, and it has been elevated from mere habit to the level of a celebrated tradition in American politics.

---

[24] These propositions find support in the conduct of Democratic primaries in the South; more factions appear in those states requiring a "run-off" primary than in those in which nomination is by a plurality in a single primary.

[25] "Theories of Electoral Systems," *Midwest Journal of Political Science*, II (November, 1958), pp. 345–376.

[26] Aaron B. Wildavsky offers a sharp criticism of Duverger for neglecting the multiplicity of factors productive of two-party politics in "A Methodological Critique of Duverger's *Political Parties*," *Journal of Politics*, XXI (May, 1959), pp. 303–318. For a general discussion of the electoral and party systems, see Avery Leiserson, *Parties and Politics* (New York: Alfred A. Knopf, 1958), pp. 108–113.

[27] Sorauf, *Political Parties in the American System*, pp. 30–31.

The Structure of American Parties

Like the over-all party system, the internal organization of each party is also shaped by the country's official electoral practices. Since the purpose of parties is to gain control of the government by winning elections, party organization is built around the electoral system. Accordingly, the formal organization of our political parties has taken on a pyramidal structure. As we shall see when we begin to identify the points of power within this structure, however, its neatness is most deceptive.

On paper, the *national committee* of each party represents the capstone of the pyramid. Actually, though, the national committee is the point of final authority only in a purely formal sense. In both the Republican and Democratic parties, the national committee is composed of one man and one woman from each state (plus members from the territories). The Republicans also give a bonus to Republican states and territories. Any state chairman gets a seat on the Republican national committee if his state voted Republican in the last presidential, gubernatorial, or congressional election. A territorial chairman is similarly a national committee member if his territory elected a Republican delegate to Congress. The national convention of both parties officially elects the two regular committee members from each state, but in reality it merely accepts the nominees submitted by the state's delegation to the convention. These nominations are made, in accordance with state law, by a primary election, a state convention, the national convention delegation, or a state committee. The duties of the national committee amount to little more than deciding when and where the next convention will meet and preparing a temporary roll of delegates—tasks that are only incidental to the chief concerns of the party.

The *national chairman* acts as the official spokesman for the party. Other party members, especially congressmen, who frequently and vociferously dissent from the chairman's pronouncements, demonstrate, however, that the party has no single voice. The national chairman is officially chosen by the national committee, but in practice he is named by the party's presidential nominee. His primary job is to manage the presidential campaign. In choosing party candidates for Congress, in executing the party program after victory, indeed even in choosing the presidential candidate, the national committee and its chairman normally play only a minor role, certainly not a role of leadership. Selected merely to oversee the presidential campaign, these party officials reflect rather than exercise the real power of the party. The great agitation among Republican leaders about removing Dean Burch as Republican national chairman in 1965 was not an effort to win a post of great power; rather, it was a move to demonstrate that the Goldwater wing was no longer in control of the party.

The national chairman and his committee lack power over their party's policies and choice of candidates, but they can sometimes play a role of real importance. Because of its limited official authority, the committee tends to be as strong or as weak as its chairman.[28] In addition to his usual role as campaign manager, the national chairman serves his party as fiscal leader and as mediator for its hundreds of state and local units as well as its major factions. An occasional chairman has the personal qualities to build considerable influence on the basis of these functions, even to the point of attempting to coordinate party policy. To get at the normal functions of the national committee, however, perhaps we should simply ask what a party would lose if its national headquarters disappeared. Hugh A. Bone, one of the few students of the national committees, supplies this answer: "If the headquarters were abolished the parties would lose an agency that has sought to coordinate the infinite variety of effort of numerous party affiliates, to raise money, and to obtain publicity for the party as a whole." [29]

Professor Bone notes, in massive understatement, that the committee has not performed its role of coordination "in a spectacular way," and he points out three weaknesses of the committee which account for this failure. First, turnover in the chairmanship is so high that an effective national office can hardly be created. From 1940 to 1962, for example, the Republicans had thirteen chairmen and the Democrats eleven. Second, the committee has no firm base in the party, with no official place in either the state or congressional party organizations. Nor do committee members normally have power as informal leaders; frequently they are relative unknowns who are selected because of financial contributions to the party. The occasional committee member who is a powerful figure in his state derives his influence from some source other than his position on the committee. Third, the national committees have no constitution or bylaws giving them definite authority and functions. The rules of the Democratic Party, for example, specifically state that the national committee has only those powers granted by the national convention and that no convention has authorized "formulation of proposals which might be construed to be in the nature of platform declarations" by the committee.[30]

Alongside the national committee in the party structure are the national *congressional* and *senatorial campaign committees*, chosen by each party's representatives in the House and Senate. Their independence of the national committee further suggests that power in American parties is dispersed. Although the demands of modern campaigning have produced an increasing amount of personalized cooperation between the various party committees, this is primarily at the staff level. "For all practical purposes both committees in both houses are autonomous," Professor Bone submits. "The four Capitol Hill com-

---

[28] Abraham Holtzman, "Party Responsibility and Loyalty: New Rules in the Democratic Party," *Journal of Politics*, XXII (August, 1960), p. 491.

[29] *Party Committees and National Politics* (Seattle: University of Washington Press, 1958), p. 123.

[30] Clarence Cannon, *Democratic Manual for the Democratic National Convention* (Washington, D.C.: Democratic National Committee, 1956), p. 9.

mittees remain jealous of their independence and are quick to resist 'encroachment' by the national committees. Especially in the realm of policy, there has been the frequent tendency of party leaders to suggest that the national committees concern themselves with raising money and let the congressional leaders determine the general policy line." [31]

Why do the Capitol Hill party committees go their own way, rather than function as units subordinate to the national committee? Most of the explanations can be attributed to the separation of powers provided by the American constitutional framework. The national committee is concerned primarily with the presidential race, so the congressman feels that he would be a party orphan without his own organization; congressional staffs are impressed with split-ticket voting and the consequent possibility of furthering their own campaigns without dependence on the presidential candidate; local appeals, which may be at variance with the party's national interests, can be better exploited through the Capitol Hill committees; the national committee favors the President's supporters but the congressional and senatorial committees are essentially service agencies, helping any member with the party label regardless of his stand on national policies; and, finally, separate committees are a way to avoid inconvenience from the three-million-dollar limit on expenditures that the law imposes on each party agency. Under these circumstances, says Bone, "One national level party committee may exert influence on another at times, but this is not the result of systematic organizational relationships. Rather, it comes from the temporary transference of personal influence of particular leaders." [32]

At the next level are the *state committees*, which reveal great variety in functions, in mode of selection, and even in title. All these committees are concerned with conducting state campaigns, but some of them also exercise control over general party activities in the state. Unlike the "higher" levels of the party structure, which are controlled only by the rules of the party, the organization of these committees is generally governed by state law. Weak or powerful, however, none of them is subordinate to the national committee.

County and *city committees* are organized around such subdivisions as townships, precincts, and wards. The chairmen of these committees often possess real power in local politics and, because of their influence over elections to national offices, they frequently make their power felt in national politics as well.

The Pattern of Power

This brief sketch of formal party organization suggests that American parties are little more than loose coalitions of state and local factions, brought together to conduct presidential campaigns and, if their party wins, to distribute public offices to loyal supporters. Except when the party's presidential candidate is seeking re-election, the national committee supports no "organization slate";

[31] *Party Committees and National Politics*, pp. 128, 150.
[32] *Ibid.*, p. 153.

nomination is controlled by unofficial and temporary alliances of state and local leaders, not by the national committee. Occasionally, some of these leaders refuse to support the party nominee, as did a number of southern Democrats in 1948 and a few in 1964. In 1964, Republican candidates in several states tried to disassociate themselves from the Goldwater candidacy, but most of them—like most southern Democrats—at least went through the formality of announcing general support for their party's ticket. Generally, the party achieves at least a surface unity during campaigns. But this unity is loose and voluntary rather than close and disciplined—the Democrats' decision in 1965 to deny seniority privileges to two representatives who had actively supported Barry Goldwater for President was the first such punitive action since 1925. Even in these cases, the representatives were not denied their status as Democrats.

Candidates for Congress are even more clearly the product of local rather than national machines. Under the Constitution, a member of the House of Representatives must be a resident of the state in which he is elected, but local machines have informally narrowed this requirement to residence in the *electoral district itself*. The national committee never boosts a promising party member by designating him as *the* party candidate for Congress, especially in a district where he does not reside. But if the Bell Telephone Company were to send a young executive from Des Moines to head its San Francisco office, no one would take offense; he would be judged—as the candidates of British political parties are—by his competence in promoting the aims of the national organization. Local biases in America are often extreme in politics, and a candidate for public office is expected to be a long-time resident of the electoral district and a product of the local party organization. Hence the route to political office—national, state, or local—is controlled by local party leaders.

The great furor over recent exceptions to this rule appears merely to demonstrate its basic validity.[33] In 1964, two prominent figures in the late President Kennedy's Administration sought election to the United States Senate in states where they had not lived for years—Pierre Salinger, former press secretary, in California and Robert Kennedy, the late President's brother and Attorney General, in New York. Although Salinger is a native Californian who had lived in the state most of his life, and although he was running as an incumbent (having been appointed in the summer of 1964 to the vacated seat under contest), he was defeated by a political newcomer and former tap-dancer, George Murphy. The outcome was attributed to the charge that he was a "carpetbagger." Robert Kennedy was subjected to the same charge (more accurately, since he had lived in New York only briefly as a child), but he won, defeating a widely respected Republican incumbent (Kenneth Keating). Both these candidacies were exceptional—they could hardly be imagined other than in the two largest and most heterogeneous states and the Kennedy victory rather than the Salinger defeat

---

[33] These exceptions could, of course, represent signs of an opposite trend. This is something to watch for in future elections.

appears truly exceptional. Kennedy received the Democratic nomination in New York without serious opposition—indeed, New York Democrats were in search of an attractive candidate to oppose Senator Keating—whereas Salinger had to defeat a leading California Democrat in a tough primary election to secure the nomination. More important, New York gave President Johnson such a tremendous majority (68 per cent) that almost any Democratic candidate could have been pulled in on his coattails. Californians gave Johnson 60 per cent of their votes, not quite enough to include Salinger in the victory. Kennedy trailed Johnson by 12 percentage points (over a million votes), whereas Salinger trailed by 11 percentage points (three-quarters of a million votes). That Salinger actually came a little closer than Kennedy to matching the Johnson vote suggests that the local route to office has not been replaced by the drawing power of a national personality and a beloved name.

To locate the real controlling power in a party, we must answer two questions: Who controls the nominations? Who controls the government when the party is in power? As we have already discovered, it is the local machines, alone or in combination, that control party nominations. Even presidential aspirants, who must ultimately win a national majority, depend initially on a coalition of state and local bosses for their nomination. No less a politician than Franklin D. Roosevelt needed the support of bosses like Mayor Frank ("I Am the Law") Hague of Jersey City and Mayor Edward J. Kelley of Chicago to win his nomination before he could appeal to the voters of the nation. The power of television, added to the decline of the old-style local boss, may modify this dependence. As of 1964, however, Senator Goldwater's careful cultivation of local Republican leaders over the preceding four years was counted as a major factor in his landslide nomination for the presidency.

A party's success in winning control of the government probably means less in the United States than in any other democracy. Since election to the presidency requires national support, the President and the chairman of the national committee stand for the views of the party as a national organization. But party members in Congress enjoy a considerable measure of independence from the national party. Since they are chosen by local organizations and depend on these same organizations for re-election, they show the parochial bias that we would expect. Local machines are more concerned with patronage and limited local projects than with national policies. Consequently, senators and representatives are largely free of any party control, either national or local, on the matters that are of greatest national importance. A variety of interest groups concerned with national policies, however, are only too happy to fill this vacuum.

While we think these statements on the distribution of party power are accurate as of the mid-1960's, we must recognize that we are living in a period of rapid political change. The state-local weighting of the American party system may be affected by changes in the direction of a more nationally oriented politics. In a brilliant essay on the anticipated effects of the Supreme Court's ruling that urban under-representation is subject to challenge as a violation of constitutional rights,[34] Martin Landau of Brooklyn College argues that "the historic function" of the decision will be "to close the gap" between state-local and national power in American political parties, "to weight the party system toward the urban-national side as against the state-local side."[35] In social and economic respects, modern means of production and communication have already reduced local peculiarities. Landau observes that, "It would be a curiosity indeed if the party system remained immune to the press of society." He submits that the function of federalism was to permit a nation to evolve despite the early insistence on states' rights; and the more we become an integrated nation, then, the less the need for federalism. Viewing our politics as an evolutionary political system, he concludes that the early demise of federalism will attest to its success in performing its function. Opponents of the Supreme Court's decision were equally convinced that it presaged the end of federalism. Representative Leslie C. Arends (R.-Illinois) said, "The Court's decision is tantamount to an abandonment of the principle of a republic of federated states."[36] Representative Arends views federalism as an end desirable in itself, whereas Professor Landau views it simply as an instrument of social change. The fact that both expect recent court decisions to transform American political parties suggests that we should watch for signs of an increasing urban-national orientation.

Party Personnel: "Members" and Leaders

The brilliant French student of political parties, Maurice Duverger, notes that the expression "party member" has different meanings in different parties and countries, and he adds in fascination, "For American parties, it even has no meaning at all. . . ."[37] What he has in mind is the lack of members in the sense that Boy Scout troops, for example, or Rotary Clubs, or college fraternities, or mass political parties in Europe may be said to have members. "Republicans" and "Democrats" undergo no official initiation (except, in some states, when they indicate their party affiliation in registering to vote), need meet no standard of fitness for membership, and pay no dues. Nor are they required to show any obligation to the party or to attend regular mass meetings. Duverger concludes, however, that there are three different degrees of participation in American parties, just as there are in parties with regular membership rolls: *electors* who vote for the party's candidates; *supporters* who go a step further by openly acknowledging their support, and who occasionally even contribute time or money to the party; and *militants* who direct the work of the party and organize its campaigns. ("Members," if we had them, would fit somewhere between supporters and militants.)

---

[34] *Baker* v. *Carr*, 369 U.S. 186 (1962). This and following cases on reapportionment are discussed in some detail in Chapter 9.

[35] "*Baker* v. *Carr* and the Ghost of Federalism," in Glendon Schubert (ed.), *Reapportionment* (New York: Charles Scribner's Sons, 1965), p. 247.

[36] *Congressional Quarterly Weekly Report*, XXII (week ending August 21, 1964), p. 1896. Representative Arends was referring to *Reynolds* v. *Sims*, 377 U.S. 533 (1964), which applied the principle of the earlier case to both houses of state legislatures.

[37] Duverger, *Political Parties*, p. 61.

It has been estimated that only about 3 to 5 per cent of the adult population in the United States are militants, or "political gladiators." [38] Lumped together as "political spectators," electors and supporters make up 60 to 65 per cent of the eligible voters. About one-third of the adult population falls completely outside Duverger's system of classification; these are the "political apathetics" who pay no attention whatsoever to politics—neither participating in nor observing the performance. For most Americans, clearly, politics is a spectator sport. If simply voting for a party makes them members of that party, then thousands of faithful fans in New York are members of the New York Mets baseball team.[39]

The passive attitude of most Americans toward party organizations is hardly surprising. Historically, the mass political parties of Europe, which actively try to organize the electorate, appeared only after extended suffrage had been achieved. Typical of these parties were the socialists, who sought both to educate the workers and to reform the existing order. In order to avoid becoming dependent on the "moneyed interests" that opposed reform, they were obliged to finance their campaigns by levying membership dues.

American workers, however, are not so class-conscious as their European counterparts, and America lacks an active socialist party. Could it be because we extended the suffrage *before* the full impact of industrialism was felt? Whatever the cause of our greater conservatism, Duverger convincingly concludes that "the archaic organization of American parties . . . seems the consequence of the essential conservatism of American politics, in the European sense of the term." [40]

The few militants who actually operate the local machines exercise the leadership of American political parties by default; indeed, for all practical purposes they *are* the political parties. What are these "political gladiators" like? What distinguishes them from the great mass of spectators who are interested enough to vote but who go no further in political participation, and from the apathetics who neither participate in politics nor observe the efforts of those who do?

In the first place, gladiators tend to occupy a higher socio-economic status than the population at large. Their larger incomes, higher-level occupations, better education, and greater exposure to group activity all serve to stimulate them to play a more active role in politics. This is particularly the case for people in *brokerage* occupations—people like lawyers, realtors, salesmen, and independent merchants, whose jobs require skills in mediating, bargaining, and negotiating with others.[41] Not only do they find these skills applicable to poli-

---

[38] Lester W. Milbrath, "Predispositions toward Political Contention," *Western Political Quarterly*, XIII (March, 1960), pp. 5–18.

[39] See Schattschneider, *Party Government*, p. 55, for a similar observation.

[40] Duverger, *Political Parties*, p. 23.

[41] The applicability of this interpretation to people in county-level public offices is demonstrated in Herbert Jacob, "Initial Recruitment of Elected Officials in the U. S.— A Model," *Journal of Politics*, XXIV (November, 1962), pp. 703–716.

tics but—unlike doctors, engineers, architects, or teachers—they also find political participation a professional asset rather than a liability.

But this is not the whole story by any means. On the basis of one of the few studies that have been made of personality and political participation in America, Lester Milbrath of Northwestern University suggests that certain personality traits are also important. Unless we take these traits into account, it is impossible to explain how one man can be so much more active in politics than a neighbor with the same background, education, occupation, income, and group contacts. This preliminary study offers several tentative generalizations about the personality dimensions of the political gladiator. He appears to be more sociable, more dominating, more confident and secure, more astute, more self-expressive, more optimistic, more self-accepting, and more responsible. As Milbrath puts it:

> . . . one gets the impression that political gladiators are persons who are particularly well equipped to deal with their environment. Most gladiators actually desire to enter the political arena and contend with their opponents. . . . Political gladiators must believe in themselves. This means they are self-accepting, confident, and optimistic; these qualities in turn, are based on their self-knowledge that they are astute, sociable, self-expressive and responsible—and these factors may find expression in a desire to dominate and manipulate other people. Most political gladiators, then, tend to have big expansive personalities which glory in political battle and are self-sufficient enough to withstand the rough-and-tumble of partisan politics.[42]

Bosses and Machines

Many observers roundly condemn American political parties for being oligarchical. But so few persons take an active part in politics that roles of leadership are amazingly easy to come by, and frequently are even uncontested. The ambitious young man with talent but without connections accordingly finds more opportunities to "make a name for himself" in politics than in private business. In grass-roots politics, the "quality" of one's connections may be less important than their quantity. Consequently, newly assimilated immigrant groups have often found politics rather than business the more open route to prestige. Each new wave of immigration has tended to be followed by a wave of political activity as soon as the new group has reached a high enough economic and social level to produce effective leaders. Until recently, the term "political boss" automatically evoked the picture of a jovial Irishman—Jim Curley of Boston, Frank Hague of Jersey City, Edward J. Kelley and Pat Nash of Chicago. Samuel Lubell, a widely read political commentator, reports that of late, however, "the plight of the Irish Democratic bosses . . . is not unlike that of the wearied rulers of the British Empire, who are everywhere on the defensive before the rising 'nationality' elements they once ruled." [43]

---

[42] *Western Political Quarterly*, XIII (March, 1960), p.17–18. Also, Jacob, "Why Men Seek Office," cited in footnote 41.

[43] Samuel Lubell, *The Future of American Politics* (New York: Harper & Brothers, 1951), p. 66.

Lubell once described Rhode Island as an illuminating case study of the rise of immigrant groups in politics. Early in 1935, the late Colonel Robert McCormick, the militantly conservative publisher of the *Chicago Tribune,* ordered one of the stars removed from the huge American flag that was displayed in the lobby of the *Tribune* building. This lordly act was to demonstrate his displeasure at Rhode Island's demonstration of unworthiness for statehood—the state had just ejected its old Yankee-Republican machine and had turned political control over to an Irish-Democratic machine. The Irish had won their success largely with the support of the Italo-Americans, who held a balance of power between the Yankee and Irish elements.

Following 1935, however, the Italo-Americans in Rhode Island "came of age," politically as well as economically and socially, and were no longer content with minor offices parceled out by the Irish. In 1946, John Pastore became the first Italo-American to be elected governor of any state and, four years later, the first United States senator of Italian origin. Pastore's rise appears to have been linked to the increase in numbers and in socio-economic status of Rhode Island's Italo-Americans. In 1907, when he was born, Italians made up only one-thirteenth of the state's population. But in 1938, the Rhode Island legislature declared Columbus Day a legal holiday, perhaps less in tribute to Columbus' discovery of America than to the discovery that every fifth voter in the state was Italo-American. With a rising middle class to provide leadership, and with money to accompany their growing voting power, the Italo-Americans in Rhode Island had arrived politically.[44]

The old-style political machine has itself been undergoing drastic change. In both national and, to a lesser degree, local campaigns, the mass media of communication have helped popular personalities to force themselves on the machine. However much they would prefer "one of their own," the machine bosses know that victory at the polling place is still their prime goal. Rising standards of living, the assimilation of immigrant groups, and the development of social welfare services under the New Deal have all militated against the continued dominance of local machines. The political boss can no longer win elections simply by distributing baskets of food on Christmas, acting as an informal employment agency, helping with citizenship papers, and talking about common ties with the "old country." A character in *The Last Hurrah,* a bestselling novel of 1956, pointed up these factors in explaining why an old party boss in Boston had finally been defeated:

> Well, of course, the old boss was strong simply because he held all the cards. If anybody wanted anything—job, favors, cash—he could only go to the boss, the local leader. What Roosevelt did was to take the handouts out of local hands. A few little things like Social Security, Unemployment Insurance, and the like— that's what shifted the gears, sport. No need now to depend on the boss for everything; the Federal Government was getting into the act. Otherwise known as a social revolution. So you can see what that would do in the long run. The

---

[44] *Ibid.,* pp. 67–75.

old-timers would still string along with the boss, of course, because that's the way they always did things. But what about the kids coming along? . . .

To begin with, they were one step farther away from the old country; he didn't have the old emotional appeal for them. You know, the racial-spokesman kind of thing. . . . And finally, most of them had never had the slightest contact with him because it wasn't necessary. When they got out of the army, for example, and needed a little spare cash to tide them over, what did they do? Did they go to the boss? Not on your life; they didn't have to. They joined the 52-20 Club and got twenty bucks a week for the next year, all supplied by good old remote, impersonal Washington. And when they went to work at last, and then got laid off for awhile, the same thing happened. No boss; Unemployment Insurance instead. It was a new era, sport. . . .[45]

If developments of this sort really serve to broaden and nationalize the political concerns of Americans, they are probably a wholesome influence. But if they mean simply that the organizational continuity and responsibility of the old party machine are to be replaced by the confusion of recurrent popularity contests, they may well create a new, less easily identifiable "machine" of professional public relations men and their employers. John Crosby, the television critic, has described this danger in the following comments on national party conventions:

The smoke-filled room is gone, possibly forever, to be replaced by the electronic living room full of 120,000,000 people. Naturally, no more cigars, no more open-necked shirts, avoid the bold patterns in [neckties] and watch those mannerisms. Well, the smoke-filled room was a deplorable political institution, but at least it was filled with human beings who smoked and chewed and spoke their minds.

There were some cussed individuals in them, but they were colorful. Now that the mass media experts have taken over, we can hardly expect horny-handed individuality. After they get the bold patterns out of the ties, the next step is to get the bold patterns out of the phrases and out of the ideas. The perfect candidate will look just like somebody out of a Chrysler ad—well-bred, well-shaved, and thoroughly antiseptic.[46]

The Doctrinal and Social Base of American Parties

The doctrines of a party reflect the needs of the groups and interests on which it tries to build electoral victories. Those who insist that parties are groups of men in agreement on basic principles are doomed to disillusionment by what must appear as unpardonable shifts in basic party policy. But it is precisely as organizations trying to win elections by fostering the aims of a coalition of interests, and not as groups dedicated to fixed principles, that American parties "make sense." After all, doctrines are created simply to serve human interests.

---

[45] Edwin O'Connor, *The Last Hurrah* (Boston: Little, Brown and Company, 1956), pp. 374–375.

[46] Excerpts from John Crosby's column, August 13, 1956, © 1956, New York Herald Tribune, Inc.

Shifts in party doctrines are the direct result of a very simple set of related factors: (1) voters try to maximize their own interests; (2) parties try to win elections; (3) to do this, parties must enlist the support of a broad coalition of interests; (4) to enlist such support, they must promote the aims of these interests; and (5) the needs of different interests undergo continuous change.[47]

We cannot undertake a history of party principles here. By comparing the present positions of our two great parties with the positions of their predecessors, however, we can suggest the extent to which changing economic and social conditions have led parties to modify their doctrines. The original party line-up in the United States found the Jeffersonian Republicans (later to become known as the Democratic Party) on one side, and the Federalists (the grandfathers of the present Republican Party) on the other. The Jeffersonians stood for the needs of an agrarian society, which they sought to foster by emphasizing the concepts of "least government" as the best government, states' rights, decentralization, *laissez-faire*, legislative rather than executive power, and economy in government. The Federalists, on the other hand, held the vision of an industrial, urban society, which they sought to foster by emphasizing the ideas of energetic government, nationalism, centralization, government intervention in the economy, executive rather than legislative power, and a managed public debt.

Notice that the two present-day parties have neatly changed positions on every one of these issues. Does this mean that they have abandoned their principles, that the Democrats have rejected Jeffersonian values for Hamiltonian values, while the Republicans were executing the reverse maneuver? We need reach that conclusion only if we confuse technique with goal, instrumental values with root values. Jefferson was imbued with faith in the masses, and, in a predominantly rural society in which the government was the only agency powerful enough to threaten popular freedoms, he was naturally suspicious of government power in almost any form. Hamilton was more impressed with the superiority of the "rich, well-born, and able," and was equally anxious to create a strong government that would reflect that superiority and would control the "unthinking majority." Now the Jeffersonian view has triumphed to such an extent that no politician would reject majority rule as such. But the Democratic Party is still more concerned with the needs of the "underprivileged," and the Republican Party, like the Federalists, is more attuned to the preser-

---

[47] Anthony Downs develops an intriguing model of party government on the basis of three fundamental assumptions: that both voters and parties behave rationally at all times, that parties are guided only by the desire to win and keep office, and that every voter tries to promote his own self-interest with the ballot. See his *An Economic Theory of Democracy* (New York: Harper & Brothers, 1957). In analyzing the actual party system of the United States, we cannot assume perfect rationality, nor can we rely on other assumptions of his model, such as that the winning party after every election takes complete control of the entire government. Nevertheless, his analysis has been most helpful to us; the analytically minded student will find it fascinating.

vation of greater rewards for the "deserving." The development of an industrialized and urbanized society has simply changed the policies that seem most appropriate for gaining these respective ends.

It was in the 1820's and 1830's, when Jacksonian Democracy promoted a great extension of the suffrage and established the President as the chief spokesman for popular majorities, that the first great shift in party doctrines occurred. The Whigs (unlike the Federalists who preceded them) rejected the idea of a strong executive and supported instead a strong legislature, in which minority interests would have more opportunity to block the majority; and the Democrats began to prefer strong executive power to strong congressional power. The rapid industrialization that took place after the Civil War concentrated private power in the hands of corporations strong enough to appear as a threat to majority interests. The Democratic Party tended to look on this concentration of private power as the chief danger to popular needs, and on the government as a means of coping with this danger rather than as a "necessary evil." Republicans, on the other hand, adopted the old Jeffersonian fear of government when, late in the nineteenth century, government began turning to such "socialistic" schemes as income taxes and business regulation.

The Great Depression that fell on the country in 1929 revealed these new orientations in a naked light. Increasing numbers of voters seemed to feel that the only way to achieve the goals of Jefferson was to adopt the techniques of Hamilton. "So the Democrats stole the Republicans' clothes, and this is always most embarrassing to the party which has gone bathing." [48] The extent of this switch in party doctrines is suggested by the roll-call votes recorded in Congress during Eisenhower's first term. Although Eisenhower himself favored such "New Deal" measures as expanded social security and higher minimum wage levels, a majority of the Republicans in Congress voted to curb executive power, to restrict government intervention in the economy, and to prevent extensions of social welfare programs. Specifically, they favored restrictions on the President's authority to reduce tariffs and supported proposals to decrease executive power in foreign relations. Similarly, they opposed government development of power projects and federal action to combat unemployment in chronically depressed communities. And they also opposed extensions of government aid in such areas as housing, education, health, and social security.[49] A majority of Democrats voted for each of these measures while a majority of Republicans voted against them.

In 1964, when the President urging positive governmental measures was a Democrat rather than a Republican, the contrast between the parties in Congress was even more clear-cut.[50] The basic differences in party doctrine still

---

[48] Roland N. Stromberg, *Republicanism Reappraised* (Washington, D.C.: Public Affairs Press, 1952), p. 13.

[49] These statements are based on roll-call votes in one or both houses of Congress.

[50] See *Congressional Quarterly Weekly Report*, XXII (week ending October 30, 1964), pp. 2593–2597.

seem to exist, then; to understand these differences, we must turn to the continuing social base of the parties.

A few years ago, when a majority of the Republicans in Congress opposed, and a majority of the Democrats supported, a move to replace a tax cut on income from stock dividends with a $100 increase in the personal tax exemption, each party was assuming its "natural" position.[51] Good arguments could be advanced on both sides: a tax cut for the small minority of the people who own corporate stock would make more money available for the investments that spur general progress; an increase in the personal tax exemption would primarily benefit those with low income, and would increase the mass purchasing power that is also essential to general prosperity. The former approach automatically made more sense to the Republicans, and the latter approach automatically made more sense to the Democrats. Why? Because the parties are identified with different social groups in the population.

The persistence with which the Democrats have looked first to the needs of those who have lower socio-economic status, and the Republicans to the needs of those who enjoy higher status, is illustrated by Wilfred Binkley's comment on the Democratic-Whig division in the nineteenth century:

> Jacksonian Democracy originated as the personal following of one who symbolized the idea of justice for the masses. He was represented as a champion of the under-dog and the Democratic Party has always relied for its voting strength primarily upon the counties with poorer soils and the crowded wards of the great cities largely populated with recent immigrant stock. . . .
>
> To the well-to-do, however, Jackson was a demagogue, a preacher of social discontent, and the prosperous became the backbone of the opposition to Jackson. The dominant elements of the Whig party consisted of the great financial, commercial, and emerging industrial interests of the East, the more prosperous agrarians of the North and the great slaveholding planters of the South.[52]

Save for the inclusion of great slaveholding planters, this statement aptly describes the bases of strength on which Democrats and Republicans rely to this day. And the heavy vote for Goldwater in the old slaveholding counties of the South in 1964 suggests that even this element might be restored to its position in the opposing coalitions of the 1830's. While the programs needed by the contending political groups in America have changed radically, each group is fairly consistent in the party it looks to for the realization of its needs.

The success with which each party has mobilized its own supporters and enticed those of the opposition into its camp has varied enough to produce

---

[51] The vote in the House was 10 Republicans for and 201 against the substitute, with 193 Democrats for and 9 against. The Senate vote on a similar measure was 2 Republicans for and 45 against, 43 Democrats for and 4 against. See *Congressional Quarterly Weekly Report*, XIV (week ending October 5, 1956), p. 1189.

[52] *President and Congress* (New York: Alfred A. Knopf, 1947), pp. 86–87.

three distinct eras of party dominance. The period from 1800 to 1860 was a time of Democratic supremacy. As the suffrage was gradually extended, the opposition was able to erase the stigma of its original distaste for democracy only twice, and then only by establishing a new party (the Whigs) and by nominating two war heroes for President—William Henry Harrison (1840) and Zachary Taylor (1848).

The Republicans enjoyed the longest period of supremacy, from 1860 to 1932. With sectional conflict over slavery disrupting the established competition between parties, the Republicans attained their first success by capturing the mass appeal the Democrats had long enjoyed. Despite its radical origins, the Republican Party emerged from the Civil War with a more "right-wing" character. "The Republican party that Grant brought out of the Civil War period was not the same Republican party that Lincoln had taken in," reports Ivan Hinderaker, a specialist on political parties.[53] "Lincoln's party had been a farmer-worker party with Declaration of Independence overtones. Grant's party from 1868 was farmer-capitalist in nature with a declaration of independence to give the capitalist a free hand in the exploitation of America's natural resources." While the Republicans were appealing to business, they also campaigned for the labor vote with the promise of a "full dinner pail." Even the "silver-tongued" promises of William Jennings Bryan, three-time candidate of the Democratic Party, were unable to win the eastern labor vote. During this period of great industrial progress, the Democrats were able to defeat the Republicans only under the leadership of Grover Cleveland and Woodrow Wilson.

The third great period of dominance returned the Democrats to power in 1932. With the severe depression that began in 1929 suddenly making the business community unpopular, the Democrats took advantage of the opportunity to label the Republicans as the party of "big business." Long-run influences that had already been working in the Democrats' favor reinforced the "no confidence" vote against the Republicans in 1932. The increased voting strength of immigrants and their children, the high birthrate of lower income groups, the shift of people from farms to cities, the increasing political awareness of ethnic minorities—all of these gave more votes to Democrats than to Republicans. Al Smith, the Democratic presidential nominee in 1928—an effective Governor of New York but, more important, a Catholic with an "East Side" New York City accent and occasional grammatical difficulties—created for many an image of the Democrats as the party of the underprivileged. The depression gave the Democrats a perfect opportunity to capitalize on this image just when it had the most appeal. Vestiges of their success can still be seen in the 1960's; many voters continue to view the Republicans as sympathizing with "big business" and the Democrats as favoring the "little man."

Eisenhower's victories in 1952 and 1956 represented a temporary "house-cleaning" in the midst of a Democratic period rather than the inauguration of

---

[53] *Party Politics* (New York: Henry Holt and Company, 1956), p. 312.

a new era of Republican control. It took a Civil War to shatter the original Democratic hold on the country, and a cataclysmic depression to terminate the Republican era. The lack of any such major upheaval in contemporary America, and the inability of the Republican Party to win control of Congress even when Eisenhower scored his second presidential victory, indicated that the Democratic tide was still running. As the representative of the majority party, John Kennedy managed to win the presidency in 1960 despite a formidable opponent and a massive resurgence of anti-Catholicism. In 1964, for the first time since 1936, short-run election forces favored the Democrats; President

"It's probably some kind of Democratic trick."

Drawing by Stevenson; © 1960
The New Yorker Magazine, Inc.

Johnson won with the greatest percentage of the popular vote in American history. In the absence of another upheaval comparable to the Civil War or the depression of 1929, the present Democratic era can be expected to continue.

Party Support Today

The two major parties still depend on electoral bases that are remarkably similar to those of the early nineteenth century. You can demonstrate this for yourself by applying the discussion on political opinions in Chapter 5 to the Republican and Democratic parties, with the Republicans as the party of the "right" and the Democrats as the party of the "left." As Duverger points out, both American parties are essentially conservative when compared with their European counterparts—our "left-wing" Democratic Party is more conservative than Britain's Conservative Party! Within the cultural context of American politics, however, the Democrats win more "leftist" support and the Republicans win more "rightist" support. In the extremely close presidential election in 1960, 55 per cent of those identified with the working class reported voting for Kennedy, in contrast to only 36 per cent of those identified with the middle class.[54] Each party tends to be relatively stronger in the major population groups indicated in Table 6-1.

TABLE 6-1   *Relative Strength of Parties in Major Population Groups* [a]

POPULATION GROUPING	DEMOCRATIC	REPUBLICAN
Sex	Men	Women
Age	Younger voters	Older voters
Religion	Catholics, Jews	Protestants
Race	Negro	White
Type of Community	Metropolitan centers	Suburban and rural areas
Education	Non-college	College
Occupation of Family Head	Unemployed, skilled and unskilled labor	Professional, business or managerial, sales
Labor Affiliation	Union	Non-union
Income	Low	High

[a] These findings may be found in almost any voting-behavior study. For a good summary, see Angus Campbell and Homer C. Cooper, *Group Differences in Attitudes and Votes* (Institute for Social Research: University of Michigan, 1956). For an analysis, see Campbell *et al., The American Voter.*

Notice that the groups are sources of *relatively* greater strength for the parties. In any given election, the Republicans might gain majority support among younger voters, for example, but they will still tend to win *a larger proportion* of the older votes. Notice, too, that none of the sources of strength represent *solid* voting blocs; with regional variations added to individual peculiarities, and with both parties using broad appeals, no social interest in the

[54] From a special tabulation furnished by the Survey Research Center of the University of Michigan.

United States can be perfectly mobilized behind either party. Unusual issues or personalities may, as they did in both Eisenhower victories, deflect substantial numbers from their normal voting habits. Finally, these general characteristics should not be regarded as the basic *determinants* of the voter's allegiance. The fact that a larger proportion of women than of men vote Republican, for example, appears to be a function of class rather than of sex differences: the general tendency of women to vote less than men is more pronounced in lower than in higher socio-economic levels; within the same class, however, the sex difference in party preference disappears.

Current trends could modify the traditional bases of party support. The increasing population shift to the suburbs, along with the tendency of the suburban vote to go heavily Republican, was spotted as one such trend during the Eisenhower era.[55] But recent analyses indicate that Republican strength increased no more in the suburbs than it did in other areas,[56] and the general decrease in Republican support in 1964 characterized the suburbs no less than other areas. The Republican environment of the suburbs accordingly seems not to affect newly arrived Democrats as much as it was once assumed to. Perhaps the children of these new residents, by virtue of their predominantly Republican environment outside the home, will be susceptible to Republican appeals. By their nature, however, gradual changes are difficult to see. Most disruptive of all to the traditional bases of party support would be a new tendency that was discernible even before Eisenhower's victories—a tendency of American voters to emphasize such personal attributes as "sincerity" to the neglect of party and of issues.[57] Although any party or policy is geared to the needs of some groups more than to those of others, personality appeals might operate in a more individualistic and unpredictable fashion. As of today, however, party identification and social class remain the most persistent factors in American voting.

Criticisms of Political Parties

Popular Complaints

The popular image of politicians and political parties is far from flattering. For those who regard politics as inherently evil, political parties are veritable cesspools of iniquity. This notion has undemocratic origins that are seldom recognized by those who hold it. At their inception, popularly based political parties were naturally opposed by those who resisted democracy and distrusted

---

[55] Louis Harris, *Is There a Republican Majority?* (New York: Harper & Brothers, 1954), pp. 123–125.

[56] Bernard Lazerwitz, "Suburban Voting Trends: 1948 to 1956," *Social Forces*, XXXIX (October, 1960), pp. 29–36; Jerome G. Manis and Leo C. Stine, "Surburban Residence and Political Behavior," *Public Opinion Quarterly*, XXII (Winter, 1958–59), pp. 483–489.

[57] David Riesman, *The Lonely Crowd: A Study of the Changing American Character* (New Haven: Yale University Press, 1950).

the masses. Since parties promise to achieve popular control, Americans who still fear "majority tyranny" are logically anti-party. But this bias is a strange one to be entertained by the majority itself, for whom parties provide a voice in public affairs.

A familiar variation on this theme is that, although parties themselves are not inherently evil, the "wrong kind of men" always seem to take over politics and turn parties into something unsavory. To test the validity of this complaint we need only refer to the studies by Milbrath and Jacob.[58] Actual investigation of the kind of people who are active in politics supports the view that they are superior in talent to the population at large. And when we compare their moral standards with those of business, labor unions, and some professions—where nepotism, lavish expense accounts, luxurious gifts from clients or customers, and vacation trips are all taken for granted—leaders of political parties come off very well indeed. True, we should apply high standards to political behavior, but we should also make realistic appraisals. After all, politicians are a product of the same society in which all the rest of us live.

A more substantial complaint is that political parties are undemocratic in their organization. Certainly the mass of Republican and Democratic voters do not maintain an active and continuing control over their parties' procedures, nominations, and policies. Democracy is rooted in the responsibility of the ruling few to the many, however, not in the actual conduct of party activities by the entire membership. Since party membership is such a vague allegiance in the United States, it is not easy to judge the extent of membership control. But the active members of political parties probably exercise as much control as union members, corporate stockholders, church members, or fraternity brothers do over their respective organizations.

We may also observe that internal democracy in political parties is not essential to popular control of the government. What *is* essential is competition *between* parties, which insures that elections cannot be won without popular candidates and policies. Even if the parties were internally autocratic, the desire to win elections would still force them to offer attractive candidates. We assume that our economic system will best serve the needs of the public if competition exists between different firms, regardless of whether the internal policies of the firms are democratic or autocratic. Surely the same assumption can be made in politics. Moreover, in politics we are more certain that competition actually exists, the public plays a greater role in the choice of the "product" to be offered, no one is allowed multiple votes, and virtually all interested adults are guaranteed an equal vote. Sigmund Neumann, a student of party systems, reminds us that in a democracy "it is the competitive scheme, the choice between at least two oligarchies, which guarantees the quality of its leadership." [59]

---

[58] See footnotes 41 and 42.
[59] *Modern Political Parties*, p. 397.

The Basic Criticism: Irresponsibility

The most valid basis for evaluating the performance of any organization is in terms of how well it performs its primary function. At the beginning of this chapter, we suggested that the central functions of political parties for a democracy are the public choice of leaders and the open and organized expression of public interests. Since these functions mark the difference between democracies and dictatorships, they offer a basis for evaluating the performance of our parties —at least for those who agree that democracy is desirable.

The popular complaints mentioned above are encouraged by those who fear that parties may do their job *too* well, and who want to foster a general anti-party attitude. A criticism based on the failure of parties to function as the essential mechanism of popular control would be more basic and meaningful. The most enduring charge of this kind is that the parties are guilty of irresponsibility. To political scientists, "Party responsibility means the responsibility of both parties to the general public, as enforced in elections." [60] In light of this simple criterion, the Committee on Political Parties of the American Political Science Association has concluded, "An effective party system requires, first, that the parties are able to bring forth programs to which they commit themselves, and, second, that the parties possess sufficient internal cohesion to carry out these programs." [61]

The great weakness of American parties lies in their failure to meet this second requirement—that is, to achieve the requisite cohesion in Congress. Although there is more straight party voting in Congress than is often recognized, party disunity is still common enough for the majority party to be uncertain about carrying through its policies. Both parties usually attain an admirable measure of cohesion during campaigns, with the rejected aspirants manfully joining in to support the party nominees. When the parties succeed in winning a majority of seats in Congress and have only to vote together in order to carry out their platform pledges, however, this unity tends to evaporate. Since state and local organizations control nominations and elections, the party as a national organization is in a poor position to demand cooperation. Consequently, congressmen often respond to the local or special-interest groups that influence the success of their efforts to be re-elected.

This failure of the parties to achieve the post-election unity they need to carry out their programs makes the general public more receptive to criticism directed against political parties. But there is a contradiction here: many voters seem to respond to criticisms of "party hacks" and to praise of "independent

---

[60] Report of the Committee on Political Parties of the American Political Science Association, *Toward a More Responsible Two-Party System* (New York: Rinehart & Company, Inc., 1950), p. 22; also see *American Political Science Review*, XLIV, Part 2 (September, 1950).

[61] *Ibid.*, pp. 17–18 (emphasis omitted).

statesmen." They condemn the congressman who is consistently loyal to his party—and thereby helps to make the election process meaningful as an instrument of popular control—and praise his colleague who responds to local or other minority pressures for his "independence." But is the real choice between statesmen and party ciphers? Or is it between control of Congress by shifting coalitions of unidentifiable minority interests and control by political parties responsible to a broader public opinion? If the party organization leaves a power vacuum, it will eagerly be filled by groups that have not been endorsed by popular election.

Some observers insist that more effective party government would decrease the freedom of the elected official to vote as he pleases—or as his conscience dictates. But even if we assume that a congressman could stand completely free of pressure from any source, this idea represents a peculiar view of the purpose of elections. Elections are held not to give a few people a chance to win popularity contests but to give the citizens a chance to influence government policy. Advocates of strong parties carry this argument a step further. If we accept the basic importance of the voter, they say our preference must be for internal party discipline. Even a nation of Einsteins could not manage to hold 535 men responsible as individuals for the enactment of legislation, but ordinary citizens *could* enforce responsibility on parties that operated as unified organizations.

Another variation on the anti-party theme is that the officeholder should respond to the views of his local constituency rather than to those of the party's national majority. Although this argument is appealing, it does not fit the facts of political life. In order for fragmented responsibility of this sort to operate, the average citizen would have to follow the performance of each individual officeholder from his district. The fact is, however, that local newspapers and radio and television stations all tend to present syndicated, nationally oriented news of party stands in Congress. It is not easy for the average voter to follow the detailed performance of his own representative and senators, even if he is interested enough to try. But he *could* get a good idea of the over-all record of his party if it operated as a cohesive, disciplined organization. Responsibility to the majority of voters cannot be effective when it is fragmented; fragmented responsibility, however, does offer advantages to pressure groups.

Ultimately, of course, one's position on this question depends on his personal values. The bias of the present party system is against rapid policy changes, whereas the bias of disciplined parties would be in favor of quicker response to public demands for new policies. Hence, most political scientists who recommend more disciplined political parties do so as a way to get reformist policies. (Those who oppose the recommendation may be equally reformist, but they regard proposals for party discipline as an unrealistic or ineffective way to get reformist policy and as conflicting with other, more important values.) The report of the Committee on Political Parties, however, is a carefully developed argument directed toward the implicit goal of reformist, majoritarian policies. Researchers have found that a large majority of political scientists are liberal or reformist in their values.[62] The endorsement of strong party government by an official Committee of the American Political Science Association thus represents an attempt to promote the values of a majority of the Association. While the values being promoted cannot be validated or invalidated by the techniques of political science, the report of the Committee can be read as a series of *prescriptive* statements: "*If* you agree on value X, then you ought to pursue course A." In this case, X equals policies responsive to the (presumably liberal) wishes of the current majority, and A equals measures designed to promote strong party government.

The Improbability of Reform

Many political scientists do not agree with the Committee on Political Parties that more "responsible party government" is desirable. Some reject X as a goal, regarding policies closely geared to the changing wishes of the majority as undesirable. Roland Pennock, a thoughtful political theorist, argues that "responsibility" in government has two meanings. In addition to answerability to the public, responsibility also means maturity of judgment, and rational actions supported by careful investigation and deliberation.[63] More of the first kind of responsibility would, Pennock thinks, mean less of the second kind—and would substitute responsiveness to momentary whims for responsiveness to settled opinions. Ernest S. Griffith, a student of Congress, strongly disapproves of the policies and techniques he associates with disciplined party government as practiced in Britain:

> A bureaucracy . . . increasing by leaps and bounds; the two parties outbidding each other with promises of governmental largesse, so as to attract marginal groups; a division of the nation along class lines; the sacrifice of independence of thought and action on the part of the individual member; the pressing home of such a drastic measure as the nationalization of steel, though a majority of the voters supported candidates opposed to it at the last election.[64]

Most dissenters from the Committee's report do not join Griffith in rejecting the goal of policies closely geared to public opinion or, for that matter, the implicit preference for more liberal policies. But they do charge the Committee with ignoring the nature of political realities in America and with overlooking the heavy price that would have to be paid for cohesive and disciplined parties. The probable price of centralized and disciplined parties, as seen by the defenders of the present system, would include: (1) the breakdown of federalism,

---

[62] Paul F. Lazarsfeld and Wagner Thielens, Jr., *The Academic Mind* (Glencoe, Illinois: The Free Press, 1958); Seymour M. Lipset, *Political Man* (Garden City, New York: Doubleday & Company, Inc., 1960), Chapter X; Henry A. Turner, "The Party Affiliations of American Political Scientists," a paper delivered at the annual meeting of the American Political Science Association, September 8, 1960.

[63] J. Roland Pennock, "Responsiveness, Responsibility, and Majority Rule," *American Political Science Review*, XLVI (September, 1952), pp. 790–807.

[64] *Congress: Its Contemporary Role* (New York: New York University Press, 1951), pp. 156–157.

(2) the deterioration of compromise among opposed groups, and (3) the development of a multi-party system.[65] The dissenters support their position with as much force as does the Committee majority. First, they argue that unitary and centralized parties are ill-suited to a heterogeneous and complex country like the United States. The great variety of interests in such a sprawling country, this argument holds, could not be accommodated in parties more cohesive than we have today. And even if such an arrangement could fit the informal power structure, the federal system of government makes it politically unattainable. Pendleton Herring, supporting the second argument, points out that the very generality and ambiguity of party platforms is what makes for peaceable compromise in this country. "The accomplishment of party government lies in its demonstrated ability for reducing warring interests and conflicting classes to co-operative terms." [66] Third, Austin Ranney maintains that unity in American parties would destroy the very two-party system the Committee on Political Parties wanted to strengthen:

> It has often been remarked that the congeries of bipartisan and intraparty "blocs" in Congress is, in effect, a multiple-party system masquerading under the labels and formalities of a two-party system. To the extent that this is an accurate description of our present national party system, it results, not from any mere organizational deficiency in our national party machinery, but rather from the diversity and multiplicity of our interest groups and the heterogeneity and complexity of the political conflict they express. So long as the basic nature of the American community remains the same, therefore, centralizing and disciplining our national parties would very likely result in a multiple-party rather than a two-party system.[67]

Despite these arguments, there are a number of ways in which party responsibility could be increased in the United States. The Committee on Political Parties recommends: the tightening of national party organization to reflect actual party support in the areas represented; the coordination of state and local party organizations by the national organization, including the "excommunication" of conspicuously disloyal groups; the release of authoritative interpretations of the platform by the national organization; the tightening of party organization in Congress by having the party caucus make binding decisions on party policy, and by selecting committee chairmen on the basis of party loyalty and service rather than on the basis of seniority. Rewards to cooperating members—in the form of campaign help and favorable committee assignments in Congress—would be stressed rather than punishment. But the Committee also advocated that discipline be applied where necessary: "It is possible to refuse to seat delegates to

---

[65] For a good summary of these arguments, see Austin Ranney and Willmoore Kendall, *Democracy and the American Party System* (New York: Harcourt, Brace and Company, 1956), pp. 527–533. Also see Ranney's *The Doctrine of Responsible Party Government* (Urbana: University of Illinois Press, 1954).

[66] *The Politics of Democracy: American Parties in Action* (New York: Rinehart & Company, Inc., 1940), p. 132.

[67] *Democracy and the American Party System*, p. 531.

the National Convention; to drop from the National Committee members representing the dissident state organization; to deny legislative committee assignments to members of Congress sponsored by the disloyal organization; and to appeal directly to the party membership in the state or locality, perhaps even promoting a rival organization. The power to take strong measures is there." [68]

The power to take these strong measures may be there, but the will to do so is not. American politics is so localized that early prospects for responsible party government seem poor indeed; the very men whom many political scientists exhort to centralize our parties are themselves products of loose alliances of local groups. If either party began to act with real unity in Congress, the voters might be so impressed that they would force the opposition to follow suit. But the centers of power in both parties appear satisfied with the present decentralized structure. The expectation of voluntary reform of the party system by congressmen ignores a fundamental law of politics: those who enjoy a form of power do not advocate reform of the system that gives them their power.

Perhaps such factors as our federal system, the separate election of President and Congress, the great variety of problems and viewpoints in the United States, and the interests that promote political localism will always forestall the unity required for responsible party government. But these factors themselves are not necessarily immutable. If recent court decisions guaranteeing urban residents an equal voice in state legislatures and in the House of Representatives effect a basic change in the balance of the federal system, other parts of the system will be modified, too.

-----

[68] Report of the Committee on Political Parties, *Toward a More Responsible Two-Party System*, p. 23.

CHAPTER SEVEN

Pressure Groups and Public Relations

We have iden-

tified a political party as a group of people who try to win

control of the government by mobilizing votes. But a good

many other organizations are also directly concerned with

political power and with mobilizing votes. In the United States,

the National Association of Manufacturers, the American Federation of Labor-Congress of Industrial Organizations, the National Education Association, the Chamber of Commerce, the American Medical Association, the American Farm Bureau Federation, and literally thousands of other groups play political roles which, at least collectively, may have a more important influence on the determination of public policy than do the political parties themselves. In 1948, for example, the platform of the Democratic Party called for compulsory health insurance, a policy that the American Medical Association (A.M.A.) denounced as "socialized medicine." The Democrats won the election, but the policy was not adopted. Clearly, public policy in this area is not determined exclusively by political parties. Organized minorities have discovered routes to power that are far more direct than submitting their policies and candidates to the electorate for approval.

The Role of Pressure Groups in Politics

Minority interests may influence policy without running their own candidates for office, but this makes it very difficult for them to frustrate the realization of long-standing majority preferences. Before World War II, for example, the A.M.A. opposed voluntary health plans like the Blue Shield and Blue Cross as un-American examples of "socialized medicine." When proposals for government-supported health care began to attract support, however, the A.M.A. embraced the voluntary plans as "the American Way" and applied the un-American label to government programs patterned on the social security system. Nevertheless, a majority of Americans have long expressed a preference for government aid for medical care, and the overwhelming victory of President Johnson in 1964 finally presaged congressional action in this area, at least for "senior citizens." The intense opposition of the A.M.A. thus delayed the program for about seventeen years. Even in apparent defeat, the A.M.A.'s opposition restricted the proposed program to the aged portion of the population.

No less important than the ability of the A.M.A. and allied groups, such as private insurance companies, to delay passage of a medicare program is the fact that some sort of program was passed over their opposition. The majority who favor government aid for medical care have been, after all, most casual in their support. Public opinion surveys have turned up sizeable majorities favoring such aid, but a "yes" response to a question of this sort implies little in the way of an active commitment. With the passive and permissive consensus of the general public intensely opposed by a well-organized minority, perhaps the remarkable thing is that any kind of medicare could be achieved. Interested minorities play important roles in American politics, then, but they cannot permanently call the tune.

The Nature and Functions of Pressure Groups

Pressure groups have much in common with political parties and even with official decision-making agencies such as the United States Congress. All fall within the general meaning of "political interest group" if we accept David Truman's definition of that concept as "a shared-attitude group that makes certain claims upon other groups in the society" by acting "through or upon any of the institutions of government. . . ." [1] Decision-making agencies like the House of Representatives or the Supreme Court are clearly distinguished from political parties and pressure groups by their official status, despite the fact that they too make claims on other groups by acting through or on government institutions. Political parties and pressure groups are both unofficial agencies but they differ on other grounds. The current practice of regarding "political interest group" simply as a more neutral way of saying "pressure group" is therefore highly misleading. The former concept includes the latter and a lot more too—such as political parties. For example, a political interest group involves "shared attitudes toward what is needed or wanted in a given situation." This is as true for the Democrats as it is for the A.M.A. The Democrats want to win elections, and the A.M.A. wants to block government health insurance. The members within each group share attitudes on what is needed. Moreover, a political interest group "makes certain claims upon other groups in the society." Thus the Democrats demand the loyalty of voters, and the A.M.A. claims support from pharmacists, patients, and physicians.

We may regard both the political party and the pressure group as political interests groups, but we must also recognize that they differ enough to require distinct labels. We have already discovered that the *purpose* of the pressure group is to achieve influence over specific policies, rather than to achieve control over the government as a whole. Another difference is in the *method* of acquiring power. The political party concentrates on winning elections, but the pressure group never submits its own candidates to the voters. It may be vitally concerned with every stage of the election process, but it does not campaign under its own banner, and it is just as interested in other means of influencing policy as it is in elections themselves.

We can define a pressure group, then, as an organized attempt to influence government policy decisions without officially entering election contests. Despite the unfavorable connotations that have grown up around the term "pressure group," we shall use it in referring to this unofficial kind of non-party political interest group.[2]

Pressure groups are based firmly on the constitutionally guaranteed freedoms of assembly and petition. Consequently, they are no less characteristic of democracy than political parties are. Freedom of speech and freedom of the press

---

[1] David B. Truman, *The Governmental Process: Political Interests and Public Opinion* (New York: Alfred A. Knopf, 1951), p. 37. Although he offers this broadly inclusive concept of political interest groups, Truman then uses it in reference only to what we call pressure groups. See, for example, his chapter on "Interest Groups and Political Parties," which suggests that political parties are not political interest groups.

[2] In a brief and penetrating analysis of pressure groups in American politics, Harmon Zeigler bows to the popularity of the term "interest groups" in his title: *Interest Groups in American Society* (Englewood Cliffs, New Jersey: Prentice-Hall, Inc., 1964). Nevertheless, his definition of pressure groups (p. 30) is virtually identical to that above.

would mean little if various interests could not translate them into organized attempts to gain recognition. And the basic function of pressure groups is just that: to give political expression to the values or interests of minority groups. Just as political parties strive to mobilize a majority of the voters, pressure groups serve to give special representation to minorities. For the political system as a whole, then, they play an indispensable part in identifying the various interests in society. Additional functions of pressure groups include stimulating interest and participation in politics and, through demands on candidates, clarifying issues during election campaigns.[3] Groups of this sort are an integral part of politics in every democracy, and even the staunchest advocate of responsible party government would not suggest that they be crushed. He would simply suggest that pressure groups should not be stronger than political parties.

Politics As a Struggle Among Groups

We opened our discussion of political parties with a recurrent theme of this book: politics is a process of interaction among groups. This point deserves emphasis, because so many of us retain eighteenth-century illusions about the nature of political power. We focus on the individual and neglect his group identifications; we tend to praise the "independent" voter and the "independent" congressman as ideal types in the exercise of political power. But in doing so we ignore the hard fact that power—the motivating force in politics—springs from organization. "In a great part of our political life the average citizen is an innocent bystander and also a bewildered one. He feels that his vote is futile, but he seldom grasps the fact that the Congress, like the state legislatures, never has functioned as a truly representative body, but only as a means of registering organized pressures. It does, in that way, represent all the forms of *organized power* in the nation. . . ." [4]

This statement appears a bit extreme, since unorganized and even latent public opinions set limits within which the power struggle tends to be confined. As we saw in Chapter 5, a basic function of political opinions is to support those policies that were so often described in the 1964 campaign as the mainstream of American politics. The boundaries of the mainstream are not precise, however, and unorganized opinions seldom have a positive influence on the direction of policy. Even if the "independent" legislator or President felt that he really owed his office to the "independent" vote, he would hardly know how to serve it, "for it is truly both dumb and divided, while the organized forces that press upon him . . . are both unified and highly articulate." [5] Here is another way of putting the point: "Organization represents concentrated power, and concentrated power can exercise a dominating influence when it encounters power which is diffuse and not concentrated, and therefore weaker." [6]

---

[3] *Ibid.*, p. 39.

[4] Harvey Fergusson, *People and Power: A Study of Political Behavior in America* (New York: William Morrow & Company, 1947), pp. 109–110 (emphasis added).

[5] *Ibid.*, p. 114.

[6] Earl Latham, "The Group Basis of Politics: Notes for a Theory," *American Political Science Review*, XLVI (June, 1952), p. 387.

In speaking of the sources of group affiliations and activities, James Madison observed in his classic *Federalist* essay No. 10 that they are ". . . sown in the nature of man." Beyond their individual peculiarities, men are conditioned by their group loyalties, contacts, and needs. No two members of any pressure group have identical native characteristics or life experiences, but their identification with a common group means that they share certain interests or attitudes. Precisely what attitudes they share may vary almost infinitely. As Madison put it,

> . . . the most common and durable source of factions has been the various and unequal distribution of property. Those who hold and those who are without property have ever formed distinct interests in society. Those who are creditors, and those who are debtors, fall under a like discrimination. A landed interest, a manufacturing interest, a mercantile interest, a moneyed interest, with many lesser interests, grow up of necessity in civilized nations, and divide them into different classes, actuated by different sentiments and views.

Although many non-economic organizations, such as the American Civil Liberties Union and the League of Women Voters, play an active role in politics, economic differences are just as predominant in the activities of pressure groups now as they were in Madison's day. Indeed, the specialization that has been brought about by our industrial economy has created so many pressure groups that we can only guess at their total number. Even according to the most conservative estimates, the number of groups active at the national level of government alone would have to be counted in at least four figures.[7] Primitive societies in which there is little division of labor have few pressure groups. But complex industrial societies tend to produce them in ever-increasing numbers.

Madison expected that a large, sprawling republic would reduce the possibility that any interest group would constitute a majority, since widely scattered individuals are unlikely to discover that any "common motive" exists among them, and, even if they do, "it will be . . . difficult for all who feel it to discover their own strength, and to act in unison with each other." Modern communications have almost nullified this expectation. The mass-circulation newspaper, cheap mail service, radio, television, telephone, railways, automobiles, and airplanes have made it possible—almost unavoidable—for people from all parts of the country with "common motives" to establish contact, to discover their shared attitudes, to form new groups.

The banker in California has more in common with another banker in New England than he has with a fruit-picker in his own county. Moreover, organizations like the American Bankers' Association keep him constantly aware of these common interests and provide a power structure through which they can be continuously represented before all the agencies of government. The fruit-picker, with no pattern of interaction with other farm laborers, seldom discovers these "common motives" and consequently has little political influence. Understandably, the legislator who is presumably representing both the banker and the

---

[7] Truman, *The Governmental Process*, p. 59.

fruit-picker is more aware of the interests of the organized group. Only if the fruit-picker's interests happen to become part of some political interest group (either a pressure group or a political party, or both) will they carry any real weight in the policy-forming process. The more nearly the fruit-picker resembles the "independent" citizen, the more completely will he find himself isolated from power.

Since Tocqueville's time, America has been described as a nation of joiners. But in focusing on the proliferation of pressure groups, we should not overstate the extent to which Americans are formally involved in such organizations. About a third of the adult population belong to no formal organizations of any kind, and another third belong to organizations that never take a stand on political questions. This leaves only one-third of the population as members of formal organizations that sometimes take a stand on housing, better government, school problems, or other public issues. Only about 2 per cent claim membership in specifically political organizations.[8] Millions of Americans are members of pressure groups, then, but equal numbers are members of no groups at all or of groups that they perceive as totally non-political. As a political resource, pressure group memberships are concentrated in a minority of the population.

Bases of Pressure-Group Strength

What makes a pressure group strong? And why is one group so much stronger than another? The lobbyist is as keenly interested in the answers to these questions as the political scientist is. Although neither has been able to establish an exact index of pressure-group strength, some of the more important factors have been identified.

The Political Environment As a Source of Strength

The strength of all pressure groups, whatever their make-up or their goals, is affected by the political environment in which they operate. In a democracy, for example, political practices make it a simple matter for different interests to advance their claims before the government. "Liberty is to faction what air is to fire," Madison observed. The techniques employed and the degree of influence achieved by pressure groups vary greatly, but these groups are at least given an opportunity to seek power in every democracy.

The formal organization of the government is a second factor that affects the strength of pressure groups. In the United States, the existence of three levels of government—federal, state, and local—and the separation of powers at each level among the legislative, executive, and judicial branches, produce many points at which government policy may be influenced. Now this system of

---

[8] Robert E. Lane, *Political Life: How People Get Involved in Politics* (Glencoe, Illinois: The Free Press, 1959), p. 75.

organizing the government works to the disadvantage of the agencies that seek control of the government as a whole—that is, the political parties. But it clearly works to the advantage of the agencies that seek only to influence specific policies —that is, the pressure groups. When a pressure group is trying to block government action that it regards as detrimental, it finds that opportunity knocks not just once but over and over again.

If a pressure group fails in one house of Congress, it can try the other. Indeed, as we shall see in Chapter 9, the manner in which Congress is organized provides pressure groups with a number of points of access in each house. Since power in Congress tends to be personalized and scattered rather than institutionalized and concentrated, to impress just one key congressman with the group's needs may be enough. If he is a member of a committee that is considering an objectionable measure, especially if he is the chairman of the committee, he may kill the measure before the membership of the house ever has a chance to vote on it.

If the pressure group fails to win the backing of any of the congressmen, it may still strive for a presidential veto. But the end of the trail does not come even there. Once a law has been passed, it is still subject to challenge in the courts, where, even if it is held constitutional, the group may succeed in having it interpreted to the group's advantage in specific cases. And when a law is put into operation, the group can continue to contact the administrators who interpret and administer the law day by day.

Our federal system offers another series of opportunities for interest groups at the state level. If a group cannot muster effective power at any point in national politics, it may still realize its ambitions in at least some of the states. The old saw, "If at first you don't succeed, try, try again," is taken very seriously by American pressure groups. If none of these efforts to influence the government is successful, the group may finally attempt to influence nominations and elections to state or federal office.

A third factor in the political environment that enhances the strength of pressure groups in the United States is the weakness of political parties. The diffusion of power in the official government structure strengthens the efforts of pressure groups to block *undesirable* policy decisions. And the weakness of political parties strengthens the efforts of these groups to promote *desirable* policy decisions. The failure of the majority party to organize Congress effectively and to act with cohesion on policy matters produces a power vacuum that tends to be filled by organized interest groups. "Because the legislator's tenure in office depends on no overarching party organization, he is accessible to whatever influences are outstanding in his local constituency almost regardless of more inclusive claims." [9] On questions that are of no direct concern to prominent interests in his locality, the weakness of party structure leaves the congressman susceptible to appeals from national pressure groups that have little or no identification with his constituency.

---

[9] Truman, *The Governmental Process*, p. 325.

In a political environment, then, in which pressure groups are free to organize, in which government power is highly diffused, and in which weak parties leave the majority largely unorganized, pressure groups have golden opportunities to reach their goals. How successful they are in taking advantage of their opportunities depends largely on the same group characteristics that determine the success of political parties—namely, organization, leaders, doctrines, and social base. All these group characteristics have a bearing on the success of a pressure group in achieving its *intermediate* objective: *gaining access to key points of decision-making in government.*[10]

Probably the most influential of all characteristics in determining the strength of a pressure group, however, is its *status.* If it occupies a position of high prestige, its leaders will enjoy an easy access to key points of decision that is denied to low-status groups. A junior legislator or administrator may actually be flattered to have a leader of a group like the American Bar Association or the American Legion come to him for help. But an organization of the far left, like the National Council for American-Soviet Friendship, or of the far right, like the John Birch Society, may find it difficult even to get a hearing. Until the 1930's, labor spokesmen generally had a hard time finding a sympathetic ear in government. This situation has changed over the decades, mainly because labor has achieved far more powerful organization and, with it, higher status. But in some sections of the country, notably in rural areas and in certain parts of the South, endorsement of a candidate by the AFL-CIO would still be a kiss of death. Consequently, the status of labor in these areas hardly insures easy access to legislators.

High-status pressure groups and their spokesmen also have the advantage of talking the same language as officeholders. Since they have similar class backgrounds, similar experiences, and similar contacts, they quickly discover similar interests. Moreover, a high-status group is able to develop common interests with other pressure groups and enlist their support in its efforts. Finally, since status is so closely tied to money in the United States, the group with greater status will almost automatically be able to command greater financial resources. And it costs money to engage in pressure politics, as our discussion of pressure-group tactics will make clear.

In addition to status, a second characteristic that influences the power of pressure groups is *organization.* The closer and more frequent the interaction among members, the more cohesive—that is, the more effectively organized—the group will be. And organization means power. Although the official organization charts of pressure groups often give the impression that they are as decentralized as political parties, they generally enjoy a much greater concentration of power at the national level. Since the leaders speak for the organization as a whole, they can command an attentive audience even when they are not accurately reflecting the opinions of many of the members. Pressure-group leaders try to

---

[10] *Ibid.,* p. 264.

avoid the localism that keeps the structure of political parties weak and that makes it difficult for anyone to speak authoritatively for the organization as a whole. Ironically, the very groups that have the highest degree of concentrated control, such as the Chamber of Commerce and the National Association of Manufacturers, are frequently the loudest champions of states' rights for political parties and the government.

A tight organization means that a pressure group can keep in constant contact with the government on impending developments. The good lobbyist works hard to gain the respect of sympathetic congressmen by offering material for speeches, data on impending legislation, detailed information on the needs of the lobbyist's clients, and other services. Conversely, the congressman can keep the lobbyist informed on new developments and on his own and his colleagues' inclinations. This kind of relationship demands time no less than skill. A lobbyist for a business group explained that he concentrated on a few strategic members of Congress because he could not maintain a sufficiently close relationship with a larger number. "To keep these friendships alive and genuine, I have to stop around to see them quite often just to say hello. For example, if I don't see . . . at least once a week, he'll say, 'Where the hell have you been? You only stop around when you want something from us.' Even a few contacts on the Hill demand a good deal of time and attention." [11] Only a group well enough organized to have a staff of spokesmen constantly on the job can hope to build this kind of mutually rewarding relationship. Another lobbyist said, "We are just getting to the point where members of Congress and agency officials come to us and seek information. This office is only ten years old, and you know it takes time to establish a reputation." [12] Without a sustained and well-organized effort, a group cannot attain this respect. It will have trouble securing even enough information to protect its interests—to say nothing of advancing new interests.

The quality of *leadership* is a third characteristic that affects the strength of a pressure group. In order to advance its claims effectively, a group needs spokesmen with official contacts and with an intimate knowledge of the political process. Many administrators and legislative assistants become lobbyists for various groups after leaving government service—a tribute both to their know-how and to their contacts. A recent study of Washington lobbyists disclosed that "over half of the lobbyists had worked for the federal government either in a staff position on the 'Hill' or in one of the agencies or as an appointive or elective officeholder." [13] Contrary to popular assumption, only a few former congressmen are found among the lobbyists in Washington. The greater reliance on people with administrative and legislative staff experience indicates the increasing importance of lobbying before administrative agencies: a lobbyist needs access

---

[11] Quoted in Donald R. Matthews, *U.S. Senators and Their World* (Chapel Hill: The University of North Carolina Press, 1960), p. 181.

[12] Lester W. Milbrath, *The Washington Lobbyists* (Chicago: Rand McNally & Company, 1963), p. 289.

[13] Lester W. Milbrath, "The Political Party Activity of Washington Lobbyists," *Journal of Politics*, XX (May, 1958), p. 346.

to administrators as well as legislators, and he must "know the ropes" well enough to take advantage of his access. To know whom to see and when to see him, what information will be most helpful, how best to advance one's case—these are invaluable assets. Many former newspapermen are also employed as spokesmen, because they have learned their way around in the formal and informal processes of government.

Unless leaders maintain cohesion within their own organization, they will have little impact in Washington even if they employ the best of lobbyists. And the greatest threat to cohesion stems from overlapping membership in various groups. Since few people are totally identified with a single group, members may be alienated or even lost from an organization if it presents too many conflicts with other loyalties. A member of the American Legion, for example, may also be a Baptist, a fisherman, a pipefitter, a father, a union member, and a Mets fan. The effective leader must somehow minimize the cross-pressures that arise from conflicting group loyalties and maximize the members' identification with his own group. To this end, skillful leaders use such devices as internal propaganda, services to members, and the maintenance of at least the appearance of membership control. Ultimately, however, the perceptive leader must sometimes recognize that other organized and potential interests among his followers impose restraints on his leadership that no skill can overcome. When John L. Lewis tried to lead the United Mine Workers into the Republican Party in 1940, the overwhelming Democratic vote that was rolled up in the mining districts was a sharp reminder of the reality of these conflicting interests.

The *social base* of a group is a fourth characteristic that affects its strength. The number of members that a group can claim is important, of course. But size does not always bestow strength, because the larger a group grows the more likely it is to become disunited. If the AFL-CIO could maintain the cohesion in politics that it does in collective bargaining, its political power would be greatly magnified. Its millions of members are pulled by so many other loyalties, however, that its power is not commensurate with its size. Actually, *cohesion* is a key determinant in every element of group strength.

The geographical distribution of the members is another important factor in the social base of a group. If members are widely scattered, the group will probably be less unified than it would be if they could frequently meet face-to-face. On the other hand, if almost all the members live in a *single* area, as importers tend to be concentrated in New York, their effectiveness before Congress may suffer. Since the importer is not an important force in most constituencies, when tariff increases are under consideration "his opposition is taken for granted, discounted in advance, and if he is heard, it is with irritation." [14] If the members of a group are fairly well concentrated in urban areas, as the members of labor unions are, the group will enjoy greater influence in the office of the President (who depends on national majorities) than in Congress (where rural areas are

---

[14] E. E. Schattschneider, *Politics, Pressures, and the Tariff* (New York: Prentice-Hall, Inc., 1935), p. 162.

over-represented). The strong influence of farm groups on Congress, conversely, springs in part from the wide geographical distribution of their members.

Finally, the *doctrines* or policy objectives of a pressure group have a direct influence on its strength. If the aims of a group fit the prevailing pattern of values in the country at large, the group will enjoy easy access to the government and cross-pressures among the members will be kept at a minimum. Everyone is in favor of good health, for example, so the American Cancer Society has the advantage of almost no opposition. (On the other hand, it may not be able to count on very strong commitment; mild approval leads to an absence of opposition but not to active support.) If the doctrines of a group run counter to prevailing values, however, its chances of attracting and holding members will be slight, and its status will suffer accordingly. Extreme examples are the communist groups in the United States today. And, despite widespread race prejudice in the South, the departure of the Ku Klux Klan from the accepted "rules of fair play" in attempting to preserve "white supremacy" has reduced it to the status of a "lunatic fringe" element in the minds of most southerners.

In order to succeed, the pressure group, no less than the political party, must be willing to modify its doctrines with changing times. Until the 1930's, the American Federation of Labor championed *laissez-faire*. But when it discovered that the government could be used to promote as well as to block its needs, and when the depression demonstrated that its needs could not be met *without* government help, it was quick to shift its support to social welfare legislation. The Minutemen organization, which claims to speak for conservatives who think that America is about to be taken over by communists, asserted in 1964 that it made an all-out effort to help elect Senator Barry Goldwater. Immediately after the election, the chief Minuteman announced that "the hopes of millions of Americans that the communist tide could be stopped with ballots instead of bullets have been turned into dust." [15] He accordingly announced a shift to the organization of "combat teams" that would employ the tactics of infiltration, subversion, and psychological warfare developed by communists. This group's doctrines are so extreme that no modification seems likely to win it much support.

The more goals a group tries to achieve, the weaker it becomes in the pursuit of any one of them. If it can concentrate on a single overriding aim, as the Anti-Saloon League did in battling for prohibition, its chances of maintaining cohesion and winning success are enhanced. The Americans for Democratic Action, on the other hand, is committed to a whole series of programs, and the diffusion of its efforts reduces its effectiveness in each program.[16] Since the pressure group is unconcerned with winning general control of the government, it need not, like the political party, develop an over-all political program for the country at large.

---

[15] *The New York Times*, November 12, 1964.

[16] Clifton Brock, *Americans for Democratic Action: Its Role in National Politics* (Washington, D.C.: Public Affairs Press, 1962).

Pressure-Group Tactics and Public Responses

The persistent efforts of pressure groups to advance their particular interests are felt at every stage of the political process. Day after day, they work to create a favorable public opinion, to influence nominations and elections to public office, and to sway governmental decisions wherever they are made. Some Americans regard these efforts as a threat to the very existence of democracy. Before we appraise the seriousness of this alleged threat, however, let us look more closely at the tactics used by these groups.

Pressure-Group Tactics

When most people think about pressure groups at all, they tend to concentrate on efforts to influence the behavior of public officials. Actually, though, pressure groups have become so aware of the importance of public opinion that they are now spending millions of dollars every year on *mass propaganda*. Not only broad groups like the National Association of Manufacturers but even individual companies maintain elaborate bureaucracies to sell "correct" ideas on general political questions along with favorable attitudes toward the company. The idea behind these efforts is that if the public can be induced to define the "American Way" precisely as the pressure group or the company does, mass support will be forthcoming whenever a critical issue arises.

The General Mills food company, for example, which most people think of as simply trying to sell Wheaties, "The Breakfast of Champions," has maintained a Director of Educational Services in its Department of Public Services. This organization has made available to secondary-school teachers, without charge, such aids as fully planned teaching units on economics, complete with comic books in color and examinations on economic questions accompanied by the correct answers. School children are consumers not only of cereals but of ideas. And if they absorb the proper beliefs along with the proper foods, they will one day grow into sturdy supporters of sound public policies.

There have been rumblings of discontent, chiefly from competing pressure groups, about these general educational campaigns. It is argued that the general public unwittingly pays for the costs of the programs. Since the costs are regarded as company operating expenses, they reduce the amount of taxes paid by the company to the government; in addition, the costs are presumably included in the price of the company's product. In 1952, Representative Robert L. Ramsay (D.-West Virginia) introduced a bill to make it unlawful for corporations to reduce their taxes by charging to "business expense" the cost of advertisements with "political purposes." In endorsing the bill, one labor publication editorialized:

> An increasing flood of this institutional advertising is pouring into newspapers, magazines, radio programs, and the mail. It can be recognized by the fact that it tries to sell—not a product—but the political and economic prejudices of a businessman or corporation. . . .

The businessmen who publish these institutional advertisements have a right to their personal opinions, but do they have a right to spread them at Government expense, which means at the expense of other taxpayers? [17]

Since labor groups cannot subsidize their own propaganda efforts in this way, it is hardly surprising that they should object to the practice. But the effectiveness of such campaigns is hard to prove,[18] and it would be difficult for legislators to frame laws that would distinguish between "product" advertising and "political" advertising. Finally—and most important—opposing groups have not managed to stir up enough public disapproval of the practice to bring about restrictive legislation.

Another tactic used by pressure groups—*electioneering*—overlaps these general educational programs. If the citizen is properly oriented on politics in general, the pressure group assumes that he will vote "correctly" in any given election. Consequently, pressure groups try to influence elections by appearing before platform committees at party conventions, by making monetary contributions to cooperative candidates, by offering propaganda services to candidates endorsed by the group, and by making direct exhortations to their members and general pleas to the public. If the right man can be elected in the first place, the group's interests will be almost automatically insured once he has taken office. In some cases, a pressure group may succeed in capturing the local party almost completely—as the United Automobile Workers have captured the Democratic Party in the Detroit area. Then it may simply install its own members in office and forget about the whole problem of influencing official decisions. Generally, however, pressure groups follow the practice of rewarding their friends and punishing their enemies, although sometimes they make contributions to both candidates in the hope that, whoever wins, they cannot possibly lose.

The tactic most generally associated with pressure politics is that of attempting to influence official decision-makers, or, more bluntly, *lobbying*. Many citizens have a lurid picture of lobbying efforts. One lobbyist reports that he once overheard a revealing conversation between two women in the Senate waiting room. One lady, apparently a resident of Washington, was pointing out the sights to her visiting friend. "That's Senator . . . ," she said in a stage whisper, "and that"—pointing to the man with whom the Senator was talking—"is . . . , the lobbyist for what's-its-name." "O-o-oh!" responded the impressed tourist. "Is he bribing him now?" [19]

Despite the negative popular image of lobbying efforts, modern lobbyists rarely resort to the use of corrupt practices or unlawful pressure. Instead, they serve as conveyors of useful information, both technical and political. The legislator and administrator must depend on the professional services of the lobbyists to

---

[17] *Congressional Record*, February 28, 1952, Appendix A1278 ("Extension of Remarks of Hon. Robert L. Ramsay"). Daily Edition.

[18] See William H. Whyte, Jr., *Is Anybody Listening?* (New York: Simon and Schuster, 1952).

[19] Matthews, *U. S. Senators and Their World*, p. 176.

keep themselves informed about the needs and preferences of important segments of the population. So the relationship is reciprocal: the official contacts the lobbyists for advice, information, or help, perhaps as often as the lobbyist contacts the official. Any pressure group that enjoys high status, cohesive organization, skilled leadership, a strategically distributed social base, and legitimate objectives requires neither ruthless pressure nor corrupt practices to achieve its ends. If the group lacks these elements of strength, it will be incapable of applying ruthless pressure. And it would have to be desperate indeed to resort to corruption.

Whenever the spokesman for a group violates the American concept of "fair play," he endangers the cohesion of the group's members—who are perhaps more committed to the general concepts of fair play than to the group itself. Moreover, he exposes the group to attack from other interests, and himself to prosecution. In 1956, for example, independent producers of natural gas seemed to have an excellent chance of winning exemption from federal rate control, a measure President Eisenhower himself had indicated he supported. Then, in the midst of debate, Senator Francis Case (R-South Dakota) announced that he had rejected a $2,500 campaign contribution from an individual who was interested in the passage of the bill, and that the offer had changed his position from probable support to opposition. "I object," the Senator submitted, to "doing something so valuable to those interested in natural gas that they advance huge sums of money as a down payment, so to speak, on the profits they expect to harvest." The Senate promptly undertook an investigation of the incident. Although little came of the investigation itself, and the bill was actually passed by Congress, it was subsequently vetoed by the President.

Here was dramatic evidence of the existence of an unorganized "majority interest" in the basic concepts of fair play. The cynic may argue that the natural-gas bill was opposed to the majority interest regardless of the tactics used to support it. He may also emphasize that the President would have signed the bill had public attention not been aroused. But the incontrovertible fact, regardless of one's views on the merits of the bill itself, is that the public interest in fair play had *set limits* that the pressure group seemed to have violated. And the President—who, more than Congress, is the spokesman for the general interest of which we are speaking—was sufficiently responsive to veto the bill because of "highly questionable activities . . . that I deem to be so arrogant and so much in defiance of acceptable standards of propriety as to risk creating doubt among the American people concerning the integrity of governmental processes." This is a point that we should keep in mind whenever we evaluate the charge that pressure groups, by themselves, can determine public policy.

The proposal of the Kennedy Administration to extend the social security system to health care for the aged (the King-Anderson bill in 1961) illustrates how pressure politics enters into the legislative process. Dozens of different organizations took formal stands and published statements, for or against the idea. A few groups with direct but different economic or professional stakes in the measure were extremely active. The American Medical Association, the American Dental Association, the National Association of Manufacturers, the Chamber of Commerce, and the insurance companies threw their combined weight on the negative side. The Americans for Democratic Action, the National Council of Senior Citizens' Clubs, and organized labor, especially AFL-CIO affiliates, worked most energetically for the proposal.

The American Medical Association is a high-status pressure group, professing to speak for about three-fourths of the nation's doctors. It opposed the Kennedy proposal on ideological grounds: "socialized medicine for the aged" would end up in "socialized medicine for every man, woman, and child in the country." It fears that "socialized medicine" might mean bureaucratic interference with the medical profession, that extension of public health service might turn the medical profession into a class of civil servants, that government payments based on "reasonable cost" might reduce doctors' fees and income. The A.M.A. maintains an aggressive lobby in Washington, with registered lobbyists paid to keep the views of the organization continuously before Congress. The central office also makes a wide appeal to the public through advertisements, "press kits" for editorial writers, and the provision of lecturers for state and county medical associations and for civic groups in general.

The most effective tactics of the A.M.A. are at the local level. The *A.M.A. News* urges physicians to tell their patients "the truth about socialized medicine, the danger in tying medical care to social security, the pitfalls in compulsory government insurance." To carry out its adverse publicity campaign, the A.M.A. furnishes suitable posters and pamphlets for the doctors' waiting rooms and texts for local television and radio spot announcements. The A.M.A. also urges its individual members not only to write personal letters to congressmen but to persuade local civic groups to join in a letter-writing campaign against "socialism."

While the A.M.A. pitches its campaign on ideological and professional grounds, its allies in the health insurance industry are frank to admit their large economic interests. Mutual of Omaha, Continental Casualty, Metropolitan Life, Aetna Life, and Equitable Life Assurance are among the companies with multi-million dollar stakes in this issue. Under medicare, these big companies feel they will lose much of the business they now get from people over 65; and if the plan were carried further to cover the health needs of people under 65, they fear that the private health insurance business would be ruined. As might be expected from their strong commitment to private enterprise, the National Association of Manufacturers and the Chamber of Commerce join in the fight against the extension of government enterprise.

Organized labor, unlike the A.M.A., has only an indirect interest in the medical aid issue. The labor unions, however, have generally supported extension of the social security system. Labor lobbyists in Washington pressure congressmen, and local affiliates are urged to write letters to their respective representatives. Many "senior citizens" have an obvious interest in the legislation, and nearly 10 per cent of the population is 65 or older. During the 1960 campaign, Senior Citizens for Kennedy were organized in a number of states. In 1961, the National Council of Senior Citizens' Clubs emerged as a broad federation that would lobby not only for medical care but for other government aids for the aged.

The failure of the Kennedy proposal for medical aid to the aged in 1961 can be attributed at least partly to the cross-currents of pressure politics. In numbers, in broad social base, the labor groups and the organized senior citizens were certainly more impressive; but their interests and their efforts were both probably too diffused. On the other hand, the high status of the opposition groups, their direct economic interest in the issue, their concentrated attack, their lavish expenditures, and their grass-roots approach to Congress seem to have been most effective.

By 1965, however, the picture had changed. The same groups played out their familiar roles once again but with different results. During the presidential campaign of 1964, the president of the National Council of Senior Citizens denounced the Republican platform as a "cruel hoax." The A.M.A. hired the firm of Fuller, Smith, and Ross to handle a million-dollar advertising campaign against medicare. The achievement of medicare under the Johnson administration cannot be attributed to a change in the lobbying forces but rather to a greater popular mandate for the President and an increase in the number of liberal Democrats in Congress. When lobbyists themselves are asked to assess the importance of different factors influencing public policy, they rank the executive branch, the composition of Congress, and voters' preferences far ahead of lobbying efforts. And the congressmen agree. Lester Milbrath of Northwestern University reports, on the basis of interviews with 101 lobbyists and 38 congressional objects of lobbying, "It is rather striking that both the practitioners and the recipients of lobbying think that lobbying is of so little importance in making public policy." He quotes one lobbyist who had great difficulty in rating the forces that operate in policy-making:

> I don't know where in the world I would fit the lobbyists as a group. Some of them have been up here for years battling for lost causes. On the whole, and speaking of all lobbyists in general, I think they are a lot less effective than most people believe.[20]

Mobilizing Majority Power

Pressure groups make several important contributions to democratic politics. They play an indispensable function in identifying the interests in society to which the political system must respond. They also serve to increase participation and to clarify issues in connection with the other great input function of the political system—leadership selection. In our single-member district system of representation, each legislator is presumed to represent everyone within a given geographical area. But political differences occur between interests that transcend district lines more often than they do between distinct territorial units. Pressure groups thus offer an important supplement to the official system of representation. By permitting a more precise expression of special interests than can be expected

---

[20] Milbrath, *The Washington Lobbyists*, p. 352. For further discussion of the influence of interest groups on welfare policies, see Chapter 14.

through the broad political parties or through a district's Representative, pressure groups may prevent a sense of alienation and enhance the stability of the system.[21]

For a number of reasons, however, pressure groups appear less satisfactory than political parties as agencies to express broad public interests: (1) all interests are not represented equally through pressure groups, especially the underprivileged and noneconomic interests; (2) the complexity of current domestic and international problems demands a coherent and stable over-all policy, and this kind of policy cannot be achieved if every problem is tackled by a different coalition of special interests; (3) since every person, no less than every district, has a variety of interests, the pressure-group leader can speak no more accurately for all the members of his group than the elected Representative can for all his constituents; and (4), most important of all, pressure groups cannot be held accountable by the general public for the manner in which they use their power, because they do not win it through popular election.

One observer of current politics, Harvey Fergusson, is convinced that we are already afflicted with pressure-group government, and that the majority interest has been frozen out in the struggle among organized minorities. Fergusson charges that "the unorganized mass of the people . . . is truly the rump of the body politic. It takes all the punishment and supports all the rest of the nation." [22] This sort of charge serves a valuable function by alerting us to the fact that organization is essential to political power. But by suggesting that policy is shaped *only* by organized pressure groups, it seems almost as unrealistic as the old interpretation of politics in purely individualistic terms. Some interests—and some social classes—do appear to be "over-represented" in the policy-making process, and the unorganized do seem to be "under-represented." This does not mean, however, that the people who are unorganized can be ignored altogether.

In our discussion of the strength of pressure groups, we have already referred to their *overlapping memberships*. These criss-crossing relationships constitute a kind of natural restraint on the power of any pressure group. Overlapping membership means that all the members of a pressure group cannot be mobilized completely on any question, for the members of any group are also involved in other groups in varying degrees. Consequently, group leaders are obliged to modify their own demands in order to accommodate the competing demands of other groups. Moreover, loyalty of members to any group varies—as in a college club, where involvement ranges from complete indifference to zealous participation by a few eager souls.

The latent power of *unorganized interests* and *potential groups* constitutes a second natural check on pressure-group power. Unorganized interest groups and potential interest groups may be aroused to counteraction if they are too flagrantly ignored. Even in a dictatorship, there are certain bounds beyond which the rulers cannot move with impunity. And in a democracy the amorphous majority interest—the underlying expectations about how the government should

---

[21] *Ibid.*, pp. 357–358.
[22] Fergusson, *People and Power*, p. 109.

operate and what sort of policies is fair—is a much more realistic check on organized minorities (remember the fate of the natural-gas bill). In a sense, then, even the submerged, potential interests enjoy a kind of representation, simply because they may organize if they are too severely mistreated. Overlapping memberships and potential, unorganized groups thus serve as natural checks on pressure-group government.[23]

Some observers of politics, either unimpressed by these natural checks or unaware of their existence, have suggested various reforms to neutralize or purify the power of pressure groups. Many of these reforms look to impractical constitutional revisions, generally in the direction of parliamentary government. James Madison and his contemporaries were relatively free to embody in the Constitution their ideas on how to cope with factions; but we have lived with the document too long and have become too attached to it for wholesale revisions to be anything other than visionary. Reformers must cope not only with the public's traditional attachment to the Constitution but also with the vested interests that grow up around any established constitutional practice. The forces working for constitutional revision must be strong indeed to surmount these obstacles. A proposal to give the President the power to "dissolve" Congress if it failed to enact his major recommendations, for example, would certainly not get much support from congressmen. So how could Congress be expected to approve such a revision by the two-thirds vote necessary to propose amendments?

More modest efforts at regulating pressure groups culminated in the Federal Regulation of Lobbying Act of 1946.[24] This law imposes no real restriction on lobbying, however, for it simply insures that the money spent by pressure groups to influence legislation be given some degree of publicity. It requires that professional lobbyists before Congress register their names and file information about themselves and their employers, and submit quarterly reports of receipts and expenditures. The Supreme Court has greatly reduced the effect of these provisions by narrowly interpreting the act to apply only to direct lobbying before congressmen.[25] The Court thus excludes from regulation the more modern technique of indirect lobbying through propaganda beamed at the general public. The failure of the act to provide an enforcement agency and the failure of the press to publicize the information that is reported further reduce the effect of the law. Obviously, this act "regulates" lobbying in name only.

We return to the political party, then, as the unofficial agency that is most capable of checking the power of interested minorities by mobilizing the power of the majority. Overlapping memberships and potential interest groups represent vital passive checks, but the political party operates as a more positive and active restraint. Only the party has a real stake in organizing the underlying majority

---

[23] Truman, *The Governmental Process*, p. 514.

[24] Title III of the *Legislative Reorganization Act of 1946*, Public Law 601, 79th Cong., 2d Sess., 1946.

[25] *United States* v. *Harris*, 347 U.S. 612 (1954). For a discussion of "The Dilemma of Lobby Regulation," see Donald C. Blaisdell, *American Democracy Under Pressure* (New York: The Ronald Press Company, 1957), pp. 82–98.

interest and in stimulating potential groups to action. Responsible party government is no panacea in itself, but it does offer the advantage of restraining organized power with greater organized power—and, what is more important, the party is *accountable to the public.*

Although American parties already restrain pressure groups to some extent, our earlier discussion suggests that we may never see really cohesive parties here of the sort, for example, that the British have developed. Where strong pressure groups in a particular constituency are opposed to the national platform of a party, it is difficult to imagine that the American legislator who represents that constituency would persist in supporting the party's position. But a judicious distribution of rewards and punishments might at least lead him to support his party more consistently on positions that are not strongly opposed in his constituency. Even now, the willingness of many legislators to jeopardize their careers in order to put the national interest first is impressive.

A fourth check on pressure group power is found in the official decision-making agencies themselves—the electoral system, the Congress, the presidency, and the courts. Only a false realism can describe the official decision-makers as passive pawns rather than as active participants in the political process.[26] Official agencies, as we said, find pressure groups vitally important sources of information and services, but not all-powerful forces before which they cringe. A leading student of Congress concludes from a study of the Senate: "Lobbying is important. The Senate could not possibly operate in the mid-twentieth century without it. But the effects of lobbying are not what most observers have assumed them to be." [27] The lobbying relationship is a reciprocal one in which the official decision-maker commands resources that give him considerable maneuverability. When pressed to support a bill, for example, the legislator may refuse, he may agree to vote for it but offer no further aid, or he may agree to lend it his all-out support. If he is known to oppose the bill, the smart lobbyist favoring passage will not even approach him, lest he lose good will and the possibility of future access to the legislator. Moreover, such futile pressure may have a boomerang effect and lead the legislator to go beyond a negative vote and actively oppose the bill.

The original ideology that the decision-maker brings to his office and the commitments he acquires during his campaign for election probably have more to do with his decisions than all the activities of pressure groups. This means that important pressure groups in his constituency may have a special claim on him— to the point where he doesn't regard their advice as "pressure"—but it also decreases the likelihood that pressure groups can do more than reinforce predispositions he already has. And remember that the decision-maker generally shares the widespread but unorganized attitudes about what constitutes fair play in American politics. In this light, pressure groups appear much less menacing than they are frequently pictured to be. Milbrath's study of the positive and negative

---

[26] Zeigler, *Interest Groups in American Society*, p. 25.
[27] Matthews, *U.S. Senators and Their World*, p. 196.

features of pressure group activities led him to conclude, "If we had no lobby groups and lobbyists we would probably have to invent them to improve the functioning of the system." [28]

Professional Public Relations

A few years ago, a survey of the unofficial agencies of politics would have come to an end with the discussion of political parties and pressure groups. But today the public relations expert is so ubiquitous in American politics that he demands special consideration. In party politics, the dominance of the local boss and his machine is on the wane; in pressure-group politics, the technique of trying to influence officials directly has begun to be overshadowed by appeals to the general public. In both cases, professional public relations organizations have been the beneficiaries of the shift and, to some extent, the agents responsible for it.

As Stanley Kelley makes clear in his *Professional Public Relations and Political Power*,[29] the new politics in America is no longer characterized by local bosses like James Michael Curley or Frank Hague, who regularly delivered the votes of their organized followers. It is characterized by public relations firms like Batten, Barton, Durstine, and Osborn, and the Joseph Katz Company,[30] whose business is to manipulate the attitudes of great numbers of voters. The tactics of pressure groups are directed less to convincing officeholders than to shaping the opinions of individuals and groups within the general public. One realistic party official, recognizing the emerging role of public relations, concludes, "If present tendencies continue, our Federal elections will increasingly become contests not between candidates but between great advertising firms." [31] Was John Steinbeck looking too far into the future when, in his novel, *The Short Reign of Pippin IV*, he described the French government as unable to employ Batten, Barton, Durstine, and Osborn because the firm was engaged on two more important accounts— rewriting the U.S. Constitution and marketing a new golf-mobile with pontoons? [32]

Madison Avenue and Modern Public Relations

Democratic politics has always dealt in relations with the public. But there is something distinctly modern in the professional public relations men who now peddle their skill in selling ideas, candidates, and causes on a mass scale for millions of dollars a year. It is this technical skill that supports the role of professional public relations in politics—a skill based on expert knowledge of the mass media

---

[28] Milbrath, *The Washington Lobbyists*, p. 358.

[29] This section is largely based on Kelley's excellent book, *Professional Public Relations and Political Power* (Baltimore: The Johns Hopkins Press, 1956). In the decade since Kelley's research, political scientists have done little to develop more systematic understanding of this subject.

[30] These two important firms were retained at one time by the Republican and Democratic Parties, respectively.

[31] Quoted in Kelley, *Professional Public Relations*, p. 2.

[32] *The Short Reign of Pippin IV* (New York: The Viking Press, 1957), p. 72.

of communication, the nature of public opinion, and techniques for manipulating attitudes.

"Madison Avenue" is a new symbol in American politics—on this famous street in New York the plush offices of the broadcasting chains, advertising agencies, and public relations firms are all clustered together. The role of Madison Avenue could not have emerged 150 years ago when there was no mass circulation press and no radio or television, when most Americans were illiterate, and when suffrage was restricted to a few. The mass media of communication, universal suffrage, and higher levels of literacy, then, are among the forces that have produced this new élite. But the more immediate explanation for the political rise of the public relations expert is, of course, his superior skill, as compared with professional politicians, in using the channels of communication.

The basic function of the public relations man is to create attitudes that are favorable to his client. As a person, he himself may have a strong preference for Ipana toothpaste over Pepsodent, or for Republicans over Democrats, but his services as a publicity expert are for sale to the highest bidder. He finds it easy to transfer his technical skill in molding attitudes from one assignment to another. The public relations director of a food company or of a health foundation may shift with equal expertise to selling a government policy or a candidate for public office. Whatever the substantive problem—the molding of proper attitudes toward toothpaste, or Democrats, or food, or Republicans, or health, or national defense—the technical problems are much the same. Thus, when President Kennedy continued Eisenhower's practice of infrequent press conferences, the critical reaction was as much in terms of the poor public relations that might result as it was in terms of the public's need for information. President Johnson's frequent unscheduled contacts with the press are similarly evaluated more in terms of showmanship than content.

The enterprising public relations expert is not content to function merely as a tactician. Nor does he consider himself simply a press agent. He has become a "practical social scientist" whose profession is "managing human relations." In business corporations, he is found more and more often as a member of the policy-making "team." And in politics, he expects to have a say in determining what issues his client will espouse as well as the manner in which the issues will be presented. Even when he does not formulate policy, he must be close to those who do in order to advise them on how to "package" their policies attractively for the public "market." In government, the public relations expert has thus turned the eighteenth-century principle of "consent of the governed" into the twentieth-century practice of "engineering consent." [33]

After he has created a popular image of the candidate—investing him with a public personality that makes him a "salable product"—the conscientious professional manager, whether his office is in Hollywood or Washington, expects his

---

[33] This term was coined by Edward L. Bernays, one of the leading public relations experts. For a fuller discussion of this topic, see his book, *The Engineering of Consent* (Norman: University of Oklahoma Press, 1955).

"star" to perform according to public expectations. But the candidate sometimes fails to cooperate. Some critics of Stevenson, for example, argue that he would have received more votes in 1952 and 1956 if he had relied more on his public relations advisers. Kelley quotes the late Clem Whitaker, at the time one of the country's outstanding public relations men, as commenting somewhat plaintively on this problem:

> . . . An automobile is an inanimate object; it can't object to your sales talk— and if you step on the starter it usually runs. A *candidate on the other hand can and does talk back—and can sometimes talk you out of an election, despite the*

Drawing by O'Brian; © 1962 The New Yorker Magazine, Inc.

best you can do in campaign headquarters. . . . We have the problem of human relations . . . his ability or inability to measure up to the character you give him by your carefully prepared build-up.[34]

Some candidates, however, have shown little inclination to "talk back." In 1951, a group of senators investigating the Maryland campaign of Senator John Marshall Butler and Jon Jonkel, his Chicago public relations counsel, remarked, "It was a matter of the campaign manager and the campaign headquarters directing candidate Butler rather than candidate Butler directing the campaign manager and the campaign headquarters." [35]

Although professional public relations firms are now a standard part of political campaigns, their efficacy may easily be exaggerated. Party identification, for example, is a stable political factor that cannot be changed by even the cleverest of gimmicks during a brief campaign. And the established records of candidates cannot be transformed to suit the ad man's schemes, even if the candidate is willing to follow all directions. Finally, the ad man's talents may not be as easily transferred from deodorants to politics as he would have his client believe.

In 1964, the Democrats relied on one of the most creative agencies, Doyle, Dane, and Bernbach, which handles the advertising campaigns of such products as Volkswagen, Avis Rent-a-Car, and Clairol. But the light touch of the Volkswagen ads was somehow missing from the material they prepared for the Democrats. The TV spot showing a beautiful little girl picking flowers in a meadow, with the scene suddenly obliterated by the mushroom shape of a nuclear blast, and the film showing a pair of hands tearing up a social security card—such flagrant biases somehow seem more appalling when they deal with the nation's future than when applied to hair rinses or automobiles. We all know the latter choices are not very serious. Somehow, the propriety of such crude emotional appeals becomes less acceptable as the seriousness of the subject matter increases. Perhaps because we are inured to it, we are not horrified to be told that the wrong hair rinse for a mother will lose both the admiration of her children and the amorous attention of her husband. But such emotionalism seems out of place when "Brand X" is identified with the destruction of mankind. Moreover, the appeal represents a level of hucksterism to which the same agency does not stoop in its commercial accounts.

On the Republican side, the 1964 advertising campaign was entrusted to a leading firm, Erwin, Wasey, Ruthrauff & Ryan. Immediately after the election, an official of the firm explained that the voters' lack of familiarity with Senator Goldwater "was but one of several problems that had to be solved in 'merchandising' him." [36] The official conceded that President Johnson's lead at the start of the campaign was probably too great for his firm to overcome even "if the problems in advertising had not existed," although he implied that the margin of defeat could have been greatly reduced. The burden of his argument was that the

---

[34] As quoted in *Professional Public Relations*, p. 222.
[35] Senate Committee on Rules and Administration, *Maryland Senatorial Election of 1950*, 82d Cong., 1st Sess., p. 9.
[36] *The New York Times*, November 5, 1964.

campaign period was too short to achieve the two objectives necessary to win the undecided vote. First, the agency had to introduce Senator Goldwater to the voters (much, presumably, as a Mr. Kleen is unveiled—a full-blown personality with no past and therefore perfectly adjusted to today's market); second, it had to tell the voters what he stood for. Capsuling these objectives into a short period produced what the ad man called a confusion of "product claims."

The confusion of "product claims" was brought into the open when Senator Goldwater repudiated a film prepared by some of his ad men and refused to let it be shown because of its blatant racism. (The film attempted to link President Johnson with race riots, nudism, pornography, and other symbols of "moral decay.") Such incidents as this may explain the complaint of an unidentified ad man to *The New York Times* that the agency is "unable to effectively choose and then capitalize on campaign issues." [37] (Perhaps the split infinitives in politicians' speeches come from their public relations men.) This complaint suggests that the parties have not turned all the issues of the campaign over to their public relations firms. The same executive's additional complaint could be turned around. He says, "Further, members of a party's national committee generally do not understand or appreciate the purpose or nature of advertising." Could it be that the advertising moguls do not fully understand or appreciate the purpose or nature of politics?

Public Relations Tactics in Politics

Some of the finest exemplars of political campaigning as a business, in the late 1950's, were to be found in the California public relations firm of Clem Whitaker and his wife, Leone Baxter, who said that they operated "just as we would if we were merchandising *commodities* instead of selling *men* and *measures*." [38] Although it would be unwarranted to speak of even the most efficient firm as the "cause" of victory, Whitaker and Baxter's record of success in about 90 per cent of their efforts for a variety of candidates and causes was highly impressive. Kelley identifies the principles that guided this firm's campaign tactics, and the most significant feature he describes is the systematic fashion in which the tactics were applied, in conformity with a meticulously planned campaign blueprint and budget.

The first principle is to conduct an offensive campaign, for this enables the firm to choose the battleground and to define the issues. In conducting a three and one-half year campaign for the American Medical Association against President Truman's proposed compulsory health insurance, for example, Whitaker and Baxter posed the issue as "Socialized Medicine" *versus* "The Voluntary Way."

Four devices are used to give a campaign its aggressive tone. First, complicated issues are reduced to simple themes or slogans—"Political Medicine is Bad Medicine!" "The Voluntary Way is the American Way!" Second, the firm uses

---

[37] *Ibid.*
[38] As quoted in Kelley, *Professional Public Relations*, p. 39.

showmanship, employing "the appeal that is beyond politics," the appeal that can compete with comics, variety shows, and murder mysteries for the voter's attention. "There are thousands of experts bidding for every man's attention—and every man has a limited amount of leisure," Whitaker warned. But, he added, "Most every American loves *contest.* . . . *So you can interest him if you put on a fight!* No matter what you fight for, *fight for something.* . . . Then, too, most every American likes to be entertained. . . . So if you can't fight, PUT ON A SHOW!" [39] Third, a "gimmick," some unusual phrase or trick, is used to command attention and "fix" a name or preference in the lazy voter's mind. Jon Jonkel employed this device effectively in his Maryland campaign by broadcasting spot announcements that droned, in the fashion of the familiar Bromo-Seltzer advertisements, "Be for Butler, be for Butler, be for Butler, be for Butler, be for Butler, be for Butler, be for John Marshall Butler, Republican candidate for United States Senator." Fourth, proper "pacing" is used to insure that the campaign will build to a climax just before election time. About 75 per cent of the total funds are spent during the last three weeks of the campaign.

A second general principle is to adapt the themes of the campaign to market conditions of time, place, and audience. Aware that society is made up of many groups, the public relations firm recognizes that no one group affiliation will dominate the average voter's preferences. If he cannot be reached as a veteran, perhaps he can be reached as a father; if not as a Methodist, perhaps as a businessman. If the various group identifications of, say, a union member, can be stimulated more than his opposing loyalties, he may even be induced to support an "anti-union" position. Public opinion polls are an invaluable aid in planning just the right appeal for different groups and places. Indeed, more empirical research in political behavior is probably being conducted by commercial agencies than by the universities.

A third general principle is to distribute the correct ideas with the maximum effect on the consumer-voter. The well-organized firm has its own apparatus for distributing pamphlets, films, and similar materials. But it is keenly interested in communicating its message through the "normal" and presumably unbiased channels of communication as well. The extent and success of its efforts to do so are suggested by the conclusion of *Fortune* magazine that almost half the contents of the better newspapers come from publicity releases.[40] Public relations experts may accomplish more by furnishing "news," by alerting editors to the importance of a problem, and by mobilizing natural allies than they can by direct propaganda.

H. Walton Cloke, coordinator of public relations for Henry J. Kaiser Corporation, has explained how his company improved its public relations program in Washington by a comprehensive information campaign.[41] The firm discovered that the fifteen states and territories in which it had plants or other facilities were

39 *Ibid.*, p. 50 (emphasis his).

40 "Business Is Still in Trouble," *Fortune*, May, 1949, p. 69.

41 Allen H. Center (ed.), *Public Relations Ideas in Action* (New York: McGraw-Hill Book Company, Inc., 1957), pp. 269–272.

represented by sixty-eight senators, congressmen, and territorial delegates in Washington. So it decided to "tell the Kaiser Story to this Congressional group." It printed a colorful brochure to celebrate its fortieth anniversary and gave copies to the congressional group in addition to 100,000 employees, stockholders, and customers. It provided each congressman with manuals to inform him on such matters as what Kaiser plants were in his district, the number of employees, and the annual payroll; it also provided him with data on the over-all corporate structure, such as a "who's who" in the management, the number of stockholders, the net earnings, and the net sales. The company put the congressmen on its mailing list for all news releases about company activities, and invited them on plant tours so that they could see for themselves how much Kaiser plants meant to their constituents. Finally, it held a public relations conference in Washington, attended by the company's top managers, and invited the sixty-eight congressmen to join in discussions of government programs affecting Kaiser business. The conference was also used to bring in several cabinet officers to talk over the general relationship of government and business. "In addition several government public relations men told the group how to work with government agencies and departments to the mutual public relations advantage of all concerned."

How extensively are such public relations tactics applied to politics? Beyond doubt, both pressure groups and political parties are increasingly relying on the public relations approach. Its influence even on the presidency is unmistakable. During President Eisenhower's first year in office, the gentleman who was chosen to merchandise his policies explained, "We all suddenly realized we were busy manufacturing a product down here, but nobody was selling it." [42] In this environment, it was not surprising that, in 1955, an unprecedented decision was made: a cabinet meeting, which never before had been opened to the public, would be televised. Given this decision, it is even less surprising that the firm of Batten, Barton, Durstine, and Osborn, with its experience in handling such hit programs as the Jack Benny show, was put in charge of the production. The day after the premiere performance, defenders of the company were insisting it was the best show they had produced, and *The New York Times* impartially reported the meeting both on its front page and in its television section. The television reviewer was the more critical, suggesting that this might be good politics, but it was poor theater.

President Eisenhower introduced the practice of having press conferences televised "on tape" for later editing and public release. President Kennedy, fresh from his success in live TV debates with Nixon, went all the way and permitted live television coverage of press conferences. Cautious observers were fearful that an ill-advised impromptu remark might jeopardize the national interest, but the presumably greater audience interest in live coverage outweighed such dangers. President Johnson appears more at home in small, informal gatherings, but the need for maximum "exposure" has led him to continue live coverage of press conferences.

---

[42] Kelley, *Professional Public Relations*, p. 2.

Shall Madison Avenue and the Singing Commercial Inherit the Earth?

What does commercialized, public relations politics portend for American democracy? While it is too early to answer with precision, we can be sure that, like any new route to political power, it will work to the advantage of some groups and to the disadvantage of others. At first, the advantage appeared to lie with the Republican Party and with business groups. The old machine politics of urban areas, however, probably worked to the advantage of the Democrats, because it was built on skills in meeting the needs of their "natural" base of support—the immigrant, the uneducated, the poor, and the underprivileged. The politics of public relations depends on quite different skills—the manipulation of attitudes among great masses of voters. The Republicans got a head start in using modern public relations techniques, partly because of their closer identification with the business community and the "businesslike" approach, and partly because they were the "outs," and more in need of a new approach, when the mass media came into their own. But the Democrats seem to have closed the gap. Their public relations counsel insisted that he conceived the idea of the first "saturation" television campaign through spot announcements before it was hit on by the firm hired by the Republicans. If the new politics does work to the long-run advantage of the Republicans, then, it will only be because the Republican Party is more successful in raising funds for this expensive type of campaigning. The ability of the Democrats to match Republican outlays in 1960 and 1964 indicates that the Republican advantage has already disappeared.

Forgetting for a moment the effect on political parties, we may credit public relations in politics with three positive gains. First, it serves to increase popular participation in elections. Since the power of the political boss was rooted in his ability to deliver a regular vote from an organized following, he preferred a low turn-out from the general public. He could always count on the "party faithful" to vote, and the larger their proportion of the total vote the more secure was the boss's position. The public relations expert, however, deals with unseen and unknown audiences to whom he has rendered no personal favors and with whom he has no personal contact. His interest is served by mass appeals that stimulate the greatest possible number to vote.

A second gain from public relations is that it tends to nationalize American politics. The political leaders of the old school, dependent on personal ties, had little interest in broad national questions. The national public relations firm, however, with its centralized and standardized approach, necessarily concentrates on broader concerns. It can hardly promise to deliver a bucket of coal, but it can promise to "deliver" a new foreign policy. Since the cost of a professional public relations approach renders it less feasible at the local level than at the national level, public relations should tend to decrease the localism that plagues American parties. If a candidate for Congress uses the advertising kit of his party's national headquarters during his campaign, he may find it embarrassing to depart from the national party line after he has been elected.

A third gain is that public relations tends to emphasize issues. The political boss was seldom interested in issues, especially not national issues. But the public relations expert is. As Stanley Kelley describes it:

> Jon Jonkel, in the Maryland senatorial campaign of 1950, had little in the way of a local organization on which to depend. In his strategy, he gave real importance to an issue and the power of that issue to determine an election's outcome. This much must be granted, whatever one may think about the way the issue was framed or the intellectual integrity of Jonkel's arguments. If there is one belief that the public relations man holds sincerely, it is his belief that words can shape men's actions and mold men's minds. He is serious about talk.[43]

Both pressure groups and political parties have become somewhat more issue-oriented as a result of the shift to public relations techniques. "This has been the chief motive back of the vast expansion of public relations programs by businesses, industries, and interest groups: to control government policy by standardizing and enforcing public opinion." [44]

Despite these apparent advantages, the threats represented by public relations politics are considerable. To begin with, access to public relations skills is highly unequal; if an individual or a group is unable to invest large sums of money in public relations, that individual or group is effectively excluded from the public "debate." Financial limitations are especially important in campaigns for nomination through primary elections; without competing party labels to help voters evaluate candidates, the citizen may be more easily influenced by propaganda through the mass media. There is no "right to counsel" in facing what Madison Avenue likes to call "the bar of public opinion."

Furthermore, public relations alters the very nature of public debate. Discussion and examination of issues are replaced by slogans, capsule notions, and "gimmicks" designed to standardize opinions. The potential voter is viewed as a victim of prejudices and intellectual laziness, uninterested in politics or in serious ideas. "Fortunately," one public relations expert submits, "the sincere and gifted politician is able, by the instrument of propaganda, to mold and form the will of the people." [45]

When Americans are faced with a problem, they usually turn to education as the route to secular salvation. Certainly a citizenry that was educated to examine ideas with critical discrimination could force the public relations expert to give political propaganda more rational content. The high sensitivity of this profession to market conditions suggests that it would quickly modify its appeals if the voters failed to respond to the current offerings. In more practical terms, however, the solution probably lies in achieving more equitable access to the agencies able to conduct large-scale public relations campaigns. Better organization of more groups, and some form of financing party and pressure-group campaigns from membership dues or contributions, appear to be the most feasible way of

---

[43] *Professional Public Relations*, pp. 217–218.
[44] *Ibid.*, p. 218.
[45] Edward L. Bernays, *Propaganda* (New York: Horace Liveright, 1928), p. 92.

assimilating modern public relations into democratic politics. For political parties, Senator Maurine Neuberger (D.-Oregon) proposed a law in 1961 that would have provided some government support of campaign activities. In addition, President Kennedy's special Commission on Campaign Costs investigated the whole problem of money in elections and recommended such reforms as tax credits for small campaign contributions.

From Unofficial to Official Input Activities

To this point, we have been talking about the input activities of the political system solely in terms of unofficial agencies—the small groups and large organizations (from the family to the mass media of communication), political parties, pressure groups, and public relations organizations through which political opinions are formed and expressed. All these unofficial agencies help to create the demands, supports, and apathy that constitute the inputs of the political system. And, in addition to their particular functions, each is involved in some degree in the broad functions of political socialization, interest identification, and leadership selection.

These are functions that we have argued are carried out, one way or another, in every political system. But the functions of leadership selection and interest identification cannot be understood, in the American context, without also including the official electoral system in the analysis. The demands, supports, and apathy that make up the input activities of American politics are authoritatively represented through the electoral system.

CHAPTER EIGHT

The Electoral System

Because of their formal and legal status, official agencies of government are easier to identify than unofficial agencies. Indeed, the first three articles of the Constitution are devoted to spelling out, at least in general terms, the structures and functions that make up the legislative, executive, and judicial agencies. Congress, the presidency, and the courts are so prominent that many people assume they are the only official agencies of the American national government. Since some parts of the bureaucracy—notably the regulatory commissions—combine legislative, executive, and judicial functions, and are not directly under the President's control, they are sometimes called the "fourth branch" of our government. But the heads of all these agencies are at least appointed by the President, so we don't have much trouble thinking of them as a part of the sprawling executive branch. Moreover, the independent regulatory commissions are not alone in combining rule-making with the application and adjudication of the rules; as we shall see in the next four chapters, each of the three principal branches of government participates in some degree in all three output functions of government—the making, application, and the adjudication of rules.

The Electoral System As an Official Agency of Government

The most common omission from lists of the official agencies of American government is the electoral system. The Constitution emphasizes output functions so heavily that we tend to overlook its official recognition of an input function common to all political systems—selection of authoritative decision-makers. Rules or policies cannot make and enforce themselves; every political system must somehow provide for the selection of those who will wield the official power of government. In the United States, this function is carried out by official agencies. True, unofficial agencies play an important role in the selection of government officials, but they also play an important role in legislation, administration, and adjudication. In elections no less than in the other functions the formal decisions are made by official agencies of government. Accordingly, the Constitution stipulates who is eligible for public office and provides means for choosing among those eligible, the two essential features of any election system.

Constitutional Provisions on Political Recruitment

The constitutional provisions on eligibility for national office are quite simple. Representatives are required to be at least 25 years old, to have been U.S. citizens for at least 7 years, and to be inhabitants of the states in which they are elected. For senators, the age and citizenship figures are raised to 30 and 9, with the same residence requirement. The President must be at least 35 and a natural-born citizen who has resided in the United States for at least 14 years. No eligibility requirements are provided for judges and other national officials appointed by the President. Such minor restrictions on eligibility represent an opposite extreme from the restrictions of some systems. Where no one is eligible for an office except a single person—the eldest male in a particular family, for example—the office may be said to be officially *assigned;* where many people are eligible, as in the United States, official status is based on *achievement* rather than official assignment.[1]

---

[1] As we shall see below, informal requirements add considerably to the restrictions on

If eligibility requirements are simple, the machinery for choosing national officials from the many who are eligible is extremely elaborate. The Constitution does not include detailed procedures: the system for choosing congressmen is left to the states, subject to alteration by Congress; election of the President must be by electors, again selected as the state legislatures may provide; judges and other officers of the United States are appointed by the President with the advice and consent of the Senate. The varying details of these procedures will be discussed later. Here we need only note that they insure a different constituency for every branch of the government. The Constitution also provides different terms of office for members of each branch—two years for representatives, six for senators, four for the President, and "good behavior" for judges.

Nominating procedures are not mentioned in the Constitution, except for the provision that the President "shall *nominate*, and by and with the advice and consent of the Senate, shall appoint" Supreme Court justices and certain other national officials. Again, diversity is assured, since the President is given no power to appoint either his successor or congressmen. Although nominating procedures for these elected officials have developed outside the written Constitution, the procedures are clearly a part of our official constitutional system. The Supreme Court has recognized the official character of the nominating system as well as of the final system of elections: "A primary election which involves a necessary step in the choice of candidates for election as representatives in Congress, and which . . . controls that choice, is an election within the meaning of the constitutional provision and is subject to congressional regulation as to the manner of holding it." [2]

The Importance of the Electoral System

If the Supreme Court has declared the entire electoral system—from nomination to final popular choice—to be an official agency of government, why has its official status been so often neglected by students of government? One reason has already been suggested: the agencies concerned with output functions are spelled out in much more detail in the original Constitution. A second reason may be that early political commentaries, such as the *Federalist* papers, followed the lead of the Constitution in de-emphasizing the electoral function of politics. Since the details of the electoral system were yet to be worked out in 1787, the authors of the *Federalist* papers can be more easily excused than later commentators. Third, the Supreme Court's inclusion of nominations along with elections as part of the official system did not come until 1941. [3]

But the most important reason for the long delay in recognizing that the electoral function is carried out by an official agency of government is *confusion*

---

eligibility—women, for example, have been effectively if informally banned from the presidency.

[2] *United States* v. *Classic*, 313 U.S. 299 (1941).

[3] The justices themselves had refused in an earlier decision to accept congressional regulation of nominations as an official part of the election process. See *Newberry* v. *United States*, 256 U.S. 232 (1921).

over what an agency is. We tend to think in concrete terms to a virtually literal extent, assuming that an official agency must be housed in designated buildings made of some durable substance. An *official agency* may be more meaningfully viewed as a structure not of concrete or steel, but of human interrelationships in which people with legal status carry out a governmental activity. The people involved in the electoral system do not meet in a single place or on a relatively continuing basis like members of Congress or of the Supreme Court. But they do have legal status, they make binding decisions, and they perform an essential function of government. Their pattern of activity accordingly makes up an official agency of government.

However occasional and dispersed its activities, the electoral system must be placed alongside the legislative, executive, and judicial systems as an official agency of government. And who can say that it is the least important? A change from achieved to assigned leaders might be more consequential than a change from a bicameral to a unicameral Congress. An election system is not an end in itself, of course; it is important for its input effect—how different interests are represented in government. But neither are legislative, executive, or judicial systems ends in themselves; they are important for their output effects—how different interests are affected by governmental policy.

The difference between a democracy and a dictatorship shows up more clearly in the selection of government officials than in any other activity. The manner in which legislative, executive, and judicial officials are chosen marks the entire political process in the United States. In the next four chapters, we shall see how their varying modes of selection, conflicts in constituencies, and differences in terms of office influence the other official agencies.

Formal Voting Requirements

In our discussion of public opinion, we implied that non-voting is voluntary, in keeping with the finding that lack of interest accounts for some 75 per cent of all failures to vote.[4] But we must remember that certain legal qualifications have to be met before a citizen can enjoy the franchise, regardless of how interested he is in politics. Residence requirements keep at least 3 per cent of adult citizens from voting in every election;[5] almost 40 per cent of the people are ineligible to vote because of their age. If the formal voting requirements of the colonial period still existed, perhaps 48 million of those who voted in 1964 would have been disfranchised.[6] Not only may formal requirements automatically exclude many

---

[4] Paul F. Lazarsfeld, Bernard R. Berelson, and Hazel Gaudet, *The People's Choice* (New York: Columbia University Press, 1948), 2nd ed., pp. 45–49.

[5] See Angus Campbell *et al.*, *The American Voter* (New York: John Wiley & Sons, Inc., 1960), p. 90.

[6] This estimate is from proportions given in V. O. Key, Jr., *Politics, Parties and Pressure Groups* (New York: Thomas Y. Crowell Company, 1952), 3rd ed., p. 602. Also see the 5th ed. (1964), Ch. 22.

people, but they may also influence the interest of those who are legally eligible to vote. Long before opinion surveys produced data on informal influences, voter registration was found to be 15 per cent higher in cities that had permanent voter registration than in cities with periodic registration.[7] Clearly, we cannot understand voting behavior without taking into account official controls over elections.

The Extension of Voting Rights

The United States Constitution provides that presidential electors shall be chosen in each state "in such Manner as the Legislature thereof may direct," and that representatives and senators shall be chosen by those voters in each state who are qualified to vote for "the most numerous branch of the State legislature." Legal requirements for voting are thus established by the states, subject to certain limitations imposed by the Constitution. Since the Constitution adopts state suffrage requirements for national elections, voting qualifications have varied from state to state as well as from time to time. And yet the history of the suffrage in the United States has been one of steady expansion, until in the twentieth century virtually universal adult suffrage has been achieved.

The first general restrictions on voting to be eliminated were religious qualifications. These qualifications prevailed in the original New England colonies, but had been generally replaced by economic restrictions before the Revolution. Somewhat slower to fall were property-holding and taxpaying barriers, but even they could not withstand the assaults of the Jacksonian Democrats; by the time of the Civil War practically all free men could vote. Today the only vestiges of the idea that men devoid of property are necessarily "devoid of principles," and that only citizens with a "stake in society" should have the right to vote, are found in provisions that restrict the vote in local bond elections to those who pay property taxes.

A third arbitrary limitation on suffrage—the denial of the vote on grounds of race or color—has resisted attacks more stubbornly. Although the Fifteenth Amendment, adopted shortly after the Civil War, forbade the states to deny the vote "on account of race, color, or previous condition of servitude," this prohibition was effectively nullified in the southern states by a variety of ostensibly legal and patently illegal devices until well into the twentieth century.

The basic subterfuge during most of the first half of this century was a device known as the "white primary." By restricting membership in the Democratic Party and participation in its primary elections to white voters, this device effectively excluded Negroes from influencing the choice of candidates in areas where the Democratic nominee always won the general election. The Fifteenth Amendment outlawed denial of the vote by *states*, but the Supreme Court viewed the Democratic Party as a private association with which the states had no concern. Consequently, the white primary seemed a perfect weapon for the guardians of "white supremacy."

---

[7] Joseph P. Harris, *Registration of Voters in the United States* (Washington, D.C.: The Brookings Institution, 1929), p. 107.

In 1944, in the case of *Smith* v. *Allwright*, however, the Supreme Court took a closer look at the situation and decided that the white primary was an integral part of a continuous process for choosing public officials.[8] Since the primary was endorsed and enforced by the state—for example, when the state certified party nominees for inclusion on the general election ballot—the Court ruled that the action of the Democratic Party constituted state action in violation of the Fifteenth Amendment. When South Carolina tried to evade this decision by repealing all laws dealing with primaries, U.S. District Judge J. Waties Waring ruled that the plan was unconstitutional, on the ground that the choice of public officials was still controlled through the primary. "It is time," said Judge Waring, himself a native of South Carolina, "for South Carolina to rejoin the Union." [9]

The effects of this Court decision provide us with an interesting commentary on the old saw, "You can't legislate prejudice out of existence." Official decisions actually do not try to regulate prejudice; they attempt to control overt acts. And illegal *behavior*, as distinguished from the attitudes that prompt such behavior, is susceptible to official modification. The estimated number of Negro voters in the South was 250,000 in 1940; the number had doubled within two years after the Supreme Court decision, in 1960 it had reached 1,414,052, and by 1964 it had climbed to 2,164,000.[10]

Ironically, in regulating behavior, court decisions may even have an indirect effect on prejudice itself. In some places, racial integration in public schools may still evoke visions of rape, bloodshed, and a steady stream of white girls marching to the church altar with Negro boys, but many southern whites who once assumed that such things would result from Negro suffrage must certainly have changed their minds. Since 1945, Negroes have been elected to scores of offices in the South, from city commission to state legislature, with every southern state having had at least one Negro in elective office. Mississippi can be included, however, only because one of its cities, Mound Bayou, has an exclusively Negro population.[11] Although Negro participation in southern politics has increased impressively, it still remains far below what one might expect from the number of Negroes in the region. Whites are still registered to vote in the South at almost twice the rate of Negroes. Part of this gap is created by outright denial of voting rights, but much of it also is created by the countless informal ways in

---

[8] *Smith* v. *Allwright*, 321 U.S. 649 (1944). In *U.S.* v. *Classic*, 313 U.S. 299 (1941), the Supreme Court had already determined that, "where the primary is by law made an integral part of the election machinery," Congress has constitutional power to regulate primary as well as general elections.

[9] *Elmore* v. *Rice*, 72 F. Supp. 528 (1947).

[10] These estimates are only rough approximations, because of the decentralized character of registration records. They are based on: Henry Lee Moon, "The Negro Vote in the South: 1952," *The Nation*, September 27, 1952, pp. 245–248; Margaret Price, *The Negro and the Ballot in the South* (Atlanta, Georgia: Southern Regional Council, 1959); *Report of the United States Commission on Civil Rights: 1959* (Washington, D.C.: Government Printing Office, 1959); and *1961 Commission on Civil Rights Report: Voting*, Book 1 (Washington, D.C.: Government Printing Office, 1961); and *The New York Times*, November 22, 1964.

[11] By the "South," we mean the eleven states of the Confederacy.

which a segregated society depresses the participation of the subordinate group.

In most of the southern states, the Negro vote has reached the point where it can be crucial to the outcome of elections. In a recent election for mayor in Atlanta, for example, the white voters were almost evenly divided between an arch segregationist and a moderate on race relations; the Negroes voted overwhelmingly for the moderate. Subsequently, the mayor of Atlanta became the only southern office-holder to testify in favor of the Civil Rights Act of 1964.

Figure 8-1

The per cent of Negroes registered was lowest— under 45—in the five states carried by Goldwater. Johnson's name was not on the ballot in Alabama. In four of the six states won by Johnson the Negro vote, almost 100 per cent of which was cast for the President, exceeded his plurality. Figures are from the Southern Regional Council.

Maps reproduced from *The New York Times*, November 22, 1964.

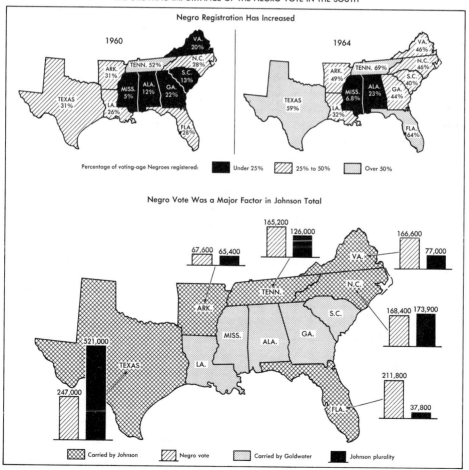

THE GROWING IMPORTANCE OF THE NEGRO VOTE IN THE SOUTH

Negro Registration Has Increased

Negro Vote Was a Major Factor in Johnson Total

As the maps in Figure 8-1 indicate, the proportion of voting-age Negroes who were registered in 1964 exceeded one-third in every southern state except Mississippi, Alabama, and Louisiana. This represents impressive increases over the level of Negro registration in 1960, when the proportion exceeded one-third in only one state (Tennessee). The general momentum of the civil rights movement, a massive Voter Education Project sponsored by the Southern Regional Council, and greater support for Negro applicants from the national government [12] appear to have been mainly responsible for these remarkable gains.

The lower map in Figure 8-1 reflects a dramatic story on the impact of the Negro vote in the presidential election of 1964. The increased Negro vote, coupled with the near-unanimous support of Negroes for President Johnson, was clearly responsible for the President's victory margin in four states (Arkansas, Tennessee, Virginia, and Florida). Indeed, Texas is the only southern state that the President could have carried comfortably without the votes of Negroes. Viewed in historical perspective, the last few years represent truly giant strides toward the long-delayed effectuation of the Fifteenth Amendment.

The fourth and last general barrier to voting—the disfranchisement of women—was not broken down completely until the Nineteenth Amendment was adopted in 1920. The struggle for woman suffrage, antedating the Civil War and closely linked to the abolition movement, had been long and ably fought. Success had been achieved in fifteen states before the federal amendment was adopted. The extremist arguments on both sides now seem amusingly anachronistic, for women have neither been "unsexed" and degraded by political participation, nor have they perfectly purified our politics by their loftier morals. According to leaders of the woman suffrage movement, however, powerful interests opposed the extension of the franchise for more practical reasons. As one of the official historians of the crusade put it, two "supreme influences were implacably opposed to suffrage for women; the corporations because it would vastly increase the votes of the working classes, the liquor interests because they were fully aware of the hostility of women to their business and everything connected with it." [13] As things turned out, the first of these groups need not have worried: women vote less than men, and the lower their economic class the less inclination they show to vote.[14] As a result, woman suffrage has probably worked to the advantage of corporate interests in politics. The liquor interests, on the other hand, did have reason to worry, for in all countries where votes can be compared in terms of sex, women appear to favor more stringent regulation or curtailment of the liquor industry than do men.

---

[12] For a discussion of the Civil Rights Act of 1964 as an output of greater Negro political power, and for more data on the growth of Negro voter registration, see Chapter 13.

[13] Ida Husted Harper, *The History of Woman Suffrage* (New York: National American Woman Suffrage Association, 1922), V, xviii. Quoted in Key, *Politics, Parties, and Pressure Groups*, 5th ed., p. 614.

[14] Angus Campbell and Homer C. Cooper, *Group Differences in Attitudes and Votes* (Ann Arbor: Survey Research Center, Institute for Social Research, University of Michigan, 1956), p. 20.

Once these general barriers had been eliminated, the right to vote in the United States became universal for all practical purposes. True, three general requirements must still be met in all the states before one can claim the right to vote, but none of these is an arbitrary denial of the franchise to a whole class of the population.

First, the prospective voter must be a citizen of the United States. Aliens were permitted to vote in twenty-two states and territories in the nineteenth century. In 1926, however, Arkansas joined the other states to make United States citizenship a universal requirement.

Second, every state has an age requirement—twenty-one years in all but four states. Georgia and Kentucky have reduced the minimum to eighteen, Alaska to nineteen, and Hawaii to twenty. Although President Eisenhower recommended a constitutional amendment in 1954 to reduce the voting age to eighteen in all states, Congress did not respond to the recommendation. In fact, however, young people are less interested in politics and less likely to vote than their elders. As a result, the drive to lower the voting age did not get far. Little has been heard about a constitutional provision to lower the voting age in recent years.

The third general requirement is that the prospective voter must have resided for a specified period in the state, county, and voting district. Although the periods required vary considerably, they are generally one year, ninety days or less, and thirty days or less, respectively. The most liberal residence requirements appear in seven states that require six months in the state and thirty days or less in the county and district.[15] At the other extreme, three southern states (Alabama, Mississippi, and South Carolina) extend the periods to two years in the state and one year in the county or voting district.[16] Since certain groups in the population—fruit-pickers, day-laborers, southern Negroes, and college professors, for example—are more migratory than others—bankers, doctors, and lawyers, for example—a long-term residence requirement may serve in some measure as a substitute for a property qualification.

In addition to these general requirements, there are several bases of disqualification that vary from state to state. Such people as the insane, prison inmates, and those convicted of specified crimes are frequently disqualified. Five southern states still require the payment of an annual poll tax of one or two dollars before a citizen may vote.[17] This requirement, generally thought to be directed against Negroes, affected enough white voters to fall into disfavor even in the South. In 1964 the ratification of the Twenty-fourth Amendment made the poll tax unconstitutional as applied to national elections. For states that retain the poll tax, this leaves two classes of voters, some qualified to vote in all elections,

---

[15] The states are Idaho, Kansas, Maine, Michigan, Minnesota, Nevada, and Oregon.
[16] For a complete tabulation of voting qualifications by state, see *The Book of the States, 1964–65* (Chicago: The Council of State Governments, 1964), pp. 24–25. South Carolina now requires only one year of residence for voting in national elections.
[17] These states are Mississippi, Virginia, Alabama, Arkansas, and Texas.

others qualified to vote only in national elections. Shortly after adoption of the Amendment, six Virginia citizens asked the federal courts to declare the state poll tax requirement unconstitutional as a form of "inherent economic discrimination." Although the United States Court of Appeals declined to rule against the Virginia poll tax, more may be heard of the argument that these citizens were denied, "solely on account of their poverty, the privilege to vote." [18]

Literacy tests are required by seventeen states. These tests were initiated in Connecticut (1855) and Massachusetts (1857) as a substitute for the property qualification, with the specific aim of denying the vote to recent immigrants. Since the ability to read is related to the ability to achieve an informed judgment, a properly administered literacy test is less criticized than a poll tax. Because of abuses of the literacy tests by election officials in some southern states, however, the Civil Rights Act of 1964 required that literacy tests must be given in writing and that a sixth-grade education shall be taken as a presumption of literacy unless the state can prove otherwise.

In at least some areas of all the states, citizens must demonstrate that they meet the voting requirements by registering beforehand.[19] In small rural communities, the election officials may know all the prospective voters and their qualifications on sight. But in the big cities some form of registration is necessary to insure that voters actually meet legal requirements.

There are two systems of registration: periodic and permanent. The periodic system seems more desirable at first glance, because it should produce a "clean" list of voters at regular intervals. In practice, however, these decentralized registrations, conducted by part-time employees chosen by party stalwarts at the precinct level, may be more conducive to fraudulent and padded lists of voters than is permanent registration. No system is foolproof, of course, but most states now use permanent registration.

The chief advantage of permanent registration is that a small, permanent staff, appropriately supervised, develops a professional spirit that reduces the chances of fraud. And the problem of revising the voting lists can be handled on a continuing basis. Such organizations as the National Municipal League and the League of Women Voters have endorsed permanent registration. But party organizations—loath to surrender the patronage accompanying the periodic employment of registration officials in each precinct—generally oppose it. Perhaps the worst system of all is the combination of permanent registration with the use of part-time political appointees to maintain the system, as in North Carolina, for example. The combination of professional, full-time personnel with permanent (but continuously revised) registration lists appears most conducive to the fair and efficient conduct of elections.[20]

All members of the official electoral agency do not work in harmony. The

---

[18] *The New York Times*, November 13, 1964.

[19] In Arkansas and Texas, payment of poll taxes is the equivalent of registration.

[20] A few urban counties of North Carolina have employed full-time personnel to "supplement" the work of precinct registrars, and they maintain accurate and up-to-date records.

federal system lends itself to departures from general legal standards whenever the dominant elements in a given geographical area are bent on imposing deviant rules. Even in the most rural, Deep-South county, however, election officials are part of a national agency. The Civil Rights Act of 1964 included specific regulations to insure that all applicants for the franchise in a county will be expected to meet the same standards and that these standards shall be reasonable.[21]

Nominating the Candidates

Over 70,000,000 American citizens were legally eligible for election as President in 1964.[22] But in the election, the voters had an effective choice between only two people. What happened to the other 70 million or more possibilities? They were eliminated by the nominating process. If nominations take care of 99.9 per cent of the political recruitment function, they are quite evidently a major part of the electoral system.

Caucuses and Conventions

The first stage in the official election process in the United States is the nomination of candidates to represent each of the parties (or independent groups) that are seeking public office.[23] In other democracies, nominations are made informally by party organizations or caucuses. But in the United States the nomination has taken on an official and elaborate form. The basic reason for this difference is probably that American political parties are less responsible as a group for the conduct of government than are the parties in other democratic regimes. Consequently, the person who seeks office under the party label takes on greater importance as an individual.

Then, too, there are the legalistic and reformist traditions that are so characteristic of American politics. Americans feel that "there ought to be a law" to deal with every problem and look askance at the practice of having candidates nominated by parties acting as private associations. Official regulation of nominations by the states was begun late in the nineteenth century at the urging of reformists who were bent on democratizing every aspect of American government. This development was particularly important in the one-party states, where nominations are tantamount to elections.

The first nominating device used by American political parties, for both national and state office, was the legislative caucus. The caucus was composed of

---

[21] See Ch. 13 for a discussion of the specific provisions of the Act.

[22] This figure is only an approximation. The 1960 census reported 76,698,688 people in the United States 35 years of age or older. We reduced this number to account for naturalized citizens, aliens, and natural-born citizens disqualified by the 14-year residence requirement.

[23] Although most states permit independent candidates to secure nomination, generally by a petition signed by a given percentage of the voters, party nominees dominate. We therefore confine ourselves to the processes of nomination by political parties.

party members in Congress (or in the legislature at the state level). But the Jacksonian Democrats denounced the caucus as an undemocratic device, and advocated the party convention as a means of insuring indirect nomination by the party rank and file. Although the convention came into universal use during the nineteenth century as the means of choosing nominees to state offices, it came to be associated with boss rule and domination by special interests during the Progressive Era in the twentieth century. Like the caucus before it, the convention was discarded for a more popular method of nomination. Today, representatives, senators, and most state officers are nominated by direct primary elections, and party conventions persist only in nominations for the presidency.[24]

The Direct Primary Election

The direct primary really serves as a preliminary official election. It is usually conducted under state laws, just as the subsequent general election is, and it provides the members of each party with an opportunity to take part in choosing the party's nominees. Aspirants to the United States Senate or House of Representatives, and to various state offices, secure a place on the primary ballot either by simply announcing their candidacy and paying a fee, or by presenting a petition signed by a required number of voters. The candidate for nomination may enter only his own party's primary, and in most states he must be able to demonstrate that he is actually a member of the party—by attesting that he supported its nominees in the last general election, for example.

A few states have permitted "cross filing" or "double filing," however, theoretically enabling a candidate to enter more than one party primary at the same time. In recent years, cross filing seems to have been unique to California.[25] For forty-six years, California permitted candidates to run in both parties' primaries, and, for most of this time, a large majority of successful candidates won the nomination of both parties. Although Democrats have far outnumbered Republicans in California since the 1930's, the Republicans had better-known leaders and a better press, so the practice of cross filing worked to their advantage. In 1958, the Democrats captured control of the governorship and both houses of the legislature for the first time in history. They were as eager to emphasize the party label as the Republicans had been to obscure it; in 1959, the legislature promptly followed the governor's request to abolish cross filing. With its elimination in California, the practice of cross filing disappeared from American politics.

---

[24] Connecticut, Delaware, Hawaii, Indiana, and New York still use conventions to nominate candidates for some or all state-wide offices. See *The Book of the States, 1964–65*, p. 20.

[25] Joseph P. Harris and Leonard Rowe, *California Politics* (Stanford: Stanford University Press, 1959), 2nd ed., pp. 2–3. Most writers refer to cross filing as the practice of "several states," but Harris and Rowe describe it as unique to California in the 1950's. It was once permitted in New York, for example, but was prohibited by a 1947 statute. See Frank J. Munger and Ralph A. Straetz, *New York Politics* (New York: New York University Press, 1960), p. 70.

Direct primary elections are either "open" or "closed." In the closed primary, a voter must be able to demonstrate that he is a party member, and he may vote only in the primary of his own party. The tests of party allegiance are often quite simple, involving merely an assertion of past, present, or future identification with the party—that he voted for the party nominees in the last general election, that he is a member of the party, or that he plans to vote for the candidates nominated by the party. In about half the states, however, his party affiliation is recorded at registration, and he is not permitted to vote in the primary of any other party. In the open primary, on the other hand, any qualified citizen may vote in the primary of any party. Party regulars resent the idea that non-members can affect the choice of party nominees and vehemently denounce the open primary as corrosive of party responsibility. Just as "cross filing" weakened the party identification of the candidate, the open primary weakens the party identification of the voter.

To what extent has the direct primary succeeded in "popularizing" party nominations? Experience with primaries suggests that they may have decreased organizational control but without bringing the promised increase in popular interest and participation. Let's look first at the effect of the primary on the party hierarchy's control over nominations. In some states, the party organization endorses a slate of candidates on the primary ballot, but these "regular" candidates meet with varying success. Even in those places where the organization is uniformly victorious, the necessity of securing the party members' approval in the primary may influence the organization's choice. Where there is no official organization slate, the primary may be fought out between fairly well-defined factions within the party, or simply between individual candidates with whatever personal organizations they can manage to put together. In any case, direct control over the choice of nominees by a few powerful leaders appears less likely than it was under the convention system.

Nomination by direct primaries has decreased the extent to which a state-wide organization can control nominations. But it has not brought the selection of candidates by a broad cross-section of party members. In the first place, participation in primaries has been disappointingly low. A study of gubernatorial elections in 15 states between 1926 and 1952 demonstrates this vividly. In a majority of the primaries, less than 30 per cent of the potential electorate voted, whereas in a majority of the general elections, over 60 per cent voted. In almost a third of the primaries, less than 25 per cent voted, but none of the general elections brought such a meager turnout.[26] In the second place, the small number who do vote in primaries do not accurately represent the entire party following. In Massachusetts, for example, the Boston area has supplied about half the Democratic Party's primary election votes but only a third of the party's general election votes. As a result, Boston—which supplied only one out of four Democratic

---

[26] The states selected were all non-southern. Turnout in general elections in the South is much less than elsewhere, but turnout in primaries is no greater. V. O. Key, Jr., *American State Politics* (New York: Alfred A. Knopf, 1956), p. 135.

nominees under the convention system—came to supply over 80 per cent of the Democratic nominees under the primary system.[27]

The great appeal of the primary is that, however small the turnout, it gives more people a chance to influence party nominations. The unexpected drawback is that, at least in two-party states, it may weaken a party's general election slate by permitting particular areas or groups in the party to create an unbalanced ticket.

The Direct Primary in One-Party Politics

Nominations are important enough in two-party areas, for they serve to reduce the voter's choice to two candidates. But in one-party areas they actually eliminate any real choice in the general election. And the one-party system—the domination of general elections by a single party—is much more widespread in the United States than is generally realized. In talking about political parties, we classified about half the states as having two-party competition because "the second party had won over 25 per cent of the elections" for President, United States Senator, and governor. This criterion leaves room, even in two-party states, for many elections to be effectively settled by the direct primary. In the forty-year period from 1896 to 1946, in the United States as a whole, over half the elections to the House of Representatives were won by a plurality of at least 20 per cent, which means that the winner received 60 per cent or more of the votes while his opponent mustered no more than 40 per cent.[28] Even with the close presidential race in 1960, a majority of the house seats were still won by the same large plurality. In 1964, 250 of the 435 congressional victories were by margins over 60 per cent.

From a functional point of view, elections are the process by which the people choose public officials, and nominations are the process by which the support of similar or allied groups is concentrated behind a candidate. In these terms, in one-party areas the primary of the major party *is* the election. What, then, constitutes the nomination in these areas? The real nomination takes place through informal bargaining in which various leaders and factions agree to support a common candidate. In some one-party states, such as Louisiana, these intra-party factions have enough continuity to resemble political parties. In other one-party states, such as Florida, nominations usually emerge from a chaotic struggle between purely personal followings.

Primary elections generally give the nomination to the candidate who receives a plurality (the largest number) of the votes. But in most one-party states a "run-off" or a "second primary" is held between the two leading candidates if neither receives a majority in the first primary. Without the primary election to give expression to political differences, the one-party system could hardly endure.

---

[27] *Ibid.*, pp. 154–156.

[28] This conclusion is based on the comprehensive analysis of Cortez A. M. Ewing, *Congressional Elections, 1896–1944* (Norman: University of Oklahoma Press, 1947), pp. 328–333. Also see Malcolm Moos, *Politics, Presidents and Coattails* (Baltimore: The Johns Hopkins Press, 1952), pp. 24–29.

In two-party states, on the other hand, the primary is much less important. Thus the few states that retain nominating conventions for state-wide offices all enjoy fairly even competition between the parties.

Although the party convention has been replaced by the direct primary in nominations for Congress and most state offices, it remains conspicuously alive in the nomination of presidential candidates. Indeed, the national nominating conventions of the political parties are regarded as no less American than baseball and hot-dogs. Foreign and American visitors to national conventions have been awed, shocked, or repulsed by the noise, numbers, and hard bargaining that characterize this quadrennial pageant of politics. Many observers regard the circus atmosphere as inappropriate to the choice of a candidate for one of the world's most powerful positions. Defenders of the convention, on the other hand, point out that the quality of American presidents has been generally competent and occasionally truly great. Like war veterans, businessmen, and other non-political conventioneers, American politicians do make a holiday of the convention, but they also manage to accomplish serious and generally successful work.

The principal function of the national convention is to nominate candidates who will serve as the party's standard-bearers in the quest for America's most prized political plum—the presidency of the United States. A second function is to create enthusiasm, both inside and outside the convention, for the party and its presidential and vice-presidential candidates. Third, the convention serves, perhaps more by the candidates it selects than by the platform it adopts, to suggest the party's position on the key issues of the day.

The selection of candidates, the creation of support, and the adoption of positions on issues are the intended consequences or the purposes of the convention. They may accordingly be called its *manifest* functions.[29] But the convention system also has latent (unintended) functions that are frequently overlooked. While the manifest functions of the convention are important primarily for the parties themselves, the latent functions are also vitally important for the political system as a whole.

Looking first at latent functions of national conventions for the parties themselves, the most important is the creation or ratification of party consensus. Through the bargains and the compromises that seem so offensive to the uninitiated, the convention serves to unite fifty state parties into a single national party, at least for the duration of the campaign. The first conventions in the early nineteenth century functioned merely to *ratify* an established consensus

---

[29] As we indicated in Chapter 1, the functions of any specified unit are understood in terms of its consequences, whether intended or unintended. This distinction between intended consequences (manifest functions) and unintended consequences (latent functions) should keep us aware that both exist. Professional political scientists sometimes become so fascinated with the discovery of latent functions that they forget the importance of manifest functions. For the distinction as we employ it, see Robert K. Merton, *Social Theory and Social Structure* (Glencoe, Illinois: The Free Press, 1949), p. 63.

on who should head the ticket, and they generally failed to create party unity in support of a vice-presidential candidate. The nomination of James K. Polk as the Democratic candidate in 1844 is cited as the first case in which a convention created "an original synthesis," nominating a candidate who received no votes at all on the first ballot and uniting the party behind him.[30] From that point on, the conventions have been able to *create* as well as merely to ratify party consensus.[31]

Occasionally, the convention fails to bring about this unity, and such failures serve to spotlight the importance of this latent function. In 1948, for example, the Democratic Party organizations in four southern states, embittered by President Truman's stand for a positive civil rights program, broke from the national party and presented a different candidate (J. Strom Thurmond, the States' Rights or "Dixiecratic" nominee) as the Democratic nominee in their states. The fact that dissension of this sort rarely develops is a tribute to the success of the convention in unifying the party behind a single candidate. The Republican convention of 1964 could be called dysfunctional so far as party unity is concerned. Even so, none of the major Republican leaders bolted the party to support the Democrats, and most manfully went through at least the motions of supporting Senator Goldwater.

As a second latent function important primarily to the parties, the convention serves as a ceremony or ritual in which the democratic nature of parties is celebrated. For a few days every four years, hundreds of minor figures enjoy the official right to decide on the destiny of their party. Although most members are committed to take their cues from their state or national leaders, any delegate may rise to challenge the vote as reported by his delegation's chairman. The exercise of this right, and the subsequent poll of the delegation, reaffirms the dependence of the leaders on their followers.[32]

Third, the national convention is one of the key devices through which political parties have democratized the choice of the President, despite the electoral college procedures prescribed in the Constitution. Here we see a latent function of great importance for the political system as a whole rather than simply for the parties themselves. The expectation of the Constitutional Convention that members of the electoral college would exercise independent judgment in voting for a President and Vice-President was quickly dashed by the development of political parties. And the convention has succeeded better than the party caucus in turning the electoral college into a recording device for

---

[30] Key, *Politics, Parties, and Pressure Groups*, p. 398.

[31] Republican conventions have more often achieved unity by ratifying consensus and Democratic conventions by creating consensus. Since the Civil War two-thirds of the Republican candidates for President and one-half of the Democratic candidates have been named on the first ballot. See *ibid.*, p. 425.

[32] In order to prevent TV-conscious delegates from delaying proceedings in order to get "on camera," the poll of delegations may now take place while the work of the convention proceeds. See Paul T. David, Ralph M. Goodman, and Richard C. Bain, *The Politics of National Party Conventions* (Washington, D.C.: The Brookings Institution, 1960), p. 388.

its choices as endorsed by the electorate. Conventions, as noisy gatherings of over a thousand of the party faithful, representing members in all the states and territories, give the party rank and file an influence that would have horrified the more genteel among the Framing Fathers, who recoiled at the turbulence of "mob action."

The nature of our national party system is a fourth consequence of the national convention. V. O. Key went so far as to imply that our national system of party government itself is a direct function of the national convention: "When the national convention was contrived to designate presidential nominees, viable national party came into existence." [33] This is probably too strong a statement, as a subsequent comment by Key himself suggests. "Without [the national convention] or some equivalent institution party government for the nation as a whole could scarcely exist." The crucial phrase here is "or some equivalent institution"—other nations without national nominating conventions have national party systems. Without this particular nominating device, we would probably also have developed some equivalents. If this line of reasoning is correct, the national nominating convention is a sufficient but not a necessary condition of national parties.

Whether necessary to the system or not, our quadrennial conventions for nominating presidential candidates have done much to shape the nature of our party system. For one thing, the national convention includes a broader base of members—and therefore of potential candidates—than the congressional caucus. Members of the losing party in congressional races would go unrepresented in a congressional caucus, but their districts are represented in the national convention. During the period when the Democrats nominated Roosevelt, Truman, and Stevenson, southerners held around 45 per cent of the Democratic seats in the Senate and about 50 per cent of those in the House, but they got only 25 per cent of the seats at Democratic national conventions. Without a non-congressional channel for advancement, such as the national convention affords, the kinds of nominations we have experienced would certainly have been quite different. Aside from the fate of the three nominees we have named, General Eisenhower could certainly not have won the Republican nomination from Senator Taft if the battle had been fought on different terrain.

The convention system has probably functioned to turn the President into the one great tribune of the people. Notice the shift from a congressional to a broad popular orientation with Jackson, the first President to capture office outside the caucus system. Granted the particularistic or local orientation of Congress, the national orientation of the presidency has probably been functional for the American system.[34]

---

[33] Key, *Politics, Parties, and Pressure Groups*, p. 431.

[34] Of course, if Congress were more directly involved in the choice of presidents, and if congressional service led more directly to the presidency, the orientation of Congress might be much less particularistic. If a national orientation is functional for the democratic polity, then, the national nominating conventions may be dysfunctional in their effects on Congress. While this reasoning is speculative, it is not entirely data-free.

Choosing Convention Delegates

The management of these great conventions is completely in the hands of the political parties, except that some states regulate the selection of delegates by law. The methods of selecting delegates vary greatly, and differences in party rules as well as state laws create an extremely complicated national picture. Fifteen states and the District of Columbia conduct presidential preference primaries in which the voters may indicate their preferences among the contenders for their party's nomination.[35] In a number of these states, however, including Illinois, Massachusetts, New Hampshire, New Jersey, and West Virginia, the outcome of the presidential preference vote is not binding on the delegates. In Nebraska, candidates for election as delegates must file affidavits pledging themselves to abide by the outcome of the presidential preference voting; but in practice this pledge has often been ignored, with the presidential primary interpreted as advisory only. In three of the states with presidential primaries—Indiana, Maryland, and Pennsylvania—some or all of the delegates are chosen by party conventions. Most of the states choose all their delegates through party conventions, but in a few they are chosen by party committees or by a combination of methods.

Most of these complications arose from attempts in the first two decades of this century to extend the direct primary to the nomination of presidential candidates. Reformers reasoned that, if the national convention could not be eliminated as the state conventions had been, at least the direct election of delegates pledged to a specific candidate would transform the national convention from a decision-making body into a mere recording device. If successful, the movement would have left the national convention with no more discretion in nominating the President than the electoral college has in electing him. By 1916, half the states were using the presidential primary in one form or another, but since that time the tide has turned back in favor of the convention. If the convention is to perform its latent function of unifying the party, as well as its manifest function of nominating candidates, the delegates must retain some freedom to maneuver, bargain, and compromise. As a result, the attempt to turn the function of the convention over to the primaries produces such complicated rules as those binding Oregon delegates. They must support the winner of the presidential preference primary until he wins less than 35 per cent of the convention votes, until he releases the delegates, or until two ballots have passed. Most of the states that bind delegates now bind them only for the first ballot.

In practice, the presidential primary may actually be more of a nuisance than an instrument of democracy. If delegates were really bound to vote only for the candidate to whom they were pledged, a failure to produce a majority on the first ballot would create a permanent stalemate. Consequently, the primary

---

See, for example, the more national orientation of the British Parliament. At minimum, it reminds us that a given institution may be functional for the system as a whole and for some of its elements while, at the same time, it is dysfunctional for other elements.

[35] *Congressional Quarterly Weekly Report*, XXII (week ending January 17, 1964), pp. 92–100.

is used chiefly as a gauge of public opinion, and in this respect it is far from satis-factory. Since the presidential primaries are held on different dates, the results in one state inevitably affect the campaign in other areas; candidates wisely refuse to enter the contest in states where they may lose more than they can gain; local "favorite son" candidates are entered in order to postpone committing the state to any national contender; grueling campaign efforts are imposed on the candi-dates; and the expense is enormous. Moreover, public opinion surveys furnish nation-wide reports on the popularity of the candidates that are probably more meaningful than the results of the scattered primaries.

Despite their limitations, presidential primaries can become important fac-tors in the battle for a party's nomination. Aside from the delegate votes they pick up, they can impress party leaders in other states with a candidate's vote-pulling power. Thus the "Minnesota miracle" in 1952, when over 100,000 voters went to the trouble of writing in Eisenhower's name in the Republican primary, gave great impetus to the Eisenhower campaign everywhere. The crucial primary for Kennedy in 1960 was in West Virginia, where he demonstrated that his Catholicism was not an insurmountable barrier to success among predominantly Protestant voters. In 1964, the California primary in effect gave the Republican nomination to Goldwater. He had garnered only 23 per cent of the Republican votes in New Hampshire and only 18 per cent in Oregon. Coupled with survey findings which consistently showed minority support for him among Republi-cans throughout the nation, these primaries were almost fatal to his chances. Even with strong support among delegates chosen through conventions, another defeat in California would probably have been ruinous. His razor-thin victory over Governor Rockefeller in California erased the stigma of defeat. Since the primaries can assume such importance, they tend to limit the field to nationally known figures and to those who can command considerable pre-convention financial backing. When Vice-President Humphrey attempted, as a Senator from Minnesota, to compete against Kennedy in the 1960 primaries, he was extremely handicapped by limited funds and by the limited organization that he could finance.

The allotment of delegates to the states and territories is controlled entirely by party regulations. Originally, it was based on the electoral college vote; for many years, each state got two convention votes for each of its electoral college votes. Then, after 1912, in order to reduce that influence of traditionally Demo-cratic states, the Republicans worked out an arrangement to give greater influ-ence in the convention to the states and districts that would actually support the Republican nominees. States with very few Republican votes are thus penalized and those with heavy Republican turnout receive "bonus" delegates. In 1964, the Republican convention included 1,308 delegates, each with a single vote. The allocation of these delegates followed this formula: *at-large delegates*—4 per state, 2 additional for each U. S. representative at large, 6 additional for each state that voted for Nixon in 1960 or that elected a Republican U. S. senator or gov-ernor in 1960 or later; *district delegates*—1 for each congressional district that cast 2,000 or more votes for Nixon in 1960 or for the Republican House candidate in 1962, 1 additional for each district that cast 10,000 or more votes for Nixon in 1960 or for the Republican House candidate in 1962.[36] This formula makes dull reading, but it is arithmetic with a message. The Republican system of at-large bonus delegates rewards Republican states and the district system punishes areas wholly dominated by the Democrats.

The Democrats have traditionally allotted delegates to every state and district, without regard to their voting records. But in 1964 they came up with a reform that carries a significance overlooked by the press. The Democrats adopted a bonus system that is designed not only to reward states which supported the preceding Democratic presidential candidate but also to reward states with a heavy turnout of Democratic votes, regardless of who carried the state. Moreover, unlike the Republican formula, the Democrats' bonus system is *keyed to the presidential race alone*. The new Democratic formula for 1964 was: 3 convention votes for each electoral vote, 1 vote for every 100,000 popular votes (or major fraction thereof) cast for Kennedy in 1960, a bonus of 10 votes if the state cast its electoral votes for Kennedy in 1960, and 1 vote to be cast by each state's national committeeman and committeewoman.[37] This system produced 2,316 convention votes to be cast by a maximum of 2,944 delegates plus 108 national committeemen and committeewomen.[38]

Because these bonuses are keyed to the presidential race only, they will not automatically accrue to southern states that frequently vote Republican in presidential contests but always elect Democrats to the Senate and governorship. Nor will they go to states that, like Mississippi in 1960, elect an unpledged slate of Democratic electors who cast the state's electoral vote for some Democrat (Senator Harry Byrd of Viriginia in this case) other than the convention's nominee. Finally, by rewarding states that turn out heavily for the Democratic presidential candidate, the new system of bonuses will work to the relative disadvantage of states with low levels of participation—and these are primarily in the South. These reforms were adopted by the Democratic National Committee in a mood that suggested they constituted the first step in a trend. Even this first step modestly shifts the relative power in the convention toward the large industrial states and away from the parochial Democrats of the South.

---

[36] *Congressional Quarterly Weekly Report*, XXII (week ending January 17, 1964), p. 84.

[37] *Congressional Quarterly Weekly Report*, XXII (week ending January 17, 1964), p. 131.

[38] This large representation was necessary so that each state could have at least as many people and votes at the convention as it had been able to send in 1960. From contact with the committee, the authors are struck with the fact that state politicians are so strongly committed to satisfying the desires of their key party members to attend the convention that they respond more to the absolute number of "bodies" they are assigned than to the more complex question of the proportionate voting strength that those bodies will wield. National party leaders are more attuned to the latter question.

The conventions meet in the summer of the election year, at a time and place designated by the national committee of each party. The preliminary work is done by four standing committees. The committee on *credentials* judges the qualifications of delegates and recommends solutions of disputes to the convention as a whole. In the convention, the "temporary roll," compiled by the national committee, determines which of the contending delegates will be seated. Bitter disputes occasionally produce a note of disharmony and an early indication of which faction controls the convention. In the Republican convention of 1964, supporters of Governor William Scranton (Pa.) offered an early motion to bar the seating of any delegate who had been selected by rules or procedures "which had the purpose or effect" of racial discrimination. This motion was supported with the charge that "forces at work in this country" want to turn the Republican Party into a "lily-white party." This statement was loudly booed by the delegates and the motion was resoundingly defeated. From this point on, it was clear that Goldwater supporters controlled the convention.

The committee on *permanent organization* nominates a permanent chairman, standing committees, and other functionaries to replace the temporary officers who were appointed by the national committee. Both the temporary chairman, whose chief function is to deliver a keynote address condemning the opposition and praising his own party, and the permanent chairman, who presides over the convention, are key officers, and their selection is another indication of what faction holds control. The President usually controls these choices for his party, but they may be hotly disputed in the opposition party.

The committee on *rules* recommends a set of rules to govern the convention. Generally, it recommends that the rules of the House of Representatives be adopted insofar as they are applicable.

The committee on *resolutions* draws up the party platform, a statement of the policies the party proposes to follow if its candidates are elected. Although party platforms are generally ignored by voters and condemned by scholars for their evasiveness and generality, they are closely watched by leaders of special-interest groups. The committee conducts hearings at which interested persons may appear, but the basic platform is settled in advance by the group in control of the convention. This group tries to bridge differences within the party by careful ambiguity. Despite these efforts, bitter floor fights—like the one on the civil rights plank in the 1948 Democratic platform—sometimes disrupt the convention.

The chief business of the convention—the nomination of a candidate for the presidency—begins with an alphabetical roll call of states. This is an occasion for florid nominating and seconding speeches in behalf of those who seek the nomination. Then the voting begins, again by the states in alphabetical order, and is continued until one of the candidates receives a majority. The Democrats formerly employed a "unit rule," under which the entire vote of each state delegation was cast for the candidate favored by the majority of the delegation. But present practice is for the convention to recognize and enforce whatever instructions have been given to the delegates by their state party agencies. Under this rule, most delegations are no longer bound to vote as a unit in Democratic conventions. The Republicans do not even honor state instructions to a delegation to vote under the unit rule.

If no candidate captures a majority on the first ballot, the negotiations between factions are intensified. At this point, minor or "favorite son" candidates often gain considerable influence—or perhaps even the vice-presidency—by shifting to the apparent winner at a propitious moment. By means of such bargaining, the convention performs its function of uniting the party behind a single candidate. The symbol of this achievement is the common practice of making the vote unanimous once the outcome has become clear.

The nomination of the vice-presidential candidate is usually a much more perfunctory matter, despite the fact that eight of the thirty-five men who have served as President have died in office. The presidential nominee, of course, has a strong voice in the selection of his running-mate, and his nod frequently goes to an opponent whose supporters helped the winner gain his majority. This is especially true if the opponent can "balance the ticket" as a spokesman for a different section, policy position, or faction of the party. Ironically, then, the vice-presidential candidate is often one of the party figures *least* likely to ensure continuity should the President die in office.

This custom may be dying out, but it may be ignored by an incumbent President more safely than by a challenger. Kennedy's choice of Johnson as his running mate in 1960 followed the theory of the balanced ticket, but it also gave him a Vice-President with great political experience. President Johnson's 1964 prospects looked so bright after the Republicans nominated Goldwater that he was under minimal pressure in his choice of a running mate. In choosing Senator Humphrey, he, too, has a Vice-President with impressive political experience. Goldwater's choice of retiring Congressman William Miller (N.Y.) clearly departed from the "balancing" theory in every sense except the geographical; Miller represented at least as extreme a form of conservatism as Goldwater himself. As the challenger of an incumbent President, Goldwater's departure from the custom of the balanced ticket may have reduced his chance of pulling an upset. The ambiguities and apparent contradictions of the usual platform and ticket were completely missing in the Republican campaign of 1964. In the 1962 edition of this book, we said, "When the chips are down in an election, party leaders can ill afford to forget the convention's function of unifying the diverse elements that make up the party." Senator Goldwater forgot this function at his own peril.

Campaigns and Elections

Campaign Strategy

Campaign strategy is designed to win elections by influencing public opinion. This strategy is directed at the processes by which the voters form their political opinions. In a pioneer study of election behavior made in 1940 in Erie County,

Ohio, the principal effects of campaign strategy were identified as reinforcement, activation, and conversion.[39] For most voters (about 53 per cent in the 1940 study), the campaign serves simply to *reinforce* preferences and intentions already formed. Most voters prefer the same party from one election to another. These members of the party faithful need only to be reassured on the rectitude of their position. Even among voters who change their party preference, more appear to switch their preference before the campaign, as a result of events since the last election, than are changed by the campaign itself. The reinforcement function is consequently central to the success of the campaign.

The campaign also stimulates the undecided or indifferent by *activating* or crystallizing latent preferences for a particular candidate or party. Without the vote of those who are only weakly attached to the party, the election may easily be lost.

Finally, the campaign tries to *convert* voters who have already decided to vote for the opposition. Although the casual observer might assume that this is the primary function of the campaign, only a small percentage of voters are actually induced to change their preference. Even the 8 per cent who switched parties in 1940 are usually enough to decide an election, however, so they cannot be ignored.

Campaigns are planned, with varying degrees of precision, to perform these three functions. Rule-of-thumb, traditional tactics may still predominate, but they are being supplemented more and more by the advice of experts in the art and science of "engineering consent." A successful campaign strategy must achieve three objectives, whether by design or by luck: (1) get the party's propaganda before the voter; (2) produce attitudes favorable to the party's candidates; (3) stimulate people *to vote*—for the right candidate. These objectives are easiest to achieve where reinforcement is all that is necessary and most difficult or impossible to achieve where conversion is required.

Getting the Message Heard and Believed

Both the traditional party institutions and the newly important public relations organizations are drawn into service in the effort to get the message heard. All the media of communication, from give-away pamphlets to television, are mobilized to make the voters familiar with the party's candidates and policies. Well-known movie stars, athletes, and scholars contribute their assorted talents. Every conceivable avenue for reaching every group of voters seems to be exploited, including the candidates' families. In 1964, Mrs. Johnson toured the southern states on a campaign train known as the "Lady Bird Special" in an effort to shore up support among wavering southerners. With Mrs. Johnson's southern charm becoming more southern at every stop, and with less gentle pressure from the White House, various southern politicians who had remained aloof during the campaign found

---

[39] Lazarsfeld, Berelson, and Gaudet, *The People's Choice*, p. 103. In addition to the 53 per cent who were reinforced and the 8 per cent who were converted, the campaign had these effects: activation, 14 per cent; reconversion, 3 per cent; partial conversion, 6 per cent; no effect, 16 per cent.

themselves climbing aboard the Lady Bird Special. Mrs. Goldwater was less active in her husband's behalf, but the Goldwater children were highly active.

Since few people vote for an unknown candidate, a politician must be known to the voters if he is to win. One of Stevenson's biggest disadvantages in 1952 and 1956 was his relative unfamiliarity as a national figure. In 1936, 1940, and 1944, Roosevelt's challengers suffered a similar disadvantage. Moreover, Roosevelt understood that it is worse for a candidate to be ignored than criticized; consequently, he avoided mentioning his opponents by name in order not to give them free publicity. Before the 1960 campaign, Nixon was a much more familiar figure than Kennedy, but Nixon's willingness to meet his opponent in the famous TV debates largely dissipated his advantage. President Johnson, wrapping himself in the duties and dignity of the presidency, refused to make the same mistake; indeed, he followed Roosevelt's lead, avoiding mention of Goldwater until very late in the campaign.

Although familiarity is an essential element in winning elections, simply becoming known is not enough for the political candidate, his party, or its policies; they must also be known in a favorable light. The manner in which a personality is projected to the voters has a great deal to do with how they evaluate him as a candidate. Because of their "double exposure," the Kennedy-Nixon TV debates in 1960 gave the candidates a unique opportunity to create favorable images in both political camps—to watch your favorite you were virtually forced to watch his opponent. Unfortunately for Nixon, his pre-debate image called for a superb competitive performance. A candidate may be admired primarily for a warm and sincere *personality* (Eisenhower), for his *political role*, such as the policies he espouses (Truman), or for his *performance* in a technical sense. The last was Nixon's forte. A *New York Times* article early in 1960 said that both Democrats and Republicans in Washington regarded Nixon as the most masterful TV performer in politics.[40] Even people who suspected his sincerity and disliked his policies admitted his skill as a campaigner. In light of these attitudes, the widespread feeling that Kennedy performed better in the first debate tended to blur and damage the Nixon image. Opponents were fortified in their anti-Nixon feelings; those who had condemned him for his consummate skill as a political infighter could now condemn him for his shortcomings as a political in-fighter. The undecided were left with a less clear or a less favorable image. And his supporters had to de-emphasize, as his opponents had previously done, the importance of mere debating skills, stressing personality or political role instead.[41]

Kennedy, on the other hand, was little known before the 1960 election. The manner in which he won the Democratic nomination gave the impression of a cool and competent, perhaps vital, young man. But his maturity was suspect, and so was his ability to "stand up to Khrushchev" as Nixon had done in an impromptu debate in Moscow. Even Kennedy's supporters expected Nixon to look more impressive in face-to-face debate, and were all set to explain that forensic

---

[40] Sidney Hyman, "What Trendex for Lincoln?" *The New York Times*, January 17, 1960.

[41] See K. Lang and G. E. Lang, "Ordeal by Debate: Viewer Reactions," *Public Opinion Quarterly*, XXV (Summer, 1961), pp. 277–288.

skills are of little importance. In the debates, Kennedy's command of facts and facility with words served to allay suspicions just where they were most acute. In addition to positive features of personality and of political role, his ability to perform under fire and to turn adversity to advantage became part of the Kennedy image.

Turning from candidates to issues, we must admit that most political argumentation takes place without the "debaters" ever getting together—either in a physical sense or in terms of the issues. Even when candidates meet face-to-face, they frequently talk past one another. In the normal campaign situation, the best way of stimulating voters to adopt the desired attitude toward campaign issues is to reiterate one's strong arguments and to ignore those of the opposition. If this appears a dubious debating practice, remember that most observers of political campaigns are partisan themselves. Voters for each party tend to ignore rather than rebut the strong points of the opposition and to concentrate on the reassuring points that support their own decision; they would be only distressed if "their" party reminded them of unpleasantries.

Timing is also important in selling a party's issues and candidates to the voters. Thus Eisenhower's last-minute promise that he would "go to Korea" in 1952 created an impression of new vigor in Far Eastern policy. On the other hand, Goldwater's promise late in the 1964 campaign that he would send Eisenhower to Viet Nam had less dramatic impact. In terms of general intensity of organizational effort, Kennedy's presidential campaign is said to have reached too early a "peak"; had a few thousand votes in the right places been cast the other way, pundits would have given part of the credit for Nixon's victory to superior timing. Both parties try to pace their efforts so as to build up to a climax in the last weeks before election. Saturation TV coverage in the last days of the campaign has now become standard practice.

Attitudes toward political parties are less amenable to good salesmanship than attitudes toward candidates and issues. Since the political parties themselves are continuing institutions, the task of changing public attitudes toward them is far more difficult. They are more vulnerable to the effect of public events that are beyond the control of campaign strategists. So the best the strategists can do is de-emphasize the importance of the party when its reputation is poor (as the Democrats did after the Civil War and the Republicans after the depression), and emphasize the importance of the party when its popularity is high (as the Republicans did during the prosperous 1920's, and the Democrats have done since the depression).

Getting Out the Vote

After the campaign strategists have caught the citizen's attention and have created a favorable attitude, their third objective is to get him to the polls. At this stage, the traditional party organization at the precinct level takes on crucial importance. Personal contact provided by good precinct captains is invaluable, especially with uninterested and undecided citizens. The mass media of communication can create a favorable general frame of reference, but they scarcely touch the indifferent. And they cannot ring doorbells, provide baby-sitters, or furnish transportation

Drawing by Stevenson; © 1962 The New Yorker Magazine, Inc.

to the polls. All political figures piously urge everyone to "vote as you please, but please vote"; nevertheless, their special efforts are naturally devoted to getting out all the votes that may be cast in their favor. Republicans worry about indifference and smugness in the suburbs, and Democrats fret about apathy and alienation in the tenements.

In our attention to mass media appeals and to responses in terms of various social characteristics, we often forget the importance of old-fashioned organizational effort at the local level. Granted the relative indifference of many citizens to politics, however, the effort of neighborhood leaders must be a crucial factor. Recent research has demonstrated that an active precinct organization can make a difference of 10 per cent in the vote division for President.[42] Good organization pays off most handsomely for the minor party in the precinct: to vote against their neighbors, people need some kind of stimulus and reassurance. Social and

---

[42] Daniel Katz and Samuel J. Eldersveld, "The Impact of Local Party Activity Upon the Electorate," *Public Opinion Quarterly*, XXV (Spring, 1961), pp. 1–24.

economic characteristics thus emerge as only partial factors in American elections. Political forces play a distinctive and independent role.

At the national level, exhortations to vote—and to vote right—reach their peak in the large doubtful states, where a shift of a few votes can radically alter the verdict of the electoral college. In 1952, for example, the Republicans blanketed forty-nine crucial counties with a last-minute "saturation" campaign of spot television appeals. One journalist, alarmed by the emotionalism, the timing, and the sheer number of these appeals, discussed them with Democratic Party officials after the election. He was surprised to hear, not an indignant complaint, but a wistful admission that the Democrats had thought of the tactic first but had lacked the money to carry it out.[43] Goldwater was criticized for making only one visit to New York during his entire campaign, but this fitted logically with his strategy—to build victory with the support of western and southern states. He made frequent appearances in California, the largest of these states.

Another common device to stimulate voters is the special appeal to the "cross-pressured"—those influenced on the one hand to vote Democratic but on the other to vote Republican. Through such organizations as "Democrats for Eisenhower" and "Republicans for Roosevelt," waverers in the opposition camp can be encouraged to think that changing their vote is not incompatible with their traditional preference. Open support from well-known figures in the opposing party can even better serve this end. Thus the switch of Senator J. Strom Thurmond of South Carolina, formerly a Democrat (and, earlier, a States' Rights candidate for President) to the Republican Party in 1964 was a boon to Goldwater in the Deep South. The Democrats effectively countered in the nation as a whole with such organizations as Republicans and Independents for Johnson, Inc., which spread the motto, "Split your ticket, not your country."

We must not forget the so-called "independent voter," that improbable hero of much of the literature on politics. Independent voters were long thought of as those who change preference or make up their minds late in a campaign, who are so interested that they wait until all the evidence is in, until they have carefully studied the platforms, until they have dispassionately weighed the relative merits of the candidates. Empirical studies show, however, that independent voters are generally the most uninformed, uninterested, confused, and uninspiring group within the voting public.[44] The "average" independent voter delays making a decision, not because he is analyzing the evidence, but because he is hardly aware that a campaign is in progress. He changes his voting preference, not because new facts force a reappraisal, but because he holds his preference so lightly that he is steered by the last person he sees on election day.

Some independent voters, perhaps including some of the professors who helped create the romanticized portrait, undoubtedly do behave according to the

---

[43] William Lee Miller, "Can Government Be 'Merchandized'?" *The Reporter*, October 27, 1957, pp. 11–16.

[44] Lazarsfeld, Berelson, and Gaudet, *The People's Choice*, p. 69; Campbell *et al.*, *The American Voter*, pp. 143–145.

myth. But if we think of those friends who are most highly interested and best informed on politics, we usually discover that they are strongly partisan rather than independent voters. A cushion of independent voters is highly useful to the democratic *system*, because they prevent the perpetuation of one party in power, but this does not mean that such voters are the best of citizens as *individuals*. For the campaign manager, of course, they are the group that respond best to last-minute—and, if possible, face-to-face—contact.

Money in Elections

Since money is crucial to all these campaign efforts, the small minority who donate large sums generally have greater access to and influence on key officials. This may be not so much a matter of "buying influence" as it is of contributing to those who are already known to hold the desired points of view. The suspicion that those who hold the purse strings control politics periodically produces regulations on campaign finances that are as well intentioned as they are in-effectual. Federal laws, for example, impose four types of regulation. First, na-tional "political committees" and candidates for the Senate and House are required to file *reports of receipts and expenditures*. These reports have not produced the glaring publicity that was anticipated, partly because journalists fail to analyze them systematically, and partly because they are realistically regarded as woefully incomplete. Political committees that operate in only one state and a great variety of "educational" committees are exempted from this requirement. The provision does not apply to primary elections or to expenditures made without the "knowl-edge or consent" of the candidate.

Second, the *amounts spent* are subject to varying limits of $10,000 to $25,-000 for the Senate, and $2,500 to $5,000 for the House, depending on the number of voters in the constituency. Again, however, the limitation applies only to gen-eral elections, to expenditures made by the candidate or with his knowledge, and only to certain types of expenses. Consequently, this limitation is as unrealistic as the $3 million annual limit that is placed on receipts and expenditures by "political committees" in a presidential campaign, a provision that has simply brought about a proliferation of committees.

Third, the *sources* of funds are also limited, with corporations and labor unions barred from contributing to campaigns for federal office. There is no limita-tion on lobbying outlays, however, nor on contributions by corporate officers or by organizations voluntarily affiliated with unions.

Fourth, the *size* of individual contributions is limited to $5,000, but a well-wisher may make any number of such donations to different election committees and, through his family, contribute much larger sums to a single candidate.

How much is actually spent? In the 1960 presidential election, national po-litical committees spent about $25 million, which represented an increase of 46 per cent over the 1956 outlay of $17.2 million.[45] Disregarding spending by labor

---

[45] The Citizens Research Foundation joined forces with the *Congressional Quarterly* to analyze 1960 reports of contributions and expenditures filed with the Clerk of the

and other non-party groups, the major parties themselves spent about $21.9 million on the national campaign. While this seems like a tremendous expenditure, it amounts to no more than 16 cents by each party to reach each voter. Considering that expenditures on commercial advertising during the same year amounted to $11.6 *billion*,[46] suspicions about an excess of money in politics appear to be exaggerated.

To be sure, the figures we have been citing do not tell the full story. If we add in the costs of nominating campaigns, and all state and local outlays for national, state, and local races, total political costs in presidential election years reach these figures: $140 million in 1952, $155 million in 1956, and $175 million in 1960. Alexander Heard, author of the most definitive study of money in elections, reminds us that "these sums result basically from the functional necessities of a democratic system of government."[47] Granted that Americans fill well over half a million public offices by popular election, and that elections call for communication between candidate and electorate, our system makes such outlays an inevitable cost of democracy.

The 1960 findings tend, as Table 8-1 shows, to dispel the idea that the Republicans, as the party of "big-money," always enjoy an advantage over Demo-

TABLE 8-1 *Summary of Political Spending at the National Level, 1960 (in thousands of dollars)* [a]

COMMITTEES [b]	GROSS REPORTED DISBURSE-MENTS [c]	KNOWN DEBT	TOTAL CAMPAIGN COSTS	TRANSFERS TO CANDI-DATES AND COMMITTEES	DIRECT EXPENDI-TURES
17 Republican	$10,600	$ 700	$11,300	$1,172	$10,128
13 Democratic	6,767	3,820	10,587	790	9,797
21 Labor	2,277	—	2,277	1,434	843
19 Miscellaneous	850	—	850	144	706
Total	$20,494	$4,520	$25,014	$3,540	$21,474

[a] Alexander, "Financing the Parties and Campaigns," in David (ed.), *The Presidential Election and Transition, 1960–1961*, p. 117.

[b] The number of national-level committees increased from 49 in 1956 to 70 in 1960, but the same criteria were used in identifying them. See *1956 General Election Campaigns*, Report to the Senate Committee on Rules and Administration, 85th Cong., 1st Sess. (1957), Exhibit 4, p. 41.

[c] Data derived from reports filed with the Clerk of the United States House of Representatives.

United States House of Representatives. Data on the 1960 election in this section are drawn largely from the analysis of the Director of the Foundation, Herbert E. Alexander, "Financing the Parties and Campaigns," in Paul T. David (ed.), *The Presidential Election and Transition, 1960-1961* (Washington, D. C.: The Brookings Institution, 1961).

[46] Bureau of the Census, *Statistical Abstract of the United States 1961* (Washington, D. C.: Government Printing Office, 1961), p. 857.

[47] The 1952 and 1956 estimates are from Heard's book, *The Costs of Democracy* (Chapel Hill: The University of North Carolina Press, 1960), p. 8. In 1961, President Kennedy appointed Professor Heard Chairman of a Commission on Campaign Costs to study this problem with an eye toward the recommendation of new national policies.

crats in campaign spending. In 1952 and 1956, Republicans did spend considerably more than Democrats, even with expenditures by labor included in the Democratic totals. For 1952, Heard finds a ratio of about 55 to 45; in 1956 it increased to about 62–38. Since about six-sevenths of all campaign expenditures are made at the state and local levels, they must also be taken into account. Heard finds that the dominant party in one-party states normally spends more than its rival, but that the Republicans usually spend more in two-party states. In 1956, the Republican advantage in the country as a whole was about the same as it was for the national campaign alone.[48]

While these were sizable Republican advantages, they did not reach the extreme proportions suggested by less exhaustive studies. Nor could the Republicans be said to have "bought" the elections of 1952 and 1956. Even if Democratic expenditures had doubled or trebled, Eisenhower could hardly have been defeated. And, in 1956, when the Republicans enjoyed their greatest monetary advantage in the country as a whole, the Democrats captured control of Congress. In 1960, with a real chance of winning the presidency, the Democrats managed to close the dollar gap. In order to do it, they had to go into debt to the tune of $3.8 million—thought to be the largest campaign deficit in American history. But a party finds it easier and more pleasant to pay off a large debt after victory than a small debt after defeat—the most expensive election is a defeat.

Another development of 1960 was the continuation of the trend toward more widespread participation in the form of campaign contributions. About 10 million people made some kind of gift to a political campaign in 1960, which was the greatest popular participation in political giving—both numerically and proportionately—in American history. In 1952, only 4 per cent of adult citizens interviewed in a national survey said they made any kind of political contribution; by 1956, contributors had increased to almost 10 per cent; in 1960, they reached 11.5 per cent.[49] This great increase in the number of people contributing to campaigns is in keeping with the needs of the candidates and, for those who believe in maximum popular participation, with the needs of the political system. But it should not lead us to believe that the "little man" is taking over the financing of campaigns. In 1960, two-fifths of the gross receipts of national organizations were reported as coming from donations of $500 or more. Big gifts, and many middle-size gifts from the same people, are still the primary source of campaign money.

Although detailed studies of 1964 outlays have not been completed, early reports indicate no changes in the basic trends revealed in Heard's exhaustive study. Among the many novel features of the 1964 election, however, was the report of a $1.2 million dollar surplus in the coffers of the losing party! [50] While

---

[48] Heard, *The Costs of Democracy*, pp. 19–22.

[49] See Alexander Heard, *The Costs of Democracy—Financing American Political Campaigns* (Garden City, New York: Anchor Books, Doubleday & Company, Inc., 1962), "Postscript." This is a paperback edition of the work cited above with a postscript on the 1960 election.

[50] *The New York Times*, November 10, 1964.

Goldwater and the chairman of the Republican National Committee pointed with pride to their budget-balancing frugality, spokesmen for the moderate wing of the party suggested that Republicans would have been better served if the surplus funds had been spent in behalf of Republican gubernatorial and congressional candidates. The Ripon Society, an organization formed in 1962 to strengthen moderate Republicanism, asked for an "independent accounting to clear the air of charges that some campaign monies have been held in reserve for post-election Goldwaterite activities." The losing party is typically plagued by re-criminations and second-guessing, but such dissension has never before centered on the problem of a financial surplus.

Campaign contributions are an advanced form of political participation. Accordingly, they show the same biases as political opinions, with officials of labor unions giving mostly to the Democrats and officials of major corporations giving mostly to the Republicans.[51] But the patterns of American politics are extremely complicated. In the 1960 election, for example, the Teamsters Union launched DRIVE—Democratic Republican Independent Voter Education—to demonstrate that labor was not solid for the Democrats. Once in office, the Democrats were in a better position to pick up corporate contributions. President Johnson took pains before the 1964 election to assure the business community that he was not anti-business. And when Goldwater won the Republican nomination, the disaffection of moderate Republicans assured Johnson of more support from corporate sources than any Democrat had enjoyed since 1932. The chairman of the Republicans and Independents for Johnson, Inc., for example, was a former president of the Pepsi-Cola Company. Neither labor nor corporate interests like to be exclusively identified with any one party even though, over the long haul, the direction of their preferences seems fairly obvious.

Since campaigns are expensive, money naturally plays a role in their outcome. If those who possess wealth usually want to avoid changes in the status quo, it is not surprising that conservative parties and conservative candidates find it easier to gain financial support than more liberal groups. But other motives, such as personal ambition or a desire to be on the winning side, complicate the picture. The power of mass organization, the influence of person-to-person contact, the impact of public events, the cohesion of social classes, and the force of effective leadership—all work to invalidate the notion that the more expensive campaign always ends in victory.

The Mechanics of the Ballot

Most Americans vote by marking secret ballots issued to them by local election officials. The ballots list a great number of offices sought by candidates whose names are usually grouped in columns according to party affiliation. Elections are conducted, according to state law, by precinct officers under the immediate, if rather casual, supervision of county or city election authorities.

---

[51] Senate Subcommittee on Privileges and Elections, *1956 General Election Campaigns*, 85th Cong., 1st Sess., 1957.

A majority of voters still mark paper ballots, but over thirty states allow local governments to install voting machines. These machines record and count the votes automatically, speed up the conduct of elections, and reduce the opportunities for fraud.

Whether by paper ballot or by machine, voting is now secret throughout the United States. In the post-Civil War period, votes were still cast by voice, or by means of easily identifiable ballots printed by the parties. But labor and other reform-minded groups, convinced that intimidation and bribery were damaging their cause, agitated for secret voting, which was generally achieved by 1900 with the adoption of the Australian ballot in a majority of the states. The Australian ballot is an official ballot which is printed by the government and lists the names of all candidates for public office.

There are two basic ways of listing candidates on the ballot. The *party-column* ballot, used in thirty states, groups the names of all candidates in columns according to party affiliation. On this ballot, it is usually possible to vote a "straight ticket" (for all the candidates of one party) by making a single mark or by pulling a single lever at the head of the column. The *office-block* ballot groups all candidates according to the office they seek rather than by party. This design forces the voter to consider who should control each individual office rather than who should control the government as a whole. Because this approach encourages split-ticket voting, the office-block ballot is deplored by party officials.[52]

While the mere mechanics of the ballot may seem dull and of little consequence, they can make a real difference in election results. One investigator argues that a referendum calling for constitutional revision in Michigan was defeated by voting machines—not machines in the sense of political organizations but machines in the purely mechanical sense![53] Perhaps such reports about voting machines help explain why, in the words of Oregon's Secretary of State, "no one is doing a bloody thing" to modify election procedures. As Oregon's chief elections officer, he hopes to introduce a 6-inch by 3-inch punch card as the ballot and make Oregon the first state with rapid, electronic computation of voting results.[54] Tennessee may represent the opposite extreme to Oregon's promised efficiency—election officials there do not even know the number of precincts in the state.

The mechanics of the ballot will not have much effect on the voting behavior of people with intense convictions. Anybody who feels so strongly that he

---

[52] In at least one state, Pennsylvania, the office-block ballot is combined with the opportunity for straight-ticket voting by a single mark or pull of the lever.

[53] Some Michigan election districts, especially in the more urban areas, have voting machines; others still use paper ballots. The urban voters tended to favor constitutional revision more than rural residents but, in the districts with machines (in contrast to rural or urban districts using paper ballots), fewer people voted on the referendum question. The study estimates that constitutional revision would have been approved had the voting machines not led to more incomplete ballots in the areas where revision was favored. John P. White, *Voting Machines and the 1958 Defeat of Constitutional Revision in Michigan* (Ann Arbor: Institute of Public Administration, University of Michigan, 1960).

[54] United Press International news item, June 8, 1961.

would go through "hell or high water" to register his views will certainly not be influenced by the mere form of the ballot. But most citizens do not have strong political convictions, and the ballot form may influence their votes.

Voting a straight ticket is easy in states with *single-choice ballots*—a ballot form that permits a single mark or the pull of a single lever to register a vote for a single party's candidates for every office. Straight-ticket voting requires more effort in states with *multiple-choice ballots*—a ballot form that requires every office to be voted on separately. A comparison of the extent of straight-ticket voting under these two kinds of ballots give us a good chance to see the influence of ballot form on voting. In those states with single-choice ballots, straight-ticket voting is significantly higher than in states with multiple-choice ballots. None of the difference is supplied, however, by people with strong party identification. When an individual's vote grows out of positive internal motivation, as it does for those with strong party identification, it is not influenced at all by the mechanics of voting. But it's a different story for those with weak party identification and, more particularly, for independents.

Table 8-2 summarizes the effect of mere ballot form on straight-ticket vot-

TABLE 8-2   *Percentage of Straight-Ticket Votes under Different Ballot Forms by People with Different Levels of Party Identification*

LEVEL OF PARTY IDENTIFICATION	SINGLE-CHOICE BALLOT	MULTIPLE-CHOICE BALLOT
Strong	77%	77%
Weak	70	55
None (independents)	48	30

Source: Survey data on 1952 and 1956 presidential elections reported in Angus Campbell and Warren E. Miller, "The Motivational Basis of Straight and Split Ticket Voting," *American Political Science Review,* LI (June, 1957), p. 307.

ing for people at different levels of party identification. Reading across the table, we see that 77 per cent of those with strong party identification vote a straight ticket regardless of the form of the ballot. Looking at independents, we see a different story: 48 per cent of them vote a straight ticket when the ballot form permits them to do so by making a single choice, but only 30 per cent vote a straight ticket when they must make multiple choices. The 18 percentage-point drop represents a sizable minority of independents who have such weak political commitments that their vote, following the principle of least effort, is determined by the form of the ballot. If they can cast a straight ticket at minimum cost of energy, i.e., by making a single choice, they vote a straight ticket. If voting a straight ticket is a costlier act, i.e., if they have to choose for each office in terms of some consistent principle like party identification, then they vote a split ticket—selecting one candidate because they have heard of him, another because they like the sound of his name, and another because his name comes first on the list. Such erratic behavior is not, of course, characteristic of most independents, but it is found in a significant minority. Again, the independent voter appears somewhat less the model citizen than political folklore might lead one to believe.

Elections and the Political System

Elections are important for what they tell us about how choices are made and how power is distributed among individuals and groups, in and out of government. But they may also be viewed in historical perspective, with each election being regarded as a single political event, as one unit in a continuing series of electoral decisions with consequences for the total political system.

Types of Elections

Elections may be classified according to two criteria. The first and most obvious is in terms of *which party wins*. If the incumbent party is retained in office, the election results in *party continuity*. If the incumbent party is defeated, a *party change* is the result. Since the question of who will control the government is the central concern during any election, this first criterion tends to dominate popular discussion. In 1928, then, the Republicans were jubilant because they retained control of the presidency by a handy margin.

A professional horse player differs from an amateur, however, in that his concerns go beyond the simple question of which horse won a particular race. He is also alert to the promise of strength in a loser and to signs of future weakness in the winner. And so it is with careful observers of elections. They are concerned with the second and less obvious criterion: whether the election reflects change or continuity in the party *preferences of significant groups* in the electorate. If deviations from the usual party preferences of major voting groups are not very great or enduring, the election may be called one of *electoral continuity*. If significant and enduring deviations occur, the election is one of *electoral change*. Viewing the 1928 election from this perspective, the Republicans seem to have won a battle while they were losing a war.

The Herbert Hoover-Al Smith presidential contest of 1928 has been called a critical election because, viewed as one in a series of electoral decisions, it accentuated and crystallized a realignment of significant groups within the electorate. Specifically, the candidacy of Al Smith intensified and solidified the movement of low-income, Catholic, urban voters of immigrant stock into the Democratic Party.[55] Because of the American penchant for viewing elections with the psychology of a novice at the races—"do they pay off on my bet?"—we forget that the long-run consequences of an election may be in terms of shifts in the electorate that do not show up in the win column. Franklin Roosevelt's vic-

---

[55] See V.O. Key, Jr., "A Theory of Critical Elections," *Journal of Politics*, XVII (February, 1955), pp. 3–18.

tory in 1932 was not the only critical election, then, for Democratic dominance during the last generation. The identification of low-income and minority groups with the Democrats was carried further in 1932, but—because almost all groups showed some shift to the Democrats in 1932—the contrast between low- and high-status groups may actually have been greater in 1928.

As far as the outcome of the elections was concerned, Eisenhower's victories in 1952 and 1956 seemed to reflect an impressive change in the electorate. But the capture of congressional power by the Democrats in 1954, 1956, and 1958— and the capture of the presidency and Congress in 1960 and 1964—demonstrates that the Eisenhower victories were based on transient appeals rather than on an enduring change in the electorate. The varying impact of these presidential elections—1928, 1932, 1952, 1956, 1960, 1964—indicates that we must distinguish between the *electoral* and the *party* implications of each election. Table 8-3 sets up four types of elections in terms of these two dimensions.[56]

TABLE 8-3   *Illustrations of Types of Elections in Terms of Consequences for the Political System*

PARTY CONSEQUENCES	ELECTORAL CONSEQUENCES	
	CHANGE	CONTINUITY
Continuity	Type A: *1928* (1796)[a]	Type C: *1964* (1864, 1900)
Change	Type B: *1932* (1860, 1896)	Type D: *1952* (1884, 1912)

[a] We are reasonably confident that the italicized presidential elections are properly classified. For earlier years, before opinion survey techniques were developed, a greater amount of guesswork underlies the classification. We enclose these dates in parentheses to indicate that the classification is only suggestive.

Change in the underlying distribution of party preferences is relatively rare, so most elections are of types C and D, with electoral continuity. The normal sequence would appear to be this: elections proceed from type A, with an underlying realignment of groups but not to the point of overthrowing the dominant party; to type B, with realignment reaching the point of a new electoral majority that puts its party into office; to type C, with the newly dominant group continuing to elect its party. Type D, in which so many people vote contrary to their party identification that the minority party wins, can intrude upon the sequence at any point, since it depends on the impact of short-run influences.

In earlier chapters,[57] we stressed the supporting function of political opin-

---

[56] Members of the Survey Research Center of the University of Michigan have also proposed a classification of elections into four types: maintaining, reinstating, deviating, and realigning. We have not adopted their system of classification because it does not consistently recognize that party and electoral consequences of an election may be different. See Campbell *et al.*, *The American Voter*, pp. 531–538; and Philip E. Converse *et al.*, "Stability and Change in 1960: A Reinstating Election," *American Political Science Review*, LV (June, 1961), pp. 269–280.

[57] Chapters 5 and 6.

ions and the moderating function of political parties. We also emphasized the impressive stability of party identification, which permitted us to divide the nation's political history into only three periods in terms of basic majority coalitions—the Democratic majority, 1800–1860; the Republican majority, 1860–1932; the Democratic majority, since 1932.

If individual elections, such as that of 1964, are viewed in the light of these stable factors, they can be understood as deviating more or less from a "standing decision" rather than as unique events. From this point of view, any Republican candidate could have been expected to lose in 1964 unless strong short-run influences worked in his favor. In 1952, Eisenhower won despite the standing decision in favor of the Democrats, because transient influences strongly favored the Republicans—his great personal appeal, the feeling that the Republican leaders would better insure peace, and dissatisfaction with alleged corruption in the Truman Administration. The first two of these forces, plus the great advantages of an incumbent, returned Eisenhower in 1956. But the lack of any basic realignment was demonstrated by the election of Democratic Congresses during six of Eisenhower's eight years in office. Again in 1960, the short-run influences—chiefly Nixon's great personal appeal and the religious issue—worked in the Republican's favor.[58] Unlike Stevenson, however, Kennedy also had widespread public appeal and, while his religious identification cost him dearly in the South, it helped him enough in other sections to reduce his net loss from the religious issue to 2.2 per cent. Granted the underlying preference for the Democratic Party, this was just about what he could afford to lose and still emerge the winner.[59]

In 1964, for the first time since the Roosevelt era, the short-run influences favored the majority party. The result was the overwhelming victory depicted in Figure 8-2, which gave President Johnson the largest vote in American history (42.1 million), the largest margin over an opponent (15.5 million), and the greatest percentage of the total vote (61.3).[60] Goldwater did not make the Republicans a minority party. He took what was already a minority party and reduced it to a minimal level of support. In addition to the debacle of his own campaign, the 1964 election gave the Democrats a 38-seat gain in the House of Representatives, which added up to the biggest Democratic margin (295–140) since 1936. The Democrats added 2 seats to their comfortable Senate majority for a 68–32 margin. The sweep of the Republican defeat is seen most dramatically in the loss of over 500 seats in the state legislatures, with most of the losses oc-

---

[58] Donald Stokes says, "The really surprising aspect of the 1960 campaign, one that faces a struggle to survive in the popular histories, is how favorable an impression Mr. Nixon made on the public." See "1960 and the Problem of Deviating Elections," a paper delivered at the Annual meeting of the American Political Science Association, September 6, 1961.

[59] Converse et al., "Stability and Change in 1960: A Reinstating Election," pp. 269–280.

[60] In percentage of the two-party vote, Johnson fell slightly below Roosevelt's 1936 percentage (62.5); the above statement refers to total popular vote, which includes minor party votes in the total.

curring in states where Goldwater's candidacy hurt Republican chances at every level of office.[61]

In effect, the Goldwater campaign challenged the moderating function of political parties and the supporting function of public opinion. His refusal to make concessions to liberal elements in his own party and his denunciation, at one time or another, of America's basic foreign and domestic policies offered a supreme test of the myth of the "hidden conservative vote." Given "a choice, not an echo," the American public resoundingly chose the echo. Indeed, the most common view of voters, few of whom had read or heard of *The Conscience of a Conservative*,[62] was that Goldwater was a "radical." His broadscale attack on policies supported by past administrations, including those of President

---

[61] *Congressional Quarterly Weekly Report*, XXII (week ending November 20, 1964), p. 2709.

[62] Barry M. Goldwater, *The Conscience of a Conservative* (Sheperdsville, Ky.: Victor Publishing Co., 1960).

Figure 8-2

Map reproduced from *The New York Times*, November 8, 1964.

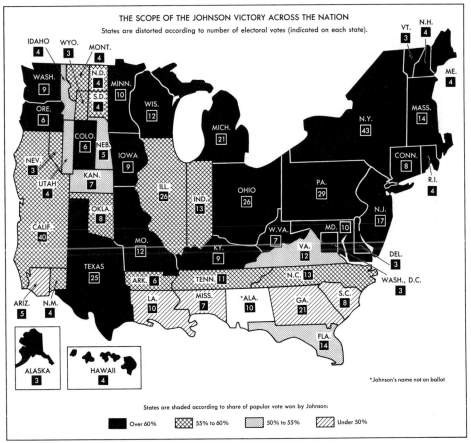

Eisenhower, struck a responsive chord only in the Deep South. His vote against the Civil Rights Act of 1964 won him Georgia and the four states that had supported J. Strom Thurmond in 1948 (Louisiana, Mississippi, Alabama, and South Carolina). And his victory margin in those states came from the tier of black-belt counties in which a majority of the population is Negro but where few Negroes vote. Had the Negroes in those counties voted, and had they supported Johnson as overwhelmingly as did Negroes elsewhere, Goldwater would have carried only his home state of Arizona.

Every election has its own peculiarities, with a new blend of events, issues, and personalities, and the short-run influences are as likely to help one party as the other. But, in the absence of cataclysmic crisis, these short-run influences act upon a standing decision that is buttressed by stable party loyalties and by support for established policies. "Other things being equal," the Democrats in the present era should win with 53 to 54 per cent of the popular vote. The "other things" were highly unequal in 1964.

The Functions of the Electoral System

From the perspective of the political system as a whole, the electoral system functions, as intended, to select the official decision-makers. It contributes less clearly to the second major input function of the polity—the identification of citizen interests. Elections often serve as quite clear judgments of past policies, bestowing either approval (as in 1924, 1936, and 1964) or disapproval (as in 1920, 1932, and 1952). But what elections demand in the way of new policies is never quite so clear. In view of the variety of interpretations that can be given to a popular mandate, it has greater clarity in retrospective terms.

In addition to these manifest functions, the electoral system has several consequences that are perhaps unanticipated. First, the entire process of popular elections serves to celebrate and to reinforce the concept of self-rule. The result is a legitimizing effect, which leads almost all citizens to recognize the right of the elected officials to make general policy. The losers of American elections are expected to show their good sportsmanship by rallying around the winner. Even the press observes a honeymoon period in which it minimizes direct criticism of the winning candidate, a practice which appears to be a conscious or unconscious effort at consensus-building.[63]

A second latent function of a system of popular elections is the extension of participation. At the outset, the right to vote may be enjoyed by selected elements of the population, such as property-owners and taxpayers early in American history. But the logic that won the franchise for some and, perhaps more important, the competition of opposing factions for votes tends to extend the franchise to new groups. A little democracy is thus a dangerous thing, exactly as anti-democrats have long argued.

Third, a popular electoral system changes the context within which public

---

[63] This statement is based on an unpublished content analysis of editorials on a series of presidents by William Blough in a graduate seminar at the University of North Carolina.

"It's exactly the kind of life I've always wanted, Yvette; it's just that I feel I ought to be home in Canton, Ohio, voting."

Drawing by Ed Fisher ; © 1964
The Saturday Review.

decisions are made. As we have seen, some elements in the population have a greater opportunity for leadership than others. But decisions on public policy in a system without popular elections are vastly different from similar decisions in a democracy. Even if elections cannot positively direct policy, decision-makers must always anticipate public reactions to their decisions. In V. O. Key's words, the suffrage means that "the wishes and probable actions of a vast number of people at the polls must be taken into consideration in the exercise of public power." [64]

To this point, we have talked about broad functions of popular elections for political systems in general. But just how do American elections serve to link public preferences and indifference to the policy outputs of government? Political opinions, political parties, pressure groups, and public relations all converge in the electoral process. Democratic theory assumes that, out of this convergence, the elected official will somehow represent the interests or views of his constituents.

At least three concepts of the relationship between constituents and decision-

---

[64] *Politics, Parties, and Pressure Groups*, p. 622.

makers have been presented as describing either the actual or the desired model. The *instructed delegate* model holds that an official acts (or should act) as a spokesman for the preferences of his constituency, following its mandate in his decisions. The view traditionally opposed to that of the instructed delegate sees the Representative performing as an *independent statesman*, acting in the interest of his constituents as he sees it, even though this may be contrary to their preferences. The *responsible party* model sees the Representative as an agent of a national rather than a local constituency. The second and third concepts both view the official as free to act contrary to constituency preferences, but they differ in that the independent statesman acts in terms of his own view of constituency or national interest rather than in response to his party's national constituency. Which of these relationships is the consequence of elections in America?

Through an imaginative combination of data on the attitudes and voting records of congressmen with data on the attitudes of their constituents and their opponents for Congress, Warren Miller and Donald Stokes have brought systematic data to bear on these concepts for the first time.[65] Miller and Stokes specify two ways in which constituency control over a congressman's voting behavior is possible: (1) the constituency may elect a Representative who shares the views of a majority in the area so that he will automatically vote their preferences in voting his own; (2) the Representative may have a reasonably accurate idea of constituency preferences which he follows regardless of his personal views. The possibility of either form of constituency control over a congressman's behavior depends on three requirements.

First, the Representative's votes must agree either with his own views or with his perception of constituency views. At first glance, this requirement might appear to be obviously met, but on reflection one recognizes that a congressman might instead follow the advice of the President, of party leaders in or out of Congress, or of pressure-group spokesmen. Examining the position of congressmen on roll call votes in three areas of legislation—social welfare, foreign involvement, and civil rights—Miller and Stokes find this first condition to be realized in all three issue areas. Even so, a minority of congressmen were found to follow the lead of the administration regardless of their own preferences or their perception of constituency preferences.

A second requirement of constituency control is that either the Representative's own attitudes or his perception of constituency attitudes must correspond with the actual opinions held in the district. This second requirement is not as well fulfilled as is the first. Congressmen most accurately perceive their constituents' preferences on the civil rights issue, but neither their own attitudes nor their beliefs about constituent attitudes are strongly related to actual constituency opinions on issues of foreign involvement or of social welfare. But

---

[65] The preceding and the following paragraphs are based on their article, "Constituency Influence in Congress," *American Political Science Review*, LVII (March, 1963), pp. 45–56. For a full report, see their forthcoming book, *Representation in Congress* (Englewood Cliffs, New Jersey: Prentice-Hall, Inc., 1965).

these are severe tests. Popular opinions on questions of foreign policy are so unstable and so poorly supported by information that the congressman could hardly be expected to have a highly accurate impression of them. And on social welfare issues, if we compare the Representative's perceptions and attitudes with the majority who supported him rather than with the entire constituency, a stronger relationship is found.

The third requirement of constituency control is that the constituency take account of the candidates' issue positions in deciding how to vote. This is the necessary condition for constituency control that is least satisfied. In contested congressional elections in 1958, only 24 per cent of the voters had heard or read something about both candidates, and only 54 per cent had read or heard something about either candidate.[66] Of those who could comment on the candidates, most offered general judgments—"he's a good man"; "he understands problems" —and only 3 per cent mentioned legislative issues of any kind. For that matter, a majority of the public could not say which party had controlled Congress during the preceding two years. If the vote was not in response to differences on issues, what was it based on? The overwhelming factor in congressional voting is *party identification*. Only one vote in twenty was cast by people with no sense of party identification and nine out of ten of these identifiers supported their party's nominee.

Despite the public's use of congressional elections as a vehicle for expressing their party loyalties, four-fifths of the congressmen who were opposed for re-election felt that the outcome was strongly influenced by their voting records in Congress. Nor are they necessarily incorrect in this estimate. In the first place, with stable party voting among most of the electorate, the congressman in a competitive district needs only to win an extra increment of votes through his record to gain re-election. Similarly, his record might reduce his stable party base enough to cost him his seat. Second, the two-step flow of communication we discussed in Chapter 5 may mean that votes apparently based purely on party identification are indirectly based on a congressman's record. Such mediating agencies as local party leaders, union or business associates, or informal opinion leaders in countless small groups react to the congressman's legislative record and pass their evaluations on to others. The ordinary member of such formal and informal groups may retain only the final evaluation—"he understands problems"—from contacts with opinion leaders, but the evaluation itself may relate back to the details of the legislative record. Third, the congressman from a safe district may correctly view his record as important in the sense that he needs to avoid becoming visible to constituents by taking a stand opposed by strong local interests. The influence of local opinions is still felt in this circumstance, most conspicuously in southern voting on civil rights.

In varying degrees, then, the requirements of constituency influence through popular elections seem to be realized. The model of constituency-representative relationship that is actually adopted varies from one issue to another. The in-

---

[66] *Ibid.*, p. 54. If non-voters were included, the percentages would be much lower.

structed delegate model appears predominant in the area of civil rights. On this issue, the congressmen's perceptions of district attitudes are twice as powerful as their own attitudes in explaining variations in their roll-call votes. The responsible party model more nearly explains the relationship on social welfare issues, where party differences have been clear enough that the voter can rely on party label as a way of communicating his preferences. Finally, the independent statesman model finds some support in congressional behavior on foreign policy questions, in the sense that the congressman does not look to his district in making up his mind. But even in this area the congressman does not make an independent decision: ". . . the reliance he puts on the President and the Administration suggests that the calculation of where the public interest lies is often passed to the Executive on matters of foreign policy." [67]

---

[67] *Ibid.*, p. 56.

Decision-Making Agencies and Activities

PART THREE

CHAPTER NINE

The
Legislators

The Constitution of the United States begins

with this declaration: "All legislative powers herein granted shall

be vested in a Congress of the United States which shall consist

of a Senate and House of Representatives." This statement has

an appealing simplicity; we like to picture government as being

neater than a confusing struggle among shifting and indistinct power groups. Generations of school children have learned that government is the business of three coordinate branches: Congress enacts laws, the President executes them, and the courts settle disputes under the law. This tells part of the story, but less than a theater program would tell a stay-at-home about the true nature of a play. The program at least gives a correct impression of the number of characters in the cast. But, as we have seen, unofficial agencies like political parties, pressure groups, and professional public relations organizations have important roles in the drama of politics. Moreover, the official electoral, executive, and judicial agencies also play important parts in influencing policy. All these agencies must be added together if we are to get a realistic roster of those who participate in legislation.

It is the congressman, however, who stands at the center of the legislative stage, the central figure on whom all other pressures converge. Popular government requires some agency to formulate policy and to work out compromises among opposing interests. And in the United States this agency is Congress. The legislator may feel a lonely responsibility in carrying out this awesome task, but at least it is the loneliness of one in a crowd. All kinds of people, with motives ranging from the best to the worst, are eager to help him carry his burden. The starting point for any realistic understanding of the work of Congress is to understand that many actors—some whose names are never even mentioned in the "list of credits"—play important roles in the drama of policy-making.

The Actors in Policy-Making

Congressmen: Heroes or Villains?

The star performers in policy-making are the congressmen. Whatever and whoever may influence them, it is they who finally cast the votes that make the laws of the United States. What sort of people are congressmen? Although we frequently hear that there is no such thing as the "typical" member of Congress, we obviously cannot discuss 100 senators and 435 representatives as 535 unique prima donnas. Nor is it necessary to do so, for we can describe the kind of people who sit in Congress in terms of age, sex, occupation, socio-economic status, family background, race, ethnic origins, education, and religion.

The average age of the people who were chosen to sit in the 88th Congress, from 1963 to 1965, was 52.7 years. The average Senator was about 57, and the average Representative was about 52. The age range was from 30 to 86 in the Senate and from 29 to 85 in the House. At least half the legislators who handle one of the most grueling jobs in the world are at an age when most men are about ready to retire. Clearly, the official policies of the United States are not made by inexperienced young firebrands. But even at their relatively advanced age, most congressmen notice that there are few women in their midst. In the 88th Congress, for example, there were only 11 women representatives and two women senators.

The fact that so many congressmen are males in their late middle age does not mean, however, that youth and women are ignored in Congress. Groups need not be physically represented in order for their interests to be recognized. Congress is not and never has been "representative" in the sense of being a cross section of the population. Leaders are different from average people almost by definition, and the characteristics of congressmen are a reflection of what Americans admire rather than of what Americans are. Most men come to Congress, as we would expect, from occupations of at least upper-middle-class standing. As Table 9-1 indicates, lawyers account for more than half the membership of Congress, and businessmen and bankers fill almost a third of the seats. Congressmen are similarly unrepresentative in family background, race, ethnic origins, education, and religion. The groups of higher social status enjoy a disproportionately large share of offices in comparison with their proportion of the total population; groups of lower status tend to be virtually excluded from office.[1]

TABLE 9-1   *Occupational Background of Congressmen*

| | 87TH CONGRESS | | 88TH CONGRESS | |
OCCUPATIONAL BACKGROUND	SENATE	HOUSE	SENATE	HOUSE
Agriculture	18%	11%	16%	10%
Business or banking	31	31	23	31
Journalism	10	8	8	8
Law	63	56	66	57
Medicine, engineering	3	2	3	1
Teaching	14	9	15	8

Source: Congressional Quarterly Almanac, XVII (1961), p. 35; XIX (1963), p. 34. Percentages total more than 100 because some members had engaged in more than one occupation.

The constitutional qualifications for congressmen are quite simple: a Representative must be at least twenty-five years of age, a citizen for seven years, and an inhabitant of the state from which he is elected; a Senator must be thirty years old, a citizen for nine years, and an inhabitant of the state from which he is elected. Any citizen can meet these requirements simply by staying alive. But various informal requirements narrow the field sharply. If one plans to be a congressman, it will normally be to his advantage to arrange to be: a late-middle-aged male lawyer whose father was of the professional or managerial class; a native-born "white," or—if he cannot avoid being an immigrant—a product of northwestern or central Europe or Canada, rather than of eastern or southern Europe or Asia; a college graduate; and a Protestant, preferably a Methodist, Presbyterian, Episcopalian, or Baptist. On church membership, for example, the religious affiliations of congressmen in 1963–65 were: Protestant, 80 per cent; Catholic, 18; Jewish, 2.[2] He should also have some political experience before

---

[1] See "Class Differences and Chances for Political Leadership," Chapter 1.
[2] Seven members whose religious affiliation was not given were excluded in figuring

seeking election to Congress—as did 98 per cent of the senators and 93 per cent of the representatives in the 88th Congress. Finally, he will do well to serve at least briefly in the armed forces—62 per cent of the senators and 68 per cent of the representatives in the 88th Congress were veterans. If, however, after going to all this trouble, he seeks office in a constituency made up principally of Negroes, immigrants from Asia and southeastern Europe, or pacifists, his efforts will have been in vain. The "typical" congressman is, after all, a product of the "typical" constituency.

These social characteristics do not determine the congressman's behavior in any complete sense, of course, but they do have an influence. For one thing, they give Congress a conservative coloration—people with backgrounds of the sort we have described are usually not wildly radical. Although many varying —and perhaps unidentifiable—factors influence the votes of an individual congressman, people whose background and interests are similar to his do enjoy an advantage in explaining their needs and ideas to him. If a Senator or Representative has the same viewpoint as an interest group, the influence of the group on his decisions is almost automatic.

The contradictory attitudes toward authority that we described before as part of the American culture are nicely illustrated by popular beliefs about Congress and congressmen. The congressman is pictured by the public as a character with a big paunch, a big cigar, and a big vocabulary, but with a small mind and a still smaller moral stature. Although this picture is highly inaccurate, the caricature is more vivid to many citizens than the photograph. Yet, even though they disparage congressmen in the abstract, most citizens are almost reverential toward Congress as an institution. Tell the average voter that Senator X is a fatuous windbag and he accepts the description as though it were a comment on the weather; but tell him that the Senate should be abolished and a one-house Congress created, and he will label you an un-American agitator. Americans may feel they would belittle themselves by looking up to the politician as an individual, but they reserve the right to stand in awe of official forms and institutions.

Life in Congress: The Demands of the Role

Congress has a group life of its own. Just as being a member of a Boy Scout troop, a neighborhood gang, or a college sorority influences a person, so does being a member of Congress. And, like any other functioning group, Congress has certain norms to which the new member must adjust. To enjoy status within this face-to-face group, the member must show respect for Congress as an institution, and he must adjust his behavior to the needs of the group. He will act, in other words, not merely as a particular kind of person with a given party identification and constituency background, but also as a member of Congress who is involved in its needs as an organization. The "club atmosphere" of the Senate is vividly demonstrated by the elaborate deference that members show

---

these percentages. The list of Protestant denominations in the preceding sentence is a ranking in order of number of members in Congress. See *Congressional Quarterly Almanac*, XIX (1963), p. 35.

to each other, even those who disagree on everything except the importance of the Senate.

What demands do the Senate and House impose on new members? These demands are not formally spelled out, but the perceptive freshman quickly learns that they are well-defined, even though informal.[3] First, he is expected to be "seen and not heard," to serve—without complaining to the "upperclassmen" —a decent period of apprenticeship, during which he performs routine chores without glory. Second, he is expected to devote himself primarily to routine legislative tasks, rather than to seek publicity by proposing major policies or by trying to dominate public committee hearings or congressional debate. Third, he is expected to specialize in the area of legislation in which his committee or constituency has a particular stake; to try to take the lead in other legislative areas would be to challenge the leadership and the special prerogatives of his colleagues. Fourth, he is expected to cooperate with his colleagues, show himself willing to "give and take" rather than insist on his own principles without compromise. His ideology may be firmly fixed on his own mind, but he must subordinate it to the legislative necessity of compromise. Finally, especially in the Senate, he is expected to show great respect for his colleagues as individuals and deep attachment to his branch of Congress as an institution.

Because these are the norms, the unofficial rules of behavior, we hear very little from new members of the Senate or House during their first years in office. Even those who have made a name for themselves before going to Congress must —if they are prudent—be content to serve a period of apprenticeship. But this is a restrictive role, and rewards and punishments are necessary to encourage conformity. These inducements are somewhat like the ones that lead fraternity pledges, and novitiates in primitive societies, to endure agonizing initiation ceremonies. Those who conform may live to be called "brother" or "true Senate men," to feel a warm slap on the back from their elders. The nonconformists, though not actually black-balled, are frowned upon for acting like "show horses" instead of "work horses" and are barred from the "inner ring" of the leaders. More tangible rewards are also offered: conforming members get the choice committee assignments, their bills receive more favorable consideration, and their states receive more favors.

The case of nonconformist Estes Kefauver (Tennessee) and conformist John Kennedy (Massachusetts) illustrates the way the system works. In 1957, both these Democratic senators sought a berth on the important Senate Com-

---

[3] Material in this and the next paragraph comes largely from Donald R. Matthews, *U.S. Senators and Their World* (Chapel Hill: University of North Carolina Press, 1960). Richard F. Fenno, Jr., finds a strikingly similar set of norms to be functional for the integration of the House Appropriations Committee and their absence to be dysfunctional for the House Education and Labor Committee. See "The House Appropriations Committee as a Political System: The Problem of Integration," *American Political Science Review*, LVI (June, 1962), pp. 310–324; and "The House of Representatives and Federal Aid to Education," in R. L. Peabody and N. W. Polsby (eds.), *New Perspectives on the House of Representatives* (Chicago: Rand McNally & Company, 1963), pp. 195–235.

mittee on Foreign Affairs. Under the normal functioning of the seniority system, the post would have gone to Kefauver because of his longer tenure. But Kefauver had conducted highly publicized investigations of crime and juvenile delinquency before each of the preceding presidential elections, and had spent considerable time campaigning, while Kennedy—although clearly ambitious—spent more time on the routine jobs of a senator. Kefauver had written a book, *A Twentieth Century Congress*,[4] in which he criticized various "outmoded" practices of Congress, including the system by which committee assignments are made on a seniority basis. Kennedy had also written a book, *Profiles in Courage*,[5] in which he eulogized the "greats" of Senate history. Kennedy got the coveted assignment. The seniority rule was relaxed—something that is rarely done—in order to keep the post from going to Kefauver, the critic of that rule, who wryly commented that he had not heard that the seniority rule was no longer in operation.

Why do the norms take the particular form we have described? Donald Matthews, a student of legislative behavior, suggests that they are highly "functional"—that is, they are necessary if Congress is to survive without major change. His remarks about the Senate may be applied with almost equal force to the House:

> These folkways . . . are highly functional to the Senate social system since they provide motivation for the performance of vital duties and essential modes of behavior which, otherwise, would go unrewarded. They discourage frequent and lengthy speech-making in a chamber without any other effective limitation on debate, encourage the development of expertness and a division of labor in a group of overworked laymen facing unbelievably complex problems, soften the inevitable personal conflicts of a problem-solving body, and encourage bargaining and the cautious use of awesome formal powers. Without these folkways, the Senate could hardly operate with its present organization and rules.[6]

Other pressures on a congressman, such as ambition for the presidency, a fixed ideology, or the peculiar demands of his constituency, are sometimes strong enough to outweigh congressional norms in governing his behavior. Behavior that is functional for Congress as a group may not be functional for an individual congressman's career—or, for that matter, for society at large. The nation needs an occasional nonconformist like the late Senator George W. Norris (R-Nebraska) even if other senators grumble that he doesn't play the game. Thus a new congressman, responding to broader norms than those of the legislature itself, may embark on a wider range of activities than his colleagues think appropriate.[7] But the majority of freshmen seem to conform.

---

[4] In collaboration with Jack Levin, *A Twentieth Century Congress* (New York: Duell, Sloan and Pearce, 1947).

[5] *Profiles in Courage* (New York: Harper & Brothers, 1958). Also published in a paperbound edition by Pocket Books, Inc.

[6] *U.S. Senators and Their World*, p. 116.

[7] See Ralph K. Huitt, "The Outsider in the Senate: An Alternative Role," *American Political Science Review*, LV (September, 1961), pp. 566–575, and Professor Matthews' letter in the following issue of the *Review*.

Actors in the Background and in the Wings

When the newly arrived congressman takes his seat in the Senate or House, he does not have to make a completely fresh start. As a mature and probably prominent person in his constituency, he has fairly well-established opinions on a variety of public problems. And he also has established contacts with different groups in his constituency who will offer cues whenever he is uncertain about his role. His role as a congressman may ultimately broaden his views, but he starts out as the representative of a particular constituency; and the problem of being re-elected by the folks back home keeps their picture bright in his mind. For that matter, his colleagues would regard him as a maverick if he forgot his constituents' special needs. Congressmen from agricultural constituencies champion price supports for farmers, those from predominantly immigrant areas favor liberal immigration quotas, those from the South oppose integration. Since these stands can be taken for granted regardless of the congressman's party or personal characteristics, the constituency is an important element in policy-making.

In a recent study of differences between Republican and Democratic constituencies, Lewis A. Froman, Jr., of the University of Wisconsin found systematic support for the long-standing assumption that the make-up of a constituency has a direct bearing on congressional voting. Democrats vote on the liberal side of social welfare questions more than Republicans not just because of their party identification or ideology but also because they come from different kinds of districts. Outside the South, Democratic districts are more urban, more racially mixed, have smaller proportions of owner-occupied dwellings, and have more people per square mile than Republican districts. Constituencies with these characteristics are generally expected to be on the liberal side of social welfare questions. The discovery that they tend to elect Democrats is therefore not surprising. But Froman goes on to demonstrate that, even when the comparison is between representatives in the same party, differences in these constituency characteristics still make a difference in congressional voting—Democrats from lower status districts vote even more for liberal measures than Democrats whose constituents are of higher status.

The finding that constituency characteristics have an influence that is independent of a congressman's party affiliation might appear to mean that representative government is simply a process through which constituency preferences are reflected by congressional agents. But this is a highly over-simplified view.[8] The two great political parties, for example, have a stake in almost all legislation—and congressmen are members of a party as well as representatives of a constituency. American parties are very loose organizations; the party as represented in Congress often cannot be identified with the party as represented by the national leaders outside Congress. Each party is an actor

---

[8] Another article by Froman demonstrates that, regardless of constituency characteristics, changes in the particular Democrat or Republican who occupies a House seat make a difference in congressional voting. See "The Importance of Individuality in Voting in Congress," *Journal of Politics*, XXV (May, 1963), pp. 324–332.

with many faces in the play of policy-making. There are the local party organizations, which are usually closely identified with constituency interests. There are national party leaders, like the President and the chairman of the national committee, who are more attuned to the interests of the urban majority. There is the face of the party presented in the platform adopted every four years at national conventions, and this image generally corresponds closely to the one presented by the President. In each of these guises, the party tries to get into the act of policy-making. The presidential interpretation of the party's role generally makes a greater public impression than the interpretations of congressmen. The party that does not control the White House has a harder time establishing its national identity, because it has no single spokesman. After their crushing defeat in 1964, competing elements of the Republican Party spoke directly to the question of the "party image" in jockeying for control.

Despite all the talk about conflicts within each party, the basic differences in Congress are between Democrats and Republicans. If a person could ask for only one fact about a congressman in order to predict his voting behavior, the knowledgeable observer would ask for his party identification. Democrats and Republicans from the same constituencies in different Congresses differ drastically in their votes on issues important for those constituencies—for example, on a larger role for the national government in the social welfare area. A recent study which made such a comparison between different party occupants of the same seats in 1957–60 and 1961–62 found that in every district the Democrat exceeded his Republican predecessor or follower in supporting a larger role for the national government; on the average the vote of the Democrats in favor of more national activity was 68 percentage points higher than that of Republicans from the same districts.[9] Although constituency characteristics have some influence independent of party affiliation, then, party affiliation has a far greater influence that is independent of constituency characteristics. Generally, of course, both forces work together: districts with "liberal" social and economic attributes elect Democrats and districts with "conservative" attributes elect Republicans. This normal congruence of constituency characteristics and party affiliation leads to great differences in party performance in Congress. Just as party identification emerged as the key explanatory variable in studying political opinions of the general public, so does it emerge as the principal factor for understanding Congress.

So many pressure groups crowd the stage that policy-making sometimes resembles a Hollywood mob scene. We usually think of a pressure group as an outside agency that is trying to influence congressmen, but often it has members and sympathizers who are also members of Congress. The veterans lobby and the farm lobby, for example, act within as well as upon Congress. On the other hand, few members of Congress have ever belonged to labor unions. A group that is not lucky enough to have members in Congress must act through sympathizers, gen-

---

[9] Clarence N. Stone, "Inter-Party Differences and Congressional Voting Behavior: A Partial Dissent," *American Political Science Review,* LVII (September, 1963), pp. 665–666.

erally from the areas in which the group is particularly strong. Experts disagree about the importance of the role of pressure groups, but no one denies that they are important characters in the cast. They are much less important in changing votes than is popularly supposed, but they play an invaluable role in furnishing information and support to those who agree with their general position.[10]

Judges are never seen on the floor of Congress or scurrying about the corridors, but they do participate in policy-making. Despite the myth that judges are neutral mediators in political wars, they help to make policy in several ways. First, every time they interpret an act of Congress they are making a declaration of policy. Legislators usually write statutes in general terms that leave room for detailed policy-making by the courts. It is hard enough to pass a new law even in a fairly general form, and if the sponsors of a bill tried to spell out every detail of application they would make their task almost impossible. So instead of alienating elements that are at least willing to go along with a general policy, they postpone the fight over specific questions until they turn up in the courts.

A second, though more negative, means by which judges influence policy stems from the power of the courts to declare state or congressional enactments unconstitutional. When a court blocks a statute, it forces Congress to follow other lines of policy, and thus has at least a negative effect on policy-formation. The Supreme Court has exercised considerable restraint in negating national laws, but the variety of state laws and practices has led to a much more active role for the Court in invalidating state actions. As has been so clearly demonstrated in the area of civil rights, the Court's review of state actions may create new national policy.

Third, the possibility that the court may declare an act unconstitutional leads congressmen themselves to think in legalistic terms. Since the courts have the power of judicial review, congressmen must worry about the constitutionality as well as the political wisdom of every statute, and this makes the judges a constant factor in policy-making. Senator Barry Goldwater (R-Arizona) thus felt free to justify his highly publicized vote against the Civil Rights Act of 1964 on the ground that it was unconstitutional, leaving in abeyance the question of its wisdom as policy. Although he did not argue that the courts would agree with his legal analysis, his explanation for his vote demonstrates the pervasive nature of constitutional requirements.

The dramatic expansion of our national and international commitments in recent years has led other governments—both local and foreign—to play a role in the policies that affect them. Should a federal housing program be handled by the national or by local government? And if by local government, should it be by state or by municipality? Which is the better policy in dealing with the communist bloc—belligerence or caution? How much and what kind of aid should be supplied to our allies in the struggle against communism? What should our policy toward the neutrals be? All the governments affected by these questions try to see that Congress comes up with the right answers. Organizations

---

[10] See Chapter 7.

like the Council of State Governments and the United States Conference of Mayors reflect the interests of state and urban governments. Foreign governments hire American lawyers, public relations men, and researchers; their lobbyists are often prominent figures with ready access to points of decision-making. In fact, the interest of foreign governments in American policy may be as great as that of many domestic governments. Although the citizens of a foreign government can hardly take an active part in our elections, their government can freely engage in most of the tactics that are so effectively used by domestic pressure groups.

Official and unofficial agencies, from the local Parent-Teachers Association to the Union of Soviet Socialist Republics, affect the policies of the United States. Russian sympathizers are a small and unpopular group, but the behavior of the Soviet government itself indirectly influences American legislators. The communist *coup* in Czechoslovakia in 1948, for example, did more to convert isolationist-minded congressmen to support of the Marshall Plan (to aid European reconstruction) than did all the arguments of American internationalists. And Russia's success in putting the first man into orbital flight in 1961 was a great stimulus to our own effort at space exploration.

The President: Director, Actor, Script-writer, Prompter

The President's role in legislation is sometimes viewed as a practice that is only partly respectable but still necessary to get the job done. Over half the bills introduced in Congress originate in the executive department. Since the first article of the Constitution proclaims that "*all* legislative powers" are vested in Congress, some observers argue that the President's participation is not strictly in keeping with the Constitution.

Defenders of presidential leadership might reply that the Framing Fathers were in error and that their intentions deserve to be ignored. Since government responds to the dominant interests of society, and since powerful urban groups have more influence on the President than on Congress, the twentieth-century expansion of the President's legislative functions would probably have occurred regardless of the Framers' intentions. So great is the American tendency toward ancestor worship in politics, however, that we are reassured to discover that the Framers of the Constitution actually expected the executive to be a legislative leader. Wilfred E. Binkley, a political historian who has studied this problem closely, reports:

> The evidence is conclusive that the fathers of the Constitution were far less fanatical devotees of the dogma of separated powers than their great grandchildren. . . . The records of the first several Congresses provide incontrovertible evidence of the framers' assumption that the department heads would provide the initiative in legislation. At any rate eighteen delegates to the Constitutional Convention later sat unprotesting in the First Congress as one out-

standing legislative problem after another was referred for study and report to the heads of executive departments.[11]

How the Constitution Makes the President a Policy-maker

The Constitution underwrites the President's policy-making role in several ways. First, the provision that "he shall from time to time give to the Congress information of the state of the union, and recommend to their consideration such measures as he shall judge necessary and expedient" thrusts the President to the front in legislation. The President delivers three regular messages every year, all more concerned with his duty to recommend than with his duty to inform. The most comprehensive of these reports is the State of the Union Message, in which the President surveys the strengths and weaknesses of the country and lays out the legislative program of his administration. In the Budget Message he presents the all-important requests for funds to carry out the programs of the executive agencies, and in the Economic Report he sets forth his recommendations for maintaining a high level of production and employment.

In these and in any special messages he may choose to deliver on specific problems, the President speaks not just for himself but for all the departments under his control. Officials of these departments, especially the Bureau of the Budget, usually participate in framing policy statements of this sort. Actually, these messages are directed to the general public or to foreign countries as often as they are to Congress itself. President Johnson chose to deliver his 1965 State of the Union Message during the prime TV hours of the evening, not because he thought congressmen would be more attentive after dinner but because he knew that millions of additional citizens would watch the presentation if it were shifted from the traditional daytime hour. Technically he was speaking to Congress; in fact he made certain that he would also speak to a maximum audience of citizens.

The Constitution gives the President power over laws from their cradle to their grave: his recommendations may create bills and his veto power may kill them. Every act must be presented to the President for his approval after it has passed both houses of Congress. Four courses of action are then possible. The President may sign the bill, and make it a law. He may hold it without taking action, in which case it becomes law in ten days without his signature. Or he may veto it and return it to the house in which it originated, along with the reasons for his disapproval. In this event, it must be repassed by a two-thirds vote in both houses in order to become law. Finally, a "pocket veto" is possible under special circumstances; if the President takes no action—that is, if he "pockets" the bill—and if Congress adjourns before he has had it for ten days, the bill is automatically killed.

The President need not actually use his veto power in order to influence legislation, for the threat or the mere possibility of a veto may serve to modify

---

11 "The President and Congress," *Journal of Politics,* XI (February, 1949), p. 69.

or even block a legislative proposal. When the President actually exercises his veto power, we have a much clearer case of policy-making than when the courts use their "veto" power through judicial review; the President can openly base his decision on policy considerations rather than on constitutionality. Thus, even in purely legalistic terms, the President is a far more important legislator than any member of Congress. He alone commands the attention of both houses of Congress in recommending policy, and he alone possesses the power to block the action of a congressional majority.

The constitutional basis of the President's legislative power does not stop, however, with his privilege of urging or vetoing bills. The Constitution also gives him the authority to convene either or both houses of Congress in special session and, if the two houses cannot agree on a time of adjournment, "he may adjourn them to such time as he shall think proper." Since the President is normally concerned with prodding congressmen rather than with cutting off their activities, the power of adjournment has never been employed. Special sessions and the threat of special sessions have, on the other hand, been useful weapons in the President's legislative arsenal. The Twentieth Amendment has, of course, lessened the need for special sessions.

Finally, the Constitution specifies that the President "take care that the laws be faithfully executed." We have seen that laws are simply broad declarations of policy when they come from Congress, and that the courts continue the policy-making function as they interpret laws in particular cases. But the executive branch plays an even greater role than the courts in filling in details and interpreting laws. Only when a policy is applied to a specific situation does it take on concrete meaning, and at this stage the intentions of the President may outweigh the intentions of Congress.

Despite Senator Goldwater's insistence that he would be constitutionally bound, if elected President, to enforce the Civil Rights Act of 1964, neither white nor Negro voters appeared to accept his protestations. (He carried the black-belt counties of the South, where white prejudices are strongest and few Negroes can vote, and he lost an incredible 90 per cent of the Negro vote nationally.) His vote against the law was a sufficient clue that it would have a different impact under his administration than under that of President Johnson. The intuitive reaction of the voters in this case could have been supported from past history: anti-trust laws have been "on the books" since 1890 but their interpretation and enforcement has varied greatly, depending on the attitudes of different presidents toward anti-trust policy.

With the growing complexity of government, Congress has openly delegated to executive officers the "quasi-legislative" power to make detailed rules with the force of law. When the President adjusts a tariff rate within the limits set by Congress, or when the Secretary of Agriculture changes the level of price supports for farm products, the ruling is as much a "law" as if Congress had incorporated it into the original statute. While many of these quasi-legislative powers are exercised by agencies that are not directly subject to presidential control, others are exercised by the Chief Executive and his direct subordinates.

The facts of political life in the United States demand that the President be a legislative leader. Even those who grumble that the separation of powers is being weakened must wonder if the Congress could really conceive legislation without being stimulated by the executive. In 1947, when the Republicans were in control of Congress, Senator Homer Ferguson of Michigan, a leading Republican critic of the Truman administration, castigated the President in this fashion: "If the President wants to tell the people that he stands for a certain thing, he ought to come to the House and Senate with a message. And he ought to provide a bill. . . ." [12] In 1957, President Eisenhower suggested that, since the government can spend money only under congressional appropriations, Congress should assume responsibility for reducing his $72 billion budget. But instead of eagerly seizing upon this responsibility, the Democratic majority in Congress protested that Eisenhower was "passing the buck."

The need for presidential leadership in legislation is confirmed by persistent complaints from congressmen about the lack of such leadership from a President of the opposite party. The organization of Congress is so diffuse that some external leadership is essential if Congress is to function as a lawmaking body. Even congressmen who regularly disagree with a President depend on him to furnish a general program that they can attack. And his followers look to him for a coherent set of objectives that they can support.

The President is chief legislator for another reason—that is the job the voters have elected him to perform. Very little is said in presidential campaigns about administrative principles. The issues the candidates do talk about, and the issues in which citizens are most interested, are questions of *policy*, not questions of administration. What policy should the country adopt on immigration, farm price supports, labor-management relations, public health, education, civil rights, military preparedness, inflation, relations with foreign nations? When a presidential candidate promises to achieve a given policy, he is in effect promising to manage Congress. Today it is inconceivable that any candidate could announce, as Admiral Dewey did in 1900, that he was unconcerned with policy questions and that he would devote himself to a disinterested enforcement of any laws that Congress might pass.

The President is not just a policy-maker; as the only official (except the Vice-President) who can claim to have a national mandate,[13] he is the *chief legislator*. Five years before he became President, Woodrow Wilson wrote:

> The nation as a whole has chosen [the President], and is conscious that it has no other political spokesman. His is the only national voice in affairs. . . . He is the representative of no constituency, but of the whole people. When he speaks in his true character, he speaks for no special interest.[14]

---

[12] As quoted in Binkley, *Journal of Politics*, XI (February, 1949), p. 74.

[13] For further discussion of the role of the President as chief legislator, see Chapter 10.

[14] *Constitutional Government in the United States* (New York: Columbia University Press, 1908), p. 68.

This portrait is somewhat idealized—and Wilson came closer to fitting it than most presidents—but in some degree it describes any occupant of the White House. Whatever the personal character of the President, the institutional forces that impinge upon him tend to align him with a broader collection of interests than any other elective official. Specifically, since his election requires support from urban majorities, the President is automatically rendered sensitive to the needs of those interests that make up a majority of the population.

The same cannot be said for a congressman, because his limited constituency leaves him more vulnerable to local interests. Calvin Coolidge, who could hardly be described as a strong President, recognized this basic difference in the orientation of Congress and the President. Shortly after he left the White House, Coolidge said, "It is because in their hours of timidity the Congress becomes subservient to the importunities of organized minorities that the President comes more and more to stand as the champion of the rights of the whole country." [15] The personal qualities of the President are important, of course, but when a man moves from Congress (or from any other position) to the White House his perspective is almost inevitably broadened. Harry Truman, for example, was never a leader for civil rights legislation as long as he was a Senator from Missouri, but once he became President he showed himself as an active champion of civil rights. As President of Columbia University, Dwight Eisenhower compared the social welfare state with a giant jail, but as President of the United States he advocated that social security coverage be extended.

The expectations and needs of both Congress and the general public, then, provide political forces that oblige the President to act as a legislative leader. These forces are strengthened by the fact that the President's purely "executive" powers under the Constitution can also be used as effective political weapons in coaxing, cajoling, threatening, and educating legislators. Among these executive powers is the President's control over patronage, funds, and projects—all matters of close concern to congressmen.

Powers of this sort are especially influential early in a new President's term, when he has many appointments to make. A President on the way out of office, on the other hand, suffers a sharp loss of influence, for everyone knows that there will soon be a new center of power. The Twenty-second Amendment, adopted in 1951, makes it unconstitutional for a President to serve more than two terms, and may thus weaken his leadership during a second term. No longer can a President keep congressmen guessing about whether or not he will run again. As soon as he begins his second term he becomes a new kind of "lame duck," an official whose successor has not yet been chosen but whose departure from office on a fixed date is assured. These expectations about the effects of the Twenty-second Amendment appear logical but their validity has not been demonstrated. President Eisenhower began his first term with a relatively deferential attitude toward Congress but gradually came to recognize the need for more executive leadership. His influence therefore did not appear to decrease in his

---

[15] As quoted in Binkley, *Journal of Politics*, XI (February, 1949), p. 73.

second term. If the interpretation is correct, however, President Johnson's effectiveness with Congress should drop if he wins a second term.

The President's status as head of his party further enhances his influence with congressmen. His party's leaders in Congress normally follow his legislative lead and rally a nucleus of the party faithful behind them. Some members of the President's party may feel that they owe their victories to his success in drawing votes to the party. If they won their seats by narrow margins and trailed behind the President in popular votes, they may find it helpful to be identified with the President and perhaps win his assistance in their efforts to get re-elected.

Unfortunately for the President, however, the key positions of power in Congress generally go to representatives and senators from constituencies in which re-election is almost assured. Thus the most prominent leaders in Congress are likely to be the very congressmen who are least dependent on the President's power as party leader. Democratic leaders in Congress, many of them permanent fixtures from the South, have frequently failed to support President Johnson. Indeed, Senator Richard Russell of Georgia went abroad on congressional business rather than help the President in Georgia in the 1964 campaign. In Eisenhower's first administration, the Republican majority leader in the Senate, William Knowland of California, publicly opposed many of the President's policies, especially in the field of foreign affairs.

Despite these limitations on his power as party leader, all the President's roles overlap to fortify him in the position of chief legislator. If he is a forceful leader, like Woodrow Wilson or either Roosevelt, he may appeal directly to the people for support in order to win still more influence over the members of Congress.

The President's Supporting Cast

The President is not just a man, he is an institution. When he speaks out on policy, he speaks as the head of the entire executive branch of the government. His policy positions are based not only on his broad responsibilities as a political leader but also on his technical experience as general manager of the national government. In a personal sense, of course, the President is no more at the point of actual contact between citizen and government than a congressman; relatively minor officials have the task of actually inspecting sanitary facilities under the Food and Drug Act, or of deciding whether an income tax return meets the requirements of the tax laws. But these people work under the President, and he can rely on their experience for a picture of how the public reacts to government policies as they are actually enforced. At their best, then, the recommendations of the President reflect the administrative experience and the technical competence of the entire civil service.

To imagine that the executive establishment speaks in one voice or even in harmonious chorus, however, is to distort reality. Some agencies that are "under" the President in the sense of being in the executive branch, notably the independent regulatory commissions, are almost completely immune to presidential control. Even regular "line" agencies that organization charts show to be directly answerable to the President sometimes develop into semi-independent little centers of power. The Army Corps of Engineers furnishes a striking example of disunity in the executive branch. The Corps, which is always eager to deepen channels, improve harbors, or strengthen levees, is closely tied to local officials and contractors, and to the congressmen from the lower Mississippi region. As part of what has been called "the lobby that can't be licked," [16] the Corps of Engineers has repeatedly and successfully ignored orders from its commander-in-chief. In 1949, the Hoover Commission [17] recommended that the dam-building functions of the Corps be placed under the Bureau of Reclamation, but the Corps continues, unscathed, to battle the Bureau for appropriations—with or without presidential approval, and always with the cooperation of interested congressmen.

Accordingly, to speak of the President's "supporting cast" is less misleading than to speak of the presidential "team." We expect supporting actors to build up their roles if they can, or even to "upstage" the leading man. But we expect members of a team to work in unbroken harmony. Every executive agency and operating division develops interests of its own, and every subordinate official is eager to preserve or extend his agency's role even while he is advising the President or interpreting his orders. Government agencies act at both the input and output stages of the lawmaking process. They recommend legislation to Congress directly and through allied interests inside and outside the government, and they interpret the existing law as they apply it day by day. Although the executive departments are all legally subordinate to the President, their influence on policy is not that of a monolithic structure. Bertram M. Gross, from the vantage point of wide experience both in senatorial committees and in the Executive Office of the President, offers this conclusion:

> A bogeyman has been created of a vast Executive bureaucracy with such power and influence that the President can use it to dominate Congress and obtain whatever legislation he wants. One reason that this is not so is that no President has ever been able to avoid or overcome serious conflicts between the heads of the various agencies. . . .
>
> . . . Many agencies themselves are established only in response to the pressure of private organizations and their representatives in Congress and can continue in existence only by working with and serving such groups. . . . As a result of these diverse and often conflicting allegiances, there are more checks and balances within the executive branch itself than the Founding Fathers ever dreamed of when they wrote the Constitution.[18]

---

[16] Robert deRoos and Arthur A. Maas, "The Lobby That Can't Be Licked," *Harper's Magazine*, August, 1949.

[17] Officially known as the Commission on Organization of the Executive Branch of the Government.

[18] Bertram M. Gross, *The Legislative Struggle: A Study in Social Combat* (New York: McGraw-Hill Book Company, Inc., 1953), pp. 104–105. Roland Young treats Congress and the President as inseparable parts of the legislative process. He notes especially the manner in which the bureaucracy advocates and defends its interests in Congress even though it is not directly represented there. See Roland Young, *The American Congress* (New York: Harper & Brothers, 1958).

The Congressional Stage: Organized Confusion

The staging of the congressional drama is complicated enough to satisfy the most "colossal-minded" Hollywood producer—and to exasperate any critic who thinks he should be able to follow the plot. The spotlights are focused on two principal scenes—the Senate chamber and the House chamber—but most of the action takes place in thirty-six scattered committees. There is no over-all plot, and the number of subplots would confuse even a Tolstoy. There is no leading man. But there are numerous "heavies," each of whom dominates a limited area of the action. It is almost as though things had been deliberately arranged to confuse the spectator-citizen. And yet, although the action is too bewildering to sustain the interest of the casual onlooker, those with a special interest, like the parents of the actors in a school play, can be counted on for attendance and close interest.

The Structure of the Congressional Scene

In simple truth, the complexity of the congressional scene was deliberately planned. The Framing Fathers had no intention of setting up policy-making organs that would give a direct and clear-cut expression of majority opinion. One of the principal reasons for establishing two separate houses in Congress, for example, was to filter out and check impetuous majorities.

The House of Representatives was conceived as the "popular" branch of Congress. Its members were to be elected directly by the people for two-year terms—or at least by the people in each state who were eligible to vote for the more popular branch of the state legislature. Each state was guaranteed at least one representative; beyond that provision, representation in the House was to be apportioned among the states according to population. Accordingly, the House was planned as the only popular agency of the national government—popular both in the manner in which the members were elected, and in the scheme of apportioning representation. The Senate, by contrast, was planned as the "non-popular," or federal, branch of Congress. Its members were to be elected for six-year terms by the state legislatures, and each state was guaranteed two senators regardless of its population.

Most of the men who wrote the Constitution were frankly opposed to the "excesses of democracy," and popular control of Congress was one of the evils they wanted to avoid. Although this view was sincerely held by many delegates, it hardly accounts for the development of bicameralism. Delegates from the more populous states, equally opposed to democracy, were satisfied with other means of controlling its excesses; they denounced the equal representation of all states as giving unwarranted power to the citizens of less populous states. Some real democrats, like Benjamin Franklin of Pennsylvania, went further and rejected bicameralism in general as an inefficient instrument of public preferences and the proposed plan in particular because it departed from the principle of popular choice of rulers. But people of Franklin's persuasion were rare in the 1780's, especially at the Constitutional Convention. Suspicion of the people was thus a convenient talking point for proponents of the federal scheme of representation, but it did not account for their success.

The hard facts of political power produced bicameralism originally, and chances are they will sustain it. All the talk about "states" having a "right" to an equal voice was and is a more attractive way of saying that people with extra power do not like to surrender it. The word "state" has no meaning except in terms of people. Political leaders from the less populous states enjoyed power at the national level disproportionate to their numbers before and during the drafting of the Constitution. And they refused to take part in the planning of the new government unless they were given a similar advantage in at least one branch of Congress. Delegates from the more populous states agreed to this hard bargain because they had more to lose under the Articles of Confederation (with no recognition of varying state populations) than under the new scheme.

Today the residents of Alaska or the residents of Nevada would hardly argue that each Alaskan or Nevadan is worth over 100 New Yorkers. But if any proposal were made to abolish the Senate, their leaders would talk about the equal rights of states, not of people, and about federalism, not about majority rule. Moreover, with the amendment plan of the Framing Fathers still intact, the senators who represent only 3 per cent of the total population could block a proposal to amend the Constitution. Politics is the quest for power, and those who enjoy power do not voluntarily surrender it. Instead, they invent ideas to justify keeping it. Bicameralism is here to stay.

Some ironic twists have radically altered the intentions of the Framing Fathers as to the roles of the House and Senate. Although the residents of less populous states continue to be vastly over-represented in the Senate, it is no longer the special champion of the "rich, well-born, and able" or of the rural interests. Since the adoption of the Seventeenth Amendment in 1913, senators have been chosen by popular election. In this regard, they are now like representatives, with the important distinction that they are chosen from a state-wide constituency. Early in the twentieth century, a majority of Americans lived in rural areas and most states were predominantly rural. Thus we became accustomed to thinking of the Senate as peculiarly responsive to rural interests and of the urban areas as finding their spokesmen in the House. But by 1950 urban residents made up a majority of the population in 30 states; and by 1960 they were a majority in 39 states. Moreover, the urban majority in 1960 included 60 per cent or more of the population in 29 states. With large, heterogeneous, and primarily urban constituencies, senators became the champions of liberal causes.

Meanwhile, members of the rural minority began to find the House peculiarly responsive to their needs. And many special interests (the modern equivalents of the "rich, well-born, and able") discovered that they were strong enough to dominate a district but not a state. The House thus became the stronghold of rural, conservative interests, blocking social welfare measures passed by the urban, liberal Senate. How did the shift come about?

Except for the guarantee of one representative to each state, representation in the House is apportioned among the states "according to their respective numbers." To keep the House representative, the Constitution further provides for the reapportionment of House seats every ten years. After taking the easy way out and permitting the membership of the House to increase steadily for over a hundred years, Congress finally called a halt at a total of 435 representatives. Since 1929, a virtually automatic arrangement has been followed. After each census, the Census Bureau calculates the number of representatives to which the population of each state entitles it, on the basis of a House membership fixed at 435. The President submits this reapportionment plan to Congress, and it automatically goes into effect unless Congress enacts a different plan within sixty days. This plan takes advantage of the difficulty of getting Congress to act— instead of requiring passage of a bill to *get* reapportionment, the procedure requires passage of a bill to *block* reapportionment.

Since 1842, Congress has required states with more than one representative to choose their representatives from single-member districts.[19] But in 1929 it dropped the additional requirement that these districts be compact, contiguous, and as nearly equal in population as practicable. In other words, Congress left the state legislatures free to handle congressional districting without guidelines. As a result, the states adopted grossly unfair districting schemes with apparent impunity.

By mid-century, the rural minority of the population held about three-fifths of the House seats, and their over-representation in most state legislatures was even greater. The demands of urban residents for an equal voice in government were loud and clear, but they could hardly become effective inputs of legislative decision-making. Both the House of Representatives and the state legislatures (which are responsible for drawing congressional districts) were controlled by the very interests which stood to lose from reapportionment. But the political system functions as a whole and its elements are so interdependent that the activity (or inactivity) of one element affects all other elements of the system. A democratic political system must somehow respond to enduring majority interests if it is to survive; if one element of the system fails to respond, another element tends to meet the need.[20] Until the 1930's, for example, American workers' efforts to organize labor unions were severely handicapped by court enforcement of "yellow-dog contracts," which bound workers not to join a union and which the Supreme Court further interpreted as forbidding union officials from trying to

---

[19] When states fail to redistrict after a reapportionment and elect their new representatives from the state "at large," the House does not refuse to seat such representatives. Alabama, which lost one representative under the 1960 census, came up with a novel plan for the 1962 congressional election. Instead of re-drawing its districts, it provided for each of its former nine districts to nominate a candidate in the first primary, and for the nominees to run in a statewide primary. The top eight in the statewide vote became the representatives. Districts were redrawn before the 1964 election.

[20] Notice the qualifying word "tends" in the proposition above. We do not mean to imply any magical process by which some element of a system will *always* compensate for the dysfunctional performance of another element. The system may be destroyed or drastically altered, but the *tendency* is for systems to maintain themselves.

organize such workers.[21] Long stymied in the courts, labor turned to Congress and won passage of the Norris-LaGuardia Act of 1932 outlawing yellow-dog contracts. Urban interests were similarly frustrated, but this time it was the legislature that appeared unyielding; they turned accordingly to the courts for relief.

A political science professor in Illinois brought the first case that promised eventual victory to urban forces. During the 1946 congressional election, he asked the federal courts to correct a situation in which one Illinois district had eight times as many people as another. By the closest of decisions—four to three—the Supreme Court refused to intervene.[22] Three members of the four-man majority based their decision on the idea that legislative districting is a "political question" with which courts cannot cope. The fourth member of the majority agreed with the three-man minority that the issue was justiciable (one that courts could properly decide), but he concurred in the decision against intervention because the timing of the case did not permit a proper remedy before the election would be held. This swing vote, added to the three-man minority holding in favor of the Court's accepting the case, actually made a majority in favor of judicial action.

In more recent decisions, the "hidden majority" which approved court action in the 1946 case has become a conspicuous majority. In 1962, the Supreme Court ruled in *Baker* v. *Carr* that federal courts have authority to review state legislative apportionments when they are challenged as violating the citizen's guarantee of equal protection of the laws under the Fourteenth Amendment.[23] The state action need not entail a direct *denial of voting rights*, as Justice Frankfurter had long insisted,[24] in order to be challenged; the charge that a state's apportionment *debased and diluted the effect of the votes* of certain citizens was enough to justify its review under the Fourteenth Amendment. *Baker* v. *Carr* has been described as second only to *Marbury* v. *Madison* in its importance for the federal system.[25] Within two years it had led to some action on the apportionment of legislative seats in 42 states. That the Baker decision would have far-reaching effects on the distribution of political power was clear from the outset, but in returning the case to the district court "for further proceedings consistent with this opinion" the Court did not spell out the criteria for legally acceptable districting.

A series of decisions in 1963 and 1964 spelled out the basic criterion in unmistakable terms: population must be the controlling factor in legislative apportionment; insofar as possible, one man's vote must be worth as much as another's.

---

[21] *Hitchman Coal and Coke Co.* v. *Mitchell*, 245 U.S. 229 (1917).

[22] *Colegrove* v. *Green*, 328 U.S. 548 (1946). At the time of the decision, there was one vacancy on the Court and one justice not participating.

[23] *Baker* v. *Carr*, 369 U.S. 186 (1962).

[24] See, for example, *Gomillion* v. *Lightfoot*, 364 U.S. 341 (1960).

[25] Robert G. Dixon, Jr., "Legislative Apportionment and the Federal Constitution," *Law and Contemporary Problems*, XXVII, Part II (Summer, 1962), p. 330. This and a number of other excellent articles are reprinted in Glendon Schubert (ed.), *Reapportionment* (New York: Charles Scribner's Sons, 1965). Also see Howard D. Hamilton (ed.), *Legislative Apportionment* (New York: Harper & Row, Publishers, 1964).

The Court first spelled out the "one man, one vote" doctrine in a 1963 decision (8–1) striking down Georgia's county unit system of voting in statewide and congressional primary elections.[26] The county unit system violated the Fourteenth Amendment because it diluted the weight of votes cast by some Georgia voters merely because of where they resided. In 1964, the same reasoning was applied to *both* houses of state legislatures. Chief Justice Warren, speaking for an 8–1 majority,[27] eliminated any remaining doubts about the court's dedication to the one man, one vote principle:

> Logically, in a society ostensibly grounded on representative government, it would seem reasonable that a majority of the people of a state could elect a majority of that state's legislators. To conclude differently, and to sanction minority control of state legislative bodies, would appear to deny majority rights. . . . Our constitutional system amply provides for the protection of minorities by means other than giving them majority control of state legislatures.
>
> We hold that, as a basic constitutional standard, the Equal Protection Clause requires that the seats in both houses of a bicameral state legislature must be apportioned on a population basis. Simply stated, an individual's right to vote for state legislators is unconstitutionally impaired when its weight is in a substantial fashion diluted when compared with votes of citizens living in other parts of the state.

Encouraged by their successes at the state level, urban residents turned again to the problem of under-representation in the national House of Representatives. In 1964, the hidden majority of 1946 appeared as a 6–3 majority.[28] Instead of the Fourteenth Amendment, the Supreme Court relied this time upon the constitutional provision that established the House as the popular branch of the national government: "We hold that, construed in its historical context, the command of Art. I, Sec. 2, that representatives be chosen 'by the people of the several States' means that as nearly as is practicable one man's vote in a congressional election is to be worth as much as another's." Speaking for the Court, Justice Black emphasized the debates in the Constitutional Convention, the early practice of statewide election of all representatives (which automatically insured an equal weight for each vote), and James Madison's emphasis in *The Federalist* on the popular character of the House in concluding that, "no matter what the mechanics of an election, whether statewide or by districts, it was population which was to be the basis of the house of representatives."

These bold pronouncements by the Supreme Court were roundly denounced by conservative interests, who correctly viewed them as threatening to change the particularistic biases that had developed within the federal system. The House of Representatives went so far as to adopt a proposal that would have denied the federal courts jurisdiction on matters dealing with state legislative apportionment. Notice that the House was more harassed by the decisions on state than on na-

---

[26] *Gray v. Sanders*, 372 U.S. 368 (1963).

[27] *Reynolds v. Sims*, 377 U.S. 533 (1964). Justice Harlan dissented; Justices Clark and Stewart agreed with the decision but not with the reasoning.

[28] *Wesberry v. Sanders*, 376 U.S. 1 (1964).

tional apportionment: the shape of congressional districts is determined by the forces that control the state legislatures. Reaction to the decisions depended heavily on party affiliation: 78 per cent of the Republican representatives and 41 per cent of the Democrats supported the anti-court proposal. If southern Democrats are separated from others, the differences are even more dramatic: for the proposal were 84 per cent of the southern Democrats, 78 per cent of the Republicans, and 9 per cent of the non-southern Democrats.[29] When the same proposal came up in the Senate, it was resoundingly defeated (56–21), with only one non-southern Democrat and four Republicans taking the anti-court position. The difference between the two houses, between the two parties, and between the two wings of the Democratic party could hardly have been more clearly demonstrated.[30]

By the time of these 1964 decisions, the House of Representatives was not nearly as stacked in favor of rural voters as it had been at mid-century. Defining urban areas as those with populations of 50,000 or more, the *Congressional Quarterly* estimated that an "ideal" apportionment—the most feasible distribution of population among the districts of each state—would result in a net change of only about 16 out of the 435 House seats. The urban areas would gain 6 additional representatives, mostly in the South, and the suburban areas would gain 10.[31] Malapportionment of the House had thus developed in such a way that it was no longer so consistently biased in favor of rural residents as it was in favor of particular incumbents, parties, and interest groups.[32] These biases were most conspicuous at the state level. Despite the changes that had resulted from *Baker* v. *Carr*, a minority of the population in 1964 could still elect a majority of the members of *both houses of every state legislative body*. Only 20 states were districted so as to require more than 40 per cent of the population to elect a majority of state senators, and 19 states to require more than 40 per cent to elect a majority of their representatives.[33]

In view of these extreme deviations from the concept of an equal weight for every man's vote, radical changes can be expected in the state legislatures and lesser changes in the House of Representatives. At the national level, these changes may not have great partisan consequences. After all, the suburban areas are those most under-represented in the House, and the Republicans are traditionally strong in the suburbs. The vote of Republican representatives to deny federal courts the authority to rule on state legislative apportionment suggests, however, that state malapportionment has worked principally to the benefit of Republicans. (The South is, as usual, an exception: southern malapportionment

---

[29] *Congressional Quarterly Weekly Report*, XXII (week ending August 21, 1964), p. 1895.

[30] *Ibid.* (week ending September 18, 1964), p. 2161.

[31] *Ibid.* (week ending February 21, 1964), p. 352.

[32] See Malcolm E. Jewell, "Political Patterns of Apportionment," in Jewell (ed.), *The Politics of Reapportionment* (New York: Atherton Press, 1962), pp. 1–48.

[33] *Congressional Quarterly Weekly Report*, XXII (week ending June 19, 1964), p. 1219.

benefits local Democrats, but southern representatives were so piqued at the Supreme Court for its civil rights rulings that they cast their votes to discredit the Court.)

Regardless of partisan implications, the consequences of a roughly equal weight for all votes will be to increase the national and urban orientation of *both* parties. When one reflects on all that would have been done about slum clearance, urban renewal, juvenile delinquency, mass transportation, and similar problems in the last twenty years if Congress had devoted the same attention to urban problems that it lavished on farm problems, the imagination is staggered. The feedback from these historic court decisions can be expected to become inputs of the greatest importance for other decision-making agencies.

Drawing by Herblock. From *Straight Herblock* (New York, Simon & Schuster, 1964).

Animal Farm

Congressional Procedure

Any aggregation of people must develop recognized leaders and rules of procedure if it is to function as a group. Just how elaborate its organization needs to be depends on the size of the group and the purpose it sets for itself. The House, for example, is more highly organized than the Senate. One reason is probably that the House is larger than the Senate. The executive branch, by the same token, is even more highly organized than the House. Administration calls for more unified and rapid action than does legislation, and the size of the executive establishment is too vast for any coherent action to be taken without a much more structured organization.

The rules of the House are therefore much more elaborate and constraining than those of the Senate, just as administrative rules are more restrictive and detailed than those of the House. In view of the large number of representatives, the House must be more tightly organized if it is to act; the smaller number of senators permits a greater emphasis on full deliberation. It is a complicated job for 435 representatives to act on any matter, even one on which a majority is in strong agreement. During the early years of the House, when its membership was small, the only important function of the Rules Committee was to report a system of rules at the beginning of each Congress. With the increase in size of the House, however, the power of the Rules Committee grew to the point where it is the key coordinating committee of the entire body.[34] If the Rules Committee opposes a bill, it may simply refuse to recommend a rule under which it can be scheduled for consideration; when it does propose a rule for the consideration of a measure, the rule may drastically limit debate or it may limit the amendments that may be offered. The members of the House may reject the Rules Committee resolution (it is not subject to amendment), but to do so is to lose the chance to

[34] Milton C. Cummings, Jr., and Robert L. Peabody, "The Decision to Enlarge the Committee on Rules: An Analysis of the 1961 Vote," in Peabody and Polsby (eds.), *New Perspectives on the House of Representatives*, p. 169.

"Next I want to sing a song about the House Rules Committee and how the legislative functions of Congress are tyrannized over by its procedural calendar, dominated in turn by an all-powerful chairman hamstringing the processes of democracy."

Drawing by Koren; © 1964 The New Yorker Magazine, Inc.

consider the measure at all and to incur the disfavor of the most powerful committee in the House. Affirmative action on the proposed rule is thus assured. The representative who gets a chance to speak for five minutes on a bill is lucky.[35]

In 1965, the Democrats enjoyed their largest majority in the House of Representatives (295–140) since 1937. Moreover, their net gain of 38 seats in the 1964 election had added liberal Democrats from outside the South; since 7 of the 9 Democratic seats lost to Republicans had been held by Democrats from Alabama, Mississippi, and Georgia who voted with the Republicans on key issues, the effective gain for the national Democratic Party was 45 votes. This was enough to win a significant reduction in the power of the Rules Committee, which had long been the burying ground for liberal legislation. On January 4, 1965, the House voted its Speaker power to speed bills from the Rules Committee. If the Committee fails to report a bill received from a policy committee for 21 days, the Speaker may recognize a member of that committee to move consideration of the bill. The Rules Committee continues to be the most powerful body in the House, but the nationalizing forces expressed in Supreme Court decisions on urban representation, in the unprecedented size of Johnson's 1964 victory, and in this reduction of the Committee's power may mean that it can no longer so blatantly thwart the preferences of the national majority.

In contrast to the House, the Senate—"the greatest deliberative body in the world"—operates under a rule of unlimited debate. A "previous question" motion enables a House majority to bring a measure to a vote, but the Senate has no previous question rule. By permitting full debate, Senate rules also permit the "filibuster," a practice that enables a minority to prevent the passage of a law by talking it to death, never letting it come to a vote. Minorities also use the filibuster or the threat of a filibuster to extract concessions from the majority.

In 1959, the Senate adopted a "cloture" rule that requires a favorable vote by two-thirds of the senators *present and voting* to close off debate. For the Senate, this represented a small step toward majority control—from 1949 to 1959, the rule was that debate could be ended only by the approval of two-thirds of the *entire membership* of the Senate. Northern and western liberals argued that the change, which restored a 1917 rule, did not go far enough. Although debate was shut off under the 1917 rule only four times, southern senators protested that its restoration was a move "to further curtail free speech in the Senate." The present cloture rule goes well beyond the attempts of the Framing Fathers to limit the majority; for the first twenty years of Senate history, debate could be ended by a simple majority vote! [36]

The anti-filibuster forces gained one concession in 1959: debate on motions to change the rules, which had been exempt from any restriction, was made sub-

---

[35] The Procedures for the conduct of business in both houses of Congress are well explained in Daniel M. Berman, *In Congress Assembled* (New York: The Macmillan Company, 1964), Chapters 6–11; and in Norman C. Thomas and Karl A. Lamb, *Congress: Politics and Practice* (New York: Random House, 1964), Chapters 4–7.

[36] See George B. Galloway, *The Legislative Process in Congress* (New York: Thomas Y. Crowell Company, 1953), p. 560.

ject to cloture. But the pro-filibuster forces won a clear victory in the provision that the rules of the Senate shall carry over from one Congress to another. Consequently, the rule permitting debate to be shut off only by a two-thirds vote is automatically in force as soon as Congress convenes. Even at the convening of a new Congress a simple majority cannot rewrite the rules in order to establish majority control in the Senate.

The House, on the other hand, organizes as a completely new body each time a new Congress convenes. But the rules of the House show special deference to the power of its standing committees. When an unfriendly committee refuses to report a measure to the floor for consideration, the only way the bill can be pried loose is by means of a "discharge petition" signed by a majority of the total House membership. Although this is not so extreme as the requirements for cloture in the Senate, respect for the committee system is so great—and absenteeism so regular—that the discharge petition is used infrequently. A majority cannot be permanently frustrated in the House, but if it is to make its will prevail it may have to mobilize its strength completely and show real determination.

Elected Party Leaders

As these key rules suggest, Congress is not dominated by strong leaders. If there is any over-all leadership, it comes from the outside, from the President. Within the Congress itself, the bicameral system, combined with the lack of solidarity in our political parties, makes any unified leadership out of the question. As we would expect from the tighter organization of the House, however, the leaders of the House have more influence on their colleagues than do those of the Senate.

The officers of each house, save for the President of the Senate, are elected by the members. In practice, this means that before Congress convenes the Republican and Democratic members of each house meet in party conferences or caucuses to select slates of candidates for the offices of their respective houses. And when it comes to backing these candidates, the party members achieve a solidarity that they rarely muster on policy questions. Voting as a bloc, the members of the majority party in each chamber always elect their slate.

In the House the principal officer is the Speaker. He is the leading member of the majority party in the House and is frequently described as "the second most powerful man in Washington." Before the powers of the Speaker were curtailed early in this century, his influence was even greater, and he exercised life-and-death control over legislation. Even today he is the strongest figure in Congress. The Speaker plays several roles: he is the presiding officer and a respected member of the House; he acts as contact man with the President when they are of the same party; and he serves as the leader of his party in the House. As presiding officer, the Speaker announces the order of business, puts questions to a vote and reports the vote, recognizes members who want the floor, interprets the rules, squelches dilatory tactics, refers bills to committees, and appoints the members of select and conference committees. While a decision of the Speaker may occasionally be overruled by the House itself, as in referring a controversial bill to a committee, his normal control over these functions gives him so much influence that even the House Rules Committee can ill afford to "buck" the Speaker. Indeed, he influences the selection of the majority members of the Rules Committee at the outset.

A liberal coalition of progressive Republicans and Democrats combined in 1911 to strip the Speaker of the House—"Czar" Joseph Cannon—of his extreme powers. But the notion of "direct democracy" failed in the House as it did in other arenas of American life. Much of the power taken from the Speaker shifted to the Rules Committee, which, as a plural body, was even less subject to control by House members. Indeed, the seniority system served to vest control of the Committee in an enduring coalition of southern Democrats and conservative Republicans. In 1961, the size of the Democrats' majority was too small to achieve a basic change in the Rules Committee's power. But the late Sam Rayburn (D-Texas) demonstrated the power of the Speaker by leading a successful move to increase the size of the Committee so that its one-man conservative majority was reduced to a one-man minority.[37] With an overwhelming majority in the 1965 House, the liberal heirs of the forces that had revolted against the Speaker's powers in 1911 voted some of them back at the expense of the Rules Committee. As noted earlier, he was empowered to bring a bill to the consideration of the membership after 21 days in the Rules Committee. In addition, he was authorized to submit to majority vote the question of referring a bill passed in different form by the Senate to a House-Senate conference committee without waiting for action by the Rules Committee. Visible and focused power has thus been recognized as, after all, more accountable than diffused power.

As a member of Congress, the Speaker is entitled to participate in debate and to vote. On the rare occasions when the Speaker descends from the rostrum to take a direct part in the debate, all the other members recognize that the issue must be an important one, and his fellow party members realize that a "wrong" vote may put them and their future projects in danger of the Speaker's disapproval. His close contact with the President lends further weight to his views. The elevation of a Representative to the Speakership, though it may not require him to be so responsive to national sentiment as the President is, does induce him to behave more as a national and less as a strictly parochial figure.

The leadership of the Senate is much harder to identify than the leadership of the House. The presiding officer, the President of the Senate, is a weak figure in comparison with the Speaker of the House. Since the Constitution stipulates that the Vice-President shall serve as President of the Senate, the Senate rostrum is occupied by a person who is not chosen by the senators, is not a member of the Senate, and is sometimes not even a member of the majority party in the Senate. The President pro tempore of the Senate, who is elected by the members to preside in the absence of the President, more accurately reflects the power structure of the chamber. The President of the Senate cannot participate in debate and can vote only to break a tie. Although he may serve informally

---

[37] Cummings and Peabody, "The Decision to Enlarge the Committee on Rules," in Peabody and Polsby (eds.), *New Perspectives on the House of Representatives*, p. 193.

as a liaison between the President and party leaders in the Senate, he is expected to preside in a more nonpartisan fashion than the Speaker of the House. His rulings on points of order may be freely appealed by any member to the entire Senate for decision, and he may even refer difficult questions to the members before making his decision. The minor officers of both houses, on the other hand, are more alike—and equally devoid of power. Such posts as clerk, sergeant-at-arms, doorkeeper, postmaster, and chaplain are held in both houses by non-members who are technically elected by the entire membership but are actually chosen by the majority party conference.

Party conferences (Democrats in the House call them "caucuses") do more than choose the official leaders in their respective houses. They are the governing bodies of the political parties in Congress. The conference is to the party in each house what the national convention is to the party in the nation; and it is almost equally ineffective as a real governing body. In addition to selecting the party leaders in each house, the conference sets up a steering or policy committee, as its executive arm, to handle strategy questions, to decide which bills should be expedited, and to steer them through the congressional maze. It also selects a floor leader who is normally the most influential spokesman for the party in each chamber (except that in the House the majority floor leader ranks below the Speaker). The floor leaders are assisted by party "whips" and assistant whips, who round up party members when a crucial vote is called and try to persuade them to vote with the party.

The party conference completes its job of selecting leaders by drawing up lists of committee assignments—through a "committee on committees"—for all members of the party. This important function is not as complicated as it might seem, however, because most members serve continuously on the same committees as long as they are in Congress. In effect, then, the task is to make decisions on requests for a shift from one committee to another, to assign new members, and to fill any vacancies that arise. The committee system is so important in the functioning of both houses that these assignments determine the fate of future legislation.

Although the party conference is supposed to make decisions on party policy as well as to allocate party and committee posts, it has been a conspicuous failure in its function as a policy-making body. If it could actually bind individual party members to accept conference decisions on important questions, then it could really organize Congress for responsible party government. In practice, however, party conferences have not served as effective governing bodies since the first administration of Woodrow Wilson. The Republicans have never regarded their members as "bound" by decisions of the party conference, but they have at least been more prone than the Democrats to call conferences to discuss the policy position of the party. Only the House Republican conference has recently shown any real interest in policy questions, in trying to mold the Republican viewpoint, and in publicizing Republican views. For the most part, party conferences, like the leadership of Congress in general, "are today dominated by men who regard their political party as a vehicle for winning elections, not for securing the adoption of a program." [38] The sectional-ideological split of the Democrats is so deep that party leaders are afraid that efforts to agree on policy would boomerang. When President Johnson was the chairman of the Senate Democratic Conference, he explained, "Party members frequently stand together for different reasons, but talking about those reasons may only open old wounds and drive them apart." His successor, Senator Mansfield, was more blunt: "I believe that caucuses are a waste of time." [39]

Seniority Leaders and the Committee System

The characteristic lack of party discipline means that party leadership in Congress is dispersed rather than concentrated. True, any list of the centers of power in Congress must include the party conferences, the steering or policy committees, Speaker of the House, the President pro tempore of the Senate, the floor leaders, and the party whips. But the list would be woefully incomplete if it stopped there, for the basic organizational units through which Congress works are the *standing committees*. Every bill that reaches the floor of Congress has first been considered by a committee. And, in contrast to the practice in most state legislatures, no bill is reported out for the consideration of all the members until it has first won a majority vote in the committee. [40] Each committee, accordingly, is a little legislature which, to reverse John Donne, is like "an island, entire unto itself." The House has twenty, the Senate sixteen, of these virtually independent centers of power, each dealing with a different policy area, such as agriculture, appropriations, banking and currency, and foreign affairs.

These committees represent the major policy areas of the national government, such as foreign affairs, taxation, armed services, and labor relations. Although they do not correspond exactly to the administrative structure, the committees do provide regular channels of communication between the executive and legislative branches in all areas of policy formation. They also provide, as Roland Young points out, a practical instrumentality through which Congress can exercise control over the administration of policy by the governmental bureaucracy. [41] In policy-making, Congress and the administration function as integral parts of a single system, sharing rather than dividing powers. Hence each committee sets up its subcommittees to work closely with counterparts in the bureaucracy. For example, the House Committee on Foreign Affairs holds formal consultative meetings of the full committee with administrative leaders in foreign policy. The Chairman of the Committee is frequently summoned to White House conferences with other top policy-makers. And the subcommittees meet regularly

---

[38] Berman, *In Congress Assembled*, p. 230.

[39] *Ibid.*, pp. 228–229.

[40] As noted above, a committee may be discharged by vote of the House or Senate from consideration of a measure, but this is a rare and difficult procedure.

[41] *The American Congress*, Chapter 3, "The Internal System of Authority." The student will find the bibliographical essay at the end of this book extremely useful in pursuing further investigations into the legislative process.

Lists of the current committees of Congress and their members may be found in the *Congressional Directory*. Some committees publish an annual survey of their activities.

with the departmental experts on particular issues. Thus the standing Subcommittee on Africa will consult with the Assistant Secretary of State for Africa, may talk with the U.S. Ambassador to Nigeria or the desk officer on the Republic of the Congo. In this kind of continuous operating relationship, the Committee has an unusual opportunity to influence political decisions, and individual members of the Committee become legislative specialists in foreign policy.

How is the membership of standing committees determined? The majority party in each house fixes the ratio of seats between the parties, always giving itself a majority in the committees roughly corresponding to its majority in the chamber. But the committee on committees in each party, which actually draws up the slates for the party conference, employs no fixed criteria in deciding which party member gets what committee assignment. Seniority is the most important qualification, although the committee on committees also takes other factors into account—reputation as a "responsible" legislator (one who is moderate in approach, politically pliant but not without conviction), for example, and the desire of congressmen to be on committees handling legislation of particular interest to their constituents.[42] The seniority principle means that the most important committees are usually dominated by congressmen from "safe" or one-party districts. Seniority comes from success in getting re-elected, and it is most easily acquired by congressmen from areas without much political competition.

Congressmen naturally go after seats on committees that deal with problems of special importance in their own locality. A committee that specializes in legislation affecting a particular economic interest tends, then, to be made up of the very congressmen who are most biased in favor of that interest. Thus the House Committee on Agriculture is controlled by representatives from predominantly rural areas; the Senate Committee on Interior and Insular Affairs, which considers laws on mining and public lands, by senators from western states; the House Committee on Merchant Marine and Fisheries by representatives from coastal regions. Although a choice committee assignment is sometimes given as a reward for party service, disservice to the party—even sabotage of the national platform—is hardly ever punished by removal from a committee. In the 1961 fight on the House Rules Committee, for example, some Democrats argued that Representative William Colmer (D-Mississippi), who had opposed his party's candidate for President, should be removed from the Committee in favor of a supporter of the party's candidate. Recognizing the traditional independence of congressmen, however, administration leaders decided that the most they could win was an enlargement of the Committee.

Just as Congress functions through its standing committees, so each committee functions through its chairman. But while the general power of Congress is scattered, committee power is concentrated in the hands of the chairman. With authority to call committee meetings, determine the agenda, appoint subcommittees, and refer bills to subcommittees, the chairman wields virtually

---

[42] Nicholas A. Masters, "Committee Assignments in the House of Representatives," *American Political Science Review,* LV (June, 1961), pp. 345–357.

autocratic power in every standing committee. As Woodrow Wilson observed, the United States government may be described as "government by the chairmen of the Standing Committees of Congress." [43] Chairman Smith petulantly demonstrated his displeasure over enlargement of the Rules Committee in 1961 by not providing chairs for the new members!

How does a congressman reach this pinnacle of power? This is one question about Congress that can be answered very simply: by staying alive and getting re-elected. Complicated questions of service to party, commitment to party platform, and competence in the subject matter of the committee have little to do with seniority; therefore they do not enter into the choice of a chairman. Once a Representative or Senator takes his place on a committee, he need only keep his seat and some day he will find himself at the head of the class. A rare exception to this rule (the first since 1925) occurred in 1965. Democrats in the House deprived two representatives (from Mississippi and South Carolina) of their committee seniority because they had openly supported Senator Goldwater for President. Even though these representatives were not denied their claim to committee assignments as Democrats, this punitive action may represent a real tendency toward the nationalization of American politics.

Despite the many critics of the seniority system—and there are more outside than inside Congress—it dominates the organization of Congress. If new members object to it, they find themselves left with the most minor committee assignments, and cut off from the essential support of the old hands in carrying out their plans. Ernest Griffith, a long-time student of Congress, concludes that "Seniority is not only a rule governing committee chairmanships, it is also a spirit prevading the total behavior." [44] The United States Congress comes closer to practicing gerontocracy (rule by the elders) than any other group in the world today, with the possible exception of the Australian aborigines, the most primitive of contemporary tribes.

This emphasis on seniority helps explain why, during the Eisenhower and Kennedy eras, the "modern" and the "new" aspects of modern Republicanism and of the New Frontier were displayed by the executive rather than by Congress. The seniority system makes it almost inevitable that committee chairmen will be out of step with the majority elements of their party. As George Galloway says, "They represent districts made 'safe' by the poll tax and other restrictions on voting, or by the monopolistic position of one party, or by the ascendancy of a major interest group, or by city or rural machines." [45] Congressmen from districts where the competition between parties is livelier, where victory shifts with national elections, simply cannot outlast their colleagues from safe districts. The Roosevelt victory in 1932 initiated an era of Democratic control in Washington, but the seniority system excluded from power the Democrats who came from the very areas that were responsible for the shift, and ensconced a number of anti-

---

[43] *Congressional Government* (Boston: Houghton Mifflin Co., 1885), p. 102.

[44] *Congress: Its Contemporary Role* (New York: New York University Press, 1956), p. 18. Also see the 3rd ed. (1961).

[45] *The Legislative Process*, p. 271.

New Deal southerners in key positions. When the Dewey-Eisenhower Republicans won in 1952, the new committee chairmen turned out to be men from "Old Guard" Republican areas who opposed Eisenhower's attempts at "modernization." No matter which party is in control of Congress, a disproportionate number of strategic committee chairmen are bound to come from one-party areas; this is particularly true when the Democrats are in power, because the "Solid South" is our largest one-party section.[46]

Consequently, the seniority system is condemned for its failure to reward competence and party loyalty and for its ruinous effects on party discipline. It is also defended, however, on two quite different grounds. First, it insures that power will be exercised by experienced hands. Second, the system works, and there seems to be no feasible alternative short of having the choice of committee chairmen made by the majority party at each new session of Congress. As with so many problems in American government, the main point of difference between the critics and the defenders of the system seems to be their attitude toward disciplined party rule. In response to attacks by Republicans in Congress on his administration's program, Eisenhower argued that if congressmen failed to support their party platform "the entire concept of party responsibility, and indeed of representative government, collapses." [47] But many agree with the Republicans in Congress, who replied that party responsibility is not essential to representative government.

The Performance

Functions of Congress

Congress was set up to represent the people in determining policy. This simple statement of manifest function leaves room for various interpretations—interpretations that are loaded with significance. First, how does the congressman "represent" the people? As we noted in Chapter 2, the "mirror" concept of representation finds more favor in the United States than the "leadership" concept. Or perhaps the two concepts are merged in the expectation that the congressman will act as a leader in helping the people get what they want from the government. We generally expect Congress to impersonate the people in formulating policy. But what about the legislator who defies public opinion in order to fight for what he regards as the best interest of the people, who depends on events or on his own powers of persuasion to change public opinion before the next election comes around? American voters may regard this as courageous behavior in the abstract, but they generally denounce it in practice as a violation of the public trust.[48]

---

[46] Marian D. Irish, "The Southern One Party System and National Politics," *Journal of Politics*, IV (February, 1942), 80–94. For a recent study of the seniority system, see George Goodwin, Jr., "The Seniority System in Congress," *American Political Science Review*, 53 (June, 1959), 412–436.

[47] *The New York Times*, June 8, 1957.

[48] See Kennedy, *Profiles in Courage*.

Second, just who are "the people" who get represented? Since there is not a single issue on which public opinion in the United States is unanimous—even a declaration of war after enemy attack is opposed by pacifists—Congress cannot possibly represent "the people" as a whole. What Americans expect is that Congress will respond to conflicting public opinions by representing the preferences held by the larger number of citizens. Only a minority of the people take an active interest in most issues, so we cannot expect Congress to represent an absolute majority of the total population. But on every issue we do expect congressmen to represent a majority of those actively concerned.

For the individual congressman this problem of representation raises another question. Assuming that he can identify majority sentiment, should he represent national interests or constituency interests? If he decides to act in favor of constituency interests, as most congressmen seem to, Congress as a whole may come to over-represent the opinions of some interests, such as those of rural areas, that have more seats than their numbers would warrant. Most voters deplore this situation, but on specific issues they invariably expect *their* legislator to reflect his constituency's preferences. "Sometimes we wish to vote for measures of national good," Representative Charles L. Gifford of Massachusetts explained to new members of Congress in 1947, "but somehow there are people back home pulling the strings, are there not? . . . Sometimes we have that appalling decision to make: shall I vote for my country as a whole or must I vote to protect my own particular district? Which should I represent? Your conscience must be your guide. But you can always educate your conscience." [49]

Most congressmen probably have less trouble with this problem than the discerning Representative Gifford; the ordinary person almost automatically sees the general interest through his own particular interest. And there is rarely a clash between constituency interest and national interest that cannot somehow be resolved. Thus, when Congress passed an act in 1953 turning the "tidelands" oil regions over to state jurisdiction, supporters of the act defended it in terms of the national interest, not self-interest. They talked about the general principles of "states' rights," not about the particular interests of the states that bordered on the oil-rich territory or of the oil companies that preferred state to federal control. Most local groups—like the oil companies—are part of national pressure groups that are active in many constituencies; few issues are purely local. The real question, then, is this: Who is going to help the congressman interpret the overlapping constituency and national interests? Greater rewards and fewer punishments seem to come from voting for interest groups powerful in the constituency. Only congressmen from some of the more populous areas—where local interests are so numerous that they include most of those found in the nation as a whole—dare to take a consistently national point of view.

As we saw earlier in this chapter, constituency interests tend to coincide with party interests often enough to make party affiliation the key factor for understanding congressional performance. And many constituencies are suffi-

---

[49] Quoted in Gross, *The Legislative Struggle*, pp. 93–94.

ciently varied so that a Democrat's view of the needs of a given district will be quite different from a Republican's view of the same district. Indeed, in considering the linkage between the electoral system and congressional performance, we found in Chapter 8 that the congressman does not have a very accurate perception of actual constituency views on social welfare issues. When his perception is compared with the attitudes only of his supporters, however, it is considerably more accurate. Where constituency opinions are clear, as on civil rights, the congressman's relationship to his constituents tends to be that of the instructed delegate. Where party differences are clear and voters tend to react to party label, as on social welfare questions, the relationship is closer to the responsible party model. Where constituency preferences are least clear, as on foreign policy questions, the congressman must look elsewhere for clues; this means largely to the President and his administration for members of the majority party. The congressman thus reflects constituent attitudes in an uneven manner, with the accuracy of the reflection on each issue depending on the extent of public information and interest.

Most studies of Congress take the roll-call vote of congressmen as the one measure of their behavior. As we have indicated, however, most of the important decisions of Congress are made in committees and subcommittees. Except for their errand-boy activities—responding to constituent requests for intervention with an administrative agency, for help in getting someone out of the army or into a job—the principal energies of congressmen are expended in their committee work. Here is where most bills are killed and others are shaped. Since the members of Congress generally accept committee recommendations, this is where most of the positive as well as the negative decisions of Congress are actually made. And this is where the norms of Congress—especially respect for seniority and specialization and the willingness to compromise—are at their strongest. Two thoughtful students of Congress independently concluded, on the basis of separate studies of major House committees, that the importance of party is greatest for the final roll-call vote on the floor, and smallest for decisions at the "working level"—that is, in the subcommittees.[50] We should not exaggerate the importance of party affiliation, then, despite its great importance in roll-call voting. This is the most public of all congressional acts. Neither should we conclude that party is of no importance "behind the scenes." The congressman will act at different stages in response to different sets of pressures. Even at the subcommittee stage, he will take his cue from his party on measures of little direct effect on his constituency. In such a case, however, he will expend less energy on the measure than if important constituency interests were directly involved.[51]

The Constitution entrusts Congress with several other responsibilities in addi-

---

[50] Richard A. Fenno, Jr., "The House Appropriations Committee as a Political System: The Problem of Integration," and Charles O. Jones, "The Agriculture Committee and the Problem of Representation," in Peabody and Polsby (eds.), *New Perspective on the House of Representatives*, pp. 79–108, 109–127.

[51] Jones, *ibid.*

tion to the basic task of legislation. Earlier, we noted that Congress initiates amendments to the Constitution by a two-thirds vote of both houses. And we have noted that when no presidential candidate receives a majority of the electoral votes, the House chooses the President and the Senate chooses the Vice-President. Congress also investigates the administration of the laws to insure that the objectives of congressional policy are being achieved. Since all executive agencies are created and supplied with funds by Congress, it has ample power to require their cooperation. As an ultimate power over other government officers, the Constitution grants Congress a judicial function, in the provision that "The President, Vice-President, and all civil officers of the United States, shall be removed from office on impeachment for, and the conviction of, treason, bribery, or other high crimes and misdemeanors." [52] Impeachment, which is similar to indictment by a grand jury, requires a majority vote of the House, and conviction on the charges requires a two-thirds vote of the Senate. Only twelve officials have ever been impeached, and only four of them convicted. Nevertheless, the impeachment power strengthens Congress in its broader function of supervising administrative agencies. Finally, the Senate approves treaties and presidential appointments.

The authoritative decisions that emerge from the responsibilities assigned to Congress under the Constitution represent its manifest function. But it also performs latent functions important for the political system. Richard Fenno, one of the ablest students of Congress, submits, "The resolution of conflict and the building of consensus are among the major functions which Congress performs for American society." [53] Conflict is not resolved in any complete sense, of course, but the decision-making activities of Congress bring it into the open, permit it to find peaceable expression, and reduce its intensity by responding to citizen demands. Similarly, actual consensus can hardly be achieved on most issues, but the emergence of a public policy from the congressional process of compromise, with the minority insured as much time in debate as the majority, serves at least to create a consensus on its legitimacy. After it has been enforced for some time, acceptance often shifts into what we termed "supportive consensus" in discussing political opinions. An additional function of Congress is implicit in the two major ones we have discussed. In resolving public conflict and in creating consensus, Congress also informs the public on public problems and governmental responses. Congress thus serves to unify the public behind the government by giving expression to differences of opinion and by turning the dominant opinions into legislation that is accepted as legitimate.

Uses and Abuses of Power: Congressional Investigations

We began this chapter with the provision from the Constitution that assigns Congress "all legislative powers herein granted." In one respect this overstates

---

[52] Article II, Section IV.
[53] "The House of Representatives and Federal Aid to Education," in Peabody and Polsby (eds.), *New Perspectives on the House of Representatives,* p. 195.

the authority of Congress. Congress hardly enjoys *all* the legislative powers of the national government; the Constitution also explicitly grants the President a role in legislation, and, since the judges must interpret the laws, they, too, get into the act. On the other hand, Congress also has *more* legislative power than the Constitution specifically assigns to it. The authority of Congress to "make all laws which shall be necessary and proper for carrying into execution" its enumerated powers has been broadly interpreted. For example, the enumerated powers over foreign and interstate commerce, taxation and appropriations, and national defense have made many kinds of other activities "necessary and proper."

One of the most important powers of Congress not mentioned in the Constitution is the power of investigation. The first congressional inquiry was conducted in 1792, when irate congressmen decided to find out why United States troops had been defeated in a battle with the Indians. Since then, there have been over a thousand investigations, with recent Congresses reaching an all-time high. The most exciting inquiries during recent years have dealt with "reds" of a different kind—communists and alleged communists.

The congressional power of investigation has never been seriously challenged, for it is evident that, as the Supreme Court put it, "the power of inquiry . . . is an essential and appropriate auxiliary to the legislative function." [54] Legislation deals with social and economic maladjustments about which congressmen are no more automatically informed than college students and professors are. In order to legislate wisely, lawmakers must be able to acquire the information they need, even if it means subpoenaing witnesses and compelling them to testify on pain of punishment for contempt of Congress. Many vital legislative reforms would never have been made if congressmen had been unable to investigate the problems beforehand. The Securities and Exchange Commission, for example, which offers what is now regarded as minimum protection to investors, could hardly have been created without the technical information and political impact produced by the Senate Banking and Currency Committee's probe into Wall Street practices in the early 1930's.

This power of inquiry also gives life and meaning to congressional supervision of the administration. Under the separation of powers spelled out by the Constitution, Congress would be hopelessly overshadowed by the executive if it had no power to call administrators to account. A law acquires meaning only as it is administered, and congressmen would be rendered almost impotent if they were denied the right to inquire into whether administrative practices and rulings are in keeping with the broad policy directives of Congress. "Instead of the function of governing, for which it is radically unfit," John Stuart Mill submitted, "the proper office of a representative assembly is to watch and control the government . . . and, if the men who compose the government abuse their trust, or fulfill it in a manner which conflicts with the deliberate sense of the nation, to expel them from office. . . ." [55] Although Congress

---

[54] *McGrain* v. *Daugherty*, 273 U.S. 135 (1927).

[55] R. B. McCallum (ed.), *On Liberty and Considerations on Representative Government* (Oxford: Basil Blackwell, 1948), p. 172.

can expel executive officers only through the laborious process of impeachment, its power of investigation, coupled with its control over appropriations, assures it the power to supervise the work of even the most powerful executive officers. Finding the system of investigation "the main guarantee against dishonesty or inefficient administration," Harold Laski, a more recent British observer, concluded, "After all, a system which drove three cabinet members to resign in 1924 and resulted in imprisonment and two suicides may reasonably claim to have a measurable public value." [56] Even the conduct of White House assistants is not safe from congressional scrutiny.

The function of informing public opinion is strengthened by the power of investigation. This informing function enters into almost everything Congress does. For example, Woodrow Wilson felt that investigations of the administration were themselves primarily important for their effect on public opinion. "The informing function of Congress should be preferred even to its legislative function," he observed. "The argument is not only that discussed and interrogated administration is the only pure and efficient administration, but, more than that, that the only really self-governing people is that people which discusses and interrogates its administration." [57] In recent years, the informing function has been extended far beyond administrative matters, as Congress has pushed its investigations into such areas as civil liberties, concentration of economic power, labor and business practices, lobbying, campaign expenditures, and subversive activities.

Like any other power, the power of investigation is sometimes abused. Rather than serving as a basis of legislation, it may be used to gain personal publicity or partisan advantage; rather than operating as a salutary check on the administration, it may become a means of usurping executive power; rather than informing the public, it may serve to confuse, mislead, and agitate. During the early 1950's, all three of these perversions of power afflicted the nation: (1) Senator Joseph McCarthy (R-Wisconsin) managed to win almost as much publicity as the President himself, and became an important force in elections far beyond the borders of Wisconsin; (2) as chairman of both the Senate Committee on Government Operations and its Permanent Subcommittee on Investigations, he invaded the executive field, as in "negotiating" an "agreement" with Greek ship-owners; (3) he was a leading exponent of the "conspiracy theory," which identified the opposition party with "twenty years of treason" and attributed communist successes anywhere in the world, not to the USSR, but to American officials who were called "soft" on communism—or worse.[58]

The term "McCarthyism" became a symbol of irresponsible self-aggrandizement, suspicion, insistence on conformity, demoralization and insubordination in the civil and military services, harassment of private citizens, and guilt by

[56] Harold Laski, *The American Democracy: A Commentary and An Interpretation* (New York: The Viking Press, 1943), p. 89.
[57] Wilson, *Congressional Government*, p. 303.
[58] See Eric F. Goldman, *The Crucial Decade: America, 1945-1950* (New York: Alfred A. Knopf, 1956), especially pp. 113-144.

accusation—all under the cloak of the congressional power of investigation. Congress was led so far afield from its primary task of legislation that people began to speak of the government as composed of the judicial, executive, and investigative branches.

The most serious abuse of the investigatory power by McCarthy and others, notably by the House Committee on Un-American Activities, is that it has been used for the "trial" of individuals before the "court of public opinion." The Constitution forbids Congress to find an individual guilty of crime, but congressmen can do by publicity what they cannot do by law. Robert Carr, a leading student of constitutional law, came to this conclusion after making a careful study of the Un-American Activities Committee:

> It is quite clear from the six-year period of the committee between 1945 and 1950 that one of its leading purposes has been to demonstrate the "guilt" of certain persons for offenses not always defined in law and to see them punished in the sense of the destruction of their reputations and the loss of their means of livelihood.[59]

The Supreme Court declared in the highly publicized *Watkins Case* in 1957: "The Bill of Rights is applicable to investigations as to all forms of governmental actions. Witnesses cannot be compelled to give evidence against themselves. They cannot be subjected to unreasonable search and seizure. Nor can the First Amendment freedoms of speech, press, religion, or political belief and association be abridged." [60] Even if the Court refuses to punish a witness for "contempt of Congress," however, he does not escape punishment in the real (as distinguished from the legal) sense. If he refuses to testify, he will be regarded by fellow citizens as guilty of some unspecified crime and he will ordinarily lose his job, whether he works for a private business or for the government.

In a democracy, protection against abuses of this type must come primarily from the voters and from the congressmen they elect. The courts have upheld witnesses in refusing to answer questions that were not pertinent to the subject under inquiry, or that were beyond the authority granted the committee by Congress. But the basic position of the courts is to "leave the responsibility for the behavior of its committees squarely on the shoulders of Congress." [61] The Supreme Court has recently held that First Amendment guarantees of private belief and association do not justify refusing to answer questions about personal beliefs and communist affiliations when such questions are pertinent to an investigation authorized by Congress.[62] Most Congressmen are scrupulous in their own use of power, and they could improve committee procedures simply by informal pressure or official regulation. The tradition of committee independence —which can be twisted into irresponsibility—is the chief barrier to this step. The

---

[59] *The House Committee on Un-American Activities, 1945–1950* (Ithaca: Cornell University Press, 1952), p. 452.
[60] *Watkins* v. *United States*, 354 U.S. 178 (1957).
[61] *Eisler* v. *United States*, 338 U.S. 196 (1949).
[62] *Braden* v. *United States*, 365 U.S. 890 (1961).

Senate censure of Senator McCarthy in 1954 ruined his influence in that body before his death in 1957, and the general fear that America is more threatened by Americans than by outsiders seemed to subside. Even so, inquiries into the beliefs of private citizens continue in a somewhat quieter vein. Organizations like the John Birch society, and a few officials like Senator J. Strom Thurmond (R-South Carolina) clamor for a return to the excitement of the McCarthy era. It is the task of Congress to bring the focus back to *problems* rather than to individuals, to *legislation* rather than adjudication.[63]

The Drama of Policy-Making

The procedure by which Congress passes a bill requires completion of eight not-so-easy steps. As we trace these steps, we will see that getting an important measure through Congress is no routine matter. Policy-making always involves the tense drama of power in conflict and compromise.

First, the bill must be introduced. This is the easiest part of all. A representative simply hands his bill to the Clerk of the House or tosses it into the "hopper," a box on the Clerk's desk. A senator must be recognized by the presiding officer in order to announce the introduction of his bill; then he gives it to the Secretary of the Senate. Of the 10,000 or so bills introduced in every Congress, each has little better than one chance in ten of becoming a law. Most of these bills are relatively trivial, and many, despite efforts to reduce their number, are "private" bills dealing with such things as individual claims against the government. Although bills are actually introduced by a congressman, most of them are probably "thought up" by other actors in the policy-making performance. Major legislation usually represents the joint efforts of many people who have been called upon by a congressman for advice or support. Just who first conceived the idea for a given bill is perhaps as unanswerable as it is irrelevant to the merits of the bill.

The second step begins when the parliamentarian of the House (under the Speaker's direction) or the President of the Senate refers the bill to an appropriate committee for consideration. This is as far as most bills get. The committee enjoys virtual life-and-death power over all the proposals that come its way: it may "pigeon-hole" a bill, disapprove it, rewrite it completely, amend it, or approve it as presented. But only if a bill wins the approval of a majority of the committee does it normally reach the floor of either house.[64] An unfriendly chairman may bury a bill by arranging the agenda so that it never comes up, or —if it is too important to ignore—by appointing an unfriendly subcommittee to consider it.

Measures that are found worthy of consideration are generally given a hear-

---

[63] This statement will be recognized as based on a value judgment—that a constitutional pattern in which the legislature deals with *general rules* and the courts with punishment of *individuals under the rules* is desirable. People who reject this value will —quite properly, from their point of view—reject the statement.

[64] Except in the rare event of a bill being reported out unfavorably or of a successful move to discharge the committee from consideration of a bill.

ing at which interested government officials, lobbyists, and other experts are permitted to testify. Next the committee members assess the technical and political implications of the bill on the bases of the hearings, their own knowledge or convictions on the subject, the results of staff research, and their individual contacts with fellow legislators, party leaders, lobbyists, and constituents. Since Congress usually goes along with what the committees recommend, the work they perform is the real heart of legislation. Aware of this fact, the sponsor of a bill tries to stimulate publicity and support from influential groups outside as well as inside Congress. The chances of passing the bill are maximized, of course, if the sponsor is a senior member or, at best, the chairman of the committee. The mere fact that Senator Robert Taft (R-Ohio), the most influential Republican in Congress, was the sponsor of the Labor Management Relations Act of 1947, for example, helped immeasurably in getting the act passed.

In the Senate, the committee phase comes to an end when a majority of the committee votes to report the bill for consideration on the Senate floor. But in the House there is a second committee hurdle for all measures except money bills.[65] Before a non-money bill reaches the floor of the House, the Committee on Rules must rule on whether, when, and under what conditions the bill may come up for floor debate. The Rules Committee may block a measure, report it to the floor with suggested amendments, recommend a substitute bill, or set up special rules to speed its passage. Since the seniority system often produces a Rules Committee that is dominated by representatives who may disagree with the prevailing sentiment of the majority party, the power of the Rules Committee over legislation has been criticized more and more in recent years. Although the critics managed for a brief period (1949–1950) to reduce the Committee's power to block legislation, it was quickly restored to a position where, in Representative Chet Holifield's words, "a few men, strategically situated in the Rules Committee, can impose their will on the Congress and prevent the enactment of legislation deemed by the House majority to be essential to the security and welfare of this Nation." [66] Congress reacted to this criticism again in 1965 by giving the Speaker power to bring bills out of the Rules Committee after 21 days.

When one of the standing committees reports a bill back to the chamber in which it was introduced, it is placed on a calendar—a list of pending bills—where it awaits the third big step, floor debate. If the bill is important enough, however, its sponsor may not have to wait for it to take its turn on the calendar. In the Senate, the Policy Committee of the majority party serves as chief traffic manager. It establishes the order in which the bills are to be brought up, either

---

[65] In addition to bills from the committees on Appropriations and Ways and Means, certain bills from three other committees—Public Works, Veterans' Affairs, and Interior and Insular Affairs—may be brought to the floor at any time. Only the Appropriations Committee takes routine advantage of this privilege. Other committees prefer to go through the Rules Committee because this leads to consideration of their bills under favorable rules. See Berman, *In Congress Assembled*, p. 204.

[66] As quoted in Galloway, *The Legislative Process*, pp. 344–345.

by unanimous consent, with the agreement of the Minority Leader, or else by majority vote. As we have seen, debate in the Senate is unlimited unless it is cut short by unanimous consent or by a vote of cloture.

In the House, departures from the calendar are made at the direction of the Rules Committee, which also provides for limitations on debate. The Rules Committee may even provide a "closed rule," which permits only members of the reporting committee to offer amendments. If a representative objects to these rules, they are referred to the entire House for a vote, but in practice such appeals are hardly ever successful. When the House sits as the "Committee of the Whole," as it does in considering appropriation bills, for example, it transforms itself into one big committee so that it can operate more informally. No record is kept of the votes, the time for debate is divided equally between opponents and proponents, and debate on each amendment is limited to five minutes.

By the time a bill is ready for the fourth step—voting—its sponsor has a fairly good idea of what its chances are. In the House, a vote may already have been taken on the rules governing debate (especially if a "closed rule" was involved), and in both chambers the votes on various amendments will have shown the alignment of the forces for and against. Indeed, the votes on crippling amendments and on the motion to recommit the bill to committee are usually more revealing than the final vote on passage. If opponents of the bill have failed in their efforts to weaken it or to send it back to committee, they know that they cannot block final passage. Accordingly, if the bill has strong popular appeal but is opposed by a strong pressure group, some of the members who have tried to defeat it at first may swing over to its support once its final passage is assured. The politics-wise pressure group will appreciate the fact that these representatives opposed the bill as long as they had any chance of defeating it. By pointing to their "yea" votes on final passage, however, they can also claim credit from the voters for *supporting* the bill.

Even after a bill has passed one house, it is still less than halfway through the process of becoming a law. We may lump together all the steps described so far as a fifth giant step—namely, the successful completion of the same steps in the other chamber. If the bill is rejected or ignored in this chamber, of course, it is dead. But if it manages to clear all the hurdles a second time, it need only be signed by the President to become a law. If it passes in slightly altered form, the house of origin must agree to the revisions before it goes to the President.

When a bill is substantially changed by the second house, it usually enters a sixth stage, in which it is sent to a conference committee made up of both senators and representatives who try to iron out the differences. The members of the conference committee are appointed by the presiding officer in each house from among the senior members of the committee that originally considered the bill. So again the cards are stacked in favor of the older members from the "safe" districts. Although technically the conference committee has no power to write a new bill, in practice its privilege of making final decisions on the contents of a bill means that the committee members exercise extraordinary power. If a majority of the members of the conference from each house agree on a compromise version, the bill is reported back to both houses in its new and final form.

If the compromise version is now approved by both houses, the bill is ready for its seventh step, presidential action. The President may allow the bill to become law without his signature, or he may indicate his approval by signing it. If he disapproves of the bill, he will refuse to sign it and will return it to Congress with a message explaining the reasons for his veto.

In this event, the bill is probably doomed to failure, although it can still become law if both houses take it through the eighth step—namely, passing it by a two-thirds vote over the President's veto. But the chances that this will happen are not good. Disapproval by the President focuses public attention on the bill, and the vote to override his veto must be a roll-call vote. Since the President is more closely attuned to national sentiments than most congressmen are, his vetoes are generally in keeping with the desires and interests of the majority. And his power as a party leader cannot be ignored, especially by congressmen who want government contracts placed in their districts, or deserving constituents appointed to federal jobs, or presidential support in their next campaign. Congressmen who are perfectly willing to support a bill the first time around, when public opinion may not be aroused and the vote may not be recorded, are often not so eager to vote to override a presidential veto.

The Critics' Reviews of the Performance

The "morning-after" reviews of the legislative performance range all the way from unstinting praise to the harshest criticism, depending on whether the critic identifies himself with interests that are being promoted or threatened. The response to practices like the filibuster, for example, seem to depend on the critic's attitude toward the measures being talked to death rather than on his general beliefs about "majority rule" or "minority rights." Thus an attack by Vice-President Charles Dawes on filibustering in 1925, when labor was opposing measures supported by a majority of senators, brought from the American Federation of Labor's national convention a counter-attack on Dawes for representing "the predatory interests." The AFL praised the filibuster for making the Senate "the only forum in the world where cloture does not exist and where members can prevent the passage of reactionary legislation." [67] By the 1940's, the political tides had changed; labor and other liberal groups were frequently in favor of measures supported by a majority of senators. The AFL accordingly reversed its position on filibusters and joined in a campaign with other liberal groups to establish "majority rule" in the Senate. The AFL is typical: the way most of us evaluate congressional procedures depends on our attitudes toward the laws being passed, not on any fixed principles about the "right" way of organizing Congress.

We may have no objective standard for saying that a given congressional practice is good or bad, but we can hope to understand why and how the practice is followed. Instead of heaping praise or blame on the congressional performance,

---

[67] As quoted in Gross, *The Legislative Struggle*, p. 418.

we may more profitably examine some explanations of the nature of that performance. Here as elsewhere, understanding should come before judgment.
Among the explanations of legislative behavior that political scientists have developed in recent years, the following five seem particularly illuminating.

First, Bertram Gross reminds us that governmental agencies—including
Congress—must be understood as contestants rather than as neutral referees in
the struggle for political power.[68] We might prefer to think that Congress makes
laws by objectively recording majority preferences. But Gross brings us back to
the realities of James Madison's query, "And what are the different classes of
legislators but advocates and parties to the causes which they determine?"[69] On
two counts, congressmen are interested parties to the causes they determine. Not
only do they belong to and represent various groups outside the government, but
they also belong to various groups within the government that have interests of
their own. As we noted at the beginning of this chapter, congressmen think and
act as members of Congress no less than as members of private groups. Even
when a congressman strongly favors a bill, for example, he hesitates to impugn
the motives of opponents in Congress lest he bring discredit to Congress as an
institution. And various subgroups within Congress—the two houses themselves,
party organizations, party leaders, bipartisan blocs, seniority leaders, committee
members, and state delegations—have their own loyalties and interests within
the larger group. Congressional organization and procedures, like laws, are never
neutral; every proposal for change is made to increase the influence of certain
groups and decrease that of others—inside as well as outside government.

Second, Stephen K. Bailey's case study of the Employment Act of 1946
demonstrates that legislation emerges as the result of a bewilderingly complex
interplay of historical, social, economic, personal, institutional, and ideological
factors.[70] Although government expresses and modifies these forces, most legislation actually has its origins outside the government. Most laws have such a
long history that the date on which they were conceived cannot be exactly identified. Bailey found the needs and desires behind the Employment Act, for example, to be as old as man's prayer, "Give us this day our daily bread." All the
forces that mold human history would have to be taken into account for a full
explanation of why men have turned to government to help meet their need for
daily bread. The final passage of a bill by Congress, then, is the culmination of
a long and complicated series of human experiences. The medieval assumption
that laws were "discovered," not "made," still has some validity.

Third, since power in Congress is scattered and personal rather than concentrated and institutional, policy is normally made by "temporary power coalitions
of political, administrative, and non-governmental interests."[71] Consequently,
the voters cannot hold any identifiable group or individual responsible for policy.

---

[68] *Ibid.,* p. 92.
[69] *The Federalist* (New York: Modern Library Series, Random House, 1937), p. 56.
[70] Stephen Kemp Bailey, *Congress Makes a Law: The Story Behind the Employment Act of 1946* (New York: Columbia University Press, 1950), p. 236.
[71] *Ibid.*

In the words of George Galloway, who has observed many legislative battles on Capitol Hill, "The total picture is one of diffusion, disunity, and disintegration —of 'a baronial system of political power'—of a mixture of legislative oligarchy and legislative anarchy." [72] With power thus fragmented, each congressman is fairly free to "vote according to his conscience." But "in behavioral terms his 'conscience' . . . may be viewed as a product of his past and present identification with the attitudes of various organized and potential groups." [73] Although his identification with the national party plays a greater role than is sometimes realized,[74] the congressman's "conscience" is also molded by the demands of his constituency and of the groups, in and out of Congress, he deals with.

From an analysis of the legislative history of ninety laws, Lawrence Chamberlain offers a fourth proposition: "In the United States, legislation is characteristically a collegial process in which the role of the Congress is no less important than that of the President. During periods when the Chief Executive assumes the initiative, the partnership between the executive and the Congress operates more efficiently." [75] Congress and the President must work together to make laws. And since no centralized leadership exists inside Congress, congressmen depend on the President to take the initiative. As Chamberlain says, "The legislative process is not like a see-saw where as one end goes down the other must automatically go up. It is, rather like a gasoline engine which operates most efficiently when all of its cylinders are functioning." [76]

Fifth, the organization and electoral base of Congress make it more responsive than the President to conservative and local interests. To say that the President speaks more for urban majorities is not, of course, to say that he is free from group pressures; but the nature of his constituency makes him more sensitive to the mass vote in the big cities across the country. Thus Truman, Eisenhower, Kennedy, and Johnson, despite differences in personality, ideas, and party, all tended to stand more for urban-supported measures like social security, more liberal immigration, and civil rights than did their respective Congresses. Wilfred Binkley, a political historian, offers a convincing explanation:

> . . . Important elements such as labor, racial and certain other groups are peculiarly weak in urging their desires upon Congress. Consequently they quite naturally and properly seek to exert a leverage on the government through their voting strength as balances of power in presidential elections. Indeed, here is a

---

[72] Galloway, *The Legislative Process*, p. 352.

[73] David B. Truman, "The Roles of Congressional Leaders: National Party vs. Constituency," *American Political Science Review*, XLVI (December, 1952), p. 1026.

[74] Julius Turner, *Party and Constituency: Pressures on Congress* (Baltimore: The Johns Hopkins Press, 1951).

In addition to the works of Gross, Bailey, Galloway, Truman, Turner, Binkley, and Lerner, cited throughout, see also Charles L. Clapp, *The Congressman: His Work as He Sees It* (Washington, D.C.: The Brookings Institution, and Chamberlain, 1963).

[75] *The President, Congress and Legislation* (New York: Columbia University Press, 1946), p. 14.

[76] *Ibid.*

counterbalance against the immense advantage the interests of property and production hold in Congress due to the underrepresentation of urban voters in Congress and to the fact that the practice of seniority in determining control of the House of Representative[s] reduces considerably the power of the urban voters. Such is the predominance of rural constituencies that the majority of Congressmen can ignore the desires of the urban masses with impunity while the President does so only at his peril.[77]

Most political scientists accept these five propositions as valid explanations of congressional behavior. Some, like Max Lerner, would add another kind of proposition: Congress has become increasingly incompetent to deal positively with the major political problems of contemporary society. Now this last proposition is the kind of broad value judgment that cannot be really proved or disproved. While we can be objective in explaining *how* and *why* Congress operates, we cannot hope for general agreement in *evaluating* that behavior.

But the evidence in support of the proposition is impressive. We have seen in this chapter that Congress cannot develop a coherent and unified approach to policy problems, largely because of the seniority system, the power of the Rules Committee in the House, the filibuster in the Senate, over-representation of rural areas, and the general lack of responsible party leadership. "Most Congressmen are neither heroes nor villains but well-meaning men caught in an almost impossible job," Lerner says. He sees Congress as facing a basic dilemma: "It is the dilemma of a body which still has, at least in theory, the control both over the purse and over the sword, both over appropriations and over the declaration of war; but which in effect finds that the decisions over great events in a complex industrial society and a world in turmoil has passed to the President and to his experts, to the bureaucrats and generals and technicians." [78]

Further support for this proposition will come in the next chapters on the President and the bureaucracy. We shall see, for example, how Congress has been forced by the complexity and the interdependence of contemporary problems to yield much of its policy-making function to the President and his managerial assistants. The service and the security state require intricate planning and expert knowledge that are beyond the capacity of Congress to supply. Consequently, Congress has been increasingly forced to depend on the President to formulate programs and, in enacting these programs, it has likewise been forced to delegate legislative responsibilities to the President.

As we mentioned earlier, however, Congress itself seems to operate most effectively when the President takes the initiative. Even if Congress does fail to provide positive leadership and even if it must delegate more and more power to the President, it still plays a key role. So long as all general laws must be enacted by Congress, and so long as Congress retains the power to investigate and supervise the administration of those laws, congressmen will remain in the center of the policy-making drama.

---

[77] Binkley, *Journal of Politics*, XI (February, 1949), p. 76.
[78] Max Lerner, *America as a Civilization* (New York: Simon and Schuster, 1957), pp. 424–425.

CHAPTER TEN

The
President

On November 22, 1963, at 2:38 P.M. CST, in

Dallas, Texas, Lyndon Baines Johnson became the 36th President

of the United States. In a crowded plane, *Air Force One*, U.S.

District Judge Sarah T. Hughes, an elderly friend of the Johnson

family, in the presence of 27 distraught witnesses, administered

the presidential oath of office. Judge Hughes held out a small black Bible and began to intone the constitutional oath, "I do solemnly swear that I will faithfully execute the office of President of the United States and will, to the best of my ability, preserve, protect, and defend the Constitution of the United States." Johnson covered the Bible with his left hand, raised his right hand, and firmly repeated the awesome charge, ending "so help me God." The ceremony took less than two minutes; when it was over, the new President gave his first order, "Now let's get airborne." The plane which carried President Johnson back to Washington to assume the great tasks of Chief Executive also bore the body of his predecessor in office. At 12:30 p.m., on that same day, President John Fitzgerald Kennedy had been shot to death as he rode in a motorcade en route to a luncheon speech at the Dallas Trade Mart. Thousands of miles from Dallas, high over the Pacific, another plane carrying Secretary of State Dean Rusk and five other members of the Kennedy Cabinet to a meeting with the Japanese Cabinet in Tokyo heard the news by radio and turned back, refueled in Honolulu, and flew to Washington. President Johnson would hold his first cabinet meeting the next day at the White House.[1]

In the second edition of this book, we described the inauguration of President Kennedy—

> On January 20, 1961, the members of Congress, the Justices of the Supreme Court, and many other important figures in American politics assembled outdoors before the snow-covered East Front of the Capitol. At 12:41 P.M., Lyndon B. Johnson was sworn into the office of Vice-President with Sam Rayburn, Speaker of the House, administering the oath. Ten minutes later John Fitzgerald Kennedy repeated after Chief Justice Earl Warren the constitutional oath of the President [exactly the same oath that Johnson would take in Dallas, November 22, 1963].

> For the first time, a man born in the twentieth century was assuming responsibilities in the nation's highest post. The new President was 43 years old, the youngest man ever elected to the presidency. By coincidence, his predecessor, Dwight D. Eisenhower, was the oldest holder of the office when he left the White House at 70. In his Inaugural, President Kennedy referred to the change in generation.

> Let the word go forth from this time and place, to friend and foe, that the torch has been passed to a new generation of Americans—born in this century, tempered by war, disciplined by a hard and bitter peace, proud of our ancient heritage—and unwilling to witness or permit the slow undoing of those human rights to which this nation has always been committed, and to which we are committed today at home and around the world.

> In the long history of the world, only a few generations have been granted the role of defending freedom in its hour of maximum danger. I do not believe that any of us would exchange places with any other people or any other generation. The energy, the faith, the devotion which we bring to this endeavor will light our country and all who serve it—and the glow from that fire can truly light the world.

---

[1] The account of this presidential transition relies principally on *The Torch is Passed*, the Associated Press story of the death of a President, 1963; and *Four Days*, the historical record of the death of President Kennedy, compiled by United Press International and *American Heritage*, 1964.

The torch was passed again on November 22, 1963. Throughout the world "the people wept, prayed, stood silent in the streets, or lit torches to parade sadly through the night." People everywhere felt a personal loss, mourned the death of a "great and good man," shared in the grief of his family and friends. Not only the American people but the whole world was bereft of a young, vigorous, and gallant leader. Governments everywhere were profoundly disturbed, deeply apprehensive, for no one knew how the assassination of an American President might affect the programs and policies of the United States government at home and abroad:

John Fitzgerald Kennedy was buried on November 25. Kings and presidents, prime ministers and chancellors, from communist and neutralist countries as well as from the free world, came to Washington to pay their last respects. De Gaulle of France, Phillip of England, Selassie of Ethiopia, Baudouin of Belgium, Frederika of Greece, in all 220 official representatives from 92 nations participated in the funeral services. Hundreds of thousands of men, women, and children lined the streets in Washington and millions more watched on television as the cortege slowly moved from the White House to St. Matthew's Cathedral, then to the National Cemetery in Arlington. All of us have poignant memories: the extraordinary procession of family, close friends, and dignitaries walking up Connecticut Avenue; a three-year-old boy called John-John who saluted the flag-draped casket of his father; a restless riderless black horse that followed the casket to the grave; the presidential salute of twenty-one guns and the final taps; folding the flag and presenting it to the young widow. Following the ceremonies at the cemetery, Mrs. Kennedy received condolences from the official guests at the White House but it was no longer her home. Presidential transition had already been accomplished.

For four days, newsmen of the press, radio, and television reported every scene and act in that "incredulous drama which combined murder and majesty." Gradually the messages changed from, "President Kennedy is dead," to "President Johnson is in control." Thus the mass media of communication played an important role in making the American people, and people everywhere, realize that presidential succession had occurred with minimum disruption of governmental activities. Tactfully, but firmly, Lyndon B. Johnson had assumed his duties as Head of State, Head of Government, in the world's oldest constitutional democracy. Symbolic of the new order, immediately following Mrs. Kennedy's personal reception at the White House, President Johnson gave an official reception at the State Department where he greeted the distinguished visitors from abroad and reassured them as to the continuity of American policies and programs.

In the initial period of succession, President Johnson felt it was imperative to continue the Kennedy Administration in toto. "President Kennedy left a program well outlined in its content. I will carry out all of the late President's commitments." Addressing a joint session of Congress in the first week of his presidency, Johnson reaffirmed the intent of his Administration to achieve the domestic and international goals of President Kennedy. "Now the ideas and ideals which he so nobly represented must and will be translated into effective action." Thus he urged prompt enactment of the pending tax cut and civil rights bills and, although Congress withheld action for the remainder of the session, continuing pressure from the White House did secure the passage of both bills in the second session.

To reinforce his pledge of continuity, President Johnson persuaded nearly all of the top men in the Kennedy Administration to remain at their posts and to help him effect the transition. In the months that followed, as the President developed his own brand of administration, he gradually moved his own men into key White House positions. But the Kennedy Cabinet remained intact until Robert Kennedy resigned in order to announce his candidacy for U.S. Senator from New York. If anything, Johnson kept in closer contact with members of the Cabinet, individually and collectively, than did his predecessor who had picked them. After the November election, however, Johnson began his own talent search for personnel to man his own Administration, the Johnson Administration.

In August 1964, the Democratic Convention, meeting in Atlantic City, noisily and enthusiastically nominated by acclamation, Lyndon B. Johnson to be the party's presidential candidate. Accepting the nomination, President Johnson asked the American people for "a mandate—not to preside over a finished program —not just to keep things going. I ask for a mandate to begin." And on November 3, 1964, President Johnson got an overwhelming "mandate to begin" on his own terms. He polled 61 per cent of the popular vote, the greatest plurality in any presidential election, bettering the 60-plus per cent of Warren G. Harding in 1920 and Franklin D. Roosevelt in 1936. He received more votes than any one candidate in American history, far surpassing the previous high of Dwight D. Eisenhower. He carried 44 states, including all of the Eastern states, even Maine and Vermont. He was endorsed by every significant racial, ethnic, and religious group in the country. He won more Roman Catholic votes than his Roman Catholic predecessor and drew over 90 per cent of the Negro votes. Ironically, the only states lost by the first southerner to become President since the Civil War were five segregationist states in the Deep South and Arizona, which narrowly supported its native son, Senator Goldwater.

On January 20, 1965, Lyndon B. Johnson again took the presidential oath of office, happily under circumstances very different from those of his earlier oath in Dallas, Texas.

The President: "An American Institution"

"Essence of the Nation's Personality"

In an entertaining and discerning study of the American President, Sydney Hyman says, "He is, or can be, the essence of the nation's personality." [2] Harold Laski, a noted British political scientist, made much the same observation in an earlier and more penetrating analysis: ". . . the essence of the presidency is the

---

[2] *The American President* (New York: Harper & Brothers, 1954), p. 13.

fact that it is an *American* institution, that it functions in an American environment, that it has been shaped by the forces of American history, that it must be judged by American criteria of its response to American needs." [3]

Earlier editions of this book stressed the personal application of presidential powers and analyzed the individual style of the man in the office. But the eventful week that followed the assassination of President Kennedy has taught us a lot more about the nature of the American presidency and its role in the continuing process of government. Because of the circumstances under which President Johnson succeeded to the office, we are now more inclined to emphasize the institutional character of the nation's Chief Executive. Each administration, however, inevitably bears the unique stamp of the President's personality and particular experience. Harry S. Truman, Dwight D. Eisenhower, and John Fitzgerald Kennedy, each had his own way of conducting the presidential business, for each was a very different kind of person. Though Lyndon B. Johnson was determined to carry on the program outlined by his predecessor, within a remarkably short time he headed a distinctively Johnson Administration which was quite different in tone and techniques from the Administration of President Kennedy.

Thirty-five men have served as President of the United States. The constitutional requirements for the nation's highest office are very modest—a President must be a native-born citizen, he must have resided in the United States for 14 years, and he must be at least 35 years old. Actually, many additional political considerations of a practical nature govern the selection of presidential candidates. But here we run into the difficulties of generalizing over a long period in American history. All our presidents, of course, have met the constitutional specifications; the practical rules that determined their ultimate "availability" as candidates have changed considerably, however, since 1789.

What makes a man available for the presidential office? First of all, the man must nominate himself: no President has ever been drafted for the office; every presidential candidate has sought the office and made his availability known to influential people in the party of his choice. Second, his party must choose him above all others who aspire to the position, presumably because he possesses personal and political attributes most likely to attract not only the popular vote but also the requisite majority of votes in the electoral college. Third, the people must elect him at the polls, preferring him to the alternative candidate who has also been selected by a major political party because of his attractive personal and political qualities. [4]

What qualifications do Americans expect in a chief executive? Nearly all of

---

[3] *The American Presidency* (New York: Harper & Brothers, 1940), p. 7.

[4] "To win the Presidency the aspirant must travel a long, hard, treacherous road abounding in bumps and quicksand and divisible into three distinct segments: the preconvention build-up, the national nominating convention, and the post-conventional electoral campaign." Louis Koenig, *The Chief Executive* (New York: Harcourt, Brace & World, 1964), p. 35. Louis W. Koenig, Professor of Government at New York University, has written what is likely to become the classic appraisal of the American Presidency. See also Chapter 8.

our presidents have been professional politicians. They have served as cabinet officers, members of Congress, and governors of their respective states. In recent years, the U.S. Senate has furnished the candidates for both parties: Richard Nixon, John Kennedy, Lyndon Johnson, and Barry Goldwater. Normally, a candidate has a better chance if he comes from a pivotal state that has a large bloc of votes and where the parties have nearly equal strength in national elections. Of the thirty-six presidential candidates put forward by the major parties from 1868 through 1964, twenty-one were from three states—New York, Ohio, and Illinois. The Republican nomination of Barry Goldwater from Arizona simply flaunted the rule, for Arizona could add but five votes to the final tally.

Until recently, candidates from southern states were ruled out of practical consideration by both parties. Neither the Democrats nor the Republicans could figure much advantage in promoting a candidate from a region that was bound to vote Democratic in any event. But ever since the Dixiecrats walked out of the Democratic Convention in 1948, protesting against Harry S. Truman's stand on civil rights, the Democratic Solid South has been crumbling. Many old-line southern Democrats became presidential Republicans in 1952, and remained such in 1956, when Dwight D. Eisenhower's record as a war hero enhanced the doctrinal appeal of Republicanism. In 1960, many southerners voted for Richard M. Nixon, partly to express their anti-Catholic opposition to the Democratic candidate, but also because the Republican Party appealed more to their politically conservative predilections.

By 1960, both parties recognized that the South had become a pivotal area in presidential politics. Unquestionably, Kennedy's choice of Lyndon B. Johnson as his running mate was intended to reassure southern moderates and to bring the defectors of 1952 and 1956 back into the Democratic camp. As Majority Leader of the Senate, Johnson was an outstanding figure in national politics, and fortuitously, he came from a southern pivotal state with 24 electoral votes. In 1964, President Johnson was in a position to nominate himself as the Democratic candidate.[5] But the fact that Barry Goldwater carried five states of the old Confederacy means that in the next presidential election both parties will be seriously considering candidates from the doubtful states of the South, certainly from Texas, perhaps from Florida.[6]

Despite the American folklore, "from log cabin to White House," less than half a dozen presidents have risen from the ranks of the very poor. Most presi-

---

[5] "When the President is sitting in the White House, the National Convention has never gone against his recommendations in the choice of a candidate or in the formation of a platform on which that Convention is to operate." Harry S. Truman with reference to his own nomination by the Democratic Convention in 1948. *Memoirs* (Garden City, N.Y.: Doubleday & Co., Inc., 1956).

[6] For further discussion see Avery Leiserson (ed.), *The American South in the 1960's* (New York: Frederick A. Praeger, 1964), especially Donald R. Matthews and James Prothro, "Southern Images of Political Parties: An Analysis of White and Negro Attitudes," and O. Douglas Weeks, "The South in National Politics." Also see Paul T. David (ed.), *The Presidential Election and Transition 1960–61* (Washington, D.C.: The Brookings Institution, 1961), especially V. O. Key, Jr., "Interpreting the Election Results," and Paul T. David, "The Political Changes of 1960–1961."

dents have grown up in the upper-middle class; a few, like George Washington, Franklin D. Roosevelt, and John Fitzgerald Kennedy, have been very wealthy. In the 1964 election, both presidential candidates were multimillionaires. Neither Lyndon Johnson nor Barry Goldwater had to worry much about personal campaign expenses or how to support a family on a government paycheck. A national election, however, costs more than even a multimillionaire can finance on his own. Before he has a chance to wage his campaign on a national scale, he must secure heavy outside financial backing.

Other factors, more or less personal, also condition the people's choice. The need to secure a majority vote in a very large and mixed electorate has prevented the candidacy of any overt representatives of special interests such as business or labor. Many of our presidents have been military leaders, ten have been army generals. President Eisenhower made his great reputation as a General of the Army, had little liking for politics, and never developed a strong sense of partisanship. Most presidents have been college or university graduates and a majority of them have been lawyers. President Kennedy majored in political science at Harvard College and his honors thesis became a best-selling book.[7] President Johnson graduated from Southwest Texas State Teachers College and taught debating and public speaking before he made politics his career. Vice-President Humphrey majored in political science at the University of Minnesota and took a master's degree in political science at Louisiana State University.

Religion and sex also enter into presidential politics. The American people are religious in sentiment if not always in behavior. Up to 1960, the Protestant tradition was strong enough to reject a Roman Catholic as President. In 1928, when Governor Alfred E. Smith unsuccessfully ran for the office, his defeat was widely attributed to his Roman Catholic faith, though other issues in the campaign becloud this conclusion. But Kennedy's 1960 victory, however close, dispelled the myth that a Roman Catholic cannot be elected to the country's highest post. In 1964, the political pundits worried whether or not it would be strategically astute for President Johnson (Christian Church) to name a Roman Catholic for second place on the Democratic ticket; he chose Hubert Humphrey, a Congregationalist. Barry Goldwater (Episcopalian) selected a Roman Catholic, William E. Miller, to be his running mate.

Custom has long excluded women from most policy positions in American government, and it will probably continue to exclude them from the office of Chief Executive for some time to come. Senator Margaret Chase Smith's decision to try for the Republican nomination in 1964 was a gallant one, but the Republican Convention at San Francisco gave her short shrift. Hitherto, a Negro candidacy has been inconceivable because of racial pride and prejudice on the part of the overwhelming majority of Caucasians who make up the electorate. But surely the time is coming when a candidate will not be barred because of sex, race, or color, just as the time finally came when a candidate was not barred because of his religion.

---

[7] *Why England Slept.*

If the President is to represent "the essence of the nation's personality," he—and his family—must appear as one of us. Though well over half the American people now live in cities, the notion persists that city men are "slickers" and "wicked" whereas rural folks are "decent and respectable." Only two of our presidents, William Howard Taft and John Fitzgerald Kennedy, were born and raised in large cities. Harry Truman from Independence, Missouri; Dwight Eisenhower from Abilene, Kansas; Lyndon Johnson from Stonewall, Texas (population about 650)—all three typify American small-town talent, the Horatio Alger tradition of "luck and pluck," "work and win." Harry Truman's whistle-stop speeches in 1948 inevitably ended, "Howja like to meet my family?" and then he would introduce Mrs. Truman as "the boss" and his daughter Margaret as "my baby." Pictures of Ike and Mamie Eisenhower in the White House were obviously made to fit into the "American album of Presidents we like"; especially appealing were those of "Grandpa Ike" and little David. The Johnsons are similarly projected. Effective public relations keeps us informed of the daily doings of the First Family and vicariously we enjoy first-name familiarity with "Lyndon," "Lynda Bird," "Luci Baines," and "Him," the beagle hound.

The Kennedys brought a new kind of sophistication to the White House. They simply could not be pictured as "an average American family from Main Street." John Fitzgerald Kennedy belonged to the "melting pot aristocracy," Boston Irish, but also of Hyannisport, New York, and Palm Beach. He had style, flair, an engaging personality, and lots of money. Youth was the hallmark of the Kennedy Administration, but not inexperienced or naive youth. The academic influence was perhaps more conspicuous in the Kennedy Administration because it had been slighted in the Truman and Eisenhower Administrations. But the New Frontiersmen were idea men rather than idealists or ideologists; most of them were also organization men, specialists in public and business administration. President Kennedy himself was a practical politician who came to the White House after fourteen years of toughening experience on Capitol Hill.

The same Madison Avenue techniques which package the presidential candidates are also used to project the popular image of the man in the White House. If the master of ceremonies were to ask, "will the real President please stand?" the American public might well be startled, and possibly more impressed. It takes character to be a President, something much more substantial and enduring than an image.

Lord Bryce, who served as British ambassador to the United States at the turn of the twentieth century, outraged the American public by devoting an entire chapter of his *American Commonwealth* to the question of "Why Great Men Are Not Chosen President." [8] He suggested several answers. First, a smaller proportion of first-rate ability is drawn into politics than into private business. Second, the methods and habits of Congress, with its emphasis on the committee system and loose party organization, offer few opportunities for personal distinction.

---

[8] James Bryce, *The American Commonwealth*, 3rd ed. rev. (New York: The Macmillan Company, 1903), 2 vols.

Third, since eminent men are more likely to make enemies than are mediocre men, political parties tend to choose safe rather than outstanding candidates.

Some years later, however, another distinguished British observer of American politics, Harold Laski, took issue with Bryce's conclusions: "On any showing, eleven American presidents have been extraordinary men whatever may be our view of the handling of their office. That is a proportion not less high than the proportion of remarkable men who have become prime minister in the same period." [9] Laski charged that it was unfair of Bryce to compare American presidents with the political leaders of England or of any other foreign government, because basically they are not comparable. A President is neither a king nor a prime minister. His single office combines the perquisites of head of the state and the powers of head of the government. In the analysis of the American presidency that follows, we shall take Laski's advice and appraise both the man and his office in terms of *American* ideology and *American* political behavior.

Presidential Transition

The inauguration of the President is an occasion for national celebration. But in the midst of celebration, the new administration is expected to carry on the business of government without crisis, without interruption. Actually, preparations for the shift in political power symbolized by the inaugural ceremony will have begun on election day and even before.

Laurin Henry, under sponsorship of the Brookings Institution, has made an historical study of how an outgoing President winds up his responsibilities as Chief Executive and how the President-elect gets ready to fill his high office.[10] Presidential transitions fall into three types: (1) when the incoming President is of a different political party from his predecessor (this has happened sixteen times, the most recent when Kennedy succeeded Eisenhower in 1961); (2) when the elected successor is of the same party as his predecessor (this has happened 11 times, the most recent when Hoover followed Coolidge in 1929); (3) when a Vice-President assumes presidential responsibilities following the death of the President (this has occurred 8 times, the most recent being the Kennedy-Johnson transition in 1963).

The first presidential transition involving party turnover in the twentieth century was from William Howard Taft to Woodrow Wilson in 1913. Laurin Henry's picture of Woodrow Wilson's inauguration offers a striking contrast to the Kennedy inauguration of 1961: the leisurely pace and old-fashioned manners, the intimate scale of government activity (including the cow on the White House lawn), President Taft and President-elect Wilson riding together in a horse-drawn carriage to the Capitol. Taft's arrangements for delivering up the office and Wilson's for taking over the administration were personal, informal, and inadequate. It is almost incredible that down past the middle of this century the American national government, ever beset by problems of increasing mag-

[9] Laski, *The American Presidency*, p. 8.
[10] Laurin Henry, *Presidential Transitions* (Washington, D.C.: The Brookings Institution, 1960).

nitude and complexity, at home and abroad, simply met the crises of executive succession on an *ad hoc*, unplanned basis. This is the crux of presidential transition as Henry puts it: "a party system that makes it both a minor miracle and a painful experience for the outparty to win a presidential election and then gives the President-elect little assistance in forming a government." [11]

President Truman made a determined effort to exit as a statesman. From his own experience, he knew how hard it was to go into the President's office without preparation. Shortly after the 1952 election, he invited the President-elect to the White House. Meantime he directed that General Eisenhower be furnished with important security information including CIA reports and policy papers of the National Security Council. The most crucial current problem was the Korean armistice negotiations. Evidently the President hoped that, in the interest of national unity, the President-elect would actually concur in foreign policy decisions. Eisenhower at once made plain, however, that he would not participate in any government decisions before taking office. As early as November, he appointed Joseph M. Dodge to be his representative to the Bureau of the Budget and Senator Henry Cabot Lodge to be his liaison with the State and Defense Departments. Their function was simply to obtain information; they had no authority to participate in fiscal or foreign policy decisions. No doubt President Truman felt rebuffed. Nevertheless, he ordered each agency to prepare "briefs" on its organization and operations so that the incoming administration could be "informed to the point of action" on inauguration day. Thus, despite some personal animosity between the two principals, and considerable partisan bitterness between the outgoing and incoming administrations, the process of transition was systematized and institutionalized. The Eisenhower-Kennedy transition, patterned after this precedent, was smoother and more effective, partly because the personal relationships were less strained and partly because the party victory was so marginal in 1960.

In the few months between election and inauguration, the President-elect must choose the key officers of his administration, his personal advisers on the White House staff, top officers in the Executive Office, the heads of departments and principal agencies, the most important ambassadors abroad. Selection of personnel, however, is only the beginning of transition. The strategy of responsible leadership means coming to grips with important issues in a specific and practical way so that programs can be produced. As Henry points out, when a presidential candidate becomes the President-elect, he can no longer lead the opposition; in his new role he must learn to identify himself with an ongoing administration and a continuing bureaucracy. "The myths of opposition must be adjusted to the hard facts of limited alternatives."

Presidential transition with a party turnover is particularly difficult. The President-elect shares responsibility with the outgoing President for an orderly

---

[11] *Ibid.*, p. 737. In order to facilitate an orderly transition, Congress passed legislation early in 1963 which authorized the outgoing administration to provide some facilities—office space, secretarial assistance and the like—so that the President-elect and his incoming administration can set up shop in Washington between election and inauguration.

shift in political power and a continuity in administration. At the same time, as leader of a victorious party, he cannot risk tarring his new administration with the policies of the old administration. Franklin Roosevelt deemed it good politics to let the Hoover Administration sweat it out even though the bankrupt state of the nation's economy called for immediate concerted effort. As a result, the Democratic Administration would not be blamed for the depression and it could take all the credit for the New Deal. General Eisenhower scrupulously refrained from assuming any responsibilities for foreign policy until he was actually sworn into office. Thus, the Truman Administration could be indicted for taking us into the Korean War; the Eisenhower Administration would be remembered for bringing peace to the nation. But such partisan restraint, to keep the two administrations distinct in the minds of the electorate, can work to the disadvantage as well as to the advantage of the incoming President and his administration. Certainly, President Kennedy's Administration was ill-starred in foreign policy at the outset—witness the Cuban fiasco—because the incumbent President and the President-elect could not assume joint responsibility for policy-making between election and inauguration.

In one sense, the presidential inauguration in January, 1965, marked the final transition from the Kennedy Administration to the Johnson Administration. President Johnson felt committed to fulfillment of the Kennedy program for the duration of what would have been Kennedy's first term. Throughout the 1964 campaign, however, Johnson made it clear that he intended to move forward with his own policies if the voters gave him a "mandate to begin." Thus the 1966 Budget, already in preparation before the election in November 1964, and presented to the Congress after the inauguration in January 1965, was designed to accommodate President Johnson's concept of "the Great Society" as well as his vision of America's role in world affairs. Moreover, in the period between election and inauguration, there were daily news reports of resignations and appointments in top policy positions. Kennedy people were moving out; Johnson people were moving in—with new loyalties, new viewpoints, new policy plans.

No incoming administration—whatever the nature of succession—can ever begin with a clean slate, however. The President and his principal policy-makers are but components in the whole political system. A transfer of power in the White House will ultimately affect Congress, the bureaucrats, and even the judges. A new administration, given time, is bound to change the policy processes and alter the policy outputs. Because the President is only a part of the whole system, the actions of his administration will in large measure be constrained by the constitutional pattern, institutional practices, environmental conditions, and the course of events.

The presidential image is sometimes distorted when it focuses too narrowly on the personal role of the President. The input of policy is a continuum of economic, social, political, and personal factors that do not automatically stop and start with the election and inauguration of a new President. When President Eisenhower came into office in January, 1953, he had to accept his legacies from twenty years of Democratic control: New Deal, Fair Deal, Korean War,

World War II, Truman Doctrine, Marshall Plan, Point Four, the North Atlantic Treaty, and Communist Containment. When the chips were down and the Republicans were actually responsible for policy making, they were not even free to repudiate the war-time agreements which they had so viciously attacked in the heat of campaigning in 1952. By the same token, when the New Frontiersmen took over in 1961, they, too, found themselves bound, inextricably committed to policies at home and abroad that were not to their liking and certainly not of their own making.[12] Johnson's inaugural speech on January 20, 1965, gave promise of new programs, but it also recognized responsibility for continuing operations—on the domestic front and in international relations.

Positions and Powers of the President

The President holds many positions, and in each position he exercises many kinds of power. He is: head of state, director of American foreign policy, commander-in-chief, chief executive, legislative director, head of the nation's economic program, party leader, and personal spokesman for all Americans.

Head of State

In an essay on British government, Ernest Barker has described the monarch as "a symbol of unity, a magnet of loyalty, and a centre of ceremony." [13] The President, as head of state, serves the American people in the same capacity. He entertains visiting royalty and heads of other governments, he receives the credentials of foreign ambassadors and ministers, he addresses Congress on the state of the Union, and he speaks to the people on crises in world affairs. As the official personification of the national character, the President must play many parts, ranging from the most solemn to the downright silly.[14] "Mr. President" is not a private person, and his time is not his own. His every waking moment is taken up with public acts; wherever he goes, he is under guard; whatever he does officially or informally is fully reported in press, radio, and TV. A steady stream of "callers" at the White House symbolizes the direct accessibility of a democratic leader to the people.

A typical presidential calendar, in any week, will include scheduled and sometimes special meetings with the Cabinet, the National Security Council, and the congressional leadership. The President will also have individual appointments with congressmen, administrative assistants, and various heads of departments. He may meet with the press in formal conference in the auditorium of the State Department, or informally as he walks about the White House grounds. He will

---

12 Marian D. Irish, "The Kennedy Administration: Appraisal at the Half-way Mark," in Jack W. Peltason (ed.), *1963–1964 American Government Annual* (New York: Holt, Rinehart, and Winston, 1963).

13 *Essays on Government* (Oxford: Clarendon Press, 1945), p. 6.

14 For a readable account of this "one-man distillation of the American people," the reader may enjoy Clinton Rossiter's *The American Presidency* (New York: Harcourt, Brace and Company, 1956), also available as a Signet Key Book.

brief American ambassadors before their departure and be briefed by them on their return from posts abroad. He will receive foreign ministers and ambassadors on their arrival, and as they leave the country. He will greet and entertain a never-ending procession of heads of states and heads of governments who want to do business with the United States. He will meet governors, mayors, bankers, defense contractors, labor leaders, military leaders, scientists, astronauts, Negro leaders, religious leaders, educational leaders—in short, all manner of spokesmen from the special interest groups that make up pluralistic America. He will usually take time out to have his picture taken with each visitor, for this is part of the presidential image—the people's chief lobbyists keeps in personal touch with all his

Drawing by Alan Dunn; © 1960 The New Yorker Magazine, Inc.

"The job's pleasant enough, except for all these comings and goings."

many constituencies. And, finally, he will be on hand for a series of social events, including perhaps breakfast with legislative leaders, a luncheon or dinner at the White House for a foreign dignitary, and, of course, the luncheon or dinner given in return by the distinguished visitor for the President.

In his role as head of state, the President has endless tasks to perform. He has monuments to unveil, medals to bestow, public works to dedicate. He has speeches to make—to the Sons of St. Patrick and the Daughters of the American Revolution, to the Veterans of Foreign Wars, and the United Cookie Cutters of America, to the members of Congress assembled in solemn session and the families of America assembled in front of their television sets. He serves as Honorary President of the American Red Cross; he chips in the first dime for the polio drive; he tosses out the first ball of the baseball season; he memorializes Washington, Lincoln, Jackson, and Jefferson on their birthdays; he joins the children hunting Easter eggs on the White House lawn; he chats with Indian chiefs, movie actresses, and America's Mother of the Year; he proclaims the Fourth of July, Labor Day, and Thanksgiving; he buys the first Christmas seals. And he struggles with a mountain of paper work, much of it before a battery of cameras. There are treaties to sign, bills to approve, bills to veto, commissions to grant, appointments to make, diplomatic reports to study, gifts to acknowledge, letters to write, budgets to revise, economic reports to digest, military reports to review, more speeches to prepare. All these are routine matters in the President's daily round of activities. As President Truman wrote in his *Memoirs:*

> One of the hardest things for the President to do is to find time to take stock. I have always believed that the President's office ought to be open to as many citizens as he can find time to talk to; that is part of the job, to be available to the people, to listen to their troubles, to let them share the rich tradition of the White House. But it raises havoc with one's day, and even though I always got up early, usually was at work ahead of the staff, and would take papers home with me at night to read, there always seemed to be more than I could do.[15]

Director of American Foreign Policy

Some years ago, Justice Sutherland of the United States Supreme Court referred to the President as "the sole organ of the federal government in the field of international relations."[16] Certainly the President has been the principal director of the nation's foreign affairs ever since the first administration of President Washington. Most of the historic foreign policies of the United States were announced originally in presidential messages and proclamations: Washington's proclamation of neutrality, the Monroe Doctrine, Wilson's Fourteen Points . . . "to make the world safe for democracy," Roosevelt's Good Neighbor policy and the "Four Freedoms," the Truman Doctrine and "Point Four," and the Eisenhower Doctrine for the Middle East.

This practice of putting full power over foreign affairs into the hands of

---

[15] *Memoirs* II, 361.
[16] *United States* v. *Curtiss-Wright Export Corp.*, 299 U.S. 304 (1936).

the President generally makes good sense. All the information that is gathered daily by our diplomatic, consular, and confidential agents abroad is made available to the President. Since national security frequently requires that information of this sort be kept secret, or that it be released only with extreme caution to appropriate authorities, the President can truly claim the most comprehensive knowledge of the conditions that prevail in every foreign country. As Justice Sutherland pointed out, "In this vast external realm, with its important, complicated, delicate and manifold problems, the President alone has the power to speak or listen as a representative of the Nation."

The Constitution, however, does not give the President an exclusive role in foreign affairs. Article II of the Constitution specifically grants to the President: (1) the power to make treaties, by and with the consent of the Senate; (2) the power to receive foreign ambassadors and ministers; (3) the power to nominate and appoint ambassadors, ministers, and consuls, with the advice and consent of the Senate; (4) the duty to report to Congress on the state of the Union and to recommend whatever measures he deems expedient; (5) and full authority as commander-in-chief over the military forces of the nation. Clearly, the Constitution provides for separation of powers and for checks and balances in foreign affairs just as it does in domestic matters; but of necessity the conduct of foreign affairs has become the primary responsibility of the President.

The President has the sole power to initiate and negotiate treaties. All the Senate can do is to approve or disapprove what the President has in effect already promised in the name of the United States. Actually, the Senate has rejected only about 1 per cent of the treaties sent to it by the President, has amended or made specific reservations in about 15 per cent, and has approved all the rest without change. The most notable rejection was the Senate's action on the Versailles Treaty that Woodrow Wilson had negotiated after World War I. Aware of Wilson's experience, Franklin D. Roosevelt was careful to include strategic members of the Senate Foreign Relations Committee in negotiations on the various treaties arising out of World War II, including the United Nations Charter. His action, however, was prompted by political wisdom rather than by any legal obligation.

The Constitution says nothing about the House of Representatives in defining the President's treaty-making powers. But Washington's second administration was nearly wrecked on this very point. Since Washington failed to inform the House on the negotiations that led to the unpopular Jay Treaty (1795), the representatives decided not to appropriate the funds he had requested to put it into operation. Washington insisted on the importance of preserving secrecy in diplomatic matters, and refused to send the House any enlightening papers or documents on the treaty. Thereupon the House threatened to impeach him. Although the House finally passed the appropriations, presidents ever since Washington's time have profited by his unhappy experience. Because the House initiates the appropriations necessary to implement a treaty, the President finds it advisable to consult with House leaders as well as with Senate leaders in his conduct of foreign affairs.

Executive agreements are actually used more often than treaties in the conduct of foreign affairs. Although the Constitution does not even mention executive agreements, the Supreme Court has declared that the President may enter into agreements with foreign governments as "a modest implied power" under his treaty-making authority.[17] Thus treaties, which must have the concurrence of the Senate, and executive agreements, which are made solely under the authority of the President, both have the force of law in the courts.

In February, 1953, Senator John W. Bricker (R.-Ohio) proposed a constitutional amendment specifying that no treaty or executive agreement could become law until it had been validated by Congress. Such a restriction would have put severe handicaps on the President's direction of foreign policy. Both President Eisenhower and Secretary of State Dulles strongly opposed the amendment, but in 1954 it came within one vote of obtaining a two-thirds majority in the Senate. The Senate apparently still remembered and resented such executive agreements as the Roosevelt-Litvinoff Agreement of 1933 by which the United States officially recognized the USSR; the "swap" of fifty American destroyers for the use of English naval bases on the eve of World War II; and the Yalta agreements, which set down the conditions under which Russia entered the war against Japan. All these agreements had been concluded by Roosevelt without consulting Congress.

The first President to leave the country in order to participate personally in treaty-making was Woodrow Wilson, after World War I. Hitherto, presidents had relied on either special agents or regular ambassadors to conduct our affairs abroad. Wilson played a leading role in the Paris Peace Conference, but this very fact was used as ammunition by his political opponents at home. Each President is said to gain a little more power by taking advantage of the precedents set by his predecessors. Certainly Franklin D. Roosevelt made frequent and dramatic use of personal conferences in arriving at international agreements of the highest import. Roosevelt and Churchill on board ship in the middle Atlantic, at Hyde Park, Washington, Casablanca, and Quebec; Roosevelt, Churchill, and Chiang Kai-shek at Cairo; Roosevelt, Churchill, and Stalin at Teheran and Yalta—these meetings heralded a new kind of top-flight diplomacy. Presidents Truman, Eisenhower, and Kennedy followed the same technique with varying degrees of success.

President Johnson, filling out the Kennedy term, carefully avoided summit conferences. As Louis Koenig observes, summit meetings are liable to score low on policy achievement and high on general failure.[18] They tend to force a President to negotiate on issues not yet ripe for diplomatic solution. At the same time, they foster moods of optimism which the realities of foreign policy may not support. Hence the public expectations, based on something as intangible as "the spirit of Camp David" (following the summit meeting of President Eisenhower and Chairman Khrushchev in 1959), may suffer a considerable let-down when the conference finally resolves itself into polite and ambiguous rhetoric. Never-

---

[17] *United States* v. *Pink*, 315 U.S. 203 (1942).
[18] *The Chief Executive*, pp. 226–228.

theless, personal meetings with heads of states serve to enhance the image of the President as "spokesman for the nation" even when the policy output is minimal or negative.

The constitutional separation of powers puts the American President at some disadvantage in bargaining directly with other heads of government.[19] When, for example, President Truman met with Marshal Stalin and Prime Minister Churchill at Potsdam in 1945, he had to explain at the outset that even though he might strongly support a proposal made at the conference, he could not guarantee that the Senate would approve of it once it was incorporated into a treaty. On matters other than treaties, however, he was fairly free to make personal commitments, either under his "war powers" or as the political leader who interpreted American public opinion. Marshal Stalin, who at that time was the Premier of the USSR, could, of course, count on the unquestioned backing of his government and presumably of his people. Ordinarily, the British Prime Minister could also depend on majority support in Parliament. As it happened, however, a British election interrupted the Potsdam conference, and the Conservatives were turned out of power. Consequently, Prime Minister Winston Churchill and Foreign Secretary Anthony Eden were replaced at the conference by Prime Minister Clement Attlee and Foreign Secretary Ernest Bevin of the victorious Labor Party. As President Truman remarked later, "It was a dramatic demonstration of the stable and peaceful way in which a democracy changes its government." We might add that the sudden change of British leadership at Potsdam suggests one marked disadvantage of the parliamentary system. When executive tenure depends on majority support in the legislature, an election that overturns the legislative majority also automatically unseats the executive; this may mean a sharp reversal of policies. The President's assurance of a four-year term, independent of Congress, does at least insure a fixed measure of stability in the conduct of policy—both foreign and domestic.

In assigning to the President the authority to receive foreign ministers and ambassadors, the Constitution implies that he also has the authority to recognize foreign governments and new states. This issue was raised in the very first administration, when Washington *received* "Citizen Genêt" and thereby *recognized* the French revolutionary government. Subsequently, Citizen Genêt abused the President's hospitality by appealing directly to the American people for intervention by the United States in the war between France and England. Exercising another presidential prerogative, Washington responded by requesting the French government to recall its overzealous representative.

During most of our history, the President has followed the customary international practice of basing the recognition of a new foreign government not on its constitutional legitimacy but on its *de facto* capacity to fulfill its international obligations. Under President Woodrow Wilson, however, the American policy of recognition took a new turn when he refused in 1913 to

---

[19] W. Y. Elliott and his associates discuss this problem in *United States Foreign Policy* (New York: Columbia University Press, 1952).

recognize the *de facto* government of President Victoriano Huerta in Mexico on the grounds that Huerta had risen to power by force and did not rule by "consent of the governed." No doubt this withholding of American recognition contributed to the downfall of the Huerta regime. Wilson used the same policy with respect to the communist government that was established in Russia in November, 1917, but this time nonrecognition by the United States did not break the new regime.

Since Wilson's time, every American President has frankly used recognition as an instrument of American foreign policy. Warren G. Harding, Calvin Coolidge, and Herbert Hoover each refused to recognize the USSR, even though the communist government continued very much in fact after 1917. Franklin D. Roosevelt's decision to recognize the USSR was based on economic rather than legal considerations, and in extending recognition he did not seek congressional approval. Hoover, and subsequently Roosevelt, withheld recognition of Manchukuo on the grounds that Japan had violated China's territorial integrity in setting up the new government. And yet President Truman recognized the establishment of Israel immediately despite protests by the Arabs that their territory had been violated. In the context of the Cold War, American presidents in the 1950's and 1960's have been quick to recognize new nations in Asia and Africa without questioning too sharply whether the peoples of these countries were ready for self-government—or whether the new governments were prepared to assume their responsibilities in the international community. On the other hand, Truman, Eisenhower, Kennedy, and Johnson each in turn have withheld recognition of the People's Republic of China for purely political reasons, since the communists without question are in actual control of the Chinese mainland, a fact recognized by most of the other nations in the world. Thus the decision to recognize or not to recognize a foreign government is a political decision that belongs to the President alone. Neither Congress nor the courts can legally force or forestall the President's decision.

The Constitution gives the President power to appoint ministers and ambassadors, but only with the consent of the Senate. He also appoints the Secretary of State, the Under-Secretary, the Assistant Secretaries, and the key figures in other departments concerned with foreign affairs, such as Defense and Treasury. All these officials constitute the "President's team" in the making of foreign policy. Just how the President uses his team members, or whether he uses them at all, depends mostly on his personal inclinations—and his capacity for statesmanship. Franklin Roosevelt became so deeply involved in foreign policy and in his role as a world leader, that he made his own decisions. In fact, Secretary of State Cordell Hull complained privately that the President scarcely kept him informed, much less sought his advice. Roosevelt personally met with other heads of state, and he usually sent his own representatives rather than the regularly appointed ambassadors to less important conferences. Apparently he trusted the on-the-spot opinions of his friend Harry Hopkins far more than the systematic studies made by the State Department.

Truman, on the other hand, who also developed a tremendous interest in and influence on the world scene, relied for the most part on the advice and judgment of his Secretary of State, Dean Acheson, who in turn worked very closely with the Policy Planning Committee in his own Department. President Eisenhower, from the outset, despite his international experience in NATO, tended to minimize his role as director of foreign affairs, leaving the formulation of policy to his Secretary of State, John Foster Dulles. Dulles had served as special adviser to Acheson in the Truman Administration, and he was determined to avoid his predecessor's difficulties with Congress and the press; hence he tended to court political advice from party leaders rather than professional assistance from career men within the State Department.

President Kennedy was never his own Secretary of State, as was sometimes charged, but he did take a direct and strong personal interest in foreign policy. He used the institutional machinery—the Cabinet, the National Security Council, the Joint Chiefs of Staff, and the Central Intelligence Agency—but less regularly and less formally than his predecessor. He exerted his personal power in foreign affairs, hand-picked most of the assistant secretaries in the State Department, and brought his own specialists into the White House Office to create what Washington observers called "the little State Department" under McGeorge Bundy. He frequently crossed departmental lines to develop a "community of policy makers," with his Secretary of State, Secretary of Defense, Attorney General, and other high officials at the core of this group. President Johnson had relatively little experience in foreign affairs, except for a few travel assignments, when suddenly he was thrust into a position of world leadership. Under these circumstances, he availed himself of the whole institutional machinery and persuaded the Kennedy team to stay with him for the rest of the term.

Whatever the President's relations with his Secretary of State or his personal advisers, every President has had to face up to the hard fact that final responsibility for every major decision in foreign affairs rests on him—and on him alone. No one can really speak for the President or make up his mind for him. President Truman described the President's plight with poignancy in his *Memoirs:* "The presidency of the United States carries with it a responsibility so personal as to be without parallel. . . . To be President of the United States is to be very lonely, very lonely at times of great decisions."

True, the President may seek moral and material support from Congress on questions of foreign policy. For example, early in 1957, President Eisenhower asked Congress to authorize his use of armed forces to secure and protect the territorial integrity and political independence of nations in the Middle East against communist agression. The Secretary of State appeared before the Senate Foreign Relations Committee to explain why congressional concurrence was needed. Although the President possesses the constitutional authority to use troops, he felt that the peoples abroad would feel more secure if the President's policy had the clear support of Congress. Congress passed the resolution granting the President the authorization he requested. But it was neither the purpose nor the effect of the resolution to add to the power of the presidency; it simply showed the world that Congress was in accord with the so-called

Eisenhower Doctrine. As director of our foreign policy, the President had formulated the doctrine; as commander-in-chief, he would have to execute it.[20]

The Commander-in-Chief

The United States was conceived as a fighting organization. The Constitution pays considerable attention to the problems of common defense and to war powers. It designates the President as commander-in-chief of the armed services of the United States and also of the state militia when it is called into the service of the United States. But the Constitution does not give the President sole or plenary powers over the military. Rather, it specifies that Congress shall have power to tax for the common defense; declare war; grant letters of marque and reprisal and make rules concerning captures on land and water; raise and support armies; provide and maintain a navy; make rules governing the armed forces; call out the state militia and provide for its training and discipline.

Although the Constitution specifically gives Congress the power to declare war, Congress has never done so except at the urgent request of the President. Indeed, as commander-in-chief, the President may dispose the armed forces in such a way that Congress has no alternative but to issue a declaration of war. The naval policies of Woodrow Wilson in 1915–17, and of Franklin D. Roosevelt in 1939–41, for example, were bound to involve this country in war. Moreover, the President may recognize a state of war, as Lincoln did in 1861, without ever asking for a formal declaration from Congress. The President may also order American troops into action to protect American citizens or American property abroad, to support our vital interests or national honor any place in the world, and to carry out America's obligations in the international community. The Marines, as we knew, have made landings "from the Halls of Montezuma to the shores of Tripoli"—they intervened in Texas in 1845, in Panama in 1903, in China in 1905, in Mexico in 1917, in Korea in 1950, and in Lebanon in 1958. These are only a few of the more than 150 occasions on which American presidents have used military forces without seeking specific authorization from Congress.

From time to time, Congress has tried, though with little success, to control the President's use of force in the conduct of foreign policy. In the 1930's, for example, after a sensational investigation of the role of munitions-makers and international financiers in World War I, Congress passed a series of Neutrality Acts designed to keep us out of "the next world war." But this legislation did not deter Franklin D. Roosevelt from making the United States "the arsenal of democracy," or from turning over American defense weapons to the nations at war with nazism. When Congress passed the Selective Service Act in 1940, it included a specific limitation on the use of American troops abroad; yet just one year later President Roosevelt sent American troops into Iceland and Greenland so that British troops could be released to fight on

---

[20] For further discussion of the foreign policy process and foreign policy output, see Chapter 15.

the German front. In the "great debate of 1951," Congress sharply attacked the President's right to station American troops in Europe in peacetime, but even in the heat of the argument the issue was really academic, for President Truman had already stationed troops there. Congress had no alternative but to appropriate the necessary funds. In situations of this sort, President Eisenhower chose to seek congressional approval in advance, both for the use of American troops to defend Formosa (1955) and to resist communism in the Middle East (1957). It would appear, however, that President Eisenhower's requests were political and, at least in the latter instance, tied very closely to economic policies, rather than to any constitutional restriction. As for the future, it seems much too academic even to discuss whether Congress or the President should be the one to declare "massive instant retaliation" if an enemy should threaten us with "instant total annihiliation." The point is dramatically illustrated by the fact that when Lyndon B. Johnson returned to Washington on that fateful afternoon of November 22, 1963, he *had* to transfer from the vice-presidential plane which had brought him to Dallas to *Air Force One*, in which his predecessor had arrived. *Air Force One* was the President's plane, with the telephone and complex communications devices that enabled him to get in touch with every sector of the globe and to give whatever commands might be necessary and proper for the national security.

The Federalist is quite frank in explaining the President's military power: "Of all the cares or concerns of government, the direction of war most peculiarly demands those qualities which distinguish the exercise of power by a single hand." Alexander Hamilton would have approved President Truman's action in removing General Douglas MacArthur from all commands in 1952 for presuming to differ publicly with his commander-in-chief. The Framing Fathers, who elected General George Washington as the first President, expected the President to assume direct command in time of war. In fact, President Washington personally headed the federal troops for a short period during the Whisky Rebellion of 1792. Abraham Lincoln frequently intervened in the operation of the Army of the Potomac until General Ulysses S. Grant finally insisted on sole command. President Wilson was more interested in "organizing for peace" than in supervising the military strategy of World War I, but President Roosevelt, along with Prime Minister Churchill, participated in all the top-level military decisions of World War II. And President Truman made the most momentous decision of any commander-in-chief in history when he gave the order to drop the first atomic bomb on Hiroshima in August, 1945.

Lincoln was the first to use his military position "to take care that the laws be faithfully executed." As commander-in-chief, Lincoln called out the militia to put down "the rebellion," paid the militia men out of the Treasury without getting any appropriation from Congress, proclaimed a blockade of southern ports, directed the seizure of rail and telegraph lines leading into Washington, suspended the writ of habeas corpus, and issued the Emancipation Proclamation. And he did all this without any authorization from Congress. In the *Prize Cases,* which upheld the blockade, the Supreme Court explained that the "Executive Chief of the Government" is not only authorized but *bound* to resist force by force, and to do so without waiting for any special legislative authority. Moreover, said the Court, the President must determine what degree of force the crisis demands.[21] Only when the war was over did the Supreme Court admonish the President that "no doctrine, involving more pernicious consequences, was ever invented by the wit of man than that any of its [the Constitution's] provisions can be suspended during any of the great exigencies of government." [22]

In World War I, President Wilson carried Lincoln's concept of the commander-in-chief still further, to embrace even more far-reaching "war powers." As Professor Edward S. Corwin points out in his classic study, *The President: Office and Powers,* the main difference between the Lincoln and Wilson patterns of administration was one of method.[23] Lincoln assumed that as commander-in-chief he had all the powers necessary to win the war, an assumption that was supported by subsequent congressional approval of his actions. In World War I, Congress moved at the outset to delegate extraordinary powers to the President. For example, the Lever Food and Fuel Control Act of 1917 gave to the President the broadest possible discretion to regulate by license the importation, manufacture, storage, mining, or distribution of necessaries; to requisition foods, feeds, fuels, and other necessaries; to purchase, store, and sell certain foods; to take over and operate factories, packing houses, pipe lines, mines, or other plants; to fix a minimum price for wheat; to limit, regulate, or prohibit the use of food materials in the production of alcoholic beverages; to fix the price of coal and coke. Other statutes gave the President power to conscript an army; to license trading with the enemy and his allies; to censor all communications by mail, cable, or radio with foreign countries; to control enemy aliens inside the country; to take over and operate the nation's water and rail transportation; to take over and operate its telephone and telegraph systems. Thus the American President, "fighting to make the world safe for democracy," had almost all the powers that a totalitarian dictator possesses—and he used most of them.

Even before American entrance into World War II, President Roosevelt began to assume "war powers." As Corwin points out, in the "Destroyer Deal" the commander-in-chief interpreted his power to *dispose* the armed services as the power to *dispose of* our armaments. The Lend Lease Act, passed by Congress nine months before we entered the "shooting war," authorized the President to sell, transfer title, exchange, lease, lend, or otherwise dispose of all kinds of "defense articles," from buttons to battleships, to any foreign government whose defense the President deemed vital to the national defense of the

---

[21] *Prize Cases,* 2 Black 635 (1863).

[22] The noble words of Justice David Davis in *Ex parte Milligan* holding unconstitutional the suspension of the writ of habeas corpus outside an actual theater of war. 4 Wall. 2 (1866).

[23] Edward Corwin, *The President: Office and Powers,* 4th rev. ed. (New York: New York University Press, 1957), pp. 237ff.

United States. Also, before we were actually at war, Congress authorized the President to procure ships and war materials; to requisition and operate any private factory for defense purposes; to modify or cancel any existing contracts that interfered with the government's defense program; to give top priority to all government defense contracts. During World War II, President Roosevelt exercised tremendous power over the national economy—price control, food rationing, rent controls, plant seizures, materials allocations.[24] All these were powers either delegated to him by Congress or implied from his position as commander-in-chief.

In some areas, notably in communications and transportation, the government's control over business was less extensive in World War II than it had been in World War I. But Franklin D. Roosevelt was much more dramatic than Woodrow Wilson in the role of commander-in-chief. The Smith-Connally Act of 1943 gave the President authority to seize private plants whenever labor troubles threatened to jeopardize strategic war production. Roosevelt had not waited for authorization from Congress, however. Six months before Pearl Harbor, asserting his authority to make a going concern of the nation's defense efforts, he had summarily stopped a labor dispute by seizing an aircraft factory in California. Before the war was over, he had made sixty such seizures, at least half a dozen of them before Congress had passed any enabling legislation. His seizure of the nation's coal mines in 1943, for example, was without congressional authorization.

Only once did industry challenge the constitutionality of these actions. When Sewell Avery of Montgomery Ward and Company refused to obey an order of the War Labor Board concerning the recognition of union representatives in 1944, he was forcibly removed from his own office on orders of the commander-in-chief, and the company's property seized by the government. By the time the case reached the Supreme Court, however, the question was settled; the government had already returned the property and Mr. Avery was back in his office. Consequently, the Court declined to pass judgment.

During the Korean War, in 1952, when the country was faced with a nationwide steel shutdown because management refused to accept a decision of government mediators, President Truman seized the steel mills. In this case, however, the Supreme Court by a vote of 6 to 3 refused to uphold the President's action.[25] Truman insisted that as chief executive and commander-in-chief he had acted to avoid national catastrophe. The six justices who ruled against the seizure all offered different reasons for their decision, but they all agreed that "separation of powers" means that Congress, not the President, is entrusted with the lawmaking

---

[24] Probably the best monograph on this aspect of presidential power is Clinton Rossiter, *The Supreme Court and the Commander in Chief* (Ithaca, N.Y.: Cornell University Press, 1951).

[25] *Youngstown Sheet & Tube Co.* v. *Sawyer*, 343 U.S. 579 (1952). For an analysis of power politics in the steel seizure case, see Richard E. Neustadt, *Presidential Power* (New York: John Wiley & Sons, Inc., 1961).

power of the nation. Justice Hugo L. Black, who delivered the opinion for the majority, explained it quite simply:

> The President's power, if any, to issue the order must stem either from an act of Congress or from the Constitution itself. . . . The order cannot be properly sustained as an exercise of the President's military power as Commander in Chief of the Armed Forces. . . . Even though "theatre of war" be an expanding concept, we cannot with faithfulness to our constitutional system hold that the Commander in Chief of the Armed Forces has the ultimate power as such to take possession of private property in order to keep labor disputes from stopping production. This is a job for the Nation's lawmakers, not for its military authorities.

Those who fear "the man on horseback" and the military *coup d'état* may find comfort not only in Black's opinion in the *Steel Seizure Case* but also in Truman's immediate acceptance of the Court's decision. On the other hand, students of constitutional law point out that, *if* it had not been so clearly the intent of Congress when it passed the Taft-Hartley Act *not* to give the President such power of seizure, some of the justices of the Court majority might very well have joined the minority who upheld the President's "war powers."

In time of war, the Supreme Court has invariably lent its support to the *military* power of the President; not till the war is over and won is the Court likely to give the highest priority to the *civil* rights of the people. A prime example is the case of the Japanese-Americans in World War II. In *Korematsu* v. *United States* (1944),[26] Justice Black, who later delivered the Court's opinion in the *Steel Seizure Case*, upheld a military order calling for the evacuation from the West Coast of all persons of Japanese citizenship or descent. The Justice regretted the "hardships" that American citizens would suffer in being evacuated from their homes and forcibly detained in relocation centers. But "the properly constituted military authorities feared an invasion of our West Coast and felt constrained to take proper security measures." Justice Felix Frankfurter concurred: "It is for the military authority, not the judicial branch to determine what means are appropriate for carrying on war." [27]

It appears, then, that the President may assume whatever powers he deems necessary to carry on a war, for neither Congress nor the Court will seriously challenge his actions so long as the nation is fighting for survival. Under such conditions, a strong President will make use of whatever powers seem to him

---

[26] *Korematsu* v. *United States*, 323 U.S. 214 (1944).

[27] Justice Owen J. Roberts dissented: "I dissent, because I think the indisputable facts exhibit a clear violation of Constitutional rights." Justice Frank Murphy dissented: "Such exclusion goes over 'the very brink of constitutional power' and falls into the ugly abyss of racism." Justice Robert H. Jackson dissented: "The chief restraint upon those who command the physical forces of the country, in the future as in the past, must be their responsibility to the political judgments of their contemporaries and to the moral judgments of history."

reasonable and realistic, whether they are plainly delegated to him by the Constitution, or only vaguely inherent, implied, or incidental to his office.[28]

The Chief Executive

Article II of the Constitution places the executive power of the federal government in the single office of the President. It was clearly the intention of the Framing Fathers, as Alexander Hamilton points out in *The Federalist*, to provide for "energy in the Executive." Hamilton considered unity the first ingredient of energy; "decision, activity, secrecy, and dispatch will generally characterize the proceedings of one man in a much more eminent degree than the proceedings of any greater number. . . ."[29] Although the Constitution itself does not give even the sketchiest outline of how the executive branch should be organized, it does empower the President to "require the opinion, in writing, of the principal officer in each of the executive departments, upon any subject relating to the duties of their [*sic*] respective offices." Apparently the Framing Fathers anticipated the establishment of executive departments to assist the President, but they could not have imagined the tremendous superstructure of administrative organization which today almost dwarfs the legislative and judicial branches. Some thirty pages in the *United States Government Organization Manual* suffice to describe the organization and activities of Congress and the federal courts. More than 500 pages are required to outline the hundreds of departments and administrative agencies that now constitute the executive branch.

The Constitution charges the President to "take care that the laws be faithfully executed." Obviously he cannot carry out this task without help. He must have assistants and, to insure their responsibility to him, he must have the power to appoint and remove them. With the advice and consent of the Senate, the President appoints "ambassadors, other public ministers and consuls, judges of the Supreme Court and all other officers of the United States" not otherwise provided for by law. But Congress may empower the President alone, or the heads of executive departments, to appoint "inferior officers" without obtaining senatorial consent. The Constitution leaves it up to Congress to draw the line between "superior" and "inferior" officers.

"Superior officers" seem to include diplomatic officers, justices of the Supreme Court, members of the cabinet, commissioners of the independent regulatory agencies, and top decision-makers in various civilian executive agencies. Whenever the President names someone to fill one of these posts, the nominee must be confirmed by the Senate. The Senate usually goes along without much debate on the President's choice of representatives overseas, members of his own cabinet, and justices of the Supreme Court. Despite the fact that President Eisenhower had to deal most of the time with a Senate controlled by the opposition party, only one of his major nominations failed to obtain confirmation, that of

---

[28] For further discussion of the role of the President in matters of national security, see Chapter 15.

[29] Alexander Hamilton, *The Federalist*, No. 70.

Lewis Strauss as Secretary of Commerce, in 1959. In other appointments, the President is expected to consult with the senators of the state in which a position is to be filled. If these senators are of the opposition party, the President consults with the state leaders of his own party before making a nomination. Whenever a President fails to observe this rule of party politics, he is likely to encounter "senatorial courtesy"—a polite way of saying that, in courtesy to their slighted colleagues, the senators will refuse to confirm the President's nominee, no matter how qualified the nominee may be for the post.

Although the President's power of patronage is now sharply curtailed by civil service regulations, thousands of presidential appointments are still made on the basis of party politics. Key offices in the administration are filled by the leaders of the party faithful, with preference going to those who backed the President most strongly during his campaign. In Chapter 8, when we discussed how a President is elected, we noted that a few persons donate large sums of money to the President's campaign. Custom reserves for these generous supporters certain positions of power and prestige, such as the ambassadorships to London, Paris, and Rome. Most presidential backers, however, prefer to take their rewards in the form of personal access to the White House or influence on administrative policies after the election has been won. Since the national parties are made up of local blocs, the President is in a unique position to pull local strings through his power to appoint thousands of tax collectors, postmasters, marshals, district attorneys, and federal judges throughout the country. And yet these same local strings are also pulling on the President. Sometimes the Man in the White House must feel that he himself is just a party puppet.

Not only party politics but special-interest groups condition the President's appointive power. Since the President's "national constituency" is formed by a winning combination of special-interest groups, we are not surprised to find that pressure politics operates on the presidency just as it does on Congress. We like to think that ours is a government of laws and not of men, yet we all know that it is men who make the laws, men who administer the laws, men who interpret and enforce the laws. The top spokesmen of business, labor, farmers, educators, racial minorities, religious groups, professional associations, patriotic societies—all the groups that helped put the President into office—are likely to be privileged callers at the White House. Because they have access to the President, they may influence his decisions.

The President's cabinet is a carefully calculated consolidation of the various groups in his national constituency; and so is the membership of the regulatory commissions and the other important administrative agencies. The influence of pressure politics extends even to the hundreds of noncareer political officers such as undersecretaries and assistant secretaries in the national administration, and to all the "inferior officers" who have any part in policy formulation or decision-making. Not even judicial appointments are immune from political considerations. Indeed, when a vacancy occurs on the Supreme Court, the representatives of special-interest groups jostle and crowd one another in their race to the White House to get their favorite nominee appointed.

President Kennedy in the first year of his administration was able to appoint more judges to the federal bench than any other President in American history. Crowded dockets had long delayed the administration of justice in the federal courts. The Eisenhower Administration had urged Congress in 1960 to increase the number of district and appeals court judges, but a Democratic Congress, mindful of the coming elections, postponed action. In 1961, a Democratic Congress readily authorized a Democratic President to fill 73 new judgeships, 63 on district courts, 10 on appeals courts. These appointments involved various political pressures. Partisan consideration was obviously paramount; no Republicans were nominated by the Democratic President (though he did renominate three Republicans serving recess appointments from President Eisenhower). President Kennedy held up most of these appointments until nearly the end of the session, probably hoping to gain maximum yardage from potential patronage. On the other hand, knowing that the Democratic Senators had virtual veto on appointments within their respective states, the President sought their political advice and consent in advance of his official nominations.

To help him supervise and control the national administration the President relies on several thousand high-level political executives. These fall into several distinct categories: (1) The President tries to place in strategic positions within the departmental hierarchies individuals whose personal loyalties will center on the chief executive. President Kennedy deliberately disrupted the orderly routine of bureaucracy in a number of agencies when he kept a direct line of communication between the White House and his personal appointees, notably with his "whiz kids" in the State and Defense departments. (2) The President must make certain patronage appointments which identify the party organization with the presidential administration. Many such appointments will have been arranged during the campaign, some of them part of the dickering and dealing before the convention. Turnover among these appointees is usually high. Many a "political executive" attracted by a high-sounding official title and a chance to advance "the New Frontier" or to help build "the Great Society" finds that the day-to-day tasks of public administration are not really glamorous and that the pay is comparably less than he could make in business or private practice. (3) The President (and his staff) is constantly engaged in a talent search to discover program executives with the special knowledge and technological background that are needed in the modern business of government. Again, turnover is high in this group, many of whom find it professionally frustrating and insufficiently rewarding to work in a political environment. (4) The continuous coming and going of political executives is partially offset by the career administrators who come up through the ranks of the civil service or foreign service. As a presidential administration settles down, presidential appointments to second and third echelons come to include an increasing number of persons recruited from the permanent bureaucracy.

Although the Constitution is fairly specific on the President's power of appointment, it is silent on the power of removal. A debate in the First Congress over whether the Senate should concur in the President's dismissal of superior officers for disciplinary reasons was resolved in favor of the executive. From that date on, the general principle has been that the President must have the power to dismiss subordinates, since he is responsible for the work of the executive departments. But the principle has not always been followed. During the serious quarrels that broke out between President Andrew Johnson and Congress in the period of Reconstruction, Congress passed the Tenure of Office Act, which provided that heads of departments should serve for the duration of the term of the President who had appointed them and one month thereafter, and that they could be removed earlier *only* with the consent of the Senate. President Johnson vetoed the act as an unconstitutional restriction on the President's power of removal, a power that had been exercised by presidents ever since Washington's time. His veto was overridden, however, and the Supreme Court managed to side-step the issue until 1926.

In *Myers* v. *United States* (1926), the Supreme Court held that Congress could not restrict the President's power to remove executive officers whom he has appointed with the consent of the Senate. In a lengthy opinion, Chief Justice Taft, who had himself been plagued by the problem during his own term as President, held invalid the Tenure of Office Act of 1867 and subsequent legislation restricting the President's removal powers. Taft took the same position that the First Congress had adopted. Since the President alone is responsible for the actions of his executive subordinates, he must have the sole power to dismiss them.

> [The President] must place in each member of his official family, and his chief subordinates, implicit faith. The moment that he loses confidence in the intelligence, ability, judgment, or loyalty of any one of them, he must have the power to remove him without delay.[30]

Not quite ten years after its firm decision in the *Myers Case*, the Supreme Court reconsidered the "constitutional principle" that the Chief Executive must have the sole power to dismiss his subordinates. This time the dispute had developed between President Roosevelt and a member of the Federal Trade Commission, Colonel William Humphrey. The President had invited Colonel Humphrey to resign from the Commission because his views differed sharply from those of the administration. When Colonel Humphrey insisted on serving out his statutory term, the President summarily dismissed him. The Supreme Court refused to uphold the dismissal, on the ground that Congress did not intend quasi-legislative or quasi-judicial agencies to be subject to the political control of the chief executive. After rereading the congressional debates of 1789, the Supreme Court decided that the President's "illimitable power of removal" extended only to "purely executive officers." [31]

---

[30] *Myers* v. *United States*, 272 U.S. 52 (1926).
[31] *Humphrey's Executor* v. *United States*, 295 U.S. 602 (1935).

Presidential Plans for Reorganization

As general manager of the executive branch, the President must have authority to control the entire national administration—the vast and complex organization of executive departments, regulatory commissions, government corporations, and miscellaneous agencies that carry on the business of the national government. The main theme of all plans to reorganize the executive branch is to make the President more effective and efficient in his role as general manager of the national administration.

The tremendous expansion of the national administration under the New Deal dramatically highlighted the President's problems of administrative management. In 1937, Roosevelt appointed a special Committee on Administrative Management headed by Louis Brownlow, a specialist in public administration. In line with the Brownlow Report, the President asked Congress for broad powers to reorganize the executive branch, a request that was angrily denied amidst political charges of presidential "dictatorship." Nevertheless, in 1939 Congress did give the President authority to propose reorganization plans which would become effective unless disapproved by Congress within 60 days. Most students of public administration agree that this statute shifted the initiative in making administrative changes from Congress to the President.

In 1945, following World War II, Congress again vested the initiative for administrative reorganization in the President, but reserved the right to override any proposed plan by majority vote in both houses. The Reorganization Act of 1945 was intended to: (1) facilitate the orderly transition from war to peace; (2) reduce expenditures and promote economy; (3) increase efficiency; (4) group agencies and functions according to their major purpose; (5) reduce the number of agencies; and (6) eliminate overlapping. Certain agencies were specifically exempted from the President's power to reorganize: the Interstate Commerce Commission, the Federal Trade Commission, the Securities and Exchange Commission, the National Mediation Board, the National Railroad Adjustment Board, the Railroad Retirement Board, and the civil functions of the United States Army Corps of Engineers. The reason behind these exemptions may have been that the agencies themselves had engaged in pressure politics; but these exemptions also reflect a deep-seated conviction in Congress that the President must share control of regulatory commissions with Congress.

In 1947, Congress created a bipartisan commission to survey the executive branch and to make appropriate recommendations for reorganization. Former President Herbert Hoover was chosen to head the Commission. Reporting to President Truman in 1949, the Hoover Commission noted that "thousands of federal programs cannot be directed personally by the President." Accordingly, the Commission recommended: (1) a more orderly grouping of the functions of government among a small number of major departments headed by the President's principal assistants; (2) clear lines of control from the President to the department heads, and equally clear lines of responsibility from these officers to the President; (3) adequate staff services for both the President and his department heads. The Hoover Commission did not, however, advocate that the politically powerful, independent regulatory commissions be abolished (as the Brownlow Committee had twelve years earlier). Indirectly, the Hoover Commission reaffirmed the *Humphrey Case* by recommending that the commissions should be bipartisan, and that the members should not be subject to removal by the President at his own discretion.

President Truman subsequently submitted to Congress a number of reorganization plans based on the recommendation of the "first" Hoover Commission. In 1955, a "second" Hoover Commission, appointed by President Eisenhower, made further reports on reorganization and executive management. These reports —a mixture of political advice, administrative recommendations, and policy analysis—followed the same line as the earlier studies by emphasizing the role of the President as "general manager of the national administration."

Like his predecessors, President Kennedy was disturbed by the confusion of responsibility in the executive branch. At his request, Congress reinstated for two years the President's power (allowed to lapse in 1959) to reorganize the administration by executive order, subject to disapproval by either house within 60 days. In his first year in office, President Kennedy submitted 7 plans for reorganization, all intended to tighten the reins of his administration. Congress rejected three of these which called for more direct executive control over the regulatory agencies, SEC, FCC, and NLRB.

An incoming administration usually has in mind some organizational changes which symbolize the transfer of power. Note, however, that the President actually has very little power on his own to make changes in the established pattern of administration. Congress determines the duties and structure of each agency, usually in some detail. In the 1953 transition, the new administration tried to emphasize its intention of "cleaning up the mess" in the State Department by bringing in a successful businessman at the rank of Undersecretary of Administration to organize the Department more efficiently. But President Eisenhower could not make the appointment until Congress first enacted a statute which authorized the new rank and title within the Department, and then not until a Senate committee held a hearing on the qualifications of the presidential nominee, after which the Senate as a whole approved the nomination. Congress keeps a tight rein on the administrative agencies, prescribes detailed procedures for their operations, sets the basic pattern of personnel practices including position classification and compensation schedules, and through its various committees continuously investigates any and every aspect of agency activities. President Johnson, who spent more than a quarter century of his political life on Capitol Hill, sees to it that his Administration works closely with Congress on personnel, programs, and budgets.

The assumption that the chief executive is a "general manager" may be misleading. With the exception of Herbert Hoover, none of our presidents has ever shown much interest in, or capacity for, administrative management. So it seems rather unrealistic to suppose that a President will necessarily be more able to manage the national administration if the main lines of authority and direction reach directly and conveniently to his office. Nor does increasing the number of special and professional assistants at the White House insure the unified and energetic executive envisaged in *The Federalist*. The essential responsibility of the President is to see that the laws are faithfully executed, and this is a problem that calls for political leadership far more than skill in administrative management. This point is best illustrated perhaps in the President's role as chief legislator.[32]

The Chief Legislator

The Constitution, as it was written, clearly intended that *all* legislative powers of the national government be vested in Congress. But the men who framed it had never been confronted with the mass vote in elections, nor with a multitude of active special-interest groups. Instead, the restricted suffrage of that day, together with the convenient device of the single-member constituency, guaranteed that middle-class farmers and merchants would be overwhelmingly over-represented in Congress. Consequently, it seemed perfectly safe to make the legislature all-powerful. Once the suffrage had become universal, the legislator, though still elected by a single constituency, was beset by the competing and conflicting claims of different groups within that constituency. He could no longer represent a single class; nor could he please or appease all the groups. The simplest solution was to pass the buck, to delegate "quasi-legislative" powers to the executive, especially in such controversial areas as social and economic policy.

James Bryce, in his study of *Modern Democracies* written shortly after World War I, observed everywhere in the world a decline of the legislature and a pathology of representative government. The great depression of the 1930's accelerated the decline, exaggerated the pathology. Overwhelmed by the complex problems of modern industrial society, the "representatives of the people" seemed more than willing to turn over the vastly expanding business of government to "the elite and the expert." And the delegation of extraordinary legislative power to the executive became a sign of the times: "executive dictatorship" in Italy, Germany, and the Soviet Union, and "executive leadership" in France, Great Britain, and the United States.

In 1933, Congress passed the National Industrial Recovery Act, which in effect empowered the major industries of the country to draw up "codes of fair competition," including minimum wages and maximum hours, provisions for collective bargaining, and the prohibition of child labor. If any industry failed to draw up such a code, the President was authorized to prescribe one for it. Judicial review, however, temporarily checked this abdication from legislative responsibility. The Supreme Court, though recognizing that a grave economic crisis had impelled Congress to delegate this policy-making authority, neverthe-

---

[32] The reader should examine for himself the Brownlow Report, and the Reports of the Hoover Commission, including the Task Force Reports. A provocative discussion on this subject is Charles S. Hyneman, *Bureaucracy in a Democracy* (New York: Harper & Brothers, 1950).

less stood firm: "Extraordinary conditions do not create or enlarge constitutional power." The Court felt that for Congress to permit either trade associations or the President to formulate and establish as law "codes of fair competition" was such a sweeping delegation of legislative power that it violated the constitutional doctrine of separation of powers. Hence, in 1935, it declared the NIRA null and void.[33]

Although the Court continues to hold that separation of powers forbids the delegation of legislative power, Congress nevertheless adds constantly to its already impressive delegations of quasi-legislative authority. For example, on several occasions Congress has passed "contingent legislation," which simply means that the executive has the power to determine when or where a situation exists that calls for putting the legislative policy into operation. The Court itself has upheld "flexible tariff" provisions of this sort, which leave to the discretion of the President the right to adjust individual items in the tariff schedules in order to keep them keyed to fluctuating costs of production at home and abroad.[34] The Court also sustained the neutrality laws of the 1930's, which authorized the President to prohibit the sale of American arms and munitions if he felt that such action would contribute to peace between belligerents.[35]

Congress also passes laws that contain only general statements of policy, leaving the executive to "fill in the details." In such cases, the Court has insisted that Congress clearly set forth the general policy and fix an "intelligible standard" for administering it. Not since the early period of the New Deal, however, has the Court been inclined to question the legislative standards too closely. It has, for example, frequently upheld such general terms as "public interest" and "public convenience and necessity." In the following chapter we shall consider some of the independent regulatory agencies to which Congress has delegated broad rule-making authority under just such general terms.

The Constitution itself sketches in certain working relations between the President and Congress. The President is required from time to time to "give to the Congress information of the state of the union and recommend to their consideration such measures as he shall judge necessary and expedient." President Washington, who thought of the President's role as somewhat like that of a monarch, delivered his messages to Congress in person, quite in the manner of the British "Address from the Throne." Thomas Jefferson, who was essentially a party President, made no such formal presentations, but he did manage to get his way in Congress by using the party organization. For example, the "floor leaders," who first appeared in Congress during Jefferson's administration, were recognized as "presidential agents." Jefferson constantly met with congressional

---

[33] See *Panama Refining Co.* v. *Ryan*, 293 U.S. 388 (1935); *Schechter Poultry Corp.* v. *United States*, 295 U.S. 495 (1935); both discuss at some length the constitutional doctrine of separation of powers. It should be noted, however, that the National Industrial Recovery Act was not invalidated on this ground alone; the Court held the act unconstitutional in so far as Congress had exceeded its commerce power and had thus invaded states rights.

[34] *Hampton & Co.* v. *United States*, 276 U.S. 394 (1928).

[35] *United States* v. *Curtiss-Wright Export Corp.*, 299 U.S. 304 (1936).

leaders, in caucus and in conference, to promote his legislative program without seeming to impose executive direction over Congress. He also devised the practice of "executive bill drafting" to make sure that Congress would know exactly what kind of legislation he had in mind. Woodrow Wilson, who was always something of a schoolmaster, often attempted to teach Congress what he thought was best for the country and, at least on domestic matters, he was very successful.[36] In Corwin's estimation, "Franklin D. Roosevelt's accomplishment as legislator first and last surpassed all previous records."[37] Roosevelt himself felt that the presidency was not merely an administrative office but primarily a post of moral leadership.

The President, then, has the constitutional right to assume legislative leadership. But Congress is under no obligation to accept what the President judges to be "necessary and expedient." Time and political circumstances, as well as the character of the President himself, determine how much influence the chief executive actually exerts as legislative leader. Franklin Roosevelt's leadership, for example, "ebbed and flowed" with events. His first administration was marked by extraordinary enterprise and energy on the part of the executive, and by remarkable docility on the part of Congress. But in the second administration, which was launched on a high tide of popular support for the New Deal, relations between the executive and the legislature dropped to a new low when Roosevelt made his ill-timed demand for administrative reorganization and announced his ill-fated court-packing plan. Presidential leadership rose to new heights in his third and fourth terms, as the commander-in-chief asked for and got what he thought was required to win the war.

Party fortunes also have a lot to do with the check and balance between President and Congress. A President can always be "strong" if he has the backing of his own party organization in both houses. He is usually "weak" when both houses of Congress are controlled by the opposing party. This was the plight of President Eisenhower for six out of the eight years of his administration. Although Eisenhower won overwhelming popular endorsement in the 1952 and the 1956 elections, his following was obviously personal, and detached from regular party politics. Indeed, his leadership toward "modern Republicanism" was as hotly contested by the so-called old-guard members of his own party as it was by the Democrats.

Constitutional separation of powers could result in a complete deadlock between the executive and the legislature. But assiduous liaison on a bipartisan basis between the Administration and Congress gave President Eisenhower a creditable score in legislative effectiveness. Through prior consultation with the congressional leadership of both parties, the Eisenhower Administration ascertained the outside limits of what it could expect from Congress and then realistically charted its program within those limits. If President Eisenhower had been

---

[36] He had written his Ph.D. dissertation in political science at The Johns Hopkins University on *Congressional Government: A Study in American Politics* (Boston: Houghton Mifflin Co., 1885).

[37] Corwin, *The President*, p. 272.

able to count not only upon a Republican majority in the 83rd Congress, but also upon a majority of "Modern Republicans," he might have attempted a more ambitious legislative program. On the other hand, if, after the 1954 elections, he had been continuously confronted with a majority bloc of liberal Democrats, he might have gotten something less than his final record. The fact that he succeeded as well as he did with a Congress controlled by "the other party" must be attributed to a coalition of Modern Republicans and Conservative (especially Southern) Democrats who went with him down the middle of the road.

The lack of party responsibility for party programming, the lack of effective discipline within each party, the crossing of party lines without pains or penalties —these make congressional government possible when the electorate chooses its President from one party and the majority of Congress from the opposition party. Because we had more congressional government than presidential government under Eisenhower, the focus of political power shifted from the White House to Capitol Hill.

President Kennedy, who had very positive ideas about the legislative role of the President, was fairly successful in pushing his New Frontier on domestic issues: a new minimum wage law, urban renewal, public housing, aid to depressed areas, interstate highways, airport construction, to name but a few of his proposals that became law. Among his more conspicuous legislative defeats were: the creation of an Urban Affairs Department, aid to the public schools, income tax reforms, medicare, and civil rights legislation. In a televised review of his first two years in office, the President attributed his legislative difficulties, not to the substance of his program, but to the way in which Congress was organized for business. He was incensed because the conservative coalition of Northern Republicans and Southern Democrats, although a minority group, was able to dominate the Rules Committee in the House and to hold the principal committee chairmanships in both houses. As he put it to his national constituency, it's not easy to move a presidential program "particularly when the seniority system may place particular individuals in key positions who may be wholly unsympathetic to your program, and may be, even though they are members of your own party, in political opposition to the President. . . ." [38]

President Johnson, rounding out the Kennedy Administration, but dealing with Congress in his inimitable way, was able to overcome some of the legislative obstacles. His most impressive achievements were getting through Congress both the tax reduction legislation and the Civil Rights Act of 1964; but he too met defeat on medicare. Democratic gains in the congressional races of 1964, however, which gave the party more than two-thirds of the membership in both houses, assured much firmer support for the Johnson Administration. Moreover, the power of the conservative coalition was significantly weakened, not only because

---

[38] The complete text of the interview broadcast of December 17, 1962, appears in *U.S. News and World Report* (December 31, 1962), pp. 54–63. For an academic analysis of the problems discussed by President Kennedy see James MacGregor Burns, *The Deadlock of Democracy* (Englewood Cliffs, N.J.: Prentice-Hall, Inc., 1963).

some northern Republicans lost their seats to liberal Democrats, but also because seven southern Democrats were removed from the Democratic Caucus by Republican gains in the South. Finally, the massive popular vote for Johnson, in contrast to Kennedy's slim margin, gave the President enormous personal power and public prestige in confrontations with Congress.

Perhaps the most distinctive feature of the American presidential system is the independent tenure of the executive, whose term of office is in no way dependent on the will of Congress. Obversely, Congress assembles at least once a year and may stay in session as long as it pleases. The President has no power to dissolve it no matter how obstreperous or disagreeable it may be with respect to the "administrative program." In the "era of normalcy" in the 1920's, when Congress kept hands off the nation's economy, sessions were fairly short. Congressmen could always count on a summer vacation and plenty of time to mend their political fences before elections. In the early days of the New Deal, however, Roosevelt kept Congress in session week after week by presenting his "emergency legislation" in serial form. Later on, when Congress was no longer so receptive to his proposals, Roosevelt reversed his tactics and urged the congressmen to go back to their constituencies. But by that time Congress had grown suspicious and was determined to stay close to Washington to check any

Drawing by Basset; reprinted from Scripps-Howard Newspapers.

'Welcome to the Great Society!'

tendencies toward executive dictatorship! The Constitution permits the President to convene Congress in extraordinary session; in case of disagreement between the two houses on whether or not they should adjourn, he may adjourn them to such time as he thinks proper. So far, however, no President has ever adjourned Congress.

The fact that Congress cannot force the resignation of an unpopular President, nor the President dissolve a recalcitrant Congress, offers both advantages and disadvantages. It may mean that a stalemate in the legislative program will be prolonged throughout the two sessions between elections; or it may promote a more practical give-and-take relationship between the President and Congress.

At this point, we need to recall that the veto power gives the President significant influence over legislation. The mere threat that he *might* veto a measure serves to moderate Congress in drawing up the bill in the first place. Once he has exercised his veto power, Congress ordinarily does not attempt to override him by passing the bill over his objections. Indeed, Congress sometimes passes a bill in the comforting anticipation that the President will veto it. This practice allows a congressman to fulfill his local commitments without jeopardizing national interests. Later on, when he is talking to his constituents back home, he can say, "*I* voted for the bill. The *President* vetoed it."

In many states today, the governor enjoys what is known as an "item veto," which means that he can veto part of a bill without rejecting the bill as a whole. President Eisenhower—and many of his predecessors—have sought the same power for the President, particularly on appropriations bills. Since the President cannot very well veto a general appropriations bill (although President Truman once did), Congress frequently attaches "riders" to them. "Riders" usually carry some policy that is repugnant to the President, a policy that he would probably veto if it were presented to him separately. Unfortunately, however, Congress can rarely be persuaded to reform the legislative process; congressmen are generally far more concerned with reorganizing the administration. Hence the item veto has not yet found substantial favor with Congress.

Head of the Nation's Economic Program

A realistic approach to understanding the President's working relations with Congress is to analyze his authority as "head of the nation's economic program." For example, in his budget message to Congress at the beginning of each session, the President specifies the major items on which he requests Congress to take legislative action. Since the President releases his legislative recommendations through nationwide networks and news services, Congress is put on the political defensive. If the congressmen cut the budget, they must explain why they dare to minimize expenditures for the general welfare or national security. If they add to the budget, they must meet the charge of "pork-barrel legislation." Thus the President, through his initiative in fiscal legislation, can almost straitjacket Congress when it comes to making economic policies and decisions on expenditures.

The Constitution does not expressly grant any economic powers to the President. The Framing Fathers believed that public finance was the major responsibility of Congress. The authority to raise revenue by taxation, to borrow money on the credit of the United States, and to appropriate money for government functions belong to the people's representatives in the legislature. For more than a hundred years Congress carried out its fiscal assignment unaided. But as the functions of the federal government expanded rapidly from year to year, there was increasing waste and extravagance, confusion and incompetence. Long after the need for more unified direction and more professional management was apparent, the President still had little influence and no supervision over the requests for appropriations or the spending practices of the various agencies of which he was "chief executive." Not until 1921 did Congress finally concede that it was unable to control the chaotic finances of the sprawling and disorganized federal government. In that year of "fiscal revolution," Congress passed a Budget and Accounting Act which provided that the President prepare and transmit an annual budget of the United States to guide Congress in making decisions on taxation and appropriations. The Bureau of the Budget established in 1921 was first located in the Treasury Department but was transferred in 1939 to the Executive Office of the President. Its location in the Executive Office gives the President both the broadest and the most specific controls, not only over public finances but indirectly over the entire national economy.

Preparing the federal budget involves not merely estimating expenditures for the year to come but also justifying the programs that are planned. It is a tremendous responsibility, and one that is not always politically palatable. In January of 1957, President Eisenhower, just beginning his second term of office, presented to Congress the highest peacetime budget that had ever been known in American history—hardly a budget calculated to please John Q. Taxpayer. On the same day, the Secretary of the Treasury told a press conference "there are a lot of places in this budget that can be cut . . . if Congress can find ways to cut and still do a proper job." It was certainly unusual strategy for a cabinet officer to assail the President's budget on the very day it went to Congress. Even more amazing was the President's own press conference three days later when he declared he was in complete agreement with the Secretary's statements. The President said he thought Congress through its committees ought to find ways to save more dollars.[39]

Since the President's Bureau of the Budget had spent months examining the estimates and justifications from all the agencies and had failed to come up with any feasible cuts, Congress was understandably reluctant to accept such a vain assignment. So the House politely passed a resolution asking the President to advise Congress where *he* thought the Budget could be reduced. The President in turn bounced the problem back to the lawmakers, again urging *them* to revise downward—if they could—such programs as defense and security, veterans' and farmers' benefits. Thereupon, the House proceeded to chop off a substantial percentage of the funds that had been requested to run the White House and Executive Office. This amusing interplay of "You first my dear Alphonse. . . . But no, you first my dear Gaston" is a good illustration of party politics in action; the people had set the stage in November of 1956 by electing a Republican President and a Democratic Congress. The attempted exchange of roles, however, was disturbing from the point of view of public administration, for it marked a retreat from executive responsibility for over-all planning.

President Kennedy, almost as soon as he entered office, revised the Eisenhower estimates upward to meet a much greater spending program. Actually, President Kennedy persuaded Congress to vote even higher appropriations in 1961 than he had initially proposed. (International crises prompted this extraordinary cooperation from Congress.) But when President Johnson took over the responsibilities as chief executive, almost his first important decision was to pare back the Kennedy Budget of 1965, then almost completed. His now famous direc-

---

[39] For a sharp analysis of this episode, see Neustadt's account in *Presidential Power*.

tive to cut down on the use of unnecessary electric lights at the White House was a piece of effective public relations which served immediately to project a new presidential image. It was not, however, a piece of fakery, as everyone in the government employ soon discovered. President Johnson intended to make frugality the hallmark of his Administration, and he succeeded in trimming the Kennedy Budget of 1965 and in holding his own Budget of 1966 to a figure even the experts in the Budget Bureau had first thought would be impossible.

Since 1946, the President has been required by law to send to Congress an annual Economic Report, and the Council of Economic Advisers was established in the Office of the President to help him prepare the report. The Economic Report is intended to be a comprehensive analysis of the current economic situation—encompassing such factors as production and employment trends, income distribution, developments in agriculture, fluctuations in prices, costs, and profits, state and local government expenditures, private investment opportunities, and foreign markets. On the basis of his Economic Report, the President may propose legislation for such purposes as strengthening the business community, maintaining sound government finances, fixing appropriate controls over credit, expanding foreign markets, conserving natural resources, and mobilizing manpower. Although the report is presented to Congress simply as information accompanied by recommendations, it places the President in a position of leadership in the planning of the nation's "free economy."

Party Leader and "Lobbyist for All the People"

What is the proper role of the President as a political leader? Certainly, during the time he is a candidate for office, he is the very personification of partisanship. To many voters, the party labels have no significance except when they are used in presidential races. With the possible exception of General Washington, every President of the United States has entered office as a party man. Yet every President who has achieved real greatness as a political leader has transcended party organization. Once elected, the President represents not only his party but the whole people. The President *is* the Head of State and the personal spokesman of "the people," even of those who voted against him and who still oppose him. Former President Truman, in a celebrated TV-radio interview with newscaster Edward R. Murrow in 1958, graphically described the President as "lobbyist for all the people."

The President is in a position to exercise political leadership for the nation at large. He is the only elected representative in the American government (except the Vice-President) who can claim a national constituency. On the other hand, as we have already pointed out, the President cannot always count on the support of his own party in Congress.[40] Each national convention drafts a party platform at the same time it chooses its presidential candidate, but candidates for Congress are neither required nor even expected to stand on the party platform. Thus a

[40] For a shrewd analysis of the relations between Congress and the chief executive, see Pendleton Herring, *Presidential Leadership* (New York: Rinehart and Company, Inc., 1940).

President who tries to follow the party standard may actually find himself out of step with the members of his own party in Congress. He may conscientiously act as spokesman for the nation, but the ears of electionwise congressmen are more likely to be turned to the parochial voices in their own constituencies.

The President is the titular "head of the party," but his political leadership is largely personal. If he is able to sell his program to Congress, it is usually because he has first been able to persuade the public that his product is what they want. This is what Woodrow Wilson tried to do—and failed—when the Senate refused to buy his League of Nations. This is what Franklin D. Roosevelt tried to do—and succeeded—when he sold the New Deal to "My Friends." The development of mass communication has favored presidential leadership. Whereas Wilson had to make a killing lecture tour across the country, Roosevelt could sit in the White House and broadcast his "fireside chats" to a nationwide radio audience. President Eisenhower was able to telecast his personal appeals under the guidance of public relations experts whose profession it is to "engineer consent." Yet Calvin Coolidge's remark is still appropriate: "A President cannot, with success, constantly appeal to the country. After a while he will get no response."

Richard Neustadt, a political scientist with staff experience under Truman and Kennedy, treats the subject of presidential power in terms of the man rather than the institution. Observing how Roosevelt, Truman, and Eisenhower performed in office, he notes that the President sits in a unique seat and works within a unique frame of reference. The power of a President is largely his personal influence upon the behavior of those who hold policy-positions in the government. Whether history rates him "strong" or "weak," "leader" or "clerk," depends most of all on the President's own character and capabilities. "The more determinedly a President seeks power, the more he will be likely to bring vigor to his clerkship." [41]

Presidential power is first of all the power to persuade, but persuasion is more than logic and charm. The authority and status inherent in the President's office give him great advantage in bargaining, which is but another facet of persuading. The bargaining power of the President is enhanced by his professional reputation and his popular prestige. These involve more than the image created by public relations experts. They stem from the opinions other men hold regarding his skill and will and also their appraisal of how his public views him. The presidency is no place for an amateur in politics; use of presidential power calls for extraordinary expertise. The way a President sees his vantage points and uses his influence to get what he wants done—"his sense of power and of purpose and his own sense of self-confidence"—these are "politics of leadership."

The fact that presidential leadership depends more on the personality of the President than on the powers of his office disturbs many thoughtful political scientists.[42] No doubt the positive and forceful character of Franklin D. Roosevelt —coupled with times of crisis—enormously enhanced the executive role in Amer-

---

[41] Neustadt, *Presidential Power*, p. 185.
[42] See Corwin, *The President*, especially his analysis of the President as a legislative leader, and particularly the résumé that follows.

ican government; but his successors picked up where he left off, each in turn adding a few more lines to the role. Paradoxically, the more popular an executive is, the graver becomes the danger of personal dictatorship. Democracy assumes, however, that the people know on whom they should bestow popularity.

As an extra safeguard against personalized power, the Constitution relies on checks and balances. A President who abuses his power may be removed from office by the process of impeachment. The President's treaty-making power is limited by the requirement that two-thirds of the Senate must concur. He may make no commitments involving expenditures without obtaining the necessary appropriations from both houses of Congress. Even his role as commander-in-chief is sharply curtailed by congressional control over the purse-strings. Congressional hearings on the executive budget are extensive and intensive, exacting and exhausting. Congressional investigations of the President's administration can be thoroughly embarrassing and utterly discrediting.

Even when Congress is inclined to delegate its legislative powers to the President, the Supreme Court can be counted upon to invoke from time to time the constitutional doctrine of separation of powers. Thus the Court has denied the President power to ignore or override the legislative will (Truman and the *Steel Seizure Case*) and has held null and void congressional delegation of legislative responsibility (Congress and the New Deal). As a further barrier to personal power, the Twenty-second Amendment provides that no person shall be elected President more than twice. But probably the most potent check on the tendency of any President to build up dictatorial powers is the American tradition itself; every incumbent has tried to live up to the honor and prestige inherent in the office.

The Executive Office of the President

So far, we have been speaking of the President chiefly as a person; but the Executive Office of the President is an institution. To appraise the presidential personality is relatively easy, since the way a President uses his constitutional *powers* and his political *influence* is closely followed by the press. To analyze the *operations* and *processes* of the Executive Office is much more difficult, for its "staff services" are covered with the cloak of bureaucratic anonymity. Not so long ago, a President was expected to handle the business of his office with the help of just a personal secretary and several clerks. Today, the institutionalized presidency includes more than a thousand permanent employees and many more thousands of part-time employees in: the White House Office, Bureau of the Budget, Council of Economic Advisers, National Security Council, National Aeronautics and Space Council, Office of Emergency Planning, and Office of Science and Technology. This somewhat amorphous organization—most of it designed and developed since 1939—presumably provides the President with the "skills and tools of management" for the highest level of our national administration.

The White House Office

In terms of prestige and protocol, the White House Office takes precedence in the Executive Office.[43] The office of Secretary to the President goes back to the first administration, when Washington, at his own expense, employed his nephew to help him with clerical chores. Not until the Buchanan Administration did Congress appropriate a salary for the President's secretary. President Hoover was the first President to appoint three secretaries, and the practice was followed by President Roosevelt. Then, in 1937, the President's Committee on Administrative Management, pointing out that the President needed more than just secretarial help, urged the addition of six administrative assistants, who were to be marked by a "passion for anonymity." The Reorganization Act of 1939 authorized these administrative assistants, and subsequent acts provided for additional special assistants.

The *White House Staff* has four main jobs: (1) to keep the President's finger on the pulse of public opinion through professional public relations advisers; (2) to brief the President on the current activities and problems of the executive departments and agencies, so that he can act as an efficient general manager of the national administration; (3) to act as liaison between the executive branch and the legislative branch so that the President can be more effective in maneuvering the administration's programs through Congress; (4) to advise the President on military matters and national security.

Truman was the first President to use the staff system in the White House. He met with the staff daily and listened to what each and all had to say, but then he retired to his office to make his own decisions. President Eisenhower, however, turned over the responsibility of chief of staff to Sherman Adams. Adams' position in the White House had no precedent. Many presidents have put unusual trust in personal advisers; Wilson had his Colonel House and Franklin Roosevelt had Harry Hopkins. But Sherman Adams as the Assistant to the President was more than a close confidant, more than an efficient chief of staff; in official circles he was the President's *alter ego*. From the outset, Adams presided over the White House staff meetings and reported to the President the consensus of the group rather than the conflicting viewpoints of the members. He also sat with the President in Cabinet meetings, in the National Security Council, and in most of the President's conferences with party and congressional leaders. Significantly, during each serious illness of President Eisenhower, the Assistant to the President rather than the Vice-President made the important executive decisions.[44]

---

[43] See Edward H. Hobbs, *Behind the President* (Washington, D.C.: Public Affairs Press, 1954); "The Office of the American Presidency," *The Annals of the American Academy of Political and Social Science*, 307 (September, 1956).

[44] For two somewhat varying accounts of the role of the White House Staff by members of the Eisenhower Administration, see Sherman Adams, *First Hand Account* (New York: Harper and Brothers, 1961); and Emmet John Hughes, *The Ordeal of Power* (New York: Atheneum Publishers, 1963). For further discussion of the White House staff system in the Eisenhower Administration, see Marian D. Irish, "The Cipher in the

President Kennedy indicated early that he would use his staff for information and counsel, but he alone would make the decisions. He apparently made maximum use of his White House Staff to assess the advice he sought from many sources in and out of the government. Today's President needs expert advice on all kinds of technical matters that bear on public policy: advice of economists on tax measures; advice of scientists on missions to the moon; advice of military men on guerilla warfare. But experts, however qualified they may be in their own fields, may be lacking in political sagacity or disinterested in policy implications. A President normally counts on his principal officers to advise him on particular policies: the Secretary of Agriculture on farm problems; the Secretaries of Labor and of Health, Education, and Welfare on urban renewal and aid to depressed areas; the Secretaries of State and Defense on world disarmament and an international nuclear test ban. But each Cabinet member has his own bailiwick to support, and he loses face within his own hierarchy if he fails to advance the departmental interests. Thus diversity of viewpoints in Cabinet meetings or in the National Security Council may represent bureaucratic parochialism or agency rivalry, and consensus from group dynamics may reflect compromise rather than rational resolution.

Theodore D. Sorensen, special counsel to President Kennedy, points up the role of the White House Staff in presidential decision-making: to review the advice of the experts and the bureaucrats within the framework of the President's perspective.[45] Responsibilities of the White House Staff are as broad as the President's: to look at the government as a whole and to view all special claims critically and skeptically. The primary assignment of the White House Staff is to serve the President's needs and to talk the President's language. Even so, the President must use his own judgment in determining whose advice to trust most in any given situation. The White House Office offers him personal loyalty but, in their zeal to serve him, staff members may sometimes be too officious. Moreover, their confidential relationship to the President may imbue them with a confidence that exceeds their competence. As Sorensen points out, a White House adviser may see a problem in a wider context than a Cabinet officer, but he may also be less knowledgeable about actual operations, about Congress, and about special interest groups.

The men who surround the President in the White House—the special counsels, the secretaries, the administrative assistants, the special assistants—are in a position to exert tremendous influence on their chief. Yet they are almost completely unknown to the public and cannot easily be held accountable for the "staff service" that they render continuously on the most important issues of the day. In the days of Franklin D. Roosevelt, political scientists were gravely concerned about the "personalized power" of the presidency; today, they are more

---

White House," *New Statesman*, December 7, 1957, pp. 761–764; also Marian D. Irish, "The Organization Man in the Presidency," *Journal of Politics*, XX (May, 1958), pp. 259–277.

[45] Theodore D. Sorensen, *Decision-Making in the White House*, (New York: Columbia University Press, 1963), especially Chapter five.

disturbed by the fear that personal leadership cannot be reasserted in view of the institutionalization of the Executive Office.

Bureau of the Budget, Council of Economic Advisers

The *Bureau of the Budget* is by far the largest and most important unit in the Executive Office of the President. Its director is one of the few top officials the President has the power to appoint without asking the consent of the Senate. Though the Budget Director is a political appointee, solely responsible to the President, the Bureau itself comprises a permanent professional staff of almost 300 seasoned and outstandingly able employees. In its impact on the government, the Budget Bureau is more powerful than any other single agency. The main business of the Bureau is to prepare the Budget of the United States for the President to submit to Congress. The President's Budget, however, is more than an accounting of estimated receipts and expenditures; it specifies the personnel and materials needed for the work to be performed by every agency in the executive branch.

No agency can request congressional appropriations without clearance by the Budget Bureau. The Bureau requires every agency in the executive branch to justify its proposed expenditures with detailed "work plans," and if the plans do not conform to the President's over-all recommendations, the Bureau returns them to the agency for revision. The Bureau also acts as a clearinghouse for any other requests an agency might make to Congress. Thus it can alert the President to the legislative needs of his administration and advise the Congress whether the agency proposals have the President's approval. In addition, the Bureau continuously scrutinizes the organization and operations of all the agencies in order to recommend changes designed to promote efficiency and economy. Since the asking budgets of the operating agencies always exceed any budget that the President can prudently recommend, the Bureau is the hatchet-man for the Administration.

The Bureau has been the target of many criticisms. The operating agencies are inclined to resent the extension of this managerial arm of the President into their "line activities" or special interests. On the other hand, Congress has sometimes felt that the Bureau has been too lenient with the agencies, more concerned with keeping books than with evaluating programs. A Task Force of the Hoover Commission (1949) reported that the Bureau had "done very little to modernize the budget document and to make it an understandable and informative presentation of the government's vast financial program." [46]

Specifically, the Hoover Commission charged:

---

[46] For further information on this subject, check *The Hoover Commission Report on Organization of the Executive Branch of the Government* (New York: McGraw-Hill Book Company, 1949); Task Force Report on *Fiscal, Budgeting, and Accounting Activities*, Prepared for the Commission on Organization of the Executive Branch of the Government (Washington, D.C.: Government Printing Office, January, 1949); and Neil MacNeil and Harold W. Metz, *The Hoover Report 1953-55* (New York: The Macmillan Company, 1956).

The federal budget is an inadequate budget, poorly organized and improperly designed to serve its major purpose, which is to present an understandable and workable financial plan for the expenditures of the government.

In 1950, Congress backed up the Hoover Report with the Budget and Accounting Procedures Act, which called for a "program and performance budget." (A program and performance budget focuses attention on the functions, activities, and projects of each agency rather than on the cost of supplies, materials, equipment, heat, and rent.) Subsequently, the Bureau itself underwent substantial reorganization in line with the Hoover Commission recommendations. Even so, Presidents find that improved procedures in preparing the budget do not lessen their political troubles in getting the budget approved by Congress.

A congressional committee, reporting in 1961, noted that the budgetary process, if employed with sophistication, could be the most discriminating and effective tool of the chief executive.[47] "It reaches deep into the activities of the great departments; it is the one Presidential management device common to all of them; it works on that most sensitive pressure point—the pocketbook nerve." But the Committee complained that the budgetary process has not kept pace with the requirements of modern government. Today's budget retains the essential format of the first budget President Harding submitted to Congress in 1921. It is a massive, exhaustive document—it takes two years to prepare—filled with obscure, archaic, fiscal jargon. But perhaps President Johnson's preoccupation with the budget, not simply as a presidential accounting device but as a tool for program planning and executive management, may bring about some of the reforms that have long been overdue.

The *Council of Economic Advisers* has a small but high-quality professional staff, mostly economists and statisticians, whose collective job it is to analyze the nation's economy, appraise the economic programs and policies of the federal government, and assist the President in his annual Economic Report to Congress. The Council consists of three members appointed by the President with the consent of the Senate. Since its own staff is small (about thirty), it relies heavily on the operating agencies to collect necessary data. Unlike the Bureau of the Budget, its recommendations tend to be general, so that it enjoys fairly cordial relations with the operating agencies. It has sometimes been accused of being too receptive to the interests of special groups (in sharp contrast with the Budget Bureau, which appears remarkably insulated from outside contacts); it has also been charged with tempering its economics with political expediency and its recommendations with too much "welfare." Nevertheless, the Council offers the President substantial assistance in program-planning for service and security. Congress itself has organized a Joint Committee to receive and act on the Economic Report that emanates from the Council.

---

[47] Subcommittee on National Policy Machinery, Senator Henry M. Jackson, Chairman for the Committee on Government Operations, U. S. Senate, *Organizing for National Security* (Washington, D.C.: U.S. Government Printing Office, 1961), Staff Reports and Recommendations, Vol. 3, pp. 89–100.

**The National Security Council, The Office of Emergency Planning,
The National Aeronautics and Space Council, The Office of Science and Technology**

The *National Security Council* is the primary policy-developing agency in the grim business of preparing this nation for any possible war. Its function is to advise the President on the best way to integrate the domestic, foreign, and military policies that relate to national security. Its members include the President, Vice-President, Secretary of State, Secretary of Defense, and Director of the Office of Emergency Planning. The President may, and frequently does, invite other strategic "decision-makers" to attend the Council meetings—the Budget Director, Chairman of the Joint Chiefs of Staff, Secretary of the Treasury, U.S. Representative to the United Nations, and others whose responsibilities are tied to national security. The Central Intelligence Agency, which coordinates all the intelligence activities of the departments concerned with security matters, reports to the Council through its director.

The National Security Council is really an interdepartmental committee at the highest policy level. No one department or agency can assume full responsibility for military preparedness. The objectives and commitments of American foreign policy must be supported by the military establishment. American foreign policy, however, must be much more, and something less, than a show of naked power. We strengthen our allies not only with military assistance, but also with economic and technical aid. We influence peoples all over the world with our overseas programs and "psychological strategy." We dare not overextend ourselves, however; we must mobilize the entire nation—not simply the military, but the industrial and civilian forces as well—all of which takes integrated planning, coordinated policy-making, and joint implementation. The President counts on the National Security Council to assist him in this difficult and complicated function.

The National Security Council is not an operating agency. It does not put any program into action; it meets only to formulate plans and to develop policies for presidential decision. President Eisenhower created the Operations Coordinating Board in 1953 to obtain coordinated implementation of the plans agreed upon in the NSC. Since President Kennedy objected to the many interdepartmental committees that had characterized the previous administration, he abolished the OCB with the explanation that he preferred to maintain direct communications with the responsible agencies "so that every one will know what I have decided."

Each President is free to use the National Security Council in the manner he finds most suitable and helpful. He is solely responsible for determining what policy matters will be brought before the Council and how they will be handled. President Kennedy chose not to meet with the Council in full session as often or regularly as did President Eisenhower. He did, however, use it for discussion of basic national policy toward a number of countries. And he sought its advice on particularly pressing decisions as well as on long-term policies. When President Johnson took office, he was inclined to call Council meetings more frequently [48] though, in part, this must be attributed to mounting crises in Africa and Asia.

The Office of Emergency Planning has gone through various statutory and administrative reorganizations. Under the Eisenhower Administration, its activities covered all aspects of civil defense and defense mobilization. Its director advised the President on how to coordinate all plans for military, industrial, and civilian mobilization. In the face of mounting international tensions, President Kennedy directed that responsibility for civil defense be transferred to the Department of Defense. Thus a civilian office in the Pentagon is now responsible for our defense preparations in such matters as health, food, manpower, and transportation. The OCDM was reconstituted as a small staff agency in the Executive Office of the President.

The Director of the Office of Emergency Planning develops over-all plans and guidelines for the national non-military defense effort. He prepares for the stabilization of the civilian economy in an emergency and plans for rehabilitation after enemy attack. Part of his preparedness operations includes determination of what kinds and quantities of strategic and critical materials must be acquired and stocked against war emergency. He is also responsible for policy standards and policy direction of the National Communications System. An Assistant Director in OEP serves as Special Assistant to the President for Telecommunications and also assists the State Department in international communications policies.

President Eisenhower, prompted by the launching of the first Sputnik, established the post of Special Assistant to the President for Science and Technology. President Kennedy upgraded the post by creating *The Office of Science and Technology*. The Director is charged with evaluating and coordinating the major policies, plans, and programs of science and technology throughout the national government and with giving them appropriate emphasis in American foreign policy and national security efforts. The Office also provides liaison between the governmental and non-governmental communities in science and engineering.

Senator Jackson's Subcommittee on Organizing for National Security, at the outset of the Kennedy Administration, strongly urged the establishment of the Office of Science and Technology in the Executive Office of the President to counteract what it considered the inevitable parochialism of scientific counsel in the government. The range of scientific and technical activities in modern government is immense, "It goes from space to sonar, from microbiology to meteorology, from symbolic logic to systems engineering." No one person in the government can begin to comprehend the whole spectrum of specialized knowledge, and yet the President as chief executive must view the national policies in the round.

---

[48] Senator Jackson's Subcommittee on *Organizing for National Security* focused much of its investigation on the role of the National Security Council. Its published study (*op. cit.*), including testimony from a variety of high officials from the Truman, Eisenhower, and Kennedy Administrations, as well as staff papers from the Committee, is a goldmine of information, observations, and critical insights. For further discussion of the policy process and policy output relating to national security, see Chapter 15 in this text.

Just as he tempers economic and military advice with over-all political considerations, so also must he keep the advance of science and technology within the context of national needs and national goals. Thus the role of the Office of Science and Technology is akin to the Role of the Council of Economic Advisers or the *National Aeronautics and Space Council* (the title of the NASC explains its functions). Each helps the President to organize highly specialized activities within an institutional framework designed to operate in the national interest, and to achieve the goals of "the great society."

Presidential Succession

The Vice-President

The Constitution provides that in case of the removal of the President from office, or of his death, resignation, or inability to discharge the powers of his office, "the same shall devolve on the *Vice-President.*" The Vice-President must meet the constitutional qualifications for the presidential office: he must be a native-born citizen, at least 35 years old, and a resident of the United States for 14 years. He may not be from the same state as the President. Both are formally chosen by the electoral colleges in separate balloting, or—if no one receives a majority of the electoral vote—by one of the houses of Congress.

In the process of nominating candidates, however, each national convention concentrates on the presidential candidate. The vice-presidential candidate is quite frankly chosen to "balance" the presidential ticket. In effect, this means that whatever the political qualifications of the presidential candidate, the Vice-President's are usually the opposite. If the President comes from the liberal, urban East, it is good politics to choose his running mate from the conservative, rural South—Kennedy vis-à-vis Johnson. If the President moves ahead of his party, his Vice-President should be a solid party man—Roosevelt vis-à-vis Truman. If the President is a senior statesman, his Vice-President should be a rising young politician—Eisenhower vis-à-vis Nixon. Although the balanced ticket is demanded by campaign strategy, it can have serious and even tragic consequences (as when Johnson succeeded Lincoln), if the Vice-President is called on to fill out the President's term.

The tragedy of Dallas, Texas, on November 22, 1963, reminds us how important it is for the nation to choose its vice-presidents with the same seriousness that it considers the presidential candidates. A Vice-President has succeeded to the presidency eight times in American history; the eight presidents who died in office served less than eight of the 32 years for which they had been elected. Fortunately, Lyndon B. Johnson, who had been a contender in his own right for the presidential nomination in 1960, was eminently qualified to take over the presidential office and was wholly committed to the fulfillment of the Kennedy program. But, for the very reason that he knew from first-hand experience the enormous difficulties that face a Vice-President suddenly called to fill the top post, President Johnson was not beguiled by the usual political advice to choose an "opposite" that would balance the Democratic ticket in 1964. He personally selected Hubert Humphrey, who had also campaigned for the presidency in 1960. In an unprecedented move in American politics, the President appeared in person before the Democratic Convention in Atlantic City to announce that Humphrey was his choice for Vice-President. Declaring that Humphrey's experience as a legislator and administrator was marked with excellence and achievement, the President said "I will feel strengthened knowing that he is at my side at all times in the great work of your country and your government. . . . This is not a sectional choice, a way to balance the ticket. This is simply the best man in America for the job."

In earlier years, the position of the Vice-President has been mostly titular.[49] The Constitution provides that he shall preside over the Senate, but allows him to vote only to break a tie. As moderator in the Senate, he merely keeps parliamentary order and may not exercise his political influence overtly. The *United States Government Organization Manual*, which describes the important officers and agencies of the federal government, has no separate write-up for the Vice-President.

President Truman, who served as Vice-President for less than three months of Roosevelt's fourth term, points out in his *Memoirs* one of the practical reasons for the anomalous position of the Vice-President. As President of the Senate, he is in between the legislative branch and the executive branch, responsible to neither, nor trusted by either. Senators rarely consult him on legislative matters; they may be outwardly friendly to him, but they do not admit him to the senatorial club. On the other hand, the President may not feel free to discuss confidential executive matters with him lest they be leaked prematurely to the congressmen with whom the Vice-President is in daily contact. Moreover, the very qualifications that made the Vice-President a good "running-mate" precluded close personal relations; Roosevelt could be cordial to Truman but not friendly.

In recent years, the Vice-President, through the invitation of the President, has begun to acquire some political status in the administration. Luckily, President Warren G. Harding had invited his Vice-President to sit in on cabinet meetings, an experience that served Calvin Coolidge well when he had to take over the President's office in mid-term. Vice-President Charles G. Dawes refused a similar invitation from Coolidge, on the ground that he did not want to establish a precedent that might be embarrassing to subsequent administrations. President Franklin D. Roosevelt devised a much more substantial role for Henry A. Wallace by naming him chairman or member of various defense agencies. Roosevelt also renewed the practice of inviting the Vice-President to sit in on cabinet meetings: Garner, Wallace, and Truman, in turn. As Truman ruefully remarked in his *Memoirs*, however, these cabinet meetings were rather formal exercises;

---

[49] See Irving G. Williams, *The Rise of the Vice-Presidency* (Washington, D.C.: Public Affairs Press, 1956). This excellent monograph by Professor Williams of St. Johns University traces the history of the Vice-President, with a running account of the personalities that have filled the office and an analysis of their political activities in that office.

Roosevelt preferred to consult his department heads individually before or after the meetings.

President Eisenhower deliberately built up the stature of his Vice-President. More conscious of the possibility of succession than his predecessors had been, probably because of his advancing age and severe illnesses, he took every opportunity to point to Nixon as "the most valuable man on my team." During Truman's Administration, the Vice-President was made a member of the National Security Council, but in the President's absence the Secretary of State presided. Eisenhower changed this to have the Vice-President preside in the absence of the President. Eisenhower also directed that cabinet meetings be held on schedule, with the Vice-President presiding, if the President could not attend. As Vice-President, Nixon was not only political spokesman and personal representative of the President in domestic politics; he also acted as the President's agent of good will in foreign affairs, making extended trips out of the country.

Vice-President Johnson profited by the more active role that Nixon enjoyed in the Eisenhower Administration. Johnson also attended cabinet and National Security Council meetings and was a bona fide member of the presidential community of policy advisers. He, too, served as a sort of roving ambassador on a number of trips abroad and undertook a number of special assignments on the domestic frontier, none more significant than his appointment to head the President's Committee on Equal Employment Opportunities. In the work of this Committee, he came to meet personally a cross-section of businessmen, bureaucrats, and civil rights leaders, an experience that paid off politically in the campaign of 1964.

Provisions for Succession

There is some academic debate whether the Vice-President actually succeeds to the office of the President or merely serves as acting President in the event of the President's disability. Eight presidents have died in office, however, and in every instance the Vice-President has succeeded to the office of the President. Thus David Fellman, an outstanding scholar of American constitutional law, remarks: "Custom has established the proposition that when a President dies the Vice-President becomes President." [50] The custom dates back to the "succession" of Vice-President John Tyler on the death of President William Henry Harrison in April, 1841, just one month after his inauguration. Refusing to consider himself as Acting President, Tyler boldly declared in his own "inaugural address" that he had been called to "the high office of President of this Confederacy." At the time, many felt that Tyler's reading of the Constitution was in error, but Congress accepted Tyler's interpretation.

Following the Tyler precedent, seven Vice-Presidents have succeeded to the presidency. Millard Fillmore took over more than half of Zachary Taylor's term; Andrew Johnson all but a month of Lincoln's second term; Chester Arthur

---

[50] House Committee Print, Committee on the Judiciary, *Presidential Inability*, 84th Cong. 2d sess., January 31, 1956. (David Fellman's reply to Congressman Emanuel Celler, Chairman, House Committee on the Judiciary.)

nearly the whole of Garfield's term; Theodore Roosevelt more than three years of McKinley's second term; Calvin Coolidge nearly half of Harding's; Truman nearly all of Roosevelt's fourth term; Johnson the last year of Kennedy's term. Corwin concludes that "Tyler's exploit . . . must today be regarded as having become law of the land for those instances in which the President, through death, resignation, removal, or other cause, has disappeared from the scene." [51] Thus where the Constitution is imprecise, time and habit provide interpretation of its meaning.

The Constitution empowers Congress to provide by statute for the exercise of presidential power when neither the President nor the Vice-President can act. When Vice-President Truman became President, he realized that the Presidential Succession Act of 1886 put the Secretary of State next in line to succeed him, followed by the cabinet officers in the order in which their respective departments had been created. But he felt it was a poor principle that permitted the President to appoint his own successor. In his opinion, the Speaker of the House was a better choice than the Secretary of State. Not only is the Speaker elected by the people of his district but by a majority of the representatives from all the districts. Following the Truman recommendation in 1947, Congress established a new order of precedence in the Presidential Succession Act: Speaker of the House, President pro tempore of the Senate, and then the members of the Cabinet in order of established rank.

The precarious state of President Eisenhower's health even in his first term focused attention on the problem of what would happen if a President is not removed from office but is nevertheless too incapacitated to perform his duties. There is no doubt, for example, that for nearly two years President Wilson was unable to meet the responsibilities of his office; yet he would not or could not designate anyone to act for him. In January, 1956, President Eisenhower asked his Attorney General to study the problem of a President's "inability to act." In April, 1957, on the basis of the Attorney General's report, the President recommended a constitutional amendment designed to meet two types of presidential inability. First, if the President should become unable to act, and so declared in writing, then the Vice-President would become acting President for the duration of the inability. Whenever the President declared his ability to act again, he would resume the powers and duties of his office. Second, if a President should be unable or unwilling to declare his own inability, then the Vice-President, with the written approval of a majority of those cabinet members who were department heads, would take over the duties and powers of the office until the President's disability was terminated. In either case, the President would resume the powers and duties of his office whenever he declared that his disability had ceased.

President Eisenhower's proposals caused a furor in the public press. Rumors immediately sprang up that the President was planning to abdicate in favor of Nixon. Congress itself regarded the recommendations coldly, and gave them

[51] Corwin, *The President*, p. 54.

short shrift. But the fact that Congress did not take action on President Eisenhower's proposals for meeting the problem of "presidential inability" does not mean that no problem exists.[52] Those of us who watched on television (or followed the press stories with photographs) are not likely to forget the picture of President Johnson making his first address to the joint session of Congress. As he tried to allay the fears of the nation—and the world—the President spoke firmly, courageously. But, immediately in the background sat the two ancient congressmen who were in direct line of succession if anything should happen to the new President. And we were all aware that President Johnson had himself suffered a severe heart attack some years earlier. The Speaker of the House of Representatives was then 75 years old; the President Pro Tempore of the Senate was 87—and there they sat, two gaunt spectres, "a single heartbeat away from the presidency."

Custom provides for the immediate succession of the Vice-President in the event of the President's death, but there is no precedent for the situation of "temporary inability." Most students of constitutional law seem agreed that, if the President is physically or mentally incapacitated, or captured by the enemy, the Vice-President on his own authority may take over the powers and duties of the presidential office. But who determines whether the President is incapacitated? And who decides if and when the President is able to resume his post? Woodrow Wilson was apparently unable to perform his presidential duties from September, 1919, to March, 1921, a crucial period in American history, especially in foreign affairs. During most of this period, he was unable to meet with his cabinet, to pass on important acts of Congress, to receive foreign ministers, or to meet his presidential obligations generally. And yet Vice-President Thomas Marshall was reluctant to assume presidential powers lest such action be construed as personal disloyalty to Wilson. When President Eisenhower was twice disabled by long illness, Sherman Adams as Assistant to the President rather than Richard Nixon as Vice-President assumed major responsibility for executive decisions.

President Kennedy and Vice-President Johnson made an informal agreement patterned on the one between Eisenhower and Nixon. President Johnson, in his turn, made an arrangement with Speaker John McCormack. In essence these provided: In the event of inability the President would, if possible, so inform the Vice-President, and the Vice-President would then serve as acting President until the inability was ended. In the event of an inability which would prevent the President from communicating with the Vice-President, the Vice-President would, after appropriate consultation, perform the duties and meet the responsibilities of the President, until the inability was ended. In either event, the President would determine when the inability had ended and would then resume his full powers as President. Since the assassination of President Kennedy, many constitutional

---

[52] For many different opinions on the issue of presidential succession and presidential inability, see the prints of the House Committee on the Judiciary: *Presidential Inability*, 84th Cong., 2d sess., January 31, 1956; *Presidential Inability* (An Analysis of Replies to a Questionnaire and Testimony at a Hearing on Presidential Inability), 85th Cong., 1st sess., March 26, 1957; *Hearing on Presidential Inability*, 85th Cong., 1st sess., April 1, 1957.

amendments have been proposed, including an elaborate one from the American Bar Association, but so far no official action has been taken. No doubt, however, the status of Vice-President and the problem of presidential succession, in the event of death or inability, is now treated more seriously by students of American government.

CHAPTER ELEVEN

The

Bureaucrats

A long-time student of comparative government, Carl Friedrich, reminds us, in a discerning observation, that public administration is the core of modern democratic government: "All realistic study of government has to start with an understanding of bureaucracy (or whatever else one prefers to call it) because no government can function without it." [1] The elected representatives set forth the ground rules for public policy, but professional administrators in day-to-day decisions determine the courses of public action. Governmental bureaucracy is organized to administer the public business, but it is more than administrative machinery. Such terms as "the executive establishment" and "the national administration" have an abstract sound to them but actually they refer to the many people, public employees, engaged in all different kinds of jobs that comprise the government at work—the mail carrier, the food inspector, the nuclear scientist, the budget analyst, the foreign service officer, and so on.[2]

The Nature of the American Bureaucracy

The Bureaucratic Model

Bureaucracy is the unavoidable consequence of bigness in our modern society. Any big organization, whether it is a big business, a big church, a big labor union, or a big government, is bureaucratic. Modern government, responsive to welfare and security needs in domestic and foreign affairs, calls for extensive public administration. A great many employees, brought together in large organizations designed to turn policies into programs, automatically constitute a bureaucracy.

Max Weber, a German economist in the early twentieth century, constructed an ideal model of governmental bureaucracy.[3] Since Weber's model serves as the basis for many studies in public administration, it may be helpful for our subsequent analysis of the American bureaucracy to indicate here the classic outlines of his bureaucratic model.

1. *Hierarchy.* The offices of government are rationally arranged in reference to each other, with lines of authority clearly drawn from apex to base, each lower office being under the constant supervision of a higher office.

2. *Position Classification.* The organization is based on a rational division of labor; every office and each position are assigned the legal authority necessary to fill their specified functions and tasks.

3. *Formal Framework.* Rules and regulations are formulated; records are written and filed; to obtain machine-like efficiency, the organization is made as neutral and depersonalized as possible.

4. *Professional Management.* An administrative class is developed, with special competencies and technical skills, to meet the qualifications required for the various positions. Bureaucracy becomes a career; entrance is by competitive examination and promotion is by merit.

---

[1] Carl J. Friedrich, *Constitutional Government and Democracy* (Boston: Ginn and Company, rev. ed., 1950), p. 57.

[2] For detailed analysis see Charles Hyneman, *Bureaucracy in a Democracy* (New York: Harper & Brothers, 1950).

[3] Max Weber, *From Max Weber: Essays in Sociology*, trans. and ed. by H. H. Gerth and C. W. Mills (New York: Oxford University Press, 1946).

Weber's model of bureaucracy was conditioned by his knowledge of European systems, which developed out of army and church organizations. Weber's concept, however, does not exactly fit the American bureaucracy. The American government expanded so fast that, like Topsy, it just "growed"; and despite recurrent reorganizations, the lines of authority blur, and functions continue to overlap from office to office. Public administration in the United States has always been touched by personal and partisan considerations. And, as we shall see later, the American bureaucracy was created largely in response to the pressure politics of interest groups seeking favors from the government. The administrative class on which Weber counted for professional management and special competency did not develop in the American civil service. Careers in the public service have never been as respected in the United States as in European countries. Weber visualized a closed career service with entrance only at the base of the administrative hierarchy. In the American system, experience in private employment can count as qualification for appointment to positions at almost any level, right up to the top.[4]

Growth of the American Bureaucracy

"That government is best which governs least" is one of the most persistent maxims in American history. And yet from the very outset American government has expanded continuously and at a steadily accelerating rate, until today its activities and services pervade the daily life of every citizen. Take, for example, the power to coin money and regulate the value thereof. Can you imagine the modern economy without the benefit of government-issued currency? The Constitution prohibits the issuance of paper money by the states. Can you visualize the confusion in the business community with different kinds of money in each of the 50 states? Providing a national currency that will serve as a relatively stable medium of exchange involves a great many governmental activities, including controls of credit and regulation of banking. Along with the power to fix the value of money, the Constitution empowers the national government to establish uniform weights and measures. This constitutional prescription of standard physical measurements underlies nearly all American industry and commerce, technology and science. Next time you go shopping, notice how many items show the marks of government standardization: men's shirts, women's dresses, automobile tires, bed sheets, canned goods, nuts and bolts, electric light bulbs, TV tubes, children's shoes—all these, and many more, come in sizes as standard as pints, pounds, and yards.

The powers actually delegated by the Constitution to the national government seem modest enough, and there have been few additions to the original list. But to set down what are regarded as the "necessary and proper" functions of our national government today would be a herculean job. Under its power to reg-

---

[4] For a brief discussion of Weber's ideal construct and its application to American bureaucracy, see John M. Pfiffner and Robert V. Presthus, *Public Administration* (New York: The Ronald Press Company, rev. ed., 1960), Ch. 3.

ulate "commerce among the states," the national government has assumed almost countless tasks—fixing rates in interstate transportation, regulating the stock markets, preventing unfair trade practices, protecting labor unions, prohibiting child labor, supporting farm prices, fixing agricultural marketing quotas, licensing radio and television stations, enforcing anti-trust laws, requiring safety devices on trains, trucks, buses, and airplanes, and forbidding the transportation in interstate commerce of lottery tickets and women for immoral purposes.

National security, military defense, diplomatic activities, foreign aid, stockpiling strategic materials, social security, public assistance for the needy, old-age and survivors' insurance, veterans' benefits, atomic research, public health measures, medical research, regulation of banking, control of credit, hydroelectric development, flood control, postal service, park services, crime prevention, administration of justice, and aids for highway construction, housing, slum clearance, disaster relief, and hospital construction—these are only a few of the activities and services now undertaken by our national government—in extension of its enumerated powers.

The national administration is organized to do many different kinds of jobs for the American people. The governmental organization varies in pattern and grows in size, in response to changing and enlarging public needs. Some Americans say, as former President Hoover once did, that the national bureaucracy is "immensely too big." But the reasons for big government today are plain enough. The extension of our national boundaries from Maine to Hawaii, Alaska to Florida, and the growth of population from under 4 million to nearly 200 million; these two factors, without any other complications, would account for a tremendous expansion in the scope of American government. There are, however, many complications in the democratic government of a modern pluralistic society.

The Industrial Revolution and phenomenal developments in technology since 1787 have caused massive changes in the social and economic life of the nation. In this new environment—urban, industrial, vastly impersonal—the individual has often been described as alone and helpless in the crowd. But individuals join in groups, and in groups they bring pressures upon the government to promote their various interests and to regulate areas of conflict. In Chapter 7 we noted some of the techniques of the many interest groups active in American politics. The mushrooming bureaucracy of the modern state is in large measure the direct result of government's attempts to accommodate such private group pressures. The Departments of Agriculture, Commerce, and Labor are impressive examples of governmental agencies established at the behest of large organized groups within the general public. The causal link between technological development and governmental expansion is obvious in the creation of such regulatory agencies as the Federal Power Commission, the Federal Communications Commission, and the National Aeronautics and Space Administration.

The development of the service state accounts for many governmental activities and hence much bureaucracy. The maintenance of national security in the nuclear age has concentrated a great deal of power in the bureaucracy. In domestic affairs, we expect our elected representatives to lay the ground rules for national policies; the bureaucracy administers what the President and Congress deem necessary and proper. The pressures in international policies are more unpredictable; they stem from events and conditions over which our country has little control. The more involved we become in the affairs of the world, the more urgent it is that the bureaucrats in the areas of national security be qualified to meet uncertain contingencies. Thus, in international affairs, we feel more secure when the professional bureaucrats—the military specialists, the atomic scientists, the professional economists, and the trained diplomats—make the strategic decisions in foreign policy and national defense.

"The Most Gigantic Business on Earth"

Nearly 2.5 million persons make up the federal bureaucracy. In 1800, the government employed only about 5,000 persons and spent less than $6 million to carry on its activities. In 1932, President Hoover's administration employed approximately 600,000 persons; urging economy in that year of depression, the President recommended an over-all expenditure of less than $4 billion. The greatest expansion in American government took place between the Hoover and Eisenhower administrations—the years of the New Deal, World War II, the Fair Deal, and the Korean War.

Democratic presidents held office between 1932 and 1952, but we cannot fairly attribute the overwhelming change in our national government to twenty years of Democratic party rule. Whether the President is Democratic or Republican, he will head a big government. President Eisenhower's budget at the beginning of his second administration was the highest peacetime budget in our history—about nine times higher than the biggest New Deal budget before World War II and twice as high as Truman's Fair Deal budget just before the Korean War. President Kennedy revised his predecessor's budget upwards by more than $4 billion just three months after he went to the White House. President Eisenhower had estimated spending to be $80.9 billion in 1962; Kennedy refigured it to be $84.3 billion. President Johnson's "austere" budget, which he had to prepare immediately on taking office in November 1963, was set at $97.9 billion.

The figures on public finances must be read in perspective, however.[5] The growth in population alone accounts for a considerable increase in demands for expenditures. In 1940, the population of the country was 133 million; in 1964 the population had increased to 193 million. Moreover, changes in the composition of the population considerably affect the demands for government services. The

---

[5] *The Budget of the United States Government* includes "historical tables." The data here are taken from *The Budget in Brief 1965*. Notice the timing of budgets. The *1965 Budget* was virtually complete at the time of President Kennedy's assassination although President Johnson did rework it and make some reductions. The "1965 Budget" was presented to Congress in January 1964 to cover the fiscal year July 1, 1964 to June 30, 1965.

"Testing—one billion . . . two billion . . . three billion. . . ."

proportion of people in urban areas increased from approximately 56 per cent in 1940 to about 70 per cent in 1964. And urban areas need more public services. The proportion of persons below 18 and over 64— the age groups that normally expect government benefits, whether for education or medicare—increased from 37 per cent of the population in 1940 to over 46 per cent in 1964. Changes in the American way of living also affect governmental costs. Americans today are not only more numerous but also more mobile, and for much of their mobility they count on governmental facilities. In 1940, about 32 million motor vehicles were registered in the United States; in 1962 there were 79 million. Obviously there is great pressure to expand the interstate highway system as well as mass transit in the urban areas. From 32,000 in 1940 airway mileage jumped to over 137,000 in 1962, which necessitated new airports and longer runways to handle jets. But population growth and social changes only partly explain zooming federal expenditures. In 1964, more than half the federal budget was allocated to the military establishment, nuclear power, the space program, international affairs, and foreign aid (especially for the developing areas of the world). In 1940 Americans were still fairly isolationist, determined to stay out of World War II; no mushroom clouds had yet been seen in any sky and the "rockets' red glare" was still only a line from "The Star Spangled Banner."

One point needs further clarification. With all the increase in federal expenditures to cover a tremendous expansion in governmental activities, the number of persons on the federal payroll has scarcely increased. In 1942, just after we entered World War II, approximately 2.3 million civilians were employed in the federal government. The figure rose to 3.7 million at the peak of wartime employment in 1945, but with the cessation of hostilities civilian employment was cut back to about where it was before the war. Ostensibly, there are fewer persons in the federal service today than there were during the first year of the Eisenhower Administration. But statistics on federal employment can be quite misleading. Actually the federal government now contracts for the services of many people outside the official establishment to perform what are essentially governmental activities. Accurate figures are hard to come by. According to one estimate, some 6 million persons are at work indirectly for the national government, which pays them through contracts, grants, and other arrangements.[6] One must also add some 3 million more men and women in the armed services, many of whom are assigned duties which might normally be performed by civil servants.

If, as we have indicated, the expansion of governmental activities is in response to new needs and increasing demands in American society, if the bureaucracy is organized to serve the people, to administer the public business efficiently and impartially, why does the specter of bureaucracy haunt American politics? Why do so many Americans use the word "bureaucratic" as a term of derision? What they are usually criticizing is not so much the employment of many people to get complicated jobs done, but the "red tape," the fixed rules, the impersonal quality of bureaucracy. If we look a little deeper, however, perhaps we can appreciate the important function that the established procedures of bureaucracy perform for us. True, the individual income tax collector or department store clerk is so bound by "red tape" that he cannot show his human kindness by dealing with you in a purely personal fashion. If you explain to him that you were just robbed of your month's wages, for example, he cannot show his sympathy by reducing your taxes or the charge for your purchase. If he were caught doing so by his bureaucratic superiors, he would be fired. On the other hand, fixed procedures protect you against the capricious and arbitrary decisions of a bureaucrat who may dislike you at sight, or simply be ill-natured. We may regret that he is not free to do us a favor, but we enjoy the assurance that he is equally unable to mistreat us.

The routine procedures of bureaucracy are necessary to insure that the decisions of those in power will be made on relevant grounds and that they will be reasonably predictable, fair, and impartial. In a small organization like a corner grocery, the owner-manager may make exceptions on a personal basis—charging less to relatives, members of his church, or anyone who strikes his fancy. But a modern supermarket is too complicated an organization to operate in such a haphazard fashion; the store manager and the sales clerks are as rigidly bound as their fellow bureaucrats in the government. The standardized procedures of bureaucracy are thus a way of trying to attain, in a large-scale organization, the ideal of fair and equal treatment for all.

---

[6] Franklin P. Kilpatrick, Milton C. Cummings, Jr., M. Kent Jennings, *The Image of the Federal Service* (Washington, D.C.: The Brookings Institution, 1964), p. 40.

The Hoover Commission in 1949 made an imposing report with many recommendations for improving the general management of the executive branch. The Commission was a bipartisan, six-man group under the chairmanship of former President Hoover, assisted by special research committees, called task forces. The Hoover Commission was officially named "The Commission on Organization of the Executive Branch of the Government." It was said at the time that Congress avoided the term "reorganization" because it recognized that the executive branch had *never* been organized. It was not organized in George Washington's day, nor in the time of Andrew Jackson. Presidents Taft, Wilson, Hoover, Roosevelt, and Truman had all tackled the job of organization, but none had really been successful.

The Hoover Commission reported in 1949 that the executive branch was "a chaos of bureaus and subdivisions." The commissioners were appalled by the number of separate agencies, the proliferation of programs, and the lack of uniformity in structure, methods, and procedures. Great confusion existed within the departments and agencies as well as in their relations to the President and to one another. The commissioners searched in vain for clear lines of authority and responsibility. They could find no common conception of the organization, functions, or mission of an executive department. They were disturbed by the various degrees of congressional control over departmental organization and management. Approximately a third of the bureau chiefs were appointed by the President with the consent of the Senate. In some instances the lack of coordination within departments was the direct result of congressional specifications on organization. Of all the departments and agencies that were operating field services, only in the Veterans Administration had field workers developed a clear line of communications with the national offices, "and there was some question whether this was working effectively." Most of the departments were weak in "top management"; department heads were in desperate need of more assistance in policy-planning, programming, and public relations.

Although the findings of the Commission and its numerous research committees appear to be entirely factual, we must be careful to interpret them within the Commission's particular frame of reference, which assumed that efficiency and economy are the paramount goals of government. The Commission endorsed centralization of responsibility, unitary organization, uniform procedures, integration of field services, and top management programming. Not all students of public administration, however, are so convinced that these principles are the *sine qua non* for good government.[7] Efficiency and economy may not always pro-

---

[7] The Hoover Commission Reports are available in 19 separate pamphlets printed by the Government Printing Office since 1949. The 19th summarizes and indexes the earlier pamphlets. It is entitled *Concluding Report: A Report to the Congress by the Commission on Organization of the Executive Branch of the Government* (Washington, D.C.: Government Printing Office, 1949). The reports of the research committees have also been printed by the Government Printing Office, designated as "Task Force Reports." For various views on administrative organization and behavior, the following books are

duce "the greatest good for the greatest number," as attested by Mussolini's corporate state in fascist Italy.

When Hoover made his second report in 1955, he estimated that the First Commission had "succeeded in about 70 per cent of its recommendations but it took six years." True, many of the Commission's specific proposals have been acted on in reorganizations of the national administration, but the over-all picture has not changed appreciably. The government is growing bigger every year and its operations are becoming more complicated. In its 1949 report, the Commission was horrified by an annual budget of $42 billion, a civil service of 2,100,-000 persons, an intricate structure of over 1,800 departments, bureaus, sections, divisions, agencies. The operating budget in 1964 was more than twice as high, many bureaus and divisions had been added to the sprawling organization, and nearly a quarter-million more persons had been put on the payroll.

A Democratic and Responsible Bureaucracy

Although the American bureaucracy is enormously big and exceedingly complicated, on the whole it is a democratic and responsible organization, dedicated to the public interest. When Tocqueville visited America in the 1830's, he was struck by the fact that "public officers in the United States are not separate from the mass of citizens. . . . No public officer in the United States has an official costume, but every one of them receives a salary." From this rather simple point of view, the American civil service is still quite democratic. American officials wear no uniforms; they form no separate class; they enjoy no special privileges or immunities; they may move freely into and out of public employment. The civil service is a classified service: positions are classified according to their degrees of responsibility and difficulty. Compensation, based on this classification, follows the general principle of "equal pay for equal work." Under a merit system, a civil servant may move steadily up the ladder of promotions. The service is open to all citizens without regard to sex, race, religion, economic status, or other distinction. Tocqueville thought it important in a democracy that everyone be paid for public services "so that everyone has not merely a right, but also the means of performing them." [8] The pay schedules for the national civil service are relatively good today, so that a person need not have an independent income to enter government work.

---

useful: Herbert Simon *et al.*, *Public Administration* (New York: Alfred A. Knopf, 1950); John M. Pfiffner and Robert V. Presthus, *Public Administration*; Leonard D. White, *Introduction to the Study of Public Administration* (New York: The Macmillan Company, 1955); Charles S. Hyneman, *Bureaucracy in a Democracy*; Marshall E. Dimock and Gladys O. Dimock, *Public Administration* (New York: Holt, Rinehart and Winston, Inc., 1964), 3rd ed.; Sidney Mailick and Edward H. Van Ness (eds.), *Concepts and Issues in Administrative Behavior* (Englewood Cliffs, N.J.: Prentice-Hall, Inc., 1962).

[8] Phillips Bradley (ed.), *Democracy in America* (New York: Vintage Books, 1954), I, pp. 214–216.

The President As General Manager

Students of American politics disagree on how the President and Congress should share the direction and control of the national administration. The important fact is that our administrative officials do serve under and are accountable to our elected political leaders. In some countries, where party government is unstable and there are frequent changes in political leadership, as in France, for example, there is a tendency for the civil service to become permanently entrenched in power and to run the country unmindful of changes at the top that presumably reflect changing public opinion.

We recognize the President's role as general manager of the government when we speak of the Eisenhower Administration, the Kennedy Administration, or the Johnson Administration. Since the President appoints most of the important officials in the executive branch—many of them his close friends, all of them presumably his political supporters—he puts a personal stamp on his administration at the very outset. This personal relationship is institutionalized in the meetings of the Cabinet and the National Security Council over which the President presides; in fact, the members of these groups are commonly called "the President's official family." About sixty key officials still report personally to the President, despite recommendations by the Hoover Commission to cut this number to a more manageable number. In practice, many of these officials deal more frequently with the White House Office than with the President himself, but the administrative responsibility is still the President's. Since nearly all presidential appointees serve at his pleasure, he is able to influence their attitudes and regulate their conduct, and even to dismiss them when their views differ too sharply from his.

Through the Executive Office, the President supervises all the activities of the executive branch. Every request for appropriations and every proposal for legislation coming from any administrative agency must clear through the White House before it is channeled to Congress. Congress has given the President authority to initiate administrative reorganization. Through the *Bureau of the Budget*, he reviews the budget estimates and apportions the congressional appropriations for each agency, and he scrutinizes the organization and operation of all the agencies in order to discover what changes are needed for economy and efficiency. All these phrases so familiar in bureaucratic circles sound bloodless and impersonal to the layman. Without using the technical language of officialese, we may simply say that the President acts as a general manager for the national government.

When a President comes into office, one of his first responsibilities is to chart the main policies of his administration. He must give his supporting officers a clear conception of what his administration proposes to achieve. And he must direct the various departments and agencies of the executive branch to prepare their work programs, with estimates of expenditures, in accordance with the overall aims of the administration. When President Kennedy immediately revised President Eisenhower's budget estimates for 1961 and 1962, he was, in effect, recommending new courses of action for the national government. The most important budget increases occurred in the programs for agriculture, labor, and welfare, and for national security. And even before the first year was half over, crises in foreign affairs made it necessary for the Kennedy Administration to request (and get) still more money for the military establishment and foreign aid.

As chief executive, one of the most complicated duties of the President is to coordinate the activities of the entire bureaucracy. The preceding chapter on the presidency called attention to the several managerial agencies in the Executive Office of the President. These included the White House Office, Bureau of the Budget, Council of Economic Advisers, National Security Council, National Aeronautics and Space Council, the Office of Emergency Planning, the Office of Science and Technology, and the Office of the Special Representative for Trade Negotiations. President Eisenhower made frequent use of the National Security Council for policy coordination in foreign affairs and military defense. For top coordination, he was inclined to rely on Sherman Adams.

President Kennedy, at the outset of his administration, hoped to cut through the red tape of countless interdepartmental committees. He was frankly not interested in "organization chart thinking." He thought that staff operations should be minimized and that the President should personally assume more direct responsibility for decisions. One of his early reorganization moves was to abolish the Operations Coordinating Board that President Eisenhower had created to insure coordinated implementation of National Security Council recommendations.[9] He seldom called a Cabinet meeting—eight times in the first six months—and only occasionally met with the National Security Council. Following the Cuban fiasco, however, he began to meet regularly with the National Security Council and appointed General Maxwell Taylor to his White House Staff to coordinate military intelligence. President Johnson maintains a close working relationship with individual members of his White House Staff, but he does not meet with them as a group. Communications to the President, even from top administrators, are normally routed through the White House Staff, though White House assistants are forbidden to interfere in the internal operations of departments and agencies.

How successful was the Kennedy Administration in cutting down the red tape? *U.S. News and World Report* states that within the first hundred days the President made some effective changes inside the White House but very little headway at the operational level in the government agencies.[10] People who do business in Washington still complain that it takes dozens of signatures and weeks of time to get the simplest of wheels to turn in government. But before we judge the bureaucracy too harshly, let us keep in mind that all this paper work with counter signatures was designed to protect the public against arbitrary, capricious, or corrupt management.

---

[9] For an exhaustive study of our national policy machinery, see the reports, hearings, and studies of the Subcommittee on National Policy Machinery, Committee on Government Operations, U. S. Senate, published in three volumes under the title *Organizing for National Security*, (Washington, D.C.: Government Printing Office, 1961).

[10] *U.S. News and World Report,* May 29, 1961, pp. 53–55.

Congressional Controls over the Bureaucrats

Congress has never been willing to give the President complete control over the administration of its policies. Congress determines the functions of the government and, accordingly, Congress also determines the tasks of the bureaucracy. It may spell out the details of administration, or it may merely supply a reasonable standard or guide for the administrator and leave the details to him. In any case, Congress possesses whatever power is necessary to keep the administrators in line with legislative policy. A large part of the *U.S. Code* is devoted to congressional prescriptions of work methods and administrative procedures to be followed by the various executive agencies.[11]

In creating agencies for the administration of its laws, Congress over the years has followed no master plan. Consequently, the administrative structure today resembles a small house to which countless rooms, even whole new wings, have been added to accommodate a growing family. All the commissions that have studied the organization of the executive branch have disapproved of the rambling, ramshackle structure and have strongly recommended more functional "architecture." Presidents Roosevelt, Truman, Eisenhower, and Kennedy all proposed and obtained some "modern improvements." But Congress retains the right to look over the plans for proposed alterations.

Congress can create or abolish any administrative unit and decide whether a new unit will be established as a department, independent agency, regulatory commission, board, or corporation. Both Roosevelt and Truman tried without success to induce Congress to establish a new Department of Public Welfare in the President's Cabinet. Then Congress accepted Eisenhower's Reorganization Plan of 1953 and created the Department of Health, Education and Welfare as an executive department responsible to the President for the administration of health, education, and social security programs. President Kennedy, in the first year of his administration, asked for but failed to get a Department of Housing and Urban Affairs. President Franklin D. Roosevelt urged that independent regulatory commissions (such as the Interstate Commerce Commission or the Federal Trade Commission) be abolished and that their functions be transferred to the major executive departments directly under presidential management. But Congress rejected the proposal and subsequently set up still more independent commissions.

How frequently an administrative organization may be reorganized is illustrated in our foreign aid program. In 1948, Congress established the *Economic Cooperation Administration* to administer the European recovery program. The Administrator was given rank equal to that of the Secretary of State, with whom he was directed to work "cooperatively." In 1951, Congress abolished the Eco-

---

[11] Joseph P. Harris, *Congressional Control of Administration*, (Washington, D.C.: The Brookings Institution, 1964).

nomic Cooperation Administration and shifted its functions, considerably expanded, to a new agency, the *Mutual Security Agency*. The Director of the MSA held a position on the National Security Council equal to that of the Secretaries of State, Defense, and Treasury. Then, in 1953, the President's Reorganization Plan abolished the Mutual Security Agency and transferred its functions to the *Foreign Operations Administration*. The Director of FOA was charged with carrying on all our foreign aid programs but under policies established by the Secretaries of Defense, Treasury, and State, and with a network of interdepartmental committees to reconcile any conflicts of interest. Nominally autonomous, the Director could be fired by the Secretary of State and actually had to take orders from subordinate officials in the State Department. In 1955, the Foreign Operations Administration was abolished by executive order and its principal functions were transferred to the *International Cooperation Administration* in the Department of State. The Director of ICA was made responsible to the Secretary of State, but an executive order again created a network of interdepartmental committees to work under, through, and above the ICA.

Early in the Kennedy Administration, the President recommended the consolidation of the principal foreign aid programs in a single agency, the *Agency for International Development*. AID was established by executive order within the Department of State. Its Administrator reports directly to the Secretary of State and the President, and he is charged not only with the direction and responsibility for economic assistance programs but also with coordinating these plans with our military assistance programs. In proposing AID, President Kennedy insisted that he was not merely reshuffling and relabeling old agencies, but that he intended to make a "fresh start under new leadership." Each succeeding administration attempts to present a new image by abolishing the old agency and replacing it with a new one. Yet a fairly permanent corps of civil servants manages to transfer from one agency to the next, thus providing administrative continuity but also constituting a core of resistance to changes in routine.

Congress placed the Budget Bureau directly under the President, but kept the General Accounting Office as a congressional "watch dog" over the Treasury. The Comptroller General, who heads the GAO, is principally responsible to Congress. Whereas the President alone can hire and fire the Budget Director, the Comptroller General is appointed with the consent of the Senate and can be removed only with the consent of both houses of Congress. The GAO has broad authority over government expenditures. Every government warrant must be countersigned by the Comptroller General. No money can be paid out of the Treasury unless the Comptroller General by his countersignature certifies the legality of the expenditure. A great deal of political and academic controversy has centered around whether the GAO should play such a decisive role in administration and yet be independent of the Executive Office. The fact remains, however, that Congress does hold the purse strings, and the bureaucrats are as conscious of congressional control through the General Accounting Office as they are of presidential management through the Bureau of the Budget.

The committee system gives Congress another way of controlling the administration. Department heads may not appear on the floor of Congress to defend or promote pending legislation, but they are regularly called into the committee rooms of Congress to explain and justify their administrative programs. When, for example, the Senate Committee on Foreign Relations chooses to consider some current problem in foreign policy, it may summon the Secretary of State, the Secretary of Defense, the Chairman of the Joint Chiefs of Staff, and sometimes a whole crew of special assistants, assistant secretaries, office directors, bureau directors, and division chiefs to explain or defend their policies.

The most effective point of congressional control over the bureaucracy is in the appropriations process. The President's budget, as he submits it to Congress, is a single document. It is not only a complete financial report but also a planned program of activities for the entire executive branch. Congress, however, never debates the budget as such. In practice, each house accepts the recommendations of its appropriations committee, paying very little attention to general policy. Moreover, each appropriations committee normally accepts the bills proposed by its respective subcommittees. In effect, this piecemeal consideration of the budget vests the power of the purse in a score of small, relatively independent subcommittees.

The subcommittees on appropriations hold formal hearings at which administrative officials must appear to justify their budgets and programs. House subcommittee meetings are usually closed and Senate subcommittees open; both, however, publish transcripts so that the public can be informed. Interrogation may not be systematic, but it can be penetrating, since continuity of subcommittee membership is bound to build up familiarity with the work of the department concerned. Members may be as concerned with programs and policies as with allocation of funds. The recommendation of the subcommittee to grant the full request for one program, to deny or cut it back for another program is, in fact, a policy decision. Members of the subcommittee frequently have special interests to protect or promote. For example, congressmen from agricultural constituencies aim for an assignment to the subcommittee that deals with appropriations for the Department of Agriculture. Members on the subcommittee for the Interior Department are likely to come from such states as Arizona, New Mexico, Wyoming, California, or Nevada. Chairmen of the subcommittees usually come from safe districts, serve for long periods, and come to have a proprietary attitude (not always kindly) toward the agencies within their jurisdiction. Representative Otto Passman (D-La.), as Chairman of the Subcommittee that considers funds for foreign aid programs, is notorious for his long-time resistance to administrative requests.

Congress also makes frequent use of its power to investigate administrative agencies. There is some doubt, however, about how far Congress can go in compelling officials to give testimony or produce documents. The courts have generally upheld the congressional power of investigation as essential to the legislative function. They have never recognized any inherent right of federal officials to withhold information from Congress (or the courts). Officials in certain departments, notably State, Defense, and Justice, have successfully claimed the "privilege" of refusing to give information on the ground that disclosure might jeopardize national security.[12] Usually, however, officials cannot afford to appear unfriendly to Congress, for the consequences might be drastic. Although Congress has no effective authority to remove officials from office or to single them out for discipline, it does have the power to abolish any agency, to eliminate specific programs, and to "reduce force." Understandably, then, most administrators are eager and cooperative when they appear at committee hearings. In fact, some departments, such as State and Defense, employ special staffs to maintain constant liaison with Congress.

Summing up the relationship of the bureaucracy to the constitutional authorities is not easy. The President, as the over-all manager, may be highly influential in top-level decisions, but the great bulk of governmental business is handled administratively. Presidential direction is nominal. And the same is generally true of the congressional controls over the day-by-day administration; they are nominal, or, more likely, non-existent. Policy-making, in fact, is a complex process of group interaction within the bureaucracy. Pinning responsibility for a particular decision is almost impossible. When President Eisenhower assumed sole responsibility for the U-2 affair in 1960 and when President Kennedy did likewise for the Cuban invasion in 1961, few people really blamed the Chief Executive personally for what was obviously lack of coordination in the administration.

"Government Under Law"

If we wanted to find the bulk of federal law that governs the country today, we would go not to the *Statutes at Large* passed by Congress, but rather to the *Federal Register*, which contains the executive orders, directives, rules, and regulations adopted by the national administration. Congress enacts general policies, but more and more it leaves the details of regulation to the administrative agencies. Beginning with the Interstate Commerce Commission in 1887, Congress has established nine independent regulatory commissions, each with rule-making authority over an important segment of the American economy, and each with what are called "quasi-legislative" and "quasi-judicial" powers. The Interstate Commerce Commission, for example, has power to fix maximum rates in interstate transportation. The Securities and Exchange Commission has power to grant or refuse approval for the offering of new securities on the stock markets. Each commission fixes standards of conduct and determines what individuals may or may not do within a specialized economic area. Clearly, this constitutes quasi-legislative administration. And each commission makes rules and hands down specific orders after conducting investigations and hearings; this constitutes quasi-judicial administration.

Many of the service agencies in the national government also perform quasi-

---

[12] The staff of the House Committee on Government Operations published a useful Committee Print on this subject: *The Right of Congress to Obtain Information from the Executive and Other Agencies of the Federal Government*, 84th Cong., 2d Sess., May 3, 1956.

legislative and quasi-judicial functions. For example, the Secretary of Agriculture regulates the marketing of basic agricultural products; the Wage and Hour Division in the Department of Labor prescribes fair labor standards for industries engaged in interstate commerce; the Fish and Wild Life Service in the Department of the Interior sets forth and polices the federal hunting regulations; the Food and Drug Administration in the Department of Health, Education and Welfare regulates the processing, packaging, and labeling of foods, drugs, and cosmetics that cross interstate lines. Today a hundred or more federal agencies are making rules that have the full force of law. Although Congress neither approves nor disapproves of all this administrative law, it does require each agency to give notice of proposed rule-making so that interested parties will have an opportunity to be heard before the rule is published. It also requires the publication of statements of general policy and procedures as well as of the rules, regulations, and orders themselves. These are published day by day in the *Federal Register* and are collected and systematized in the *Code of Federal Regulations*.

Government control of the modern economic system calls for highly technical knowledge and professional experience. Consequently, the administrators, who are appointed to furnish general policy leadership, must rely heavily on specialized staffs in making rules and quasi-judicial decisions. For example, a corps of lawyers, accountants, engineers, and other specialists is required to work out a railroad schedule that will meet the Supreme Court's requirement of a "fair rate of return on the fair value of the property." Another corps of technicians and specialists is required to allocate radio frequencies, to decide which sector of the broadcast band will be allotted to television, to assign specific frequencies to individual applicants, to check whether this station or that network is complying with the rule that calls for a balanced presentation of controversial public issues.

In America, the administrative expert is not immune from ordinary law. Any citizen who believes that an administrative order or rule is unjust, discriminatory, or a denial of his legal or constitutional rights may take his case into the ordinary courts. The Administrative Procedures Act of 1946 provides for judicial review of administrative decisions. A complainant, of course, is expected to seek redress in the administrative agency before resorting to court action. The courts, to protect themselves against a flood of litigation, may refuse to review questions of fact that do not also involve questions of law or questions of statutory or constitutional authority.

In practice, however, the administrative agencies do enjoy a large measure of independence from judicial review. Because the administrator knows that his actions may be subject to judicial review, he consults continuously with the attorneys in his agency to be sure that he is acting in a legal manner. This very fact often discourages the private citizen from seeking legal redress. The great number of lawyers in the public service means that the individual has little hope of bucking the bureaucracy without high-priced legal counsel. Washington is full of lawyers who make a lucrative living by guiding clients through the procedural maze and legalistic ways of administrative agencies. But most people cannot afford the large fees of lawyers and the high costs of litigation, and the average citizen may lose rather than profit by a "rule of law" that is beyond his means.

Moreover, judicial restraint tends to favor the administration. The same reason that impelled the legislature to delegate rule-making authority makes the courts reluctant to review administrative decisions: the subject matter is often so technical that it is beyond the competence of the lay judges. Even when the courts do attempt review, they must listen to expert versus expert and then decide. Yet there is comfort in the democratic theory that no official is above the law, that all must operate within the law, and that any private citizen has the right to go to court and seek redress against arbitrary or excessive bureaucracy.

Government Services and "Special Interests"

The Hoover Commission reported to Congress in 1955 on "services, activities, and functions not necessary to the efficient conduct of government" and "nonessential services, functions, and activities which are competitive with private enterprise." To illustrate this basic theme the Commission compiled a great many data on the industrial and commercial enterprises operated by the Defense Department and by the federal civilian agencies:

> The Federal Government today operates over a hundred business-type activities. It is, among other things, the largest electric power producer in the country, the largest insurer, the largest lender and the largest borrower, the largest landlord and the largest tenant, the largest holder of grazing land, the largest holder of timberland, the largest owner of grain, the largest warehouse operator, the largest shipowner, and the largest truck-fleet operator.[13]

The Commission discovered that the military establishment owned and operated thousands of commercial and industrial facilities, employing more than half a million people, in such varied activities as laundry service, dry-cleaning, meat-cutting, coffee-roasting, bread-baking, clothing-manufacturing, shoe-manufacturing, retail-store service, and food-servicing. Outside the Defense Department, the Commission found a miscellany of big-business enterprises owned and operated by the government, such as the TVA fertilizer program, the postal savings system and parcel post service in the Post Office, the Alaska Railroad, the Virgin Island Corporation, the National Park Concessions, the Federal Prison Industries, and the Government Printing Office.

Assuming that the private enterprise system is best for the national economy, the Commission was inclined to regard government in business as "creeping socialism." So we can understand how the Commission came to the conclusion that the federal government should get out and stay out of business as much as possible. It took its political cue from President Eisenhower:

---

[13] Director of the Bureau of the Budget, A Speech to the Conference of the National Association of Bank Auditors and Comptrollers, New York City, December 7, 1954, cited by the *Commission on Organization of the Executive Branch of the Government, Subcommittee Report on Business Enterprises of the Department of Defense* (Washington, D.C.: Government Printing Office, 1955), p. 1.

To bring Government closer to the people we will set up these principles and adhere to them: that no Federal project, large or small, will be undertaken which the people can effectively do or be helped to do for themselves; that no Federal project will be undertaken which private enterprise can effectively undertake.[14]

Though the average citizen also professes to believe in private enterprise, he demands a great many public services that in 1790 were either nonexistent or left to private entrepreneurs. When the Framing Fathers traveled to the Constitutional Convention in Philadelphia, they had to stop all along the way to pay tolls for private roads, bridges, and ferries. Today American government at every level is expected to provide good roads—graded, drained, hard-surfaced, with two to six lanes, or whatever else the traffic demands. When our Constitution was written, the majority of the population was too illiterate to read it; only those who could afford to pay tuition in the private schools, "the rich and well-born," could expect to become "well educated." Today, public education is free and compulsory in every state.

Whether a business is operated under private enterprise or as a public service is determined by changing economic and political conditions, not by any static economy theory. A great social and economic revolution has totally changed the American environment since 1790—from a scattering of primitive rural communities to an urbanized industrial nation. What was good enough for our fathers is no longer good enough for our children—open wells and outdoor privies, kerosene lamps and lightning rods, vigilantes and volunteer firemen, local almshouses for the orphans, widows, aged, needy, and friendless, muddy roads and the pony express. We demand all kinds of public works—public reservoirs, sewage disposal and garbage collection, police and fire service, rural electrification and telephone service, public hospitals and public health clinics, school doctors and visiting nurses, old-age and survivors' insurance, and public assistance for the indigent.

The Hoover Commission insisted that the government ought not to operate any public business in competition with private business. But some activities can be carried on only as public services—those that are necessarily monopolistic or those that are highly desirable for the general welfare, yet too expensive or too unprofitable for private business to undertake. Moreover, when private enterprise fails to satisfy the public needs, either in terms of performance or costs, the people are likely to use their political power to get what they want out of the government.

Often, however, minority pressures rather than public opinion create the demand for government services. The federal bureaucracy is generally organized on the "functional principle"—subordinate agencies carrying on similar activities and having common objectives are grouped in a single department. But the very fact that the government is organized on a functional basis makes the bureaucrats susceptible to the influence of private groups with corresponding interests. Thus the Department of Agriculture works closely with the Farm Bureau, the Depart-

---

[14] President Dwight D. Eisenhower, in 1952, *ibid.*, p. 1.

ment of Commerce with the Chamber of Commerce, and the Department of Labor with the AFL-CIO. Indeed, the working relationship is frequently so close that a line cannot be drawn between the objectives of the public agency and the private organization. This identification of the general welfare with special interests is the more complete where there is considerable mutual membership or overlapping personnel in the public agency and the private organization. For example, members of the National Education Association are constantly in and out of the

Drawing by D. Ruge ; © 1964 The Saturday Review.

". . . and, in return, I'd be happy to vote against any further centralization of power in the hands of federal agencies."

Office of Education; members of the American Legion hold key positions in the Veterans Administration.

These personal contacts—the result of a natural affinity of interests—between the administrative agency and its private counterpart are calculated to produce agreeable working relations. Consultants, "dollar-a-year men," and semi-official advisory committees attached to many of the public agencies represent the special interests of organized groups in labor, business, and agriculture. Such pressure politics is the more difficult to check, because it is covert rather than obvious. Lobbyists who try to influence the legislative process at least receive a certain amount of publicity; but public attention is rarely focused on special interests that work to influence the administrative process.

The bureaucrat has a natural tendency to believe that his own vested interests coincide with the public interest. Any agency that develops a sense of mission and *esprit de corps* will expand its own small bailiwick into a sizable empire if given the time and opportunity. We have noted that the most obvious characteristic of our national administration is its immense size. We might also observe that many bureaucrats agree with Galbraith; social balance in "affluent" America requires increasing public service. In Chapter 14, we shall take a closer look at how administrative agencies sometimes act as pressure groups in the legislative process.

Whether or not a particular government agency serves the public interest depends on what it regards as its "public." The public is rarely if ever an organized majority with a single common interest; rather it is a changing coalition of many groups with various special interests. The administrator may think he is doing the best he can to serve the public if he simply satisfies his own clients. If, for example, the Farm Bureau is happy with the services and activities of the Department of Agriculture, the bureaucrats may assume that they have won the "consent of the governed." And yet there is a larger, inarticulate, unorganized public—the consumers—who must also be considered. The functional agencies, left entirely to themselves, tend to give all their energies to the objectives that constitute their *raison d'être*. But the private citizen has a right to expect top management to subordinate the special interests of pressure groups and the vested interests of bureaucratic agencies to the broader public interest.

Organization and Management in Government

The Constitution does not spell out how government activities should be organized and managed. It simply says that the President "may require the opinion in writing of the principal officer in each of the executive departments upon any subject relating to the duties of their respective offices." Today, however, many important federal activities are carried on outside the executive departments—in regulatory commissions, corporations, and other independent agencies.

428

The government now has ten executive departments: State (1789), Treasury (1789), Defense, (1947), Justice (1870), Post Office (1872), Interior (1849), Agriculture (1862), Commerce (1913), Labor (1913), and Health, Education and Welfare (1953). Each executive department is headed by a Secretary appointed by the President with the consent of the Senate. The ten Secretaries are recognized as the top political figures in the national administration; they are in the so-called line of succession to the presidency; they sit in the President's Cabinet; each heads a large and important operating agency; and next to the President and Vice-President, they earn the highest salaries in the administrative hierarchy.

Historically the President's Cabinet dates back to the first administration of George Washington. Washington had been snubbed when he tried to use the Senate as an advisory council, and had been rebuffed when he went to the Supreme Court for an advisory opinion. So he turned for collective advice to his principal administrative officers (the Secretary of State, the Secretary of Treasury, the Secretary of War, and the Attorney General). This was the informal beginning of the President's Cabinet. Soon it was institutionalized and given regular status, but not until the second administration of Theodore Roosevelt was it mentioned in federal law (1907). The Senate customarily confirms the President's nominations to his Cabinet, though the Senators occasionally question a nominee's qualifications, as when they questioned the business interests of Charles E. Wilson, Eisenhower's nominee for the Secretary of Defense in 1953.

Since cabinet positions are regarded as top prizes in national politics, party loyalty figures high in the appointments. Sometimes for strategic reasons, however, a President will make at least a pretense of bipartisanship, as when Franklin D. Roosevelt appointed two distinguished Republicans, Henry L. Stimson and Frank Knox, to serve in his wartime Cabinet as Secretaries of War and Navy.[15] President Eisenhower thought it good politics to recognize the "Democrats for Eisenhower" by naming a Texas Democrat, Mrs. Oveta Culp Hobby, as his first Secretary of Health, Education and Welfare.

The construction of President Kennedy's Cabinet involved a variety of political as well as personal considerations. No doubt the narrow margin of his party victory in 1960 induced the President to name two Republicans to key posts in the New Frontier—the Secretary of Treasury, Douglas Dillon, and Secretary of Defense, Robert McNamara. Though a President has a fairly free hand in the selection of his cabinet, certain demands are bound to limit his choice. It is politic, for example, to include representatives from various sections of the country; as it is politic also to recognize the major religious groups. President Kennedy planned to name a Negro as head of the proposed new Department

[15] Announcement of these "patriotic" appointments was made on the eve of the Republican National Convention in 1940. Angry Republicans cried "double cross" and demanded that Stimson and Knox be "read out of the party." On the other hand, Democratic party regulars like Jim Farley denounced the "party betrayal."

of Urban Affairs, but the refusal of Congress to establish the new department precluded this move. Designating his brother Robert as Attorney General was obviously a personal matter.[16]

On the assassination of President Kennedy, Lyndon Johnson declared that he wanted no immediate innovations in the Kennedy Administration. "President Kennedy left a program well outlined in its content; I will carry out all of the late President's commitments." To achieve this end, he felt that continuity of personnel was essential. Hence he urged all of the principal officers, including members of the Cabinet, to stay at their posts. He made the appeal partly on personal grounds but also in terms of the nation's needs.

Just how effectively the President and his Cabinet work together depends largely on their personalities. Franklin D. Roosevelt met regularly with his Cabinet, and played on rivalries among members to draw forth their conflicting views. But he never really used his Cabinet for collective policy-making. On such important matters as the "court-packing plan" and the development of the atomic bomb, he neither consulted with nor informed them in advance. President Truman introduced the device of a prepared agenda for cabinet meetings, discussed all general policies with his Cabinet, and made a point of summarizing their collective judgment. Nevertheless, he made it clear that the Cabinet must follow the direction of the President. He simply would not brook public opposition from any cabinet member. As he expressed it,

> When a cabinet member speaks publicly, he usually speaks on authorization of the President, in which case he speaks for the President. If he takes it upon himself to announce a policy that is contrary to the policy the President wants carried out, he can cause a great deal of trouble.[17]

President Eisenhower attempted to turn his Cabinet into a "political team." He established a cabinet secretariat to deal with interdepartmental affairs, circulated a prepared agenda before meetings, called for "briefs" on different points of view, tried to achieve collective decisions, and authorized the release of "major policy statements" after cabinet meetings. It does not appear, however, that this approach resulted in any greater sense of collective responsibility, for the Eisenhower Cabinet from the outset was marked by public bickering, which the Presi-

---

[16] Candidate Kennedy promised during the 1960 campaign that "all appointments, both high and low, will be made on the basis of ability." President Kennedy was criticized for appointing his younger brother Robert as Attorney General, his brother-in-law Sargent Shriver as Director of the Peace Corps, and another brother-in-law, Stephen Smith, as consultant to the Development Loan Fund. But these family appointments proved themselves on ability. And it is part of the President's prerogative to choose as his closest advisers persons whose judgment he can trust and whose personal loyalty he need never question. One remembers that President Eisenhower used his brother Milton on various confidential assignments and that he brought a number of his former military aids into the White House circle. See Marian D. Irish, "The Kennedy Administration: Appraisal at the Halfway Mark," in Jack W. Peltason (ed.), *1963-64 American Government Annual*, (New York: Holt, Rinehart & Winston, 1963), pp. 33-60.

[17] Harry S. Truman, *Memoirs* (Garden City, N.Y.: Doubleday & Company, Inc., 1955), I, 329.

dent usually tolerated with rare good humor. President Kennedy in an early TV talk to the public on how he expected to run his administration explained that he preferred to meet with individual Cabinet members on particular problems and to keep in daily contact with the separate departments. He felt that large, formal, and regular meetings were "unnecessary and involve a waste of time." [18] When President Johnson suddenly was called to take charge, he relied much more on the cabinet as an institution. Whereas Kennedy preferred dealing with cabinet members individually, Johnson found greater support in collective meetings.

The prestige enjoyed by the American Cabinet seems to spring more from political tradition and protocol than from actual power in the government. Individual Secretaries may be very important to the President, as Acheson was to Truman, Dulles to Eisenhower, and Robert Kennedy to his brother. But they have no responsibility as a group for furnishing broad political leadership. Moreover, the independent regulatory commissions and such important agencies as the Veterans Administration and the Tennessee Valley Authority are excluded from the Cabinet. President Eisenhower frequently invited to cabinet meetings such officials as the Chairman of the Civil Service Commission, the American Ambassador to the United Nations, the Director of the Budget, and the Assistant to the President, but this never became a regular practice. The Cabinet seldom gets any further than discussing interdepartmental matters; its decisions are not binding even on its own members; and neither the President nor Congress is bound to heed its "major policy statements."

Many political scientists have proposed ways of strengthening the Cabinet's role in government. Some have suggested that cabinet members be invited to sit in Congress and participate in debates that concern their particular departments. Senator Estes Kefauver long urged that Congress follow the British practice of a "question hour" in which congressmen could call on cabinet members to answer questions about the executive policies of the day. Still another suggestion is that the cabinet membership be expanded to include key congressmen who could then participate in policy discussions. The Constitution, however, forbids congressmen to hold posts in the administration.

Some political scientists have urged fundamental constitutional reforms in the relations between the executive and legislative departments to provide for real cabinet government, in which the heads of executive departments would be collectively responsible for policy decisions. W. Y. Elliott, for example, advocates that the Constitution be amended to give the President the right to designate ten to twenty of his principal department or agency heads to sit and vote in both the Senate and the House. Elliott argues that this reform would strengthen the President's prestige in Congress and "bridge the appalling gap that exists between the two ends of Pennsylvania Avenue—the White House and the Capitol." [19]

---

[18] *The New York Times*, April 12, 1961.

[19] William Y. Elliott, Chairman, *United States Foreign Policy*, Report of a Study Group for the Woodrow Wilson Foundation (New York: Columbia University Press, 1952), p. 259.

Since "separation of powers" has created separate vested interest in the executive and legislative branches, however, constitutional reform of the Cabinet seems unlikely.

Even a brief description of the organization and functions of each of the departments in the cabinet takes up some 300 pages in the *United States Government Organization Manual*. Obviously it would be pointless to try to round up this sort of readily available, currently changing, factual information here. If you are interested in how the departments operate and finance their programs, you will find the accounts of hearings before congressional appropriation committees a mine of information.

The typical pattern of organization is hierarchical, with a single administrator at the top of the pyramid. Each department carries on activities that are more or less related to a single major function. Thus the Department of State is mainly concerned with the conduct of foreign affairs, and the Department of Agriculture with the welfare of farmers. Some departments, however, perform a variety of only distantly related functions. The Department of Interior, for example, is charged with Indian affairs, the conservation and development of natural resources, and the government of the territories outside the United States.

The *State Department* is a good example of departmental organization. It is the oldest department in the national administration, having been created by the Continental Congress in 1781 and reconstituted without interruption of functions by an Act of Congress signed by President Washington in 1789. At the head is the Secretary of State, who sits in the President's Cabinet and usually acts as the President's right-hand man on all matters relating to foreign affairs. Sixty-three men have served as Secretary of State, from Thomas Jefferson in 1790 to Dean Rusk. Six of these later became President of the United States (Thomas Jefferson, James Madison, James Monroe, John Quincy Adams, Martin Van Buren, and James Buchanan); two were later appointed Chief Justice of the Supreme Court (John Marshall and Charles Evans Hughes). General George Marshall was the only non-civilian to hold the office.

The Secretary of State is responsible for all the activities of the Department (see Figure 11-1). His alter ego is the Under Secretary, who is Acting Secretary in the Secretary's absence, a frequent occurrence in this era of summit diplomacy. An Under Secretary for Political Affairs serves as principal coordinator for the regional bureaus. Five regional bureaus, each under an assistant secretary, give specialized attention to the major areas of the world: the American Republics, Europe, the Far East, the Near East and South Asia, and Africa. The regional bureaus are further subdivided into "offices" and "desks." Thus "Mister N" is on the Norway *Desk*, in the *Office* of the British Commonwealth and Northern European Affairs, in the *Bureau* of European Affairs; his job is to know all there is to know about Norway that will in any way affect our relations with that country. Other assistant secretaries, advisers, heads of missions, and administrators handle a variety of duties ranging from liaison with Congress to developing educational and cultural exchange programs. A Deputy Under Secretary for Administration is responsible for the internal management of the department.

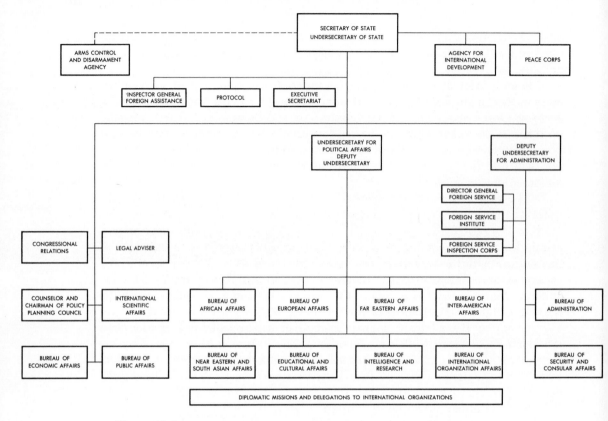

Figure 11-1

The principal officers in each of the great departments are political executives, appointed by the President with the consent of the Senate, serving at the
pleasure of the President. Such political appointments reach down to the second
and third echelons. Presumably these are the policy-makers within the Department. Below them is the permanent bureaucracy in the classified civil service.
Incoming political executives, eager to make policy changes, are likely to view
the massive and seemingly immovable bureaucracy with dismay. Like the military
conquerors of Old China, who were ultimately absorbed by the culturally im-
penetrable mass of Chinese, so the new "principal officers," especially in old-line
departments like Agriculture and Interior, inevitably discover that they can get
little done unless they work through the usual channels and adapt their ways to
the departmental mores.

On the organization charts it is relatively simple to distinguish between
political executives and career administrators. In the policy process, however,
political executives and professional bureaucrats work closely together. Moreover, as one administration draws to a close, and vacancies occur at the top of
the departmental hierarchies, the outgoing President is likely to fill the vacancies
with professional bureaucrats who forego their permanent status while holding

a political appointment. An incoming President takes his time in designating his second and third "teams," so that the career officers are generally responsible for carrying on governmental activities during presidential transitions.

In the State Department, foreign service officers, who constitute a professional corps apart from the regular civil service, do double duty representing the United States abroad and also serving at home in the departmental hierarchy. Unlike the civil servant whose rank, salary, and status depend on the specific job he holds, the foreign service officer takes his rank, salary, and status with him to whatever post he is assigned. During the period of presidential transition, when continuity in foreign policy is crucial for our international relations, distinguished foreign service officers usually command most of the top posts in the State Department. As the new administration learns to make its own way in foreign policy, foreign service officers yield to political appointees and again take their tours of duty abroad. Although the organization of a department makes a nice chart for the Appendix of the *Organization Manual*, actually the skeletal structure derives its vitality from the people who fill the specific positions. A former Secretary of State, from his own experience at the head of the hierarchy, reminds us that "the work of the Department is performed by many thousands of trained, intelligent, and devoted men and women in all parts of the world and in Washington." Commenting on the notion that "policy originates at the top and is passed down," Dean Acheson agrees that "great decisions are, for the most part, made at the top"; but he insists that, in the sum total of departmental decisions, "the springs of policy bubble up, they do not trickle down." [20]

In Chapter 15, which deals with the policy process in foreign affairs, we shall find that the "community of decision-makers" is at considerable variance with the traditional models of administrative hierarchies. When President-elect Kennedy made a point of naming an Assistant Secretary of State, an Under Secretary of State, and the Ambassador to the United Nations *before* he designated the Secretary of State, he was in effect announcing his intention of directly injecting presidential power at the second and third echelons of the Department. Each nomination was prefaced with a statement that the "post" was "second to none in importance." As President, Kennedy remained personally accessible to

---

[20] *The New York Times*, October 11, 1959. Recurrent crises in foreign affairs in the Eisenhower Administration provoked much debate in professional and political circles—how best to reorganize the State Department. The American Assembly discussed the problem from various points of view in its national meeting, October, 1960: *The Secretary of State*, The American Assembly, edited by Don K. Price (Englewood Cliffs, N.J.: Prentice-Hall, Inc., 1960).

The Senate Committee on Foreign Relations sponsored a series of 13 studies in connection with its over-all examination of U.S. foreign policy authorized by the Senate in 1958. No. 9 in the Series, "The Formulation and Administration of United States Foreign Policy," by the Brookings Institution, discusses the organizational structure and administrative procedures that are involved in the conduct of American foreign policy. The Department of State is one unit in the over-all flow of policy-making in foreign affairs. See *United States Foreign Policy Compilation of Studies*, prepared under the direction of the Committee on Foreign Relations, Senate Document No. 24, 87th Cong., 1st Sess., March 15, 1961 (Washington, D.C.: Government Printing Office).

many persons whose offices were far from the top of the administrative hierarchy; the emphasis was on personal relations rather than on bureaucratic channels. In a television interview at the end of his second year in office, the question was asked, "Is it true that during your first year, sir, you would get on the phone personally to the State Department and try to get a response to some inquiry that had been made?" The President replied, "Yes, I still do that when I can, because I think there is a great tendency in government to have papers stay on desks too long. . . . After all, the President can't administer a department, but he can at least be a stimulant." [21] President Johnson has also established a strong personal role for himself. He is more inclined, however, to stimulate the policy process at the points of formulation rather than implementation. Thus the Johnson style of administration calls for a great many phone calls to old colleagues in Congress rather than to the lesser bureaucrats.

Independent Regulatory Agencies

The *United States Government Organization Manual* lists more than 40 independent agencies that function outside the departmental organization. Some are small and obscure; others are large and powerful. In the latter category are the regulatory boards and commissions whose services and activities affect vital areas in our national economy: Interstate Commerce Commission (created 1887), Federal Reserve Board (1913), Federal Trade Commission (1915), Federal Power Commission (1920), Federal Communications Commission (1934), Securities and Exchange Commission (1934), National Labor Relations Board (1935), Civil Aeronautics Board (1938), Atomic Energy Commission (1946). All have certain features in common. All are headed by boards or commissions having from five to eleven members. All are outside the executive departments and are free from direct responsibility to the chief executive. All engage in policy-making and regulatory activities, mostly in the economic sphere. All have quasi-legislative and quasi-judicial powers. Taken together, these commissions exercise tremendous authority over transportation by railroad, bus, truck, pipeline, merchant marine, and airlines; communication by telephone, telegraphy, radio, and television; hydroelectric development, interstate electric power, water resources, flood control, and interstate transportation of natural gas; unfair trade practices in industry and commerce; unfair labor practices in labor-management relations; banking practices, credit policies, issuance of securities, and trading in the national stock markets.

Many reasons are suggested for setting up the independent regulatory commissions outside the departmental structure. Since the commissions have quasi-judicial duties, such duties can best be performed by independent and impartial persons. Also, since regulatory tasks often involve rule-making authority—quasi-legislative power which has the force of law upon business and industry—such rule-making functions should be handled by a plural body in which several points

---

[21] Louis W. Koenig, *The Chief Executive* (New York: Harcourt, Brace, & World, Inc., 1964), p. 175.

of view may find expression. A more philosophical justification stems from the concept of separation of powers; because the regulatory commission exercises judicial, legislative, and executive functions, it ought not to be put wholly under the chief executive. In the more experimental and exploratory stages of regulation, Congress has thought it wiser to create new and independent agencies in order to insure maximum leeway in the development of new procedures and standards of administration. In some fields of policy-making, where regional representation seems desirable, the plural commission rather than the departmental unit more easily secures geographical distribution of decision-makers. Many of the tasks of regulation are complicated and technical, and experienced experts are more readily recruited if they are offered freedom from political pressures and partisan control. The Interstate Commerce Commission, first of the independent commissions, was considered generally successful; this encouraged Congress to continue the pattern and to promise the regulatory commissions their "independence from politics." [22]

Actually, the independence of the regulatory commissions has been overrated. Presidential appointment of commissions is certainly not free from politics. Executive review of commission budgets and congressional control of appropriations inevitably give both the President and Congress considerable influence over the commissions. Moreover, Congress has the power of investigation, which may lead to the abolition or complete revamping of an agency, or turn the heat of pitiless publicity on individual commissioners. Finally, the courts may exercise judicial review to insure due process of law in commission procedures, and to see that the commissions do not overstep the powers delegated to them by Congress.

Experts on public administration disagree on whether or not the commissions should retain their independence. President Roosevelt's Committee on Administrative Management in 1937 referred to the commissions as "the headless fourth branch of the government," and recommended that they be integrated into the executive departments and made clearly subordinate to the chief executive. The Hoover Commission in 1949 also had many complaints about the commissions. Since the members' terms of office are longer than four years, the make-up of the commissions does not change when a new President takes office. Appointees are not always of the highest caliber, partly because of low salaries, but even more because the President may fail to realize what high qualifications are needed in a good commissioner. The commissioners are usually so busy with the immediate problems of regulation that they have no time for any long-range planning. Coordination between the commissions and the related departments is "loose and casual and sometimes non-existent." For example, the National Labor Relations Board has no close relationship to the Department of Labor, and the

---

[22] Robert E. Cushman sums up the more important reasons that led Congress to establish the commissions outside the departmental structure. See his Special Study, *The Problem of the Independent Regulatory Commissions*, in Report with Special Studies, President's Committee on Administrative Management (Washington, D.C.: 1937). A brief adaptation of the study is found in Dwight Waldo (ed.), *Ideas and Issues in Public Administration* (New York: McGraw-Hill Book Company, Inc., 1953), pp. 138–155.

Federal Trade Commission has little to do with the Department of Commerce. Despite these complaints, the Hoover Commission concluded that "the independent regulatory commissions have a proper place in the machinery of our Government." [23]

Before President Kennedy assumed office, he requested James M. Landis, former Dean of the Harvard Law School, former Chairman of the Securities and Exchange Commission, and a former Chairman of the Civil Aeronautics Board, to study the independent agencies and to make appropriate recommendations for streamlining. The Landis Report criticized the agencies more in terms of performance than of administrative structure. President Kennedy early in his Administration urged Congress to provide for greater coordination among the agencies, and for a more hierarchical pattern in the executive branch. He recommended that: the Chairman of each agency serve at the pleasure of the President; the Chairman have greater authority over his agency's budget and staff; the commissioners be able to delegate more of their work to the technical staff. He singled out the Federal Communications Commission for specific reform. But the Kennedy Administration came up against the same facts of political life that had defeated earlier efforts to bring the independent agencies into the executive hierarchy. The interest groups that are most directly affected fought to maintain the "independence" of the agencies that regulate them.

Both the Committee on Administration Management in 1937 and the Hoover Commission in 1949 were concerned with the organization through which independent commissions work. Neither tackled the really tough problem of evaluating the results achieved by the commissions. But the objectives are surely more important than the organizations through which the objectives are sought. Consideration of the commissions in this broader sense would lead to questions about the working relations between the regulators in government and the "regulated" in private life. Can the regulators be counted on to represent the public interest as vigorously as the regulated represent their own interests? Problems of this sort are settled by politics, not by organizational forms.

We have already seen that the regulatory commissions are never outside politics. The Senate has always felt free to criticize presidential nominations to the regulatory commissions. When senators hold committee hearings on appointments, they never limit themselves to discussing the technical qualifications of the nominee or his professional fitness for the job. Senators are frankly interested in the nominee's political views, his economic and social philosophy, his sympathy with the objectives of the law he is to administer, his attitude toward those whom he is to regulate. Congressional lobbyists for interest groups do everything they can to make sure that new appointments are "favorable." A glaring example of what this sort of pressure can lead to was the Senate's refusal to confirm President Truman's reappointment of Leland Olds to the Federal Power Commission

---

[23] The most useful exposition of independent regulatory commissions from an organizational standpoint is the *Task Force Report on Independent Regulatory Commissions*, prepared for the Commission on Organization of the Executive Branch of the Government, March 1949, p. 3.

in 1949. During his ten years on the Commission, Olds had bucked the public utility industry by pressing for price-fixing and federal regulation of natural gas. So the gas and oil lobby went to work on the senators to make sure that he would not serve a third term, with the result that the Senate rejected the Commissioner's reappointment.[24]

Every one of the commissions was born in a hotbed of politics and has grown up in an environment of conflicting pressure groups. "The spirit and enthusiasm of a commission depends to a large extent on the general political setting." [25] When a commission is first set up, the public always shows a lively interest in its activities. This is the period when the commission can apply public policy most vigorously because public support is at its peak. As the public interest wanes, however, the political leaders tend to relax, leaving the agency to take care of specific problems as they arise. The commissioners in turn lose their initial zeal and settle into rules of procedure that are neither too arduous nor too disagreeable to either the regulators or the regulated. "Perhaps the most marked development in a mature commission is the growth of a passivity that borders on apathy." [26] The mature commission rarely goes out looking for new business. Since initiative and enterprise only stir up controversy, the commissioners are inclined to wait for private parties to bring in new cases.

At the outset, a new commission is operating in an area where public policy is inevitably rather experimental and exploratory. The commission's "experts"— most of them lawyers, engineers, and accountants—gradually work out the rules of conduct. As Marver Bernstein points out, however, "Expertness plays into the hands of the regulated interests." [27] The preponderance of lawyers is likely to give a strong legalistic flavor to commission activities. They tend, for example, to regard the special interests who are supposed to be regulated as clients who need to be protected from governmental attack. This was the issue between President Franklin D. Roosevelt and Chairman William E. Humphrey of the Federal Trade Commission. Although the Commission was supposed to promote and enforce codes of fair competition, Humphrey was reluctant to crack down on long-time friends who failed to meet the New Deal standards.

The organization and activities of each of the regulatory agencies is outlined in the *United States Government Organization Manual.* We cannot repeat all the details here, but we can take a closer look at the National Labor Relations Board by way of illustration.

The *National Labor Relations Board* was established as an independent

---

[24] See Joseph P. Harris, "The Senatorial Rejection of Leland Olds: A Case Study," *American Political Science Review,* XLV (September, 1951), p. 674.

[25] For a realistic study of the "life cycle of regulatory commissions," see Marver H. Bernstein, *Regulating Business by Independent Commission* (Princeton: Princeton University Press, 1955), p. 83. Cornelius P. Cotter, *Government and Private Enterprise* (New York: Holt, Rinehart and Winston, 1960), treats government regulation of business in terms of policy-making and administrative processes. The emphasis is empirical, with background materials on the principal regulatory agencies.

[26] Bernstein, *Regulating Business,* p. 88.

[27] *Ibid.,* p. 118.

agency in 1935 by the Wagner Act, and was reorganized in 1947 by the Taft-Hartley Act. In these two acts, Congress established the general policy and the major functions of the agency: to assure labor the right to bargain collectively through unions of their own choosing, and to prevent unfair labor practices by either workers or their employers. The Board, appointed by the President, with consent of the Senate, consists of five members with staggered terms of five years. The General Counsel, also a presidential appointee, directs the enforcement of the law, largely through regional and field offices; the Board itself is primarily judicial, and hears the cases that arise under the law. Hearings on unfair labor practices in a particular plant or industry are ordinarily conducted by trial examiners in the regions where the unfair practices occur. After the hearing, the trial examiner issues a decision which includes his findings of fact, his conclusions, and a recommended order. Unless contested by either party, the trial examiner's recommendation takes effect as a Board order and the entire proceeding is ended. Though cases may be appealed from the regional offices to the General Counsel, to the Board, and subsequently to a United States court of appeals, most cases are settled in the regional units.

This institutional description of the NLRB tells us how the agency is supposed to act according to the law. But if we look at the NLRB as one of the component parts of the political system, we should have a more realistic understanding of the why—and how—of official decision-making in labor-management relations.

Like every government agency, the NLRB operates within the current economic, social, and political environment. Changes in the environment usually presage changes in public policy. The NLRB was set up under the Wagner Act (National Labor Relations Act) in 1935, one of the early pieces of New Deal legislation. For more than a decade, Board decisions showed a bias toward labor unions as, no doubt, the framers of the Act intended. But, in 1946, a Republican Congress was elected with adverse views toward the position of organized labor in the national economy. By passing the Taft-Hartley Act (Labor-Management Relations Act) in 1947, Congress substantially altered the Board's procedures and reformed its mission. The Wagner

Drawing by Herblock. From *Straight Herblock* (New York: Simon & Schuster, 1964).

"I surrender, dear."

Act had forbidden management to engage in unfair labor practices in interstate commerce; the Taft-Hartley Act put a similar prohibition on the unions. Thus, under the Taft-Hartley Act the Board reversed its bias and began to act more as an advocate of management. After the Republican victory in 1952, as more conservative Republicans were named to the Board, the NLRB began to narrow its definition of interstate commerce and to limit its jurisdiction. In 1959, the Taft-Hartley Act was amended to eliminate the "no-man's land" for regulation of labor-management relations in industries which do not substantially affect interstate commerce, with the result that an increasing number of labor-management disputes were turned over to state agencies for adjudication. But, in 1961, with the beginning of another Democratic Administration, the NLRB once more became a focal point for contending forces in the economic life of the nation. The agency expanded its activities in many areas and began to process more cases on an accelerated schedule. (Among other causes, growth of the economy, geographic shifts of industry, and the development of automation also help explain the increased volume and complexity of NLRB's case load.)

If we look at the demands and supports for the NLRB, we find that these too change with the times. In 1935, organized labor was a relatively weak interest group. At the outset of the New Deal, the labor movement was in precipitous decline, with less than 3 million members in the American Federation of Labor. We cannot claim, therefore, that the demands of labor were sufficiently strong to produce a New Deal for labor. Moreover, President Roosevelt, as chief strategist for the New Deal, was not particularly pro-labor and gave no support to the Wagner Act until after it had passed the Senate. The effective demands seem to have come from a handful of congressmen, notably Senator Robert Wagner of New York, and from some young lawyers in the executive branch.

Despite the personal drive on the part of a few officials, and the spokesmen for that small sector of the laboring force that was organized, the Wagner Act owed its acceptance mainly to public apathy. It was passed in a period of depression when the business community was at its lowest ebb in public esteem. The fact that organized business, like the National Association of Manufacturers, opposed the Wagner Act probably encouraged public apathy. At that time, most Americans were quite convinced that what was good for business was bad for the country! But, in 1947, when the Taft-Hartley Act was passed, the relative status of labor and business interests was reversed. Though labor unions had more than quadrupled their membership and were now powerful political organizations, a series of nation-wide strikes after the war lost them considerable support with the general public. Hence the efforts of labor to fight off the Taft-Hartley Act met with public apathy. On the other hand, the production record of business during World War II and general economic prosperity after the war made people believe that what was good for business might really be good for the country. Thus, Congress passed the Taft-Hartley Act with large majorities in both houses and overrode President Truman's veto, apparently with public approval.

Within the changing environment (regional as well as national), and subject to changing demands, supports, and apathy, the NLRB makes decisions that become the national policy in labor-management relations. But other factors also complicate the decision-making process within the agency. Members of the Board do not react automatically to the inputs of the political system; they too are individuals whose professional judgments are conditioned by personal interests, biases, and values. Moreover, they are subject to inputs within their own agency. To study decision-making at the top of an agency, without regard to activities in the lower rungs of the hierarchy or out in the field, is like taking a picture of the tip of the iceberg that shows above the sea. As we have already seen, most cases in the agency never reach the top offices. Bureaucrats in the NLRB try to perform their assignments objectively, professionally, in strict neutrality. Even so, personal factors are bound to enter into the decision-making process at every level in the hierarchy. And granted that the over-all policy of the NLRB is oriented toward the public interest, we find it difficult to ascertain just where decision lines are drawn that differentiate accommodation toward the special interests and concern for the general welfare.

The policy process is much the same in every government agency. Certainly other regulatory commissions are just as caught up in politics as the NLRB. No part of the economy can be divorced from politics simply by putting its regulation in the hands of experts in an independent agency. As Bernstein points out, "Independence, in practice, means that the commissions are enjoined not to consider the impact of their decisions on other industries and industrial practices or the economy as a whole. . . ." [28] Government by commission means that regulation is fragmented—a situation that plays straight into the hands of organized minorities. By emphasizing the technical and professional aspects of administration we obscure over-all public policy—namely, to plan and promote the interests of majority coalitions.

In many of our earlier discussions, we have stressed the role of organized groups in the political process, and nowhere is their effectiveness more obvious, their pressure more persistent, than in administrative regulation. But it is unlikely that the commissions will soon be integrated into executive departments directly responsible to the political leadership, for special interests strongly prefer, and with good reason, "government by commission."

Government Corporations and Other Businesslike Agencies

The government corporation is another device for carrying on public business with a minimum of presidential direction or congressional control. The government corporation is organized much like its counterpart in private business, and its function is much the same—to conduct an economic enterprise. Since most government corporations have been creatures of war and depression, they have been rather short-lived experiments. Actually, however, the corporation is one of the oldest forms of federal administration. It dates back to the Bank of North

---

[28] *Ibid.*, Chapter 10, "An Appraisal of Regulation by Commission," p. 283.

America, chartered by the Continental Congress in 1781, and to the United States Bank, chartered by Congress in 1791.

In 1936, the President's Committee on Administrative Management listed 93 government corporations, presumably the peak number. The Committee spoke favorably of the "freedom of operation, flexibility, business efficiency, and opportunity for experimentation" that were possible in these autonomous, business-like organizations. Typically, the government corporation of that time was created by Congress with an act of incorporation that defined its functions and placed it under an independent board of directors. The corporation was generally given capital to carry on its activities, authority to borrow money, freedom to buy and sell commodities, the right to sue and be sued, and exemption from many overhead controls in budgeting, accounting, and personnel management. Powerful business groups, however, objected to the competition of these public corporations. Moreover, the bureaucrats in top management pressed for the adoption of the same procedures and practices required of other agencies, "coordination" with the rest of the executive branch.

The *Corporation Control Act of 1945* subjected government corporations to most of the fiscal controls applied to other departments. Under this Act, both the General Accounting Office and the Bureau of the Budget have some control over the corporations: they must submit to a "customary commercial corporation audit" by the GAO, and must channel their budgets to Congress through the Budget Bureau and the President. The corporations must have specific congressional authorization for capital expenditures; and no corporation may be created except by Congress, thus ending the earlier practice of establishing them by executive order. Finally, whereas some federally owned corporations had previously been incorporated under state charters to escape close federal controls, they must now be incorporated by the federal government itself. In addition to these restrictions imposed in 1945, other laws have further reduced the autonomy of government corporations. Most have been placed under the Civil Service Commission, for example, thus depriving them of their discretionary power in hiring and firing.

As a result of these changes, it is hard to distinguish most government corporations from agencies in the regular departments. Indeed, many corporations are now pocketed away in the executive departments. The Farm Credit Administration in the Department of Agriculture is a holding company for all the government agencies that lend money to farmers. Federal Prison Industries, Incorporated, is located in the Department of Justice. Only a few corporations retain their independent status—the Export-Import Bank of Washington, the Federal Deposit Insurance Corporation, the Panama Canal Company, the Public Housing Administration, the St. Lawrence Seaway Development Corporation, the Tennessee Valley Authority. The TVA has proved especially hardy, for it has survived suits in constitutional law, investigations by Congress, internal dissension, and constant criticism from privately owned public utilities.

Much of the public business is carried on by agencies other than corporations. The *Post Office*, for example, one of the world's largest businesses, is organized as an executive department. This is one department that the Hoover Commission, with its emphasis on "economy and efficiency," thought should be operated as a revenue-producing, self-supporting enterprise. The Commission did not go so far as to suggest that the Postmaster General be removed from the President's Cabinet, but it did recommend that "the Post Office should be taken out of politics" and that the Postmaster General should not be a political party leader. Nevertheless, President Eisenhower followed party custom by naming his 1952 campaign manager as Postmaster General, and Postmaster General Arthur Summerfield in turn rewarded thousands of the party faithful with local postmasterships.

The Post Office Department finds itself in one financial difficulty after another, and Congress has to bail it out every year with appropriations to meet the deficit. Thus the Hoover Commission recommended that the Post Office Department be placed under the provisions of the Corporation Control Act of 1945, which call for businesslike budgeting, accounting, and auditing. In fairness, however, we must realize that the unbusinesslike showing of the Post Office springs largely from organized pressure groups which condition both the policies of Congress and the regulations of the Department. The "junk mail" delivered at rates below cost to the "occupant of the household" means that the taxpayers are actually footing the bill for multimillion-dollar schemes to promote new soaps, detergents, powdered coffee, tooth paste, and insurance. And through second-class mailing privileges, the Post Office is subsidizing the news and magazine business and much of the big business advertising that goes into nationwide circulation. Finally, the Post Office Department has noncommercial objectives that cannot be measured in profit-and-loss statements. True, it does lose money delivering rural mail and reading matter in general, but Congress feels that the widespread dissemination of ideas in a democracy is important. As a monopoly, the Post Office could raise prices to a level that would guarantee huge "profits," but only at the cost of severe social "losses."

One of the most obvious examples of group politics in the federal government is the *Veterans Administration,* established during the Hoover Administration. This independent agency is headed by a Director appointed by the President with senatorial consent. Although the Director does not have cabinet status, he enjoys direct access to the President, acts as adviser to the President on veterans affairs, and administers the vast program of benefits for veterans and their dependents and beneficiaries. The Veterans Administration employs more civilian employees than any other federal agency except the Post Office and Defense departments. Over $5 billion of the 1965 Budget, exclusive of expenditures for national security, was allocated for veterans benefits and services.

The Veterans Administration receives its strongest support from the American Legion and the Veterans of Foreign Wars, which have a membership of well over 3 million. The veterans have a special kind of appeal in pressure politics— a patriotic appeal that no other pressure group can match. The "professional veterans" in the veterans' lobby may put too much emphasis on pensions and bonuses and too little on benefits related to actual military service, but no congressman can afford to disregard the claims of those for whom the lobbyists profess to speak.

Management, Housekeeping, and Paperwork

The most remarkable expansion of the federal bureaucracy in recent years has been in management and housekeeping services for the executive branch as a whole. For nearly a hundred years, each department managed its own activities, with only intermittent direction from the President and occasional investigations by Congress. Then, in this century, government suddenly grew immensely big, and the very size and complexity of the public administration meant that overall managerial aids had to be provided for the political leaders. We have already seen how the President looks to the Bureau of the Budget for help in planning his fiscal program, how Congress expects the General Accounting Office to act as a watchdog over the Treasury. But the President also needs managerial assistance to achieve economy and efficiency. The General Services Administration and the Civil Service Commission are intended to meet this need.

The *General Services Administration*, created in 1949, has direct or supervisory authority over the purchasing, storage, buildings, documents, and paperwork of the national government. What do these responsibilities mean? Among its many other jobs, this little-known agency operates a central purchasing service and develops standards for all government purchasing. It has the task of collecting and storing a variety of items, from strategic materials to government records. It manages government buildings and supervises the planning and construction of new buildings. It preserves and publishes such documents as acts of Congress, executive orders, and administrative regulations. And it plans the forms to be used in the paperwork essential for large-scale government programs.

The General Services Administration gives us a striking illustration of bureaucratic "red tape." None of this agency's activities touch the general public, for it operates solely to manage the "housekeeping" of other administrators. It is a tremendous organization, employing thousands of persons in the District of Columbia and in ten regional offices. Standardized specifications, centralized purchasing, routinized procedures, and uniform practices seem as necessary to the federal government as to any large-scale business. Volume purchasing lowers operating expenses, and centralized control of supplies and equipment guards against fraud and favoritism. But overhead controls of this sort also mean more bureaucracy and more paperwork.

The Hoover Commission of 1955 prepared a special report on "paperwork management" in the federal government.[29] A few sentences taken from the *Report* suggest the extent of the problem:

---

[29] *Task Force Reports on Paper Management* are in two parts: Part I, "In the United States Government," January, 1955; Part II, "The Nation's Paperwork for the Government, an Experiment," (June, 1955). The Commission Reports on *Paperwork Management* are also in two parts (Washington, D.C.: Government Printing Office, January, 1955, and June, 1955).

The Government creates and handles some 25 billion pieces of paper each year, exclusive of the tons of paper used in printing technical manuals, pamphlets, periodicals, and the like. This requires the services of more than 750,000 full-time employees and an expenditure of more than $4 billion annually, a sum about equal to the whole Federal Budget prior to 22 years ago. . . . The Federal offices turn out more than a billion individual letters each year. Office space for full-time paperwork employees costs the Government $180 million. There are more than 24 million cubic feet of Federal agency records, enough to fill 7 buildings the size of the Pentagon. . . . The 18 billion printed or mimeographed forms used by the Government in a year include tax returns, statistical data, requests for economic and social information, personnel information, procurement, inventories, etc. . . . The Government requires about 25,000 different reports annually from its units in the field. . . . The Government's office machines, valued at several hundred million dollars, have a replacement and annual rental cost of about $100 million . . . ranged from annual typewriters to giant mechanical brains which cost more than $1 million each. . . .

The Hoover Commission was overwhelmed by the volume of paperwork in Washington. Paperwork, however, is not peculiar to government bureaucracy. It is the "curse of bigness." The "red tape" and paperwork in the federal government are not very different from those of big business:

One of the ten largest companies advertised in October 1954 that if all its products now in use were placed one in front of the other they would stretch around the world 1½ times. The official inventory of this company's files also shows that if its business papers were set end to end they would reach around the world twice.[30]

The only cure for the evils of bureaucracy seems to be more bureaucracy. So the Hoover Commission recommended that a Paperwork Management Service be set up in the General Services Administration. This new managerial unit would provide "a broad-scale approach to the paperwork problems of the government," and would put an end to "the mass of uncoordinated, conflicting, and overlapping instructions which bewilder the public and confuse, instead of assist, the individual at the receiving end." The Commission conceded, however, that no amount of "paper-work management" could really reform the government. Rather it put its trust in "qualified personnel," in the millions of men and women who constitute the civil service.

The Civil Service

"The Spoils System"

When President Washington made his several hundred appointments to the federal service, he declared that he had chosen from among the best qualified persons for each job. As his Administration became increasingly pro-Federalist,

---

[30] *Ibid.*, p. 4.

however, it turned out that the "best qualified" were usually Federalists and, when Thomas Jefferson became President in 1800, he found that nearly all the jobs in the federal service were held by Federalists. As leader of the Democratic-Republican Party, Jefferson felt obliged to dispense what patronage he could to friends in his own party who had personally worked for "the great victory." Invoking a rule of "due participation" by both political parties, he immediately removed a great many Federalists to make room for Democratic-Republicans. But he explained that as soon as his party appointees equaled the number of Federalists already in office, he would "return with joy to that state of things when the only questions concerning a candidate shall be, Is he honest? Is he capable? Is he faithful to the Constitution?"

When Andrew Jackson became President in 1829, he at once threw out of office about 10 per cent of the 10,000 employees in the civil service. His enemies charged him with introducing a "spoils system," although Jackson chose to call it "rotation in office." Jackson feared the bureaucracy, convinced that no man could long hold public office without being corrupted. He opposed the development of an officeholding class, and urged Congress to limit all appointments throughout the federal service to four-year terms. In his first annual message in 1829, Jackson made his position clear:

> The duties of all public officers are, or at least admit of being made, so plain and simple that men of intelligence may readily qualify themselves for their performance; and I cannot but believe that more is lost by the long continuance of men in office than is generally to be gained by their experience.

There is still something to be said for "due participation" of the parties and "rotation in office." It is a democratic approach to self-government based on faith in the ability of the common man. It is also a practical way of strengthening the party in power and of achieving more direct political responsibility to the people. James Farley, Postmaster General and Democratic National Chairman during Franklin D. Roosevelt's first term, justified the spoils system as "fair, reasonable, and intelligent." He thought that merit and politics could well be wrapped in the same package. In passing out 150,000 federal jobs to deserving Democrats in the first year of the New Deal, he followed two simple rules: First, is the applicant qualified? Second, is he loyal to the party and sympathetic toward the program of Franklin D. Roosevelt? This was Farley's point of view:

> Patronage is a reward to those who have worked for party victory. It is also an assistance in building party machinery for the next election. It is also—and this the public usually forgets—the test by which a party shows its fitness to govern.[31]

But as the federal government grew bigger and bigger over the years, and as its functions became more and more specialized, due participation of the parties

---

[31] James Farley, "Passing Out the Patronage," *American Magazine*, August, 1933, p. 21.

and rotation in office were no longer enough to insure an effective public service. The mob scenes that occurred in Washington with every change of party fortunes in the presidency reached a tragic climax in 1881 when President Garfield was shot by a disappointed office-seeker. To meet these evils, a movement for civil service reform had been spearheaded by the National Civil Service Reform League, aided by such persuasive periodicals as *Harper's Weekly* and the *Nation*. At first, the politicians scorned the "snivel service reform" advocated by civic groups, but they finally yielded to pressure politics. At last, in 1883, the Pendleton Act established a classified civil service under a Civil Service Commission.

The Competitive System

The Pendleton Act, sometimes called the "Magna Charta" of the civil service, originally affected some 14,000 positions, about 10 per cent of the federal service in 1883. The classified service has since been extended "upward, outward, and downward," until today 80 per cent of federal employees fall under the rules and regulations of the United States Civil Service Commission. Most of the few agencies that do not come under the Commission have established their own merit systems, as in the Tennessee Valley Authority, the Atomic Energy Commission, the Federal Bureau of Investigation, and the Foreign Service. When the Democrats returned to power in 1960, the *Congressional Quarterly* estimated that the political turnover in the national administration would affect around 61,000 officials, representing a payroll of $54 million.[32]

Almost every kind of vocation and profession is represented on the federal payroll: astronomers, bakers, clerks, draftsmen, economists, foresters, guards, historians, internal revenue agents, librarians, mail handlers, nurses, personnel officers, radar instructors, secretaries, truck drivers, veterinarians, X-ray technicians, zoologists. And this is only a sample. During World War II, the federal payroll reached a peak of over 3 million persons; the figure keeps changing, but for some time it has been around 2.5 million. Only about one in ten of the federal employees works in the District of Columbia. The rest are in the "field"—in navy yards, arsenals, post offices, veterans' hospitals, agricultural experiment stations, and regional and local offices of national agencies. A little less than half work as civilian employees for the armed forces, and nearly a fourth are in the postal service. One out of four is a woman, and seven out of ten are white-collar workers. More than half the federal employees have veteran preference.

The Classification Act of 1949 groups and grades positions in the civil service according to duties, difficulty, responsibility, and qualifications required. There are 18 grades in the General Schedule, with "equal pay for equal work" within each grade. The largest single group of workers in the classified service is in the administrative, clerical, and office positions, approximately six out of ten. The next largest group is in accounting and fiscal services, but these represent less than six out of a hundred. Blue-collar workers are not covered in the General Schedule; they are paid according to the rates prevailing in the local market.

---

[32] *Congressional Quarterly*, XIX (January 20, 1961), pp. 80–82.

The public service is open to all, without regard to sex, marital status, race, creed, color, or political affiliation. At least, that is what the law says. In actual practice, certain preferences and some discrimination do exist. Approximately two-thirds of the sub-professional, white-collar workers are women, whereas only a handful of women hold top jobs. Figures are not available on racial and religious backgrounds of civil servants, but in recent years strong political pressure has been exerted to give minority groups more visible representation in administrative and professional positions. In the Kennedy Administration, departmental agencies vigorously competed with one another to attract qualified Negroes, especially for front offices. In the Johnson Administration, when word went out that "the Chief" wanted more women in top jobs, suddenly an impressive number of qualified women were found deserving of promotion.

A team of researchers at The Brookings Institution, a major research foundation in Washington, recently surveyed national samples of the general employed public, academic groups, groups in business, general federal employees, and special groups in the federal service, to ascertain what images come to people's minds at the mention of "federal civil servants." The single trait most frequently cited by the general public was "good personal character." Business groups, who rendered the least favorable over-all reactions, frequently mentioned such qualities as "inordinate concern with security" or "lack of ambition and initiative." In answering why people enter the federal service, an overwhelming majority of the general public replied, "security and fringe benefits." Academic groups, particularly college teachers and high school and college students, stressed the possibilities of service to others as well as security. Answers by the government workers may or may not reveal their own motives; at any rate they echoed the general public in emphasizing security and fringe benefits. But high-level federal employees offered a wide range of motives besides the security explanation, such as specific job opportunities, desire to be of service, and opportunities for self-advancement.

The Brookings staff was impressed by what the respondents did *not* say as well as by what they did say. Apparently, most Americans do not think that a person enters the federal service because it offers a prestige career. On the other hand, they do not believe that federal officials are attracted primarily by love of power. And there were virtually no attributions of low or bad personal character, from which we may infer that there is no widespread concern about corruption in the federal service.[33]

---

[33] Franklin P. Kilpatrick, Milton C. Cummings, Jr., and M. Kent Jennings, *The Image of the Federal Service.* See also the companion volume, *Source Book of a Study of Occupational Values and the Image of the Federal Service* (Washington, D.C.: The Brookings Institution, 1964), which presents the detailed data for the entire study.

Adventures in Public Service, edited by Delia and Ferdinand Kuhn, (New York: The Vanguard Press, 1963) offers a different approach to understanding why persons are attracted to and choose to remain in the federal service. The book denies the familiar stereotype of a bureaucrat, "a grubby individual wrapped in yards of red tape with only vision enough to see as far as the boundaries of his own department." It highlights the careers of eight men who have won the Rockefeller Public Service Awards.

The Brookings study identifies a number of basic changes in the federal civil service since 1789. Among these are:

1. *Increase in numbers.* In 1801, it is estimated that one American in 2,000 worked for the national government; by 1957, one American in every 80 was a federal employee. Of every 30 members of the civilian labor force, one was employed by the national government. The number of federal civil service employees has remained constant in recent years, but the federal government now farms out many of its activities through contracts, grants, and other arrangements, thereby reducing the official payroll.

2. *Changing social composition.* In the early years, the federal service was principally attractive to members of the socio-economic upper class. Democratization of our political system, however, has promoted the recruitment of government workers from the total spectrum of American society.

3. *Increased need for specialists and technicians.* Public administration in the eighteenth century, before the age of industrialization and urbanization, was a relatively simple matter. Today, because of the magnitude and complexity of governmental activities, the federal civil service has a high proportion of managerial, professional, technical, and scientific personnel. In 1960, one in every fifty employees in non-government service was engaged in scientific and engineering tasks; in the federal work force the ratio was one in fourteen.

4. *Changed ratio of military to civilian services.* Traditionally, the American people have been averse to a large-size, peacetime military force. Only during wartime did many Americans wear uniforms. Ever since the end of the Korean War in 1953, however, the number of persons in the military services has exceeded the number of persons in the civil service.

5. *Increased fringe benefits.* With the creation of a federal retirement program in 1920, the federal service has developed a comprehensive system of fringe benefits that now include: provisions for retirement, vacation and sick leave pay, group life insurance, health insurance, career development programs, in-service training, and compensation schedules that, except at the very top, compare favorably with those in private enterprise.

The *United States Civil Service Commission*, set up in 1883, is bipartisan and composed of three members, only two of whom can be from the same political party. For many years, the Commission had two major assignments: (1) devising tenure regulations to insure continuity in administration and to protect civil servants from political pressures; (2) establishing a system of merit examinations to recruit qualified persons into a classified civil service. Over the years, the agency has developed a highly effective system of personnel management that covers the whole range of problems involved in a modern big bureaucracy: recruiting and examining, career development and training, incentive awards, pay and position classification, development of tests and standards, inspection and appraisal of personnel programs, investigations and security appraisals, appeals, retirement, and judicial review of administrative actions.

The Civil Service Commission acts as the central recruiting agency for the entire executive branch. Compared with the spirited brochures used in military recruitment, the announcements of civil-service openings seem very dull indeed. They are usually posted in such public buildings as post offices, although form letters are sometimes sent to organizations and institutions that might be able to contact prospective applicants. Recently, however, the Civil Service Commission has made a special effort to attract college-trained persons into the federal service, recruiting them on the basis of a "government career" rather than for any particular position. Since 1955, it has offered the Federal Service Entrance Examination several times a year. In the words of the Civil Service Commission:

> The objective is not merely to fill current needs, but to bring into the Federal service a number of highly qualified, career-minded people who have the potential to grow and develop within the service and become the career managers, skilled technicians, and professional leaders of tomorrow.[34]

Examinations for the classified service are generally of a practical sort to test the applicant's ability to fill a particular position. Different tests measure aptitude, achievement, and specific skills; the nature of the examination depends on the specific duties and responsibilities of the position. Oral tests may be given to check on personal characteristics that do not show up on written work: appearance, manners, mannerisms, facility in speaking, ability to react in a given situation—whatever the examiners feel is pertinent. Those who fail do not appear on the register of candidates eligible for appointment. Veterans and their families are given preferential treatment. All veterans receive 5 points in addition to their earned ratings on civil service examinations, and disabled veterans and their wives, widows, and mothers receive a bonus of 10 points. Since 1953, however, all veterans must make the passing grade of 70 before they become eligible for the additional points. Veterans with service-connected disabilities of 10 per cent or more automatically go to the top on many "registers" or lists of eligible job applicants. After World War II, Congress ordered that many examinations be open only to veterans, but since 1952 most of these have been reopened to nonveterans. Preference is also given to veterans when there is a "reduction in force"; the order of "separation" from the service is determined by length of tenure, efficiency ratings, and veteran or non-veteran status.

Before World War II, the Commission itself did most of the testing and made up the registers from those who passed. During the war years, when activities were still highly centralized under the Commission, so many bottlenecks built up that the Commission had no choice but to delegate more and more authority to the personnel offices of the individual agencies. Now the agencies, subject to standards fixed by the Commission, do almost all their own hiring, firing, promoting, demoting, and classifying.

Before a civil-service appointment becomes official, the applicant must swear that he will support and defend the Constitution, that he is not a com-

---

34 See U.S. Civil Service Commission, *Federal Careers* (Washington, D.C.: Government Printing Office, 1956), p. 3.

munist or fascist or a member of any other organization that advocates the overthrow of the government by force or violence, and that he will not strike against the government or belong to any organization of federal employees claiming the right to strike against the government. The Commission itself conducts a routine investigation of every applicant, checking references and making pointed inquiries to local law enforcement agencies, former employers and supervisors, school authorities, and even neighbors. If the position involves "national security," the investigation is more extensive, probably including a full field investigation by the FBI. The Commission acts as a central clearing house for all loyalty and security information on persons in the civil service, maintains central reference files and records, reviews derogatory information resulting from inquiries, and checks with other investigatory agencies such as the Department of Justice and military intelligence.

Political and Civil Rights of Public Employees

The original purpose of the merit system was to take politics out of the public employment. Appointments and promotions were to be based on relative fitness for positions without regard to political affiliations. Demotions and dismissals were to be made only on the grounds of incompetence, inefficiency, or moral turpitude. Over the years, civil service rules and congressional legislation have increasingly restricted the political activities of public employees. The *Hatch Act* of 1939 forbids any officer or employee in the classified federal service to take an active part in party politics or political campaigns. In 1940, a second Hatch Act extended this prohibition to state employees whose salaries are paid wholly or in part by federal loans or grants.

The Commission has worked out specific rules on what employees may or may not do in politics. The civil servant may vote, express his personal opinions, make voluntary political contributions, put stickers on his private car, and wear political badges or campaign buttons when off duty. He also may: hold such local offices as justice of the peace, member of a school board, and member of a library board, or serve on any other civic but nonpartisan boards. He may write his congressman or sign a non-partisan petition to Congress, and attend political rallies and join political clubs if he does not hold office in them. The civil servant may not run for any national or state office, solicit others to become candidates for such offices, campaign for or against any political party, distribute campaign material, march in any political parade (except when playing an instrument in the band!), solicit or receive political assessments, make or receive any political contributions in a federal building. If he violates any of these rules, he is subject to penalties ranging from 90 days' suspension to actual removal.

The purpose of these restrictions is to protect federal employees from political coercion and to protect the public from the spoils system. In 1947, the Supreme Court upheld the Hatch Act as a proper regulation designed to promote efficiency in the public service.[35] In a dissenting opinion, however, Justice Hugo

---

[35] *United Public Workers* v. *Mitchell*, 330 U.S. 75 (1947).

L. Black pointed up the fact that the act does deprive public employees of basic civil rights:

> It relegates millions of federal, state, and municipal employees to the role of mere spectators of events upon which hinge the safety and welfare of all the people, including public employees. It removes a sizeable proportion of our electorate from full participation in affairs destined to mould the fortunes of the nation. It makes honest participation in essential political activities an offense punishable by proscription from public employment.

In his zeal for "the preferred freedom," the Justice may have overstated the case—and yet there is a case. It is ironical that the very people who are most familiar with the operation of our government should be prohibited from participating freely in the political activities that give it shape and substance.

The public expects its public service to be reliable, trustworthy, of good conduct and character, and loyal to the United States. After World War II, the mounting fear and suspicion of the international communist conspiracy, the disclosure that spy rings and espionage agents had operated in the top grades of our government and in strategic areas of our national defense, the rise of "McCarthyism" and the turn of public opinion to conservatism—all these developments led to the establishment of loyalty and security programs in the federal service.

In March of 1947, by executive order, President Truman launched the first full-scale, peacetime loyalty investigation in American history. The "loyalty" of every person in the federal service as of October, 1947, and of every person who was employed in any federal agency after that date, was checked and verified. Activities that could be considered as evidence of disloyalty included sabotage, espionage, treason, sedition, advocacy of revolution or violence, intentional and unauthorized disclosure of confidential documents to foreign agents, and serving the interests of another government. More questionable criteria included membership in, affiliation with, or sympathetic association with any organization designated by the Attorney General as totalitarian, fascist, communist, or subversive. The machinery for settling individual loyalty cases consisted of a hierarchy of loyalty boards in the various agencies, and a Loyalty Review Board in the Civil Service Commission to which appeals could be taken from adverse findings in the agencies.

The "witch-hunting" sometimes went to incredible lengths. Loyalty boards actually reviewed such "derogatory information" as the books bought by a suspect, the magazines to which he subscribed, the pictures he hung in his living room (Picasso?), the records he played on his hi-fi (Prokofiev?), the friends he made in college, and the textbooks he was required to study in his undergraduate courses. And yet, in September, 1951, after the public servants whose loyalty was open to reasonable doubt had been dismissed, it was found that they amounted to about one one-hundredth of 1 per cent of all who had been screened.[36]

---

[36] Federal Personnel Counsel, U.S. Civil Service Commission, *Facts About Government Work and Workers*, Revision No. 1 (Washington, D.C.: Government Printing Office, April, 1952).

Normally a civil service employee has permanent tenure. Under the rules of the Civil Service Commission he may be discharged only "for such cause as will promote the efficiency of the service"; and he may appeal his discharge from any agency to the Civil Service Commission for review. In 1950, however, Congress authorized the heads of certain agencies to dismiss summarily any person whose employment they deemed not "in the interest of the national security of the United States." Congress placed under this authorization all "sensitive" agencies whose activities are directly related to the country's security, such as the Departments of State and Defense and the Atomic Energy Commission. Under the loyalty program set up by Truman's executive order, employees charged with disloyalty could appeal from agency action to a central loyalty review board. But under the 1950 statute, employees who were dismissed from the "sensitive" agencies as security risks had no such right of appeal.

The Republicans who came into office in 1953 decided that the Truman loyalty program was far from adequate. Almost immediately after his inauguration, President Eisenhower replaced it with a much broader "security" program. To the existing loyalty tests were added such new grounds for dismissal as "any behavior, activities, or associations which tend to show that the individual is not reliable or trustworthy," and "any facts which furnish reason to believe that the individual may be subjected to coercion, influence, or pressure which may cause him to act contrary to the best interests of national security." As Leonard D. White, a former member of the Civil Service Commission, observed, "The new tests of reliability were extraordinarily vague and pervasive." [37]

Responsibility for initiating investigations of both incumbents and applicants was left to the Civil Service Commission. Then, if the Commission discovered any derogatory information, the FBI was to undertake a field investigation. After evaluating the Civil Service and FBI reports, a security officer (one was required in each agency) could recommend immediate suspension. The suspended employee was entitled to a hearing before an *ad hoc* board nominated by the Civil Service Commission from a roster of government employees, none of whom could come from the agency involved. But the opinion of the board was advisory only—the agency head had final authority to exonerate, transfer, or remove the employee.

In effect, the Eisenhower security program extended the congressional legislation of 1950 to all government employees. In 1956, however, the Supreme Court held that Congress had not authorized such a sweeping presidential extension of its national security requirements. In *Cole v. Young* (1956), the Court considered the case of a food and drug inspector who had been dismissed as a security risk from the Department of Health, Education and Welfare. A majority of the Court found that the act of 1950 applied only to security risks in sensitive positions and that the President had acted beyond his powers in

---

[37] White, *Introduction to the Study of Public Administration* (New York: The Macmillan Company, 1955), 4th ed., p. 446. The reader will do well to consult White's entire chapter on "Loyalty and Security." White wrote from long-time, firsthand experience.

extending the criteria of "security" to all employees in all agencies. Three members of the Court vigorously dissented: "We believe the Court's order has stricken down the most effective weapon against subversive activity available to the government." [38]

Reports of the Civil Service Commission give no statistical breakdown of the number of persons who have been removed for security reasons. The Supreme Court decision in 1956 has no doubt cut down on the number of summary dismissals. We must not, however, misinterpret the Court's position. In previous cases, the Court had upheld the right of the President to remove disloyal persons from the government services through proper procedures.[39] *Cole* v. *Young* holds that the President may not authorize dismissals without review except from those sensitive positions specified by Congress. The Civil Service Commission still professes, and can uphold by proper procedures, the principle that the public's business must be conducted properly and by people of unquestioned loyalty and integrity.

Political Executives and Career Administrators

The merit system is extended by the shift of positions from a patronage basis into the classified service. When this is done, the incumbents acquire permanent status, despite their original patronage appointment. During the period from 1933 to 1953, when the Democratic Party was in power, some 193,000 employees acquired permanent status noncompetitively. Most of them, however, were required to meet some noncompetitive standard of fitness in order to achieve permanent status.

When the civil service was first established, certain positions were included in the classified service—that is, they carried tenure—but were not subject to competitive testing. Since 1902 these "excepted positions" have been listed in "Schedule A." For many years Schedule A was restricted mostly to attorneys, employees in foreign countries, certain confidential and private secretaries, and some patronage jobs in customs, internal revenue, and the post office. Following an executive order of President Roosevelt in 1938, a number of "policy-determining" positions were added to Schedule A. Then, in 1940, the competitive service was extended under the *Ramspeck Act*, and most of the agencies responded by shifting many high-ranking positions into Schedule A. Under the Truman Administration, either by executive direction or legislative action, many of these top-grade jobs were removed from Schedule A and put back into the competitive service. But when the Republicans entered office in 1953, they claimed to be appalled at the number of "Democrats who had been covered into the civil service improperly," particularly in the higher grades. Almost no patronage had been left to the victorious party. President Eisenhower promptly

---

[38] *Cole* v. *Young*, 351 U.S. 536 (1956).

[39] *Bailey* v. *Richardson*, 341 U.S. 918 (1951). See also Justice Frankfurter's concurring and dissenting opinion in *Garner* v. *Board of Public Works*, 341 U.S. 716 (1951), involving a California loyalty test. "The Constitution does not guarantee public employment."

requested the Civil Service Commission and the heads of all agencies to determine whether additional positions should be added to Schedule A.

In March, 1953, President Eisenhower by executive order created a new Schedule C for those positions in the policy-forming and confidential categories that had formerly been in Schedule A. All the agencies were directed to submit to the Civil Service Commission requests for additional positions that they would like to have in Schedule C. The Commission was flooded by requests to add chiefs and assistant chiefs of bureaus, departmental directors of information, general counsels, heads and assistant heads of planning and legal staffs, and special aides or assistants to the political executives. Although the Commission manned the dikes with heroic resistance, a great many holes appeared in the merit system in the next two years. As of September, 1954, 1,098 positions had been placed in Schedule C and 350 more positions had been added to Schedule A. In percentages, these "exceptions" from the competitive service seem very small indeed. "But numbers alone do not tell the whole story," observed a Hoover Commission task force in 1955. "In importance of positions affected, Schedule C and the recent enlargement of Schedule A represent the most significant cut-back of the competitive service in its history." [40]

Since all public administration is laced with politics, it is almost impossible to draw a sharp line between "political executives" who help make policy and "career administrators" who carry out policy. The Hoover Commission regarded the two types as complementary. The political executives help make the policies of the Chief Executive and with him assume responsibility for the government. They come and go with the party in power—"Their expendability is an essential element in representative government." The career administrators, on the other hand, provide a reservoir of knowledge and managerial competence based on long-time experience. Politically neutral, they serve anonymously in the public service. Their main concern is with organization, methods, procedures, techniques; they are the professional experts who know *how* to do *what* the political executive decides should be done.[41]

Following the Kennedy victory in November, 1960, the Democrats were at once confronted with patronage possibilities. The Senate Post Office Committee published a 141-page book listing likely job openings in the new administration. Schedule C included over 1,200 policy-making positions. These are the political executives who make up the President's team: heads of departments, under secretaries and assistant secretaries, members of the regulatory boards and commissions, key officers in the Executive Office of the President, and so on.

---

[40] Commission on Organization of the Executive Branch of the Government, *Task Force Report on Personnel and Civil Service*, February 1955, p. 192.

[41] Warner W. Lloyd, Paul P. Van Riper, Norman H. Martin, Orvis F. Collins, *The American Federal Executive* (New Haven: Yale University Press, 1963), is an important contribution to the literature on the American bureaucracy. It surveys the careers of nearly 13,000 civilian and military executives, "the elite" of all federal agencies, old and new, who hold political appointments or career positions at the level of GS-14. The statistical evidence includes social and personal data and points up the complicated and conflicting demands of the executive role in the federal service.

As top men on the President's team, they share his political responsibility for the national administration. They have a representative role, and in that role they are expected to equate the public policy with the public interest.

A political executive, however, soon discovers that he is an organization man. He cannot make policies on his own, but must enter into the institutional process of decision-making. Administrative activity is group activity, and administrative decision-making is largely collective behavior. The head of a department may direct its activities, but he in turn is influenced by its activities. This is especially true in those governmental agencies where technical skill and expert intelligence are requisite to rational decisions—for example, in the Defense Department. Paradoxically, the development of technology and the emphasis on specialization in our modern society have decentralized and diffused decision-making.[42]

In the administrative hierarchy, the crucial point of contact between the political executive and his operational staff is with the career administrators, who are not only experienced in programming for the department, but have also acquired know-how in governmental relationships with Congress and with other agencies. Political executives, new to their jobs, must lean heavily on the career administrators in their organization. When party changes bring hundreds of new political executives to Washington, the career administrators are important in furnishing continuity to governmental operations.

To survey the American bureaucracy in one chapter is obviously impossible. We have considered only its basic features. Our national administration is a complicated, almost chaotic structure of departments, bureaus, divisions, boards, commissions, corporations, and other independent establishments. But it is a responsible bureaucracy sensitive to political direction, even though the President and Congress sometimes pull in opposite directions. The bureaucracy is under the rule of law, though it has quasi-legislative and quasi-judicial powers of its own. Because citizens have increasingly discovered the usefulness of the service state, the American bureaucracy is engaged in great public enterprises; we still assure ourselves, however, that we really believe in and prefer private enterprise. Presumably the American bureaucracy operates in the public interest, though pressure politics often promotes private interests of a restricted scope.

The Constitution does not authorize any particular pattern of administration. The secretaries of the principal departments sit together in the President's Cabinet, though the practice is based on custom rather than law. They have no responsibility as a unit for the top-level decisions of the administration. The National Security Council, which has been set up by statute, does have interdepartmental and collective responsibility for the problems of total war. Some of the most powerful regulatory agencies are outside the cabinet departments and relatively independent of presidential direction and congressional controls. They are not, however, "out of politics"; politics pervades the whole administra-

---

[42] See J. Pfiffner and R. Presthus, *Public Administration*, Ch. 6, for a discussion of administration in the behavioral context, and the bibliographical essay in this text.

tion, as it must in a democratic bureaucracy. Some of the public business is carried on by government corporations, much of it is not; although there are both advantages and disadvantages to the corporate form, there is no rhyme or reason why the TVA is incorporated and the Post Office is not. Recently, the most phenomenal development in the federal bureaucracy has been in the area of management and housekeeping services, and in the piling up of paperwork tied with government red tape.

Today, the public servant must have all kinds of specialized, professional, and technical competence. Nearly the whole of the federal service is now organized into a great competitive service, operating under a merit system. The United States Civil Service Commission sets the standards for personnel management, but in recent years it has given the agencies considerable freedom in implementing Commission regulations. Congress gears the general schedule of compensation to position classification, with "equal pay for equal work." Salaries have long been good in the lower grades. The Government Employees Salary Reform Act of 1964—providing the largest single pay raise ever granted to federal executives, $10,000 for cabinet members and comparably high raises for the second and third echelons of government managers—now puts the whole federal service on a fairly competitive basis with big business.

CHAPTER TWELVE

The
Judges

On May 17, 1954, the Supreme Court of the United

States announced its decision in the case of *Brown* v. *the Board*

of Education. Though the occasion was momentous, the Court

followed its usual "decision-day" routine. Promptly at high noon,

the nine justices in their flowing black robes entered the great

courtroom. Parting the red velvet curtains behind the bench, they entered simultaneously and took their seats according to protocol, with the Chief Justice in the center and the Associate Justices on each side in the order of appointment. This was the highest court of the land, dedicated to "equal justice under law." Lawyers, sightseers, casual spectators, and reporters packed the courtroom. None of the spectators knew what decisions the Court would announce on this particular Monday. But every case the Court decides is of "paramount public importance," and decision day is always fraught with excitement.

At 12:52 P.M., the Chief Justice began to read the unanimous opinion of the Court in the *Brown Case*. The acoustics were poor in the marble-columned, high-ceilinged room. The Associate Justices leaned forward in rapt attention. Everyone in the courtroom strained to hear the reading: "We conclude that in the field of public education the doctrine of separate but equal has no place. . . . Segregation is a denial of the equal protection of the laws." The reporters rushed out of the courtroom and the news was flashed around the world.

Public Reactions to Judicial Decisions

On May 18, 1954, *The New York Times* ran its headlines clear across the front page: HIGH COURT BANS SCHOOL SEGREGATION 9 to 0 DECISION GRANTS TIME TO COMPLY. How did the public react to this momentous decision? The *New York Herald Tribune* editorialized, "The Supreme Court of the United States squared the country's basic law with its conscience and its deepest convictions." The *Washington Post* declared the decision "an occasion for pride and gratification." The *Cincinnati Enquirer* observed, "What the Justices have done is simply to act as the conscience of the American nation." The *Baltimore Sun* foresaw "powerful implications." The *Richmond Times Dispatch* cautioned its readers that this was "a time for unhysterical appraisal." The *Atlanta Constitution* also warned that it was "no time for hasty and ill-considered actions."

From the outset, however, the "sociological" nature of the decision caused some adverse reaction. James Reston, in his column in *The New York Times*, wrote, "The Court founded its segregation ruling on hearts and minds rather than laws." It is true that the Court did footnote its opinion rather generously with references to journals of psychology and sociology and to such studies as Witmer and Kotinsky's *Personality in the Making* and Gunnar Myrdal's *An American Dilemma*. The "sociological decision," however, was not unprecedented in law. Although the *Brown Case* reversed *Plessy v. Ferguson* (1895), in which the Court had upheld the doctrine of "separate but equal," the justices were merely extending the reasoning of more recent decisions. Indeed, their decisions did not come as a surprise to anyone who had been following the rulings of the Supreme Court in recent years. The Court had consistently viewed racial discrimination as a denial of equal protection of the laws. It had already decided against segregation in public transportation, had ruled against the exclusion of Negroes from jury lists and party primaries, and had nullified zoning laws and restrictive covenants relating to race. In education, it had already abandoned the separate but equal doctrine as applied to public institutions of higher learning.

Before making its final decision in the school segregation cases, the Supreme Court had ordered reargument preceding implementation. Counsel for the original parties were joined in the reargument, on invitation of the Court, by the Attorney General of the United States and several Attorneys General from the segregation states, as well as various interest groups in the role of *amici curiae* (friends of the court). One important change had taken place in the personnel of the Court; Justice Jackson, who had died, was replaced by John Marshall Harlan, grandson of the lone dissenter in *Plessy* v. *Ferguson*.

On May 31, 1955, the Supreme Court was ready with its "implementation" decision. A new amplifying system had been installed in the Supreme Court room, and this time there was no straining to hear the clear, firm voice of the Chief Justice reading the again unanimous opinion of the Court. The cases were returned to the local courts "because of their proximity to local conditions and the possible need for further hearings." The states were ordered to "make a prompt and reasonable start toward full compliance" with the ruling of May 17, 1954. The Court warned, "The vitality of these constitutional principles cannot be allowed to yield simply because of disagreement with them."

Public comment on the "implementation decree" followed the same pattern it had followed the year before, when the constitutional decision had been announced. *The New York Times* was less excited, and its headlines covered only three columns: HIGH COURT TELLS STATES TO END PUPIL SEGREGATION WITHIN REASONABLE TIME. In an editorial it observed, "We are on the way to a more perfect democracy." Public reaction was generally more favorable outside those communities in which the decision offended the local mores. But we must remember that the decree was counter to the laws and customs in 21 States and the District of Columbia.

The South was "shocked" and "angry." Governor Herman Talmadge of Georgia declared, "It won't be feasible in Georgia for a long, long, long time." Attorney General Eugene Cook of Georgia predicted that the decree "opened the door for perhaps a century of litigation." As if to confirm these predictions, Negro leaders from all over the South met immediately in Atlanta, Georgia, to plan their strategy of litigation. In a special session of the Florida legislature, one representative remarked, "It may be feasible in Florida in the next 50 to 100 years. No one would say it is feasible now."

Many white southerners felt that the Supreme Court had not acted in a judicial manner, but rather had assumed legislative power in ruling against segregation. Extremists were determined to resist the decree even if it meant closing the public schools. Others thought that "every lawful means" should be used to hold off implementation for as long as possible. Official resistance almost reached the point of nullification in the "interposition resolutions" which state after state south of the Mason-Dixon line sent to Congress and the Supreme Court. Arguments in constitutional law that had not been heard since before the

Civil War were dusted off and shined up. The Union became a compact of states: "The Supreme Court is not a party to the compact, but a creature of the compact." [1] The Court was without jurisdiction, because "the great subjects of the controversy are of legislative character, and not a judicial character." The Court was without power, authority, or jurisdiction to base its opinions on "the inexact and speculative theories of psychological knowledge." Thus, "It is the duty of the State in flagrant cases such as this to interpose its power between its people and the effort of said Court to assert an unlawful dominion over them."

Much of the public reaction to the *Brown Case* was steeped in emotionalism. A great deal of the animus that was aroused against the Supreme Court, in this case and in others, is based on public misconceptions of the role of the justices in decision-making. Inaccurate and inadequate reporting by the press is possibly the greatest barrier to public understanding of judicial functions. Most newspapers give cursory consideration to judicial decisions; the texts of judicial opinions are usually treated like routine government releases. *The New York Times* performs a public service when it prints in full the major decisions of the Supreme Court. (Notice how much coverage your local newspaper gives to the *content* of Supreme Court opinions.) NAACP WINS AGAIN or COMMUNISTS FREED BY SUPREME COURT, those are typical headlines which excite more than they inform. The complicated reasons why the Court has reached its decisions are usually left out of the news report or the accompanying editorials.

Philip B. Kurland, Professor of Law at the University of Chicago Law School, claims that the deficiencies of the Bar are a major factor contributing to the lack of understanding of the Supreme Court. [2] The public naturally assumes that practicing lawyers in the community are most competent to judge the decisions of the justices. What the public does not realize is that many lawyers are not conversant with Supreme Court business and only a few are qualified to practice before the highest Court. Yet, because lawyers are influential in the community, their off-the-cuff views, reflecting local prejudices, may be taken as professional opinions. Thus, the public is unduly alarmed when the newspaper adds fuel to the fire: BAR ATTACKS COURT.

A third factor in the public misunderstanding of the Court stems from the reactions of Congress. A certain antagonism is inherent in the relationship between Congress and the Court, because the power of judicial review can nullify congressional legislation. Congress is inclined to be wary of the power even when the Court professes to exercise judicial restraint. Frequently, in cases involving statutory construction, the Court is charged with trying to supersede the lawmaking branches when it attempts to decide in a specific case what the legislature or Congress meant in a general law. Sometimes outright hostility is

---

[1] The quotations in this paragraph are from a legislative resolution in Florida. They are selected simply to illustrate the points of controversy.

[2] Philip B. Kurland, "On Misunderstanding the Supreme Court," *The University of Chicago Law School Record*, IX No. 1 (1960), p. 13.

evident, as when the Senator from Mississippi is Chairman of the Senate Committee on the Judiciary at a time when the Court persists in anti-segregation opinions! The public too often mistakes the voices of a few unhappy congressmen for congressional reaction in general. The "Declaration of Constitutional Principles," prompted by the Court's opinions on desegregation, represented less than one-fifth of Congress in 1956.

Critics of the Court sometimes deliberately misinterpret judicial decisions and then make political capital of the misinterpretations. In 1962, for example, the Court held that it was unconstitutional for the New York State Board of Regents to prepare an official prayer to be said aloud in unison by students in New York public schools at the beginning of each school day.[3] Justice Black, who delivered the opinion, declared that the official establishment of religious services in public schools was a violation of the establishment clause of the First Amendment. If one reads what Justice Black actually said, one knows that his opinion was in no way hostile toward religion or prayer. On the contrary, he made it perfectly clear that he was in accord with the Framers of the First Amendment, "Those men knew that the First Amendment which tried to put an end to governmental control of religion and of prayer was not written to destroy either." Nevertheless, the decision evoked demagogic misinterpretation. One southern congressman claimed, "They put the Negroes in the schools and now they've driven God out of them." Another declaimed, "The Court has now officially stated its disbelief in God Almighty." Others charged that the justices were trying to "abolish God." Depicting the decision as "the most tragic one in the history of the United States," a congressman from New York State introduced a constitutional amendment to sanction religious exercises in the public schools. Though these charges were absurd and had no basis in fact, many people, who never read any part of Justice Black's painfully conscientious opinion, were convinced that the Court was hell-bent on striking all vestiges of religion from public life.

Unlike other agencies of government, the Supreme Court has no office of public information and no public relations officers to bridge the gap between official action and public understanding. The nine justices have a tremendous responsibility. They must decide some of the most complicated and difficult social and economic problems of the day; they have no staff services, no field services, no special consultants; they are expected to do their own work. They speak only in their official capacity, though not necessarily with one voice. They are frequently divided among themselves, and any given case may include not only a majority opinion, but also concurring opinions and dissenting opinions. The justices cannot enter into the general arena of politics, but they have considerable discretion in what controversies they will hear. Though technically their decisions settle only the specific cases before them, their opinions may actually have sweeping effects on the nation's economy, on political practices

---

[3] *Engel* v. *Vitale*, 370 U.S. 421 (1962). For further discussion of the Court's views on religion in the public schools, see Chapter 13. For public reaction to the New York Regents' prayer case, see James E. Clayton, *The Making of Justice* (New York: E. P. Dutton Co., 1964), pp. 17–23.

in all states, or on civil rights for minority groups. The justices are constrained by judicial protocol not to speak unofficially about what they have done officially. No matter how much abuse the public heaps on the Court, as in campaigns to "Help Save America, Impeach Earl Warren," the Chief Justice may not go on TV with a fireside chat explaining his own position or the actions of his Court. Judicial decisions speak for themselves.

In this chapter we shall try to examine objectively and dispassionately some of the general questions involved in judicial decision-making. What is the meaning of law? What is constitutional law? What is the judicial process? What is the role of judges (and lawyers) in the rule of law? What is the role of politicians in the administration of justice?

The Rule of Law

Meaning of Law

The law is many paradoxes. The law must be known, though most of us are ignorant of it. The law must be certain, though it is usually written with convenient vagueness. The law must be uniform, but it classifies dissimilar things for different treatment. Law is what a reasonable man would think just; but, when this is translated from the ideal to the practical, it means that the will of the dominant political group will prevail. Law is the prerequisite of liberty, but laws promote liberty by the exercise of authority. Law is necessary to keep the peace, but the law is upheld by force. Law is all the rules of government which determine our conduct in society. It forbids us to do this; it requires us to do that. But it never tells us what we ought to do, nor what would be good or wise or even decent for us to do.

To most laymen the law is something to avoid. It's the highway patrolman lurking behind the billboard. It's the fine print in the insurance policy. It's the long delay in settling a small estate. It's the dog catcher when you've let your dog slip his leash. It's the game warden when you've shot one duck too many. It's the process-server with the jury summons for the week you planned to spend at the beach. It is prohibition and prosecution. It is words and phrases that only a lawyer can read and write. It is lawyer's fees and court costs. The power of the law is a policeman in uniform. The majesty of the law is a judge in black robe.

The law is described in many ways. In Gilbert and Sullivan's *Iolanthe* the Lord Chancellor sang:

> The law is the true embodiment
> Of everything that's excellent.
> It has no kind of fault or flaw,
> And I, my Lords, embody the Law.

Tennyson wrote of the "lawless science of the law":

> that codeless myriad of precedent,
> that wilderness of single instances.

Dr. Samuel Johnson said, "Law is the last result of human wisdom acting from human experience for the benefit of the public." But Mr. Bumble in *Oliver Twist* described it more graphically, "The law is an ass, an idiot."

Professional students of the law have also viewed it in quite different ways. The nineteenth-century British scholar, John Austin, held that every law is a command from a political superior that is binding on inferiors—"superior" in this context signifies the power to force compliance. The "Austinians" concede that custom may serve as a rule of conduct in society, but argue that it becomes positive law only when it is adopted as such by the courts of justice and only when the judicial decisions based on it are enforced by the power of the state.[4]

Other political scientists, from the time of Aristotle to the present, have noted, "The law has no power to command obedience except that of habit, which can only be given by time." In this same vein, followers of the "historical school" reject the concept that law is a command, for they believe that law springs from the customs of society. To them, government does not *make* law but *guarantees* it. In *The Web of Government*, Robert MacIver describes "the firmament of law" as vastly greater and more intricate than could ever be devised by government. The "firmament of law" is derived from custom, cultural tradition, settled modes of procedure, and religious precepts, as well as from political rules. People observe the laws by "doing what comes naturally" rather than in compliance with a command. Thus the real origins of the law are found through anthropology, history, and even psychology rather than through contemporary political science.

There are still other approaches to the meaning of law. The "idealists" insist that laws have validity only if they are intrinsically just, only if they accord with the "laws of nature and of nature's God." The idealists compound justice with morality—what is good, and what is right, for men to do one to the other.

Justice Benjamin Cardozo, in deciding a case before the Supreme Court, once referred to "some principles of justice so rooted in the traditions and conscience of our people as to be ranked as fundamental."[5] Justice Felix Frankfurter holds that law is "deeply rooted in reason," that it cannot be arbitrary, capricious, or whimsical. What "shocks the conscience" or runs counter to the "decencies of civilized conduct" cannot be upheld as due process of law.[6] Arthur Sutherland of the Harvard Law School notes, "Reasonableness is one of the commonest tools in the American lawyer's kit."[7] To some, *stare decisis* (following the rules laid down in previous cases) is the "unrolling of reason in history"; since human nature is rarely original, almost any case that comes to court is bound to have a legal precedent. Thus law is the logical outcome of past experience.

---

[4] See "The Definition of Law," in *Lectures on Jurisprudence*, 1832, as given in excerpt by Margaret Spahr, *Readings in Recent Political Philosophy* (New York: The Macmillan Company, 1935).

[5] *Snyder* v. *Massachusetts*, 291 U.S. 97 (1934).

[6] Frankfurter in *Rochin* v. *California*, 342 U.S. 165 (1952).

[7] See Arthur E. Sutherland, *The Law and One Man Among Many* (Madison: University of Wisconsin Press, 1956), for a brief, original, and provocative discussion, "Perception of Justice."

Jerome Frank, a legal realist and a distinguished federal judge, wrote a great deal about the "Law"—"that vague and troublesome word"—but eventually he tired of the "silly word-battle." "For I think that one may say of 'Law' what Croce said of the word 'sublime'; it is 'everything that it is or will be called by those who have employed or will employ that name.'" Frank preferred to discuss what he called courthouse government, the pattern of social control that is imposed on us by lawyers and judges.[8] Justice Oliver Wendell Holmes once commented, "The prophecies of what the courts will do in fact, and nothing more pretentious are what I mean by law." To Justice Frankfurter, due process of law is "compounded of history, reason, the past course of decisions, and stout confidence in the strength of the democratic faith which we profess." [9]

The legal realists are less concerned with the origins and precedents of law than with its current impact. They regard the law as a social science, and their real interest is in fact-finding, in arriving at conclusions supported by current evidence. Skeptical of legal magic, scornful of the "ancient word," they would make law serve its social purpose in the everyday world. In their approach to law, they study not only the statute books, the court reports, and the legal text-books; they also dig into the data of economics, sociology, psychology, and political science. It is, for example, not enough to know the rules of bankruptcy "from time immemorial." They feel that it is much more significant to understand the personal and the institutional causes of bankruptcy, and the social, economic, and psychological causes of bankruptcy within a given period. Laws are not discovered but rather must be made for a particular time in a specific place.

The legal realists (or the sociological school) reject the old saw, "More important that a case be settled than that it be settled right." Although *stare decisis* offers the advantage of certainty and stability, "outworn concepts which no longer fit the facts must be vacated. The judge should fit his decision to the facts; if he cannot find the precedents he must create new precedents." [10]

The principal purpose of law is to control relations among human beings. Law exists to settle disputes and to maintain order. Most people are naturally social and as a matter of habit abide by the Golden Rule, "Do unto others as you would have them do unto you." People have very different interests, however, and when these interests come into serious conflict, the self-interest of the strongest or the smartest is likely to prevail. This is jungle law. Civilization, however, is designed to establish justice in which the community secures the rights of individuals and promises each man his due under law. The very core of law is the relationship between rights and duties. That is why so many of the titles in the statute books have to do with reciprocal relations: husband and wife, parent and

---

[8] See *Law and the Modern Mind* (New York, Coward-McCann, Inc., 1930); *If Men Were Angels* (New York: Harper & Brothers, 1942); *Courts on Trial* (Princeton: Princeton University Press, 1950).

[9] *Joint Anti-Fascist Refugee Committee* v. *McGrath*, 341 U.S. 123 (1951).

[10] William O. Douglas, "Stare Decisis," *Columbia Law Review*, XLIX (1949), p. 735.

child, guardian and ward, landlord and tenant, master and servant, vendor and purchaser, principal and agent.

Law does not exist in the abstract. Nor does it consist of absolute or immutable rules, for it is a product of changing human relations. In effect, law is what the government enforces at a particular time in a specific place. Traffic rules have changed considerably since the days of the one-hoss shay; and even today the rules must vary from throughways to city streets, from mountain roads to desert flats. What law the government chooses to enforce depends largely, of course, on the cultural context and the politics of the time.

In a democracy, the laws presumably reflect what the majority of the people believe is right or good for the greatest number. Having read this far, however, you will be on guard against presumptions of this sort. The government itself, under separation of powers, may have

Drawing by Herblock. From *Straight Herblock* (New York: Simon & Schuster, 1964).

"You know what? Those guys act like they really believe that."

not one but several wills—especially if the executive and the legislature are under separate party management, or if the judiciary consists mainly of the appointees of the preceding administration. Moreover, as we discovered in our discussion of pressure politics, organized and articulate minority groups, rather than an amorphous and incoherent majority, normally formulate the law and determine how it will be enforced in the areas of their special interests.

Did the Supreme Court in the *Brown Case* hand down a sociological opinion or a decision in law? The answer depends on which definition of law we accept. Though race relations is a subject of increasing controversy in this country, it is reasonable to assume that it can and will be settled peaceably and equitably under law. To say that law cannot change or control human behavior is to deny the high purpose of law. Whether the law is effective, however, depends on its suitability to the facts of contemporary society. Race relations in this country are not what they were in 1790, or in 1865, or even in 1896; and the law that governs them today must be keyed to the changes that have taken place. In 1896, the Court was satisfied that "separate but equal" was justified by "the nature of things." In *Brown* v. *the Board of Education*, it sought more modern authority. Was the Court of 1954–1955 less judicial because it chose to verify the "nature of things" with more recent data from social science? [11]

Constitutional Law and Judicial Review

The most difficult kind of law to define is constitutional law. The primary base of constitutional law is, of course, the Constitution—as it was written in 1787 and as it has since been formally amended. This Constitution is more than a philosophical declaration or a statement of principles. All laws passed by Congress must be "in pursuance of the Constitution." The President of the United States, sworn to uphold the Constitution, may veto any act he considers beyond the constitutional powers of Congress. All administrative rules and regulations are governed by constitutional limitations. In short, every public act—national, state, or local—must conform to constitutional requirements. Because the Constitution is "the supreme law of the land," it is binding on all parts of the American political system and must be enforced in all the courts of the country, "anything in the Constitution or laws of any State to the contrary not withstanding."

The legal character of the Constitution has given rise to the practice of judicial review. *Judicial review* is the power of the courts to declare "null and void" any act of the national government or the states which is contrary to the Constitution. Any court, national or state, may exercise judicial review, but because the Supreme Court of the United States is at the top of the judicial hierarchy, its judgment in constitutional law is final in any given case. It is not left to the judges, however, to pick an issue and start a case. What the judges think is unconstitutional may not at all affect actual practice unless someone takes the trouble to challenge the constitutionality of a particular act in the courts.

In the American system, the judges rather than the legislators have the final word in deciding what is constitutional law. The constitutionality of any statute may be challenged in the courts, and if the judges find it repugnant to constitutional law, they will invalidate it. (In Great Britain, where there is no single written constitution similar to ours, Parliament determines what is constitutional and legislates accordingly; the courts are then bound to accept Parliament's legislation as constitutional. Legally, the British Parliament is omnipotent.) In the United States an act that has been passed by both houses of Congress and approved by the President may still be declared null and void by the judiciary. And an act passed by a state legislature under the state's own constitution may be invalidated by the United States Supreme Court if a majority of the justices agree that the act conflicts with national law or contravenes the national Con-

---

[11] We shall consider later in this chapter the charge that the Court was not "judicial" because it "made" its own law without waiting for congressional legislation. For the meaning of law, there are many books that may be read with profit: Benjamin Cardozo, *Law and Literature* (New York: Harcourt, Brace and Company, 1931); Roscoe Pound, *An Introduction to the Philosophy of Law*, rev. ed. (New Haven: Yale University Press, 1954); Roscoe Pound, *Justice According to Law* (New Haven: Yale University Press, 1951); William Seagle, *Law, the Science of Inefficiency* (New York: The Macmillan Company, 1952); Carl J. Friedrich, *The Philosophy of Law in Historical Perspective*, 2nd ed. (Chicago: University of Chicago Press, 1963).

stitution. Although the President—and the fifty governors—are actually interpreting the Constitution when they issue executive orders, their orders may be invalidated if the Supreme Court makes a different interpretation.

Thus in law the Constitution becomes "what the judges say it is"—for the time being. The Court may later reverse its own decisions. Or "We the People" may overrule the Court's judgment by constitutional amendment. The Eleventh and the Sixteenth Amendments attest to this ultimate power retained by the people.

The great precedent for judicial review is the case of *Marbury* v. *Madison* (1803), in which the United States Supreme Court declared invalid a part of the Federal Judiciary Act of 1789.[12] Before President Adams left office in 1801, he had appointed some sixty Federalists to newly created judicial positions. Among them was William Marbury, who had been appointed as a justice of the peace for the District of Columbia. Marbury's appointment had been approved by the Senate and his commission to office had been signed and sealed. But Madison, Secretary of State for President Jefferson, refused to deliver this commission and others, for he recognized them as a last-minute "court-packing" effort on the part of the Federalist Party. Marbury went directly to the Supreme Court for a writ of mandamus (an order from the court) to compel Madison to deliver his commission. Chief Justice Marshall—himself a leading Federalist politician—declared that Marbury had a lawful right to his commission, and that it was quite proper for Marbury to bring his suit directly into the Supreme Court. The Federal Judiciary Act of 1789 had authorized the Supreme Court to issue writs of mandamus in cases of original jurisdiction (original jurisdiction refers to cases brought to the court in the first instance). After so scolding the administration, however, Marshall's opinion took a surprise twist and announced that the Judiciary Act was itself unconstitutional. Since the original jurisdiction of the Supreme Court is clearly defined in the Constitution, Congress has no power to enlarge this jurisdiction to include mandamus cases. The Court held that the act was repugnant to the Constitution and dismissed Marbury's petition for want of jurisdiction.

And yet we must not assume that in *Marbury* v. *Madison* Chief Justice Marshall simply seized for the federal judiciary supreme power over interpreting the Constitution. His argument for judicial review is entirely reasonable. If the Constitution is the supreme law of the land, and if it is the function of the Court to settle all controversies in law, it is the Court's duty to decide in favor of the Constitution when any conflict arises between the Constitution and ordinary law. Marshall's thesis was that this principle is essential to all written constitutions— namely, that any law contrary to the Constitution is void.

This thesis was not original with Marshall; Marshall's opinion shows striking similarity to Hamilton's words in *The Federalist* (Numbers 78 and 80). Although the Framing Fathers did not spell out the power of judicial review in the Constitution, they probably intended the judiciary to have such power. Back in the

---

[12] *Marbury* v. *Madison,* 1 Cranch 137 (1803).

colonial period, the British Privy Council had established the precedent of judicial review over acts passed by the colonial legislatures. More influential perhaps was the fact that the courts in ten states prior to 1803 had already exercised the same power. Lower federal courts had also "reviewed" both state and national laws. But *Marbury* v. *Madison* was the first case in which a federal court actually decided that an act of Congress was unconstitutional.

The power of judicial review has been used sparingly and with restraint. Chief Justice Marshall never declared an act of Congress unconstitutional again after the *Marbury* v. *Madison* case. No other act of Congress was ruled invalid until the eve of the Civil War when Chief Justice Taney, in the *Dred Scott Case*, held the Missouri Compromise unconstitutional after it had been in operation more than thirty years.[13] The Supreme Court has more frequently declared state laws unconstitutional. When we remember that the states enact thousands and thousands of laws every year, however, it becomes clear that the courts rarely overrule the legislators. Nevertheless, both the Supreme Court and lower federal courts *do* have the power, and they *can* use it when they see fit. As a result, legislators may sometimes be as concerned over the constitutionality of a proposed law as they are over its real merits.

Justice Roberts once explained that when the United States Supreme Court considers a constitutional question, it "has only one duty, to lay the article of the Constitution which is involved beside the statute which is challenged and to decide whether the latter squares with the former."[14] But this explanation is much too simple. Every case that goes to the Supreme Court involves a controversy of paramount national importance. Probably every case in constitutional law that has been decided by the United States Supreme Court could reasonably have been decided otherwise. How else can we explain that the state legislatures or Congress—whose members are all sworn to observe and uphold the Constitution—have already passed the laws which the courts are asked to review? How else can we account for the frequent disagreements among the justices themselves and the Court's not infrequent departure from its own previous decisions? The idea that the Constitution clearly dictates the Court's decision in each case is a myth.

Quite obviously when the Court engages in judicial review, it is actually determining public policy and, in effect, making political decisions. We shall examine the Court's role in policy-making at a later point in this chapter.

Constitutional Law and Non-judicial Interpretations

The delegates at the Philadelphia Convention in 1787 were principally concerned about the "forms" and the "framework" of government. Not that they were unaware of "the plain facts of political life"—the economic, social, psychological, and cultural forces that shape every government. But they hoped to contain these within a carefully contrived political pattern.

Almost immediately, however, the pressures and tensions of politics altered

---

[13] *Dred Scott* v. *Sandford*, 19 How. 393 (1857).
[14] *United States* v. *Butler*, 297 U.S. 1 (1936).

the original "forms" and "framework." Indeed, the structural metaphor is no longer apt. Now we speak of the "living Constitution" and say that constitutional law is "organic law." This change in metaphor is significant. That which "lives" and is "organic" is constantly growing, and it changes as it grows. The Framers themselves did not suppose they had fixed a *status quo* when they wrote the Constitution in 1787. "Time and habit," said Washington, the presiding officer of the Convention, "are necessary to fix the true character of government." Consequently, the Constitution is neither quite what the Framers intended nor just what the judges say it is.

The Constitution says nothing at all about political parties, but political parties manage our elections. They nominate the candidates for public office, they write the political platforms, they conduct the political campaigns, and they get out the vote. They elect the President and the Vice-President, and they man the policy positions in the executive offices. They organize both houses of Congress, devise the congressional rules of debate, and write most of the laws. Not infrequently the same party controls both houses of Congress and the presidency. When one party occupies the presidency for several terms, it usually has a chance to appoint many federal judges, including justices of the Supreme Court, thus increasing the likelihood that judicial review will follow the election returns. Political parties have almost erased the separation of powers and checks and balances that the Framers devised to prevent "the excesses of democracy." In our time, we are grateful to the political parties for making democracy work, for organizing the electorate, for presenting alternative policies to the people, for registering the popular will at the polls—in short, for promoting free discussion of issues in the public forum and seeking majority rule in the government. Parties have thus become an integral part of our constitutional system without being mentioned in the Constitution itself.

The Constitution provides for separation of the branches of government; the parties have served to unite them. Political parties have likewise tempered the divisive character of federalism, the distribution of power between the national government and the states. On the same ballot we find the party's candidates for national, state, and local officers. In a presidential election year, one party frequently sweeps the country, winning not only the presidency but also a majority of state governors and a majority of state legislators. Political parties have accordingly given the real constitution—our customary political practices—a meaning different from that of the official document.

Political parties have not only grown up outside the Constitution; they also have changed the meaning of that document. The Constitution calls, for instance, for the President to be chosen by electoral colleges in the states. But the parties have changed this to have the President chosen by the voters from candidates that the parties present to the whole nation. Some of the Framers said they expected that no candidate for President would receive a majority of the electoral votes in most elections, so that the final choices would be made in the House of Representatives. Since the parties reduce the number of real candidates to two, however, the House has not made the final choice for well over a century.

The structure of the national government, as outlined in the original Constitution, has also been modified. Partly as a result of presidential interpretation and partly as a result of congressional enactment, the President of the United States is advised by a cabinet. The Constitution gives no details on how the executive branch should operate, except to note that the President may require written opinions from the principal officers in each of the executive departments. Ever since Washington's first administration, however, the President has called the heads of executive departments together for their collective advice.

Article II of the Constitution, which describes the executive branch, mentions only the President. But the executive branch today includes the Executive Office of the President, ten executive departments, and many independent agencies. None of this superstructure is part of the original constitutional framework; it has all been added by congressional action or executive order. Our modern bureaucracy, which employs almost as many persons as there were in the entire country during Washington's first administration, would have been quite beyond the comprehension of the Philadelphia delegates.

Concerned as they were with "forms" of government, the Framing Fathers would be surprised, perhaps aghast, to learn that some of the most important activities of the national government are today carried out by independent regulatory agencies with executive, legislative, and judicial powers all woven together. The National Labor Relations Board, the Interstate Commerce Commission, the Federal Communications Commission, the Federal Power Commission—all have jurisdiction over vast and complex problems that could not even have been imagined in 1787. Moreover, these commissions are almost entirely independent of the President and Congress. But they have been developed by presidential and congressional interpretations of the Constitution. The simple contrivance of the Framing Fathers—the separation of powers with checks and balances—has proved too cumbersome and slow-moving to keep up with the modern pace of government regulation.

The Kinds of Law in Federal Courts

Because cases in constitutional law usually involve controversies of paramount public importance, we tend to focus our attention on them and in so doing we overlook all the other kinds of cases that call for judicial decisions. Actually, most of the business of the federal courts—except the Supreme Court—is not concerned with constitutional law but rather with statutory law or common law, criminal law and civil law, and equity.

The notion that legislatures make the law and that judges merely apply it to specific disputes does not give a true picture of law in the making. As a matter of fact, the great body of law in this country, in all states except Louisiana, is the *common law.*[15] This is the law that has governed Englishmen everywhere "from

---

[15] Louisiana, originally a French colony, still maintains a separate system of law based on the Napoleonic Code.

time immemorial." Common law is judge-made law as distinguished from *statutory law*, which is enacted by the legislature.

"From time immemorial" dates from about the twelfth century, when Henry I attempted to regularize the administration of justice in England. The king's justices, who rode on circuit from one community to another, were instructed to apply the king's justice uniformly in all the king's courts. This meant that they were to render similar judgments in similar cases throughout the realm. In making a decision, each judge would refer to other cases he had decided elsewhere on the circuit, or to the precedents set by judges on other circuits. Contrary to popular misconception, common law is not unwritten law; it is very much written, for it has been recorded for hundreds of years in court reports. The origin of common law is to be found in customary law (the customs of the community), canon law (the laws of the Church), the Roman codes (for the Romans occupied Britain for a longer period than white men have lived in the Western Hemisphere), and merchant law (the laws developed in commercial transactions).

Since human beings tend to fall into the same kinds of trouble in every age, many of the cases heard in American courts today are not too different from the disputes decided long ago by the king's judges in England. Here are some familiar cases in court, any place, any time: the neighbors who argue over boundary disputes (*his* oaktree puts *my* rosebed in too much shade; the eaves of *his* house trespass upon *my* property; *his* well is drawing *my* water; *his* chickens wake *me* at the crow of dawn)—the husband and wife who find marriage disagreeable (*he* won't support me and the children; *she* doesn't understand me; *he* deserted me; *she* wouldn't leave her mother; *he* ran after another woman; *she* "entertained" while I was at work). Judges have been settling such disputes for centuries; there is no end to the legal precedents. But if an entirely new kind of case does happen to arise, one that cannot be settled by turning to precedent, under common law the judge may use right reason and decide "what a reasonable man would think just." Without benefit of any legislative law at all, judges have always been "making" the everyday law for the community. Moreover, since common law exists and grows within the cultural context, most people abide by it habitually and conscientiously, without ever realizing that they are obeying the law.

Human nature may be much the same in the twentieth century as it was in the twelfth, but social and economic conditions are vastly different. In an era of atomic energy, the wheels of civilization turn infinitely faster than in the days when the king's justices rode on horseback from village to hamlet. To wait for the slow accretion of common law, case by case, seems too inefficient and cumbersome for modern society. Today we look less to the judges and more to the legislators to "make" the law.

Statutory law embodies the prevailing public policy—that is, the will of the dominant group in the community. In a democracy, then, statutory law should represent the will of the majority, even though minority groups frequently obtain what they want through pressure politics. Statutory law deals with general problems rather than with specific disputes between individuals, however, so that the judges must still "find" the statutory law, the general rule, which best applies to a particular case.

Past experience is sometimes useless in settling current problems. Consequently, we must have statutory law to supplement and replace the common law, especially in the complicated situations that arise in an urban, industrial society. Under the common law, for example, a worker was expected to assume the risks of his trade. If he was injured on the job, he could win a suit against his employer only if he could prove that (1) he himself had not been negligent, (2) his fellow workers had not been negligent, and (3) his employer had been negligent.

These common-law defenses against employer liability—"assumption of risk," "contributory negligence," and "fellow servant's negligence"—may have been reasonable in days when master and servant worked side by side in the home or backyard shop. But in the twentieth century, in huge and hazardous industries—in steel mills or coal mines, for instance—it is almost impossible to blame any one person for accidents on the job. The separation of ownership from management in corporate business has destroyed the personal relationship between employer and employees. Few stockholders have ever seen "their" company's employees at work, and few ever ask managment about the safety or sanitary conditions in the company from which they draw their dividends.

Industrial accidents and occupational diseases have become a tremendous social problem. Injured workers who are unable to pay the costs of their disability may become burdens on private or public charity unless the government helps them to secure compensation. This is why legislatures have passed workmen's compensation laws requiring employers to make financial compensation—no matter who was at fault—to workers who are injured or incapacitated on the job. The Supreme Court has sustained such statutes even though they run counter to the old common-law rules on liability.[16] Statutory law simply supersedes any common law with which it conflicts.

Federal law is statutory law. It is made up of the laws passed by Congress and the rules and regulations that administrators make in carrying out those laws. When the federal courts hear cases that involve citizens of different states, however, they must apply the common law of the state where the controversy arose if that state has no specific statute to govern the case. For more than a century, federal judges were free to use their own judgment in the absence of state statutes, and had built up a body of federal common law. In 1938, however, in a decision that reversed precedent and practice dating almost from the beginning of our history, the United States Supreme Court ruled: "Except in matters governed by the Federal Constitution or by acts of Congress, the law to be applied in any case is the law of the state. . . . There is no federal general common law." But this "reform" has created a problem, for now the same federal court may

---

[16] The Supreme Court discusses the problem in *New York Central Railroad Company* v. *White*, 243 U.S. 188 (1917).

have to apply different laws in deciding cases with identical facts because the cases arose in states with different laws on the subject.[17]

Criminal law is concerned with offenses against the public—that is, crimes. A major offense that is punishable by death, imprisonment, or a heavy fine is called a felony. A minor offense that is punishable by lesser fines or a short jail sentence is a misdemeanor.

Many kinds of crime make the front page of the newspapers: assault and battery, mayhem, rape, prostitution, abortion, bigamy, kidnapping, arson, burglary, larceny, embezzlement, robbery, forgery, counterfeiting, bribery. All these and many more are serious offenses against the public. In most states, criminal law is now generally covered by statutes that define the offense and prescribe the penalties. But any offense against the public morals, safety, or peace is "against the law" even if not in the statutes; the judge can always go back to the common law.

In the presidential election of 1964, the Republicans campaigned vigorously against crime in our cities and "moral decay" in the nation. It was never made clear, however, just how the Republican candidate, if elected, proposed to use his office in tackling what is admittedly a nation-wide problem. Our federal system vests primary responsibility for the maintenance of law and order in our state and local authorities. Since we have no national common law, offenses against the national government are limited to violations of federal statutes and administrative orders. Every year, Congress passes hundreds of statutes and the administrative agencies prescribe thousands of rules which have the force of law. Hence federal criminal law touches on everyday activities in every community. The Department of Justice, which is charged with enforcing federal criminal law, prosecutes individuals for violations of civil rights acts, internal security statutes, and antitrust laws; evasion of federal taxes; fraud in elections; adulteration of food, drugs and cosmetics; violations of the narcotics, liquor, and gambling laws; fraud against the government; and fraud by mail. The Department of Justice enforces more than 600 federal criminal statutes covering treason, espionage, sedition, labor racketeering, bank robbery, bankruptcies, extortion, kidnaping, counterfeiting, transporting stolen motor vehicles across state lines, and many other offenses.[18]

In criminal law, the government prosecutes; the case in court is heard as "The State of Minnesota against John Doe" or "The United States against Jane Roe." If the defendant is found guilty, he is punished. In civil law, one citizen is in dispute with another; the plaintiff is the one who brings suit, usually in order to get compensation for damages done to his person or property. In civil cases, although the government provides the court, the litigants must pay the court costs.

A single deed may involve both a crime (an offense against the public) and a civil offense (a wrong done by one person to another). For instance, the Sher-

---

[17] See *Erie Railroad Co.* v. *Tompkins,* 304 U.S. 64 (1938), reversing *Swift* v. *Tyson,* 16 Pet. 1 (1842).

[18] See *Annual Report* of the Attorney General.

man Act makes combinations in restraint of trade both a criminal and a civil offense. Under criminal law, the federal government may prosecute a business that is engaged in unfair and unreasonable monopolistic practices. Under civil law, the small businessman who is being ruined by such competition may bring a suit for damages or seek an injunction—a court order—to prohibit the continuance of such practices. Although the same court may hear both the civil case and the criminal case, they are totally different cases.

Cases in civil law do not usually make the front page of the newspapers. Most citizens, however, seem to get involved in civil litigation at some time or other even when they stay home and mind their own business. If you fail to keep up the payments on your house or car, if your dog nips the newsboy or chases your neighbor's chickens, if your car even so much as dents the fender of another, you may find yourself the defendant in a civil suit. Or you may find it necessary to appear as plaintiff in a suit for libel, violation of contract, or abatement of nuisance.

The United States courts hear a great many civil suits involving federal laws on such matters as copyrights, patents, trademarks, fair labor standards, labor-management relations, and civil rights. Then, too, even though no federal law is at issue, citizens of different states may bring their controversies into federal courts. For example, a citizen of Georgia may sue a citizen of Vermont, or a corporation organized in Delaware may bring suit against a corporation organized in Illinois. Many such suits go to federal courts under "diversity of citizenship," and in these cases the federal judges apply state rather than federal law. The increasing number of civil cases in both state and federal courts suggests that Americans are a very litigious people.

Still another kind of law that is found in both the federal and state courts is called *equity* (or the rules of *chancery*). Like the common law, equity has its roots in medieval England. Both the common law and equity stem from ancient doctrines—"the king can do no wrong" and "the king is the fountain of justice." Thus, if the king's subject could not find justice in common law under regular court procedures, he could appeal to the king's person to redress the wrong and to order that "justice be done." Eventually this personal approach to justice also became systematized in precedents, formalized in procedures, and institutionalized in the courts.

Equity still remains, however, a distinct kind of law. In common law, the remedies for private wrong usually take the form of monetary compensation for damages suffered. But the remedies in equity take the form of court orders to prevent the wrong from occurring. For example, a person may sue a trespasser for damages; or he may go to court in equity to obtain an order (or injunction) to stop the trespassing. Among the more common cases in equity are: abatement of nuisances, divorce decrees, suits for alimony, foreclosure of mortgages, garnishment of wages for debts, injunctions against trespass, disposition of estates, receiverships in bankruptcy.

Federal courts handle cases both in law and equity. For example, enforcement of the Civil Rights Acts may involve prosecution for violation of the criminal code or it may prompt a variety of suits in equity. Thus a court may order a registrar to place on the voting rolls certain Negroes found to have been discriminated against in the registration process. Or it may issue an injunction against a state official attempting to interfere with school desegregation decrees.

The Rulers of Law

Lawyers and Judges

Americans are fond of saying that we have "a government of laws and not of men." But the fact is that all laws are made by men to rule other men. Although the United States has less than a quarter of a million lawyers, their influence in all branches of the government is great, and they have practically taken over the judiciary completely. In Anglo-Saxon countries especially, where respect for law is a tradition, lawyers enjoy a special status in society, because only they know how to read and write the language of the law. Whereas the law is unintelligible to laymen, hereinafter called the party of the first part; and whereas only lawyers, hereinafter referred to as the party of the second part, know what the law says or how to obtain standing under the law in the courts of justice; and whereas ignorance of the law is no excuse to the party of the first part; be it understood therefore by all those present that the party of the first part has the right, privilege, and every necessity to seek the advice and counsel of the party of the second part in due process of law and administration of justice.

When Tocqueville visited the United States, he was impressed by the conspicuous leadership of lawyers in American society. Everywhere he went, he found that the legal profession constituted a sort of privileged body, a political aristocracy that could be counted on to brake the excesses of democracy. "Men who have made a special study of the laws derive from occupation certain habits of order, a taste for formalities, and a kind of instinctive regard for the regular connection of ideas, which naturally render them very hostile to the revolutionary spirit and the unreflecting passions of the multitude." [19] Tocqueville thought that the emphasis which Anglo-Saxon law puts upon precedents had a distinct effect on the character of its lawyers:

> In the mind of an English or American lawyer a taste and a reverence for what is old is almost always united with a love of regular and lawful proceedings. . . . A French observer is surprised to hear how often an English or an American lawyer quotes the opinions of others and how little he alludes to his own, while the reverse occurs in France. . . . This abnegation of his own opinion and this implicit deference to the opinion of his forefathers, which are common to the English and American lawyer, this servitude of thought which he is obliged to profess, necessarily gives him more timid habits and more conservative inclinations in England and America than in France.[20]

[19] Alexis de Tocqueville, *Democracy in America, 1830*, edited by Phillips Bradley (New York: Vintage Books, 1954), I, p. 283.
[20] *Ibid:* I, pp. 282–290 *passim*. See also Heinz Eulau and John D. Sprague, *Lawyers in*

More recently, Jerome Frank has criticized the "cult of the robe" in the United States. To Frank, the medieval black robes worn by our federal judges (and by many state judges) "symbolize the notion that courts must always preserve the ancient ways; that the past is sacred and change impious . . . the judge's vestments are historically connected with the desire to thwart democracy by means of the courts." [21] Judge Frank (who wore the black robes of a federal judge for many years) holds that "In a democracy, the courts belong not to the judges and the lawyers but to the citizens." His *Courts on Trial* is an attack not only on the conservatism of judges but on the backwardness of the whole legal profession. Conceding that tradition is "the prime support of social stability," and admitting that stability has its good points, he scorns judges who are willing to sacrifice justice on occasion so that their law may remain "certain." He felt that a little uncertainty is a healthy sign in any progressive society, and that judges (and lawyers) should speak more plainly and candidly. Minutely distinguishing the "true rule" from the "dicta" of the precedents; stuffing the words of an old rule with new and different meanings; turning out oblique and evasive opinions intended to disguise departures from precedents—Frank saw these simply as legal trickery designed to fool the public. He quoted his longtime friend, Justice William O. Douglas: "The more blunt, open, and direct discourse is truer to democratic traditions. . . . A judiciary that discloses what it is doing and why it does it will breed understanding. And confidence based on understanding is more enduring than confidence based on awe." [22]

The Framers of the Constitution had no intention of making the courts responsible to the people. On the contrary, in the original design of the Constitution, the judges were three steps removed from direct election. They were appointed by the President (who was indirectly chosen by the electoral colleges), and were confirmed by the Senate (which was appointed by the several state legislatures). And they could stay in office during "good behavior." As we have seen before, the Framing Fathers took a dim view of direct democracy. Hamilton, in *The Federalist*, counted on the judges "to do their duty as faithful guardians of the Constitution, where legislative invasions of it had been instigated by the major voice of the community." Hamilton anticipated that the legislature, as representatives of the people, might respond to the majority will of the moment and be persuaded into "dangerous innovations in the government." Therefore he put his trust in the "independency of the judiciary"—independence, that is, from popular control.[23]

No public officials of course are ever completely independent. All of them

Politics (Indianapolis: The Bobbs-Merrill Co., 1964), pp. 22–27. On the basis of an empirical study of the lawyer-legislators and non-lawyer legislators in four states, the authors find little evidence of difference in ideological stance. They suggest that the argument about the "conservatism" of lawyers is "a hazardous inference from unsubstantiated assumptions."

[21] Frank, *Courts on Trial*, pp. 254–255.
[22] *Ibid.*, p. 289.
[23] Alexander Hamilton, *The Federalist*, No. 78.

are conditioned by the social and economic environment in which they live and work, and their decisions are bound to represent some of those attributes which we call character in a man. Judges are perhaps less free than legislators or bureaucrats to inject their personal opinions into the decision-making process. The high priests of the law are traditionally impersonal and rational in their professional stance; any deviation from strict neutrality or departure from *stare decisis* calls for extraordinary justification. Nevertheless, judicial behavior remains human behavior. Judicial decisions often reflect the emotional biases, personal values, and policy predilections of individual judges. Moreover, decisions that emerge from group dynamics, as "bloc voting" on the Supreme Court, show definite patterns of personal interactions. Thus, to understand how the Court has reached a particular decision, or to predict how it may decide a pending case, the student needs information about the judges as persons, as well as knowledge of the legal precedents.

John R. Schmidhauser, of the University of Iowa, has done a pioneering job of data-gathering on the social and political backgrounds of the justices of the Supreme Court, 1789–1959. "The picture that emerges in the pattern of recruitment of Supreme Court justices is one which emphasizes the intimacy of judicial and political affairs." [24] Schmidhauser assumes that the social and economic backgrounds of the justices, especially family attitudes, "may be accounted subtle factors influencing the tone and temper of judicial decision-making." Only a handful of the justices were of essentially humble origin. Most of them came from politically active families in comfortable economic circumstances, from the gentry and professional classes. Only six of the justices were born abroad, five of these in the British Isles, Felix Frankfurter in Austria. In ethnic origin, nearly all the justices have been of British descent; only five of them of central, eastern, or southern European descent; no person of Asian or African descent has ever been nominated. The largest percentage of justices have been Protestant, mainly Episcopalian, Presbyterian, Congregational, and Unitarian. Only 10 per cent have been Roman Catholic, Jewish, or Quaker. All the justices have had legal training of some kind, all practiced law at some stage in their careers, nearly all of them made law their major occupation. Up to 1861, most of the justices had pursued primarily political careers before appointment. Between 1862 and 1933, the percentage of judicial careerists increased considerably. In the whole history of the Court, over 50 per cent of the justices had prior judicial experience, although only slightly more than 25 per cent had really extensive judicial careers.

The reference to judicial experience of Supreme Court justices reminds us that the judicial process begins in the state courts and lower federal courts. It is relatively simple to gather biographical data on the 92 justices who sat in

---

[24] John R. Schmidhauser, *The Supreme Court: Its Politics, Personalities and Procedures* (New York: Holt, Rinehart and Winston, 1960), p. 57. See also by the same author, "The Justices of the Supreme Court—A Collective Portrait," *Midwest Journal of Political Science*, III (1959), pp. 1–57. The article contains extensive charts detailing the social and economic variations in judicial selection.

the Supreme Court between 1789 and 1959. It would be a Herculean task to do as much for all the state and federal judges whose decisions have settled the law in various ways, at different times, in different sections of the country. Only a small fraction of 1 per cent of the controversies heard in the courts of the land percolate up to the highest court. Because the Supreme Court justices are few in number, they are inevitably the target of political attack (and an endless subject for academic studies), although, in fact, most law-making by judges occurs in the lower courts. For a more complete understanding of the human factor in judicial decision-making, we need to scrutinize the social, economic, and political background of *all* the judges.

Federal judges "hold their offices during good behavior," which usually means for life or until they retire in old age. Consequently, appointments to the judiciary have great political significance. Because President John Adams had appointed John Marshall as Chief Justice of the Supreme Court, the Federalist Party remained entrenched in the national government for many years after the Federalists had ceased winning national elections. Indeed, every administration has tried to extend its political power through its appointment to the federal judiciary. The Constitution fixes no qualifications for federal judges. But the method by which they are selected—presidential nomination and senatorial confirmation—makes their political views a paramount consideration.

Certainly politics has always governed appointments to the Supreme Court. Roger B. Taney, who succeeded John Marshall as Chief Justice in 1836, had been a member of Andrew Jackson's cabinet, and he carried his political views along with him when he went to the Court. Constitutional law was considerably revised as the Taney Court emphasized states' rights and "dual federalism" instead of the strong national government that the Marshall Court had supported. Even more dramatic was the revolution in constitutional law that was staged in the 1930's. President Roosevelt's New Deal was blocked at the outset by the "nine old men" of the Court, the political appointees of previous administrations. Roosevelt eventually succeeded in replacing eight of the nine with his own appointees, who were imbued with "the new constitutionalism," and the "Roosevelt Court" soon discovered dimensions in the federal system that made it possible to constitutionalize the national welfare state, without any formal amendment.

Franklin D. Roosevelt's unusual difficulty with the judiciary was in part simply a matter of bad luck; he had to wait four years to make his first appointment to the Supreme Court. As Robert A. Dahl notes in his revealing study of the frequency of presidential appointments to the Supreme Court, "Over the whole history of the Court, on the average of one new justice has been appointed every twenty-two months. Thus a president can expect to appoint about two new justices during one term in office." Given even average luck, Roosevelt would have made two appointments in his first term and might have been able to avoid the head-on collision with the Court that occurred over the New Deal. A President does not normally appoint justices whose views on public policy are hostile to his own. Nor are the senators likely to confirm the nomination of a man whose stance on key questions is flagrantly at odds with the majority of the Senate. In other words, most justices are selected not so much for their "judicial" qualifications as for their "political" views. Hence Dahl draws the logical conclusion: ". . . the policy views dominant on the Court are never for long out of line with the policy views dominant among the lawmaking majorities of the United States." [25]

"The good that Presidents do is often interred with their Administration. It is their choice of Supreme Court justices that lives after them." [26] President Eisenhower in his first administration had an opportunity to reshape constitutional law through his appointments to the Supreme Court. In making appointments to the Court, it is customary for the President to consider such political factors as party affiliation, geographic background, religion, and political and social beliefs even more than legal training and judicial experience. The Eisenhower appointments followed the custom. His first appointment was Earl Warren as Chief Justice. This obviously fulfilled a party, and possibly a personal, commitment. Warren—three times Governor of California, and a vice-presidential candidate in 1948—was a national figure in Republican politics. Moreover, he had contributed substantially to the Eisenhower victory in the West in 1952. Eisenhower's second appointment to the Court, John Marshall Harlan of New York, was also political. Harlan had served less than a year on the federal bench, but he was a personal friend of Governor Thomas E. Dewey, to whom Eisenhower was indebted for the eastern campaign in 1952.

Almost immediately, the Warren Court had to decide a number of extremely controversial issues, involving such questions as segregation, sedition, and control of natural gas. Those who disliked the decisions criticized the justices for being "unjudicial." Some members of the American Bar Association were especially vocal in complaint. They managed to get introduced into Congress various proposals that would require more judicial training as a qualification for nominees to the Supreme Court. Individual congressmen joined in the complaints against judicial forays into policy-making, but Congress took no official action to change the composition or ways of the Court.

President Eisenhower, however, did respond to public opinion. Instead of replacing Justice Sherman Minton, who had resigned, with another midwestern Republican, he appointed William Joseph Brennan, Jr., a member of the New Jersey Supreme Court with ten years of experience on the bench. Since this appointment was made on the eve of the 1956 elections, some cynical commentators noted that Brennan was a Catholic and a Democrat, and hinted that the

---

[25] Robert A. Dahl, "Decision-Making in a Democracy: The Role of the Supreme Court as a National Policy-Maker," *Journal of Public Law* (Emory University Law School), VI (1957), pp. 279–295. This same volume contains a symposium, "Policy-Making in a Democracy: The Role of the United States Supreme Court," written by well-known political scientists and lawyers.

[26] Editorial, *The Nation*, January 14, 1939, p. 52, on the occasion of Justice Frankfurter's appointment to the Supreme Court.

appointment might have been calculated to bring some of Brennan's faith and party into the Republican fold. Eisenhower's fourth appointment did go to the Midwest, to a lawyers' judge, Charles E. Whittaker. For twenty-five years, Justice Whittaker had been a successful trial lawyer; he had served as president of the Missouri State Bar Association; and he had sat for over three years as a federal judge. The retirement of Justice Harold Burton in the fall of 1958 gave President Eisenhower the opportunity of naming a fifth justice of the Court. He chose Potter Stewart, a judge of the U.S. Court of Appeals since 1954. Known as a "liberal" and a "humanitarian," Judge Stewart also admitted to "being a Republican" from Ohio.

In his less than three years in office, President Kennedy made two appointments to the Supreme Court, both in 1962. The first appointment went to Byron R. White, following the retirement of Justice Whittaker. The new justice was known to many Americans as "Whizzer" White, an All-American football star in the 1930's; but he was also a Rhodes scholar, a graduate of the Yale law school, a law clerk of Chief Justice Fred Vinson, and a successful corporation lawyer. Probably more pertinent to the appointment, he had campaigned for Kennedy in 1960; and in 1961, as Deputy Attorney General, he had successfully handled the problem of attacks on "Freedom Riders" in Alabama. The chance to make a second appointment came with the resignation of Justice Frankfurter, who had suffered a number of heart attacks in the spring and summer of 1962. The President named Arthur Goldberg, then Secretary of Labor, who had achieved his professional reputation as a labor union lawyer.

No doubt the selection of White and Goldberg was calculated to tip the balance of power toward the "liberals" on the Court and to assure the President that he would have at least two justices on the Supreme Court who were in accord with the policies of the New Frontier. Some commentators on the Goldberg nomination, however, recalled the circumstances under which his predecessor had arrived on the Court. In 1939, Professor Frankfurter's appointment was generally regarded as part of President Roosevelt's strategy to pack the Court with "left-wing radicals"; but in 1962, when the Justice ended his long and distinguished career on the Court, it was the conservatives who felt they had lost their most effective spokesman.[27]

The fact that judges are selected on a political basis does not mean that they become stooges for the administration that appoints them. The members of the "Roosevelt Court" followed no White House party line, or any other one political line. In fact, they frequently disagreed with one another—Frankfurter versus Douglas, Jackson versus Black. The "Truman Court" turned on the administration in the *Steel Seizure Case*, when two out of four of Truman's personal appointees voted against his action. So when we speak of the "political"

[27] James E. Clayton, on the staff of *The Washington Post*, has given a non-technical account of the October Term of 1962 in *The Making of Justice—The Supreme Court in Action* (New York: E. P. Dutton & Co., Inc., 1964). The account is particularly discerning because of its vignettes of the people who participate in the judicial process.

character of the Court, we do not mean that the judges make decisions in the manner of party hacks, or that their opinions simply reflect their personal prejudices. Most judges observe the ethics of their profession, and will not consciously use their position on the bench to advance their private views or even to support popular policies. Justice Frankfurter, who was regarded as a political appointee of President Roosevelt, asks this question: "Does a man cease to be himself when he becomes a Justice? Does he change his character by putting on a gown?" And he answers the question in the same way most of his colleagues would answer it:

> No, he does not change his character. He brings his whole experience, his training, his outlook, his social, intellectual, and moral environment with him when he takes a seat on the supreme bench. . . . To assume that a lawyer who becomes a judge takes on the bench merely his views on social or economic questions leaves out of account his rooted notions regarding the scope and limits of a judge's authority. The outlook of a lawyer fit to be a Justice regarding the role of a judge cuts across all his personal preferences for this or that social arrangement.[28]

The Constitution provides that the President shall appoint judges of the Supreme Court with the advice and consent of the Senate, but it does not spell out how judges of the inferior courts are to be selected. Legally, the President appoints *all* federal judges with the advice and consent of the Senate; actually, the roles of the President and Senate vary considerably according to the level of appointments under consideration. Since lower federal courts handle about a hundred thousand cases in a year and since only about 3 per cent of federal cases ever get beyond the trial courts (the Supreme Court ordinarily gives full review to less than 200 cases), we need to take a closer look at how district judges and judges of the circuit courts gain their positions as decision-makers in the federal judicial system.

In President Kennedy's first year, Congress created 73 new federal judgeships, 10 in the circuit courts of appeal, and 63 in the district courts. President Eisenhower had urged the preceding Congress to authorize additional judgeships in order to alleviate overloaded federal dockets. The Democratic Congress determined to hold off, however, until a Democratic President could dispense the luscious patronage plums. However able and qualified the candidates for judicial office, the appointment process begins with political considerations. The Kennedy Administration made no bones about its policy of rewarding the party faithful, especially those who had worked for the nomination as well as the election of the President.

In George Washington's time, perhaps the President could be expected to know personally who was qualified and available for judicial appointments. But the modern President is much too occupied with policy matters to spend his

---

[28] "The Judicial Process and the Supreme Court," a paper read at the Annual Meeting of the American Philosophical Society, Philadelphia, 1954. Reprinted in Philip Elman (ed.), *Of Law and Men* (New York: Harcourt, Brace and Company, 1956).

time seeking out and screening candidates for lower level appointments. Thus it is now customary for the President to rely on the Department of Justice, and particularly the Deputy Attorney General, to organize the selection process.

Many different pressures enter into the selection of federal district judges. Though the Constitution does not specify any residence requirements, it is understood that judgeships in any given state will be filled by local candidates. Aspirants to judicial office normally seek the endorsement of their local and state party leaders and bar associations. A senator usually feels obliged to collect information on several contenders for judicial positions within his state. Operating on the old saw that "in making an appointment you make fifty enemies and one ingrate," most senators are inclined to suggest a number of "acceptable" candidates and then leave it up to the Department of Justice to take its pick for presidential consideration.

Since 1945, the American Bar Association, acting through a Standing Committee on the Federal Judiciary, has undertaken to pass on the qualifications of nominees. It offers an informal report to the Department of Justice on any person being seriously considered for nomination. After carefully investigating, it will rate the person in question as "Exceptionally Well Qualified," "Well Qualified," "Qualified," or "Not Qualified." The President is not bound by ABA ratings, but no administration can afford to recommend candidates whom the ABA calls "Not Qualified." As a matter of routine, the Department of Justice runs an F.B.I. investigation on all persons under consideration for judicial posts; like Caesar's wife, federal judges are supposed to be above suspicion. Finally, the President, on advice of the Deputy Attorney General, sends a formal nomination to the Senate. The Senate Committee on the Judiciary may hold a hearing on the presidential nominee, though such a proceeding is usually perfunctory since clearance is almost always worked out informally before the President acts officially.

Harold Chase, at the Brookings Institution, has made an extensive study of the federal judicial appointments.[29] He points out that the custom of senatorial courtesy gives the individual senators considerable influence in the selection of district judges within their respective states. But when it comes to appointments in the Courts of Appeal, the balance of power shifts to the presidential side. No one senator, or pair of senators, can claim a vital interest in a judicial appointment within a circuit that covers several states. Senatorial courtesy may be invoked by a senator of the state from which the nominee comes, but this is a rare occurrence. Ordinarily clearance on all nominations—including ABA ratings, FBI checks, and party endorsements—has been settled before the President takes any public action.

The Constitution provides that "the judges, both of the supreme and in-

---

[29] We have here leaned on Professor Chase's preliminary study of "Federal Judges: The Appointing Process," a paper delivered at the 1964 annual meeting of the American Political Science Association. But see also John R. Schmidhauser, *Constitutional Law in the Political Process* (Chicago: Rand McNally & Co., 1963), Ch. 6, "The Selection of Federal Judges."

ferior courts, shall hold their offices during good behavior," but neither the Framing Fathers nor the Congress have deemed it fitting to establish the kind of career service which characterizes judicial systems in the continental countries. As we have just seen, local political influence plays a large part in the selection of the district court judges. A considerable number of judges on the courts of appeals have been recruited from the trial courts, but the American judicial hierarchy has no tradition of promotion from one rung to the next. Relatively few justices in the history of the Supreme Court have had judicial experience before their appointment to the top tribunal. If judicial experience had been a requisite for Supreme Court appointments, the Court's roster would never have included such distinguished names as John Marshall, Roger B. Taney, Morrison R. Waite, Melville Fuller, John Harlan, Edward S. White, Louis Brandeis, Charles E. Hughes, George Sutherland, Harlan F. Stone, Robert H. Jackson, Fred Vinson, or Felix Frankfurter.

Justice William O. Douglas refutes the myth that prior service on other courts or a long-time practice in law gives the "judicial" attitude and legal experience necessary for the work of the Supreme Court. He points out that most law firms, large or small, do not attempt to cover the wide range of problems with which the Supreme Court must deal. Most lawyers tend to become specialists, in patents, admiralty, bankruptcy, taxation, and the like; many law offices never take a case in civil rights. The bulk of litigation in the lower courts is not concerned with paramount public issues but rather with the settlement of specific and technical legal questions. Justice Douglas, from his own experience, avers that it takes a decade or more for a justice on the Supreme Court to "run the length of the course and become familiar with its various features." [30] Certainly, the breadth of knowledge and wide experience in the law are desirable qualities in any judge. But since the courts play a positive and creative role in policy-making, it is also important for judges to have a broad understanding of public policy and a realistic concept of the impact of law on the social structure. Judges who have reached greatness have balanced law and politics in their administration of justice.

The Federal Courts

Under the Constitution, the "judicial power" of the United States extends broadly to two kinds of cases:

1. According to the *nature of the controversy*
   a. Cases arising under the Constitution, laws, and treaties of the United States.
   b. Cases under admiralty and maritime law.
2. According to the *nature of the parties*
   a. Cases affecting ambassadors and other foreign diplomats.
   b. Controversies to which the United States is a party.

---

[30] Justice William O. Douglas, "The Supreme Court and Its Case Load," speech to the Cornell Law School, Ithaca, New York, April 8, 1960.

c. Controversies between two or more states.

d. Controversies between citizens of different states.

We have seen that the Constitution defines the original jurisdiction of the Supreme Court. Otherwise the Constitution leaves it up to Congress to determine the jurisdiction of the federal courts.

The only federal court the Constitution mentions by name is the Supreme Court. The Constitution did, however, give Congress power to create any other courts that may be needed. The Constitution merely says, "The judicial power of the United States shall be vested in one Supreme Court, and in such inferior Courts, as the Congress may from time to time ordain and establish." Under this provision Congress has established a complete hierarchy of courts (see Figure 12-1): (1) District Courts of the United States, (2) United States Courts of Appeal, and (3) the Supreme Court of the United States. Congress has also established other courts, such as the courts of the District of Columbia and various special courts.[31]

In 1965, there were 87 *District Courts of the United States*.[32] These are trial courts for both criminal and civil cases. That is, they are courts of original jurisdiction—cases begin in these courts. There are one or more District Courts in each state, with one to twenty-four federal judges assigned to each court, depending on how congested the docket is. In 1963 there were 287 federal district judges in the States and 15 in the District of Columbia. That year more than 36,000 defendants were prosecuted for criminal offenses in the District Courts and nearly 64,000 civil cases were commenced in these same courts. Each year the statistical reports show an increase in the volume of both criminal and civil proceedings. Clearly the case load is heavy at the district level. Heavy case

---

[31] Congress has created a number of special courts: *The United States Court of Claims* handles claims cases in which the United States is being sued; the *Court of Customs and Patent Appeals* reviews decisions of administrative agencies in certain types of questions arising under the customs laws, patents, and trademarks; the *Customs Court* reviews appraisals of imported merchandise and decisions of collectors of customs; the *Court of Military Appeals* is the final appellate tribunal in court-martial convictions. Since all these "congressional courts" are outside the regular judicial hierarchy, constitutional provisions with respect to the appointment and tenure of federal judges need not apply.

The *Administrative Office of the United States Courts* was created by act of Congress in 1939. Its Director, appointed by the Supreme Court of the United States, is the administrative officer for all the federal courts. He works under the direction and supervision of the *Judicial Conference of the United States*.

The Judicial Conference is an annual meeting to which the Chief Justice of the Supreme Court summons the chief judges of the judicial circuits. The Conference keeps an eye on the volume of business in the federal courts, assigns judges to district and circuit courts according to how much judicial business is anticipated, and suggests to the various courts how they might expedite their business. The Chief Justice may invite the Attorney General to report to the Conference on court cases in which the United States is a party.

[32] The factual data on the court system in this section are taken from the *Annual Report of the Proceedings of the Judicial Conference of the United States* (Washington, D.C.: Government Printing Office, 1964). To bring these data up to date, consult the most recent *Annual Report*.

loads always mean "justice delayed" and "justice delayed is justice denied."

In criminal proceedings, the largest number of prosecutions are for auto theft, violation of liquor laws, forgery, counterfeiting, and tax frauds. Other federal offenses tried in the District Courts include: violations of the Selective Service Act, illegal use of service uniform, white slave traffic, and narcotics cases. In 1963, approximately 85 per cent of the criminal defendants were convicted and sentenced. About half of these received prison sentences; about a third were placed on probation or given suspended sentences; others were fined.

The constitutional rights of defendants in federal courts include: the guarantee against unreasonable search and seizure; the right to indictment by grand jury; the writ of habeas corpus; protection against double jeopardy; security against self-incrimination; the right to a speedy and public trial by an impartial jury; the right to be informed of the nature and cause of the accusation; the right to have witnesses subpoenaed; assistance of counsel; and protection against excessive bail, excessive fines, or cruel and unusual punishments. And yet, with all these rights and guarantees, less than 25 per cent of those who are charged with federal offenses choose to be tried in the federal courts. When we find

Figure 12-1

JUDICIAL SYSTEM OF THE UNITED STATES

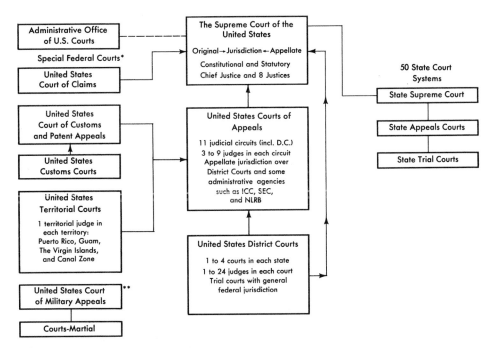

* Created by Congress to perform special judicial functions
** Independent of the judicial system but highest tribunal for Courts-martial

that 75 per cent of the accused plead guilty before trial, we are impressed with the efficiency of the law-enforcement officers in arresting the right persons!

More than half the cases in the federal District Courts are in civil law. The government may bring suit in land condemnation or civil rights cases, or it may appear as plaintiff under such federal laws as the Fair Labor Standards Act, the Taft-Hartley Act, or the Food and Drug Act. The government may appear as defendant in tax suits, personal injury claims, or suits to enjoin federal agencies. In cases where the United States is a party, the government lawyers are notably successful in getting their cases settled before they reach the trial stage. About three-fifths of the civil cases in federal courts involve private litigation between individuals. Some civil suits arise from disputes over "federal questions," such as anti-trust laws, labor laws, patent, copyright, and trade mark laws. Actually, diversity of citizenship cases—that is, controversies between citizens of different states—account for the greatest amount of court activity. Nearly four-fifths of all jury trials in civil cases in the federal courts do not concern the federal government and do not even involve a federal question.

The United States is divided into 11 judicial circuits. In each circuit, there is a *United States Court of Appeals*. The District of Columbia constitutes one circuit; the states and the territories are grouped in the ten remaining circuits. In 1961, from three to nine circuit judges were assigned to each Court of Appeals, depending on how much work had to be done. The chief judge of each circuit summons all the circuit and district judges to an annual conference to discuss and plan the year's business in the circuit. The chief judge also represents the circuit in the Judicial Conference of the United States (see footnote No. 30).

The Courts of Appeals have appellate jurisdiction—that is, they hear cases on appeal from the District Courts. A Court of Appeals may review either the facts in controversy, or the lower court's interpretation of the law. They also hear cases on appeal from various administrative agencies, such as the U.S. Tax Court and the National Labor Relations Board. The Courts of Appeals are the last resort for diversity of citizenship cases if no federal law or constitutional rights are involved, and for criminal cases in which less than $1,000 is at stake. No case can be appealed from the state courts to the federal Courts of Appeals.

Appellate judges also enjoy tenure during good behavior. A federal judge may retire at 70 if he has served for 10 years or at 65 if he has served for 15 years. But he is not compelled to retire. All federal judges are subject to impeachment for misbehavior in office. It speaks well for the honor of our federal judges that since 1790 only four have been impeached. The caliber of federal judges has been, and is, uniformly high.

The *Supreme Court of the United States* is the highest tribunal in the land. Congress fixes the number of Supreme Court justices. Since 1869, there have been nine justices on the Court at any given time, but the number has changed half a dozen times in the Court's history, ranging from as few as five to as many as ten. We have already noted the furor that arose when President Roosevelt tried to "pack the Court" in 1937 by adding one justice for each justice on the Court over 70. Since six of the nine justices were then over 70, Roosevelt's plan would have enlarged the Court to 15. The Court had come to enjoy such high prestige by this time—especially in the conservative press—that Congress refused to endorse the plan despite the President's smashing victory at the polls in 1936.

Under the Constitution, the Supreme Court has both original and appellate jurisdiction. Its original jurisdiction extends to: (1) all cases affecting ambassadors, other public ministers, and consuls; (2) all cases in which a state is a party. In *Marbury* v. *Madison* (1803), Justice Marshall held that Congress does not have the power to extend this original jurisdiction. And the decision still stands. The Court hears perhaps one or two cases in original jurisdiction during each term.

Congress fixes the appellate jurisdiction of the Supreme Court. Under present law, the Supreme Court may review cases both from state courts and from lower federal courts. The Court must hear appeals from any lower court decision that invalidates an act of Congress. It must also hear appeals from final judgments of the highest courts in the states if: (1) the question involves the validity of a federal law or treaty and the decision has been against its validity; (2) the state court has upheld the validity of a state statute alleged to be in violation of federal law or contrary to the Constitution. The Supreme Court of the United States will not review any cases from state courts, however, unless federal law or constitutional rights are involved.

The greatest number of Supreme Court cases reach the Court by means of the writ of *certiorari*, a court order calling a case up for review. Under certiorari, the Supreme Court may call up any federal case that at least four of the justices feel is of sufficient national importance to warrant the Court's attention. The writ is entirely discretionary, which means that the Court is free to deny most petitions for review. In a single Court term (a term runs between October and June) some 2,000 appeals and petitions for certiorari may appear on the Court's docket. But the Court will give full review to less than 10 per cent of these cases. Notice, however, that when the Supreme Court decides not to review a case, it is nevertheless making a decision—in effect it is deciding to affirm the judgment of the lower court.

To watch the Supreme Court in action is an impressive and dramatic experience. During a Court term, the Supreme Court hears cases Monday through Thursday, holding its conferences on Friday. This routine is followed for two weeks, then the Court recesses for two weeks to write its opinions. Since the oral proceedings are now mostly questions and answers between the justices and attorneys on points of law, there is no opportunity for the impassioned pleas and bursts of oratory of a Daniel Webster or a Charles Pinckney that marked Court proceedings in days gone by. Before coming into court, counsel on both sides have filed voluminous briefs with supporting data which the justices presumably study before they grant a hearing. The proceedings are public but, because the courtroom is small and the rules of order strict, the audience is hushed and duly decorous. While the page boys prime the justices with glasses of water, and the learned lawyers privileged to practice before the Supreme Court Bar present their cases, the sightseers and friends of the participants may gaze on the panels of art around the room—"Powers of Evil" and "Defense of Virtue"—or lift their eyes upward to the murals of the historic lawgivers—Menes, Mohammed, and Marshall. We are reminded of John Winthrop's words in 1644, "Judges are gods upon earth."

"Judgment Day" occurs on three Mondays in each month during Court term. A decision requires a majority vote of the justices. If the justices disagree, and they frequently do, those who differ from the majority may prepare a dissenting opinion. Sometimes the justices reach even a majority decision by different lines of reasoning, and then they prepare separate concurring opinions. In the *Steel Seizure Case* in 1952, for example, six of the justices decided that the President had acted beyond his authority. Justice Black read the opinion of the Court. Justices Frankfurter, Jackson, Douglas, Burton, and Clark each gave separate concurring opinions. And Justice Vinson, joined by Justices Reed and Minton, submitted a dissenting opinion.

The frequency with which the justices of the highest Court disagree has caused complaint and even consternation among both laymen and lawyers. Many people feel that the Court should develop a greater corporate spirit and should function "institutionally." Such is the opinion of Carl Swisher, professor of constitutional law at The Johns Hopkins University:

> We have a Court of nine justices not for the purpose of getting nine opinions in each case, or six or four opinions, or even two, but for the purpose of pooling into a unified decision and a unified statement of law the best that nine justices can offer. The people do not give the justices positions for life with guaranteed salaries merely to provide them with a forum for display of their individuality. The purpose is to build an institution.[33]

On the other hand, the late Justice Robert H. Jackson defended the practice of presenting dissenting opinions. Pointing to dissents of such great names in the Court's history as Oliver Wendell Holmes, Louis Brandeis, Benjamin Cardozo, and Harlan F. Stone, Justice Jackson observed: "The right of dissent is a valuable one. Wisely used on well-chosen occasions, it has been of great service to the profession and to the law." He continued more critically, "But there is nothing good, for either the Court or the dissenter, in dissenting *per se*. Each dissenting opinion is a confession of failure to convince the writer's colleagues, and the true test of a judge is his influence in leading, not in opposing, his court."[34]

Justice Frankfurter, writing a concurring opinion in an important tax case in the late 1930's, expressed his preference for individual opinions from the justices in every case, a preference he himself has put into practice many times since:

---

[33] *American Constitutional Development* (Boston: Houghton Mifflin Co., 1954), 2d ed., p. 1085.

[34] Robert H. Jackson, *The Supreme Court in the American System of Government* (Cambridge: Harvard University Press, 1955), p. 19. This brief book, delivered as "The Godkin Lectures on the Essentials of Free Government and the Duties of the Citizen," is a perceptive and firsthand approach to an understanding of the Supreme Court as a unit of government, a law court, and a political institution.

The volume of the Court's business has long since made impossible the early healthy practice whereby the justices gave expression to individual opinions. But the old tradition still has relevance when an important shift in constitutional doctrine is announced after a reconstruction in the membership of the Court.[35]

To the layman, however, who looks for certainty and security in the supreme law of the land, too many dissenting and concurring opinions are unsettling. One of the unique features of the segregation case with which we introduced this chapter was that the decision was unanimous. If the justices could achieve a single opinion in an issue as controversial as this, surely with a little more reflection and deliberate effort they might more often arrive at consensus in constitutional law. Too many dissenting opinions serve to discredit the Court; too many concurring opinions tend to obscure the law.

The Judicial Process

The courts provide the institutional framework within which the judges establish the rule of law. Organizational charts, jurisdictional lines, and statistics on case loads do not tell us much, however, about the nature of the judicial process. In the next part of this book, when we examine the policy outputs of the political system, we shall see that judicial decisions have been very important, not only in settling specific controversies but also in shaping the main lines of public policy. The federal judges have played a dominant role in maintaining individual rights and liberties; and to a considerable extent they have also determined the constitutional limits of economic and social policies in the states as well as in the national government.

The Supreme Court As a Decision-maker [36]

In our diagram of the basic features of a political system in Chapter 1, we represented all of official decision-making activities by a neat circle. We noted then that the simplicity of the diagram should not suggest perfect homogeneity among decision-makers. In fact, they are not only often in conflict, but the outputs of one decision-making unit may also be the inputs of another. Despite the ideal of an independent judiciary, the Supreme Court does not operate in a vacuum. The justices live and work within the contemporary social, economic, and political environment; their decision-making is influenced by that environment and their decisions affect that environment.

Inputs for judicial decision-making include demands, supports, and apathy. Constitutional arrangements insure the Court a position of relative independence from direct inputs of the electoral system or of unofficial agencies like parties

---

[35] *Graves* v. *New York ex rel O'Keefe*, 306 U.S. 466 (1939).

[36] For a more sophisticated discussion of material in this section see Walter T. Murphy, *Elements of Judicial Strategy* (Chicago: University of Chicago Press, 1964), especially Ch. 1.

and pressure groups. The demands to which the Supreme Court responds come from, or are filtered through, other official agencies. Appeals and petitions for certiorari from litigants in the lower courts constitute the bulk of direct demands upon the Court, though occasionally states or foreign diplomats demand the Court's attention in original jurisdiction. The controversies which these litigants bring to the Court frequently involve public issues of national magnitude. Hence the Court's docket, in any term, is likely to include demands for judicial arbitration from a variety of organized interest groups with conflicting claims— for example, in race relations, labor management disputes, or church and state problems. When the government appears as party to a case—whether as plaintiff, prosecutor, defendant, or amicus curiae—in effect it, too, is making demands for judicial support of its activities.

The supports for the Supreme Court as a decision-maker are both institutional and unofficial. The jurisdiction of the Court has been firmly established by the Constitution and by congressional statutes. But the judicial power is more than a matter of legal prescription. From the days of Chief Justice John Marshall, the Court has generally been supported by popular esteem. The high prestige of the Court can be attributed in part to a well-earned reputation for legal skill and professional integrity; but it is also a matter of tradition and habit for people to respect the judgments of the Court.

Since the Court considers only real controversies, it is bound to please one side, and to displease the other when it makes a decision. The interests favored by Court decisions are always the champions of judicial review. Between 1900 and 1935, when the Court consistently resorted to *laissez-faire* arguments to invalidate social and economic legislation, it won considerable support from the business community. On the other hand, in the 1960's, while the Court is actively trying to maintain equal protection of the laws for minority groups, its greatest support comes from "liberals" and various groups in the civil rights movement.

Apathy is a significant input of judicial decision-making. Most people, if they are not directly involved in litigation before the Court, tend to accept the Court's opinion because of ingrained respect for the law. Hence most litigants who lose their cases before the highest tribunal are not likely to win much sympathy or political backing from the general public. Paradoxically, seeming apathy on the part of public officials toward judicial decisions may represent a positive attitude. For example, congressmen, or the President, sometimes find it advantageous to let the Court serve as a scapegoat for decisions which they may want to accept but which they dare not, for political reasons, directly espouse. Thus, for nearly a hundred years after the Civil War, largely because of the apparent apathy of the political branches, the Court was left to make most of the policy decisions on civil rights. Similarly, within the local community, school officials who would not have had the nerve to initiate integration readily comply with court orders; local merchants who hesitated to affront local mores may be quite willing to accept a court decision that enables them to serve all customers without discrimination.

Each of the nine justices perceives his environment within the limits of his own experience and according to his personal values. As individuals, the justices may react quite differently to the demands, supports, and apathy that constitute the inputs of the judicial process. But as Professor Swisher has pointed out, the Court is certainly more than nine individual justices; it is a venerable institution, and all the justices are constrained to act within the institutional framework, according to its customary way of doing business.

We do not have much information on how the justices act in their conference sessions; such meetings take place behind closed doors and there are no reports to the press. We know that the Chief Justice presides, that he summarizes each case and indicates how he thinks it should be decided. Each of the judges, usually in order of seniority, expresses his separate view. During this presentation, however, some consensus is likely to emerge. When the members are ready to vote—the order is now reversed, with the junior justice voting first and the Chief Justice last—a majority of judges decide who wins (enjoys rewards) and who loses (suffers deprivations).

If the Chief Justice has voted with the majority in a case, he assigns the writing of the opinion to one of the judges in the majority—or chooses to write it himself. If the Chief Justice has voted with the minority, the senior justice in the majority makes the assignment. The writing of judicial opinions is not intended, however, to be a prima donna performance. Opinions are circulated, and re-circulated, in the hope that all or most of the justices will be persuaded to join in "the opinion of the court." The ability of a justice to write an opinion which is reasonably attractive to all his colleagues on the bench is regarded as a mark of judicial craftsmanship. Many concurring and dissenting opinions in any given term underscore the lack of unanimity on the Court. Nevertheless the *total output* of the Court represents collegial responsibility. Many opinions, embracing composite views, indicate that the justices have responded to group dynamics.

The impact of a Supreme Court decision is difficult to assess. Most cases do not begin in the Supreme Court; by the same token, most of them do not end there. Many decisions go back to the lower courts for further judicial proceedings. In the school desegregation cases of 1954–1955, the Supreme Court did not make a final disposition of the issue. Quite the contrary, after stating the "fundamental principle that racial discrimination in public education is unconstitutional," the Supreme Court remanded the cases to the federal district courts "because of their proximity to local conditions." [37] When the Supreme Court declared that the New York State prayer program in the public schools violated the establishment clause of the First Amendment, and therefore the Fourteenth Amendment, it remanded the case to the New York court where the case originated.[38] In 1962, when the Supreme Court held that a state's failure to reapportion its legislature may constitute denial of equal protection of the laws, it did not require all state legislatures immediately to reapportion. It simply found that the issue of reapportionment was justiciable and that, in this case, the complainants from Tennessee

---

[37] *Brown* v. *Board of Education*, 349 U.S. 294 (1955).
[38] *Engel* v. *Vitale*, 370 U.S. 421 (1962).

—which had failed to reapportion its legislature since 1901—were entitled to a trial and decision in the federal District Court in Tennessee.[39] In all these cases, though the Supreme Court stirred the whole country to action—and reaction— it simply stated the constitutional principle and then left the problems of policy implementation to the local authorities.

Judicial Activism and Legal Realism

Mr. Justice Douglas reminds us that "each age brings the Court its own special worries, anxieties, and concerns." The main outlines of the life of the nation are mirrored in the controversies which the Court is called upon to decide. It is expected to hand down final answers to "questions in which important blocs of opinion in the nation have fixed and set opinions that no amount of argument would change. . . . The Court sits in a maelstrom which has increased in intensity with the growth of blocs and pressure groups." [40] The economic, social, and religious groups that press their claims to the highest court represent increasingly well-organized interests. They come before the Court not only as individual contestants, but also on behalf of those in similar situations. The frequent appearance of *amici curiae* before the Supreme Court indicates that many judicial opinions concern more than the parties named in a suit. In cases involving racial restrictions in housing, for example labor organizations, neighborhood protective associations, real estate interests, and civil liberties organizations, no less than racial and religious groups, may enter briefs as *amici curiae*.

"The law is not made by judge alone, but by judge and company." [41] Here is a partial listing of *amici curiae* for a recent term of the Supreme Court: Religious Freedom Committee, American Civil Liberties Union, Railway Labor Executives Association, American Federation of Government Employees, National Association of Life Underwriters, Prudential Insurance Company of America, Chamber of Commerce of Metropolitan St. Louis, National Association of Retail Grocers of the United States, American Patent Law Association, Royal Netherlands Shipowners Association, American Committee for Protection of Foreign Born, American Federation of Labor and Congress of Industrial Organizations, Bureau of Information of Eastern Railways, the Southern California Gas Company, and the Chase Manhattan Bank. Many agencies of the federal and state governments also appeared as *amici curiae*, representing official special interests. This miscellaneous collection of "friends of the court" suggests the variety of company which may counsel the Supreme Court in a single term.

How does the Supreme Court reach judgment in areas of general controversy represented in specific cases? What are the criteria that govern the justices when they exercise judicial review? What is meant by judicial restraint and judicial activism? Unfortunately, these questions cannot be answered simply and precisely.

---

[39] *Baker* v. *Carr*, 369 U.S. 186 (1962).

[40] Speech to the Cornell Law School, *op. cit.*

[41] A remark by Jeremy Bentham amplified by Paul Freund in his essays *On Understanding the Supreme Court* (Boston: Little, Brown and Co., 1949).

Many scholarly studies have been written on individual justices; but to read these is to discover that each justice goes about his business in his own way. Justice Robert Jackson wrote, "The Court functions less as one deliberative body than as nine, each justice working largely in isolation except as he chooses to seek consultation with others. These working methods tend to cultivate a highly individualistic rather than a group viewpoint." [42] Nevertheless, patterns of group behavior have been found in judicial decisions. Herman Pritchett's succession of studies on the Roosevelt Court, the Vinson Court, and the Warren Court have stimulated further analyses of bloc behavior among the justices.[43]

"Libertarian activism" is a term used by Professor Pritchett to identify a bloc of justices active in the 1940's—Black, Douglas, Murphy, and Rutledge—"libertarian" because these four evinced a high level of support for civil liberties, "activism" because they also tended to favor a broad scope of judicial review. By contrast, although Frankfurter was a libertarian in his personal sympathies, he was a believer in and practitioner of judicial self-restraint; he would defer to legislative policy and avoid the constitutional issue if at all possible. "Libertarian restraint" or "restrained libertarianism" would seem to characterize his position.

Judicial activism is certainly not new in the history of the Supreme Court; it goes back to the time of Justice Marshall. Liberals (or libertarians) have no monopoly on this approach to constitutional law. Conservatives found judicial activism a highly effective technique around the turn of the century, and even into the 1920's and '30's. Most of the early labor and welfare legislation passed by Congress or the states was struck down by the Court. When Justice Holmes dissented in these cases, he pitched his liberalism on grounds of judicial self-restraint. In 1924, the La Follette Progressives advocated "a constitutional amendment providing that Congress may by enacting a statute make it effective over a judicial veto." In the 1930's, when the conservatives on the Court invalidated most of the initial measures of the New Deal, liberals protested the judicial activism of the Nine Old Men. In the 1950's, when liberals on the Court narrowly interpreted or invalidated legislation restricting civil rights, conservatives protested judicial legislation.

When the Court exercises judicial review, it engages in policy-making. Charles Black, distinguished professor of law at Yale, offers a thought-provoking analysis of judicial review within the context of legal realism. "Once it is recognized that judicial decisions are not the mechanical exercises they were once thought to be, it is clear that all judges, in all cases, make policy to some degree, and that the Court, so long as it performs the task of judicial review, must function to some extent and in some ways as one of the policy-making organs of the nation." [44] As Black sees it, the Court participates in public policy whether it in-

---

[42] Jackson, *The Supreme Court in the American System of Government*, p. 16.

[43] Glendon A. Schubert, *Constitutional Politics* (New York: Holt, Rinehart and Winston, 1960); and Murphy, *Elements of Judicial Strategy*.

[44] Charles L. Black, *The People and the Court* (New York: The Macmillan Company, 1960), p. 167.

validates ("checks") or validates ("legitimates") the political actions of our government. He finds no antithesis between the legal (or judicial) and the political functions of the Court. He is inclined to emphasize the affirmative or legitimating work of the Court, which he regards as a "people's institution." The people rely on the Court not only to nullify what is unconstitutional, but also to uphold what is constitutional. When the Court upholds governmental actions, we can all "breathe the sweet air of legitimacy."

Black stresses the concept of the Constitution as law, but he does not divorce law from policy. He talks about "vigorous judicial review," "a living body of constitutional law," and law which has "no demonstrable existence outside the facts of life." Judicial decision-making calls for technical competence and for expert knowledge of statutes, precedents, and procedures. "Law is and forever will be technicality. But law is also insight and wisdom and justice." [45] More than a technical lawyer is therefore needed to decide whether Congress has the constitutional right to appropriate public money for parochial schools or to regulate wages and hours in a western lumber camp, or whether the states can provide separate but equal education for Negro and white children, or remove smutty literature from drugstore magazine stands. In most cases that come before the courts, the controversy turns not upon the rule of law, but upon its application to the facts.

We began this chapter with reference to the *Brown Case* and the sociological approach of the Supreme Court justices. The sociological approach is one which stresses fact-finding and fact-selecting in the judicial function. The Court did not single out the school segregation issue for unusual treatment; the sociological approach did not begin with 1954. The Brandeis Brief, filed in 1908 in a case involving hours regulation for women in industry, included a great many background facts on the economic and social conditions of women workers.[46] The Brandeis Brief has become the prototype of numerous briefs and judicial opinions; lawyers and justices alike recognize the relevance of business facts, economic data, political practices, and social customs, as well as legal precedents, in settling controversies of public importance.

Because the facts are apt to be central to judicial decision-making, a principal strategy of litigants is to help the judges "find the facts." When the litigants represent interest groups, we note a special kind of pressure politics: organized research, systematic collection of data, and dissemination of the "facts," preferably in the professional and legal periodicals that are likely to be read by the justices. The NAACP frankly admits that this has been one of its educational techniques. Other interest groups have used similar tactics to influence judges and win decisions.

---

[45] *Ibid.*, p. 182.

[46] This brief was prepared by Louis Brandeis, then counsel before the Court, later one of the justices. (*Muller* v. *Oregon*, 208 U.S. 412.)

Robert McCloskey, Professor of Government at Harvard University, places the exercise of judicial review close to the mainstream of American politics. The Court is continuously forced to decide specific controversies within the broad context of the great issues that confront the nation: federal-state relationships, business-government conflicts, police power and private rights, national security and individual liberties. McCloskey repudiates the "myth of a perfect judiciary perfectly administering a perfect Constitution." At the same time, he discounts the view of the legal realists who treat the Court "as if it were not a court at all, as if its 'courthood' were a pure façade for political functions indistinguishable from those performed by the legislature." [47]

To begin with, the Constitution was never perfect, and no amount of judicial review by mortal judges will make it so. Conceived in ambiguities, the Constitution never lent itself to a single, consistent interpretation. In Chapter 1, on "the cultural context," we pointed up some of the many ambivalences of the American character. The Convention of 1787 exemplifies our national inclination, even determination, not to choose but to compromise. The Framers were gentlemen of principle *and* property. They created a more perfect union *and* they conserved the states. They granted great powers to the national government *and* put various vague limitations upon it. They specified the powers of Congress *and* authorized additional necessary and proper powers to carry into execution "all other powers" vested in the government of the United States. They established a bicameral Congress—the House to represent the people in proportion to their numbers *and* the Senate to give the states equal representation. The familiar words and phrases throughout the document bespeak the many compromises that made the Constitution acceptable to factions that disagreed on basic principles and practices. The Framers gave Congress the power to regulate commerce *among* the states; the preposition made a nice distinction, something more than *between* the states, something less than *in* the states. They referred to "privileges and immunities of citizens in the several states" but nowhere did they define citizenship, either in the United States or in the several states, and nowhere did they attempt to spell out the meaning of privileges and immunities.

The article on the judiciary represents extreme forbearance on the part of the Framers. "Judicial power of the United States," surely a momentous power, is not defined. "Inferior courts" are neither prescribed nor described. What, then, could be more fuzzy and uncertain than the "appellate jurisdiction" of the Supreme Court? Assuming that Marshall's logic was good and his interpretation of the Framers' intentions reasonably accurate in *Marbury* v. *Madison*, how are the courts expected to exercise judicial review? What did the Convention really mean when it wrote so impressively, "This Constitution . . . shall be the supreme law of the land"?

---

[47] Robert McCloskey, *The American Supreme Court* (Chicago: The University of Chicago Press, 1960), p. 19.

McCloskey calls our attention to the continuing and countervailing approaches to American constitutionalism: the rule of law *and* the will of the people. Although the Framers honored both doctrines, they accepted them side by side and not in synthesis. And this posed from the outset a dual development of constitutional interpretations. We believe that certain principles of government must be upheld as fundamental to a free society even when sometimes they are contrary to current popular opinions. But we also believe in the practice of majority rule and trust that the popular ideas will not really deviate too far from the constitutional tradition. Thus we expect the President and Congress to act in a political capacity to turn public opinion into public policy, "in pursuance of the Constitution." And we expect the Court to act in a judicial capacity, sustaining the supreme law of the land, observing "the imperatives of public opinion."

The Constitution is what the judges say it is, but the judges must be careful what they say. When the judges expound the Constitution, they are not only exercising judicial review but are also engaged in policy-making at the highest levels of statesmanship. The Court must draw a discreet line between what lawyers call "judicial activism" and "judicial restraint." It must not be too modest. "America needs the Court's advice and control to help mitigate its own extravagances." [48] We are an impulsive nation; sometimes we act too much and too soon, and think too little and too late. We count on the Court to remind us of what is fundamental in our public philosophy. The Court must not be too aggressive. As McCloskey points out: "No useful purpose is served when the judges seek all the hottest political caldrons of the moment and dive into the middle of them." We count on the Court to blend its orthodox judicial opinions with a mixture of reasonably popular ideas. The function of the Court is so to interpret the Constitution as to maintain the stability and continuity of our fundamental principles and at the same time to permit necessary flexibility for changing times and new ideas.

As Justice Frankfurter once observed, the Court is the undemocratic organ in American government. The justices are not truly political agents within the democratic framework in that they are not accountable or responsible to any general body of constituents. The President and Congress are elected to office for limited terms; if their record as policy-makers does not meet with popular approval, they can expect to be defeated in the next election. Judges, on the other hand, may be appointed on political grounds, but once they sit on the bench they are there to stay during good behavior. They do not have to court public opinion or concern themselves with majority preferences. By constitutional design, they are insulated from most political pressures. They do not have to fight for appropriations to carry on their activities, and their compensation will not be cut if they invalidate laws passed by Congress and approved by the President. And *amici curiae* behave much more respectfully than the lobbies which clamor for congressional attention or the interest groups that continuously besiege the executive offices.

---

[48] *Ibid.*, p. 20.

Because the Court does enjoy a specially protected position in the political system, judges are careful not to overplay their parts in the policy process. In the past, the Court has exercised its power of judicial review to check or sanction policies originating in the political branches. Only recently has the Court extended its decision-making to *initiate* political reforms and to force far-reaching changes in prevailing social behavior. This new role of the Court has stirred much public controversy and has disturbed some thoughtful political scientists.[49]

Administration of Justice

Under the Constitution, the federal courts have jurisdiction only over "cases" and "controversies." Judicial review is the most important and delicate duty of the courts, yet the judges may not take the initiative in passing upon the constitutionality of any statute. They may not render advisory opinions even at the request of the President or Congress, nor may they hear any case that is not a real contest between parties in conflict. The courts can only judge "real, earnest, and vital" controversies in which the legal or constitutional rights of the litigants are actually at stake. Even when grievous wrongs exist between individuals, the courts can do nothing about them unless the aggrieved parties present their cases for settlement. Lawlessness may exist in the community but, unless the officers of the law bring the offenders into court, no judge can pronounce sentence. Judges may decide on cases, but they themselves have no power to enforce their decisions. Here we turn briefly to the *administration* of justice on which the courts must depend.

The Department of Justice

Enforcing federal laws is the job of the Department of Justice. The head of the Department, the *Attorney General of the United States*, is also a member of the President's Cabinet and the chief legal counsel for the President and the executive departments. This is an important political position, and it often leads to a career on the bench. Several Attorneys General in recent years, for example, have been appointed to the Supreme Court: Wilson appointed his Attorney General, James McReynolds; Coolidge appointed his Amherst classmate, Harlan F. Stone, first as Attorney General, then to the Supreme Court; Roosevelt appointed Robert H. Jackson; Truman appointed Tom Clark.

The *Deputy Attorney General* supervises all the major units in the Department of Justice, including the Executive Office for United States attorneys. This office provides administrative assistance and supervision to the United States Attorneys in each federal judicial district. We noted earlier that the Deputy Attorney General plays a key role in the selection of federal judges.

---

[49] Charles S. Hyneman, distinguished professor of government at Indiana University, and past president of the American Political Science Association, raised some fundamental questions about the Court's new activism in *The Supreme Court on Trial* (New York: Atherton Press, 1963).

The *United States District Attorney* represents the United States in all cases initiated in the federal district court; he files suits on behalf of the United States in civil cases, and he conducts the prosecution in criminal proceedings. The *United States Marshal* in each district performs duties similar to those of the sheriff in state courts. He arrests and holds in custody persons accused of federal offense, summons jurors, serves subpoenas to witnesses, and executes the judgments of the courts. The *United States Commissioner* in each federal judicial district resembles a police magistrate or a justice of the peace. He issues warrants, holds preliminary hearings, fixes bail or holds suspects in jail pending trial in federal court. A *Clerk of the Court* keeps the records in each district. All these officers of the courts are political appointees. Their positions are covered neither by constitutional provisions for "independence of the judiciary," nor by civil service regulations. The President fills them with members of the party faithful.

The *Solicitor General* represents the federal government in Supreme Court cases and, when requested by the Attorney General, he may conduct and argue cases in any federal court. He directs the activities of federal law officers throughout the country. When the United States District Attorney loses a case in the District Court, he may not appeal to a higher court except with the permission of the Solicitor General.

Figure 12-2

Source: *United States Government Organization Manual.*

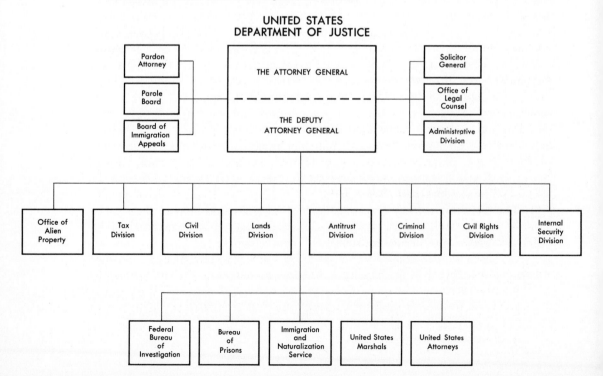

There are several major divisions in the Department of Justice, each in charge of some particular aspect of law enforcement: the Antitrust, Civil Rights, Civil, Criminal, Internal Security, and Tax Divisions. Three important bureaus are also in the Department: the Federal Bureau of Prisons, the Immigration and Naturalization Service, and the Federal Bureau of Investigation. The work of each bureau is briefly described in the *United States Government Organization Manual.*

Every movie, radio, and TV fan is familiar with the super-exploits of the FBI in crime detection. In its Identification Division, the FBI has a file of the fingerprints of all known criminals in the United States, as well as the fingerprints of members of the armed forces, government employees, aliens, persons employed on classified projects, and citizens who have volunteered their fingerprints. The facilities of the Laboratory Division of the FBI, which are almost as elaborate and ingenious as Dick Tracy's, are available to all federal, state, and local officers of the law. In recent years, the FBI has engaged in a never-ending battle against communist subversion. It investigates the activities of known or suspected communist fronts and other subversive organizations. Federal prosecutions under the Smith Act of 1940, the Labor-Management Acts of 1947 and 1949, and the Internal Security Act of 1950, depend largely on evidence obtained by FBI agents.

In its investigations of espionage, sabotage, subversive activities, and related matters, the FBI has relied heavily on "the invaluable assistance rendered by confidential informants who have first hand knowledge of the Communist Party." In 1957, in the case of Clinton Jencks, a New Mexico labor leader who had been convicted of filing a false noncommunist affidavit under the Taft-Hartley Act, the Supreme Court upheld Jencks' contention that at the trial he should have been allowed to see reports filed with the FBI by two witnesses.

The Court held that it was more important that justice be done than that the United States win its case. The government cannot deny the consitutional rights of the accused, and it is a constitutional right of the accused "to be informed of the nature and cause of the accusation and to be confronted with the witnesses against him." [50] If the government feels that the disclosure of its source of evidence would not be in public interest, then the government must let the accused go free. The press described the Supreme Court decision as a "blockbuster" that would shatter the FBI's tactics in its war against subversives. But the only dissenter on the Court was Justice Tom Clark, who no doubt recalled his own problems when as Attorney General he was responsible for the FBI.

The Civil Rights Act of 1960 made significant additions to the FBI's jurisdiction. Among the activities prohibited by this law are:

---

[50] *Jencks* v. *United States*, 353 U.S. 657 (1957). Glendon Schubert comments on this decision: "In order to uphold the claim of civil right, the Court had to challenge both political branches of the government on an issue that was inescapably political as well as legal. . . . In thus vetoing J. Edgar Hoover, the Court had made a political decision that no President in recent years would have felt politically strong enough to resist." Schubert, *Constitutional Politics,* p. 595.

1. Interference with any federal court order requiring a public school to desegregate.

2. Interstate flight to avoid prosecution or giving testimony in cases involving willful damage to any religious or educational institution.

3. Interstate transportation of any explosive for purposes of damaging educational, religious, charitable, residential, business, or civic property.

4. Use of the mails, telephone, or telegraph to convey threats of damage to such property.

These prohibitions were aimed to put an end to waves of violence in the wake of the school desegregation orders in some southern communities.

The FBI is the investigative arm of the Department of Justice as well as the primary civilian intelligence agency in the nation. Its investigations cover many fronts: crimes against banks; escapes across state lines; interstate transportation of stolen property; white slavery; kidnapping and extortion; labor and management offenses; fraud against the government; espionage and sabotage. It also offers a wide variety of services to other federal agencies in intelligence matters, including security investigations of individuals in government jobs.

Politics Seasons Justice

We began this chapter with a case in constitutional law, an interpretation by the Supreme Court of the meaning of "equal protection of the laws" as applied to racial segregation in the public schools. And we found that the meaning of law, in a general way, is the application of social policy in specific controversies. We turn now to the political context in which law is enforced.

Courts do not initiate cases. The segregation cases were brought to court by private litigants who felt that their constitutional rights were abridged by state laws. Individual Negro children had been barred from entering "white" schools in their localities; their parents went to court claiming that the children had been denied equal protection of the laws. The Supreme Court recognized the importance of these cases and called them up for review by granting writs of certiorari. We have noted that the parties who lend their names to litigation often represent special-interest groups. In the segregation cases, for example, Thurgood Marshall, then top-flight legal counsel for the National Association for the Advancement of Colored People (NAACP), represented the Negro litigants before the Supreme Court. The student of practical politics finds it most revealing to note the *amici curiae* in judicial proceedings. Pressure politics, which leaves an imprint on all legislation and administration, also has its impact on the judical process. This is politics.

On the government side, the Department of Justice is responsible for all cases in which the federal government is a party or has an interest. The degree to which a law is enforced depends generally on the attitudes and habits of the community and particularly on the activities of the law-enforcement officers. If the marshal, or the FBI, makes the arrest; if the commissioner who holds the preliminary hearing holds the accused for trial; if the district attorney decides to prosecute—then and only then does the federal court have before it a case in criminal law. Whether a case that the government loses in the trial court is ever taken "clear up to the Supreme Court" is also largely up to the Department of Justice. We have already mentioned that no case is appealed by the government except by permission of the Solicitor General. The district attorney, however, is really the key figure in the administration of federal justice. He directs the grand jury to bring in an indictment. He can dismiss charges and refuse to prosecute without giving any reason. He can bargain with the accused to forego trial and to plead guilty to a lesser offense. And the district attorney, holding a party patronage job, is in politics.

The "independent judiciary" actually depends on political figures in the administration of justice. Why arrests are made or not made, why some cases are prosecuted more vigorously than others—these may be largely matters of politics. In one administration, word goes down the political line to "bust the trusts" or to hit the "economic royalists"; in another administration the heavy guns are turned on the "labor hoodlums and union racketeers." This is politics too.

Certain types of crime provoke better publicity than others. "Human-interest" stories can build political careers; run-of-the-mill cases make no head-lines. The ambitious district attorney with his sights on Washington, perhaps on the White House, may pick and choose his cases according to their public relations values.

Even the constitutional requirements for "due process of law" may become the football of politics. In the general animus against communism, the guarantee against self-incrimination has fallen into such political disrepute that it is in danger of being abolished. When the Supreme Court tries to hold the fort for the Bill of Rights, it is charged with comforting communists, and individual justices are threatened with talk of impeachment.

Uncertainty about the meaning of law, heavy congestion in court dockets, cumbersome trial procedures that were devised in the days of duels and ordeals by combat, brutality in law-enforcement procedures, high fees for lawyers and heavy costs in courts, lawyers and judges touched with the bias and prejudice of class, the whole administration of justice seasoned with politics, from deputy marshal to Chief Justice of the Supreme Court—all these charges have been made against the judiciary. The administration of justice is a constitutional function of democratic government and as such, it is inseparable from responsible politics. We can congratulate ourselves, however, that we live in a country that takes for its norm "liberty and justice for all under law."

We do not have concentration camps; the writ of *habeas corpus* is a constitutional guarantee available to all. We have no gestapo; when law-enforcement officers act too brashly or brutally, their cases fail in court. Due process of law is written into the supreme law of the land. We have no secret trials, no mass trials. Every man accused is entitled to a speedy, public, and impartial trial. He is entitled to know the charges against him, to be confronted with the witnesses and the evidence against him; and the government will subpoena witnesses for him. The federal system still holds to the grand jury, indictment by a representative body of the community, and trial by one's own peers. Over every court presides

"His Honor, the Judge." "Judges," observed Justice Douglas in a contempt-of-court case, "are supposed to be men of fortitude, able to thrive in a hardy climate." Taking them all in all, federal judges are "men of fortitude"; they have to be, in the hardy climate of today. More than that, they are generally men of "right reason" devoted to their calling. And the law they serve is "What a reasonable man would think just."

Outputs of the Political System:
Rewards and Deprivations

PART FOUR

CHAPTER THIRTEEN

Individual Rights and Liberties

In the American political system, individual rights and liberties are a matter of public policy. If you have followed the theoretical framework of this text, you will recognize that public policy is the output of the whole political process. We entrust our official decision-makers—the legislators, the chief executive, the bureaucrats, and the judges—with authority and power to determine and implement the public policy. But decision-making always occurs within an environment which conditions the official actors.

The political environment within which governmental decisions are made is an integral part of the whole society which constitutes the American way of life. The purposes, goals and objectives toward which governmental activities are directed—and it is essential that public policies have such rational direction—are deeply rooted in the cultural values, the political traditions, and the legal norms of the American people. Official actors make the authoritative decisions, but in a democratic system they are not likely to act without prompting from their various constituents. Public policies are never permanent; they must continuously reflect changes in the social environment and also react to changing demands and supports for governmental action within the community.

Since World War II, American public policy on individual rights and liberties has assumed great significance in international politics as well as in the domestic arena. The rising expectations of people in the new nations have inevitably focused attention on the output of the first democratic nation in the modern world. How has the American government fulfilled the original intentions of the Constitutional Convention of 1787, "to secure the blessings of liberty to ourselves and our posterity"?

The Rights and Liberties of All Persons

"Unalienable Rights" and the Puritan Tradition

The American Declaration of Independence holds that *all men* are "endowed by their Creator with certain unalienable rights, that among these are Life, Liberty and the pursuit of Happiness." The Constitution declares that *no person* shall be deprived of life, liberty or property "without due process of law" and further provides that no state shall deprive *any person* within its jurisdiction of "the equal protection of the laws." This is the American tradition and the supreme law of the land—that every individual possesses basic rights and liberties simply because he is a human being entitled to decent respect from his fellows.

The American government was instituted "to secure these rights" but the rights are *unalienable*; they may not be abridged by official decisions and they are deliberately placed beyond the reach of the current majority. These beliefs, which the authors of the Declaration of Independence proclaimed as self-evident "truths," still stand as the dominant rationale for our national policies in the area of civil rights.

The ideas of John Locke—philosopher of the Puritan Revolution, "The Glorious Revolution," in seventeenth-century England—permeate both the Declaration of Independence of 1776 and the Constitution of 1787. To Locke, man was amenable to reason and susceptible to the claims of conscience. Endowed by his Creator with these potentialities, man can shape his role in society and determine the kind of government to which he will give his consent. Locke believed that the good society is a free society in which men live by "right reason." The best kind of government is the one that governs least in matters of mind and spirit. When God gave Adam reason, he gave him freedom to choose, for reason is but choosing —so the great Puritan poet, John Milton, brought reason and freedom together in *Areopagitica* when he spoke for liberty of the press before the English Parliament: "Man is born free and rational." This basic tenet of the Puritan Revolution was also the basic tenet of early American political theory. Thus the approach of our forebears to civil rights was presumably both intellectual and moral: government must above all guard the institutions of freedom.

As we observed in Chapter 3, however, the delegates to the Philadelphia Convention were more concerned with economic security than with political democracy. This concern also was in the Puritan tradition. Most of the God-fearing Puritans whose cause John Locke so rationally espoused were rich and powerful merchants. True, they put an end to the divine right of kings and advanced the cause of representative government. But their main objective was to insure that their business interests could be asserted in a parliament that had supreme power over the nation. Locke himself was quite frank: "The reason why men enter into society is the preservation of their property." We must remember, however, that to Locke the general term "property" encompassed the "lives, liberties, and estates" of every man. This explains, at least superficially, why Locke appealed both to the "radicals" of the American Revolution, who were primarily concerned with safeguarding personal liberties, and to the "conservatives" at the Philadelphia Convention, who were more concerned with protecting private property.

The doctrines of limited government and unalienable rights were not meant to imply license or absolute liberty, with every man free to say and do what pleases him personally. Civil rights were conceived in a moral context; the individual not only has a legal right but also a moral responsibility to seek the truth and to act according to "right reason." Moreover, every individual is constrained by the society in which he lives; he has a moral commitment as well as a legal obligation to respect the rights and liberties of his neighbor. Thus all rights and liberties, even those we regard as fundamental, are relative in practice. "No man is an Island, intire in itselfe"—no one of us can live alone. Clearly no individual has an absolute claim to a right if it is in conflict with a neighbor's claim; every personal liberty is restricted to certain ends and limits fixed by society. Though the individual may claim freedom of speech, he has no right to slander his neighbor, to incite his fellow citizens to rise up against the state, or to urge extremism that provokes mob action, even in defense of rights or liberties. As Justice Oliver Wendell Holmes once observed, "The most stringent protection of free speech would not protect a man in falsely shouting fire in a theatre and causing a panic." Liberty of conscience and freedom of worship are fundamental in a democratic society, but not even in the name of religion may American citizens engage in disorderly conduct, perpetrate fraud, or indulge in polygamy. Freedom of press is a primary right in our democracy, but it gives no license to publish what is seditious, obscene, malicious, or libelous.

Within the moral context of the Puritan tradition, our individual rights and personal liberties carry with them corresponding responsibilities and obligations. Thus the claim to liberty of conscience assumes that each citizen has an obligation to make ethical decisions. The right to full and free discussion is tempered by the moral maxim that reasonable men may reasonably disagree—but they must stay within the bounds of reason. The right to publish books, newspapers, and magazines without censorship carries an obligation to inform, not inflame, public opinion. The right of the individual to read whatever he chooses implies some obligation to choose wisely—to read for information and counsel as well as for relaxation and diversion. If we believe that "the market place of ideas" should be open to all, then we must count on the conscience and common sense of our citizens to reject the shoddy and false, to hold out for the good and true. Thus, the democratic creed depends on both the intelligence and the moral character of citizens.

Civil Rights in Constitutional Law

The appeal to morality as a basis of individual rights and responsibilities is seemingly not so persuasive today as it was to our forebears. Supposedly unalienable rights have been alienated in so many parts of the world that we are less certain about the self-evident nature of our truths. Nevertheless, the fact that the Framing Fathers implanted their notion of unalienable rights in our constitutional law gives to *civil rights* an exalted position in our political and legal system.

After the American colonists had broken away from the British Crown, the Continental Congress advised them to organize "conventions of the people" that would provide permanent constitutional government in each of the new states. Virginia was the first state to draft a constitution, a constitution prefaced by a Declaration of Rights that became the model for lawmakers in the other states.[1] The delegates to the Constitutional Convention in Philadelphia felt that these new state constitutions adequately protected the fundamenal rights of the individual; they decided it would be superfluous to attach a detailed Bill of Rights to the federal Constitution.

They did, however, put a few restrictions on both the national and the state governments with respect to personal liberties. Thus, Congress was forbidden to suspend the writ of habeas corpus except in case of rebellion or invasion. Both Congress and the state legislatures were forbidden to enact bills of attainder, to pass ex post facto laws, or to impair the obligation of contracts. Treason was carefully defined, and punishment was limited to the life and person of the traitor. Finally, religious tests were banned as a qualification for any office or public trust under the United States. The inclusion of these few restrictions, and the exclusion of other and more important ones, served to strengthen the popular

---

[1] See Allen Rutland, *The Birth of the Bill of Rights*, 1776–1791 (Chapel Hill: The University of North Carolina Press, 1955), for an objective and accurate historical account of the background of the Bill of Rights. Authorship of the Virginia Declaration of Rights is attributed principally to George Mason and Patrick Henry—the same Colonel Mason who refused to sign the Philadelphia Constitution because it did not include a similar Bill of Rights for the whole people—the same Patrick Henry who refused to attend the Convention of 1787 because he "smelt a rat."

demand for a comprehensive Bill of Rights as an integral part of the federal Constitution. If promises had not been made in the state conventions assuring that such a Bill of Rights would immediately be added to the original text, the Constitution would certainly not have been ratified.

During the fight for ratification, more than a hundred civil rights amendments were proposed to the various states. In the first Congress, James Madison introduced a series of amendments to reassure the people that the new government had no intention of denying or disregarding "those rights of persons and property which by the Declaration of Independence were affirmed to be unalienable." The House actually passed seventeen of these amendments, although two of them were rejected by the Senate. The remaining fifteen were consolidated into twelve and then submitted to the state legislatures. Ten were ratified. These first ten amendments constitute the "American Bill of Rights," though only the first eight actually detail the rights of individuals.

The Bill of Rights, then, is an integral part of the Constitution. These amendments reveal what the eighteenth-century champions of popular freedom regarded as the most precious rights and liberties of the individual—the rights that must be most carefully guarded. In brief, these are: the free exercise of religion, freedom of speech and press, rights of assembly and petition (Amendment I); the right of the people to keep and bear arms (II); protection against quartering of soldiers in private homes (III); protection against unreasonable searches and seizures of persons, houses, papers, and effects (IV); the procedural rights of persons accused of crime and guarantees of due process of law with respect to life, liberty, and property (V); further rights of the accused, including trial by jury and the right to assistance of counsel (VI); provisions for trial by jury in civil cases (VII); and the prohibition of excessive bails or fines and of cruel or unusual punishment (VIII).[2]

Among the amendments that Madison originally proposed as part of the federal rights, one would have provided: "No State shall infringe the right of trial by Jury in criminal cases nor the rights of conscience, nor the freedom of speech, or of the press." Although this proposal was rejected by the Senate, Madison evidently wanted to place restrictions upon the states as well as upon the central government. At the time, four of the states had no Bill of Rights, and some of those that were adopted by the other states he judged "not only defective, but absolutely improper." Madison's proposal was probably defeated by senators from states whose established churches would presumably have been outlawed by this amendment, since these churches would probably have been held to infringe rights of conscience. In any case, the rejection indicated that Congress intended the first eight amendments to restrict only the central government. Thus, the First Amendment begins, "Congress shall pass no law . . . ," an implication that the Bill of Rights was designed to restrict only the national government. This interpretation was made constitutional law when Chief Justice Marshall

---

[2] The incorporation of the Bill of Rights has already been discussed in Chapter 3, pp. 107–115.

in the case of *Barron* v. *Baltimore* (1833) firmly rejected the proposition that the Bill of Rights applied to the states as well. If Congress had so intended "they would have declared this purpose in plain and intelligible language." [3] This interpretation was to be repeated in many cases over the next quarter century.

The addition of the Civil Rights Amendments—the Thirteenth, Fourteenth, and Fifteenth—after the Civil War considerably complicated the pattern of federalism in the area of civil rights. In their historical context, these amendments were specifically concerned with the Negroes who had recently been freed in the southern states. The Thirteenth Amendment, prohibiting slavery, was intended to affirm the Negro's constitutional status as a freedman. The Fourteenth was intended to define his citizenship and to guarantee his privileges and immunities as a United States citizen; no state may deny him equal protection of the laws or deprive him of life, liberty, or property without due process of law. The Fifteenth was intended to guarantee that his right to suffrage would not be abridged because of race, color, or previous condition of servitude.

Congressional debates on the introduction of the Fourteenth Amendment show the intent, at least on the part of those who spoke out, to make the entire Bill of Rights applicable to the states. Immediately following the adoption of the Thirteenth Amendment, Congress had enacted the Civil Rights Act of 1866, which conferred citizenship on the newly freed Negroes and provided that Negroes should have "full and equal benefit of all laws and proceedings for the security of person and property as is enjoyed by white citizens." President Andrew Johnson vetoed the bill on the ground that it was beyond the constitutional power of Congress to "repeal all state laws discriminating between whites and blacks. . . ." Congress passed the Civil Rights Act over the President's veto but meantime, to make legitimate national legislation in the broad area of civil rights, Congress introduced the Fourteenth Amendment. Unquestionably, the framers of the Fourteenth Amendment hoped to overrule the decision of *Barron* v. *Baltimore* and to bring the states under the same limitations as the national government with respect to individual rights and liberties. On the other hand, those who opposed the Amendment were just as certainly antagonistic to any transfer of responsibility for civil rights from the states to the national government.

In our complicated political system, no single set of decision-makers has the last word on public policy. No sooner was the Fourteenth Amendment ratified than the Supreme Court began to interpret its meaning without reference to the pertinent congressional debates. Within a decade the expressed intentions of the Congress were interred in a series of judicial decisions which in effect denied to Congress the power to pass general legislation on civil rights. The Court invalidated the Civil Rights Act of 1875 which had prohibited discrimination in public accommodations.[4]

---

[3] The Chief Justice was not usually such a stickler for strict construction; see *Marbury* v. *Madison* (1 Cranch 137), *McCulloch* v. *Maryland* (4 Wheat. 316), and *Gibbons* v. *Ogden* (9 Wheat. 1).

[4] See the *Slaughter House Cases* (1873), which virtually negated the privileges and immunities clause of the new Amendment (16 Wall. 36); and the *Civil Rights Cases* (1883), which declared void the Civil Rights Act of 1875 (109 U.S. 3).

In drafting the Fourteenth Amendment, Congress unfortunately failed to express its "purpose in plain and intelligible language." The Amendment was written and adopted in a period of intense emotionalism and extreme partisanship in American politics. In the years since, it has been left largely to the courts to determine in the light of current controversies what Congress meant by such pregnant phrases as "citizenship," "privileges and immunities," "due process of law," and "equal protection of the laws." As the judges have tried to settle specific controversies that have arisen under these amendments, the original intentions of Congress have been much altered and vastly expanded. All kinds of people have insisted on their civil rights, taking their cases clear up to the Supreme Court—butchers of New Orleans, Chinese laundrymen of San Francisco, Jehovah's Witnesses from Alabama, Roman Catholic Sisters in Oregon, communist propagandists from New York, a newspaper in Minnesota, and a chambermaid in Washington, as well as business corporations, railroads, public utilities, and labor organizers in every state. All these and many more have sought judicial opinions on the relationship of the Fourteenth Amendment, which restricts the states, to the Bill of Rights, which limits the central government.

When, however, we view policy as a continuing sequence of activities, we perceive that the passage of time inevitably changes the public policy. As Justice Holmes put it, time has upset many "fighting faiths." What men once thought most important may seem insignificant, even dangerous, to their children's children. What Americans most want today may not have occurred to our forebears. A democratic system is naturally resilient. In the political process, the majority continues to have its way; but as the majority itself changes in character so do the decision-makers respond to new pressures and different circumstances. In 1954, in the momentous case that held segregation in the public schools unconstitutional under the Fourteenth Amendment, Chief Justice Earl Warren declared, "We cannot turn the clock back to 1868 when the Amendment was adopted." As we discuss current and specific policies in civil rights, we cannot turn the clock back to 1787 when the Constitution was designed, to 1787 when the Bill of Rights was introduced, to 1868 when the Fourteenth Amendment was adopted, or even to 1964 when Congress passed the first great Civil Rights Act since 1875. The output of any decision becomes part of the input for the next decision.

Civil Rights and Fair Procedures

Mr. Justice Frankfurter once said that "the history of liberty has largely been the history of observance of procedural guarantees." The constitutional requirements of due process of law in the Bill of Rights are quite specific. They represent the usages and the modes of procedure under English common law that the eighteenth century considered basic to a "government of laws and not of men."

These requirements are: *The right of the people to be secure in their persons, houses, papers, and effects against unreasonable searches and seizures . . . issue of a warrant only upon probable cause, supported by oath or affirmation, and particularly describing the place to be searched and the persons or things to be seized* (Amendment IV); *indictment by grand jury for capital or otherwise infamous crime . . . the restriction upon double jeopardy . . . immunity against self-incrimination* (Amendment V); *the right to a speedy and public trial, by an impartial jury in the state and the district wherein the crime was committed . . . the right to be informed of the nature and cause of the accusation . . . the right of the accused to be confronted with the witnesses against him . . . and the right to have compulsory process for obtaining witnesses in his favor . . . the right to counsel* (Amendment VI); *. . . protection against excessive bail, excessive fines . . . and cruel or unusual punishments* (Amendment VIII).

How many of the procedural guarantees in the Bill of Rights are carried forward by the Fourteenth Amendment into the states? The Court has refused to give any definitive answer, preferring to consider each case on its merits. Until recently, the centrifugal forces of federalism have tended to prevail over the logic of uniformity. At one time or another the Court has held various guarantees in the Bill of Rights to be unnecessary for due process of law in the states—the right to trial by jury, indictment by grand jury, protection against double jeopardy.[5]

Justice Black and other justices have argued that the basic standards of justice should be the same in all courts, federal and state.[6] More and more the Court has been inclined to incorporate the mandates of the Fourth, Fifth, and Sixth Amendments within the meaning of due process of law in the Fourteenth Amendment. Thus the Court has declared that search and seizure may not be such as to outrage the canons of decency; the accused has the right to counsel—even before trial—if necessary, at public expense; the defendant cannot be compelled to testify against himself and confession may not be coerced; the accused is entitled to a hearing before an unbiased judge; and a speedy and public trial is essential. Presumably, these procedures represent what Justice Benjamin Cardozo had in mind when he referred to principles "so rooted in the tradition and conscience of our people as to be ranked as fundamental."[7]

When we search for some clear guide to the line of division between what is basic and what is not in court procedures, however, we are bound to be frustrated. Since the Court refuses to accept *all* the procedures outlined in the Bill or Rights, it has been obliged to invoke some sort of "natural law"—call it "civilized decency," "the conscience of the community," or "a sense of justice"—to rationalize its selection of *some* criteria for "fundamental justice" which must not be denied in any

---

[5] *Walker* v. *Sauvinet*, 92 U.S. 90 (1876); *Hurtado* v. *California*, 110 U.S. 516 (1884); *Palko* v. *Connecticut*, 302 U.S. 319 (1937).

[6] Since the adoption of the Fourteenth Amendment, at least ten justices have felt that it protects from infringement by the states *all* of the privileges, protections, and safeguards granted by the Bill of Rights—but at no time have a majority of justices on the Court commanded this view. The justices: Field, Harlan (the first), Bradley, Swayne, Murphy, Rutledge, Jackson, Black, Douglas, Harlan (the second).

[7] *Palko* v. *Connecticut*. For a succession of cases illustrating judicial application of Bill of Rights guarantees for due process of law in state administration of justice see: *Tumey* v. *Ohio*, 273 U.S. 510 (1927); *Powell* v. *Alabama*, 287 U.S. 45 (1932); *Rochin* v. *California*, 342 U.S. 165 (1952); *Gideon* v. *Wainright*, 372 U.S. 335 (1963); *Escobedo* v. *Illinois*, 378 U.S. 478 (1964); *Malloy* v. *Hogan*, 378 U.S. 1 (1964).

court. Notice the vague contours of Justice Felix Frankfurter's definition of due process: "Representing a profound attitude of fairness between man and man, and more particularly between the individual and government, 'due process' is compounded of history, reason, the past course of decisions, and stout confidence in the strength of the democratic faith which we profess." [8]

The confusion resulting from a "double standard of justice" in federal and state courts is illustrated by the long uncertain status of the Fourth Amendment, which prohibits unreasonable searches and seizures. In 1914, the Supreme Court held that evidence secured by illegal search and seizure could not be used in federal prosecution. [9] Thirty-five years later, the Court for the first time discussed the effect of the Fourth Amendment on the states. Justice Frankfurter stated as a general principle that the Fourteenth Amendment prohibits unreasonable searches and seizures by state officers. "The security of one's privacy against arbitrary intrusion by the police . . . is basic to a free society. It is therefore implicit in 'the concept of ordered liberty' and as such enforceable against the States through the Due Process Clause." [10] But, at the same time, he declared that the Fourteenth Amendment did not require state courts to follow the federal rule that excludes evidence secured by unreasonable searches and seizures.

In a 1961 case, Justice Clark, who had considerable experience with the practical side of administering justice when he was Attorney General, observed that the exclusion in court of evidence illegally obtained "makes very good sense. . . . There is no war between the Constitution and common sense." [11] Furthermore, unless this rule of exclusion is applied equally in federal and state courts, the fruits of an unconstitutional search and seizure could be traded back and forth between federal and state agents, thus encouraging disobedience to the Constitution by officers of the law. If the federal agent obtained evidence illegally that he could not use in federal courts, he could hand it over to the state agent for use in state courts; and if a state agent made an illegal seizure, he could carry the evidence across the street to the federal attorney. Mindful of these practical problems in law enforcement, the Supreme Court now holds that evidence obtained by unconstitutional means cannot be used in either federal or state courts.

The uncertain status of the Fourteenth Amendment vis-à-vis the Bill of Rights does not mean that the states have shown no concern for civil rights except those enforced by federal power. Indeed, some states go well beyond the guarantees of the federal Constitution in the protection of individual rights. Yet Justice

---

[8] *Joint Anti-Fascist Refugee Committee* v. *McGrath*, 341 U.S. 123 (1951).

[9] *Weeks* v. *United States*, 232 U.S. 383 (1914).

[10] *Wolf* v. *Colorado*, 338 U.S. 25 (1949).

[11] *Mapp* v. *Ohio*, 81 S. Ct. 1684 (1961). The impact of a Supreme Court decision is not always as impressive as a mere reading of opinions might suggest. Before the adoption of the exclusionary rule for federal courts in 1914, twenty-seven states admitted evidence illegally seized by state officers in their own court proceedings. In 1960, eleven years after the Court declared that unreasonable searches and seizures by state officers were constitutionally prohibited, twenty-four states still admitted evidence obtained by such illegal mehods.

William J. Brennan observes from his own experience on the United States Supreme Court:

> Far too many cases come from the states to the Supreme Court presenting dismal pictures of official lawlessness, of illegal searches and seizures, illegal detentions attended by prolonged interrogation and coerced admissions of guilt, of the denial of counsel and downright brutality. Judicial self-restraint which defers too much to the sovereign powers of the states and reserves judicial intervention for only the most revolting cases will not serve to enhance Madison's priceless gift of 'the great rights of mankind secured under this Constitution.' [12]

To understand due process of law, of course, we must look to more than constitutional declarations, legal codes and judicial opinions. The administration of justice, as a matter of public policy, involves a great many actors—policemen, lawyers, judges, lesser court officials, jail guards, prison wardens, and others— who play specific roles. All of these figures are actors-in-an-environment, and the environment includes the unofficial norms, the conscience and culture (or lack thereof) of the community. Most persons haled into our criminal courts are "unrespectable" defendants—murderers, rapists, thieves, arsonists, dope peddlers, gangsters, racketeers, and just bums. Because they generally are such unsavory characters, the community is not likely to protest if some of those accused get short shrift, something less than due process of law, between arrest and imprisonment or execution.

Equal protection of the laws may be denied simply because many people cannot afford to pay for justice under our legal system. In 1963, the U. S. Supreme Court considered the petition of Clarence Gideon, a prisoner in Florida who had been sentenced to serve a five-year term after he had unsuccessfully tried to conduct his own defense in a jury trial on the charge of breaking and entering a poolroom with intent to commit a misdemeanor. Without funds of his own, he had been unable to hire a lawyer, and under Florida law only a person charged with a capital offense was entitled to a public defender. The Supreme Court of the United States which received Gideon's petition (in forma pauperis) recognized that "in our adversary system of criminal justice, any person haled into court, who is too poor to hire a lawyer, cannot be assured a fair trial unless counsel is provided for him." [13] Gideon's case was remanded to the Florida court for retrial with counsel, and subsequently Gideon was found not guilty. In the wake of Gideon's case, however, came a flood of similar petitions; the good citizens of Florida were shocked to learn that of the 7836 inmates currently

---

[12] Justice William J. Brennan, "The Bill of Rights and the States," reprint of the James Madison Lecture, New York University Law Center, February 15, 1961, at page 24.

[13] *Gideon* v. *Wainright,* 372 U.S. 335 (1963). Gideon had made his petition to the Supreme Court in a handwritten note on prison stationery. *In forma pauperis* is a proceeding whereby any citizen has a right to proceed in any federal court without payment of fees upon execution of a pauper's oath. The Supreme Court annually receives over a thousand petitions for *in forma pauperis,* and grants about 3 per cent. Gideon's case was argued before the Supreme Court by one of Washington's most distinguished attorneys, appointed by the Court.

serving time in the state penitentiary, 5093 had been tried and convicted without counsel and were expecting to be freed as a result of Gideon's case.

Defendants associated with unpopular causes may find justice hard to get at any price. Obviously, defendants need lawyers to guide them through the intricacies of courtroom procedures. But atheists, communists, civil rights demonstrators, extreme rightists, and political assassins may be denied due process of law because they cannot secure adequate counsel. The civil rights drive in the South has dramatized this special problem; local lawyers have been most reluctant to take cases involving racial issues, especially if the accused were Negro or northern integrationists. Similarly, persons accused of being security risks or subversives (especially from the Left) have found it difficult to obtain counsel. Lawyers know that if they take such cases they may be accused of being sympathetic with the client's cause, which could seriously injure their professional status and practice in the community.

The Bill of Rights and the Military Establishment

The civil rights of persons in the military establishment is now a major problem. The Constitution gives to Congress power "to make rules for the government and regulation of the land and naval forces." During the Administration of President Washington, the problem was insignificant; Congress authorized an army of 840 men but less than 700 were actually in uniform. The situation today is vastly different. Some 2.5 million persons are now serving in the armed services of the United States, and every resident male is a potential member. The average male citizen may spend 4 per cent of his adult life in active military service and his reserve obligations may extend over 10 per cent of his lifetime. Veterans number approximately 23 million.

Congress has exercised its constitutional power by enacting the Uniform Code of Military Justice. Generally the judicial power of the civil courts does not extend to the treatment of military personnel under this code. The Supreme Court has made it plain, however, that court martial proceedings can be challenged through habeas corpus [14] proceedings in the regular courts if a defendant has been denied his fundamental rights. As Chief Justice Warren puts it, "Our citizens in uniform may not be stripped of basic rights simply because they have doffed their civilian clothes." [15] The Court of Military Appeals acts as a sort of civilian "supreme court" over military proceedings to insure fairness in courts-martial. That few appeals are ever taken from the Court of Military Appeals may be a tribute to its success in securing due process of law in the courts-martial.

The constitutional rights of persons overseas presents a special problem. Early in the nation's history, the Supreme Court generally held that the Constitu-

---

[14] The writ of *habeas corpus* is perhaps the most basic of all procedural rights, requiring the release of the accused unless just cause for detention be shown to the satisfaction of the court.

[15] This discussion on the application of the Bill of Rights to the military borrows from Chief Justice Earl Warren, "The Bill of Rights and the Military," 37 *N. Y. U. Law Review*, 181, 186–188, 190–195 (1962).

tion was inoperative beyond the nation's boundaries.[16] Americans abroad—tourists, traders, students, merchants, and missionaries—accepted the fact that when they entered a foreign country they were subject to the law of that country and could not claim privilege and immunities of United States citizenship.

The tremendous expansion of American military bases around the world after World War II substantially changed this simple picture. Members of the armed forces, wherever stationed, are, of course, governed by military rules and regulations and subject to court-martial jurisdiction. But what about the status of the hundreds of thousands of civilian employees and civilian dependents who are attached to the armed forces overseas?

Congress gave one answer in the aforementioned Uniform Code of Military Justice, an Act passed in 1950, effective in 1951. Briefly, this Act established United States military jurisdiction over all civilian employees and civilian dependents of the armed forces when stationed in foreign nations. The Act was implemented in 1953–1954 through the Status of Force agreements with those countries where the United States maintained military communities. These agreements permitted the United States to exercise extra-territorial jurisdiction over all persons covered by the Uniform Code of Military Justice, including the civilian employees and civilian dependents.

Shortly thereafter, numerous appeals reached the United States Supreme Court challenging the right of military tribunals to try civilian persons. One of the first of these cases involved a civilian in the United States, Robert Toth, who had been discharged from the Air Force five months when American military authorities in Korea discovered evidence implicating him in the murder of a Korean national. Toth was arrested while at work in Pittsburgh and flown to Korea to stand trial by court-martial. The Supreme Court, in a six to three decision, ordered his release on writ of *habeas corpus*. Justice Black spoke firmly: civilians like Toth cannot be subjected to trial by court-martial. He declared invalid that part of the Uniform Code which extended court-martial to civilians charged with offenses committed during military service.[17]

Within months of the highly publicized *Toth Case* (1955), other civilians who had been court-martialed for offenses overseas were claiming a constitutional right to trial by jury and other procedural rights. The cases presented a variety of problems: capital cases involving civilian dependents; non-capital cases with civilian dependents; capital cases with civilian employees; non-capital cases with civilian employees. The issues were numerous, complex, and technical. Suffice it to say that in January, 1960, the Court declared invalid that section of the Uniform Military Code which provided for courts-martial of civilians in the overseas military establishments. Four cases were settled simultaneously, and in each case the civilians were freed. Justice Clark gave the opinions for the Court, but some justices concurred or dissented in every case.[18]

---

[16] *In re Ross*, 140 U.S. 453 (1891), and *Downes* v. *Bidwell*, 182 U.S. 244 (1901).

[17] *Toth* v. *Quarles*, 350 U.S. 11 (1955).

[18] *Kinsella* v. *U.S. ex rel Singleton*, 361 U.S. 234 (1960); *McElroy* v. *U.S. ex rel Guagliardo*, 361 U.S. 281 (1960); *Grisham* v. *Hagan*, 361 U.S. 278 (1960); *Wilson* v. *Bohlender*, 361 U.S. 234 (1960).

The Court has obviously thrown a monkey wrench into the military machinery overseas. No doubt the maintenance of discipline in the military community was easier when all persons, military or civilian, were subject to courts-martial. But ours is a constitutional system, a government of laws, in which the individual is guaranteed his civil rights. The subordination of the military establishment to civilian authority is deeply rooted in the American experience. To treat the military establishment as an enclave outside the constitutional guarantees would be contrary to our long-established tradition.

First Amendment Freedoms

The Court has been reluctant to accept the proposition that the Fourteenth Amendment makes the whole of the Bill of Rights applicable in the states. Before World War I it was generally believed that the First Amendment did not restrain the states. But during the "red scare" after the war and in the early 1920's, when a number of legislatures tried to curb political expression, the Court began to reinterpret the First Amendment precisely as if it read "Neither Congress nor any state shall make any law restricting freedom of religion, speech, press, peaceable assembly and petition of the people for redress of grievances." In 1925, in a case involving freedom of speech and the press in New York, Justice Sanford simply *assumed* that the fundamental freedoms of the First Amendment were incorporated in the personal rights and liberties protected by the due process clause of the Fourteenth Amendment from impairment by the states.[19]

Liberty of Conscience.   The First Amendment, which has been called "the First Article of our Faith," says, "Congress shall make no law respecting an establishment of religion, or prohibiting the free exercise thereof." The primary purpose of this amendment was to prohibit the establishment of a national church with a preferred status, such as the Anglican Church in England. Since tax-supported religious institutions did exist in several states, however, it was generally understood that the First Amendment left to the states full power and free policy in religious matters. The Anglican Church had been disestablished in Maryland, the Carolinas, Georgia, and Virginia when the colonies' political ties with England were severed. But all the New England states except Rhode Island continued to give preferred status to the Congregational Church. Not until 1833 did Massachusetts amend its constitution to place all religious denominations on an equal footing. For many years, New Hampshire, New Jersey, Massachusetts, and North Carolina required that office holders be Protestants. Delaware and even Pennsylvania, which had a Bill of Rights affirming the unalienable right of all men to worship God according to the dictates of their own conscience, still disqualified Jews and non-Christians for public office.[20]

The Founding Fathers for the most part were religious men. As Justice Story observed in his commentaries on the Constitution (1840),[21]

---

[19] *Gitlow* v. *New York*, 268 U.S. 652 (1925).

[20] The most complete study on this topic is Anson Phelps Stokes, *Church and State in the United States* (New York: Harper & Brothers, 1950), 3 vols.

[21] Joseph Story, *A Familiar Exposition of the Constitution of the United States: Containing a Brief Commentary* (New York: American Book Company, 1840), p. 261.

> Probably, at the time of the adoption of the Constitution, and of the [First] amendment . . . , the general, if not the universal, sentiment in America was, that Christianity ought to receive encouragement from the State, so far as such encouragement was not incompatible with the private rights of conscience, and the freedom of religious worship.

As a matter of fact, through the years, the American government has officially encouraged religious practices and has offered special concessions to churches. By act of Congress, the pledge of allegiance to the United States is made to "one nation under God." The currency of the country carries the national motto, "In God We Trust." The Supreme Court of the United States opens each session with the intonement, "God save the United States and this Honorable Court." Each house of Congress appoints a chaplain who invokes divine blessings and prays for God's guidance in the daily proceedings. Chaplains are attached to all the armed forces of the United States; Sunday attendance at chapel exercises is compulsory at West Point, the Air Academy, and Annapolis. Church property and income are generally exempt from federal and state taxes. Sunday is legally recognized as a day of rest in every state. Thanksgiving, Christmas, and Easter are observed in every community in the country. The Bible is commonly used in taking court oaths, "So help me God." In some states, custody and adoption laws are tailored to religious beliefs.

The Supreme Court has assumed that "liberty" under the Fourteenth Amendment includes all the basic freedoms specified in the First Amendment. Thus the fundamental relationship between church and state, which is defined for the national government in the First Amendment, is also implicit for the state governments in the Fourteenth. In other words, neither Congress nor the states may establish a church or prohibit the free exercise of religion. This does not mean, however, that government cannot regulate religious practices that may offend public morals, jeopardize public health, or in other ways endanger the public welfare. For example, the practice of polygamy, the sacrifice of virgins, or wrestling with rattlesnakes may be forbidden without violating constitutional rights. State university students may be required to take ROTC training; first-graders may not be admitted to public schools without vaccination against smallpox; a couple may have to take blood tests before obtaining a marriage license. These and many similar provisions come under the police power of the state, which is paramount to the dictates of individual conscience.

Thomas Jefferson was frequently criticized by clergymen for talking about a "wall of separation" between "Church and State." Especially in the sensitive area of public education the controversy is still acute. For example, the Roman Catholic Church maintains parochial schools so that Catholic children may receive regular religious instruction along with the usual secular education. These parochial schools have given rise to many constitutional issues. Some years ago, Oregon passed a law requiring that all children attend the Oregon public schools; in effect, this law would have eliminated all private and parochial schools. Without referring directly to any religious rights involved, the United States Supreme Court held the law invalid under the Fourteenth Amendment on the grounds that it was a seizure of private property without due process of law.[22] In Louisiana, where there are many Roman Catholics, the state provides free textbooks for parochial and public schools alike; this policy has been upheld as an aid to school children rather than a public assistance to church schools.[23] The Supreme Court has also, on the grounds of public safety, sustained a New Jersey statute permitting free bus transportation for school children traveling to either parochial or private schools.[24]

The problem of "released time" for religious instruction in the public schools is still not solved, despite two key decisions on the issue. In 1940, members of three major faiths, Jewish, Roman Catholic, and Protestant, joined together in Champaign, Illinois, to provide for the religious instruction of school children. Classes were arranged in the regular public school classrooms; separate groups were taught by Protestant ministers, Roman Catholic priests, and Jewish rabbis; students attended only with parental consent; those who did not choose to take religious instruction were required to stay in study rooms. Mrs. Vashti McCollum, a parent, brought suit against the Champaign Board of Education; she did not wish her child to be subjected to religious instruction, nor did she wish him to be embarrassed because he was not receiving such instruction. The Supreme Court sustained Mrs. McCollum on the grounds that a state may not utilize its public school system to promote religious education. Justice Hugo Black, speaking for the Court, repeated the thought of Thomas Jefferson, "The First Amendment has erected a wall between church and state which must be kept high and impregnable." [25]

The *McCollum Case* stirred wide debate, not only among interested church groups, but also among scholars on historical and constitutional grounds, who felt that the Court had gone well beyond the intent of the First Amendment. Four years after the *McCollum Case*, the Court reconsidered the problem of "released time." [26] The New York public schools were releasing students during the school day to permit them to go to religious centers for instruction. Students were released only on parental request; those who were not released remained in the classrooms. No expenditure of public funds was involved, and no religious instruction was offered in the public school buildings. Justice William O. Douglas, while reaffirming the doctrine of separation of church and state, nevertheless justified the New York system, in which "the public schools do no more than accommodate their schedules to a program of outside religious instruction. . . . We are a religious people whose institutions presuppose a Supreme Being. We cannot read into the Bill of Rights . . . a philosophy of hostility to religion."

The number of church-state questions that go into court attest to the many and deeply devisive opinions that Americans hold on the meaning of religious freedom. In 1962, the Supreme Court declared that it was unconstitutional for the

---

[22] *Pierce* v. *Society of the Sisters of Holy Names of Jesus and Mary,* 268 U.S. 510 (1925).

[23] *Cochran* v. *Louisiana State Board of Education,* 281 U.S. 370 (1930).

[24] *Everson* v. *Board of Education,* 330 U.S. 1 (1947).

[25] *Illinois ex. rel. McCollum* v. *Board of Education,* 333 U.S. 203 (1948).

[26] *Zorach* v. *Clauson,* 343 U.S. 306 (1952).

New York State Board of Regents to prescribe a "prayer" as part of the daily exercise in the New York public schools.[27] Even though the Board of Regents claimed that the prayer was "non-denominational" and even though students who did not wish to participate in the exercise were permitted to remain silent or be excused from the schoolroom, the Court held that such an officially established prayer program violated the Establishment Clause and also the Free Exercise Clause of the First Amendment.

In 1963, the Court struck down a Pennsylvania statute which called for "at least ten verses from the Holy Bible to be read without comment, at the opening of each public school on each school day." Any child was excused from the exercise upon written request of his parent or guardian. The Court also held unconstitutional a similar requirement in the public schools of Baltimore—"reading without comment, of a chapter in the Holy Bible and/or the use of the Lord's prayer." In both cases the Court held firmly that the Establishment and Free Exercise Clauses of the First Amendment require the government to be strictly neutral in matters of religion, "protecting all, preferring none, disparaging none." [28]

Drawing by Herblock. From *Straight Herblock* (New York: Simon & Schuster, 1964).

"I'll get you in there if it kills you."

The Court's decisions in the prayer cases—"taking God out of the schools"—outraged many people and stirred heated controversy in press and pulpit, in Congress and in state legislatures. Some groups have advocated passing a constitutional amendment to prohibit the Court from interfering with state educational policies so that school children will not be deprived of their religious heritage or deprived of moral instruction. On the other hand, spokesmen of the

[27] The prayer in question read, "Almighty God, we acknowledge our dependence upon Thee, and we beg Thy blessings upon us, on our parents, our teachers and our country." *Engel* v. *Vitale*, 370 U.S. 42 (1962). Mr. Justice Stewart who was the lone dissenter in the case said, "I cannot see how an 'official religion' is established by letting those who want to say a prayer say it. On the contrary, I think that to deny the wish of these school children to join in reciting this prayer is to deny them the opportunity to share in the spiritual heritage of the nation."

[28] *School District of Abington Township* v. *Schempp*, 374 U.S. 203 (1963).

major denominational groups have generally supported the Court's doctrine of governmental neutrality with respect to religious activities. The separation of church and state, they point out, does not prevent people from praying at any time, nor from going to the church of their own choice. But because we are a religious people, a people of many different faiths, public policy—whether it is policy from the bench, the legislative chamber, or the office of the state superintendent of instruction—is not likely to settle the ancient issues of church, state, and school relations.

In the first edition of this book (1959), in discussing qualifications for the presidency, we pointed out that the Protestant majority had always insisted that the President, as a symbol of the national character, be at least nominally a Protestant. But the election of John F. Kennedy in 1960 dispelled the myth that a Roman Catholic could not hope to reach the White House. Ironically, the Kennedy Administration almost immediately ran into a very bitter religious controversy when it proposed federal aid to public elementary and secondary schools, for classroom construction and for teachers' salaries. Even before the hearings on the bill began in Congress, bishops of the Roman Catholic Church insisted that federal aid to education should also be extended to private (that is, parochial) schools. President Kennedy told Congress that he thought federal aid to church-sponsored schools would violate the constitutional separation of church and state. Representative John W. McCormack, Democratic Floor Leader, expressed a contrary view, supported by a legal opinion from Professor Arthur Sutherland of the Harvard Law School.[29] Meanwhile, Catholic Church officials publicized numerous instances of federal funds used for church aid. Under the GI Bill of Rights, veterans had used federal grants to attend Catholic colleges. Under the National Defense Act, passed in 1958, students in Catholic colleges could obtain federal loans and scholarships. Catholic parochial schools were included in the federal free lunch and school milk programs.

The great debate over federal aid to education in 1961 was not entirely fought on religious grounds. The Catholic hierarchy was joined by some southern leaders who hoped that if federal funds could be used by parochial schools, they might also be used for private schools set up to avoid integration. Many persons, like Senator Barry Goldwater, opposed the idea as another money-spending plank in the welfare program. Others fought the extension of federal power over an area traditionally reserved to the states. President Kennedy was in a peculiar spot: as the first Catholic President, he could not risk the charge of pushing the Roman Catholic position; on the other hand, he did not want to jeopardize the whole program of federal aid to education by refusing any aid to the parochial schools. As the battle moved to a climax in Congress, the White House remained aloof from discussion. No one following the congressional debates on federal aid to education, or the resultant editorial opinions in the newspapers, could remain

---

[29] Excerpts of Professor Sutherland's opinion were published. See Arthur E. Sutherland, "Does the Constitution Really Ban U.S. Aid to Parochial Schools?" *U.S. News and World Report*, April 3, 1961, p. 109.

under any illusion that church and state are separate in American politics and that religious prejudices do not enter into public policy.

Freedom to Differ. Most eighteenth-century Americans believed that the good society was a society in which every man was free to think for himself and to express his thoughts to others. They could put their trust in the consent of the governed so long as every man was free to follow the dictates of his own conscience and to form his opinions in full and free discussion with his fellows. This is the simple philosophy that underlies the First Amendment, "Congress shall make no law . . . abridging the freedom of speech, or of the press; or the right of the people peaceably to assemble, and to petition the Government for a redress of grievances."

In his great essay, *On Liberty*, John Stuart Mill said, "If all mankind minus one were of one opinion, and only one person were of the contrary opinion, mankind would be no more justified in silencing that one person, than he, if he had the power, would be justified in silencing mankind." Justice Holmes expressed this same sentiment: "If there is any principle of the Constitution that more imperatively calls for attachment than any other it is the principle of free thought, not free thought for those who agree with us but freedom for the thought we hate." [30]

The principle of free discussion was put to a severe test in the first decade of the Republic when the Federalists attempted to squelch the rising opposition of the Jeffersonian Republicans through the Alien and Sedition Acts of 1798. The victory of the Jeffersonian Republicans and the election of Thomas Jefferson in 1800 put a quick end to these acts. Not until World War I would Congress again try to control freedom of political expression. In 1917, Congress passed an espionage act that was intended to restrict political dissent while the nation was at war.

In 1940, Congress passed the Smith Act, the first peace-time sedition act to be put on the books since the Alien and Sedition Acts of 1798. This Act forbids both the advocacy of the violent overthrow of the government and conspiracies designed to cause this overthrow. After World War II, as the international conflict of ideologies grew sharper, Congress turned its attention to the problems of "psychological warfare." To avert the dangers of subversion, and especially to guard against communism, Congress began to take steps toward the control of political thinking that was directly inimical to "Americanism." As early as 1947, Congress included in the Taft-Hartley Act a provision that required officers of labor unions to swear they were not members of the Communist Party or any organization that believes in or teaches the overthrow of the government by force or by other illegal methods.

Also in 1947, President Truman by executive order prescribed "Procedures

---

[30] The case, *U.S.* v. *Schwimmer*, 279 U.S. 644 (1929), involved a 49-year-old Hungarian woman, a professional pacifist, who was seeking U. S. citizenship. The majority of the Court refused to grant citizenship to a person who refused to bear arms in defense of the U. S. Though Holmes himself was no pacifist, he strongly dissented from the majority views.

for the Administration of an Employees' Loyalty Program in the Executive Branch of the Government." A network of Loyalty Boards was established to investigate every employee in the federal service. Membership in organizations listed by the Attorney General as totalitarian, fascist, communist, or subversive was an important fact in determining "disloyalty." Following a "hearing," many government employees were suspended, discharged, or resigned under fire, because their political views made them "security risks." At the same time, Congress was investigating un-American activities and subversives in all sectors of American society—university professors and public-school teachers; Hollywood actors, writers, and directors; news reporters and editors; clergymen; and especially ex-New-Dealers. A motley parade of informers and witnesses, many of them ex-communists, appeared before congressional committees to give testimony about communists, communist sympathizers, fellow-travelers, and "liberals." Individuals who refused to cooperate with the committees were liable to be held in contempt of Congress, and those who failed to tell the whole truth about their past or present political associations could be tried for perjury. The most celebrated case of the early 1950's was that of Alger Hiss, who had had a high post in the State Department; he went to prison not because he was found guilty of espionage or even disloyalty, but because he perjured himself before the House Committee on Un-American Activities.

In 1950, Congress passed the comprehensive Internal Security Act. This Act set up a Subversive Activities Control Board charged with determining, at the request of the Attorney General, whether a particular organization is communist "action," communist "front," or communist "infiltrated." It required every communist organization to: register annually with the Attorney General; report the names of its officers, the names of all its members; identify the sources of all its funds; and label as "communist propaganda" all its publications sent through the mails or across state lines. Also according to this Act, members of communist organizations may not obtain passports, hold elective federal positions, serve as officers or employees of a labor union, or work in a defense plant.

In the 1954 Communist Control Act, Congress went even further by virtually outlawing the Communist Party as a political organization. Thus, the Party can no longer place its candidates on official election ballots.[31] Membership in the Communist Party per se is not illegal, but communists are natural targets of the Smith Act, which makes it a crime to be a knowing, active, and purposeful member of a group advocating the violent overthrow of the government.

How effective has all this legislation been in combating communism? The Communist Party has not put forward a presidential candidate since Earl Browder in 1940. Its membership in 1961 was estimated at around 10,000. It held a national convention as late as 1959 from which the press was excluded. Its overt activities have nearly reached the vanishing point. The requirement that communists be registered was intended to make it easy for the government to prosecute Party

---

[31] About half the states also have statutes in effect barring the Communist Party from the ballot.

leaders and most active members.[32] So far, the total number of communists actually convicted stands at less than fifty. But we do not know how potent the communist underground apparatus is or how effective its alliance with the Kremlin.

In 1950, organized labor argued before the Supreme Court that the non-Communist affidavit provision of the Taft-Hartley Act was a violation of the First Amendment guarantee of free speech. But Chief Justice Vinson upheld the Taft-Hartley provision as a necessary and proper method for removing political obstructions (communist-inspired strikes) to the free flow of commerce. Although he paid tribute to "the high place in which the right to speak, think, and assemble . . . was held by the Framers of the Bill of Rights," he did not think that the First Amendment restrained Congress from making a legitimate attempt to protect the public from noxious ideologies. Only Justice Black dissented; he could not agree with the assumption that individual freedom can be abridged whenever a majority of the Court is satisfied with the nature or purpose of the abridgment. The Court must hold strictly to the constitutional guarantees.[33]

The Supreme Court upheld the Smith Act in the highly dramatic *Dennis Case* (1951), which sprang from the conviction of the eleven top communists in the United States for violating the act. The majority of the Court viewed the role of the Communist Party in the United States as "a well organized, nationwide conspiracy." The Court held that it was not necessary for the government to wait until a *putsch* was about to be executed, with the plans laid and the signal awaited. It accepted the formula that Judge Learned Hand had applied in the Court of Appeals: "In each case [courts] must ask whether the gravity of the 'evil,' discounted by its improbability, justifies such invasion of free speech as is necessary to avoid the danger." In effect, this decision bestowed on Congress the power to determine when it is reasonable to restrict freedom of speech to safeguard public security.[34]

Justices Black and Douglas dissented vigorously in the *Dennis Case.* Black pointed out that the communist leaders had been charged neither with any attempt to overthrow the government, nor with any overt acts designed to overhrow it Rather, they had been charged with something three steps removed from such an attempt—they had been charged with conspiring to advocate the overthrow of the government. Douglas could see no "clear and present danger" in the Communist Party: "Some nations less resilient than the United States, where illiteracy is high and where democratic traditions are only budding, might have to take drastic steps and jail these men for merely speaking this creed. But in America they are miserable merchants of unwanted ideas; their wares remain unsold." The

---

[32] In *Aptheker* v. *Secretary of State* (12 L. ed. 2d 992 (1964)), the Court held unconstitutional a section of the Subversive Activities Act which prohibited members of any registered communist organization from applying for or using passports to travel abroad. The Court held that the section too broadly and indiscriminately restricted the right to travel and thereby abridged the liberty guaranteed by the Fifth Amendment.

[33] *American Communications Association, C.I.O.* v. *Douds,* 339 U.S. 382 (1950).

[34] *Dennis* v. *United States,* 341 U.S. 494 (1951).

majority of the Court, however, were unconvinced, unimpressed. The Smith Act was allowed to stand.

In 1957, the *Dennis Case* was somewhat modified by the decision of the Supreme Court in the *Yates Case*.[35] A group of California communists had been tried and convicted in the lower federal court on the charge of advocating the forcible overthrow of the United States government. The opinion of the Supreme Court was written by Justice John Marshall Harlan, who pointed out that "the Smith Act does not denounce advocacy in the sense of preaching abstractly the forcible overthrow of the government." Thus, in order to convict the communists under the Smith Act, the government would have to show that the defendants had advocated *overt action* toward the forcible overthrow of the government. Advocacy, said the Court, is criminal only if it urges persons to *do* something rather than merely to *believe* something. The Court therefore ordered a retrial of the California communists in line with this interpretation. Justices Black and Douglas dissented in part; they would have reversed the convictions and acquitted the defendants on much the same line of reasoning they had used in the *Dennis Case*: ". . . the present type of prosecutions are more in line with the philosophy of authoritarian government than with that expressed by our First Amendment."

In 1961, the Court considered the membership clause of the Smith Act. In a lengthy and complicated opinion, Justice Harlan upheld the conviction of an *active* member of the Communist Party, who had *knowledge* of the Party's illegal purpose and specific intent to overthrow the government of the United States. Justices Black, Douglas, and Brennan and Chief Justice Warren dissented on various grounds. Justice Douglas charged the majority with making "a sharp break with traditional concepts of First Amendment rights." Justice Brennan argued that the Internal Security Act of 1950, requiring Communists to register, was intended to give them immunity from prosecution under the Smith Act.[36]

In the same term, the Court also upheld the registration requirements of the Internal Security Act of 1950.[37] Justice Frankfurter, speaking for a majority of five, found that the Act neither violated the First Amendment freedoms nor constituted a bill of attainder. His opinion took cognizance of the world communist movement. He pointed out that the special requirements of registration, disclosure of membership, filing of financial statements, and identification of publications did not apply to all political groups but only to foreign-dominated organizations. Mr. Justice Black in dissent pressed the argument that "freedoms of speech, petition, and assembly guaranteed by the First Amendment must be accorded to the ideas we hate or sooner or later they will be denied to the ideas we cherish." In 1964, in a case already cited, the Court apparently has indicated that it will not countenance prosecution or restriction of activity simply on the fact of membership in a registered organization.[38]

---

[35] *Yates* v. *U.S.*, 354 U.S. 298 (1957).
[36] *Scales* v. *U.S.*, 367 U.S. 203 (1961).
[37] *Communist Party of U.S.* v. *Subversive Activities Board*, 367 U.S. 1 (1961).
[38] *Aptheker* v. *Secretary of State*, 12 L. ed. 2d 992 (1964).

The Fourteenth Amendment has brought many cases of "thought control" by state governments to the Court. In the case of *Gitlow* v. *New York*, to which we have already referred, the Court declared that the fundamental freedoms contained in the First Amendment must be construed as part of the "liberty" that the Fourteenth Amendment guaranteed against restrictive state legislation. Under this interpretation, the Court held the states to the general principle that they may not pass any law that curbs freedom of speech or freedom of the press. In the Gitlow case, the Supreme Court upheld the conviction of Gitlow, who was charged with "criminal anarchism" under the New York law. Gitlow had published a *Manifesto* which the majority of the Court felt went well beyond academic discussion; indeed, they felt that it advocated revolutionary mass action. The Court found that New York State, in convicting Gitlow, had exercised its police power in a reasonable manner to suppress danger at the outset. Justice Holmes dissented, on the grounds that Gitlow's *Manifesto* offered no "present danger" to New York. Holmes felt that the minority has the right not only to discuss but to incite: "Every idea is an incitement. It offers itself for belief, and, if believed, is acted on unless some other belief outweighs it, or some failure of energy stifles the movement at its birth." [39]

The Court has sometimes been accused of favoring the Radical Left. This is probably because in recent years cases that have gone up to the Court have more often involved the Radical Left than the Radical Right. On the record, however, it appears that the justices are more concerned about the constitutional rights than the political views of the individuals whose cases they decide. For example, in the *Terminiello Case*, the Court declared a Chicago ordinance unconstitutional because of the manner in which it had been interpreted by the enforcement agencies. Under the ordinance, Father Terminiello, an extreme Rightist, had been found guilty of disorderly conduct in criticizing certain racial and religious groups and stirred his audience to anger, turbulence, and violence. Justice Douglas, usually identified with the "liberal bloc," spoke for the majority: "A function of free speech under our system of government is to invite dispute. It may indeed best serve its high purpose when it induces a condition of unrest, creates dissatisfaction with conditions as they are, or even stirs people to anger." [40]

Supreme Court decisions are generally popular when they uphold the political views of the dominant majority. When the Court validated the membership clause of the Smith Act and the registration provisions of the Internal Security Act, Arthur Krock, veteran correspondent of *The New York Times*, congratulated the majority of the justices for "strengthening the defenses of the nation." And in this vein, he chided the dissenting justices for their persistence in interpreting the guarantees of the First and Fifth Amendments as absolutes, thus permitting the communist conspiracy to hide behind a shield of constitutional guarantees.[41] Editorial opinion across the country was generally pleased with the decision.

---

[39] *Gitlow* v. *New York*, 268 U.S. 652 (1925).
[40] *Terminiello* v. *Chicago*, 337 U.S. 1 (1949).
[41] *The New York Times*, June 6, 1961.

The judicial opinions reflect basic controversies in our current politics. Many people believe that the whole problem of national security, even national survival, is tied to the world communist movement. They say the American Way of Life can continue only if communism is stopped in America and contained in the world. Many persons are alarmed by what they regard as widespread un-American activities and disloyalty. Some have a tendency to equate opinions with which they disagree or practices of which they disapprove with "un-Americanism" or "communism." Others, perhaps not so many, are seriously disturbed by what they regard as ever-increasing abridgment of their constitutional rights and liberties.

In the interest of national security, the official policy-makers, national and state, have cracked down on communists and communist organizations, in effect not only outlawing communist activities but also severely restricting any expression of communist views. Numerous citizens' groups have recently appeared in the public forum eager to battle against communism in a much wider arena than is now covered by official policies. The best known of these groups is the John Birch Society, though there are others with ideas even farther to the right. In general, these groups contend that the greatest danger to national security is from subversion and infiltration at home. They are prone to attack military expenditures and foreign aid programs as wasteful and "phony defense." They are inclined to equate communism with socialism and socialism with liberalism. Their program of massive inoculation against communism has both an economic slant and a patriotic appeal. They view Americanism mainly in terms of the free-enterprise-competitive economy. They are likely to attack, in the name of Americanism, an odd assortment of persons and programs: beatniks and textbooks; pacifists and scientists; the Supreme Court and the Peace Corps; public libraries and the registration of firearms; preachers and professors. Their exuberant evangelism and vigilantism have had an increasing effect on public opinion. They have been successful in organizing adult discussion groups, projects, rallies, and freedom forums, and have even promoted their cause in public school education.

How has the general public reacted to the charges of communists in government? Apparently few votes have been influenced by such accusations. Though the extreme Right went all out to support the Republican presidential candidate in 1964, President Johnson was overwhelmingly re-elected. Indeed, a Louis Harris survey reported that 45 per cent of the eligible voters regarded Goldwater as a radical, while only 1 to 3 per cent considered themselves or Johnson to be radical. (Johnson was predominately viewed as "middle of the road" or as "liberal" whereas Goldwater was predominately described as at the extremes— "radical" or "conservative.") For the ideologically pure, "radical" may suggest socialist or even communist economic policies, but it's just another term for "extremist" to many voters.

How do people react to governmental action to meet the "communist threat"? On the basis of a nationwide survey, conducted during the height of alleged anti-communist hysteria, Samuel Stouffer, a public opinion analyst, found very few Americans either worried about the internal communist threat or deeply concerned over any loss of civil liberties. Community leaders, particularly the better educated, were found to be relatively more tolerant than the general population was of such unpopular groups as suspected communists, socialists, and atheists.[42] Do Americans really believe that no matter what a person's political beliefs are, he is entitled to the same legal rights and protections as anyone else? A recent study by a group of political scientists indicates an overwhelming affirmative consensus. Americans strongly support the idea of liberty in the abstract, though the average citizen is less likely than the political activist to support specific applications of civil rights. For example, about half of the general electorate but less than 20 per cent of the political activists sampled in a national survey felt that "a book that contains wrong political views cannot be a good book and does not deserve to be published." [43]

Freedom of Speech and Press—and the Mass Media

Many Framers of the United States Constitution were frankly skeptical of democracy—and with good reason, for in their time a majority of the people were illiterate. For them to base the future of the Republic on the consent of the governed was for their time a remarkable expression of faith in the common sense of the people. In the generations since, free public schools and mass media of communication have virtually eliminated the technical reasons for mass ignorance. In our time, people throughout the country have every opportunity to become well-informed. Never before has so large a part of the population been able to read and never before have they had so much to read.

The Framing Fathers believed that consent of the governed should rest on full and free discussion. To this end they wrote into the Bill of Rights the guarantee of a free press. On the whole, to this day, the press as well as newer media of communication are free from governmental censorship, and the public is relatively free to make its own choice in the vast "market place of ideas." Neither the press nor the public, however, takes full advantage of this constitutional freedom.

The newspaper is certainly an influential instrument in forming public opinion. National and international news services bring the news of the world into every American community almost constantly. We must remember, however, that newspapers are in business to make money. They make their real money out of advertising, and the greater their circulation the more advertising revenue they enjoy. Freedom from government control does not leave them free to inform the public as they please. They have found that the easiest way to increase circulation is not to print more news or to improve their editorial policy, but to add special features—keyhole columnists, sportswriters, and syndicated comic strips.

How does the public take advantage of a free press? Most adult Americans

[42] See Samuel A. Stouffer, *Communism, Conformity and Civil Liberties* (Garden City, N.Y.: Doubleday & Company, Inc., 1955), p. 230.
[43] Herbert McClosky, "Consensus and Ideology in American Politics," *American Political Science Review*, LVIII (June 1964), pp. 361–382.

read a daily newspaper but few of them read the news columns attentively enough to develop alert and intelligent opinions on the issues of the day. The typical American citizen, "reading" his daily paper, scans the headlines, looks at the comics, reads the sports page, and checks the list of births, deaths, hospital admissions, and police blotter cases. Even less can be said for the public's choice of books and magazines. The books that we read are mainly fiction, not the great novels of the world's literature but the current best sellers—books that titillate and entertain, not books that enlighten. On the non-fiction list, we choose books on cooking, gardening, home repairs, care of pets, and popular psychiatry; rarely books on public finance or foreign policy! In magazines, the biggest sale is in "pulps"—movie magazines, police gazettes, detective stories, "true confessions," scandal, and sex. At neighborhood drugstores, local chain groceries, five-and-ten-cent stores, and bus and train terminals, Americans by the millions pick their "paper-backs" from among the scores of covers that promise "blood and lust," "brutality and depravity." Children of all ages, who can't or won't read, buy the "comics" of "sex and sadism."

It has always been a point of common law—and the First Amendment incorporates this point—that neither speech nor press may offend public morals or public decency. It is within the police power of government to forbid the publication of whatever is "obscene," "lewd," or "lascivious." But we have seen how difficult it is to apply the formula of "clear and present danger" to political thinking, and it is even more difficult to test "evil thoughts" in the field of public morals. Many people feel that the sharp upswing in sex crimes and juvenile delinquency can be attributed to the current popularity of lurid literature—particularly to what the poet, E. E. Cummings, once called "uncomic non books." But no one has yet been able to tell us how to control the situation without violating civil liberties.

In 1948, the United States Supreme Court held invalid on the ground of "vagueness" a New York statute that prohibited publications "having a tendency to encourage or incite commission of any crime." With apparent regret, the Court declared that it did not know how the public could protect itself from sanguinary and salacious reading matter. Explained Justice Stanley Reed, "Though we can see nothing of any possible value to society in these magazines, they are as much entitled to the protection of free speech as the best of literature." [44] Walter Gelhorn, a learned champion of civil rights, comes to this conclusion in a discerning essay on restraints on book reading: "What we need in this country is not less reading, but more; not fewer poor books, but more good books; not repression, but liberation." [45]

Although the federal government possesses no police power to protect public morals, it has attempted to do so under various powers enumerated in the Constitution. The power to regulate foreign commerce has been used to prohibit

---

[44] *Winters v. New York,* 333 U.S. 507 (1948).
[45] Walter Gelhorn, *Individual Freedom and Government Restraints* (Baton Rouge: Louisiana State University Press, 1956), p. 104.

the importation of obscene pictures and obscene literature. But enforcement has been rather inept, since it is sometimes difficult to distinguish between art and pornography! [46] Congress forbids the use of the mails for a long list of purposes, including the shipping of dead animals, explosives, obscene and seditious matter, and anything fraudulent or tending to incite arson, murder, or assassination. The Postmaster General may revoke the second class mailing privileges of publications which, after a hearing, he finds obscene or seditious. He may not, however, as the Postmaster tried to do in the case of *Esquire* (1946), deny second-class privileges to a publication simply because in his opinion it does not "contribute to the public good and the public welfare." [47]

The First Amendment specifies freedom of the press but as a matter of policy—legislative, administrative, and judicial—this point has been construed fairly broadly to include all the mass media of communication which have been developed since the eighteenth century. Federal control over radio and television, however, is necessarily extensive. The Federal Communications Commission is obliged to license radio and television stations simply because there are only a limited number of broadcasting hours in a day and only a limited number of wave lengths that can be assigned. Licenses are granted "in the public interest, convenience and necessity." Since they may be rescinded for failure to operate in the public interest, and must be renewed periodically, indirect censorship may sometimes come into play. In fact, although the Federal Communications Commission will not censor programs for obscenity, it gives fair warning that it may not renew the license of a station that broadcasts objectionable matter. The Commission requires balanced presentation of controversial issues and specifically forbids stations to censor political broadcasts. Since radio and television stations are engaged in interstate commerce, their control is preempted by the federal government and they cannot be censored by the states.

Nine out of ten American households possess both radio and TV sets. All these people have a vested interest in the kind of programs that come over the air-waves. But who speaks for this silent audience? The Chairman of the Federal Communications Commission told the National Association of Broadcasters:

> We all know that people would more often prefer to be entertained than stimulated or informed. But our obligations are not satisfied if you look only to popularity as a test of what to broadcast. You are not only in show business; you are free to communicate ideas as well as relaxation. You must provide a wider range of choices, more diversity, more alternatives. It is not enough to cater to the nation's whims—you must also serve the nation's needs. The people own the air.[48]

But the Commissioner's admonition fell flat. When a government agency presumes to judge how much entertainment, how much information, how much editorializing shall be done through the mass media, the First Amendment is at issue.

---

[46] As an illustration of this point, there is amusement as well as edification in *United States* v. *One Book Entitled Ulysses*, 72 Fed. 2nd 705 (1934).

[47] *Hannegan* v. *Esquire*, 327 U.S. 146 (1946).

[48] Newton M. Minow to the Annual Meeting of the National Association of Broadcasters, May, 1961.

The Supreme Court has always stood firm against "prior censorship" of the writer, publisher, and bookseller.[49] But licensing and prior censorship of movies and plays have long been practiced, especially at the local level. New York law, for example, until it was cut down by judicial review, provided that no film should be licensed for showing if it was "obscene, indecent, immoral, inhuman, sacrilegious or . . . of such character that its exhibition would tend to corrupt morals or incite to crime." Under this statute, the New York Board of Regents decided in 1950 that the Italian film *The Miracle* was "sacrilegious" and directed that its license be rescinded. The United States Supreme Court reversed the order, however, on the ground that "it is not the business of government in our nation to suppress real or imagined attacks upon a particular religious doctrine, whether they appear in publications, speeches, or motion pictures." [50] Shortly thereafter, the Supreme Court again reversed the New York Board of Regents for having refused a license for the French film *La Ronde* on the grounds that it was "immoral and tended to corrupt morals." [51]

Although moving pictures are included under the category of the press, whose freedom is guaranteed by the First Amendment,[52] the Court has been inclined to admit prior censorship of films. In a 1961 case,[53] the Court upheld a Chicago ordinance that required the submission of films to city officials, who had to grant a permit before they could be exhibited. This was a 5–4 decision in which the minority spoke out strongly against the "vice of censorship through licensing" and the "evil of previous restraint." Chief Justice Warren, who prepared the dissenting opinion, offered an astonishing list of films banned in various communities on different grounds: Chicago censors banned a scene depicting the birth of a buffalo; Memphis banned a film because it contained scenes of white and Negro children in school together; a Pennsylvania censor disapproved the duration of a kiss.

We are concerned primarily with official policies and government protection of the rights and liberties of the individual, but we must remember that private groups exercise a great deal of control which is no less effective or pervasive. Radio, television, and movies have set up their own self-imposed codes of censorship in order to avoid offending the sponsors, the buying public, or the box office. Church groups sometimes act as self-appointed guardian angels. The Roman Catholic Legion of Decency has been in the vanguard of those who are anxious to insure "clean literature" and "family-type" entertainment. It was not so long ago that Protestant fundamentalists were leading the crusade to keep "dangerous heresies" such as the theory of evolution out of the public schools. Patriotic

---

[49] See *Near* v. *Minnesota*, 283 U.S. 697 (1931).

[50] *Burstyn* v. *Wilson*, 343 U.S. 495 (1952). *The Miracle* had treated the Annunciation and Nativity in such a way as to offend many Christians.

[51] *Commercial Pictures Corp.* v. *Regents of New York*, 346 U.S. 587 (1954).

[52] *United States* v. *Paramount Pictures*, 334 U.S. 131 (1948). The real controversy in this case involved charges of monopoly in distribution. The statement cited is dictum only, the Court's opinion but not the basis for its decision in the particular case.

[53] *Times Film Corporation* v. *City of Chicago*, 365 U.S. 43 (1961).

groups such as the Daughters of the American Revolution and the American Legion have been vigilant in screening school books and public libraries for "un-Americanism." Ethnic groups have fought to eliminate from the public forum any derogatory reference to their respective races or nationalities.

Outright censorship is rare in American government. Much more difficult to determine or appraise is official management of the news. A few months after President Kennedy went in to office, he summoned a representative group of newspaper editors and publishers to the White House. The purpose of the meeting was to urge the American press to use more "self-restraint" in handling news stories affecting national security. The President pointed out how different was the situation in the enemy camp: "Communist preparations are concealed, not published. Its mistakes are buried, not headlined. Its dissenters are silenced, not lionized. No expenditure is questioned, no rumor is printed, no secret is revealed." The President, of course, was not suggesting that these were desirable conditions, but he did make clear that an irresponsible press could seriously embarrass the Administration in its Cold War maneuvers.

Publicity about scientific developments, new weapons, or defense plants might result in giving information to the enemy. Leaks to the press from executive sessions of congressional committees, or from meetings of the National Security Council, could involve a damaging breach of intelligence. Sensational headlines, premature speculations in the syndicated columns or editorial pages, sharp criticism of administrative policies, all can handicap our bargaining power in foreign policy. Even so, the American press prides itself on a tradition of "publish and be damned . . . the people have the right to know." The press did not take kindly to President Kennedy's lecture, the more so because he delivered it upon the heels of the Cuban invasion fiasco, which had been lambasted by nearly every newspaper in the country. Thus, President Kennedy found no easy way out of the dilemma that has plagued every administration since George Washington's: how to restrain a critical press without aggravating it.

The dilemma is almost inescapable, especially in the area of foreign policy and national security; privacy has always held high priority in diplomacy but full and free information is essential in democratic government. The news reporter and the government official are likely to view the problem of publication from different vantage points. The reporter demands maximum disclosure of official activities and expects to use his own judgment in publishing what he thinks the public should know. The government official looks on the mass media as a means of engineering consent of the governed: to this end he may withhold as well as give out information; the important consideration is to secure public support. To put it bluntly, full information and free discussion of governmental activities will not enable the general public to decide many of the crucial issues of our times. The intrusion of public opinion could even be disastrous at some stages in the policy process. In the space age, many governmental decisions are necessarily made by scientists and specialists. Shall we rocket to the moon, convert atomic power to industrial use, give developmental aid to the newest African nation, or recognize the People's Republic of China? Equating public opinion with public policy today is a vastly different and much more complicated operation than it was at the founding of the Republic.[54]

Thomas Jefferson once made this claim for the University of Virginia, which he had founded: "This institution will be based on the illimitable freedom of the human mind. For here we are not afraid to follow truth wherever it may lead, nor to tolerate an error so long as reason is free to combat it." If there is any place that should be free from propaganda and indoctrination, it is the university. Both professors and students must have the utmost freedom to find out all they can, to examine every doctrine and idea, to test out all opinions. This is the only way in which men can pursue the truth that makes them free.

We have heard much about the infiltration of communism into our colleges and universities. But, as Justice Douglas has pointed out, the communists have been for the most part "miserable merchants of unwanted ideas." Actually, other groups have been far more successful in peddling their wares in our educational system. Business has a point of view that it wants taught—the doctrines of *laissez-faire* and private enterprise. Labor wants recognition of its rights to collective bargaining, maximum hours, minimum wages. Patriotic societies want to promote their ideas of 100 per cent Americanism. Church groups are eager to strengthen "moral and spiritual values" on every campus. And so it goes—parents, alumni, taxpayers, special-interest groups—all have something to say about what professors should and should not teach, about what students should and should not learn.

The federal government has no jurisdiction over colleges and universities. Nevertheless Congress, through its investigations of communism and un-American activities, has been able to curtail academic freedom perceptibly and substantially. Professors who fail to cooperate with investigating committees, who invoke their constitutional immunity under the Fifth Amendment, have been dismissed from their teaching positions. Tax-supported colleges and universities especially have been subjected to "loyalty programs" and popular agitation against "radicalism." Loyalty oaths are now rather generally required as evidence of fitness to teach both in the public schools, and in the state institutions of "higher learning." The oaths vary in form and content, from a simple declaration that one supports the national and state constitutions to swearing that one is not now and never has been a member of any organization described as subversive by attorneys general, legislative committees, or other authorities.

Common practice throughout the country is to fire—or refuse to hire— any admitted communist on the grounds that, aside from being a dangerous political character, a communist is too biased to be able to teach objectively and impartially. The Feinberg Act in New York State carries this presumption one

---

[54] See Bernard Cohen, *The Press and Foreign Policy* (Princeton, N.J.: Princeton University Press, 1963), for a carefully researched and perceptive study of the interaction between the press and government officials.

step further by making membership in a "subversive organization" *prima facie* evidence of disqualification as a teacher. Under this act, the New York Board of Regents is authorized to make a listing, "after full notice and hearing," of subversive organizations. The Feinberg Act was upheld with unusual alacrity by a majority of the United States Supreme Court called upon to make a "declaratory judgment" even before the law actually became operative. Justice Sherman Minton, for the Court, pointed out that a state has a vital concern in the manner in which schools shape the minds of young people. He was not at all disturbed by the implication of "guilt by association." On the contrary, "One's associates, past and present, as well as one's conduct, may properly be considered in determining fitness and loyalty. From time immemorial, one's reputation has been determined in part by the company he keeps." [55]

Justice Douglas dissented from the majority, along with Justice Black. Their minority opinion made a strong case for academic freedom:

> Where suspicion fills the air and holds scholars in line for fear of their jobs, there can be no exercise of the free intellect. Supineness and dogmatism take the place of inquiry. . . . This, I think, is what happens when a censor looks over a teacher's shoulder. . . . It produces standardized thought, not the pursuit of truth. Yet it was the pursuit of truth which the First Amendment was designed to protect. . . . The Framers knew the danger of dogmatism; they also knew the strength that comes when the mind is free, when ideas may be pursued, wherever they lead. We forget these teachings of the First Amendment when we sustain this law.

In the early 1950's, Senator Joseph McCarthy (R-Wis.) constituted himself a one-man crusade against communism on every front. As Chairman of both the Senate Committee on Government Operations and its Permanent Subcommittee on Investigations, he conducted a spectacular campaign against subversives in government. But, in 1954, a Senate Resolution censured the junior Senator from Wisconsin for his abuse of legislative power and demagogic tactics. So ended "McCarthyism." The public gradually began to make more vigorous protests against the violation of civil rights. Legislative hearings showed more regard for due process of law—even the Supreme Court was inclined to reappraise its previous opinions. Thus, in May, 1956, Justice Tom Clark (who as Attorney General of the United States had been largely responsible for launching the federal loyalty program) said for the Court that the City of New York could not summarily dismiss a professor at Brooklyn College for having invoked the Fifth Amendment before the Internal Security Subcommittee. The Justice sharply rebuked those who followed "the practice of imputing a sinister meaning to the exercise of a person's constitutional right under the Fifth Amendment." The Court could not say whether the professor in question, after teaching German for twenty-seven years in the state schools, was qualified for his position. It could—and did—say that his claiming a constitutional privilege before a congressional committee could not be converted into a presumption of guilt warranting dis-

---

[55] *Adler* v. *Board of Education*, 342 U.S. 485 (1952).

missal from public employment.[56] Two years later, however, the Court upheld the discharge of a public school teacher in Philadelphia who had refused to answer questions put to him by the Superintendent of Education relative to membership in an allegedly subversive organization.

In *Sweezy* v. *New Hampshire*[57] the Court made its strongest statement in support of academic freedom (although the decision was not based on this ground). It reversed the contempt conviction of Sweezy, who had refused to reveal his knowledge of the 1948 Progressive Party movement in New Hampshire or to disclose his personal beliefs on a wide range of subjects raised by the Attorney General. Chief Justice Warren declared:

> Merely to summon a witness and compel him against his will, to disclose the nature of his past expressions and associations is a measure of governmental interference in these matters. These are rights which are safeguarded by the Bill of Rights and the Fourteenth Amendment. We believe that there unquestionably was an invasion of petitioner's liberties in the areas of academic freedom and political expression—areas in which government should be extremely reticent to tread. . . . Scholarship cannot flourish in an atmosphere of suspicion and distrust. Teachers and students must always remain free to inquire, to study and to evaluate, to gain new maturity and understanding; otherwise our civilization will stagnate and die.[58]

Communism as an issue in public education has turned out to be mostly a bugaboo. More insidious and pervasive is the problem of sterilized instruction. John Milton wrote in *Areopagitica*, "Where there is much desire to learn, there of necessity will be much arguing, much writing, many opinions; for opinion in good men is but knowledge in the making." Nevertheless there is great pressure on teachers, especially in tax-supported schools, to keep controversial issues out of the classroom. For the administrator, this is safe public relations; for the teacher, it is realistic self-defense; but for the student it is not good instruction.

The political process by which textbooks are adopted in the secondary and elementary schools involves a kind of pre-censorship which is all the more dangerous because it is scarcely suspected by the public. No publishing house can afford to print a textbook for secondary or elementary schools that will not sell in large quantities across the country. This means that no house is likely to publish anything that will displease any section of the country or any special-interest group that might be influential in "book-rating." A high-school textbook in American government, for example, must be acceptable to, or at least it must not antagonize, such diverse groups as the American Medical Association, the National Association for the Advancement of Colored People, the Daughters

---

[56] *Slochower* v. *Board of Higher Education of New York City*, 350 U.S. 551 (1956).
[57] *Sweezy* v. *New Hampshire*, 354 U.S. 234 (1957).
[58] This strong statement is, however, considerably toned down by the long-drawn-out case of Dr. Williard Uphaus, who languished in New Hampshire jails for refusing to tell Attorney General Wyman who attended the summer camp of World Fellowship. The United States Supreme Court upheld his contempt conviction. *Uphaus* v. *Wyman*, 360 U.S. 72 (1959).

of the American Revolution, the American Federation of Labor, the National Association of Manufacturers, the Roman Catholic Church, the American Legion, the Jews, the Christian Scientists, the Italian-Americans. Since the public pays the bill for "free textbooks," the public pipes the tunes that accompany the textbooks into the schools. Thus, in order to offend no local prejudices, to affront no special interest, public-school textbooks are almost always (just as the students say) colorless, opinionless, dull.

A More Positive Concept of Civil Rights—Equal Protection

So far in this chapter, we have been concerned with our "American heritage," the blessings of liberty that are specifically guaranteed in the Constitution. You may have noticed that most guarantees of these individual rights are negative in character: "government *shall not do* this or that to any person." In recent years, however, a more positive concept of human rights has developed: "government *must do* this and that for all of us." For example, a whole new area of social security has been added to the conventional liberties and rights of the individual. President Franklin D. Roosevelt included in the Four Freedoms: (1) freedom of speech and expression, (2) freedom to worship God, (3) freedom from want, (4) freedom from fear.[59] President Truman's Committee on Civil Rights declared that four basic rights were most important in the American Way: (1) the right to safety and security of the person, (2) the right to citizenship and its privileges, (3) the right to freedom of conscience and expression, (4) the right to equality of opportunity.

The concept of "equal protection of the laws," stated in the Fourteenth Amendment, has undergone major surgery over the years. The Fourteenth Amendment was designed to extend the same civil rights to all persons without regard to race and color.[60] Specifically, Congress intended to remove any doubts about the constitutional validity of the civil rights legislation that had been passed during Reconstruction to protect Negroes. Ironically, the Supreme Court subsequently denied this specific intent in the *Civil Rights Cases* (1883).[61]

In these cases, the Court held unconstitutional the Civil Rights Act of 1875, which affirmed the right of all persons within the jurisdiction of the United States to the full and equal enjoyment of accommodations and advantages in hotels, public conveyances, theatres, and other places of amusement. In its decision, the Court made two important points. First, the Fourteenth Amendment gives Congress no

---

[59] See his Annual Message to Congress, January 6, 1941.

[60] Although the Fourteenth Amendment was undoubtedly intended to protect human persons only, very shortly the Supreme Court extended its coverage to "artificial persons." In 1886, Chief Justice Waite refused to hear argument on whether equal protection of the laws should be given to corporations; he simply announced, "We are all of the opinion that it does." See *Santa Clara County* v. *Southern P. R. Co.*, 118 U.S. 394 (1886). Roscoe Conkling, who had been a member of the Joint Committee on Reconstruction, had as counsel before the Court very plausibly argued this point of view a year or so earlier. Conkling's argument gave rise to the so-called "conspiracy theory" of the Fourteenth Amendment, that a joker had been deliberately slipped into the Constitution without the people's knowledge to give extraordinary protection to corporations.

[61] *Civil Rights Cases*, 109 U.S. 3 (1883).

positive powers over civil rights; Congress simply has the power to enact corrective legislation that is necessary to counteract state laws which violate privileges
and immunities, due process, or equal protection. Second, the Fourteenth Amendment guarantees protection only against aggression by the states; it does not
protect rights against encroachment by individuals unless such individuals are
acting for the state. The Court's decision in these cases—a decision that in effect
marked the end of Reconstruction—was widely applauded. The southern states
were especially grateful for the institution of judicial review, since it allowed
the "sound judgment" of the Court to reverse the "radical views" of the Congress.

In denying Congress the power to establish a national policy with respect to
civil rights, however, the Court in effect assumed for itself final authority over
civil rights in the states. In matters of race relations, the Court was inclined to
follow the path of least resistance, leaving this peculiar problem to local custom.
For many years, the southern states counted on the courts to hold that laws
requiring separate but equal facilities for "white" and "colored" met the constitutional standard of "equal protection of the laws." The leading case was *Plessy*
v. *Ferguson* (1896), which involved a Louisiana statute that required separate railway carriages for white and colored passengers. Plessy, a citizen of the United
States, described as of "seven-eighths Caucasian and one-eighth African blood,"
attacked the constitutionality of the act. Plessy had been arrested for refusing to
leave a coach designated for whites and to take a seat in another coach assigned
to Negroes. He claimed that such a legal requirement violated his constitutional
rights under the Fourteenth Amendment. The Court upheld the Louisiana law,
declaring that *"in the nature of things* [the Fourteenth Amendment] could not
have been intended to abolish distinctions based upon color, or to enforce social,
as distinguished from political, equality, or a commingling of the two races upon
terms unsatisfactory to either." [62]

The justices of the Court made no effort in *Plessy* v. *Ferguson* to document
their own sense of "the nature of things" with the findings of sociology, psychology, or philosophy. Instead, they upheld the practice of segregation on the basis
of their own rule-of-thumb proposition that social prejudices cannot be overcome by legislation. Justice John Marshall Harlan, as the lone dissenter, was
"of opinion that the statute of Louisiana is inconsistent with the personal liberty
of citizens, white and black, in that state, and hostile to both the spirit and letter of the Constitution of the United States." Little more than half a century later,
Justice Harlan's grandson, also named John Marshall Harlan, was to join in a
unanimous opinion of the Supreme Court in 1955 which turned the "brooding
spirit" of his grandfather into the "intelligence of today." [63] The doctrine of separate but equal, established in *Plessy* v. *Ferguson*, long gave constitutional sanction,
however, to the Jim Crow laws of southern states which required racial segregation
(with "equal accommodations") in public transportation, public schools, and public meeting places.

---

[62] *Plessy* v. *Ferguson*, 163 U.S. 537 (1896).
[63] 349 U.S. 294 (1955). This was the implementation opinion for *Brown* v. *Board
of Education*, 347 U.S. 483 (1954).

Beginning in the 1930's, under the impetus of the New Deal, Negro interest groups began to press their claims for equal protection of the laws through systematic litigation. The first major break-through came in the field of public education. In the *Gaines Case* (1938), the Court held that a state must offer equal educational facilities to Negroes and whites and do so within the state. This obligation could not be fulfilled by providing tuition scholarships for Negroes to go out of state to obtain professional training available to whites within the state. The Court ruled that a state must accord all citizens within its jurisdiction equality of privileges regardless of race.[64] The effect of this decision was to improve educational facilities for Negroes in the southern states, though the facilities were still kept separate.

In 1950, the Supreme Court virtually abandoned the doctrine of separate but equal in higher education. It upheld the contention of a Negro graduate student at the University of Oklahoma that he had been denied equal protection. Although the Negro had been allowed to attend the university, he had been required to sit apart from the white students in the classrooms, the library, and the cafeteria. Conceding that these restrictions were "in form merely nominal," the Court nevertheless felt that the student had been substantially handicapped in the pursuit of his graduate work, since so much of education consists of discussion and association with fellow students.[65] In the same year, the Court held that the establishment of a separate law school for Negroes in Texas did not provide "equal protection," since the University of Texas Law School for whites and the new law school for Negroes were not substantially equal. In judging the Negro school inferior, the Court employed such criteria as the prestige of the faculty and the position and influence of alumini.[66] Under criteria of this sort —the intangible factors considered by any prospective student—*no* racially segregated school could possibly meet the equal protection standard. Racial separation had not been rejected as such, but it had been subjected to a test that it could never pass in a specific case.

The Supreme Court heard five cases in 1952 that involved segregation in public schools below college level. In the earlier cases on higher education, the Court had avoided passing directly on the equal but separate doctrine. In these new cases, however, the Negroes did not contend that facilities were unequal, but that they were separate. The Court's decision, stated by Chief Justice Earl Warren in 1954, was unanimous: "We conclude that in the field of public education the doctrine of 'separate but equal' has no place. Separate educational facilities are inherently unequal." The opinion reads much like an academic term paper replete with footnotes from the "learned journals" in sociology and psychology. The Court firmly rejected *Plessy* v. *Ferguson*, but strategically left to the following term its "decree on implementation." [67] The states were thus given time to

---

[64] *Missouri ex rel. Gaines* v. *Canada*, 305 U.S. 337 (1938).
[65] *McLaurin* v. *Oklahoma State Regents*, 339 U.S. 637 (1950).
[66] *Sweatt* v. *Painter*, 339 U.S. 637 (1950).
[67] *Brown* v. *Board of Education*, 347 U.S. 483 (1954).

argue before the Court how they thought the judicial decision could be translated into specific and detailed court orders for desegregation.

Finally, in May, 1955, the Court handed down its implementation decrees in the anti-segregation cases. It ordered a "prompt and reasonable start toward full compliance" but left it to the federal district courts to supervise this process in the local communities. No deadline was fixed and the Supreme Court's dictum that desegregation must proceed "with all deliberate speed" evoked more deliberation than speed. Not one school district in the former Confederate States was integrated during the 1954–1955 or 1955–1956 academic years. In 1956–1957, only 108 school districts, about 5 per cent of all bi-racial districts in the region, opened their doors to one or more Negro children. Five years later the number of desegregated school districts had approximately doubled. In 1964, ten years after the historic repudiation of the separate but equal doctrine, in seventeen states and in the District of Columbia, out of 5,973 school districts, 1,282 had been "desegregated."

As the "Southwide" row at the bottom of Table 13-1 indicates, progress toward desegregation has been slow, but the rate of progress has clearly accelerated. The actual number of Negro children in desegregated schools in the South is still small—about 2 per cent of all Negro pupils.[68] Nevertheless, ten years produced at least some integration in every southern state. Only 58,000 Negro children attending schools alongside whites may not seem like many, until one recalls that *no* Negro child attended a white public school in the South before the Supreme Court's historic decision. Moreover, if one takes account of the immediate desegregation that occurred in the District of Columbia and the border states —which also had segregation laws prior to 1954—the impact of the judicial decisions is impressive.

Even after desegregation was established as national policy, many citizens felt that "all deliberate speed" would mean at least a generation in Deep South states like Mississippi. And the data in Table 13-1 reflect great unevenness in the response of different states to the new policy. Three years after the initial decision, only Texas, Arkansas, Tennessee, and North Carolina had admitted any Negro children to formerly white schools. The last states to acquiesce were South Carolina, Alabama, and Mississippi. But they did acquiesce. The old notion of *Plessy* v. *Ferguson* that "you can't change human nature" by legal actions was simply bypassed. Without demanding that human nature should be changed, the political system did change human behavior. (And one may assume that the change in behavior will lead to some change in the attitudes described as "human nature.")

In this transformation of southern practice, the federal courts continued to play a key role. In 1958, the Supreme Court unanimously reaffirmed the "correctness" of its opinion in the *Brown Case*.[69] The School Board of Little Rock,

---

[68] This figure is for the 1964–1965 school year. See *Southern School News*, September, 1964, p. 11. If we look at the figures for the District of Columbia and the border states, which were also affected by the 1954 decision, the actual number of Negro children in school with white children in 1964 was 379,321, about 10.8 per cent.

[69] *Cooper* v. *Aaron*, 358 U.S. 1 (1958).

TABLE 13-1 *Percentage of Bi-racial School Districts Desegregated in 11 Southern States, 1956–64*

STATE	1956–57	1957–58	1958–59	1959–60	1960–61	1961–62	1962–63	1963–64	1964–65
					ACADEMIC YEAR				
Mississippi	0	0	0	0	0	0	0	0	2.7
Alabama	0	0	0	0	0	0	0	3.5	7.0
South Carolina	0	0	0	0	0	0.5	0	0.9	14.8
Georgia	0	0	0	0	0	1.5	0.5	2.2	5.5
Louisiana	0	0	0	0	0	1.5	1.5	2.9	4.5
Florida	0	0	0	0.5	0.5	7.5	14.9	23.9	31.3
Virginia	0	0	2.3	4.7	8.6	14.7	23.5	42.9	62.5
North Carolina	0	1.7	2.3	4.0	5.8	6.4	9.2	23.4	35.7
Tennessee	0.7	1.4	2.1	2.8	4.2	9.1	17.5	37.7	40.8
Arkansas	1.8	3.1	2.6	3.5	4.4	4.4	5.3	5.7	9.2
Texas	12.3	14.6	17.3	17.6	18.1	23.0	18.9	27.1	32.0
Southwide	4.9	6.1	6.7	7.3	8.4	10.3	11.8	18.8	25.3

Sources: Derived from statistics in Southern Education Reporting Service, *Status of School Segregation-Desegregation in the Southern and Border States,* Nashville, Tenn., 1960; *Southern School News,* December 1960, p. 1; *ibid.,* December 1961, p. 1; *ibid.,* December 1962, p. 1; *ibid.,* December 1963, p. 1; *ibid.,* September, 1964, p. 11; Southern Regional Council, *School Desegregation: The First Six Years,* Atlanta, Ga., 1960.

Arkansas, pleaded that its efforts toward gradual integration had produced "intolerable" conditions of tension in Little Rock's Central High School. In special session, the United States Supreme Court upheld the lower court in denying the school board's plea. Chief Justice Warren's opinion was even more explicit than in the *Brown Case:*

Drawing by Herblock. From *Straight Herblock* (New York: Simon & Schuster, 1964).

"You don't understand, boy—you're supposed to just shuffle along."

State support of segregated schools through any arrangement, management, funds, or property cannot be squared with the Amendment's command that no State shall deny to any person within its jurisdiction the equal protection of the laws. The right of a student not to be segregated on racial grounds in schools so maintained is indeed so fundamental and pervasive that it is embraced in the concept of due process of law.

In 1963, the Supreme Court refused to stay an order of the U.S. Court of Appeals requiring the School Board of Mobile, Alabama, to make "an immediate start in the desegregation of schools." The Board had complained that even token integration in the existing climate of opinion in Mobile would be detrimental to the Negro children. Justice Black, himself a native of Alabama, indicated his impatience that, nine years after the Supreme Court had declared segregation in the public schools unconstitutional, Mobile had not taken a single step toward desegregation.[70] In 1964, the Supreme Court ordered the School Board of Prince Edward County in Virginia to reopen its schools on a desegregated basis. Prince Edward County had closed its public schools in 1959 rather than comply with an integration order of a federal district court. Justice Black, who gave the opinion of the Court, pointed out that it was a denial of equal protection of the laws for Virginia to treat the school children of Prince Edward County differently from the way it treats the school children in all other counties of the state.[71]

The *Brown Case* focused on segregation in public schools. One week after that decision, however, the Court projected the principle of desegregation to other public facilities such as parks, theatres and playgrounds.[72] Earlier it had held state segregation laws an unconstitutional burden on interstate transportation.[73] Obviously, the Court was giving general application to a policy decision—that segregation under color of law, wherever applied, is a denial of equal protection of the laws. Enforcement of this policy has had nationwide repercussions, but its most massive impact was on the southern states. Full implementation promises radically different patterns of behavior in the social and economic, no less than in the political, practices of the region.

At the outset of this chapter, we emphasized the point that public policy is the output of the whole political process. The Supreme Court is but one agent within the American system of self-government. How did other decision-makers within the system react to the desegregation policy declared by the courts? And what kinds of supports and demands were prompted by the Supreme Court decisions?

At first, southern political leaders uniformly opposed desegregation. The issue thus did not lend itself to political compromise. The token responses to the new law of the land that did occur could be explained more in terms of the social and economic characteristics of southern counties than in terms of their political

---

[70] *Board of Commissioners of Mobile County v. Davis,* 84 S. Ct. 10 (1963).
[71] *Griffin v. Cy. School Board of Prince Edward Cy.,* 84 S. Ct. 1226 (1964).
[72] *Muir v. Louisville Park Theatrical Association,* 347 U.S. 971 (1954).
[73] *Morgan v. Virginia,* 328 U.S. 373 (1946).

characteristics. So far as school desegregation was concerned, southern communities showed little political variation.

A statistical analysis of community characteristics related to school desegregation found that such non-political factors as the degree of urbanism and the extent of Negro freedom from economic depression were most important. Political characteristics, such as the degree of party and factional competition, were relatively inconsequential.[74] These findings might suggest that local responses to the output of national decision-making agencies are determined more by social and economic than by political factors. But a companion study of variations in Negro voter registration in southern counties found that political factors were as important as social and economic factors.[75] Rather than conclude that political variables are unimportant, then, we must conclude that their importance varies from one issue to another. We can infer that their importance also varies from time to time. Perhaps we could say that the degree to which a society has achieved democracy can be judged by the number of issues that are responsive to political solution. Twenty years ago, variations in Negro voter registration probably depended on social and economic factors rather than on political considerations. By the same token, school integration is probably becoming more and more responsive to political considerations. But this is a question for future research.

How did the southern states express their opposition to desegregation? In 1956, a hundred congressmen from eleven southern states presented Congress with "A Declaration of Constitutional Principles." In the nature of a manifesto, this document excoriated the Court—"the naked judicial power"—"the clear abuse of judicial power"—"the unwarranted decision" which is "in derogation of the authority of Congress" and which "encroaches upon the reserved rights of the states and the people." It commended "the motives of those states which have declared their intention to resist forced integration by any lawful means."

With Alabama and Virginia in the lead, most of the southern state legislatures proceeded to draft declarations of "interposition." The right to interpose state sovereignty and to nullify national laws that go beyond constitutional limits has been claimed at one time or another (albeit always unsuccessfully) by states in every section of the country. Hitherto, state interposition had been posed against acts of Congress; southern interposition resolutions in the late 1950's reflected determined and massive resistance to desegregation by federal judicial decrees. White Citizens Councils and other groups were organized to enlist public opinion against official compliance. Hundreds of new laws and ordinances were passed throughout the Deep South to prevent, restrict, or control school desegre-

---

[74] Donald R. Matthews and James W. Prothro, "Stateways Versus Folkways: Critical Factors in Southern Reactions to *Brown* v. *Board of Education*," in Gottfried Dietze (ed.), *Essays on the American Constitution* (Englewood Cliffs, New Jersey: Prentice-Hall, Inc., 1964), pp. 139–156.

[75] Donald R. Matthews and James W. Prothro, "Social and Economic Factors and Negro Voter Registration in the South," *American Political Science Review*, (March, 1963), LVII, pp. 24–44; and "Political Factors and Negro Voter Registration in the South," *ibid.*, (June, 1963), LVII, pp. 355–367.

gation. A variety of tactics were used to circumvent integration in other public facilities. Public golf courses were converted to private clubs; public swimming pools were closed for extended repairs; picnic facilities were removed from public parks.

Racial tensions grew more critical within the region, although there was relatively little violence. Unfortunate incidents occurred—in Little Rock, Arkansas, where Governor Orval Faubus defied a federal court order by calling out the National Guard and instructing the guardsmen to prevent Negro students from entering the white high school; in New Orleans, Louisiana, where irate housewives resisted the entrance of Negro first-graders into the white elementary schools; in Athens, Georgia, where Klansmen and others joined in a violent student demonstration against the enrollment of two Negro undergraduates; in Oxford, Mississippi, where some "Ole Miss" students and assorted hoodlums followed Governor Ross Barnett's policy of defiance to engage in a pitched battle with United States marshals over the admission of James Meredith, a Negro, to the University of Mississippi. These isolated instances, played up by the mass media, disturbed many people in America and around the world. In general, however, both parties to this interracial cold war followed a strategy of non-violent resistance. As white southerners counted on legislation, so Negro southerners countered with litigation, bringing hundreds of suits in federal and state courts on segregation, desegregation, and related issues.

In the summer of 1958, the Conference of State Chief Justices by vote of 43 to 1 passed a series of temperately worded resolutions, rebuking but not attacking the Supreme Court. "We believe that . . . the Supreme Court has too often tended to adopt the role of policy-maker without proper judicial restraint." The Conference earnestly urged the Supreme Court to exercise firmly its tremendous, strictly judicial, powers but to eschew as far as possible "the exercise of essentially legislative powers when it is called upon to decide questions involving the validity of state action, whether it deems such action wise or unwise." [76]

What about the President and Congress? How did they react to judicial desegregation? In the Little Rock crisis, President Eisenhower ordered the use of federal troops to enforce federal court orders. Disclaiming any personal opinions as to integration, desegregation, or segregation, the President explained that drastic action was necessary because normal processes had failed. His action created a great furor; a nation-wide debate raged over whether the President had exceeded his constitutional powers as Chief Executive. Federal troops arrived in Little Rock, however, and there they stayed, to afford military protection throughout the year to the handful of Negro children permitted to attend Central High School by court orders.

In September, 1962, President Kennedy took similar action when the Governor of Mississippi personally barred the entry of a Negro student at the University of Mississippi despite a federal court order requiring his admission.

---

[76] Full text of the Resolutions, with report on the conference, appears in *U.S. News and World Report*, October 3, 1958.

President Kennedy televised a message to the nation: "Americans are free to disagree with the law but not to disobey it. For in a government of laws and not of men, no man, however prominent or powerful, and no mob, however unruly or boisterous, is entitled to defy a court of law." Under presidential orders, U. S. marshals, and for a time regular U. S. troops, enforced the court order which admitted the first Negro student to the University of Mississippi. Little Rock, Arkansas, and Oxford, Mississippi, dramatically illustrate the exercise of presidential power to secure obedience to federal court decrees. They were, however, isolated incidents. Certainly neither President Eisenhower nor President Kennedy used full presidential powers to bring about desegregation of the public schools in line with Supreme Court decisions.

As for Congress, it simply sat tight, taking no action, though individual members expressed strong opinions pro and con in continuous debates. Less than a fifth of Congress joined in the celebrated Southern Manifesto which represented the official southern viewpoint. When Senator Jenner (R-Ind.) tried to capitalize on widespread dissatisfaction with various judicial decisions relating to communists, subversives, and labor organizers, as well as racial minorities, Congress rejected his bill to curb judicial power and restrict jurisdiction of the Supreme Court. Indeed Congress not only took no direct stand on the issue of desegregation and integration, but also continued to authorize and appropriate grants-in-aid to the states and local communities for health, education, and welfare projects which would operate on a segregated basis. Congress did pass in 1957 and 1960 two modest Civil Rights Acts which pertained mainly to rights of suffrage and discrimination in voting practices. But not until 1964, a decade after the initial decision in the *Brown Case*, did Congress attempt to back up court decrees, executive orders, and administrative rules with a comprehensive Civil Rights Act that would make equal protection of the laws a positive national policy.

The Civil Rights Act of 1964

The final passage of the Civil Rights Act of 1964 is a striking example of public policy viewed as an output of the whole political process. It represents new demands and supports for governmental action in the rapidly changing contemporary environment. The congressional decision to take affirmative action reflects mounting pressures in international relations as well as in domestic politics. The year 1960 was crucial. It was the year that sixteen African nations entered the United Nations and drastically altered the balance of power in the Cold War between East and West. The rising tide of color in world politics inevitably had a considerable impact on American foreign policy, and those entrusted with our policies abroad were extremely concerned about how racial relations at home would affect our status and bargaining power in the international community.

Also, 1960 was an election year which returned the Democrats to power in the White House and in Congress. The Democratic campaign on civil rights had been unequivocal and the Negro electorate, which was especially strong in the big cities in the pivotal states, supported the Democratic candidate. President John F. Kennedy and his brother, Attorney General Robert Kennedy, were both personally committed to the principle of equal protection of the laws. Hence, it was to be expected that the Kennedy Administration would make every effort to push for a national policy on civil rights to be proclaimed as the law of the land. Moreover, Congress itself was subject to increasing demands from its grass-roots constituencies. The civil rights movement was stepping up its protests and expanding its demonstrations to a national scale. The NAACP continued its persistent course of litigation; other organizations, like CORE, sponsored more dramatic activities—student sit-ins, freedom rides, peaceful picketing, and local boycotts. The whole movement reached a climax in the impressive March on Washington, August 1963, which was fully reported by all the mass media of communication. Not only the Negro organizations but dozens of church groups, labor organizations, and others, such as the American Civil Liberties Union and the American Friends Service Committee were actively enlisting the support of public opinion.

President Kennedy had made civil rights legislation a primary objective of his administration; he died perhaps a martyr to this cause. But his assassination strengthened the determination of his successor to obtain a comprehensive civil rights act. In his first State of the Union Message, President Johnson pleaded with the Congress: "Today Americans of all races stand side by side in Berlin and Viet Nam. They died side by side in Korea. Surely they can work and eat and travel side by side in their own country." It was not easy to get a civil rights bill through Congress, given the customary mutual distrust of Democrats and Republicans in an election year, as well as a marathon southern filibuster in the Senate. The Johnson Administration and a bipartisan congressional leadership, however, worked with parliamentary skill and consummate political strategy to enact the bill with a minimum of personal bitterness between proponents and opponents.

The Civil Rights Act of 1964 committed the national government to:

1. enforce the constitutional right to vote for public officials;

2. secure full and equal enjoyment of goods, services, and facilities in all places of public accommodation (hotel, motel, lunch counter, cafeteria, motion picture house, theatre, sports arena, etc.);

3. give the U. S. Attorney General power to initiate legal proceedings on behalf of persons denied equal utilization of any public facility, including the public schools;

4. authorize the U.S. Commissioner of Education to assist local communities in the various problems that arise from desegregation of public schools;

5. expand the activity of the Commission on Civil Rights as a national clearing house for information on denials of equal protection of the laws in the fields of voting, education, housing, employment, use of public facilities, transportation, and the administration of justice;

6. forbid discrimination, on the ground of race, color, or national origin, in all federally assisted programs;

7. make it an unlawful employment practice for an employer or a labor organization to hire or fire employees, or in any way to segregate employees, because of an individual's race, color, religion, sex, or national origin;

8. create the Equal Employment Opportunity Commission to help police discriminatory employment practices;

9. authorize the Secretary of Commerce (in connection with the decennial census) to compile registration and voting statistics;

10. establish as part of the Department of Commerce a Community Relations Service to help local communities resolve disputes, disagreements, and difficulties relating to discrimination based on race, color, or national origin.

The most controversial provisions of the Act are those relating to fair employment practices and equal accommodations. Fair employment practices is not novel as a national policy, and it has long been public policy in many of the states. Early in World War II, President Roosevelt established a Fair Employment Practices Committee to receive and investigate all complaints about discrimination in defense industries. Furthermore, an executive order required all federal agencies to include in all outside contracts a provision obligating contractors not to discriminate against workers on grounds of race, color, creed, or nationality. Nothing like 100 per cent compliance with this order was ever achieved, but it did cause many wartime industries to abandon anti-Negro, anti-Jewish, and other unfair employment practices. After World War II, the Federal Fair Employment Practices Committee went out of existence, for all efforts to retain it as a permanent agency were cut short by filibustering in the Senate. Several of the states, however, led by New York, enacted their own fair employment practices legislation patterned after the federal program.

President Truman made a stubborn effort to have wartime fair employment practices carried over into peacetime. His Committee on Civil Rights reported in 1947 that equality of opportunity is a vital part of our American heritage: "We abhor the totalitarian arrogance which makes one man say that he will respect another man as his equal only if he has *my* race, *my* religion, *my* political views, *my* social position." The Committee declared:

> It is not enough that full and equal membership in society entitles the individual to an equal voice in the control of his government; it must also give him the right to enjoy the benefits of society and to contribute to its progress. The opportunity of each individual to obtain useful employment, and to have access to services in the fields of education, housing, health, recreation and transportation, whether available free or at a price, must be provided with complete disregard for race, color, creed, and national origin.[77]

When President Truman insisted that the 1948 Democratic platform incorporate his views on civil rights, he met tremendous opposition inside his own party. Southern delegations actually walked out of the nominating convention, an act that both reflected and deepened the cleavage within the Democratic Party. Although President Truman was elected in 1948, his party made no effort to carry out the civil rights plank on which he had campaigned.

The Eisenhower Administration followed a policy of nondiscrimination in business covered by government contracts, though the policy was one of executive

---

[77] Report of the President's Committee on Civil Rights, "*To Secure These Rights*" (Washington, D.C.: Government Printing Office, 1947), pp. 9–10.

directives without legislative mandate. The Kennedy Administration also campaigned against job discrimination in government agencies and in private firms holding government contracts. The President's Committee on Equal Employment Opportunity was established by executive order early in 1961. This Committee had specific powers to make the campaign against discrimination effective. Government contractors were required to file compliance reports with the government; employers who cooperated were awarded Certificates of Merit. The Committee had power to investigate and to hold public hearings for the purposes of compliance, enforcement, or education; criminal proceedings could be instituted against contractors furnishing the Committee with false information. The Committee could cancel contracts of companies that refused to comply. To give the Committee initial status, Vice President Lyndon B. Johnson was named Chairman. Chairman Johnson, on accepting this assignment, indicated that in most cases the tactics of the Committee would be those of persuasion and appeals to good will: "This is not a persecuting committee or a prosecuting committee." As President, Johnson's task under the Civil Rights Act is to see that the law is faithfully executed.

The provision respecting public accommodations was opposed by many persons who were otherwise well-disposed toward strengthening the national policy on civil rights. The question whether "Mrs. Murphy's boarding house" is a public accommodation or a private enterprise is a difficult one to answer. The Constitution draws no line between, but rather brackets together, personal and property rights—no person shall be deprived of liberty or property without due process of law. But how does one resolve the conflict constitutionally when personal rights collide with property rights? Mr. D., who owns a small lunch counter on Main Street, may feel that business will improve if he reserves the right to serve an "exclusive clientele." Prior to passage of the Civil Rights Act, the Supreme Court had held that a privately operated restaurant within a public facility (a bus and parking terminal) could not discriminate among would-be customers.[78] It also determined that a privately owned restaurant could not choose to serve only white customers even though public policy in the local community, express or implicit, required or permitted segregation.[79] The courts, however, had not made a final decision on what constitutes trespass in a private establishment when no official action is involved. But, in December 1964, the Supreme Court unanimously upheld the public accommodations section of the Civil Rights Act of 1964. The Court's action cleared the way for full-scale enforcement of the Act. Lawyers in the Justice Department and conciliators in the Community Relations Service of the Commerce Department had anxiously been waiting the decision.

One thing is certain—passage of the Civil Rights Act of 1964 and its full enforcement will not produce the millenium in American race relations. The

---

[78] *Burton* v. *Wilmington Parking Authority*, 365 U.S. 715 (1961).

[79] *Lombard* v. *Louisiana*, 373 U.S. 267 (1963). The first decision upholding the Civil Rights Act of 1964 appears in *Heart of Atlanta Motel* v. *U.S.* (December 14, 1964).

outbreaks of violence and mob looting in Harlem, Bedford-Stuyvesant, and up-state Rochester, New York, within a month after passage of the Civil Rights Act reveal the many frustrations of the Negro even in a state with a strongly affirmative policy on individual and minority rights. A survey conducted in the New York area immediately after the 1964 street riots suggests that most Negroes regard civil rights as a minor public problem compared to economic complaints: low-grade, low-paid jobs; unemployment; bad housing, high rents, and over-crowded conditions.[80] Most of the Negroes polled indicated that they want their children to go to integrated schools with white children. They want to live in an integrated neighborhood with white families. On the other hand, most of them said they did not really like whites. Here is probably the crux of racial relations, the difficulty in attaining mutual respect between the two races, for bigotry exists on both sides of the color line. The Civil Rights Act cannot be relentlessly en-forced; it can succeed only through voluntary compliance that stems from good will. As one perceptive journalist has observed, the act of Congress must find its ultimate legitimacy in the ethical realm.[81]

Privileges and Immunities of Citizens

So far we have been discussing the civil rights of individuals as *persons*. Not all persons in the United States, however, are *citizens of the United States*. Citizen-ship implies more than residence in the country; it means membership in the political community and such membership carries with it significant privileges and immunities.

Citizens of the United States

The Articles of Confederation mention "the free inhabitants of these States," "free citizens in the several states," and "the people of each State." The Constitution of 1787 speaks of "citizens of each State" and "citizens in the several States," but it adds a new phrase and a new concept: "citizens of the United States." Not until the adoption of the Fourteenth Amendment in 1868, however, do we find a con-stitutional definition of United States citizenship: "*All persons born or naturalized in the United States, and subject to the jurisdiction thereof, are citizens of the United States and of the state wherein they reside.*"

Under international law, each nation decides for itself who shall be counted as citizens. Until the adoption of the Fourteenth Amendment, the prevailing view was that United States citizenship was derived from state citizenship. Thus, after the Declaration of Independence, all persons born in a colony or naturalized there became citizens in the new state. And, under the Constitution of 1787, the citizens in each state also became citizens of the United States. In the famous *Dred Scott Case* (1857), Chief Justice Taney argued that "citizens of each state"

[80] *The New York Times*, July 27, 1964.
[81] Max Ascoli, *The Reporter*, July 16, 1964, p. 18.

meant citizens of the United States as understood at the time the Constitution was adopted and that Negroes then were not considered capable of citizenship.[82] The Dred Scott decision was one that only the Civil War could reverse. When the war was over, Congress faced the problem of defining the status of the freed Negro. Through the Fourteenth Amendment, it deliberately overturned Taney's judgment in the Dred Scott case.

A nation may establish the citizenship of its people under two general principles of international law: (1) *jus soli* (law of the land) and (2) *jus sanguinis* (law of blood). Under *jus soli*, the place, the country in which a person is born, determines his citizenship; under *jus sanguinis*, the citizenship of the parent is transmitted to the child. The Fourteenth Amendment adopts the policy of *jus soli*, citizenship dependent on the place of birth.

The United States Supreme Court has ruled that the Fourteenth Amendment means just what it says: *All* persons born in the United States are citizens of the United States. In the case of *U. S.* v. *Wong Kim Ark* (1898),[83] the Court held unconstitutional an attempt by Congress to exclude the children of aliens who themselves were ineligible to become citizens. Regardless of the race or nationality of their parents, then, all persons born in the United States are citizens of this country. On the other hand, since corporations are created by law and are not natural-born persons, they cannot have the status of citizens. This particular interpretation has been important in excluding corporations from the constitutional privileges and immunities of United States citizenship. "Subject to the jurisdiction thereof . . ." has undergone both political and legal refinement. In brief, persons born in any of the states, in the District of Columbia, Puerto Rico, Guam, the Virgin Islands, American territorial waters, American missions abroad, and American public vessels—all are "subject to the jurisdiction of the United States."

Although the Fourteenth Amendment makes *jus soli* the basis for United States citizenship, Congress has by statute also adopted the policy of *jus sanguinis*. Thus a person born abroad of American parents may also be an American citizen. Under present law, a person born abroad of American parents is an American citizen (1) if either of his parents is a citizen who has resided in the United States for at least ten years, five of them after the age of 16, and (2) if he himself resides in the United States for at least five years between the ages of 13 and 21.

Since other countries also define citizenship on the basis of *jus soli* or *jus sanguinis*, or both, many persons actually have dual citizenship. This dual citizenship may involve an individual in problems of conflicting jurisdiction in matters of military service, tax obligations, political activities, and protection in foreign countries. So far, however, the nations of the world have not been willing to accept any single, uniform basis for citizenship.

---

[82] *Scott* v. *Sandford*, 19 How. 393 (1857). Justice Curtis disagreed with Taney, asserting that as a matter of fact there were free Negro citizens in 1789 and that it was then understood that a state was free to extend citizenship to new classes of persons within its borders.

[83] *United States* v. *Wong Kim Ark*, 169 U.S. 649 (1898).

The Fourteenth Amendment prohibits the states from abridging the privileges and immunities of citizens of the United States. But nowhere in the Constitution is there any complete listing of these "privileges and immunities." From time to time, however, the Supreme Court has tried to enumerate some of them. In *Crandall* v. *Nevada* (1868), a case decided while the Fourteenth Amendment was before the states for ratification, the Court identified various "citizen rights": to have access to the government, to transact business with it, to seek its protection, to share its offices, to engage in administering its functions, to have entrance into its courts of justice and free access to the seaports.[84]

The first Supreme Court ruling on the meaning of the "privileges and immunities" mentioned in the Fourteenth Amendment was handed down in the *Slaughter House Cases* (1873).[85] These cases, which involved the validity of a Louisiana statute, offer an excellent example of how vague and confused Supreme Court decisions can sometimes be. Under the state's power to protect public health, the Louisiana legislature authorized a slaughter-house monopoly in New Orleans. The independent butchers of New Orleans, in turn, protested that the monopoly deprived them of their privileges and immunities as United States citizens. The Court's decision was close—five to four. Justice Samuel F. Miller, speaking for the majority, held that when Congress framed the Fourteenth Amendment it had no intention of making any radical change in the relations between the state governments and the federal government, or in the relations of either of these governments to the people. The Justice "ventured to suggest" that Congress had considered the privileges and immunities of United States citizenship mainly as those that owe their existence to the federal government or that arise out of the nature and essential character of the national government. Quite understandably, the Court did not feel that butchering fell into this restricted category.

The decision in the *Slaughter House Cases* was hailed by the proponents of states' rights, especially in the South. According to the Court's interpretation, the Fourteenth Amendment gave the national government no additional positive power over civil rights. This interpretation also meant that the privileges and immunities of citizens of the United States which no state may abridge are the same as and no more than those which belonged to United States citizens before the amendment was adopted. The Court's list of such rights in *Crandall* v. *Nevada* was certainly scanty and unimpressive. But a citizen of the United States is also a citizen of the state in which he lives. The decision in the *Slaughter House Cases* reinforced this concept of dual citizenship: the Supreme Court's ruling left it up

---

[84] Nevada had levied a head tax on every person leaving the state by public transportation. The Court held that since it is the right of the citizen to move freely from one state to another, a state tax restricting such movement was unconstitutional. 6 Wall. 35 (1868).

[85] *Slaughter House Cases*, 16 Wall. 36 (1873). Some constitutional authorities accord the *Slaughter House Cases* as much importance as *McCulloch* v. *Maryland* and *Gibbons* v. *Ogden*. Whereas Marshall's great decisions enhanced the power of the national government, the decision in the *Slaughter House Cases* preserved the prestige of the states in the Union.

to the states to protect the everyday privileges and immunities of citizens within the local cultural context.

Some students of constitutional law feel that the Court's decision in the *Slaughter House Cases* virtually nullified the privileges and immunities clause of the Fourteenth Amendment. True, the decision severely limited the privileges and immunities of *national* citizenship, but by the same token it gave greater emphasis to the privileges and immunities of *state* citizenship. The American citizen today looks to his state—not to the national government—to give him free schooling, to protect his home and other property, to grant his marriage license, his automobile license, his occupational license, his hunting and fishing licenses, and eventually to issue his burial permit!

Many people would still prefer to have the privileges and immunities of citizenship the same in every state and so guaranteed by the federal government. Some argue that this is what Congress actually intended when it wrote the Fourteenth Amendment. Justice Stephen J. Field, who dissented in the *Slaughter House Cases*, thought that the Fourteenth Amendment meant that, "The fundamental rights, privileges, and immunities which belong to him as a free man and a free citizen, now belong to him as a citizen of the United States, and are not dependent upon his citizenship of any state. . . ." This interpretation has not prevailed, however. Just as rights of *persons* vary from state to state, so also do the rights and privileges of *citizens* in the several states.

The Freedom Riders of the 1960's tested the rights of *persons* to move freely in interstate commerce without discrimination as to race and color. The constitutional questions, however, were similar to those presented by the "okies," indigent migrants from the Dust Bowl in the depression years. In *Edwards* v. *California* (1941),[86] the Supreme Court considered a California statute which prohibited the entrance of indigent persons into the state. The Supreme Court unanimously found the California statute unconstitutional: five of the justices said the prohibition imposed an unconstitutional burden upon interstate commerce; four thought the prohibition violated *the privileges and immunities of citizenship*. Justice Douglas was especially keen on this latter point: "The right of persons to move freely from state to state occupies a more protected position in our constitutional system than does the movement of cattle, fruit, steel, and coal across state lines. . . . The right to move freely from State to State is an incident of *national* citizenship, protected by the privileges and immunities clause of the Fourteenth Amendment against state interference." Whether one argues from the position of the majority or of the concurring four in the *Edwards Case*, it seems clear that the Constitution protects personal freedom of movement from state to state, without discrimination, both under the commerce clause and under rights of national citizenship.

The privileges and immunities of citizens of the United States may be vague and uncertain within the states. But outside the country, United States citizenship is of primary importance. When an American goes abroad, his right to full pro-

---

[86] 314 U.S. 160 (1941).

tection of the United States government comes from national, not state, citizenship. The passport of the individual American citizen abroad is an impressive document: "I, the undersigned Secretary of State of the United States of America hereby request all whom it may concern to permit safely and freely to pass and in case of need to give all lawful aid and protection to the above named citizen of the United States." Indeed, the United States government sometimes seems much more zealous in protecting its citizens overseas than at home.

Immigrants

America is a land of immigrants. Not until the latter part of the nineteenth century did this country begin to close its gates against certain classes of strangers. Some of the states, under pressure from vested social and economic groups, had earlier attempted to control the admission of "undesirable" aliens, but the Supreme Court declared all such state laws unconstitutional.

Congress passed its first major immigration act in 1882, barring the entrance of idiots, lunatics, convicts, and paupers. In the same year it enacted the first Chinese Exclusion Law, a controversial statute that was not repealed until World War II, when China was one of our allies. In 1885, largely at the behest of organized labor, Congress prohibited the importation of contract labor. Up to World War I, Congress continued to place qualitative restrictions that excluded such undesired persons as the feeble-minded, professional beggars, anarchists, and polygamists. (This specific exclusion suggests that these groups had been freely admitted previously.)

A phenomenal increase in immigration in the opening decades of the twentieth century—more than a million immigrants in a single year—caused great concern in many quarters. Organized labor thought that the flood of cheap labor aggravated unemployment and lowered wages. Increasing immigration from southern and eastern Europe posed new problems in social and political assimilation. Earlier immigrants, and their descendants, from northern and western Europe were determined to protect "the American heritage"—that is, their own background. A Presidential Study Commission, appointed in 1907, produced a 42-volume report in 1911. Congress took no action until 1917, however, when it established a simple literacy test for all immigrants and excluded virtually all immigration from a designated zone comprising most of Asia and the Pacific Islands.

Not until after World War I, when immigration from Europe was reaching the proportions of an invasion, did Congress impose quantitative limits. The Quota Act of 1921 permitted the annual admission of 3 per cent of the number of persons of each nationality in the United States in 1916. In 1924, Congress established the quota system as a permanent policy for immigration. The total annual immigration was fixed at approximately 150,000, a mere fraction of the hundreds of thousands of pioneers and settlers who once came to our shores every year. This total was broken down into quotas based on "national origins": the number of immigrants admitted from any foreign country in any given year was reduced to one-sixth of 1 per cent of the number of persons in the United States in 1920 whose "national origin" could be attributed to that country. The "national origins" policy was designed to admit the largest number of immigrants from northern and western Europe, the smallest number from southern and eastern Europe. (The combined quotas for the British Isles and Germany accounted for nearly three-fourths of the legal total.) There are many arguments for this policy of "national origins," but most of them sound like a page out of Hitler's *Mein Kampf.*

The Immigration and Nationality Act of 1952 (popularly known as the McCarran-Walter Act) repealed most of the old laws and codified old and new policies. It is the basic immigration statute under which we now operate. The quota system according to national origins is retained. The total annual quotas for each country remain about the same, with preference up to 50 per cent given to highly skilled or educated persons whose immigration would "be beneficial to the economic or cultural interests of the United States."

The tides of immigration to this country have turned in large measure upon economic and political conditions in this country and abroad. Our country has always been "the land of the free" for the politically oppressed or pursued, "the land of opportunity" for the economically depressed and ambitious. Even under the quota system, this pattern has prevailed. In the 1930's, the largest proportion of our immigrants came as refugees from Nazi Germany. But the 1930's left immigration generally at a low ebb, because the Great Depression in this country made us economically less attractive to settlers than at any other time in our history. World War II virtually stopped all immigration, but in 1946 we welcomed the influx of war brides—German, Japanese, Korean, from wherever our young soldiers had been stationed. Also, acting on humanitarian and political grounds and out of strategic motives arising from the Cold War, Congress has made special and temporary provisions for displaced persons and political refugees from behind the Iron Curtain.

Until 1952, nearly all immigration to the United States from Asian countries was barred on racial grounds. Since that time, racial barriers as such have been eliminated, but the policy of national origins continues the exclusion in practice. In the 1950's, the total immigration from all Asian and Near Eastern countries was less than 10 per cent of the European immigration, and this includes the many war brides whom our soldiers brought back from Japan and Korea. Immigration from the Western Hemisphere is not controlled by the quota system, but immigration from Latin America is surprisingly negligible despite our "good neighbor policy."

There was a time when America was proud of its international population, of its being the "melting pot of the world." Ironically, at this point in our history, when keeping friends and allies abroad is so essential to our national interest, national pride and prejudice have caused us to enforce immigration and alien control laws that embarrass our diplomats and make most difficult their tasks abroad. When President Harry S. Truman vetoed the McCarran-Walter Bill in 1952, he declared that its provisions were "insulting to large numbers of our finest citizens, irritating to our allies abroad, and foreign to our purposes and ideals."

Nevertheless, Congress passed the bill over his veto. Presidents Eisenhower, Kennedy, and Johnson, each in turn, have requested Congress to modify our immigration laws, but the basic policies remained unchanged.

Aliens and Naturalized Citizens

Although the Constitution does not mention immigration, it does specify that Congress shall have power to establish uniform rules of naturalization. In his first annual message, President Washington urged Congress to determine by law "the terms on which foreigners may be admitted to the rights of citizens." Congress passed the first Naturalization Act in 1790, making naturalization an activity of the federal and state courts. Until early in the twentieth century, Congress left the procedures of naturalization largely to the discretion of state and federal courts.

With little central control, standards were not uniform and procedures were often extremely lax. During those decades, when millions of immigrants were pouring into this country, political machines in many cities helped produce new citizens—and first voters—on a mass-production basis. On election eve, party workers rounded up aliens and rushed them into local courts where, after perfunctory hearings, they would be granted "final papers" just in time to vote for the machine's candidates at the polls. To correct such abuses—undignified and sometimes fraudulent—Congress in 1906 provided for special examiners to assist the courts with naturalization and placed the Bureau of Immigration and Naturalization in the Department of Commerce and Labor.

When the Department of Labor was created in 1913, a Bureau of Immigration and a Bureau of Naturalization were reorganized within the new Department. We were still welcoming immigrants in great numbers and looked upon them as a continuing source of labor power for the nation. In 1940, the Immigration and Naturalization Service was removed from the Department of Labor and transferred to the Department of Justice. By then, we were more distrustful of the strangers who came to our shores, more inclined to regard them with suspicion as potential subversives.

Under present law, naturalization of individuals is still a judicial process, usually in a federal court.[87] An examiner from the Immigration and Naturalization Service makes the preliminary investigation to determine whether the applicant meets the various legal requirements for admission to citizenship. Most judges do not question applicants in court, but accept the recommendations of the Immigration and Naturalization Service. Nevertheless, the court procedure is generally impressive and the ceremony of induction to citizenship is a solemn and memorable occasion for most of our naturalized citizens.

There are two stages in the formal process of naturalization: (1) the applicant files a petition with the court for an examination; (2) after a public hearing

---

[87] Congress has extended collective naturalization by treaty to the people of the Louisiana Territory (1803), Florida (1819), and Alaska (1867); and by statutes to the Indians (1924) and to the people of Hawaii (1900), Puerto Rico (1917), the Virgin Islands (1927), and Guam (1950).

before a naturalization examiner, the court grants him "final papers." Any alien who has been lawfully admitted to the United States and who has resided here for five years may petition for American citizenship. He files an application with the nearest office of the Immigration and Naturalization Service, giving such personal information as marital status, employment record, and organization affiliations. Subsequently, he appears before an examiner with two United States citizens who can testify to his good character and loyalty. He must swear that he is not a polygamist, an anarchist, a communist, or a supporter of any totalitarian government and that he intends to reside permanently in this country. The final hearing is held in open court not less than 30 days after the preliminary examination.

An alien applying for naturalization must be "attached to the principles of the Constitution of the United States and well disposed to the good order and happiness of the United States." When the court grants his petition for naturalization, the applicant renounces allegiance to the foreign state of which he has been a citizen and promises to bear allegiance to the United States of America. Here is the legal crux of differentiation between the citizen and the alien—*allegiance*. The citizen is required to defend his country and to support its constitutional principles; he must be "loyal." Between World War I and World War II, in a series of naturalization cases, the Court persistently held that a person who refused to take an oath to bear arms in defense of the United States could not become an American citizen. Rosika Schwimmer, a 49-year-old Hungarian woman whose case we have already mentioned; Marie Bland, a Canadian-born, devout Episcopalian who had served as a nurse with the American Expeditionary Forces in France; Douglas MacIntosh, Dean of the Yale Divinity School, who had served as chaplain in the Canadian Expeditionary Force—all were denied citizenship because of their pacifist views. Then, in 1946, the Supreme Court reversed itself and sustained the application of James Girouard, a Canadian conscientious objector, who refused to fight but was willing to accept non-combatant assignments.[88] Finally, in 1950 and 1952, Congress cleared up the judicial confusion by exempting conscientious objectors from the requirement that a new citizen must prove his loyalty by willingness to bear arms in defense of the United States. The "conscientious objector" who believes in a Supreme Being may now meet the

---

[88] *United States* v. *Schwimmer*, 279 U.S. 644 (1929); *United States* v. *Bland*, 283 U.S. 636 (1931); *United States* v. *MacIntosh*, 283 U.S. 605 (1931); *Girouard* v. *United States*, 328 U.S. 61 (1946). Every American draft law since the first one passed in 1917 has exempted conscientious objectors from military service. Nevertheless, local draft boards are frequently unimpressed by claims for exemption on religious grounds. Robert E. Cushman, an authority on civil liberties, reports that about six thousand conscientious objectors were sent to prison during World War II. As convicted felons, they were then subject to such disabilities as loss of suffrage, denial of driver's license, and barriers to certain professions; the penalties varied from state to state. The Selective Service Acts have made certain concessions to conscientious objectors who believe in a "Supreme Being," but not to those whose objections are based on a "mere personal code" or on "political, sociological or philosophical views." In 1952, Congress provided that those whose consciences will not permit them to serve in the armed forces must work for two years as civilians in an approved governmental or non-profit agency.

naturalization requirement by promising to perform non-combatant service in lieu of military duty.

In 1952, all racial barriers to naturalization were removed. The law now requires that the candidate be able to speak, read, and write simple English, and that he have some knowledge of the history, principles, and form of our government. In most countries, a married woman takes the citizenship of her husband. Under American law, however, an American woman who marries an alien does not (since 1922) lose her American citizenship even though under the laws of her husband's country she acquires his citizenship. Similarly, an alien who marries an American citizen does not acquire American citizenship, though the process of naturalization is shortened and simplified for the alien spouse. This practice of separate citizenship for husband and wife often creates problems of dual citizenship. Since many of our troops abroad are now marrying foreign women who immediately lose their original citizenship without gaining United States citizenship, many of these brides cannot claim citizenship anywhere.

In the thirty years between 1930 and 1960, about four and three-quarter million aliens became citizens through judicial naturalization. The Alien Registration Act of 1940, restrictive actions against enemy aliens in World War II, and various psychological and economic pressures during the War, brought about a record upswing in individual naturalizations, nearly half a million in 1944 alone. Over the whole thirty-year period, British, Italians, and Germans have comprised 52 per cent of all aliens naturalized in this country; during World War II, Germans and Italians, designated as enemy aliens, could not apply for citizenship; but immediately following the war, they were back at the top of the list. The removal of racial restrictions during this period resulted in the naturalization of some 78,000 persons from Asian countries, including 16,000 Chinese, 20,000 Filipinos, and 28,000 Japanese. Since World War II, about a million and a half persons have gained citizenship by naturalization; of these about three-fifths were in the working force. Here, we note a sharp increase in the percentage of professional persons and skilled labor, with a corresponding decrease in service workers, indicating special selection of the displaced persons and political refugees whom we admitted under emergency immigration provisions.

Naturalized citizens enjoy the same constitutional privileges and immunities as native-born citizens. There is only one exception: a naturalized citizen is not eligible to be elected President or Vice-President of the United States. A naturalized citizen of the United States automatically becomes a citizen of the state in which he resides. No state may deprive either a native-born or a naturalized citizen of his United States citizenship. It is nothing more than a popular misconception that a person who is convicted of felony thereby loses his citizenship. It is true, however, that a felon may by law be deprived of such privileges of citizenship as officeholding and suffrage. Whatever civil rights are implied as part of national citizenship—such as the right to participate in elections or to move without restrictions from state to state—belong equally to those who acquired citizenship by accident of birth and to those who acquired it by choice through naturalization.

Expatriates and Denaturalized Citizens

The Constitution says nothing about expatriation or deprivation of citizenship. In 1868, Congress declared that the right of expatriation was "a natural and inherent right of all people." This was a fitting policy for a nation of immigrants who could acquire American citizenship only by severing ties with their native lands.[89] The same policy was also extended to any person who wanted to renounce American citizenship. In 1907, Congress defined the grounds for loss of citizenship: (1) naturalization in a foreign state; (2) taking an oath of allegiance to a foreign state; (3) marriage by an American woman to an alien (a provision repealed in 1922). In addition, residence by a naturalized citizen in a foreign state for five years, or in his native country for two years, produced a presumption that his American citizenship had ceased. This, in brief, was our policy until the Nationality Act of 1940 expanded the grounds for expatriation to include: foreign military service, voting in a foreign country's political election, formal renunciation, conviction for desertion from U.S. military forces, or treason.

A number of Supreme Court decisions have recently turned on the issue of expatriation. In 1958, the Court upheld the constitutionality of forfeiture of citizenship for voting in a foreign election. Chief Justice Warren and Justices Black and Douglas dissented; they felt that Congress lacked even implied power to denationalize a citizen without his consent. "Citizenship, like freedom of speech, press, and religion, occupies a preferred position in our written Constitution. . . . The power of Congress to withhold it, modify it, or cancel it does not exist." [90] In a second case, decided at the same time, a majority of the Court invalidated the statutory provision for expatriation upon conviction for desertion during time of war. Five justices repeated the views of the dissenters in the first case: that Congress could not expatriate individual citizens. In 1963, the Court struck out the section of the statute which automatically deprived a person of his citizenship if he left the United States or remained outside the country during wartime or in a national emergency in order to evade military service.[91] In 1964, the Court held that a naturalized citizen could not be divested of his citizenship because he chose to reside more than three years in the country of his birth. The Court held, "This statute proceeds on the impermissible assumption that naturalized citizens as a class are less reliable and bear less allegiance to this country than the native born." [92]

The general policy of the United States is not to force naturalization on any alien lawfully admitted to this country. Immigrants in this country may retain their alien status indefinitely. True, since 1940 the Smith Act has required that all aliens be registered and fingerprinted. And, as part of its internal security program,

---

[89] On the other hand, English common law—and most of our immigrants were still coming from England at that time—regarded allegiance to one's native land as immutable. This conflict in principle was one of the issues in the War of 1812.

[90] *Perez* v. *Brownell*, 356 U.S. 44 (1958); *Trop* v. *Dulles*, 356 U.S. 86 (1958).

[91] *Kennedy* v. *Mendoza*, 372 U.S. 144 (1963).

[92] *Schneider* v. *Rusk*, 84 S. Ct. 1187 (1964).

in 1952 Congress provided that the Justice Department should maintain a central file with information on all aliens in the United States. Aliens must notify the Department of any change of address and must file certain information with the Attorney General each year. Otherwise, however, except in time of war, aliens are under no great disability in this country. Although they do not enjoy special privileges and immunities, as persons they are entitled to the same fundamental civil rights as citizens.

The basic civil rights guaranteed by the American Constitution belong to all *persons*, not just to *citizens*. This policy is expressed in the Fifth and Fourteenth Amendments. In everyday affairs, then, the status of the alien is not very different from that of the citizen. He must obey the laws, pay his taxes, and send his children to school. He has access to the courts and, if he is prosecuted or sued, he is entitled to the same fair procedures and due process to which a citizen is entitled. And yet the courts have upheld many special restrictions on aliens, especially in the economic field. For example, most states have laws that bar aliens from various licensed occupations and professions. The Supreme Court has ruled, however, that a state may not go so far as to bar aliens from *all* opportunities to earn a living.[93] Some states have prohibited land from being owned by aliens who are ineligible for naturalization. The purpose was to bar Asians. With the racial barriers now removed from naturalization, however, the point of such restrictions is lost. Some states deny aliens a share in welfare benefits, such as old-age assistance and workmen's compensation. All states now prohibit aliens from voting and generally bar them from public office. Finally, aliens are ineligible for most positions in the federal civil service.

In one respect, the status of the alien in this country is totally different from that of the citizen. The alien has no *right* to stay in the United States. The Internal Security Act of 1950 codified the various grounds for deportation of aliens. Subject to deportation are those aliens who: (1) have entered the country unlawfully; (2) were admitted for a specific time or purpose and who subsequently violated the conditions of their admission; (3) have been lawfully admitted, but who have proved themselves to be undesirable residents through criminal, immoral, or subversive acts.

Deportation proceedings are handled by the Immigration and Naturalization Service, subject to review in individual cases by a Board of Immigration Appeals. In cases of subversion, the Attorney General has almost unlimited discretion. Most deportation cases are routine—catching up with the stowaways or those who have slipped across the borders. The most flagrant class of violators are Mexican nationals who steal across our southern border every year by the thousands.

The most difficult deportation cases are those involving aliens who "at the time of entering the United States" or "at any time thereafter" have been members of the Communist Party. These cases, though few in number, are likely to be dramatized with pathos and political overtones. Even though the alien has no right to stay in this country, he does have the right to notice and a hearing before he is

---

[93] *Truax* v. *Raich*, 239 U.S. 33 (1915).

deported. The proceedings, however, are administrative. Although judicial review is possible, the Supreme Court has not been inclined to question the constitutionality of deportation, and it has generally upheld the administrative fact-finding. For example, it has upheld the right of Congress to deport an alien for past membership in the Communist Party without requiring proof that the member actually advocated the overthrow of the American government.[94]

Voting Rights and Political Freedom

Universal suffrage is generally regarded as one of the basic tests of democracy. We have already mentioned that the Constitutional Convention of 1787 could not come to agreement on this crucial test. Their decision was to leave it to the states to decide who should have the right to vote in the new Republic. Thus the members of the House of Representatives, according to the Constitution, are chosen by the same electorate in each state which votes for "the most numerous branch of the state legislature." Even to this day, we have no national policy with respect to congressional or presidential elections except in a negative sense. The states still determine voting qualifications subject to the restrictions of the Fifteenth, Nineteenth, and Twenty-Fourth Amendments. No state may deprive any person of the right to vote because of race, color, sex, or failure to pay a poll tax. In all the states, citizenship is the prime prerequisite for voting. This is perhaps the most important right which a citizen can claim and which an alien cannot exercise today. This, however, is a consequence of state policy rather than constitutional law or national policy.

The first major step of the Supreme Court toward ending racial discrimination was in protecting voting rights, which the Fifteenth Amendment says "shall not be denied or abridged by the United States or by any state on account of race, color, or previous condition of servitude." Beginning in the 1890's, the southern states developed various devices designed to exclude Negroes from the polls—"grandfather clauses," educational qualifications, registration requirements, poll taxes, and white primaries. In 1915, the Supreme Court held invalid a provision of the Oklahoma Constitution that required a "literacy test" for suffrage but waived the test for any person who had been entitled to vote in 1866, or who had resided at that time in a foreign country, and for any lineal descendant of such persons. This was one of the so-called "grandfather clauses." Since Negroes were obviously the only persons who could not be excused from taking the test, the Court regarded this device as a flagrant violation of the Fifteenth Amendment.[95]

For many years, the most successful technique for disfranchising Negroes was the Democratic white primary. In some southern states in the 1920's only white persons were admitted to membership in the Democratic Party. Since only members of the party were permitted to vote in the primaries, only white persons could vote in the Democratic primaries. Negroes were not only denied the privilege of voting in the Democratic primaries but, since the Democratic Party was

---

[94] *Niukkanen* v. *Alexander*, 382 U.S. 390 (1960).
[95] *Guinn* v. *United States*, 238 U.S. 347 (1915).

the only party in most southern precincts, there were no candidates of other parties for whom they could vote in the general elections. Then, in 1927, the Supreme Court held unconstitutional a Texas statute that barred Negroes from the Democratic primaries. Speaking for the Court, Justice Holmes declared, "We find it unnecessary to consider the Fifteenth Amendment because it seems to us hard to imagine a more direct and obvious infringement of the Fourteenth. . . . Color cannot be made the basis of statutory classification." [96]

The wave of dismay felt in the southern states when this decision was announced was accompanied by grim determination to keep the Negroes from voting. If *statutory* exclusion was out, they asked, what about party action? Apparently the Court was ready to accept this alternative, for in 1935 it upheld the "white primary" setup by the Democratic Party in Texas without any statutory support.[97] Nine years later, however, the Court (albeit with some changes in personnel) reversed its earlier ruling to declare that the right to vote in a primary for the nomination of congressional candidates, no less than the right to vote in a general election, is secured by the Constitution.[98] The great increase in Negro voting in the South following this decision has helped promote equal protection in other areas—public transportation, public schools, and so on. As such, it is a dramatic reminder of the basic importance of suffrage in securing all other rights. People who can and do vote are in a position to get what they want from government.

In the summer of 1957, Congress passed the first national civil rights legislation since the Reconstruction Era. The act offered immediate and practical assistance to any person deprived of suffrage on grounds of race or color. Hitherto a Negro denied his right to vote had no recourse except to file suit in court to obtain his ballot. Such a suit would usually be beyond his financial means; and even if he could afford to go into court and did win his case, judicial relief would come too late to permit participation in the election. The Civil Rights Act of 1957 authorized the Attorney General of the United States to file a civil suit against any state officer who deprives any person of his constitutional voting rights. This meant that a person who was unlawfully barred from the polls could appeal directly to the Attorney General. The Attorney General would then seek a court injunction to compel the officer in question to cease his violation of civil rights. An officer who disregards such a court order may then be tried for contempt of court, but trial by jury is required.

The Civil Rights Act of 1957 provided for a continuing federal interest in state voting practices. It authorized a civil rights division in the Department of Justice and set up a Civil Rights Commission not only to investigate discrimination in voting, but also to study other aspects of "equal protection of the laws." The Commission, comprising three northerners and three southerners, issued a lengthy report in 1959, pointing out discrimination in such matters as voting,

---

[96] *Nixon* v. *Herndon*, 273 U.S. 536 (1927).
[97] *Grovey* v. *Townsend*, 295 U.S. 45 (1935).
[98] *Smith* v. *Allwright*, 321 U.S. 649 (1944).

housing, and education. The report was important, because it forced both parties to show an active interest in civil rights prior to the presidential election of 1960. After considerable filibuster, another Civil Rights Act was passed in 1960. This Act further implemented the 1957 Act. Briefly, if the Department of Justice sued a voting official to compel registration of persons who had been disqualified because of race, and if it obtained a court finding that a "pattern or practice" of racial discrimination existed in any district, the federal court could name voting referees in that district to secure the registration of Negro voters.

These acts laid important groundwork for correcting arbitrary denials of voting rights, particularly in authorizing the federal government to bring suits against state officials who engage in discriminatory practices. Even so, such blatant discrimination continued in some areas that the U.S. Civil Rights Commission concluded in its annual report for 1963 that "The right to vote in large sections of the South is still denied to many citizens, solely because of race."

How could such discrimination persist despite the reinforcement of constitutional prohibitions in the Fourteenth and Fifteenth Amendments (almost 100 years old) by statutes only a few years old? A complete answer to such a question is not possible in a few pages, but we can conclude that local political systems will tend to resist disruptive changes, however unimpeachable the legal sources demanding reform. The outputs of the national political system—whether in the form of court decisions, legislative enactments, or presidential orders—do not become inputs of local political systems without modifications.

Crayfish County, Mississippi—a place where no Negro has ever voted—demonstrates the point in dramatic fashion.[99] The county is part of a state political system which includes the largest proportion of Negroes and the smallest proportion of Negro voters of any state in the nation. Mississippi laws are designed to maintain the latter distinction. Mississippi has more demanding residence requirements, for example, than any other state: the prospective voter must have lived two years in the state and a full year both in the city or town and in the precinct where he hopes to vote. Thirty-five states require a precinct residence of only a month or less, and only two other states (Maryland and New Hamsphire) require as much as six months.

In addition to its uniquely stringent demands as to residence, Mississippi law imposes a poll tax of $2.00, the highest price for voting in the nation.[100] Moreover, the tax can be paid during only eight weeks of the year, between December 1 and February 1, and the new voter must also pay for the preceding year. This is the season of the year when Mississippi sharecroppers are least likely to have cash and most likely to devote any money they can get to Christmas gifts for their children. Four dollars is 10 per cent of the monthly income of the average Negro *family*

---

[99] The material on Crayfish County is from Matthews and Prothro, *Negro Political Participation in the South* (New York: Harcourt, Brace, & World, Inc., 1966), Chapter 5. "Crayfish" is a pseudonym.

[100] The Twenty-fourth Amendment bans the poll tax only as applied to election of federal officials.

in Crayfish County. The poll tax is collected by the sheriff, a public servant with whom few Crayfish Negroes would voluntarily seek contact.

The function of voter registration itself is performed by the clerk of the circuit court. If a Negro decided to register, he would have to appear in person before this official; he would first have to demonstrate that he had paid his poll tax before February first, and then he would face a literacy test. If he succeeded on both these counts, more difficult obstacles would follow. The applicant must "demonstrate" to the county registrar a reasonable understanding of the duties and obligations of citizenship under a constitutional form of government." If this test, too, were passed, the applicant's problem would be to convince the registrar that he is of "good character." If he reached this stage, his name would be published in the local paper for two weeks, according to state law, and any qualified Crayfish voter would have the right to challenge his good character by filing an affidavit with the registrar within the next fourteen days. It would be up to the applicant to ascertain whether he had passed or not. This discussion of the registration process in Crayfish has to be put in hypothetical terms because no Negro voter has ever gone beyond the first step!

Crayfish County should not be regarded as typical of the South. On the contrary, it represents conditions of repression as extreme as one could find anywhere in the region. Even so, it suggests why President Johnson called for legislation to protect voting rights in the Civil Rights Act of 1964. Table 13-2 suggests

TABLE 13-2 *Estimated Percentage of Voting-Age Negroes Registered in the South, 1940–1964*

STATE	1940	1947	1952	1956	1960	1964
Mississippi	a	1	4	5	6	7
Alabama	a	1	5	11	14	22
South Carolina	a	13	20	27	c	34
Louisiana	a	2	25	31	31	32
Georgia	2	20	23	27	c	39
Arkansas	3	21	27	36	38	42
Florida	3	13	33	32	39	51
Virginia	5	11	16	19	23	28
Texas	9	17	31	37	30 b	58
North Carolina	10	14	18	24	38	45
Tennessee	16	25	27	29	48 b	67
Southwide	5	12	20	25	28	39

a Less than 0.5%.
b Incomplete data; the data for Tennessee are especially unreliable.
c No data.

Sources: Derived from U.S. Census data on nonwhite population and Negro registration estimates in G. Myrdal, *An American Dilemma* (New York: Harper and Brothers, 1944), p. 488; M. Price, *The Negro Voter in the South* (Atlanta: Southern Regional Council, 1957), p. 5; U. S. Commission on Civil Rights, *1959 Report* (1959 Commission on Civil Rights Report) (Washington, D.C., 1959), and U.S. Commission on Civil Rights, *Voting* (1961 Commission on Civil Rights Report) (Washington, D.C., 1961); Southern Regional Council data reported in *The New York Times*, August 23, 1964.

another reason: as a result of Supreme Court decisions and congressional and presidential acts, and as a result of tremendous efforts by Negro leaders, the number of Negro voters in the South has steadily increased since 1940. Indeed, just before the election of 1964, the Southern Regional Council announced that the number of Negro voters in almost every southern state exceeded the margin by which the winning candidate for President had carried the state in 1960.[101] The director of a massive Voter Education Project conducted under the auspices of the Council reported that 1,937,982 Negroes were registered, an increase of 527,934 over 1960. (After the election, the Council raised its estimate of Negro registration in the South to 2,164,000.) As of 1964, this meant that 39 per cent of all eligible Negroes were registered to vote in the South. While this was scarcely more than half the proportion of southern whites who were registered, it was enough to mean that Negroes would play a significant role in the input processes of politics.

These registration figures for southern Negroes represent both outputs and inputs of the national political system. The increasingly firm position of the national government that began with the Supreme Court's 1944 decision outlawing the "white primary" has helped produce dramatic increases in the proportion of Negro voters in the former Confederate states. In 1948, V. O. Key's classic study of *Southern Politics* reported that the South contained too few Negro voters for an analysis of their behavior to be possible.[102] From an inconsequential number to 2,000,000 is an impressive measure of the impact of national policy and of Negro responses to it. But the feedback process goes from output to input. In and outside the South, Negroes began to command enough votes to constitute an important factor in election outcomes. And their demand for equal rights commanded the support of increasing numbers of whites, especially those seeking public office in close contests.

The passage of the Civil Rights Act of 1964 can be described as a product of what we have called the *demand function* of public opinion—not among the entire public but among Negroes and white "do-gooders." On this issue, Negroes were as united as any sizeable segment of the electorate can get, and they demonstrated their demands in no uncertain terms. Many whites, especially church groups, joined the Negro demands. On the whole, however, white opinion could probably be described as performing the *permissive function*—they were ready to see Negro rights recognized but they were not sufficiently exercised to threaten the congressman who failed to support the effort. A small minority of whites, primarily in the South, were as strident in their demands for preserving segregation as civil rights groups were in their insistence on integration. Within this complex, with a permissive majority in general support of the American creed, and with an intense minority demanding implementation of the creed opposed by a smaller but equally intense minority, some positive action was clearly necessary. Our

---

[101] *The New York Times*, August 23, 1964.

[102] V. O. Key, Jr., with the assistance of Alexander Heard, *Southern Politics* (New York: Alfred A. Knopf, 1949).

political system would have been severely strained had the action not favored civil rights.

As we have said, the most consequential provisions of the Civil Rights Act dealt with public accommodations and fair employment practices. But voting rights were buttressed by several additions to the 1957 act:

1. No individual can be required to meet standards or undergo procedures different from those required of other individuals within the same county or similar political subdivision (such as being disqualified for inabilitiy to name the number of bubbles in a bar of soap).

2. No one can be denied the vote because of immaterial errors in his application (such as underlining rather than circling the "Mr." in the "Mr.-Mrs.-Miss" set of choices).

3. All literacy tests must be administered in writing, with the individual having the right to receive a copy of the papers (although the Attorney General may enter into agreements with state or local authorities that their tests are fairly administered and need not be given in writing).

4. A sixth-grade education (in the English language) is made a presumption of literacy which local authorities must rebut if they deny literacy.

5. The Attorney General, in filing suits under the 1957 act, may request that the case be heard by a three-judge federal court (which means that the decision can be immediately appealed to the Supreme Court).

6. Cases under the Act must be heard "at the earliest practicable date and . . . be in every way expedited."

However stilted the legal phrases, they represent the continuing response of the political system to the varying nature and intensity of demands, support, and apathy among different elements of the population. And the story of civil liberties tells us that the output of rewards and deprivations embodied in the phrases will affect the future input processes through which the political system works.

CHAPTER FOURTEEN

General Welfare and Common Defense

What do we mean by public policy? As a rational concept it is relatively easy to define. It refers to the course of action taken by the government to achieve an objective or purpose. Notice that policy implies more than a set of governmental activities; it is a series of related activities that are goal-oriented. Notice also that the policy base for governmental action, in any area, on any issue, involves significant decisions both as to means and ends. The decision-makers in American government—the Congress, the presidency, the bureaucracy, and the courts—determine the courses of action within an institutional framework. But the institutions of government are conditioned by the whole social environment, which embraces values, beliefs, ideas, and interests as well as the sensate, or material, culture of the people.

No policy is perfectly fixed or permanent, because politics—the attempt to influence policy—never ends. It never ends because laws are never neutral. The conflicting needs and views that various groups try to express in policy are constantly changing. Since every election, every law, every administrative ruling, and every court decision reflect some combination of conflicting claims, they are bound to please some political interest groups and to displease others. And in a democracy the losers are free to do what they can to modify or change the decision. Although this practice may distress those who seek permanence or at least neutrality in government, it is the essence of politics.

General Welfare in the Changing Environment

The Constitution of the United States was ordained and established to achieve certain great objectives, among these to "promote the general welfare." As a means to this end, the national government was given a variety of powers and Congress was specifically empowered to lay and collect taxes to provide for the general welfare of the United States. Nowhere in the Constitution, however, is general welfare defined or limited.

General welfare is in fact a social idea rather than a legal term and because the American society is highly pluralistic, our ideas of general welfare vary considerably. In an open society, many different groups pursue political power for their own ends. The public interest—or the general welfare—appears as an accommodation of many different, competing, and conflicting interests. The policy base for governmental activities at any given time generally represents the goal orientation of the dominant or prevailing interests. All groups do not have equal power over every decision of government; policies therefore affect various interests differently. Since few groups in a democracy are willing to accept a subordinate role—or a "raw deal"—forever, policy becomes a nucleus around which politics continuously revolves. As the balance of power shifts within the political system, as it must in any dynamic society, governmental activities, in so far as they are goal-oriented, reflect continuously changing policies. As we said, politics knows no end.

In this chapter we propose to examine the policies of the national government within the expansive range of general welfare (and, less fully, of the common defense). To do this realistically, we must keep in mind the changing social environment which conditions the entire policy process. We shall look for guidelines in the constitutional background, for an ideological orientation as well as for institutional prescriptions. We shall take a hard look at the input of policy-making, at the many and diverse unofficial agencies in our political system which are so influential in stimulating or blocking government action. Finally, we shall focus on the official decision-makers and their decisions which constitute the public policies, particularly with respect to the various roles of government in the economy.

Constitutional Background: Ideological Orientation and Practical Accommodation

If we look at the bare text of the Constitution, we see that the Philadelphia Convention was practically concerned with the relations between the political order and the economy. In Article I, Section 8, about half of the powers enumerated to Congress pertain to economic matters: *to lay and collect taxes . . . ; to borrow money on the credit of the United States; to regulate commerce with the foreign nations, and among the several states . . . ; to establish . . . uniform laws on the subject of bankruptcies throughout the United States; to coin money, regulate the value thereof, and of foreign coin, and fix the standard of weights and measures; to provide for the punishment of counterfeiting the securities and current coin of the United States; to establish post offices and post roads; to promote the progress of science and useful arts . . . ; and to make all laws which shall be necessary and proper for carrying into execution the foregoing powers. . . .* If we analyze this listing of national powers, we see that the original document (a) authorized the national government to engage directly in business enterprise (postal services); (b) provided that the government furnish certain basic instrumentalities for business (currency, weights and measures, patents, trademarks and copyrights, and also communication and transportation facilities); (c) empowered the government to police the market (control bankruptcies, impose tariffs) and to regulate foreign and interstate commerce.

We may also infer from the Constitution certain principles that have a direct bearing on the relation of government to business: (1) the sanctity of private property; (2) the concept of limited government; (3) the federal pattern. Article I, Section 9, places specific limitations on the national government: no tax or duty shall be laid on articles exported from any state and no preference shall be given to one state over another in any national legislation on commerce or revenue. Section 10 puts other restrictions on the states: they may not coin money, issue bills of credit, or make anything but gold and silver legal tender; they may not pass laws impairing the obligation of contracts; and they may not levy taxes on imports or exports from out of state or out of the country. The Fifth Amendment prohibits the national government from depriving any person of property without due process of law and just compensation; the Fourteenth Amendment imposes a similar prohibition on the states. These provisions, within the federal system, limit both the national government and the states. On the other hand, the Sixteenth Amendment, which authorizes Congress to lay and collect income taxes, gives to the national government almost unlimited power to redistribute the wealth of the country. Attach the Sixteenth Amendment to the original power of Congress to lay and collect taxes for the general welfare and the national policy with respect to the economy becomes as pervasive as the prevailing concept of general welfare.

We do not find in the text of the Constitution any of the verbalisms which the business community likes to associate with the American Way: private enterprise, free enterprise, freedom of contract, freedom of competition, or the separation of government and business. Neither do we find any specifications about labor relations: the right to organize and to bargain collectively, the right to work, fair labor standards, or fair employment practices. There is no mention in the Constitution of profits, prices, income (except that it may be taxed from whatever source derived), interest rates, full employment, or wage controls. Observations of this sort led Mr. Justice Holmes to remark that the Constitution embodies no particular economic theory.[1]

By coincidence, Adam Smith, a Scottish professor of moral philosophy, published his book *The Wealth of Nations* in the same year that the United States proclaimed its independence from British colonialism and mercantilism. The doctrine of Adam Smith became a kind of economic theology for the American business community. Basically, what Smith said was that every man works best in his own interest, and therefore *laissez-faire* ("hands off") is the best kind of government. In terms of economics, Smith preached the message of the free market. The free market implies a self-regulating, self-adjusting economic system that operates under the "iron law" of supply and demand without need of governmental intervention. The doctrine was particularly appealing to American businessmen in the early years of the Republic. Adam Smith's natural law of economics was cut out of the same cloth as Thomas Jefferson's natural laws of politics. The free market offered "adventure, romance, and risk"; as one modern businessman explains it, "the market system fits the temper and character of the American people."[2]

From the beginning, however, the American people were able to keep both their political and economic ideologies comfortably apart from everyday activities. They might proclaim and even fight for the unalienable rights of all persons and still maintain the institution of slavery. They might talk about the free market and the strict separation of economics and politics and still use government to provide subsidies and other benefits to business. And, if they were troubled by logical inconsistency, apparently they were soothed by the felicitous thought which Grover Cleveland expressed so neatly, ". . . it is a condition that confronts us, not a theory."

The American economy *is* a condition, not a theory. It is not today—and it never was—the output of policy-planning either by business or by government. In *The Politics of Industry*, Walton Hamilton, an outstanding political economist, wrote about "the great transformation" in the socio-economic environment. "The

---

[1] *Lochner* v. *New York*, 198 U.S. 45 (1905); a dissenting opinion.
[2] John R. Bunting, *The Hidden Face of Free Enterprise* (New York: McGraw-Hill Book Company, 1964), p. 21. Mr. Bunting is vice-president of the Federal Reserve Bank of Philadelphia. His book is a candid discussion of the businessman's views toward government and its role in the economy.

machine process, the assembly line, the huge factory, the chain of stores, the speedy movement of commodities down the channels of merchandise, and the rise of corporations blessed with assets in excess of those of most of the states of the Union"—Hamilton attributed these modern economic phenomena to the scientists, the technicians, and the business executives who inadvertently fashioned a new order "with little thought of the impact of their innovations upon the established ways of society." [3]

A basic function of government is to deal with the conflicts and controversies that arise in society and to respond with policies that tend to promote order by distributing rewards and deprivations among the contending interests. As the character of society changes, as economic forces take new shape, new problems spring up for government to tackle. Thus what we regard as necessary and proper political regulation today is likely to be very different from what the Framing Fathers felt was appropriate for the circumstances that conditioned their thinking. It is pointless for us to argue whether the Constitution of 1787 was intended to regulate marketing quotas in agricultural products, to promote old age and survivors' insurance, to guarantee collective bargaining in industrial relations, and to develop public power projects. What is important to us is whether Congress and the courts can or should interpret the Constitution broadly enough to authorize such policies today.

The Constitution of the United States has survived because Americans have always been able to interpret it to meet current needs. To have held constitutional law to the literal "words and phrases" of the Framing Fathers would have rendered their work obsolete almost as soon as their signatures were dry. For instance, the Framers of the Constitution gave Congress the power to regulate commerce. The only instrumentalities of commerce they knew were sailing ships, stage coaches, and pedestrian traffic. But this does not mean that Congress is without power to regulate more modern instrumentalities of commerce like steam vessels, railroads, telegraph and telephone, air lines, trucks and buses, radio and television. Similarly, we cannot look in the dictionaries of 1790 to determine whether "due process of law" applied to wire-tapping and lie-detectors; whether "stomach pumps" come under the prohibition of "unreasonable search and seizure" or fingerprinting and alcoholic meter tests under "self-incrimination"; whether death in the electric chair or in the lethal gas chamber constitutes "cruel and unusual punishment." We must interpret the ancient words and phrases within the modern context.

We have seen that the Constitution itself reflects a continuous struggle over policy. The Framing Fathers simply began the debate over the meaning of the Constitution—they did not complete it. The Antifederalists denounced the document, warning that it would bring about the complete consolidation of the states into a unitary government. Once the Constitution had been adopted, however, they reversed their argument and insisted that the Constitution was really only a

---

[3] Walton Hamilton, *The Politics of Industry* (New York: Alfred A. Knopf, 1957), p. 33.

compact among states that still retained their sovereignty. Ever since, the dominant groups in each generation of American politics have interpreted the document to correspond to their views. Minimum-wage laws were regarded as unconstitutional in the 1920's, not so much because of the "intention of the Framers" or the objective meaning of the Constitution, as because of the way in which the coalition then controlling American politics viewed the public interest—and their own. Minimum-wage laws finally became constitutional in the 1930's, not because of any change in the intentions of the Framers or in the words of the Constitution, but because of the Supreme Court's response to the new conditions and the new power relations that had developed during the current generation.

The Right to Private Property

If any one economic principle is imbedded in our political philosophy and our constitutional law, it is the right to private property. Blackstone, the great English law commentator, speaks of "the rights of persons and the rights of things." There is a tendency today to sharpen this dichotomy, to draw a line between *personal* rights and *property* rights. In the Lockean ideology, however, the rights of man include "life, liberty, and property" in indissoluble union. As John Taylor, principal theorist of Jeffersonian Republicanism, explained in considering the "principles of our revolution": "The rights to life, liberty and property, are so intimately blended together, that neither can be lost in a state of society without all; or at least, neither can be impaired without wounding the others." [4] John Adams, exponent of Federalist philosophy, wrote: "Property is surely a right of mankind as real as liberty. . . . The moment the idea is admitted into society, that property is not as sacred as the laws of God, and that there is not a force of law and public justice to protect it, anarchy and tyranny commence." [5]

But if we look carefully at the wording of the Constitution, we find that the protection of private property, as envisaged in the Fifth and Fourteenth Amendments, is conditional, not absolute. *A person* may not be deprived of property without due process of law, but a reasonable implication is that he *may be deprived of property with due process of law*. *Private property* may not be taken for public use without just compensation but it *may be taken for public use with just compensation*. No person has a claim of absolute right to private property against a counter-claim of his government that the property is needed for public use. Eminent domain—that is, taking private property for public use—is an inherent and essential power of government. Though not specifically delegated to the national government, the power of eminent domain is implied as an attribute of government.

Just what constitutes public use at any given time depends largely on the

---

[4] John Taylor, *From Construction Construed and Constitutions Vindicated* (1820), excerpt in Francis Coker, *Democracy, Liberty and Property* (New York: The Macmillan Company, 1942), p. 496.

[5] In *Works*, VI, 8–9; excerpt in Coker, *ibid*, p. 464.

prevailing concept of what governmental activities are proper and necessary. Thus, today, private property may be taken over to make way for *public roads* (including superhighways, bridges, tunnels, and roadside picnic areas); *public buildings* (including fire houses, police stations, courthouses, hospitals, libraries, and slaughter houses); *public schools* (including cafeterias, bookstores, auditoriums, and stadiums); *public recreation facilities* (including ball parks, botanical gardens, zoos, swimming pools, skating rinks, and golf courses); *public works* (including water reservoirs, sewage-disposal plants, power plants, and gas works); and *conservation projects* (irrigation and drainage ditches, fish hatcheries, bird refuges, and forest preserves). There is almost no limit to the list.

In recent years, the national government has taken over a great deal of private property for military establishments and for huge hydroelectric and atomic energy installations. Several states and municipalities have taken private property in order to operate port facilities, piers, and warehouses. The Port of New York Authority, for example, exercised eminent domain on a gigantic scale to build the Holland and Lincoln tunnels, the George Washington Bridge, a huge railroad freight station, a large motor-truck terminal, a central bus terminal, and the great airports at LaGuardia Field, Queens, Teterboro, and Newark. Many other cities have condemned private property to build airports, to clear slum areas, to construct civic centers. Although the courts still maintain that the question of public use may be settled by litigation, in practice judges tend to accept whatever the local political authorities decide. In effect, the courts have conceded that "public use" is a matter of social philosophy rather than a legal concept.

A decision of the United States Supreme Court illustrates how broad the current construction makes the power of eminent domain. In 1954, Justice Douglas upheld a slum-clearance and redevelopment project that had been enacted by Congress for the District of Columbia. A department store in the area protested the condemnation proceedings, arguing that the redevelopment project would simply shift its property to different private management. The Court, however, went no further than to affirm the initial public purpose: "a beautiful, healthy, spacious, clean, well-balanced, carefully patrolled" community. The Court regarded as immaterial the fact that Congress chose private enterprise, rather than public ownership or even government operation, as the means of accomplishing this purpose. Since the Court found the requisite public purpose in the housing project, it could then conclude: "The rights of these property owners are satisfied when they receive that just compensation which the Fifth Amendment exacts as the price of the taking." [6]

The tremendous expansion of government activities in recent years has vastly enlarged the judicial concept of public use. Since any property may be taken for public use, just compensation remains the sole legal bulwark of private property rights against eminent domain. Politically, of course, property owners are in a good position to demand protection of their interests by their elected

---

[6] *Berman* v. *Parker,* 348 U.S. 26 (1954).

representatives. The guarantee of just compensation is explicit in the Fifth Amendment with respect to the taking of private property by the federal government, and it is implicit in the due process clause of the Fourteenth Amendment with respect to the taking of private property by state or local governments. In general, the courts have held that just compensation represents "the fair value" of the property at the time it is taken, and fair value is usually regarded as the market value. If the owner of the property is not satisfied with the initial price offered by the government, due process provides that he be given a fair opportunity to present his case at some point during the condemnation proceedings. Public officials whose tenure depends on good will in politics are more inclined to be generous than otherwise with the taxpayers' dollars in these condemnation cases. In other words, the government price will more likely overvalue than undervalue the private property in most cases of eminent domain.

Determining what constitutes "fair value" is not always a simple matter. For example, in a 1956 case before the Supreme Court, a private power company protested the value that the federal government had fixed on lands taken for the development of the Clark Hill project on the Savannah River. This project was intended to serve several purposes—hydroelectric power, flood control, and navigation. The power company thought that "fair value" should be based on what the land would have been worth *if* the power company itself had been allowed to develop water power. The majority of the Court held that water power is not a "compensable interest" under the Fifth Amendment when the United States asserts its right to improve navigation. A minority of the Court, however, felt that the government should have paid a higher price for the land which lay along the river even though all riparian water-power rights under the law now belong to the federal government.[7]

Finally, the government is not always obliged to compensate the owner when it takes private property. For example, in exercising police power to protect public health, safety, or morals, the government is not required to compensate private owners for the seizure and destruction of such property as illegal slot machines, bootleg liquor, lottery tickets, adulterated food or drugs, diseased or pest-infested plants, and substandard fertilizer. When national prohibition went into effect after World War I, the federal government offered no compensation to the distillers and brewers whose billion-dollar business had been closed out by the law.[8] Early in World War II, the military situation in the Philippines seemed so hopeless that the United States Army demolished a considerable amount of private property in Manila to prevent it from falling into enemy hands. The Caltex Company, whose terminal facilities and petroleum stock were destroyed, later demanded compensation, but the Supreme Court held that there was no constitutional right to compensation for property taken over by the military in wartime.[9]

---

[7] *United States* v. *Twin City Power Co.*, 350 U.S. 222 (1956).
[8] See *Hamilton* v. *Kentucky Distilleries and Wine Co.*, 251 U.S. 146 (1919).
[9] *United States* v. *Caltex, Inc.*, 344 U.S. 149 (1952).

As we pointed out in the preceding chapter, the Constitution draws no line between personal and property rights—no persons may be deprived of liberty *or* property without due process of law. But what happens when claims to personal rights collide with claims to property rights?

The right to private property and free enterprise may be cardinal principles in American economic theory, but no one is free to use his property or carry on his business contrary to public policy. And in the final analysis it is the government that has authority to determine and enforce the public policy. If the law says (and it does) that an employer may not oppose labor union activities or refuse to bargain collectively with representatives chosen by his employees, then an employer is not free to obstruct unionism in his business even though privately he thinks labor unions are un-American. If the law says (and it does) that an employer may not discriminate in hiring or firing employees, or segregate them in any way because of race, color, sex, religion, or national origin, then the employer is not free to engage in discriminatory practices even though he may be anti-semitic or segregationist in his private views.

In the 1960's the civil rights movement precipitated countless clashes between claims of private property rights versus personal liberties. The private motel on the interstate highway refused accommodations to Negroes. The gas station on the edge of town opened its "comfort room" to white customers only. The proprietor of the small lunch counter on Main Street maintained service for "exclusive clientele—whites only." The manager of the local movie house reserved the right to seat whites only, or to seat Negroes in a segregated section of the theatre. When the Negroes staged sit-in demonstrations, picketed, or marched en masse to the tune of "We Shall Overcome," in many communities they were arrested for trespassing on private property or for disturbing the public peace.

Now the Civil Rights Act of 1964 makes it unlawful—as a matter of national policy—for any private business that offers public accommodations (hotel, motel, lunch counter, cafeteria, motion picture house, theater, sports arena) to deny goods, services, or facilities to anyone on grounds of race, color, religion, sex, or national origin. The Act was passed principally under the power of Congress to regulate commerce among the states. Public policy, however, is always open to challenge and changing interpretations. No one institution in American government ever has the last word on public policy. Test cases to determine the constitutionality of the 1964 Civil Rights Act were brought into court almost before the President had finished signing the Act. Segregationists who had been criticizing the courts for usurping the legislative power now counted on judicial review to invalidate congressional action!

The first two cases involving the 1964 Civil Rights Act to reach the Supreme Court came from a barbecue drive-in in Birmingham, Alabama, and a motel in Atlanta, Georgia. A federal district court in Alabama held that the public accommodations section of the Civil Rights Act was unconstitutional when applied to a local and private business. Meantime, a federal district court in Georgia had upheld the public accommodations provision when applied to the Atlanta motel, most of whose guests were admittedly travelers in interstate commerce.

When the attorney for the Atlanta motel argued his case before the United States Supreme Court, he indicated that the fundamental question was whether the Congress has the right to deny the owner of a private business freedom to run his firm as he wishes and to choose his customers. "The fact that Negroes are involved in this case is purely incidental," he said. "If Congress has the power to take away the personal liberty of the individual business man, there is no limit to the power of Congress." But Mr. Justice Black refused to enjoin enforcement of the Civil Rights Act of 1964 pending final determination of the constitutionality of the Act. In December 1964, the Supreme Court upheld the public accommodations provisions of the Act under the commerce power of Congress. Justice Clark, who delivered the opinion of the Court, observed, "Congress could have pursued other methods to eliminate the obstructions it found in interstate commerce caused by racial discrimination. But this is a matter of policy that rests entirely with Congress, not with the courts." [10]

Economic Policy in the Social Context

Marshall Dimock has recently attempted a "synthesis of politics and economics" in *The New American Political Economy*. He complains at the outset that "what America lacks is a policy base from which to reach sound decisions that are consistently right in the long run." [11] But a society which is (1) pluralistic, (2) dynamic, and (3) democratic does not expect its government to operate from any one policy base "in the long run." Government acts at any time in response to the combination of elements that make the most powerful demands on the decision-makers. Since the social and economic environment constantly changes, government policies must also undergo never-ending change. For one thing, new conditions may lead the powerful interests themselves to change their minds about what they once championed as desirable policy. So they change their means or their goals, or both. But meantime, economic and social changes may give rise to new interests with different demands and new coalitions may become sufficiently influential and powerful to redirect policy to their own ends.

In the early days of the American republic, the Hamiltonians wanted a strong national government that would provide a national market, a national currency, a national transportation system, and protection for the sanctity of contracts and the right to private property. The Jeffersonians, who came to power after the elections of 1800, represented rival economic interests and different social values. The policy base of Hamiltonianism was intended to promote the interests of manufacturing, commerce, and urbanism; the policy base of Jeffersonianism was intended to protect the interests of the rural communities and citizen farmers who believed "that government is best which governs least."

But the application of technology to industry transformed the socio-political environment and reversed the position of the classical antagonists. Big business no

---

[10] *Heart of Atlanta Motel, Inc.* v. *U.S.*, 85 S. Ct. 1 (1964); 85 S. Ct. 348 (1964).

[11] Marshall Dimock, *The New American Political Economy* (New York: Harper and Brothers, 1962), p. 17.

longer needed the help of government and so it embraced the Jeffersonian doctrine of *laissez-faire*. On the other hand, the farmers, workers, and the less privileged elements of the general public tried to combat the new plutocracy by challenging big business with big government. Spokesmen for these groups, who had championed "strict construction" of the Constitution while government powers were being used to promote commercial interests, turned to "liberal construction" when they needed government to match the power of private economic interests. Whereupon the business community, which had once advocated a strong national government, began to espouse the "principle" of states' rights.

Power divided among the several states could hardly cope with or control economic operations which were nation-wide, or even international in scope. Once American resources and technology had developed powerful economic interests that wanted merely to continue established aids to business, and once American politics had extended the franchise to masses of people who felt a need for the government to curb those economic interests, the about-face in opinions on the role of government in economics swiftly followed.

The policy base for government's role in the economy logically shifts as the nature of the economy changes. In the American economy, the most striking change has occurred in the institution of private property. When Tocqueville visited America in the days of "coonskin democracy," he observed that "as every one has property of his own to defend, every one recognizes the principle upon which he holds it." At that time, private property was held in an economic system that was vastly different from the one in operation today. The wealth of the country was mainly in land, and most of the population were yeoman farmers. Business was indeed a matter of private enterprise, for it was conducted on a small scale by shopkeepers and mechanics in the scattered villages and towns. The usual form of ownership was the single proprietorship. There were few corporations, several hundred at most, and these were principally in transportation and banking. Freedom of competition, liberty of contract, and *laissez-faire* were the "principles" that governed the conduct of private business in those early days.

Today, however, the majority of Americans live in industrial, urban areas. Less than 10 per cent of them are self-employed; three-fourths of them are working for wages and salaries in private industry; the rest are government employees. The corporation, with multiple ownership, dominates the nation's business. There are more than half a million corporations doing business today in this country, many of them multi-million dollar enterprises such as Armour and Co., Alcoa, American Telephone and Telegraph, United States Steel, General Motors, General Electric, Eastman Kodak, Standard Oil of New Jersey. About 8 per cent of the population shares in the corporate ownership of public utilities, communications, transportation, manufacturing, finance, and trade. The ownership of shares by millions of persons in these great corporations—the New York Stock Exchange calls it "people's capitalism"—is something quite different from the private enterprise of the individual entrepreneurs in the time of Tocqueville. Modern business is carried on by a complex organization of promoters, investment brokers, lawyers, bondholders, stockholders, advertisers, public relations men, management, and labor. It has become public business in which the owners assume no personal responsibility for the quality of the products, the fairness of the price, the conditions of labor, or the soundness of securities.

After the mid-nineteenth century, in response to the rapid spread of the Industrial Revolution, European governments generally went into the business of providing the basic public utilities, especially in communications and transportation. In this country, however, there was almost no advocacy of socialism. Given the character of the American people, their belief in individualism and their idea of progress through free competition, few in the United States wanted to substitute governmental enterprise for private business. On the other hand, a firm belief in equality, along with a deep-rooted humanitarianism, was also a part of the American democratic tradition. Gross abuses of economic power by individual tycoons and oversized combinations in restraint of trade, monopolistic tendencies that belied the free market, discriminatory practices that denied fair play, distressing working conditions, and extremes of poverty and riches prompted many people to press for governmental regulations of the economy.

Meanwhile, the democratization of the suffrage, increasing pluralism in the electorate, and the extension of public education were changing the nature of the political arena. As in Europe, an awakening social conscience and rising expectations were parts of the output of the Industrial Revolution. Mass production and urbanization tended to shift the political emphasis from individual civil rights to social and economic reforms. In this country, the "revolt of the masses" took the form of populism and progressivism. Organized and articulate groups representing various sectors of the economy demanded that the police power of the state be used to promote the public health, safety, and morals and, indeed, to meet all public needs. The business community, outnumbered in the electorate, hence less influential in the legislative constituencies, counted more and more on the courts to protect the rights of private property and to brake the new "liberalism."

Although corporate business had revolutionized the American economy by the end of the nineteenth century, the courts continued to apply the principles of private property that had once protected the single proprietor, the individual entrepreneur. The courts still held that the due process clauses of the Fifth and Fourteenth Amendments restrained both the federal and state governments from regulating "private business." The first noteworthy break in this interpretation occurred in the 1870's when organized pressure from mid-western farmers who were dedicated to "raising less corn and more hell" forced state legislatures to regulate the railroads.

In *Munn* v. *Illinois* (1876), Chief Justice Morrison R. Waite declared that "when private property is devoted to a public use, it is subject to public regulation." He found that, since grain elevators were devoted to a public use, their rates and service could be regulated by the state legislature. Justice Stephen J. Field, however, took sharp issue with the Chief Justice. In Field's opinion, the due process guarantee extended to the use of property and to the fruits of that use: "The same liberal construction which is required for the protection of life and liberty . . . should be applied to the protection of private property." Field did not want property, any more than life or liberty, to be subjected to the will of the legislature, even when the legislature acted "under pretense of providing for the common good." [12]

For a half-century following the *Munn Case*, Field's views rather than Waite's tended to prevail in the courts. For example, the early attempts of the states to regulate hours of labor were frustrated by narrow judicial interpretation of due process of law. In *Lochner* v. *New York* (1905), the Supreme Court invalidated a New York statute which, under the guise of protecting public health, limited the work of bakers to sixty hours a week. Justice Holmes dissented in vain. Distressed by his colleagues' tendency to look to the *laissez-faire* ideas of the popular English writer, Herbert Spencer, rather than to the Constitution, Holmes sharply reminded them, "The Fourteenth Amendment does not enact Mr. Herbert Spencer's Social Statics." Insisting that the public interest was "not in the slightest degree affected by this purely labor law," the majority of the Court gave the highest priority to "liberty of contract." [13] They believed that the liberty of workers and employers to contract with each other could not be regulated by the government. The high-water mark for this judicial concept of liberty of contract was approached in *Adkins* v. *Children's Hospital* (1923) when in a five-to-four decision the Court declared that a congressional act establishing minimum wages for women in the District of Columbia was a violation of the due process clause of the Fifth Amendment. The Court took a purely formal view, regarding the charwoman (Adkins) and the corporation (the Children's Hospital) as "persons" under the law, able to bargain as equals, both entitled to liberty of contract.[14]

Not until the 1930's, when the Great Depression forced the Court to face the facts of economic life, was there a turning of the tide in judicial interpretation of "business affected with a public interest." In the case of *Nebbia* v. *New York* (1934), the Supreme Court upheld a New York State statute regulating milk prices. Although the Court recognized that the milk business was in no sense a public utility, it nevertheless affirmed the right of the state to control any business for the public good. It found nothing "peculiarly sacrosanct" about the price a man may charge for what he makes or sells. It saw no reason why a state should not be free to adopt whatever economic policy it deemed necessary to promote the public welfare—including price-fixing—if the legislature thought such a regulation appropriate. Four justices dissented, subscribing to the dire warning of Justice James C. McReynolds that to adopt the majority view was "but to declare the rights guaranteed by the Constitution exist only so long as supposed public interest does not require their extinction." [15]

---

[12] *Munn* v. *Illinois*, 94 U.S. 113 (1877).

[13] Subsequently the Court did retreat from this extreme position with respect to hours legislation. It later upheld an Oregon statute regulating hours of labor for women, and then a general hours law for men and women. *Muller* v. *Oregon*, 208 U.S. 412 (1908); *Bunting* v. *Oregon*, 243 U.S. 426 (1917).

[14] *Adkins* v. *Children's Hospital*, 261 U.S. 525 (1923).

[15] *Nebbia* v. *New York*, 291 U.S. 502 (1934).

As constitutional law now stands, the protection of liberty and property under the due process clause of the Fifth and the Fourteenth Amendments does not forbid reasonable regulation of the economic system. In *West Coast Hotel Co. v. Parrish* (1937), Chief Justice Hughes specifically overruled the *Adkins Case* and sustained a minimum-wage law passed by Washington. In *Olsen* v. *Nebraska* (1941), Justice Douglas reversed another earlier decision by upholding the regulation of rates charged by employment agencies.[16]

This shift in judicial interpretation does not mean that business no longer has any constitutional protection against unreasonable, capricious, or confiscatory action on the part of government. Rather, it means that business can no longer claim complete immunity against the government's exercise of police power in the public interest.

Federalism and "Commerce among the States"

In 1787 the Constitutional Convention had to make some momentous decisions. Given the contemporary social and economic context—a vast territory sparsely populated, an economy predominantly agricultural, and a people with as yet very little sense of national identity—the Philadelphia Convention could hardly justify a strong unitary national state. On the other hand, an aggressive business community, bent on developing a national economy, was frustrated by legislative policies in the states—steep taxes to pay off revolutionary debts, paper currency and inflation, statutory relief for debtors even to the point of liquidating debts, and tariff barriers at state boundary lines. The farmers were active in state and local politics, but the national leadership came almost wholly from the business community. Hence the Framing Fathers, appraising the alternatives, chose the ambiguous pattern of federalism which would permit the development of a strong national government and at the same time recognize the continued existence of the states as political entities.

The identification of the business interest with the national interest—and of the national interest with the business interest—was most evident in the early days of the Republic. President Washington's selection of Alexander Hamilton as Secretary of the Treasury set the tone of the First Administration and established policy bases which persist to this day. Hamilton proposed that the new national government assume all the public debts, national and state, at face value. By this refunding of all public debts, he established the credit of the United States and at the same time gained the support of its creditors. All those who hold government securities, and there are proportionately many more today than in the 1790's, have a vested interest in the national government. Hamilton proposed the establishment of a national bank as well as a national mint so that the national government could control the currency and regulate the fiscal policies of the country. Despite mounting opposition from the Antifederalists, the Hamiltonian system became national

---

[16] *Olsen* v. *Nebraska*, 313 U.S. 236 (1941); *West Coast Hotel Co.* v. *Parrish*, 300 U.S. 379 (1937).

policy, enacted by the Congress and implemented by the Washington Administration.

The Jeffersonian Republicans, who opposed the Hamiltonian system, represented a variety of interests—small farmers, frontiersmen, some town laborers and mechanics—the rank and file of citizens. Since most of them distrusted a government designed to build a national economy, in which they saw no direct benefits for themselves, they attached the principle of states' rights to a policy of minimum government. The victory of the Jeffersonian Republicans in the election of 1800 was a popular revolution, but the checks and balances in the constitutional system enabled the Federalists to retain a defensive position within the judiciary. The business community, however, would never again have the positive influence in the national government that it enjoyed in the first formative years. During the 1920's, Republican Presidents still held that "the business of American government is business," but by that time business leaders were mostly interested in blocking government action, not in working for policies that would benefit them directly.

When an American political party loses control of Congress or the Presidency, it often looks to the courts to fight a rear guard action against major policy innovations by the incoming party. Since judges are appointed for life, the longer a party has been in power the more entrenched are its appointees in the judiciary. Thus, despite the overwhelming victory of the Jeffersonian Republicans over the Federalists in 1800, the federal judges who had won their appointments before the Republicans took over were able for many years to legitimate the doctrines of the defeated Federalists. Not until 1812 did the Jeffersonians obtain a dependable majority on the Supreme Court.

Chief Justice John Marshall's greatest decisions illustrate how a Federalist on the Court was able to advance his party's ideas—to strengthen the national government and to protect the interests of private property.[17] In *Marbury* v. *Madison* (1803), he claimed for the judiciary the power to declare an act of Congress unconstitutional. In *Fletcher* v. *Peck* (1810), he gave a narrow and literal translation of the constitutional provision that prohibits any state law from "impairing the obligation of contracts." His Court refused to sanction an act passed by the Georgia legislature rescinding past grants of public land that had been obtained by private companies through corrupt practices. The Chief Justice, who had the highest esteem for private rights, declared that once such rights were vested they could not be violated even by legislative action. In *McCulloch* v. *Maryland* (1819), Marshall developed the doctrine of implied powers under which the activities of the national government can be indefinitely expanded so long as congressional policies appear "convenient and useful" in carrying out the constitutional powers. And in *Gibbons* v. *Ogden* (1823), he gave a broad and expansive interpretation to the commerce clause; the case concerned conflicting national and state rights to regulate steamboat navigation on the Hudson River. In upholding the congressional

---

[17] *Marbury* v. *Madison*, 1 Cranch 137 (1803); *Fletcher* v. *Peck*, 6 Cranch 87 (1810); *McCulloch* v. *Maryland*, 4 Wheat. 316 (1819); *Gibbons* v. *Ogden*, 9 Wheat. 1 (1824).

regulations, Marshall rejected the proposition that national power over commerce must stop at state lines.

Marshall's successor, Roger Taney, born of southern landed aristocracy, did what he could to emphasize states' rights; since he was on the Court nearly thirty years (1836–1864), he was fairly successful in his efforts. Taney countered Marshall's earlier opinions on national power by building up a positive concept of police power in the states. (Police power is construed as the inherent power of the state to protect the general welfare of its citizens.) Without denying the supremacy of the national government in the use of its delegated powers, Taney stressed the Tenth Amendment as a guarantee of states' rights. In contrast to Marshall, who assumed that Congress had exclusive power over commerce among the states, Taney believed that a state had the right to protect the health, safety, and convenience of its own citizens even if this meant regulating interstate commerce. He would not declare a state statute unconstitutional unless it seriously conflicted with an act of Congress. But his most famous decision, the *Dred Scott Case* (1857), invalidated the Missouri Compromise on the grounds that Congress had no power to prohibit slavery in a territory since such a prohibition amounted to taking "property" without due process of law.[18]

Actually Congress made little use of its power to regulate commerce among the states until near the end of the nineteenth century. For the most part, litigation under the commerce power was initiated by businessmen who appealed to the principle of national power over commerce in order to resist state regulations. As long as Congress remained silent and did not try to use its power affirmatively, free enterprise could flourish. Eventually the strategy backfired, however. Midwestern farmers, outraged by railroad extortions ("all the traffic would bear"), organized politically as the National Grange to secure state regulation of railroad rates and services. Such legislation, as we have already mentioned, was upheld in *Munn* v. *Illinois* (1877) as a reasonable regulation of a business affected with a public interest.

In 1886, the Supreme Court struck down an Illinois statute forbidding unjust rate discriminations by railroads. It held that legislation which restricted interstate commerce went beyond the state's authority; only the Congress of the United States could regulate interstate commerce.[19] An aroused public demanded that Congress act immediately. At that time, Congress had a choice of several courses of action. Like the European countries, it could have embarked on a policy of governmental ownership and management, but as we know, the American people have always opposed the idea of socialism. It could have continued private ownership and management with government intervention to insure free competition, but this recourse would not have been economic. Students of the problem argued that the country really needed a unified transportation system that could offer adequate service even to sparsely settled and widely scattered communities. But the practical solution as Congress viewed it then—and now—was to leave the railroads under

---

[18] *Dred Scott* v. *Sandford,* 19 How. 393 (1857).
[19] *Wabash, St. Louis and Pacific Ry.* v. *Illinois,* 118 U.S. 557 (1886).

private ownership and management and to place them under national regulations which would protect the public against unreasonable rates. Thus, the Act of 1887 created a national regulatory commission, the Interstate Commerce Commission, and established as national policy that railroad rates must be reasonable and just, and discrimination between places, persons, or commodities prohibited.

Congress has always shown special concern for the development of national transportation. The very first Congress in 1789 provided various benefits for shipping concerns, and the American merchant marine is still heavily subsidized by the national government. The improvement of rivers and harbors and the construction of roads have been major activities of the national government. Both the national government and the states provided substantial subsidies for the construction of railroads in the nineteenth century and for the development of commercial aviation in the twentieth century. Partly because of its importance for national military strength, transportation has received more direct federal aid than any other industry. Nevertheless, the industry has taken countless cases to the courts, claiming the rights of "free enterprise." Over the years the judges have gradually sanctioned the national power to regulate the rates and services of railroads, bus lines, and airlines, not only in interstate commerce but also in related intrastate commerce.

A second landmark in the extension of positive national power over commerce among the states was the passing of the Sherman Anti-trust Act in 1890. By the end of the nineteenth century, giant industrial corporations and great financial holding companies threatened to dominate the entire economy. Huge combinations in restraint of trade were driving small businesses to bankruptcy in every community. In the 1880's, the same political forces that had secured the Granger legislation against the railroads—farmers, workers, and consumers—also sought legislation against the corporate monopolies. Obviously, however, a single state, or several states acting independently, could not begin to control the multi-million dollar combinations that were turning into industrial and financial empires. Thus Congress was forced to take action on a national basis.

The Sherman Act (1890) declared unlawful "every contract, combination in the form of trust or otherwise, or conspiracy in restraint of trade or commerce among the several states, or with foreign nations." Congress could only declare the public policy, however; to put the policy into operation required supporting action from the other branches of the government. Judicial interpretations almost immediately nullified the original intent of Congress. As early as 1895, in the *E. C. Knight Case*, the Supreme Court held that the Sherman Act was not meant to regulate monopoly in manufacturing since manufacturing is not part of interstate commerce.[20] Pursuing this construction, the Court decided that a corporate combination with a monopoly on the manufacture of 90 per cent of the sugar refined in the United States could not be prosecuted under the Sherman Act.

Whatever Congress had expected to accomplish by the Sherman Act, the executive and judicial branches offered little support. Although the Supreme Court

---

[20] *U.S.* v. *E. C. Knight Co.*, 156 U.S. 1 (1895).

ruled almost immediately that the Act could not apply to manufacturing, it was quite willing to entertain suits brought by the Justice Department against labor organizations attempting to boycott manufacturing companies. Not until 1914, and then only after considerable pressure from organized labor, did Congress specifically exempt labor unions (and also agricultural and horticultural organizations) from the provisions of the anti-trust legislation. Meantime, "judge-made" law continued to alter congressional output with respect to restraint of trade. The Court held that Congress did not intend to make *every* combination in restraint of trade unlawful (as the law plainly stated) but only *unreasonable* combinations. In the long-drawn-out case of *U. S. v. United States Steel Corporation* (1920), the Court decided that mere size was not a criterion of unreasonable restraint. It found that the U. S. Steel Corporation was not an unreasonable restraint, that the U. S. Steel Corporation was not an unreasonable combination, even though it had the largest capitalization of any single corporation in the country, over a billion dollars, and was the leading producer (though not the only one) in its field.[21]

So far we have said little about the role of labor in determining the national economic policy. In fact, the labor movement in the United States was much less aggressive than its counterparts in other industrial countries. The Knights of Labor in the 1880's represented an attempt by American workingmen to organize in one large national union, something comparable to the farmers' organization of the National Grange. But the Knights soon became embroiled in a succession of violent strikes, culminating in the disastrous Haymarket Riot in Chicago. In 1886, the Knights had planned a May Day demonstration to promote the cause of the eight-hour working day. In the course of demonstrating, the Knights tangled with a group of foreign-born anarchists and, when the Chicago police tried to break up the melee, a number of people, including several policemen, lost their lives and many were wounded. Organized labor was blamed for the bloody incident and the discredited Knights lost most of their membership almost overnight.

The American Federation of Labor (AFL), much less radical than the Knights, appeared next on the scene. Appealing to trade unions whose members were mostly skilled workers, the AFL worked for such general goals as the eight-hour working day, the six-day work week, decent wages, sickness and unemployment benefits, and restrictions on child labor. Not the least interested in forming a separate political party, the AFL supported candidates and platforms of any party that promised to promote labor interests. Though not inclined to violence, the AFL was prepared for direct action, to strike or boycott to gain its objectives. Under the leadership of Samuel Gompers, AFL membership increased from about 150,000 in 1886 to nearly 2 million at the outbreak of World War I.

Organized labor even in the 1930's was mainly concerned with better working conditions and higher wages for workers, especially skilled craftsmen. In the mid-1930's, John L. Lewis, head of the United Mine Workers, formed a Committee for Industrial Organizations (CIO) which undertook to unionize mass-

---

[21] *U.S. v. United States Steel Corporation,* 251 U.S. 417 (1920).

production industries on a vertical basis, thus bringing into the labor movement hitherto unorganized, unskilled workers. The AFL fought the CIO for a number of years, but the CIO succeeded in building powerful unions in the steel, automobile, rubber, maritime, coal, electrical, and other industries. In 1938, the CIO became a permanent organization, the Congress of Industrial Organizations. In the 1940's, the CIO, through its Political Action Committee, was active in politics, getting out the mass vote and promoting candidates and policies favorable to labor. In 1948, the AFL also set up a political committee, the Educational and Political League (EPL); both the AFL and the CIO campaigned vigorously for President Truman's re-election (and even more vigorously against the Republican candidate who had co-authored the Taft-Hartley Act in 1947). By the 1950's, the American labor movement was ready to accommodate both the horizontal crafts organization (AFL) and the vertical industry organization (CIO); the merger was officially accomplished as the AFL-CIO in 1956.

On the whole, American labor has had no quarrel with capitalism, nothing approaching the Marxist notions of the class struggle that motivated many labor movements in Europe. Even so, the reactions of American business were extremely hostile to labor union activities. As the labor unions learned to play the game of politics more effectively, they began to get what they wanted out of government. To offset the growing influence of labor among elected officials, businessmen counted on the judges, especially those appointed for life, to resist the pressures of "socialism" and "anarchism."

In 1914, under pressure from labor interest groups, Congress restricted judicial injunctions in labor disputes (Clayton Act) but not until 1932 (Norris-LaGuardia Act) did "the public policy of the United States" recognize the workers' need to organize and to bargain through their own representatives on the terms and conditions of their employment.

Although the national government had no positive labor policies until the mid-1930's, in many instances federal judges were able to govern labor relations by use of injunctions. If labor called a strike, the employer could seek an injunction ordering the strikers to cease and desist their interference with private business or their trespass on private property. To get the case into a federal court, it was not necessary to prove that the business in question was part of commerce among the states; if the parties to the suit came from different states, the federal judge could take jurisdiction under diversity of citizenship.

Before World War I the opponents of labor unionism used all kinds of tactics, legal, extra-legal, and illegal, to resist the organization of workers. A favorite device was the "yellow-dog contract," which required a job applicant to abandon his labor union membership as a condition of hiring and made return to labor union membership a basis for firing. Prompted by labor lobbyists, especially by the brotherhoods of railroad workers, Congress (1898) made it a criminal offense against the United States for a railroad carrier in interstate commerce to discharge an employee simply because of his membership in a labor organization. A decade later, the Court held the provision to be an unconstitutional invasion of personal liberty as well as of the right of property guaranteed by the Fifth

Amendment. Mr. Justice Harlan, who delivered the opinion of the Court (1908), professed that the employer has a legal right to discharge an employee, and an employee has an equal right to quit his job, "and any legislation that disturbs that equality is an arbitrary interference with the liberty of contract which no government can legally justify in a free land." As to whether Congress could prohibit yellow dog contracts under the commerce power, Justice Harlan asked, "but what possible legal or logical connection is there between an employee's membership in a labor organization and the carrying on of interstate commerce?" [22]

For more than three decades following the turn of the twentieth century the Supreme Court construed the commerce power narrowly to keep national regulations at a minimum. Despite Justice Holmes' protest that the Constitution does not embody a particular economic theory, the Court managed to inject Adam Smith's concept of the free market into the supreme law of the land. Thus, in 1918, the Court held that, since manufacturing is not part of interstate commerce, Congress may not forbid interstate commerce in goods manufactured by child labor. And, in 1923, the Court invalidated a minimum wage act for women in the District of Columbia after finding that such legislation interfered with freedom of contract implied by the due process clause of the Fifth Amendment.[23] Meantime, the Court went even further in limiting the powers of the states over the business community. Citing the due process clause of the Fourteenth Amendment, in case after case, the Court prevented the states from restricting working hours, setting minimum wages for women, forbidding mining operations that endangered dwelling places, regulating fees charged by private employment agents, and fixing the prices of gasoline to prevent cut-throat competition.

The crash of the New York stock market in 1929, which signaled the beginning of the Great Depression of the 1930's, brought about a revolution in the relations between government and business in the United States. Between 1929 and 1932 the national income was cut approximately in half; the big factories cut down production and slashed their payrolls; mines were closed or worked only part time; stores closed for lack of customers with cash; thousands of banks failed or suspended operations; millions of savings accounts were wiped out; nearly a hundred thousand business firms folded within three years; over 15 million persons were unemployed; millions of home and farm mortgages were foreclosed because people out of work could not keep up payments; people to whom normalcy meant prosperity stood in breadlines and many who couldn't stand the change in material circumstances committed suicide. Economists are still arguing among themselves just what happened to the American economic system and why. But at the time, most Americans seemed to think that the government ought to do something to meet the distressing situation.

When Franklin D. Roosevelt was inaugurated as President of the United States on March 4, 1933, the people were ready for a New Deal. The incoming

---

[22] *U.S.* v. *Adair*, 208 U.S. 172 (1908).
[23] *Hammer* v. *Dagenhart*, 247 U.S. 251 (1918); *Adkins* v. *Children's Hospital*, 261 U.S. 525 (1923).

President told the nation that he would ask the Congress for "broad executive power to wage a war against the emergency, as great as the power that would be given to use if we were in fact invaded by a foreign foe." His first action was to proclaim a bank holiday, call a special session of Congress—"The Congress of the Hundred Days"—and place the banks under national control. In a relatively short time, the New Deal constituted a kind of grand design for national recovery. It was not, however, so much a systematic national policy as it was a sequence of ad hoc reactions to pressing circumstances.

Though President Roosevelt had bipartisan support in both houses of Congress and overwhelming popular endorsement, the major policies of his first administration came to grief in the courts. Between 1934 and 1936, the Supreme Court invalidated the major acts of the New Deal. In 1935, the Court struck down the National Recovery Act, which was a package deal to establish codes of fair competition for every major industry in the country. For those industries which could not work out their own codes, the President was empowered to impose a "blanket" code prohibiting child labor, establishing maximum hours and minimum wage scales, and guaranteeing labor's right to organize and bargain collectively. By unanimous vote the Court held that such legislation exceeded the power of Congress to regulate commerce among the states and also violated the constitutional separation of powers by delegating legislative powers to the President.[24] In 1936, the Court nullified the Agricultural Adjustment Act, which proposed to regulate agricultural production as a way of raising farm prices and thus increasing farm incomes. Referring to "the accepted doctrine that the United States is a government of delegated powers," the Court decided (six to three) that the right to regulate agriculture was reserved to the states.[25] And a few months later, the Court (again six to three) invalidated the Bituminous Coal Act; commerce among the states could no more apply to mining operations than it did to manufacturing.[26]

But the Constitution is more than what the judges say it is. It too reflects the social context and in the long run it stands for what the people think is necessary and proper for the general welfare. Two months after the Supreme Court nullified the NRA, Congress passed the National Labor Relations Act, sometimes called the Magna Carta of American Labor. The Act created a national regulatory agency, the National Labor Relations Board, prohibited certain unfair labor practices, and reaffirmed labor's right to collective bargaining. Though the U. S. Chamber of Commerce, the National Association of Manufacturers, the Iron and Steel Institute, and similar interest groups were strongly opposed, organized labor,

---

[24] *Schechter Poultry Corp.* v. *U.S.*, 295 U.S. 495 (1935).

[25] *U.S.* v. *Butler*, 297 U.S. 1 (1936). In this case, Justice Roberts refused to ascertain the scope of the phrase "general welfare" or to determine whether an appropriation in aid of agriculture falls within it. It is difficult for the layman to perceive how the Justice, simply by laying the AAA alongside the Constitution, could be so sure that aid to agriculture was not in keeping with the national power to tax for the general welfare but rather a violation of the Tenth Amendment.

[26] *Carter* v. *Carter Coal Co.*, 298 U.S. 238 (1936).

by then a potent force in national politics, more than counteracted the pressures from the business community.

Judges may be somewhat lagging in their responses to new demands and supports, but in the long run they too are sensitive to shifts in public opinion. All policy-making, including judicial decisions, is conditioned by the dominant interests in the community. In 1937, the Supreme Court upheld the National Labor Relations Act. As Chief Justice Hughes, speaking for the majority of the Court, explained it, the judiciary had finally opened its eyes to "the plainest facts of our national life." [27] In 1937, in the face of stormy controversy, especially from the South, Congress enacted the Fair Labor Standards Act, which fixed minimum wages and maximum hours for persons engaged in interstate commerce, including manufacturing. The Court also upheld this legislation in 1941, and in doing so flatly overruled its previous decisions.[28] By 1941, however, a "Roosevelt Court" was in operation; seven of the nine justices had been appointed since 1937.

One looks in vain for a consistent policy base in the interplay of executive, legislative, and judicial decisions. The economic battles of American history are fought within the constitutional framework of federalism and a government based on the concept of separation of powers. But, in any given period, the antagonists seem to capitalize on national power, advocate states' rights, or insist on *laissez-faire* not so much as a matter of constitutional law or political theory as of economic interest.

The General Welfare: Demands, Supports, and Apathy

In the preceding section, we scrutinized the changing social environment for clues to power shifts within the American political system. From an historical perspective, we observed how various economic interests have appealed to American ideology and constitutional principles to support quite different goals. We have also seen how the framework of federalism has been used over the years to accommodate quite different views of national power and states' rights with respect to interstate commerce. As we narrow our focus to policy-making in its contemporary context, we shall examine the inputs affecting specific issues to discover who wants what. For this purpose we have singled out national tax policies and national spending policies to see how public demands and supports are brought to bear on official decisions.

The National Tax Policy

The most revolutionary change in our national economy has proceeded from a broad construction of the fiscal powers granted by the Constitution to the federal government—"To lay and collect Taxes . . . to pay the Debts and provide for

---

[27] *National Labor Relations Board* v. *Jones and Laughlin Steel Corporation*, 301 U.S. 1 (1937).
[28] *United States* v. *Darby Lumber Co.*, 312 U.S. 100 (1941).

the common Defense and general Welfare [and] To Borrow Money on the Credit of the United States." From the first days of the Republic, Congress has used the taxing power not only to support the costs of government but also to carry out social and economic policies for the whole country. When Hamilton proposed a protective tariff in Washington's first administration, he was interested not only in raising revenue but also in promoting and encouraging infant industries in the new nation.

Since Hamilton's day, Congress has used its taxing power to promote many other policies. Tax laws with policy objectives beyond the mere raising of revenue have included taxes on state bank notes, on colored oleomargarine, on dealers in such firearms as sawed-off shotguns and machine guns, on narcotics, on the "occupation" of gambling, and so on. Congress thus uses its tax power to carry out various policies that are not specifically included among its delegated powers. In doing so, it expands the meaning of the Constitution.

How far can Congress go in using taxes to enlarge its other powers? We have seen that the Constitution describes the taxing power in the most sweeping terms, authorizing Congress to tax "for the common defense and general welfare." But the Supreme Court in the 1920's and early 1930's imposed a "judge-made" limitation on the taxing power, holding that Congress could not use taxes to achieve purposes not included in its enumerated powers. It invalidated a tax on mines and mills that used child labor, a tax on coal operators who refused to accept the price-fixing and fair labor provisions of a New Deal code, and a tax on processors of agricultural products from which the proceeds were to be used for grants-in-aid to farmers cooperating in the agricultural program of the New Deal. In recent years, however, the Court seems to have returned to the Hamiltonian view that Congress has the broad power to tax for the "general welfare."

As a matter of fact, all taxes, even those exclusively intended to raise revenue, have other effects as well. Excise taxes on liquor, gasoline, tobacco, cosmetics, and other products, which bring in nearly 10 per cent of the federal revenue, raise the prices of these commodities. This effect on prices amounts to penalizing the consumers of these products, a penalty that is justified from various policy positions—that these products are non-essential, that they are injurious or perhaps even sinful, that excise taxes are "hidden" from citizens in the prices of products they purchase, and that, as an alternative to the income tax, excises decrease the burden on people with large incomes. No provision in the Constitution gives Congress direct power to penalize such things as fondness for "non-essentials," self-indulgence, or sin, but such penalties are very much a part of our constitutional practice. On the ground that these taxes are regressive (imposing greater proportionate burdens on the poor than the rich), President Lyndon Johnson recommended the repeal of several excise taxes in 1965.

The most regulatory tax of all—the one with the greatest policy implications and the greatest effect on the people—is, of course, the federal income tax. The Sixteenth Amendment authorizes federal taxes on "income from whatever source derived." The estimated revenues from income taxes make up about 80 per cent of the total federal receipts. The very fact that the income tax produces so much revenue makes it an effective governmental tool for redistributing the national wealth and for directing the nation's economic policy.

Changing tax laws bring into sharp focus the connection between policy and socio-economic divisions among the voters. Citizens have always had an intense interest in, not to say aversion for, taxes. In Biblical days, suppressed populations warmly loathed the tax collector and his arbitrary ways; American colonists protested against "taxation without representation"; the small farmers of western Pennsylvania reacted to Hamilton's excise tax on whisky with the "Whisky Rebellion" of 1794; nor does the country ring with shouts of joy when Americans file their income tax returns today. No tax could ever be devised that all citizens would accept as fair and neutral; hence the government tends to follow the tax principle of "plucking the goose that squawks the least."

Until the twentieth century, the political power structure of the United States meant that the principal tax burden fell on those with low incomes. Duties on imports (tariffs) and domestic taxes on special commodities (excises) were the principal sources of revenue for the national government. Taxes of this sort have the same regressive effect as a sales tax: by raising the price paid by consumers for the items affected, they extract a greater percentage of income from the poor than from the rich. Ten dollars out of the weekly income of some consumers may mean little or nothing; but it may be a big slice out of the income of others. This is the principle Jesus applied when he pointed out that the contribution of "two mites" by a poor widow was "more" than larger contributions from the wealthy.

This system of taxation met with some resistance from low-income groups, as the Whisky Rebellion demonstrates. And yet the groups that held political power were able to keep it in force, for two reasons: many people in the low-income groups were disfranchised by the property qualifications required for voting; these same people were deficient in education and organizational skills, and consequently were not always aware of just how the taxes affected them.

When the suffrage was extended and workers and farmers began to organize, the tax base was shifted. In 1890, as a concession to the Populists—the most radical political force of the time—a 2 per cent tax was levied on incomes over $4,000 a year. But the sentiment of the people had not yet become the sentiment of the Supreme Court. In an 1895 decision almost openly based on their attitude toward conflicting political forces, the justices corrected what they called "a century of error" in court interpretations of Congress' tax power and declared the income tax unconstitutional.[29] But the Court could not permanently substitute its own class biases for those of a newly restive majority of the voters. What had seemed a sudden outburst of class conflict to the Court had merely been the organization of new forces to give more effective expression to the views of people with lower socio-economic status. In 1913, the Sixteenth Amendment permitted the income tax to become the law of the land, and since then the geese with the most feathers have been regularly plucked.

---

[29] *Pollock* v. *Farmers' Loan and Trust Co.*, 157 U.S. 429 (1895).

When the Sixteenth Amendment was proposed, it was bitterly attacked in Congress and in the state legislatures as socialistic. Today, however, the idea of a progressive tax on personal and corporation income seems firmly written into the public policy. The rate of taxation goes up as income goes up; the upper limit is now 70 per cent. Those with the highest incomes protest against "confiscatory" taxation; those with low incomes claim the exemption base of $600 is unreasonably low. Notice that most arguments today focus on how to reform the tax structure rather than on the merits or demerits of the income tax *per se*.

One of the major goals of the Kennedy Administration was to secure an equitable revision of the income tax law. Within a few months after his inauguration, President Kennedy directed the Treasury Department to prepare recommendations for a comprehensive tax reform bill. The Treasury Department took 21 months to work out technical changes in the income tax system that would (1) broaden the tax base (2) remove certain inequities and loopholes and (3) permit tax reductions on both individual and corporate income. President Kennedy incorporated the Treasury recommendations in his tax message of January 1963. The House Committee on Ways and Means and the Senate Committee on Finance held hearings and listened to hundreds of important witnesses, representing many different and influential groups in the economy.[30] Obviously all of the opinions expressed could not carry equal weight with Congress. If you were a conscientious congressman anxious to please your constituents and to serve the national interest—not always the same thing—how would you weigh these opinions?

The Chamber of Commerce of the United States, representing some 3400 local and state chambers of commerce and trade associations, argued that tax cuts were imperative but that reduction of federal expenditures was equally imperative. According to its spokesman, the Chamber opposed "the political arithmetic of rate making" and the popular philosophy of "tax and tax and spend and spend and elect and elect." Arguing that the present tax structure was one to encourage consumption and to discourage investment, the Chamber urged that immediate tax cuts be made in the top-income brackets to encourage "job making investments." On the other hand, the AFL-CIO, presenting its demands on behalf of 13 million industrial and trade workers, favored immediate tax cuts for the low-income brackets but claimed that it would be disastrous to make such tax cuts conditional on reduction of federal expenditures. In fact, the AFL-CIO advocated greater government spending, especially for public works, as a means of relieving the unemployment situation. The AFL-CIO argued that low-income people would be sure to spend their tax savings, thus stimulating production and creating new jobs. It also insisted that the $600 basic deduction for dependents was unrealistically low, and suggested that, if the base were raised to $1000, the tax loss from this move could well be offset by closing the present loopholes with respect to mineral depletion allowances, dividend credits, and capital gains on transfer at death.

---

[30] The excerpts of testimony that follow on the Internal Revenue Act of 1963 are from the *Hearings* before the Senate Committee on Finance. 88th Congress, 1st Sess., (Washington, D.C.: Government Printing Office, 1962).

Here then are two viewpoints, diametrically opposed, one from an influential organization of businessmen, the other from a powerful organization of industrial workers. How to reconcile their divergent views in the public policy?

Those who appeared before the congressional committees represented a variety of interests. The Independent Petroleum Association of America (6000 independent oil and gas producers) pleaded with Congress, for example, to take no action as regards the special depletion allowance for oil and gas producers. The Association claimed that the oil and gas business was in such a state of decline, as to prices, employment, and business generally, that the atmosphere for capital investments in oil and gas production was already most unfavorable. Lest the industry appear too selfish, the Association spokesman pointed out how vital petroleum production is to the economic life of more than half the states and thousands of communities and also how important oil is in the national defense. The American Automobile Association testified on behalf of the millions of American motorists; its pitch was to include state gasoline taxes, car registration fees, and licenses as deductible items in the national income tax levy. The Association was indignant at the very idea that use of an automobile should be put in the same taxable category as consumption of alcoholic beverages; and it argued plausibly that, if the national income tax permitted deductions for furs, jewelry, and other items of luxury, then surely it could do no less for such a needed item as gasoline. A more modest request came from the National Federation of the Blind—an additional tax exemption for a taxpayer supporting a blind dependent. How would you have reacted to these specific requests from special interests?

The Farm Bureau Federation, representing 1.6 million farmers, told the Senate Finance Committee that any tax reductions not tied to reduced expenditures would be fiscally irresponsible. It stated unequivocally that it was opposed to any general tax reduction until the federal government was prepared to cut its expenditures. It was also opposed to raising the minimum standard deduction since this was bound to reduce the number of people who pay taxes and at the same time increase the number of voters who would feel free to demand and support additional programs to be paid for by others. On the other hand, the National Farmers Union, also representing farmers, offered complete support to President Kennedy's tax proposals. Believing that the basic cause of unemployment is underconsumption, it counted on tax cuts for the wage earners to increase their ability to purchase the goods and materials they produce. It was not in favor of allowing wealthy individuals to use farm losses to escape payments on off-farm income and it was opposed to the various loopholes which allowed great foundations to evade taxes.

The President of the National Association of Manufacturers pointed out that excessive income tax rates constitute a roadblock to the development of our entire national economy. He felt strongly that steeply graduated rates of income taxes contradict the principle of incentive which is vital in the free enterprise system of compensation. His Association urged tax cuts, especially in the middle- and upper-income brackets. It opposed high rates on corporate income as stifling capital formation and it specifically opposed repeal of the 4 per cent dividend credit which exempts a portion of income from corporate dividends. Voicing similar views, the President of the Junior Chamber of Commerce spoke for 225,000 young men and their families, in 4900 communities, dedicated to the creed "economic justice can best be won by free men through free enterprise." He advocated tax cuts, especially for the middle-income brackets, the able and energetic people whom he saw as contributing most to the expanding economy.

The Americans for Democratic Action decried the excessively heavy tax burdens borne by persons in the lowest income brackets, which lend a strong regressive bias to the national tax system as a whole. It also deplored the loopholes through which billions of dollars in income, mostly in the high-income brackets, evade taxation. It clearly expressed itself as opposed to any attempt to offset the loss of revenues from tax reduction by curtailing government expenditures. In support of this viewpoint, it called attention to the enormous unmet needs of the nation for increased public outlays for schools, public welfare, housing, urban redevelopment, water supply, mass transit, highways, and health and recreational facilities.

The American Bar Association, with a membership of 114,000 lawyers, many of them tax specialists, favored broadening the tax base, reducing income rates, simplifying technical provisions, simplifying administration, and easing the burden of compliance. Since it would take time to achieve these ends, the lawyers said it would be better not to tinker with piecemeal reforms. On the other hand, the Business Committee for Tax Reduction in 1963, whose membership included upwards to 2000 of the big names in big business, board members and officers of such firms as Ford Motors, Pennsylvania Railroad, American Telephone and Telegraph, Chase Manhattan, American Can, Commonwealth Edison, Westinghouse Electric, and others of similar magnitude, demanded across-the-board reductions on individual and corporate incomes. The Committee insisted that immediate tax cuts would not only stimulate consumer spending but also encourage business investment. Though it was opposed to deficit financing, it left it up to Congress to decide where and how federal expenditures could be cut; it was not willing to take a position on any particular items. If you were on the Congressional committee, whose advice would you have heeded, the lawyers who counseled a wait-and-study period, or the businessmen who insisted on immediate action?

In the next section of this chapter, we shall be looking at official decision-makers and their policy outputs. Who makes policy is always open to argument. In this text, we have taken the point of view that the unofficial agencies furnish important inputs in terms of demands and support, but policies are made by the official agencies. One bit of testimony before the Senate Committee on Finance relating to the 1963 Revenue Act suggests, however, the close interaction between the official and unofficial agencies. Following the presentation of the Business Committee for Tax Reduction in 1963, the senators' interrogation revealed that the idea for such a committee actually originated in the Treasury Department, which was sponsoring the proposed legislation. Five or six key businessmen had been invited to meet with Treasury officials to talk over the strategy of getting an omnibus tax bill through Congress in 1963. Subsequently, this small group divorced itself from the Treasury Department, organized on its own as a lobby to work on Congress, extended its membership, and sought and obtained financial contributions from hundreds of companies—insurance, utilities, distillers, automobile manufacturers, banks, department stores, iron and steel, coal and coke, oil, bus lines, air lines, ship-building—in short, a cross section of the nation's business. Was the Treasury Department indirectly engaged in lobbying?

The national political parties gather together a full range of issues and present them as platforms to the electorate. But because each party writes so many different planks into its platform, official policy-makers cannot always tell which issues are most influential in deciding the outcome of the national elections. Moreover, because congressional candidates frequently do not stand on the presidential platform of their party, and also because many citizens split their ballots, policy-makers are likely to be more responsive to the specific pleas of organized interest groups than to the confused and multiple party lines.

The Federal Regulation of Lobbying Act (1946) requires all lobbyists to register themselves and their activities with Congress. But judicial interpretation of the Act limits its application to those in "direct communication with members of Congress." Hence, interest groups, however active in politics or persuasive in molding political opinions, do not come under the lobbying act unless they attempt to influence the legislative process directly. Even so, more than 300 interest groups are registered as congressional lobbyists, and their demands and supports constitute a major input in setting policy goals and in formulating programs and operations. The *Congressional Quarterly Almanac* every year publishes a "Lobby Round-up," listing the registered lobbyists by category and indicating the amount of money reported as spent by each lobbyist in efforts to influence congressional decisions. The table below is based on the reports for 1963:

TABLE 14-1   *The Lobby Round-Up, 1963*

NUMBER OF LOBBYISTS BY CATEGORY		REPORTED AMOUNT SPENT FOR LOBBYING ACTIVITIES
170	Business	$1,836,125.93
50	Citizens	531,001.82
37	Labor	945,206.18
22	Farmers	412,523.97
6	Military and veterans	141,990.83
19	Professions	344,455.24
Total 304		$4,211,303.97

Source: *Congressional Quarterly Almanac*, XIX (1963), p. 1038.

The activities of lobbyists frequently go well beyond their special interests. As we have seen on the tax hearings, labor had much to say about business, and vice versa; farmers talked about business conditions and labor problems; consumer groups and veterans covered the whole range of legislation. The views of the larger number of apathetic or uninformed citizens constitute effective inputs only as potential demands or supports that might be created by the feedback of policy outputs. Weighing all of these expressed and potential interests, Congress must discern the common interest and promote the general welfare.

Federal Spending

The constitutional power to tax—to pay the debts and provide for the common defense and general welfare—implies the power to spend the public monies for these ends. How official policy-makers decide to spend the public monies reaches to the very heart of politics—who gets what. In a democracy, all official policies are supposed to reflect the needs and goals as well as the opinions and votes of the citizens. But citizens have many conflicting viewpoints. Moreover, different political opinions and behavior are not randomly distributed through the population. These matters are still far from perfectly understood, but such variables as socio-economic status seem to have a weighty and persistent influence on the political preferences of voters. The perspective of a business executive gazing at the world through the tinted windshield of his chauffeur-driven limousine is likely to be quite different from that of an employee riding home on a bus or subway.

President Franklin D. Roosevelt's New Deal in the 1930's began as a great national effort to meet the exigencies of depression. Local charity and state activities had not been able to cope with the nation-wide emergency. Most Americans did not want outright relief; government handouts belied the American tradition of individual self-reliance. Work relief seemed a more respectable alternative to the dole. Hence the Roosevelt Administration tried out various public works programs to put millions of unemployed people into useful jobs. No doubt there was some "boondoggling" or useless work in the hastily designed public works programs. But Arthur Schlesinger, Jr., historian of the period, reminds us that the Public Works Administration put up the Triborough Bridge in New York, built a new sewerage system for Chicago, a municipal auditorium for Kansas City, a water supply system for Denver; it rebuilt the Los Angeles schools after the earthquake of 1933 and constructed the bridges and highway between Key West and the Florida Mainland; it helped build the Tennessee Valley Authority, the Grand Coolee and Bonneville Dams on the Columbia, Fort Peck Dam on the Upper Missouri, and Boulder Dam on the Colorado. Between 1933 and 1939 it spent about $6 billion dollars and in those few years it helped construct 70 per cent of the nation's new educational buildings, 65 per cent of the court houses and city halls and sewerage disposal plants, and 35 per cent of all the roads, bridges, and subways. As Schlesinger observes, all this must be counted a "prodigious accomplishment." [31]

Whether the PWA, and all the other alphabetical spending agencies of the New Deal, took us out of depression and up the road to recovery is still open to

---

[31] Arthur M. Schlesinger, Jr., *The Coming of the New Deal* (Boston: Houghton Mifflin Company, 1959), p. 288.

argument. To understand the New Deal, however, one must realize the full impact of nation-wide social and economic distress; unprecedented conditions called for unprecedented government action. But in 1939, World War II totally changed the national as well as the international environment. Thus, the "welfare state" of the 1930's became the "warfare state" of the 1940's and thereafter.

When the Republican Party returned to power after World War II, the Eisenhower Administration carried forward its activities in a social and economic context vastly different from the early years of the New Deal. America was once more prosperous. American business had developed its technology and stretched its industrial capacity to win World War II and in doing so it entered into an entirely different relationship with the national government. The war effort had called for gigantic spending programs for military purposes as the government contracted with private enterprise to provide the weapons and materials for total war.

From *What's Got Your Back Up?* Copyright © 1961 by Bill Mauldin. Reprinted with the permission of Harper & Row, Publishers.

"Who's livin'?"

The Cold War, which followed shortly after the end of World War II, kept the government spending for national security at levels hitherto unimaginable in the American economy. Moreover, the three top industries of the country—modern weaponry, atomic energy, and space exploration—owed their very existence as well as spectacular development to government policies. The great spending programs of the government in the 1950's and 1960's were largely directed into these three industries. Government was in business in a big way but business was also in government in a big way. Again the magic nexus between government and business was in the form of profitable government contracts for private enterprise. As business prospered, the gross national product zoomed and American consumption patterns for family living were keyed to the economy of abundance. Science and technology in the service of government and business had made us the most "affluent society" in the modern world.

It came then as a sort of shock when the Johnson Administration launched its "war on poverty" as a national policy. Some people, and not just Republicans, thought that the poverty issue was cooked up for the 1964 elections. It was hard to believe that poverty was, in fact, a widespread condition of living in the richest country in the world. But the millions of Americans who live in poverty are generally invisible to us who live fairly comfortably. Poverty exists off the beaten track, in the city slums where we seldom venture, in the mining towns off the main highways, in the backwoods country. Many of the very poor are old people, many are children, most of them are unemployable. As Michael Harrington points out in *The Other America*, these people at the bottom of our society rarely speak out for themselves—"The people of the other America do not, by far and large, belong to unions, to fraternal organizations, or to political parties. They are without lobbies of their own; they put forward no legislative program. As a group, they are atomized. They have no face; they have no program." [32]

Specific reactions to President Lyndon Johnson's plans for helping what Harrington calls "the other America" illuminate the nature of inputs affecting national spending policies. The specific demands and supports through which social interests are identified come from the decision-makers themselves no less than from groups outside the government structure. President Johnson first declared all-out war on poverty in his State of the Union message in 1964. In March 1964, the House Committee on Education and Labor began hearings on the Economic Opportunity Act, "a bill to mobilize the human and financial resources of the nation to combat poverty in the United States." [33] The Administration plan, incorporated in the Act, was to test out a variety of programs in Appalachia, between the Eastern Seaboard and the Mid-West Farm belt: basic education programs, community action programs, and special programs to combat poverty in rural areas. Adam Clayton Powell (D-NY), as Chairman of the Committee, introduced the Act as a first step toward helping "one fifth of our nation's population who have been left out of the flowing stream of prosperity." The Republican member from New Jersey countered, "We Republicans are unanimously of the opinion that it is unwise and a mistake to use an omnibus approach to this so-called war on poverty." Throughout the hearings, party lines were more evident than usual, because 1964 was an election year and both parties were alert to campaign issues.

The Administration's initial presentation was by Sargent Shriver, Director of the Peace Corps and later head of the Poverty Corps when that agency was authorized. He told the Committee that in planning the proposed programs he had consulted with many different persons—college presidents and professors, prominent businessmen, representatives of foundations, labor leaders, state and local officials, and also with a task force from concerned agencies in the national government. Subsequently, every member of the President's Cabinet, except the Postmaster General and the Secretary of State, appeared before the Committee to explain how the proposed programs tied in with their particular areas of concern.

---

[32] Michael Harrington, *The Other America* (Baltimore: Penguin Books, 1963), p. 13. For further data on the extent of poverty, see Chapter 1.

[33] The excerpts of testimony that follow on the Economic Opportunity Act of 1964 are from the Hearings of the ad hoc sub-committee of the House Committee on Labor and Education, 88th Congress, 2nd Sess. (Washington, D.C.: Government Printing Office, 1964).

Drawing by Herblock. From *Straight Herblock* (New York, Simon & Schuster, 1964).

"Ah, dying is hard for both of us."

Then began the parade of witnesses speaking for the pluralistic interests of America.

Though labor leaders strongly supported the idea of a government war on poverty, they emphasized that the Appalachian project was only a small beginning. The President of AFL-CIO, for example, took the opportunity to plug for extension of fair labor standards, claiming that more than a million Americans still earn less than fifty cents an hour. He also urged extension of federal aid to primary and secondary education, federal aid for area redevelopment, federal aid for urban mass transit facilities, and federal standards for unemployment compensation. The President of the United Auto Workers made the same pitch. Since Congress was then considering medicare under social security, he added that item to labor's demands—"we are doing less to meet the medical care needs of our older citizens than any industrialized nation in the world on either side of the Iron Curtain."

Spokesmen for farm groups expressed different opinions. The National Grange favored the program, "the first time we have taken a broad look at the whole problem of American poverty." The National Farmers Union likewise gave all-out support. But the more conservative Farm Bureau was adamantly opposed to any additional federal spending until the federal budget could be balanced.

Strongest opposition to the anti-poverty program came from the National Association of Manufacturers and the Chamber of Commerce of the United States. The Director of the Economic Research Department for the Chamber of Commerce questioned the statistical basis of the government's assessment of poverty in the country. "It goes without saying that our nation's level of living is the highest in the world." He pointed out that the federal government was already supporting more than 40 programs related to the problems of poverty and the results were not impressive. He suggested that the President's concern with poverty was an election gimmick and that Congress should delay legislation until it could engage in "operational thinking." On specific questioning by Edith Green, the Democratic Representative from Oregon, the Chamber of Commerce spokesman expressed opposition not only to the Economic Opportunity Act but also to federal spending for urban renewal, public housing, area redevelopment, mass transit, accelerated public works, hospital care for the aged under social security, public education, the

Youth Employment Act, the Domestic Peace Corps, public power projects, TVA, the National Defense Education Act, and school construction. The Chamber favored tax cuts, fast tax write-offs, subsidies to air lines, and the trade expansion act.

Republican members of the Committee frequently raised the issue of states' rights. And a number of witnesses objected to the national government bypassing the states to work directly with the local communities. Democratic members of the Committee argued that the problem of poverty had become too large for states and localities to solve without financial support from the national government. Governors from New Jersey, Kentucky, North Carolina, Indiana, and California appeared before the Committee to plead for the Act. Speaking for one of the largest and richest states, the Governor of California assured the Committee that his state not only needed help but was prepared to implement the federal programs at once in its own battle against poverty. When a Republican member of the Committee intimated that the Act would allow "no role for the state government to play at all," the Governor replied that in his experience federal agencies could be depended on to work cooperatively with state agencies. A succession of mayors—from New York City, Chicago, Detroit, St. Louis, and Syracuse—offered similar testimony, that their cities needed and wanted the kind of federal assistance promised in the Act.

How then do policy-makers arrive at reasonable decisions in the public interest when the input of political opinions is so strikingly divergent? That government must rest on consent of the governed is a fundamental principle of democracy, but how can our official representatives ascertain what all the people, or most of the people, really need or want?

Decision-Makers and Their Decisions: General Welfare and Common Defense

Thus far in this chapter we have focused on the cultural, social, and economic factors that condition the political environment within which our policy-makers determine what governmental actions are necessary and proper to promote the general welfare. We have observed especially the impact of science and technology on the economy and the consequent development of new inputs for the political system. We have looked at the changing demands and supports from the unofficial agencies in the policy process—political parties, pressure groups, opinion leaders —trying to influence the government to pursue this, or that, or still another kind of activity. Now we reach the authoritative decisions, the policy process itself. Here we attempt to identify the principal actors in the current policy process, not only the decision-makers within the constitutional and institutional setting but also the various "communities" of policy specialists. Finally, we take stock of the major policies which seem to be goal-oriented toward the general welfare, keeping in mind that such policies emerge as outputs from the entire political system.

All authoritative decision-making in American government takes place—or is supposed to—within the constitutional framework. In a democracy, it is assumed that every governmental activity may be rationalized, if not always justified, as directed toward the general welfare. Within this broad interpretation, every congressional statute, every executive order, every judicial decision relates to some aspect of the general welfare.

In discussing governmental policies, the traditional approach is to set up a number of "areas" and then to summarize the laws that fall into each—business, agriculture, labor, social welfare, finance, and foreign relations, for example. For this approach, the current *United States Government Organization Manual* is a convenient source. It indicates the constitutional and statutory authority of each agency, sketches the organization, outlines the official responsibilities and duties of each operating unit, and lists the principal officers. Its appendix includes a set of "organization charts" which point up the bureaucratic hierarchy in each major agency. What the *Manual* does not do is tell us how or why the decision-makers in each agency determine to take (or not to take) certain courses of action. Obviously in the remaining few pages of this chapter we cannot examine the policy process in every government agency whose activities contribute to the general welfare. For illustrative purposes, we select the agencies that deal directly with social security to show how they operate within the institutional setting.

If we put policy-making in the context of politics, the summary descriptions and neat charts in the organization manual will not tell us who really made specific decisions or why one program got a green light and another got a stop signal. In the actual policy process, the official hierarchy may not be so important as an ad hoc "community of policy makers." Membership in the community of policy-makers varies considerably according to the content of the policies under consideration. The community of policy-makers is a flexible concept, which in effect may disregard the constitutional designs for federalism or separation of powers or the institutional setting prescribed by statutes. Personal considerations may become more significant than official positions and bureaucratic channels.

Social Security

How social security was established as a national policy is a long story that dates back to the beginning of the New Deal. The Democratic Platform of 1932 had declared, "We advocate unemployment and old age insurance under state laws." The official decision, however, provided for a much more complicated federal system. The Social Security Act of 1935 was a three-in-one package, and a prime example of that "cooperative federalism" we discussed in Chapter 4. (1) It provided for a national system of social insurance against old age financed through national taxes and administered directly by the national government. (2) It provided for a nation-wide plan of public assistance financed in part by matching grants-in-aid to the states, administered in state agencies under certain conditions specified by the national government. (3) It provided for a nation-wide scheme of unemployment insurance, financed through national taxes with tax credits to the states, but administered under state plans approved by the national government. Congress has since made many changes in the original act that extend the coverage and liberalize the conditions under which benefits may be claimed. National administration of social security legislation has been reorganized in successive presidential administrations, but the whole social security system still operates in a pattern of working cooperation between the national government and the states.

Who made the initial decisions? The formulation of public policy always involves a variety of official actors. In this case, the principal actor was President Roosevelt, who was personally committed to the idea of public insurance.[34] We do not, however, attribute the specific programs to the President; a number of different bills had been proposed in Congress in 1933 and 1934 dealing with unemployment compensation, old age pensions, and assistance to the needy aged. The President asked Congress (June 1934) to delay action on piecemeal legislation until his Administration could work out (1) a truly federal program that would involve both the national government and the states; (2) a comprehensive measure that would be actuarially sound, financed by contributions rather than by any increase in general taxation. Meantime the President appointed a Committee on Economic Security, headed by the Secretary of Labor, Miss Frances Perkins, to formulate an over-all program.

The Committee on Economic Security comprised a group of "experts," drawn from the public (national and state) and private (labor and management) sectors of the economy, who represented a variety of views on how to set up, finance, and administer a social security system. Some advocated an exclusively national system; others preferred separate state systems; some urged financing by governmental contributions raised through general taxes; others thought that employers only should contribute since they could and presumably would shift payroll taxes to the consumer; others argued that employees ought to contribute so that they could more surely claim their benefits as earned rights. The President leaned toward the last view, not so much on the basis of economics, as on political grounds. Some time after the decision was made to finance old age insurance by joint contributions of worker and employers the President explained privately, "We put those payroll contributions there so as to give the contributors a legal, moral, and political right to collect their pensions and their unemployment benefits. With those taxes in there, no damn politician can ever scrap my social security program."

Recently Governor of New York State, Franklin Roosevelt was inclined to favor a state system of administration; but as President of the United States, confronted with a nation-wide depression, he recognized the need for national planning and national action. On January 17, 1935, he sent his message to Congress requesting national social security legislation. Senator Robert Wagner of New York (D) and Representatives David J. Lewis (D) of Maryland and Robert L. Doughton of North Carolina (D) introduced draft bills for the Administration in the Senate and House respectively. Hearings began at once in the House Ways and Means Committee. A battery of witnesses from the Administration, including

---

[34] The account of the New Deal period is borrowed largely from Schlesinger's *The Coming of the New Deal*.

members of the Committee on Economic Security and Henry Morgenthau, Secretary of the Treasury, discussed alternative programs and problems of financing and defended the compromise position of the Administration. Interest groups, for and against, made their views known through committee hearings and with individual members of Congress. The business community generally viewed with alarm the ultimate outcome of such a socialist venture—". . . the result would be moral decay, financial bankruptcy, and the collapse of the republic." Many Republicans, first in committee sessions, then in floor debate, reflected the views of the business groups. Representative John Taber of New York (R) declaimed, "Never in the history of the world has any measure been brought in here so insidiously designed as to prevent business recovery, to enslave workers, and to prevent any possibility of the employers providing work for the people." But when the chips were down, and the people's representatives had assessed the weight of political opinions in their own constituencies, the House passed the bill 371 to 33 and the Senate, 76 to 6. Thus the principle of public insurance became a national policy as a result of many interactions, public and private, and with many persons officially and unofficially in the act.

But policy involves more than endorsement of principle; it must be made operative. At the national level, the social security system was off to a poor start when a Huey Long filibuster in the Senate blocked the necessary appropriations. After consulting congressional leaders of both parties, President Roosevelt determined to finance the new social security agency from NRA and WPA funds. With the advice and consent of the Senate, he named three members to the new Social Security Board. The first Chairman was John G. Winant, a Progressive Republican, who had been Governor of New Hampshire, and who had also served on the Advisory Council of the Committee for Economic Security.

Enactment of the Social Security Act and the establishment of the national agency was only the beginning. The initial decision—not to set up a unitary national system but rather to work through a federalized pattern—meant that actual implementation of the social security program was more or less left up to decision-makers in each state. It took some doing to get all the states into the system. When Congress passed the Social Security Act in 1935, only Wisconsin had an unemployment compensation plan. Most states did not support statewide welfare organizations, and less than half the states offered any kind of pensions or old age assistance and these plans applied only to the indigent. Though every state was persuaded to participate, the decision to participate had to be made within the constitutional and political framework of each state. To this day, our federalized social security system resembles a crazy quilt of varying state standards as to procedures, coverage, and benefits. And if we attempt to identify the principal actors in the policy process as well as in the institutional setting, we find a sort of interlocking directorate among the official decision-makers—national and state, executive and legislative, political and bureaucratic.

Even the judges got into the act through judicial review and in doing so sanctioned the basic policy decisions. The constitutionality of cooperative federalism was thoroughly discussed by Justice Benjamin Cardozo in the case of

Steward Machine Co. v. *Davis* (1937), involving the validity of the federal unemployment tax as applied to employers in Alabama.[35] The Court held that the tax did not involve national coercion of the states and did not invade powers reserved to the states under the Tenth Amendment nor violate any other restrictions implicit in American federalism. The Court agreed with the supporters of the Social Security Act "that its operation is not constraint, but the creation of a larger freedom, the states and the nation joining in a cooperative endeavor to avert a common evil." Congress passed the Social Security Act in a time of urgent national economic distress, and Justice Cardozo handed down his decision while the country was still emerging from a great economic depression. But the country has shown little inclination since then to repeal the congressional policy or to reverse the Court's opinion.

Old age, survivors, and disability insurance is financed through special taxes levied by Congress under its power to tax for the general welfare. All persons covered by the Act—nearly all workers, including self-employed persons, except doctors of medicine and federal government employees—pay their social security taxes to the Director of Internal Revenue. The Treasury Department maintains separate trust funds from which the benefits and administrative costs of the program are paid. The Social Security Administration in the Department of Health, Education and Welfare administers the program through some 600 district offices. For most Americans this compulsory federal insurance constitutes the first line of defense against dependency in old age. The process of maintaining records of the lifetime earnings in more than 100 million active accounts is almost completely automated. Yet the main function of this vast and impersonal mechanism is to insure the economic independence of each individual to the end of his days.

Social security in the form of a basic retirement income is now an accepted national policy. Though many Republicans regarded the policy as socialistic in the early days of the New Deal, the return of the Republican Party to power in 1953 did not spell the end of social security. To the contrary, President Eisenhower's Administration considerably extended coverage and increased benefits under social security. By 1960, however, nearly 10 per cent of the population were over 65—thanks to improved sanitation and medical advances. Most of these old people depend on social security income to meet day-to-day living expenses; about 90 per cent of the population over 65 now claim social security benefits. But old people are prone to serious and expensive illnesses which involve major medical charges that cannot be met with social security checks. The Kennedy-Johnson Administration proposed that social security insurance be expanded so that people could build up earned protection against the high costs of hospitalization and medical care bound to come with old age. This is the program familiarly called medicare.

Medicare has long been an issue in American politics. Vice-President Hubert Humphrey introduced a medicare bill as his first major measure when he was a freshman Senator from Minnesota back in 1949. Senator Kennedy led a floor fight

---

[35] *Steward Machine Co.* v. *Davis*, 301 U.S. 548 (1937).

for medicare in the summer of 1960 and, on being defeated in the Senate, took the issue to the polls as the Democratic presidential candidate that year. As President he made medicare an urgent policy recommendation of his Administration. President Johnson made a heroic effort to get the medicare program through the second session of the 88th Congress and almost succeeded. But at the very end of the session, the medicare amendment to the social security program bogged down in a conference committee. Meantime an impatient Congress, eager to begin campaigning back home, left the issue wide open for the 1964 elections.

Medicare was not the most crucial issue in the presidential election but certainly it was one that swayed many votes—and the voters had a clear choice. The Junior Senator from Arizona had made a special flight from Phoenix to Washington in order to register a vigorous "No" when the Senate voted for medicare. As Republican presidential candidate he continued his campaign against socialism. (Toward the end of his campaign he was trying to explain rather frantically that he really was in favor of social security, if not medicare.) He gained favor among those groups that had been pressuring Congress not to pass medicare—the American Medical Association, the American Dental Association, and various business people who were opposed to any increases in governmental expenditures for welfare purposes. On the other hand, the groups that had been lobbying with Congress to support the Johnson Administration on medicare—the AFL-CIO, Americans for Democratic Action, the National Council of Senior Citizens, and others—urged the electorate to vote for the Democratic candidate who spoke firmly for increased social security benefits including medicare. Johnson and Humphrey won the election. Did the voters choose medicare?

In his 1965 State of the Union Message, President Johnson offered the 89th Congress a blue-print for legislative action to achieve "the Great Society." He indicated that he would submit a number of special messages with detailed proposals for national action in specific areas. First, in the promised series, was the President's "health message" which called for a hospital insurance program to be administered by the social security system. (Other proposals in the President's health package included: a national network of regional medical complexes to bring together the latest medical technology for combating heart disease, cancer, stroke, and other major diseases; comprehensive health services for preschool and school age children; improved services for the mentally retarded; and a variety of programs intended to protect the health of the American people.) And the first bill introduced in the House and in the Senate in the 89th Congress was for medical care for the aged. (The administrative bills also called for an increase in social security retirement benefits and an increase in the federal share in state public assistance programs.)

Public assistance was once the most urgent operation in the social security system. In the 1930's millions of Americans, most of them through no fault of their own, lacked the barest essentials of existence—food, clothing, and shelter. Local charity and state welfare programs could not begin to cope with all the hardship cases occasioned by the nation-wide depression, but the Social Security Act offered the advantages of cooperative federalism. Making full use of its power to tax the general welfare, Congress extended federal grants-in-aid for state programs of public assistance. The Act, many times amended since 1935, now provides for grants-in-aid to the states for five major categories of public assistance: aid for the needy aged, medical assistance for the needy aged, aid to the blind, aid to the totally and permanently disabled, and aid to needy families with dependent children. Minimum standards for such assistance programs are specified by the national government, although state programs reflect considerable difference in historical background, social custom, and degree of community concern. The Welfare Administration in the Department of Health, Education and Welfare is responsible for seeing to it that the state plans meet and maintain the basic federal prescription.

National expenditures for grants-in-aid to state public assistance programs are mounting every year. This fact is exploited by those who attribute the rising costs of government to socialism in Washington. Keep in mind, however, other statistical trends that help explain why expenditures for public assistance programs continue to increase even in these times of prosperity: the over-all increase in population, the higher proportion of people over 65 in the population, the increased cost of living, higher costs of medical care, and higher charges for hospitalization. Actually, less than 5 per cent of the population receives any kind of public assistance. Since the depression years, emphasis in the social security system has shifted from giving relief to the dependent to building up earned rights to independence.

Unemployment insurance was an urgent issue in the 1930's when millions of Americans were out of work. Economists, labor leaders, businessmen, social workers, and New Deal politicians all insisted that the government work out a long-range national insurance program to protect workers from the hazards of unemployment. Since Wisconsin was the only state in 1935 to have an unemployment compensation plan in operation, it became the model for the federal program. Under the Social Security Act, the national government levies a tax on industrial and commercial employers; but if they contribute to a state unemployment insurance system, they may claim a tax credit with the federal government. This federal tax credit has been an important fiscal device in the development of cooperative federalism. Briefly, state taxes paid for the support of approved unemployment compensation plans are credited against the federal employers tax. Thus, if a state has no approved plan, the federal taxes must still be paid by employers in the state even though the workers receive no unemployment compensation. If a state does have an approved plan, costs of administration will be paid out of federal grants-in-aid. Obviously the federal tax credits and the grants-in-aid have been persuasive factors in obtaining the desired state laws. The laws differ widely in coverage, benefits, eligibility, and disqualification requirements, but all of them must meet a minimum federal standard if the state is to receive the federal tax credits. The Bureau of Employment Security in the U.S. Department of Labor reviews and approves the state programs.

What did the Framing Fathers have in mind when they established a new republic with the avowed national purpose, "to promote the general welfare"?

Remember what the country was like in 1790. Of its 4,000,000 inhabitants, only 3 per cent of the population lived in towns of 8000 or more; 750,000 were Negro slaves. It is safe to say that the Framing Fathers did not worry about such problems as slum clearance, area redevelopment, mass transit, or public housing projects. Certainly they were not then concerned with national public health programs or anything resembling medicare. Public sanitation, as well as personal hygiene, were simply primitive, symbolized by the privy in the backyard. Medical science still endorsed such practices as cupping, bleeding, purging, and dosing with calomel, ipecac, opium, and mercury. Neither anaesthesia nor antisepsis existed. Obviously President Washington had no thought of including a Secretary of Health, Education and Welfare—or for that matter a Secretary of Agriculture, or Commerce, or Labor—among the principal officers of his Administration. In those days, paupers—the very young, the very old, the morons, the lunatics, and the totally disabled—were dumped in local jails or almshouses. But the most remarkable attribute of the American Constitution is its flexibility; it does not bind us to live as our forefathers had to live; succeeding generations of Americans have been—and will be—free to interpret "the general welfare" within the contemporary environment.

In his 1965 State of the Union message, President Johnson recognized "the great upward surge of well-being" that characterizes modern America. And he made it clear that his Administration was determined that Americans should not "live in the midst of abundance, isolated from neighbors and nature, confined by blighted cities and bleak suburbs, stunted by a poverty of learning and an emptiness of leisure. . . . Our basic task is three-fold: First, to keep our economy growing; to open for all Americans the opportunity that is now enjoyed by most Americans; and to improve the quality of life for all."

Strategic Defense

No analysis of policies or policy-making in the national government is complete without some consideration of the overriding factors of "common defense." In the next chapter, we will turn our attention to foreign policy, and in doing so, we will examine the changing bases of our national security policies. But we cannot conclude this chapter without observing, at least briefly, the impact of war and defense policies on the political economy and the general welfare. Moreover, the community of strategic decision-makers affords a striking example of the national policy process uninhibited by institutional boundaries.

The United States was conceived as a "fighting organization," and nearly half of the powers of Congress enumerated in Article I, Section 8, relate directly to problems of common defense and the conduct of war. The Framing Fathers could have had no foreboding of modern warfare, with its techniques of mass extermination and total destruction. But they did give the national government all the powers necessary and proper to raise and support armies, to provide and maintain a navy, to call out the militia, to train the militia according to the discipline prescribed by Congress, to make rules for the regulation of land and naval forces, to declare war and make peace, to levy taxes for the common defense.

Congress has declared war five times—in 1812, 1848, 1898, 1917, and 1941; the President has twice recognized a "state of war"—in 1861 and 1950; and there have been numerous minor expeditions of American troops abroad. With muskets and rifles replaced by thermonuclear weapons and guided missiles, the concept of war has become increasingly total in scope.

The demands of war have inevitably led to the broadest interpretation of the Constitution. The Constitution, of course, gives no direction on how the government shall meet a civil war. When the southern states seceded from the Union in 1861, President Lincoln established a blockade against the southern ports; and the Court held in 1863 that as commander-in-chief the President had the power to determine what measures were necessary to suppress an insurrection.[36] Later on, as a "war measure," without any authorization from Congress, President Lincoln issued the Emancipation Proclamation freeing all slaves in the rebellious states. The Constitution gives Congress the power to coin "money," but in order to support the Union armies in the field Congress authorized the printing of "greenbacks," and made them legal tender in the payment of debts. In 1870, after the War was over, the Supreme Court declared that the greenback issue was unconstitutional; one year later, after President Grant had filled two vacancies on the Court, it reversed its decision and declared that the issue was constitutional.[37] Today we simply accept the practice of printing money as an implied power of Congress.

During World War I, the national government assumed unprecedented powers over the economy of the country. Congress authorized the President to regulate the importation, manufacture, storage, mining, or distribution of essential materials; to requisition foods, feeds, and fuels; to take over and operate factories, packing houses, pipelines, mines, or other plants; to fix a minimum price for wheat; limit, regulate, or prohibit the use of food materials in the production of alcoholic beverages; to fix the price of coal and coke and to regulate their production, sale, and distribution. Other statutes gave him power to take over and operate the rail and water transportation system and the telephone and telegraph systems of the country. You will not find in the Constitution any such sweeping powers granted to Congress or to the President. The explanation is simple, as Chief Justice Hughes put it: "The power to wage war is the power to wage war successfully."

Some of the acts passed by Congress during World War I were still on the books at the outbreak of World War II, and Congress enacted new ones to facilitate the defense effort. It set up rationing for consumers, control of industrial materials and production, and even empowered the President to seize plants where production was endangered by strikes. It also authorized price and rent controls. None of these provisions was ruled unconstitutional. Whatever economic theory the Court has used to interpret the Constitution in time of peace, in time

---

[36] *The Prize Cases*, 2 Black 635 (1863).
[37] *Hepburn* v. *Griswold*, 8 Wall. 603 (1870); *The Legal Tender Cases*, 12 Wall. 457 (1871).

of war it has generally upheld the plenary power of the Congress and President to mobilize and to command the total resources of the nation—not only to draft men for the armed forces but also to regulate the entire economy.

During World War II, Congress delegated such broad authority to President Roosevelt, not only over military matters but over the whole economy, that his powers under the Constitution approached those of *Il Duce* and *Der Führer* under dictatorship. On the other hand, during the Korean crisis in 1952, when President Truman ordered the Secretary of Commerce to take possession of the steel mills in order to avert a shutdown of the mills, the Court returned to the doctrine of "separation of powers." It held that, though the "theater of war" is an expanding concept, the commander-in-chief even in a military crisis cannot take possession of private property in order to keep labor-management disputes from stopping production. The Chief Justice and two of his associates in a dissenting opinion insisted that the majority was wrong to deny the President the exercise of "extraordinary powers" for "extraordinary times." [38] Apparently, then, the Constitution can be interpreted not only to give tremendous war powers to the national government but also to put a limit on such war powers.

Since World War II, the determination of the United States to maintain a strong defense posture as a deterrent to communist aggression has called for a tremendous military establishment at home and abroad. We also give military assistance to more than 40 nations with whom we are joined in mutual security pacts. Moreover, our peacetime policy of keeping our armed services strong and up to date has created an armaments industry of vast proportions.

President Eisenhower, in his televised farewell address to the American people, soberly warned of "the acquisition of unwarranted influences whether sought or unsought by the military-industrial complex." As he saw it, from his own experience, "the total influence—economic, political, even spiritual—is felt in every city, every statehouse, every office of the Federal Government." To put it more concretely, the Defense Department spends billions of dollars annually for services and the procurement of guns, missiles, airplanes, electronic devices, vehicles, tanks, ammunition, clothing, and other military goods. What to buy and how much to buy (aircraft carriers or strategic bombers, nuclear submarines or spaceships to the moon) involve military decisions; where to procure items and from whom to buy involve business arrangements, contracts with industrial corporations. The Defense Department has billions more to invest in real estate developments, for training camps, air bases, naval bases, arsenals, proving grounds. Where to locate them is a military decision that also concerns congressmen and their constituents, who are more likely to be interested in the local economic benefits resulting from a military establishment.

Concerned as they were with "forms" of government, the Framing Fathers would be surprised, perhaps aghast, to learn that some of the most important activities of the national government are carried on without regard to the careful contrivance of checks and balances in the Constitution. Nowhere is this more

---

[38] *Youngstown Sheet and Tube Co.* v. *Sawyer*, 343 U.S. 579 (1952).

dramatically evident than in the policy process for national security. The Constitution gives to Congress, and only to Congress, the power to declare war; but the strategy of war in the nuclear age outmodes lengthy political deliberations. National security in the era of ICBM's and H-bombs calls for split-second decisions based on top-level military planning and highly confidential intelligence. How far decision-making can go without engaging the attention or authorization of Congress is illustrated by the "invasion" of Castro's Cuba in 1961. Apparently Congress had no knowledge of the role of the State Department, the Pentagon, or the CIA in this expedition until after the fiasco.

Don Price, Dean of Harvard's Littauer School of Public Administration, maintains that "as a matter of practical politics, we have fortunately recognized that the basic framework can be preserved best if we do not worship all the incidental apparatus and procedures that the Founding Fathers had in mind." He reminds us that technical advances in the twentieth century have broken down most of the old boundaries between peace and war, domestic and foreign problems, public and private affairs, which were implicit in the written constitution of the eighteenth century. Hence it has been "quite necessary, in order to maintain the general spirit of the Constitution, to work out an unwritten Constitution on new lines." [39]

Providing for the common defense has become the nation's biggest business. Multi-million dollar defense industries are almost wholly dependent on government contracts—and this in time of peace. Small business as well as big business vies for its share of military procurement. The Pentagon contracts with private firms for more than 2 million items a year, "from shoelaces to submarines." Adhering to the ideology of "free enterprise," the government calls on private contractors to design, develop, and produce the weapons systems that defend the free world—on a cost plus basis. But once a private firm enters what President Eisenhower called the "military-industrial complex," it is no longer engaged in much free enterprise. In order to insure uniform security practices within industrial plants, educational institutes, or other organizations working with classified materials, the Pentagon issues a bulky manual of detailed instructions and admonitions similar to those it issues to military installations. And these security regulations cover several million defense workers who are employed in private business under government military contracts. [40]

The national economy is wholly involved in modern war. Hence it is reasonable that the Pentagon should seek advice and assistance from the nation's top industrial leaders. It is not surprising that the Secretary of Defense is usually

---

[39] Don Price, "The Secretary and Our Unwritten Constitution," in the American Assembly, Columbia University, *The Secretary of State* (Englewood Cliffs, N.J.: Prentice-Hall, Inc., 1960), p. 171.

[40] Jack Raymond, reporter on defense affairs for the *New York Times*, discusses many important implications of the defense policies in *Power at the Pentagon* (New York: Harper and Row, 1964). See especially chapters on "Research and the Federal Government," "Free Enterprise and National Defense," "The Military Lobbies," and "Questions of Probity."

chosen from top management in private industry. Nor is it difficult to understand why a rather large number of the country's military experts, former top-ranking military officers, are now employed by the country's leading defense industries. Military and industrial leaders have a mutual concern with the whole spectrum of military operations.

In his farewell address, President Eisenhower called attention to the link between our "industrial-military posture" and modern science and technology. In the atomic age, research has become more formal, complex, and costly. It calls for big organization. The Defense Department alone planned to spend $7 billion on research and development in 1963; and the Atomic Energy Commission $1.4 billion. Before World War II, most government research was done in the government's own laboratories, but after the war the government began to contract for research to be done outside—on the university campuses and in non-profit organizations.

Government sponsored research in the universities and in private non-profit institutions has some disturbing implications for the policy process. Roughly, out of a total expenditure of $22 billion for research and development, the national government accounts for $15 billion.[41] The national government has long operated its own laboratories; for example, in the Bureau of Standards, in the Coast and Geodetic Survey, in the Food and Drug Administration, and in the Department of Agriculture. The National Institutes of Health in Health Education and Welfare conduct studies on every major medical research problem in their own laboratories and clinical center. They also make extensive grants for outside research; about 40 per cent of medical research in the country is sponsored by NIH; in the universities, about 40 per cent of federal research funds come from NIH.

Government grants to the universities for research in particular areas has far-reaching consequences for higher education. Approximately a billion dollars a year of the federal tax monies now go for research fellowships, construction of facilities, education and training in the colleges and universities. But only a handful of universities—MIT, Harvard, University of California, Johns Hopkins, and a few others—get the really big grants. Every university wants, and needs, more money than it receives from endowment funds or public appropriations to meet the pressures of increasing enrollments and the rising costs of higher education. Huge grants from Washington are sorely tempting. Grants-in-aid for very specific purposes can, however, cause acute imbalance in a university system. And when the grants are accompanied by tight security checks, as they must be in many cases, then such grants may indeed jeopardize the traditional role of the university—to be free and unfettered in the search for truth. If, as it is reported, a single university receives more federal funds for research than the entire judicial

---

[41] It is difficult to get exact figures on research contracts; what is "research" has various connotations. These figures are from Paul J. Piccard's "Issues in the Study of Government and Science," a paper presented at the Southern Political Science Association meeting at Durham, November 13, 1964.

branch (or the TVA, or the Department of Labor), then that university may have to operate like a government agency, more bureaucratic than academic.

Even more controversial is the proliferation of private non-profit institutions with multimillion dollar government contracts engaged in the design, development, and production of our weapons systems. Several hundred such organizations, employing the nation's top scientists and engineers, have come into existence since World War II; some of them are sponsored by the government, some by universities, others by otherwise profit-seeking corporations. Best known is the Rand Corporation, established in 1948, with money from the Ford Foundation, to help the Air Force. The Sandia Corporation, a non-profit subsidiary of Western Electric Company, has worked on nuclear bombs. The Applied Physics Laboratory at Johns Hopkins works for the Navy. The Operations Evaluations Group at MIT also serves the Navy. The Institute for Defense Analyses was set up by the Defense Department as a kind of holding company for eight colleges and universities to make vital studies in disarmament, civil defense, and various weapons sites.

When the Kennedy Administration first came to office, it was dismayed by the number of private corporations handling top confidential assignments in national security. David Bell, then Director of the Bureau of the Budget, reported that "there have been instances—particularly in the Department of Defense—where we have come dangerously close to permitting contract employees to exercise functions which belong to our Government officials." [42] No doubt these contract arrangements between the government and private organizations are somewhat synthetic. Their purpose, in part, is to circumvent the civil service regulations with respect to salary limitations in order to secure the best brains in the nation to work on the toughest problems that confront us in the age of atomic energy and space science. As far as business is concerned, the arrangement offers extraordinary opportunities; the government takes the risk and the industry gets the profit. On the other hand, a business that becomes wholly or significantly dependent on contracts may suddenly find itself in difficulties if for any reason the government shifts its research and development interests or changes its production plans.

Military leaders, defense contractors in big corporations, scientists and engineers in organized research have become influential in shaping, as well as in implementing, the policies of national security.[43] Obviously, this integration of public and private business, outside the constitutional framework, raises many questions about conflict of interest and personal loyalties. Dean Price suggests some of the far-reaching consequences of this breakdown in the old boundaries between public and private affairs.

---

[42] See Jack Raymond's commentary on the Bell Report in *Power at the Pentagon*, p. 149–151.

[43] For informed analyses of this development in policy-making, see *Public Policy*, published annually by the Graduate School of Public Administration, Harvard University, edited by John D. Montgomery and Arthur Smithies (Cambridge, Mass.: Harvard University Press, 1964), Vol. XIII. See especially Wesley W. Posuar, "The Impact of Strategy Expertise on the National Security Policy of the U.S."; and Bruce L. R. Smith, "Strategic Expertise and National Security Policy: A Case Study."

If anyone doubts that the boundaries are different today, let him reflect on the facts that Mr. Francis Powers, who flew the ill-fated U-2 over Russia, did so (or so the NASA announced) on the payroll of a private aircraft company; that technical assistance and international educational exchanges, which have become important arms of foreign policy, are largely conducted by universities and private institutions under contract for the government; and that some of the most important strategic studies are being made for the military not by staff officers in uniform but by a series of private institutions which began work under the somewhat narrower concept of operations research.[44]

Our enormous commitments in international relations, the total involvement of our economy in the national defense, and the unprecedented role of science in both military and industrial technology—these require a great deal of skill in policy-making, top-level planning, and technical coordination in public administration. Again, the trend in modern government is to go outside the constitutional system for consultants and advisers. Henry A. Kissinger, one of the most astute observers in the area of foreign policy, discusses this problem in *The Necessity for Choice*. "Crucial policy advice is increasingly requested from ad hoc committees of outside experts, as for example, the Gaither Committee on national defense or the Draper Committee on economic assistance or the Coolidge Committee on arms control." [45]

The ad hoc committee approach to public administration and what Kissinger aptly calls "the conversational approach to policy" pose new problems in American government. Our constitutional system is based on the proposition that those who exercise power can be held responsible, both legally and politically, for their public acts. But when power is achieved through the back door, as it were, by the private consultant, the technical adviser, or, on a broader scale, by the "community of strategic expertise," the constitutional guarantees are difficult to maintain. In the next chapter, we shall explore further some implications of policy-making that cut across institutional lines and constitutional barriers in foreign policy and national security.

To guard against abuses of power by men in government, the Framers established a republic, with representative government, separation of powers, checks and balances. But how effective—or desirable—are these relatively simple devices of the eighteenth century in the turbulent world of today?

---

[44] The American Assembly, *The Secretary of State*, p. 169.

[45] Henry A. Kissinger, *The Necessity for Choice* (New York: Harper and Brothers, 1960), p. 346.

CHAPTER FIFTEEN

Foreign Policy and National Security

A month or so after he had come into office, Secretary of State Dean Rusk gave an informal talk to the policy-makers in the Department of State on how to think about foreign-policy problems. "The problem . . . begins to take shape in a galaxy of utterly complicated factors—political, military, economic, financial, legal, legislative, procedural, administrative—to be sorted out and handled within a political system which moves by consent in relation to an external environment which cannot be under control." [1] This chapter considers first the context of foreign policy, the external environment as well as the domestic setting. It examines values, interests, and objectives not only in terms of the national policy process but also in relation to the dynamics of international politics. Since this is a chapter on American *foreign* policy, we are primarily concerned with how the American political system is geared to secure the national goals *beyond the territorial limits of the United States.*

The International Environment of American Foreign Policy

Charles Burton Marshall, a member of the Policy Planning Staff of the State Department in the 1950's, stresses "the obvious but often overlooked externalness of foreign policy." [2] Most of the world lies outside our own borders, and it is not a world of our own making. This is the fundamental and enormously complicated factor in the conduct of foreign policy. Our policy-makers must determine national goals primarily within the context of national values, interests, and objectives. In the formulation of policy, those who make the decisions may be most attentive to the demands and supports of their own constituents. But foreign policy as an effective course of action, must be implemented in an external environment which is beyond the reach and influence of the American political system. American foreign policy is almost wholly a matter of international interaction— WE and THEY. THEY comprise approximately 3 billion people, most of them colored and non-American, in nearly 150 diverse nations and territories. American foreign policy, whether we look at it from the standpoint of input and formulation or of output and implementation, is in large measure shaped by actors and actions outside the United States.

Development of United States Diplomatic Relations

The development of U. S. diplomatic relations reflects not only the changing role of the United States in world affairs but also the kaleidoscopic changes in the international community. When General George Washington became first President of the United States, the new Republic maintained diplomatic representation in only two countries, France and Spain. By the time Thomas Jefferson was President, the number of American missions abroad had increased to six, adding the Netherlands, Great Britain, Portugal, and Prussia. A seventh mission was

---

[1] Selected papers, prepared by the subcommittee on National Security Staffing and Operations, 87th Cong., 2d Sess. *Administration of National Security* (Washington, D.C.: Government Printing Office, 1962), Committee print, p. 23. Informal remarks made to the policy-making officers of the Department of State, February 20, 1961, by the Honorable Dean Rusk.

[2] Charles Burton Marshall, *The Limits of Foreign Policy* (New York: Rinehart and Winston, Inc., 1954), p. 15.

established in 1809 when President John Quincy Adams appointed an American minister to Russia. In the 1820's, the United States recognized the young revolutionary governments in Latin America and quickly established diplomatic and consular ties with its sister republics in the Western Hemisphere. Then to forestall any future European intervention in the area, President Monroe, in 1823, unilaterally declared that the United States intended to stay out of European affairs and expected the European powers in turn to keep out of the Western Hemisphere. By 1843 our eyes had turned toward Asia. In that year a diplomatic mission was established in China, and in 1859 a similar mission was opened in Japan.

The traditional principles of American foreign policy were established during the presidency of George Washington: to maintain "a liberal intercourse with all nations," to "steer clear of permanent alliances to any portion of the foreign world," and to remain aloof from wars that beset the rest of the world. As a new nation we had tasks enough at home to confront without becoming embroiled in the problems of other countries. Taking full advantage of our "detached and distant situation," we steadfastly, and sometimes aggressively, pursued a policy of continentalism, to build a free nation—one nation—from the Atlantic to the Pacific. To say that the American people achieved their "manifest destiny" by a policy of isolationism from the rest of the world, however, is to contradict the facts of our history. The United States continuously extended its diplomatic and consular representation to all parts of the globe (approximately 50 countries on the eve of World War I), principally to backstop American business abroad but also to serve a variety of national interests, political and cultural, public and private.[3]

The United States entered World War I buoyed by a catchy slogan, "to make the world safe for democracy." When the war had ended, however, the world was not inclined to make itself over in the image of Woodrow Wilson's democratic ideals. In 1917, Marxist communists overthrew the would-be moderate government that followed the Czarist regime in Russia. The ensuing "dictatorship of the proletariat" turned out to be a ruthless personal dictatorship, first under Lenin, then under Stalin, in a one-party, totalitarian system of government. The communists not only revolutionized Russian society but also planned revolution against capitalist economies and democratic governments everywhere in the world. Counter-revolutionary forces immediately developed—anti-communist and anti-democratic. In Italy, the Fascists took over as early as 1922. In Germany, the National Socialists stamped out the Weimar Republic, though not until 1933. Communism professed to be an international movement; fascism was aggressively nationalistic. But whether the take-over was communist or fascist, totalitarian governments were threatening the safety of democratic governments throughout the world.

---

[3] William Barnes and John Heath Morgan, *The Foreign Service of the United States* (Washington, D.C.: Historical Office, Bureau of Public Affairs, Department of State, 1961). Offers a factual account of the origins, development, and functions of the American Foreign Service.

To Woodrow Wilson, the most important point in the peace settlement after World War I was a League of Nations which he believed would keep the peace of the world and "afford mutual guarantees of political independence and territorial integrity to great and small states alike." Ironically, the United States was the only power of any consequence that refused to join the League. At one time or another, over 60 nations of the world were members. Although the League failed in its most important function—to prevent another world war—it did make headway in developing economic, social, and cultural foundations for the international community.

Wilson's insistence on "national self-determination" as a guiding principle in the territorial settlements of 1919–1920 produced an independent Poland and new states in the Balkans. These were duly invited to join the League, as were the new states that were formed from the non-Turkish territories of the Ottoman Empire. As part of his democratic idealism, Wilson had urged the League to include not only legally independent states but also fully self-governing colonies or dominions. Thus, Canada, Australia, India, and others, were admitted as original members of the League; within a few years they were proclaiming their equal and independent status as members of the British Commonwealth of Nations. Here then is the paradox of the period; while the League was stressing the universality of world concerns, the proliferation of national states was actually developing a new pluralism within the international community.

Pluralism in One World

The League of Nations after World War I, the United Nations after World War II, represent the aspirations of people everywhere "to save succeeding generations from the scourge of war . . . to practice tolerance and live together in peace with one another as good neighbors. . . ." Extraordinary advances in communications and transportation since the mid-nineteenth century have made the concept of "one world" technically feasible. When the United States entered the community of nations, peoples could not speak to peoples. The largest audience reached by the human voice could be counted only in the thousands, and would have to be gathered in one place. Today radio and television carry the voice and image of nations' spokesmen to hundreds of millions of people in all parts of the globe, simultaneously listening and watching. Sailing ships were the principal links between nations when George Washington was President of the United States. But the maps that sailors used in the eighteenth century bear little resemblance to the navigation charts of today's air and space pilots. The arctic regions which were not navigable in the age of seapower are the shortest commercial and strategic routes today between many nations in the Northern Hemisphere. On old Mercator maps, the United States is separated from Europe and Asia by vast oceans and seas; but if we place the North Pole at the center of our maps, then our "detached and distant situation" appears as an optical illusion.

Notwithstanding modern technology in communications and transportation, the dream of one world has yet to materialize. Indeed, the premise of unity is implicitly denied in the Preamble to the Charter, "We the peoples of the United

Nations." Most nation-states, including the United States, now belong to the United Nations, but some states like Communist China, Viet Nam (North and South), Korea (North and South) and Germany (East and West) have been denied admission for political reasons related to the Cold War. On the other hand, Switzerland—one of the oldest nation states in the world—has refused to enter the United Nations lest international commitments jeopardize its own policy of neutrality.

The United Nations boasts a membership about twice the size of the old League of Nations, but perhaps more significant is the increasing heterogeneity of the membership. Thus the paradox which appeared in the League is exaggerated in the United Nations. The more universal the membership in the international organization, the more difficult it becomes to maintain common interests and to work toward common goals. The League of Nations, though ostensibly world wide in membership, was actually dominated by the European powers and generally operated within the fairly homogeneous Western community. The United Nations has developed into a very different kind of organization. The extension and diversification of membership since 1945, especially the admission of many Asian and African states, have inevitably shifted the balance of power away from the traditional Western complex.

The United States plays an important role in the United Nations, but it also goes its own way in the pluralistic world of nation-states. By 1950 the United States was maintaining diplomatic relations with 74 countries; a decade later the number had jumped well over the hundred mark. The task of American policy-makers is to influence decision-makers in all of these countries in order to protect and promote American interests.

Legally, the actor-states on the international stage are sovereign. "Sovereignty" in its original context denoted absolute power, authority without accountability. The concept was developed toward the end of the Middle Ages to make legitimate the ruling claims of various temporal authorities and to justify their break from the Holy Roman Empire. First conceived as a personal attribute of the monarch, the doctrine of sovereignty was soon employed to rationalize the independence of nation-states in international affairs. Thus the government of a sovereign state—whether democratic or totalitarian, republican or monarchical, federal or unitary—has complete dominion over the land and people within its boundaries. No outside authority has a right to intervene in the domestic affairs of a sovereign state. Since sovereignty implies the idea of absolute power, all sovereign states enjoy equality under international law. Medieval as this idea may sound, the Charter of the United Nations nevertheless still proclaims: "The organization is based on the principle of the sovereign equality of all its members."

Sovereignty is essentially a Western concept with many overtones from the prevailing natural law, "the law of nature and of nature's God." When we discussed the philosophical justification of individual rights, we mentioned that some rights are regarded as "unalienable" because they are viewed as the endowment of the Creator. In like manner, a nation possesses "fundamental rights." Just as the individual looks to his government to guarantee his rights to life, liberty, and property, so each nation expects to have its rights to *existence, independence,* and *territorial integrity* respected in the international community.

If you read the above paragraph carefully, you will discover a significant discrepancy in the analogy between individual rights *guaranteed* and nations' rights *respected.* Within a nation, the government possesses the power to enforce civil rights and to punish those who violate public policy. It cannot, however, legally exercise such powers outside its borders even though it might wish to do so in pursuit of the national interest. Within the international community, no government has the authority to legislate on national rights or to punish transgressors. Thus the United Nations cannot establish international policy for any independent nation. It offers various facilities for peaceful settlement of disputes and may invoke certain sanctions intended to deter aggression, but it lacks the ultimate power of coercion. One has only to look at the current news maps of "trouble spots in the world" to realize that the United Nations is not an international government; it cannot make authoritative decisions and carry them out by force except with the consent of the nations involved.

Sovereignty is certainly not the essence of national independence. Neither can it be dismissed as myth or metaphysics. It sums up in one word, "an aggregate of particular and very extensive claims that states habitually make for themselves in their relations with other states." [4] Each nation or nation-state relies on devices of self-help to protect its fundamental rights (or habitual claims) as well as to advance its own international interests. And self-help is a matter of relative *power* in international politics. In large measure, the conduct of foreign policy is the pursuit of power and the use of power by each nation bent on getting what it needs and wants in the world. In the context of power politics, the concept of equality among sovereign nations, although it is logical, is not realistic.

International Power Politics

Once we depart from the logical equality of sovereign nations, we are faced with the problem of determining what makes a country powerful or influential in the world. It is fairly easy to list the basic ingredients of national power: (1) geography and topography; (2) natural resources; (3) degree of economic development; (4) stage of political development and morale; (5) military strength; (6) friends, allies, and enemies. But this is like writing out a cake recipe: (1) eggs; (2) milk; (3) sugar; (4) flour; and (5) baking powder. Any cook would immediately ask whether this was a recipe for sugar cookies or angel food, and would then want to know specifically how many cups of flour, how many eggs, the order of mixing, the oven temperature, and the time for baking. So it is with countries, only on a much more awesomely complicated scale. What kind of country do you have in mind—a Switzerland content to be neutral in international relations and prosperous at home, or a Soviet Union determined to be

---

[4] J. L. Brierly, *The Law of Nations* (London: Oxford University Press, 1955), p. 48. Brierly's discussion of "The Character of the Modern State System," from the legal standpoint, is excellent.

top power in the world and to bury the capitalist countries under communism, or an India that wants merely to modernize its society and to keep peace with its neighbors?

The geography and topography of a nation are still important, though not so critical as they once were in conditioning foreign policy. The great undeveloped land mass between the Atlantic and Pacific made it possible for millions of Americans throughout the nineteenth century to pursue the course of Westward Ho. Because our continental security seemed so impregnable before World War I, the United States could assume a stance of "neutrality" and even "isolation" from time to time in international relations. The English Channel long served as a strategic defense for England against the land armies of European powers. Nations once fought for rivers as natural boundaries—the Rhine, the Rio Grande, and the Yalu. But the development of air power and nuclear weaponry has drastically reduced the significance of natural defenses. On the other hand, conflicts in international relations can be resolved only once by all-out nuclear war. Meantime, the location of a country, its size, its accessibility by land and sea, and other geographic factors are still strategic in conventional warfare and guerilla fighting, as evidenced in the Congo and Viet Nam.

Natural resources are basic for military and industrial power. A nation need not possess all the essential resources within its boundaries (no nation does), but it must have access to them in order to develop a modern economy and to maintain national security. No nation in the world has been so richly endowed and no nation has made more use of its natural resources than the United States. But even the United States is not self-sufficient; it must go into the world market for many strategic and critical materials such as chromite, tin, industrial diamonds, manganese, platinum, uranium, and plutonium. To secure these vital imports has been a prime concern of American foreign policy.

The riches of this earth have not been equitably distributed over all parts of the world. It is oversimplifying the issue to divide nations into the "haves" and "have-nots"; but on the basis of such a rough classification, it is the "have" nations that are generally trying to maintain the status quo and the "have-nots" that are attempting to break it. Being rich in certain natural resources is no assurance, however, that a "have" country will remain one. New developments in technology may lessen the demand for certain natural resources or even render them useless. For example, in the jet age navigable rivers are not the crucial assets they once were in a nation's trade and commerce; and in the atomic age, access to plutonium is more critical perhaps than natural water power.

The most important natural resource any nation can possess is its people. We assess the power position of any state on the basis of quantitative and qualitative population data. There are more Chinese, Indians, and Russians than there are Americans. But mere numbers are not so significant today as when they represented potential military and industrial manpower. In the era of atomic fission and increasing automation, what really counts for military and industrial power in a nation is the number of its scientists, engineers, and technicians rather than the gross number of its soldiers and workers. The U. S. and the USSR are well matched in natural resources. The USSR has the larger population and its government is putting tremendous stress on science and technology to insure the specialized skills which are basic to modern, diversified military and industrial power. But because the Industrial Revolution reached the United States years before its influence was felt in Russia, the United States still seems to have the edge in the competition.

Many of the new African and Asian states have a wealth of natural resources; but so did the American Indians, who had neither the inclination nor know-how to use them. The less developed nations comprise approximately two-fifths of the world's population and their lands include a third of the globe's surface. The average per-capita income of the approximately 1 billion people who live in these countries ranges from $50 to $100 per year, against an average per-capita income of $1,000 annually for the approximately 400 million people living in the modern industrial nations of Europe and North America. These new countries, as yet relatively untouched by the scientific revolution, stand in acute need of development technologies. An important aspect of American foreign policy—and of Soviet policy, too—is to help these countries develop appropriate technologies for modern living conditions. In one respect the Cold War is a race which will decide whether the promises and performance of democratic capitalism or of Marxist communism will modernize the backward areas of the world.[5]

The great enigma in the external environment of U. S. foreign policy is the Peoples' Republic of China. Since the Communist regime of Mao Tse-tung came to power in 1949, we have almost no first-hand accounts by Westerners of Chinese scientific and technological progress. We know that China possesses massive natural resources, and we also know that the Chinese periodically embark on a "Great Leap Forward." It is reported that Communist China now stands fifth in coal production (following the United States, the Soviet Union, Western Germany, and Great Britain) and sixth in steel production (only slightly behind Japan). We are told that China is making great strides in the production and consumption of electrical power, in agricultural production, and in weather prediction. The Soviet Union, until recently, has been China's foremost technological mentor, but as China has begun to catch up with the rest of the world, the USSR has been less inclined to be helpful. Given the militant cast of Chinese communism, its overwhelming hostility toward Western capitalism, the most agonizing question we ponder is how the Chinese will employ the nuclear power on which they have been so desperately working.

The political development of a country is perhaps more important than its economy in the conduct of diplomacy. American foreign policy must be carried on within the constitutional framework and political institutions of the American system. By the same token, the American diplomat abroad must operate within the constitutional and political pattern of the foreign government which he seeks

---

[5] Caryl Haskins, President of the Carnegie Institution of Washington, discusses the implications of science and technology in world politics, especially with reference to the new nations, in *The Scientific Revolution and World Politics* (New York: Harper and Row, 1964).

to influence in favor of American interests. Since personal and institutional sources of power vary from one country to another, a considerable part of the continuing intelligence and research that underlies American foreign policy is to determine who are the decision-makers in foreign governments, what supports, demands (or apathy) can be expected vis-à-vis policies that concern the United States.

In some ways, it is easier to do business with a totalitarian government where power is obviously located than in a democracy where public opinions may reflect a confusion of popular views. It is, for example, sometimes difficult for foreign diplomats to discover who speaks authoritatively on American foreign policy—the President, the Secretary of State, the Secretary of Defense, or any one of 535 congressmen in the mood to make a speech on the Berlin Wall or Viet Nam? Or perhaps the Governor of Florida on Cuba? On the other hand, there will be some diffusion of power even in a dictatorship, and not all the members of its power elite may be known abroad. Outsiders cannot easily assess the amount or type of rapport which exists between government and governed. We tend to underestimate the support which citizens in totalitarian systems give to their government, because we think morale in such an environment must be low. Our fact-finders and diplomats must guard against projecting their own values into a foreign situation. Most of them do, which is precisely what distinguishes the foreign policy expert from the average man in the street.

We have said that, in the absence of an international government, each nation must fend for itself. As a last resort (it is rarely the only resort) military strength may be crucial, depending on what a nation wants in the world and who has it. Military strength refers to many factors—military manpower, trained and in reserve; armaments up-to-date and ready for use; an industrial establishment geared for war; a civilian population prepared for defense against attack; a nation with the will to fight, an ideology to defend or extend. In the nuclear age, the ultimate weapon, given the capabilities, is the will to escalate the use of force even to all-out nuclear war. No matter how massive the deterrent, it will not deter unless it conveys credibility that it will be used if necessary to maintain a commitment.[6] No doubt the installation of Soviet missiles in Cuba was based on the assumption that the United States would not risk direct confrontation and nuclear war. By the same token, the withdrawal of the missiles was dictated by the reverse belief, when Chairman Khrushchev realized that President Kennedy was not bluffing.

The two great nuclear powers, the Soviet Union and the United States, clearly do not want to test the consequences of nuclear strategy in action over Korea, Laos, Viet Nam, Cuba, or Berlin. Both negotiate from the strength of nuclear capability but prefer to fight with conventional and counter-insurgent weapons. The choice will not remain for long with the U. S. and the USSR. The bipolarity of nuclear power ended when the French exploded their own nuclear bomb in the Sahara desert. The most delicate issue in our NATO alliance is the

---

[6] W. W. Rostow, Chairman of the State Department's Planning Council, candidly discusses "American Strategy on the World Scene" in *View from the Seventh Floor* (New York: Harper and Row, 1964).

degree of partnership which the United States will tolerate in the nuclear enterprise. Fifteen nations in the Atlantic Community are committed to mutual defense, in a military alliance of sovereign states, all of whom (including the United States) resist the idea of a unified sovereign institution over all.

W. W. Rostow, Chairman of the State Department's Policy Planning Council, raises pertinent questions: "Whose finger will be on the trigger; whose finger on the safety catch? Could the European forces fire their atomic weapons without the the agreement of the United States? Could the United States fire without the agreement of Europe? Could individual nations within the Alliance veto firing by others?" [7] And the American presidential campaign of 1964 added still more confusing questions: Should the President of the United States have sole authority, or should military officers have a decisive role in initiating the use of nuclear weapons? Should the choice be left either to civilian or to military officers in each, and all, of the 15 member states of NATO? On the other side of the potential confrontation, only the USSR possessed a nuclear capability for many years, but an aggressive and hostile Communist China now poses another potential threat.

So far we have viewed the world as a highly pluralistic society of sovereign nations, each seeking its own interests. But no nation is sufficiently strong, or independent, to rely wholly on its own resources. The history of international relations has been largely a pattern of shifting alliances, whereby nations with like interests and common causes join together. The idea of a League of Nations, or a United Nations, looks to a multilateral equilibrium of nation states, a world-wide organization, to keep the peace. But because all nations insist on sovereignty retained, the organization cannot make authoritative decisions and cannot function as an international government. The alternative is to establish a balance of power whenever divisive forces split the international community.

The Balance of Power Since World War II

In the period since World War II, the most divisive factor in the world has been the Cold War, the struggle for power and influence between the Communist Bloc led by the Soviet Union and the Western Bloc led by the United States. For nearly the whole of its history the United States had abjured the balance of power system, following the advice of Washington and Jefferson against any "permanent" or "entangling" alliances. A revolution in American foreign policy occurred during World War II when the United States, under President Franklin D. Roosevelt, became deeply involved in the power politics that would shape the postwar era. At Casablanca, Cairo, Teheran, and Yalta, President Roosevelt entered into pivotal decisions on postwar settlements: unconditional surrender of the Axis powers and a succession of territorial arrangements in the Far East and in Eastern Europe. And at Potsdam, President Truman helped to draw up the final and fateful arrangements for a totally defeated Germany and Japan.

---

[7] *Ibid.*, p. 64.

622

The wartime and immediate postwar agreements engaged the United States in world affairs to an extent hitherto unimaginable to the American people. As late as 1951, Senator Robert Taft could stage a "great debate" in the American Senate on whether the President of the United States could or should send troops to Europe in peace time. But the die had been cast. American frontiers had already moved to the Elbe, the Black Sea, the Himalaya, the Mekong, and the China Sea. During the postwar period the United States would enter into a network of defensive alliances with more than 40 countries in Europe, the Middle East, Latin America, and the Far East, some multilateral, some bilateral. It would back up its vast new commitments with almost astronomical expenditures for military establishments and foreign aid programs. The American people would come to accept military conscription, overseas service, continued mobilization of the domestic economy, and even rockets to the moon as normal peacetime requirements for the national security. They would barely complain when annual defense expenditures comprised more than half of the national budget.[8]

The revolution in foreign policy was rationalized by most Americans as a necessary defensive measure against "the enemy." Just as they had subscribed to the "devil theory" when they fought the war against fascism and national socialism, so Americans were now psychologically prepared to battle communism. A distinguished Secretary of State in the 1950's persuaded himself—and officially acted according to this persuasion—that WE were the free world and THEY were the communist menace and that all who did not join with us must be against us. By the 1960's, however, it was clearly oversimplification—as most scholars and statesmen now attest—to regard the world as divided into two, or even three, "power blocs."

The war-torn countries of Western Europe to which we had extended aid under the Marshall Plan and a succession of European recovery and mutual security programs had miraculously recovered. Meantime, they had also established new and integrated economic systems. Six of them—France, West Germany, Italy, Belgium, Holland, and Luxemburg—traditional rivals in business, had formed a Common Market. Another seven had united in a European Free Trade Association: Britain, Denmark, Norway, Sweden, Portugal, Switzerland, and Austria. And it was predicted that by the mid-1960's the two organizations might merge into a European community that would raze all internal tariff walls in Western Europe. Moreover, as the peoples of Western Europe prospered, as business boomed and unemployment all but disappeared, American influence, which had been so all-pervasive immediately after the war, began to wane. The United States, which had once made the political unity of Europe a major goal in foreign policy, now found itself on the outside of what was largely its own creation. Furthermore, the Western European powers, increasingly engaged in their own foreign policies in Europe and abroad, resented American influence.

[8] William G. Carleton, *The Revolution in American Foreign Policy* (New York: Random House, 1963) narrates and interprets the course of American foreign policy since 1945 and views the contemporary situation from the perspective of history.

The ideological conflict between the Free World and the Communist Bloc, so pronounced in the early 1950's, was much less distinct by the mid-1960's. The Soviet Union had met NATO with a counter alliance, the Warsaw Pact, comprising the communist countries of Eastern Europe. But just as the situations of the West European countries were changing, so the East European countries were becoming more pluralistic under a variety of pressures. The break between Marshall Tito and Marshall Stalin occurred as early as 1948 when Tito was excluded from the Cominform and Yugoslavia defected from the Soviet system of satellites. Despite the fact that ideologically all are Marxist oriented, Poland, Czechoslovakia, and Hungary have begun to differentiate considerably in their practice of communism. Albania has recently been extremely critical of the Kremlin. Peking and Moscow were closely linked in the 1950's, but in the 1960's relations between the two have become more and more strained. Differences in ideology account in part for the rift, but power politics also explains the break in partnership. The USSR has not been willing to share its nuclear power or to give as much economic assistance as China had expected from her ideological comrade.

Among our NATO allies in the "Free World," Portugal, Greece, and Turkey could hardly be called democratic. In the OAS (the Organization of American States), the United States is joined with the Latin American countries to resist the advance of communism in the Western Hemisphere, but most of our Latin American allies are in fact run by military or personal dictatorships. SEATO (the South East Asia Treaty Organization) was established to defend the newly independent Asian countries from communist aggression, but so far most of the new nations of Asia (and Africa) have shown little understanding in either the principles or practices of democratic government.

We now realize that the unconditional surrender of the Axis powers did not put an end to fascism in the world. In Spain, the corporate state continues in a form almost identical to that of Mussolini's pre-war Italy with General Franco retaining strict political discipline through a one-party system and military control. The Portuguese corporate state, adopted by popular vote in 1933, also survived into the 1960's under the dictatorship of Prime Minister Salazar. But both Spain and Portugal have been welcomed into the Free World: Portugal is a full-fledged member of NATO and Spain has a special military agreement with the United States. All this shows that we tend to overemphasize a phrase, oversimplify a concept—such as "Free World"—when we are actually concerned with an exceedingly complex situation.

Most of the new African and Asian countries that have emerged since 1945 have rejected both democracy and communism. The very factors which led to their fight for independence tend to promote a kind of fascism: bitter anti-colonialism, anti-Westernism, strong nationalism, and racism. Nearly all of them are underdeveloped. To modernize as quickly as possible, they have counted more on government planning than on free enterprise. Most of them, in Asia, the Middle East and Africa, are fragments of disintegrating colonial systems. The masses of the people are illiterate and politically inexperienced. Many of the new states are operating under one-party or personal dictatorships. Determined to become strong and independent nations in the modern world, they need a great deal of help from the older and more advanced countries not only in the technological processes of modernization but also in the psychological aspects of political socialization.

Russia's leaders talk much about the "socialist camp," meaning the Communist-Socialist Bloc. But most of the camp members do not call themselves communist; they prefer to style themselves "democratic" or "peoples' republics." Witness: the German Democratic Republic (communist East Germany), the Peoples' Republic of China (Communist China), the Rumanian Peoples' Republic (communist Rumania), and the Democratic Republic of Viet Nam (communist North Viet Nam). Notice, however, that, like the USSR, every peoples' republic in the communist-socialist bloc is still ruled by a totalitarian dictatorship. In every instance, the communists have seized power through revolution or force and have stayed in power through force. No totalitarian state has run the risk of tolerating competing parties, free elections, or free speech and free press.

When we look at the world in terms of rival ideologies, we do not find two competing camps sharply distinguished one from the other. We see more than a hundred different independent countries each with its own national traditions, its own kind of government, its own economic system. Not all the countries in the Free World follow the American Way. The United States is the leading exponent of "free enterprise," but many of its allies are well advanced toward socialism. Indeed, socialism made its most spectacular gains in Europe following World War II when victors and vanquished alike required a great deal of government planning, government aid, and government controls to recover from wartime destruction. Not all the countries in the Communist Bloc follow the Kremlin Way. Among the European communist countries, as they begin to prosper under planned industrialization, the pressures of liberalism and individualism appear to be making headway. The cleavage between the USSR and China dramatizes the pluralistic consequences of the uneven development of industrialism in the communist world.[9]

But among all the peoples, in varying degrees, in all the countries, under totalitarian and democratic governments, under whatever economic system, the revolution of rising expectations is changing the relationships between the public and private sectors of society. Everywhere people (including most Americans) look to their governments to get what they need or want at home and abroad— and everywhere governments are getting bigger, more bureaucratic, more impersonal. This then is the external environment in which American foreign policy must be conducted. It is a complex world that cannot be comprehended with clichés and abstractions, influenced or conquered by slogans, or effectively

---

[9] *World Pressures on American Foreign Policy*, edited by Marian D. Irish (Englewood Cliffs, N.J.: Prentice-Hall, Inc., 1964), examines the impact of international politics and external forces on American foreign policy. See especially Henry B. Mayo, "Theory, Ideology, and Foreign Policy"; Merle Fainsod, "The Future of the Communist Bloc and American Foreign Policy"; and Frederick M. Watkins, "Colonialism, Dictatorship, and the American Political Tradition."

projected by "images." There is no simple model for making or implementing foreign policy in the modern world. Decision-making in foreign policy—if it is to succeed in terms of goals and objectives, general or specific, long-range or immediate, strategic, political, economic, or cultural—calls for all kinds of highly specialized intelligence and the most sophisticated judgments.

The Domestic Environment of American Foreign Policy

Policy-making in a reasoned framework means choosing among alternative courses of action after carefully calculating the probable rewards and deprivations. Since the United States (or any country) must pursue its foreign policy in the external environment, the outside world in all its complexities conditions the policy-choices of our decision-makers. The range of alternatives available is further limited by the domestic environment, by the ideological orientation of the people and their sense of national purpose, by constitutional and traditional prescriptions, and by the input of domestic politics and the pattern of interests within the political system. Most of this book has been given over to a general analysis of these factors. Here it should suffice to point out some of the data which are particularly pertinent in the formulation and the implementation of foreign policy.

Ideological Orientation

The ideological orientation of the American people, as in any country, is rooted in historical experience. We are a revolutionary people and because of this we are inclined to be sympathetic toward the revolutionary nations in today's world. We were once an exploited colony and because of this we profess to dislike colonialism and imperialism even when practiced by our friends and allies. We entered the international community as an underdeveloped country and because of this we feel obliged to give our aid and technical know-how to the less developed countries of today. As a constitutional democracy we identify ourselves with the Free World and expressly oppose totalitarianism, whether fascist or communist. Because we are a peace-loving nation, we are committed to the principles of international law and support the peace-keeping operations of the United Nations.

Every nation attempts to justify its foreign policy in sweeping ideological terms. This is effective strategy in modern psychological warfare but it is not a new tactic. The American Declaration of Independence was consciously written with "a decent respect to the opinions of mankind." It is important, in domestic politics as well as in international relations, that a government appear to be acting in accord with the basic beliefs and moral convictions of its people. Political ideas which appeal to the minds of men and capture their imagination also move them to action. That an idea does not perform as promised does not necessarily detract from its function. For example, a great many Americans went into World War I "to make the world safe for democracy" and a great many more since 1947 have been stationed in military posts all over the world to "contain communism."

Hans Morgenthau, best known for his debunking of "moralism" and "sentimentalism" in American foreign policy, nevertheless insists that "in order to be worthy of our lasting sympathy, a nation must pursue its interest for the sake of a transcendent purpose that gives meaning to the day-by-day operations of its foreign policy." [10] To Morgenthau, the fundamental and minimal purpose of America is to maintain "equality in freedom" in the United States. To others the national purpose may appear in a less liberal guise. As long as the purpose is conceived in broad generalities, consensus is possible; when stated in specific terms, the whole spectrum of disagreement is soon manifest.

Toward the end of the 1950's some high-ranking policy-makers became alarmed that the American people had lost their sense of national purpose. President Eisenhower actually commissioned a dozen distinguished citizens, representing a cross-section of leadership in American society, to set up a series of "Goals for Americans" both on the home front and in foreign affairs. Members of the Commission reached consensus on such generalities as "The basic foreign policy of the United States should be the preservation of its own independence and free institutions" and "Our principles and ideals impel us to aid the new nations." When the recommendations got down to brass tacks, however, individual members began to voice dissent. The Commission agreed that "The healthiest world economy is attained when trade is at its freest," but not all members would go along with the specific recommendation that the United States should gradually reduce its tariffs and quota restrictions. The Commission agreed that the United States should stand firm and strong against communist aggression and subversion. The majority thought we should be prepared to negotiate on a reasonable basis and to try continuously for mutual tolerance. The representative of labor, however, took exception to a specific suggestion that we enlarge personal and cultural contacts with the peoples behind the Iron Curtain because he feared that, given an opportunity, Soviet trade unionists would attempt to subvert American labor organization.[11]

About the same time as President Eisenhower appointed his Commission, the Senate Committee on Foreign Relations requested the Council on Foreign Relations (a general interest group) to make a study of the "basic aims of American foreign policy." An ad hoc group of members, after examining the historic aims of American foreign policy, concluded that foreign policy in practice rarely corresponds fully to broad statements of aim and principle; decisions are made and actions taken on the basis of "calculations of national interest in the specific circumstances." The Council's report to the Senate Committee covered diverse official policies: building an international order, strengthening the Atlantic Community, economic and technical assistance for the less developed areas, military needs to meet the communist challenge, limitation and control of armaments. The Report also underscored the massive unofficial contacts which Americans make today

---

[10] Hans J. Morgenthau, *The Purpose of American Politics* (New York: Alfred A. Knopf, 1960), p. 8.

[11] The President's Commission on National Goals, *Goals for Americans* (Englewood Cliffs, N. J.: Prentice-Hall, Inc., A Spectrum Book, 1960).

with peoples all over the world (trade relations, tourism on a grand scale, exchange of professors and students, exchange of scientific findings, and the movement of ideas across national frontiers via press, radio, and motion pictures). And it made the important point that the "national purpose," as judged abroad, is determined by the actual conduct of the American society. Moreover, "As a free and pluralist society America speaks not with one voice but with many." [12]

Diplomats and scholars both agree that competing ideologies have a part in contemporary international relations, but we find widespread disagreement concerning the actual influence of ideology in the making or implementing of policy. Henry Mayo, in a perceptive analysis of "theory, ideology, and foreign policy," suggests that abstract theory may be relevant but as a political force it is never enough to control policy.[13] But whether or not ideology is a controlling factor in policy-making, public opinion at home and expectations abroad require every nation, and certainly a world power, to stand for something more than "national interest" or "national security and economic well-being." Thus the United States, as the oldest constitutional democracy, claims leadership of the Free World; the Soviet Union, as the most successful exponent of Marxism, heads the Communist Bloc. It is, however, unrealistic to view world politics as a grand confrontation of two opposing ideologies. As Professor Mayo observes, the decision-makers in the Kremlin have "on the record adjusted Marxist ideology to their practice rather than the other way around." Over the years, Soviet foreign policy has been primarily directed toward strengthening the Soviet Union and only secondarily toward promoting world revolution. We have already mentioned that the Free World has not subscribed wholly to the American Creed. The so-called Free World has no agreed definable doctrine except perhaps a basic belief in the right of every nation to go its own way and for all to exist in diversity.

A political ideology intended for export is not likely to be persuasive unless it is geared to the experiences of the people whom it endeavors to reach. This is the basic dilemma in American foreign policy: How to convey the American appreciation of due process of law and the blessings of liberty to people who most of all seek equality and especially equality in the economic sphere? How to explain the advantages of democratic capitalism over totalitarian communism to a people who are not prepared for self-government and whose economy is far from modernized? On the other hand, the communist line comes closer to the aspirations of the new nations, challenging the inequities of the status quo and promising to raise the standards of living for the underprivileged masses. The Soviet Union, which has developed into a modern industrial state and acquired great power and prestige on the world stage within a single generation, becomes the very prototype of communism. In the long run, constitutional democracy, with its respect for individual rights and human dignity, may be more impressive but meantime the

---

[12] Council on Foreign Relations, *Basic Aims of United States Foreign Policy*. This is No. 7 in *United States Foreign Policy, Compilation of Studies* prepared under the direction of the Committee on Foreign Relations, U.S. Senate. (Washington, D.C.: U.S. Government Printing Office, 1961.)

[13] *World Pressures on American Foreign Policy*, p. 26.

new countries are most eager to improve their material conditions and to modernize their society in this generation. Hence, American foreign policy toward the underdeveloped countries is a sophisticated mix of economic assistance and technological aid, along with information and propaganda to publicize the American ideology.

Constitutional Prescription and the Pattern of Federalism

Looking at the Constitution of 1787 we are struck by the Framers' preoccupation with foreign affairs. More than half of the powers enumerated to the Congress in Article I, Section 8, are related to problems of national security or international relations. Congress has power to: provide for the common defense; regulate commerce with foreign nations; regulate the value of foreign coin in the United States; establish uniform rules of naturalization; define and punish piracies and felonies committed on the high seas and offenses against the law of nations; declare war; make rules concerning captures on land and water; raise and support armies and a navy and make rules for governance of the armed services; provide for the organization, arming, and training of a militia. Add to this specific enumeration all the powers necessary and proper (or convenient and useful) to carry out the foregoing powers and you see that Congress carries a considerable weight in foreign policy.

On the other hand, Article II of the Constitution gives to the President the initiative and primary authority in foreign policy. In Chapter 10, we pointed out the President's various roles as head of state, commander in chief and director general of foreign policy. Unquestionably, the constitutional separation of powers between Congress and the President, complicated by checks and balances, tends to provoke confusion, dissension, and deadlock both in formulating and in implementing foreign policy. In the continuing process of decision-making, however, there is actually a great deal of inter-institutional collaboration. Fairly effective working relations between the executive and legislative policy-makers, particularly in the area of foreign policy, have developed a "community of policy-makers," constitutional barriers notwithstanding. We shall take a closer look at this community of policy-makers in a later section of this chapter.

The American pattern of federalism poses another set of problems in the foreign policy process. The Constitution makes it quite clear that, when it comes to international relations, the national government has complete power. Since this power has not been granted by the states, they cannot recover it at any time. International law reinforces the Constitution on this point: under international law, every independent and sovereign nation has the inherent power to engage in foreign affairs. As Justice Sutherland pointed out, sovereignty in world affairs passed directly from the British Crown to the government of the United States in 1776.[14] None of the states (except Texas and Hawaii) has ever exercised independent power in the international community. Furthermore, the Constitution specifically forbids the states to enter into any agreements with foreign nations.

---

[14] *United States* v. *Curtiss-Wright Export Corporation*, 299 U.S. 304 (1936).

The states may retain power over certain domestic matters, but they can claim no power over foreign affairs.

The treaty power of the national government, for example, is *plenary*, or absolute, and it is an *exclusive* power that is not shared with the states in any way. As early as 1796, and again in 1816, the Supreme Court declared that a treaty held good even if it conflicted with laws passed by the states. In the 1816 decision, when the Supreme Court overruled the highest court of Virginia, it touched off a storm of protest from advocates of states' rights. The Virginia court angrily responded that the Supreme Court did not have the authority to reverse a state court, for the sovereign states had created the Constitution and they had reserved to themselves the right to settle their own problems. Justice Story, speaking for the Supreme Court, rejected the idea that the Constitution is a compact among sovereign states and declared it to be a supreme law created by the people themselves. He gave short shrift to the argument that the Supreme Court did not have the right to review actions of state courts.[15] Without such review the nation would have no supreme law. A treaty is superior to any state law, then, and the Supreme Court has the authority to enforce it as part of the "supreme law of the land."

Unlike the laws of Congress, which must be made "in pursuance" of the Constitution, treaties are made "under the authority of the United States." In a recent case involving an executive agreement with Great Britain, Mr. Justice Black points out that the Framers used this particular wording so that agreements made by the United States under the Articles of Confederation would remain in effect.[16] The Justice declared that it would be "manifestly contrary to the objectives of those who created the Constitution" for the United States government to make agreements without observing constitutional prohibitions. He judged it "completely anomalous" to say that a treaty need not comply with the Constitution.

The states have claimed time and time again that the treaty power ought not to be used to abridge their powers reserved under the Tenth Amendment, but this seems to be wishful thinking on the part of states'-rights advocates. For example, in the case of *Missouri* v. *Holland* (1920), the Supreme Court upheld a treaty between the United States and Great Britain calling for the protection of migratory birds in Canada and the United States.[17] Earlier, the Court had rejected a law passed by Congress to protect migratory birds, claiming that it was an invasion of the police power of the states to protect game within their respective jurisdictions; the Court could find no delegated or implied power under which Congress could enact such a law. Once the treaty had been concluded by the national government, the Court accepted substantially the same legislation, on the grounds that Congress had power to implement the treaty. In *Reid* v. *Covert*, Mr. Justice Black in effect reconfirms *Missouri* v. *Holland*: "To the extent that

---

[15] *Martin* v. *Hunter's Lessee*, 1 Wheat. 304 (1816).
[16] *Reid* v. *Covert*, 354 U.S. 1 (1957).
[17] *Missouri* v. *Holland*, 252 U.S. 416 (1920).

the United States can validly make treaties, the people and the states have delegated their power to the national government and the Tenth Amendment is no barrier."

The Constitution requires the consent of two-thirds of the Senate before the President can ratify a treaty. This provision assures the states some control over the manner in which the national government uses its treaty power. But they have no such control over "executive agreements" as a means of conducting foreign policy. The President may conclude an executive agreement with a foreign government without obtaining the consent of the Senate, and such an agreement is just as binding on the states as a treaty. In 1933, for example, President Roosevelt concluded an executive agreement with the Soviet government to settle claims and counterclaims arising out of the Communist Revolution of 1917. Under the terms of this agreement, the United States government was assigned a considerable amount of property rights in this country claimed by the Soviet government under its nationalization decrees. New York State, however, refused to recognize the extraterritorial effect of the Soviet decrees on the grounds that confiscation of private property was contrary to the public policy of New York. Hence, when the United States government sued to recover the assets of the New York branch of a Russian insurance company that had been "nationalized," the New York courts refused to turn the property over to the national government. But the Supreme Court of the United States ruled against New York:

> No state can rewrite our foreign policy to conform to its own domestic policies . . . the policies of the States become wholly irrelevant to judicial inquiry when the United States, acting within its constitutional sphere, seeks enforcement of its foreign policy in the courts.[18]

National supremacy in the foreign affairs of the United States is incontestable. These Supreme Court decisions make several points clear: (1) the United States has plenary and exclusive power over foreign affairs; (2) this power is not shared with the states and need not be exercised so that it conforms to state policies; (3) Congress may exercise powers in carrying out a treaty that are neither delegated nor implied in the Constitution itself; (4) the President is our principal agent in foreign affairs and may make far-reaching agreements without even consulting Congress or obtaining its consent; (5) Congress may not, however, use the treaty power in violation of constitutional principles. So long as the United States followed a policy of continentalism, the states had little reason to be alarmed over all this latent power in the national government. In recent years, however, the United States has taken the lead not only in international politics but also in social, economic, and humanitarian movements the world over. Spokesmen for states' rights have been anxiously seeking to curb the treaty powers of the United States.

The position of the United States on the International Covenant of Human

---

[18] *United States* v. *Pink*, 315 U.S. 203 (1942).

Rights, drawn up by the United Nations in 1947, illustrates the problem. In line with its penchant for "sentimental moralism," the United States took a leading part in the drafting of a preliminary Declaration of Human Rights. The draft, which Mrs. Franklin D. Roosevelt, as Chairman of the Human Rights Commission, presented to the United Nations General Assembly, is a rousing piece of prose in which we join the peoples of the world in expressing our faith in fundamental human rights. But when it came to drafting the actual Covenant of Human Rights, which would have committed the nations to implement these "human rights," the American delegation was forced into an obstructionist role.

While the United States advocated personal and private property rights, it was reluctant to include some of the social and economic rights now widely accepted by nations that are moving toward socialism. Furthermore, the United States insisted on adding a federal-state article to the Covenant. Such an article would permit a federal government like ours to leave enforcement of the Covenant up to its states or provinces. Even this concession was not enough to satisfy the states'-rights champions in the United States, who feared that the national government might use the Covenant to claim greater control over civil rights. And so we finally explained to our associates in the United Nations that the policy of the United States is to support the principles of the Declaration but to abstain from support of the Covenant. Thus, as a matter of practical politics, the proponents of states' rights within the United States made it impossible for the United States to pursue the foreign policy that would have done much to bolster our position as leader of the free world.

Constitutionally, under the treaty power, the United States could have pledged its support to the Covenant of Human Rights; and Congress could then have passed laws to implement the Covenant—laws that might have revolutionized the protection of civil rights in the United States by centering them under the national government. To make sure that the pattern of federalism would never be disrupted in this way, Senator John W. Bricker (R-Ohio), joined by fifty-eight of his fellow senators, introduced an amendment to the Constitution in 1952. As approved by the Senate Judiciary Committee, the Bricker amendment would: (1) nullify any treaty that conflicted with any provision of the Constitution; (2) permit a treaty to become internal law only through legislation that would have been valid if there had never been such a treaty; (3) give Congress the same power over executive agreements with any foreign power or international organization that it has over treaties.

This attempt to restrain the President's hand in foreign affairs, particularly in making executive agreements, met with top-level opposition. President Truman and his Secretary of State (Dean Acheson), and President Eisenhower and his Secretary (John Foster Dulles), were equally firm in insisting that primary responsibility for making foreign-policy decisions must rest with the President. And yet the discussion went on for several years, even provoking a nationwide campaign against "un-American internationalism." Debates in Congress reached a sharp peak early in 1954 when both houses several times appeared on the verge of mustering the two-thirds vote needed to pass the amendment; the consent of three-fourths of the state legislatures was virtually assured. Then, in the show-down vote in the Senate, the necessary two-thirds majority was missed by only one vote.

Even in defeat, however, the states'-rights proponents scored a partial victory, for during the debates on Bricker's proposal, Secretary of State Dulles publicly conceded that the United States had no intention of adhering to the Covenant of Human Rights. In fact, the Senate has frequently added a "federal-state clause" to treaties specifying that they shall not empower Congress to exercise powers otherwise reserved to the states under the Tenth Amendment. Thus, even in the conduct of foreign affairs, where the intent of the Constitution is to give the national government exclusive and plenary power, the states sometimes share in the making and shaping of policy, at least in a negative fashion.[19]

The Inputs of Foreign Policy: Demands and Supports

The play of domestic politics and the pattern of interests (active or apathetic, public or private) within the political system inevitably affect the course of foreign policy. Foreign policy issues have always engendered sharp dissension in public opinions. One can trace the continuity of disunity from the Washington Administration to the Johnson Administration and the recurrence of party battles over American foreign relations in every election from 1800 to 1964.

Political Parties and Bipartisanship [20]

In modern times we recall the fierce partisan quarrels immediately following World War I when Woodrow Wilson as the outgoing Democratic President tried and failed to persuade a Republican-controlled Congress to consent to United States membership in the League of Nations. Certain influential senators were personally piqued because they felt the President had slighted their con-stitutional prerogatives to advise and consent. The President had not fully dis-cussed with the Republican leadership problems likely to arise in the Paris peace settlements. He had not been sufficiently politic in his personal relations with the Senate to include the Republican Senator from Massachusetts, Henry Cabot Lodge, in the official entourage that went to Versailles. Subsequently, the Repub-licans capitalized on the League issue and the war-weariness of the American people to win the presidential election of 1920. Warren G. Harding, the Repub-lican Senator from Ohio who had participated in the partisan attack on the Covenant, succeeded Woodrow Wilson as President. And the American refusal

---

[19] See "The Problem of the Federal State in Foreign Affairs" by Noel T. Dowling in *Federalism Mature and Emergent*, a symposium edited by Arthur MacMahon (Garden City, N.Y.: Doubleday & Co., Inc., 1955).

[20] Cecil V. Crabb, Jr., *American Foreign Policy in the Nuclear Age* (Evanston, Ill.: Row, Peterson and Company, 1960) includes an excellent chapter, "Executive-Legislative Relations and Bipartisanship." See also Crabb's *Bipartisan Foreign Policy: Myth or Reality* (Evanston, Ill.: Row, Peterson and Company, 1957).

to join the League would have fateful consequences not only for the American people but for the entire world.

The controversy over the League points out several significant aspects of policy-making. First, the constitutional prescription of separation of powers enhances the possibilities of institutional discord between the official decision-makers, President and Congress. Second, partisan interests may be more influential than the so-called national interest when issues in foreign policy can be used to stir the electorate, turn out the party in power, and win the presidency for the opposing party. Third, interpersonal relations among the policy-makers may be crucial even in decisions of paramount public importance. Fourth, and perhaps most important, the policy process is no more rational than the men who sit as policy-makers.

The League fiasco taught the Roosevelt and Truman Administrations some very practical lessons in how to conduct foreign policy more effectively during World War II and in the postwar period. The idea that the leadership of both major parties should rise above partisan politics in the area of national security was consciously institutionalized. The American delegation to the Bretton Woods Conference in 1944, which laid the foundations for the International Bank and the International Monetary Fund, included bipartisan representation from both houses of Congress. Before President Roosevelt went to Yalta, he held a special bipartisan meeting with key members of the Senate to discuss with them what kind of world organization should be established and how we might go about settling some of the postwar problems of Eastern Europe, including our relations with the Soviet Union.

The organization and operation of the United Nations is a conspicuous example of bipartisan foreign policy. The United States delegation to the San Francisco Conference that drafted the Charter included Democrats and Republicans from Congress. Before the delegation went to San Francisco, the State Department offered bipartisan briefings and during discussions and decision-making at the Conference the American delegates participated fully on a bipartisan basis. When the Charter was brought back to Washington, the Senate approved it by the overwhelming bipartisan vote of 89–2. Since San Francisco, American participation in all aspects of the United Nations organization and activities are deliberately bipartisan. Thus, two members of Congress—one Democrat and one Republican—are appointed in alternate years from the House and Senate to sit in the United States delegation to the General Assembly. President Truman, who strongly stressed bipartisanship in foreign affairs, appointed Warren Austin, former Republican Senator from Vermont, to head the U. S. Mission to the United Nations and to represent us in the Security Council. President Eisenhower was more partisan in designating Henry Cabot Lodge (grandson of the Senator who fought the League) to succeed Austin, and President Kennedy was just as partisan when he named Adlai Stevenson to the post.

In all important foreign policy decisions since World War II, the community of decision-makers has been bipartisan. Specific practices that set the pattern of bipartisan collaboration include: prior consultation between the Chief Executive and the congressional leadership on all measures that will call for legislative action or an outward show of internal unity; official briefings and continuous liaison between the Secretary of State, the Secretary of Defense and other executive agencies with such congressional committees as the Senate Committee on Foreign Relations, the House Committee on Foreign Affairs, and both the House and Senate committees on the Armed Services; close working relations between the congressional subcommittees and the geographical and functional divisions of the Department of State and operating agencies in foreign affairs, particularly aid and information. Since the congressional leadership and the congressional committees are bipartisan in composition, these practices of executive-legislative liaison insure bipartisan collaboration. Another significant practice is the appointment of negotiators, consultants, and advisors from both major parties to insure bipartisan participation in important international conferences and to promote bipartisan support for the ensuing agreements.

Arthur Vandenberg, the Republican Senator from Michigan, was one of the principal architects of postwar bipartisanship. President Truman counted on the influential Senator to swing his fellow Republicans into line in support of the Marshall Plan, the Truman Doctrine, the China Aid Bill of 1948, the North Atlantic Treaty, the Mutual Defense Assistance Program, and the various economic and technical assistance programs under Point Four. Over and over Senator Vandenberg told the American public—and thus the world—that most Republicans were proud to join the Democrats in a show of national unity on major problems in foreign policy. The ideal, he said, is "an unpartisan American foreign policy—not Republican, not Democratic, but American—which substantially unites our people at the water's edge in behalf of peace."

American foreign policy—under Presidents Roosevelt, Truman, Eisenhower, Kennedy, and Johnson—has been largely bipartisan in planning, negotiating, deciding, and programing.[21] Nevertheless, every national election since World War II has focused on foreign policy as a major partisan issue. How then do we reconcile the continuous practice of bipartisanship with recurrent, fierce to vicious, partisan attacks on formerly agreed policies? First, in all honesty we must say that not all Republicans were glad to join with Senator Vandenberg in support of President Truman's foreign policy. Senator ("Mr. Republican") Robert Taft from Ohio launched an all-out attack in 1951 on the entire range of Truman's foreign policy, hitting especially hard the "troops-to-Europe" decision which the Administration found necessary to implement the NATO agreement. President Truman's dismissal of General MacArthur for failure to support the official and political policies of his own government (and of the United Nations) touched off a highly partisan investigation and full-scale foreign policy debate that furnished much of the grist for the Republican campaign in 1952.

Second, personal relations as well as partisan considerations enter into the

---

[21] See *Review of Bipartisan Foreign Policy Consultations Since World War II* by John Sparkman, 82d Cong., 1st Sess., Sen. Document, No. 87. (Washington, D.C.: U.S. Government Printing Office, 1952.)

political situation. President Truman bitterly resented General Eisenhower's use of the Korean War as a campaign issue in 1952. President Truman had made General Eisenhower Chief of Staff of the U. S. Army and subsequently Commander of the Allied troops in Europe. In fact, Eisenhower had appeared as a witness for the Administration in the congressional hearings on the troops-to-Europe issue. At the outset of the campaign, the President had offered the General complete and confidential briefings on matters of national security, thereby hoping to maintain the posture of national unity in foreign affairs through the election period. The General for his part became increasingly sensitive as President Truman's salty comments rubbed him the wrong way. Because the principal actors in the situation were hardly on speaking terms after the election, the 1953 transition from Democratic to Republican power in the White House had rough going, with unfortunate repercussions in foreign policy.

John Foster Dulles, who had been an influential member of President Truman's community of foreign policy advisers and who had negotiated the Japanese Peace Treaty for the Administration, was chief strategist for the Republican Party on foreign policy issues in 1952. The Republicans charged the Democrats with plunging us into the Korean War, abandoning the friendly nations of East Europe to communist rule, permitting the communists to take over China, and in general blamed the Roosevelt and Truman Administrations for all the troubles in Latin America, the Middle East, the Far East, and Africa. After the Republicans clinched their victory at the polls, Dulles appeared before the Senate Committee on Foreign Relations as the President-elect's choice for Secretary of State. Responding to questions from committee members about how the election returns would affect the course of foreign policy, Dulles explained that a political campaign is like a legal contest. The parties play the role of lawyers rather than judges; they represent their clients in court and use what tactics are necessary to win their case. When the case is settled, the opposing lawyers can shake hands in professional fellowship. Thus, when a national election is won, campaign charges can be dropped. Said the incoming Secretary, "I believe we should try to work together on a bipartisan basis." [22]

In January 1960, when the junior Senator from Massachusetts announced his candidacy for the Democratic presidential nomination, he attacked the Republican Administration for the whole sorry state of the world. The attack, however, was on the *style* rather than the substance of administrative policy. This was the Kennedy image sustained throughout the campaign (and the less than three years he would be in office): a young man born in this century, dedicated to the public service, experienced in the political process, ready to make the most of presidential powers, alert to the crucial issues of our times, prepared to open and keep open the channels of communication between the world of thought and the world of action.

---

[22] Hearing before the Committee on Foreign Relations, U.S. Senate, 83rd Cong., 1st Sess., on nomination of John Foster Dulles, Sec. of State designate, Jan. 15, 1953. (Washington, D.C.: U.S. Government Printing Office, 1953.)

The record of bipartisanship throughout the Eisenhower Administration was blurred by a series of mishaps and unfortunate events in May and June 1960 which gave the Democrats all the campaign material they needed to disparage the incumbent Republicans: the downing of an American U-2 plane inside Russia, President Eisenhower's assumption of personal responsibility for the incident, Chairman Khrushchev's angry reaction and the subsequent fiasco of the Paris Summit Conference, and finally the cancellation of President Eisenhower's projected visit to Tokyo to celebrate the newly ratified mutual security pact between the United States and Japan because of violent anti-American demonstrations that jeopardized his personal safety. Actually, the presidential candidates in 1960 were not too far apart on issues of foreign policy, not even in the "great debates" before the nation-wide television audience. They clashed over Quemoy and Matsu and over Castro and Cuba. Nixon seemed farther out on the first and Kennedy seemed farther out on the latter, though each in turn later denied that he meant to go so far. Both wanted adequate military strength, atomic and conventional; neither would abandon Berlin or Taiwan; both supported controlled and supervised disarmament; both would fight to contain communism. No one could really judge from this split-screen drama how either candidate might perform as the nation's chief policy-maker when he would be expected to act deliberately on the basis of all the intelligence available to this office.

The incoming Kennedy Administration stressed the "leadership of change" and in the revolutionary world of the 1960's certainly change was the order of the day. But the Kennedy Administration had to learn (as every administration must) that the central themes of American foreign policy are more or less constant regardless of the party in power. National traditions, historical precedents, legal principles, strategic interest, and policy commitments continue to shape the national policies from one administration through the next. Party changes in the American political system may affect the external environment but only incidentally. The pattern of cross-purposes in the international community is determined by the ideas, interests, and institutions that condition policy-makers in more than a hundred independent nation-states.

In all policy planning, events have a way of altering the input even before the planners have had time to assess their data. The death of Premier Joseph Stalin in March 1953 was probably the most significant event in the first year of President Eisenhower's Administration. Policy-makers in Washington had nothing to do with reorganizing the party and state apparatus in the USSR, but the new regime in Moscow immediately affected the plans of the Eisenhower Administration to carry psychological warfare behind the iron curtain. Early in the Kennedy Administration, Fidel Castro joined Cuba to the Communist Bloc; the rift widened between the Soviet Union and the Peoples' Republic of China; the East German government built a concrete wall that sealed off East Berlin from the West; Dag Hammarskjold, Secretary General of the UN, killed in a plane crash in the Congo, was replaced by U Thant, Burmese Ambassador to the UN, thus symbolizing the new Afro-Asian balance of power in international diplomacy; Russian troops, then Russian missiles, appeared in Cuba. To these events—and to many more in the world outside—the Kennedy Administration had to react and the sum of the reactions became a large part of American foreign policy.[23]

"New frontiers" were established in the Kennedy Administration, such as the Alliance for Progress and the Peace Corps, but the grand design of foreign policy was not radically changed. As in every administration since World War II, national security was—and continues to be—the main objective. President Kennedy had no difficulty in obtaining bipartisan support for increased expenditures for military purposes, including a build-up in conventional weapons to implement a policy of "limited war" as an alternative to nuclear confrontation. When President Johnson, in his first budget, attempted to cut expenditures at points where he thought our defenses were already powerful, congressmen from both parties and in all parts of the country protested on behalf of constituents who had economic interests in defense installations and defense contracts.

As in the Truman and Eisenhower Administrations, the second line of defense was—and continues to be—foreign aid, with emphasis shifting in the Kennedy and Johnson Administrations from military to economic assistance, especially for the underdeveloped countries. Each year debates on foreign aid get rougher, however, as Congress becomes increasingly reluctant to appropriate the taxpayers' money for overseas projects. Nevertheless, on the record, both Democrats and Republicans voted for—and against—foreign aid programs in the Truman, Eisenhower, Kennedy and Johnson Administrations.

An incoming administration cannot start with a clean slate. It must begin with the policies and commitments of its predecessor. In the 1952 election, the Republicans claimed that if they were returned to power they would "repudiate all commitments contained in secret understandings such as those of Yalta." But, in fact, President Eisenhower found himself constrained to observe all agreements made in good faith by his predecessors in office. *Pacta sunt servanda* (agreements are observed). Even if the American President had wanted to undo the political and military decisions taken at Yalta and Potsdam, he could not have turned back the sequence of past events in countries outside the United States. Likewise, when President Kennedy took office he inherited policies and programs from the Eisenhower Administration. Secretary Dulles had tied the United States into a network of mutual defense arrangements with more than 40 different nations. Secretary Rusk accepted these treaties with all their implications as part of continuing American foreign policy. An incoming administration may reverse its predecessor on domestic policies, but in foreign affairs it cannot disrupt the *continuum of policies* which involve international agreements or commitments. Notice, however, that continuum of policies is not a static concept. The new party in power will have an opportunity to make its own choices of action as new events and new actors change the external environment and the domestic situation.

---

[23] See Marian D. Irish, "The Kennedy Administration: Appraisal at the Halfway Mark," in the 1963–64 *American Government Annual* edited by Jack W. Peltason (New York: Holt, Rinehart, and Winston, 1963).

Interest Groups in Foreign Policy

The continuity of bipartisanship in American foreign policy suggests the existence of considerable consensus in American public opinion. This is because American political parties, as well as the electorate, generally view foreign policy as a grand design to insure *national* security and *national* well-being. But if we look at foreign policy not so much in terms of high-level diplomatic relations but rather in the context of day-to-day operations from country to country, then we perceive that specific programs represent a wide range of special interests, rival interests, and conflicts of interest. In Chapter 7, we have already discussed how the activities of interest groups enter into the policy process. It would be remiss, however, not to point out some of the diverse demands and supports that press upon decision-makers in *foreign* policy. The accommodation of various special interests within the framework of "national interest" explains what might otherwise seem to be an incoherent approach to national policies.

We began this chapter by stressing the "externalness" of American foreign policy. At this point, again we stress the obvious. Just as the United States maintains diplomatic missions in more than a hundred different countries for the purpose of advancing *our* national interests (and the interests of American nationals), so do these same hundred and more countries maintain *their* diplomatic missions in the United States to advance *their* national interests (and the interests of *their* nationals). In Washington, there is continuous traffic between the foreign embassies and the various administrative agencies in Washington that deal in foreign affairs—State, AID, the Export-Import Bank, and so on.

The diplomat's job is a politically delicate one. He is expected to provide his own government with maximum intelligence about the country to which he is accredited. This means he must seek authoritative information. He is expected also to negotiate for whatever policies (programs) that might benefit his own government. He must therefore have access to those in authority and in a position to carry out commitments. Because diplomats are formally accredited to heads of states, it is generally understood that they will pursue their missions with the executive branch of the government, not with the legislative branch.

International law accords the diplomat many privileges and immunities which facilitate his mission, but it also places him under various restrictions. Thus it is not proper for a foreign diplomat in the United States to seek an engagement with a congressional committee even though the committee may be considering a program very important to his country. By the same convention, a congressional committee may not invite foreign diplomats to testify even though such testimony might be the shortest cut to first-hand information which the Committee needs to suggest intelligent legislation. On the other hand, congressmen and foreign diplomats may meet "for lunch" and talk on any topic. The constant round of social life in Washington affords congressmen, foreign diplomats, and other key actors a non-official setting where they can get together on matters of common interest. Who influences whom and how much depends on many factors.

That diplomatic missions try to influence American decision-makers is so obvious that it is often overlooked in analysis of inputs in the foreign policy process. Another set of influentials, usually not so obvious in their activities, are the many (about 500) non-diplomatic individuals and organizations who act within the United States as private agents of foreign governments and interests.[24] Since 1938, these foreign agents have been required by law: (1) to register with the Attorney General; (2) to identify the foreign governments or foreign interests which they serve; (3) to account for the activities they undertake on behalf of their foreign principals; and (4) to indicate any foreign propaganda which they circulate in the United States. Since these foreign agents are not diplomats, they do not have special privileges and immunities, but neither are they subject to the restrictions of international law. Provided that they declare their activities, they are legally free to influence legislative or executive decision-makers.

The number of foreign agents in the United States has increased in recent years, partly because the number of countries in the world has increased and also because many of the new nations do not have sufficient native talent for export. They frequently find it more effective to supplement their rather small diplomatic corps with American citizens paid to perform specific services. The Attorney General's list indicates that the largest number of such foreign agents in the United States are engaged in public relations, publicity, and information activities. The second largest group provides legal services; some of the most distinguished law firms in the United States are on the payrolls of foreign governments or foreign interest groups. The third largest category includes economic consultants, financial advisers, and trade promoters, the kind of experts most needed by the under-developed countries. These foreign agents work to influence governmental activities on behalf of their clients; they also may provide liaison between interest groups in this country and groups with similar interests in the country which they represent.

Gabriel Almond in his study of *American People and Foreign Policy* identifies and classifies American interest groups that influence foreign policy: (1) labor groups (AFL-CIO); (2) business organizations (U.S. Chamber of Commerce, National Association of Manufacturers); (3) agricultural groups (American Farm Bureau Federation, National Grange); (4) veterans' groups (American Legion, Veterans of Foreign Wars); (5) women's groups (League of Women Voters, American Association of University Women); (6) religious groups (Federal Council of Churches of Christ, specific church groups such as Methodists, Presbyterians, Roman Catholics, etc.); (7) ethnic groups (Jews, Germans, Poles, etc.). Here we add (8) government groups (vested and special interests *within* the government agencies).[25]

Government agencies, especially bureaucrats with specialized interests, do

---

[24] See *Activities of Non-Diplomatic Representatives of Foreign Principals in the United States*, Hearings before the Committee on Foreign Relations, U.S. Senate, 88th Cong., 1st Sess. (Washington, D.C.: U.S. Government Printing Office, 1963).

[25] Gabriel Almond, *American People and Foreign Policy* (New York: Harcourt, Brace and Co., 1950), Chapter VIII. See also Charles O. Lerche, Jr., *Foreign Policy of the American People* (Englewood Cliffs, N. J.: Prentice-Hall, Inc., 1961), Chapter 2.

what they can to influence the political process in order to further particular programs to which they are professionally committed. The Pentagon, for example, effectively lobbies on military issues; AID on foreign aid; and USIA on information programs. Most administrative agencies now maintain a professional staff whose task it is to sell administrative programs. The Department of State has an Assistant Secretary of State whose job it is to handle "congressional relations" not only for the Secretary of State but also for all the various bureaus and offices in the Department. The Department of Defense also has an Assistant Secretary whose office manages legislative affairs for the many components within the Pentagon. But when congressional committees are asked to authorize and to appropriate for specific programs and particular operations, it is the bureaucrats most concerned who really put mind and heart into "justifications."

Outside the government, the line-up of pressure groups varies considerably according to issues. In January 1957, President Eisenhower laid before a joint session of Congress his proposal for American action to deter communist aggression in the Middle East. This proposal, now called the Eisenhower Doctrine, immediately activated many different groups with special interests in the Middle East: the military establishment because the proposal was to authorize military assistance to Middle East countries needing help to combat communist aggression; area specialists in the State Department who backstop the community of policy-makers on all matters pertaining to the Near East; Arab groups in the United States who felt that the United States had no right to make a unilateral policy which would affect the lives and fortunes of 50 million Arabs in the Middle East; Zionist groups who urged that the United States refuse aid to any Arab nation unwilling to make peace with Israel; supporting groups for the United Nations who urged that the United States not by-pass the United Nations in pursuit of unilateral objectives; representatives of major oil interests because the Middle East contains 70 per cent of the world's known oil reserves and supplies 20 per cent of the oil used by the "Free World" and 75 per cent of West Europe's oil imports. Thus, congressional decision-makers had to consider the wishes and positions of a number of conflicting public and private interests and opinions.

A more recent and dramatic illustration of pressure groups in action during the course of decision-making occurred in the late summer of 1963 when the Treaty of Moscow was before the Senate. The treaty, which culminated long-time negotiations between the United States and the Soviet Union, forbade participants to conduct nuclear weapons tests or nuclear explosions in the atmosphere, in space, in territorial waters, or on the high seas. The senate committees on the Armed Services and Foreign Relations held joint hearings over several weeks so that many interested individuals and organizations, official and non-official, could present their dissident views. Two groups with professional stakes in the issue, the militarists and the atomic scientists, divided among themselves, with spokesmen supporting and opposing the treaty. Among those pressuring for ratification were the United World Federalists, the American Friends Service Committee, SANE, Methodist church organizations, and other religious groups. The American Legion endorsed the treaty subject to certain reservations, whereas the Veterans of Foreign Wars opposed it. A Citizens Committee for Nuclear

Test Ban, comprising 167 distinguished citizens, including 13 Nobel Prize winners), coordinated the activities of approximately 25 interest groups in a nation-wide campaign to influence public opinion to influence congressmen. Congressional offices reported an unusually heavy barrage of letters, telegrams, and personal visits from constituents. Thanks to the efforts of the Citizens Committee, support was focused, whereas the opposition, though also intense, was not organized. The Treaty of Moscow was ratified by a bipartisan vote, 80 to 19. Among the 19 Senators voting against it was Barry Goldwater, Republican Senator from Arizona, a vote which Johnson and Humphrey exploited in the 1964 campaign as an indication that the Senator was out of "the mainstream" of both parties.

Public Opinion in Foreign Policy

Consent of the governed is a tradition of American government as old as the Republic. But applied to foreign policy, the function of the tradition is at least open to question. In the fall of 1958, Secretary of State Dulles was engaged in "brinkmanship" over Quemoy and Matsu, two small islands offshore from the China mainland claimed by Chiang Kai-shek. From time to time, the Chinese Communists had pressed counter claims by bombarding the islands. In September 1958, following such a bombardment, Secretary Dulles announced that the United States intended to use force if necessary to defend the off-shore islands for Chiang. To underscore the Secretary's announcement, the United States forthwith began to concentrate its powerful air-naval fighting force in the Pacific. Letters to editors, the White House, the Secretary of State, and to congressmen immediately reflected an increasingly adverse public reaction to the Secretary's statement of policy. Editorials across the country, TV and radio commentators, paid ads by interest groups, and a number of public opinion polls expressed a trend definitely opposed to the Secretary's announced policy. In press conference, Dulles was asked whether he thought the reaction of the public, on one side or another, was important to the implementation of the policy. He replied that a policy involving grave decisions for the country should have the support of the American people "so far as practical," but he insisted that final decisions in foreign policy must rest with the President and his advisors, regardless of public approval or disapproval.

At the crest of public reaction to the Quemoy-Matsu affair of 1958, a subordinate in the State Department "leaked" to the *New York Times* a report that 80 per cent of the 5000 letters received in the Department were critical of the administrative position. This report touched off another phrase in the debate when Vice President Nixon said he was "shocked" at such a disclosure by a government employee. Secretary Dulles stood his ground, that "public opinion is always important because obviously you cannot carry out effectively a public policy without the support of public opinion. The question is always present as to whether the public opinion is sound or not. Certainly you cannot allow your foreign policy to be dictated by public opinion." [26]

---

[26] For an extended discussion see Marian D. Irish, "Public Opinion and the Quemoy Crisis," *Political Quarterly*, XXXI (1960), pp. 151–161.

Fortuitously, the crisis over Quemoy-Matsu blew itself out and the public almost forgot about the offshore islands until they were featured once again in the Kennedy-Nixon debates of 1960. Many questions raised in the 1958 incident remain unanswered, however. We do not know whether all the sound and fury in the public forum, especially in the press, altered the conduct of official policy. We do not know whether the barrage of letter writing (if 5000 letters, without regard to quality, constitutes a barrage) reflected opinions held by the general citizenry, by special groups, or by an assortment of aroused individuals. And we cannot say whether the Administration would have been better advised if it had responded more sensitively to the opinions expressed in the press and mass media. Dorothy Fosdick, onetime member of the State Department's Policy Planning Staff,

Drawing by Herblock. From *Straight Herblock* (New York: Simon & Schuster, 1964).

"Absolutely! We should stay out of foreign affairs and we should make other countries do as we say."

reminds us that "the wisdom of a policy bears no direct relation to the number of people favoring it." [27]

The making of foreign policy is a tortuous process involving many factors not only within the domestic arena but also in the external environment, factors which the man on the street cannot know, much less appraise. The public, comprising many different groups with many different interests, cannot decide foreign policy by plebiscite or polls. Foreign policy may be a paramount issue in a presidential election or in congressional elections, but the many studies on how America votes (including Chapter 5 of this book) indicate that such factors as family background, class, residential and ethnic identifications, and party regularity are more likely to determine voting behavior than reasoned choices in foreign policy. In the final analysis, citizens must leave policy decisions up to their public officials. On the other hand, public officials in a democracy are constrained to consider the value judgments of the whole people from whom they receive their legitimate power. Alexander Hamilton wrote in *The Federalist* (No. 70), even as he was defining the concept of a vigorous and strong executive, "The circumstances

---

[27] Dorothy Fosdick, *Common Sense and World Affairs* (New York: Harcourt, Brace and Company, 1955), p. 188.

which constitute safety in the republican sense are, first a due dependence on the people, secondly a due responsibility."

The problem of communications between the governors and the governed is especially difficult in the area of foreign policy. "Open covenants openly arrived at" is more convincing as a slogan than as a diplomatic practice. By definition, foreign policy involves more than one government, more than one people. The American government is not free to disclose to the American people the full story of its relations with another country unless the government of that country is equally ready and willing to tell all. Moreover, an important part of decision-making, in the context of the Cold War, and especially in programs of counter-insurgency, is the gathering and analysis of strategic intelligence. And, understandably, it is not always feasible to offer up for public debate the top-drawer plans of the State Department, Pentagon, or the CIA. Sometimes it may even be necessary, as a part of strategy, to withhold information from the public or to manipulate news, as the Kennedy administration felt impelled to do during the Cuban missiles crisis in 1962.

American public officials, traditionally sensitive to public opinion in foreign as well as domestic policy, generally try to provide the public with adequate information regarding governmental activities in foreign affairs. The Bureau of Public Affairs in the Department of State maintains day-to-day relationships with the news media of the world; press, radio, and TV networks; motion pictures; and photographers. It also conducts a variety of programs that reach opinion leaders and groups especially interested in international affairs; arranges policy information conferences and briefing sessions in Washington and throughout the country; sends out knowledgeable speakers for all kinds of public forums, from civic luncheons to academic commencements and veterans' conventions; and handles a great deal of personal correspondence on international affairs both for the Department and for the White House. A similar Bureau in the Department of Defense performs informational and public relations services for defense policies, plans, and programs.

The Bureau of Public Affairs in the State Department is charged with interpreting to the Department and to the Foreign Service what appear to be the demands and supports within the American public for American foreign policy. The Bureau of Public Affairs in the Defense Department carries out a similar responsibility with respect to defense policies and plans. Communications as an aspect of policy-making is a two-way activity: (1) the government provides the public—or opinion leaders and interest groups—with information on public policies and programs; (2) the public—or interested individuals and groups—responds in various ways to the government policies.[28] Probably the weakest side in the communications system between the public and its officials is the feedback process —the way in which the government agencies attempt to ascertain public opinions

---

[28] For a first-hand account of how the Bureau of Public Affairs in the State Department operates, see Andrew Berding, *Foreign Affairs and You* (Garden City, N. Y.: Doubleday and Company, Inc., 1962). The author was Assistant Secretary of State for Public Affairs in the Eisenhower Administration.

and the way in which they respond to what they apprehend as public opinion. A soap company about to market a new detergent—or an oil company researching customer reactions to credit cards—does a much more sophisticated kind of analysis and a much more effective job in public relations than either the State Department or the Pentagon about to market a new look in foreign policy or national defense.

Congressmen are seemingly even more casual and haphazard than the administrative agencies in the way they sample public opinion. One researcher reports that a number of congressmen told him the best guides to public opinion are letters from constituents, chats with callers who happen into the office, and occasional visits with the folks at home. Congress has generally frowned on any systematic polling by government agencies.

Ernest May, a professor of history at Harvard who has done some recent research on the role of public opinion in foreign policy-making, finds that not only the congressmen but the President and high-ranking officials in administrative circles, looking for clues to public reactions, are inclined first of all to look in the daily mail bag and then at the editorials and comments of their favorite columnists.[29] Bernard Cohen of the University of Wisconsin, who has also recently made a study of *The Press and Foreign Policy*, declares that most officials in the State Department use newspapers as their "daily measure" of how the American people are reacting to the course of foreign policy.[30] For students of political science who like to observe political behavior in a reasoned framework, it is somewhat dismaying to notice how our top decision-makers calculate public opinion—and make judgments accordingly—in the age of computer science!

Decision-Makers and Their Decisions in Foreign Policy

In Part 3 of this book we looked at the decision-makers in American government within the institutional frame of reference—Congress, the presidency, the bureaucracy, and the courts. When we focus on decision-making within particular policy areas, we discover that membership in the community of policy-makers varies considerably according to specific situations.

Decision-Making

In so far as decision-making in the international community affects national policies in the member states, we must count many persons outside the United States as influential participants in the shaping of American foreign policy. Syngman Rhee in Korea, Konrad Adenauer and his successor Ludwig Erhard in the German Federal Republic, deGasperi in Italy, Charles de Gaulle in the Fifth French Re-

[29] Ernest R. May, "An American Tradition in Foreign Policy: The Role of Public Opinion," in *Theory and Practice in American Politics* edited by William H. Nelson (Chicago: University of Chicago Press, 1964).

[30] Bernard C. Cohen, *The Press and Foreign Policy* (Princeton, N. J.: Princeton University Press, 1963).

public, Nikita Khrushchev in the USSR, Nehru and Shastri of India, Chiang Kai-shek in Formosa, Mao Tse-tung and Chou En-lai in the People's Republic of China, the Diem family in Viet Nam, Fidel Castro in Cuba, Willy Brandt of Berlin, Kwame Nkruma of Ghana, Harold MacMillan of the United Kingdom— all these and many more have played key roles in the international situation. *Their* activities on behalf of *their* respective governments—and the reactions of *our* decision makers in defense of *our* national interests—have in large measure determined the course of American foreign policy since World War II. American foreign policy has frequently been little more than *ad hoc* reactions to actions taken in the international situation. Witness the recurrent crises over Berlin where communist maneuvers, Soviet and East German, have generally set the pattern for American policies.

Many actors on the stage of international politics, both friends and enemies, influence the course of American foreign policy. While, however, such powerful and high-ranking statesmen as President de Gaulle and former Chairman Khrushchev influence American foreign policy, they do not make it. A policy-maker holds a position of authority—to determine goals and to prescribe courses of action toward those goals—within a political system. American foreign policy-makers derive their authority, and exercise it, within the constitutional and institutional pattern of American government. Without authority to implement policies outside the United States, they determine the goals and strategy of American foreign policy in terms of our national interests. The President of the United States, certainly one of the most powerful men in the world, is a policy-maker at home, but only an influencer abroad. The same holds true for President de Gaulle, Prime Minister Wilson, and all the others who figure so prominently in international affairs. However influential they may be in international politics, they are policy-makers only within their own country, where each is accountable and responsible within the constitutional, institutional, and political framework of his own government.

From an institutional standpoint, it is relatively easy to identify the major units within the national policy machinery concerned with American foreign policy. (See Part 3.) For the most part, the principal American actors in the policy process hold official positions within these major units. Thus, for the same reason that we have excluded influential foreign statesmen from the category of policy-makers, we also exclude many influencers of domestic affairs—spokesmen for interest groups, opinion leaders, consultants of all sorts. Only those who hold official positions are the accountable and responsible decision-makers.

If we look at foreign policy, at the highest level of decision-making, we find that the top group of policy-makers represents a relatively small cluster of official positions. The President, of course, is pre-eminent; in the final analysis he is solely responsible. But the President needs, and gets, a great deal of help in making decisions. Within the Executive Office he can count on professional and political assistance from members of the White House office staff, the National Security Council, the Bureau of the Budget, the Council of Economic Advisers, the National Aeronautics and Space Council, the Office of Emergency Planning, and the

Central Intelligence Agency.[31] Each of these agencies has become bureaucratized and some of them are large. To be realistic, we should probably include only the heads or directors of these presidential agencies in the category of policy-makers who meet together with the President to consider major policy decisions.

Also within the executive branch, but outside the Executive Office of the President, we include the heads or directors of the major agencies directly involved in foreign policies and national security. The Secretary of State is officially the principal adviser to the President in the determination and execution of the foreign policy of the United States. The Secretary of Defense is the President's principal assistant in all matters relating to defense and national security. Because American foreign policy since World War II has been tied into a world-wide network of defense agreements, guaranteed by military commitments, and because continuous brush fires constantly threaten to turn the Cold War into a hot war, the Chairman of the Joint Chiefs of Staff almost always sits with the top policy-makers to represent professional military opinions which are crucial in many foreign policy decisions. Because the military assistance programs and foreign aid operations call for vast outlays of public expenditures, the Secretary of the Treasury and the Director of the Budget also belong in the top group; their advice on financial matters is at the very center of most policy decisions today. Since Hiroshima, atomic warfare has been accorded high priority in all considerations of military strategy, particularly during the Eisenhower Administration when the decision was made to rely on nuclear deterrents rather than to build up conventional armaments and also during the Kennedy and Johnson Administrations, as the presence of the Chairman of the Atomic Energy Commission at high-level policy meetings signifies.

The Central Intelligence Agency is attached, but does not seem to be specifically responsible, to the National Security Council. Ostensibly, the CIA is a service unit, an interdepartmental clearing house for all intelligence relating to national security. But the CIA is also an operating agency whose operations are not controlled by, and frequently not even known to, the regular departments. Its activities—in Latin America, East Europe, and Southeast Asia—only occasionally reach the headlines, as during the Bay of Pigs invasion or the overthrow of the Diem government in Viet Nam. Thousands of high-grade specialists and professional people are employed in its huge steel and concrete establishment in Virginia, a few miles out of Washington; the nature of their employment is never discussed and the place is guarded against visitors. An unknown number of CIA agents overseas are engaged in activities which are never mentioned in the public records, although it is evident, from time to time, that the agency has a decisive influence on the mainstream of American foreign policy. Enough has been said to indicate that the Director of the CIA is a key officer in American foreign policy.

---

[31] The current *United States Government Organization Manual* (Washington, D.C.: U.S. Government Printing Office) describes each agency and briefly outlines the assigned activities of its component units. The student should use the *Manual* as a reference for further information on each of the major units in the national policy machine.

The top group of policy-makers for the most part comprises heads of major units in the national power structure; they have direct access to the President and meet with him frequently, as a group and/or individually. Within the executive community of policy-makers, there exists a kind of pecking order; some positions (and some persons) are more equal than others. A step down from the top level policy-makers we find a second group of high-ranking policy officers who frequently meet together (but rarely with the President) for interagency planning and interagency programming. In the Eisenhower Administration the Operations Coordinating Board was an attempt to formalize and institutionalize such interagency coordination. President Kennedy early in his administration abolished the OCB because he preferred to keep the policy process more flexible. As it turned out, however, those who now fill the positions formerly in OCB still find it convenient and fruitful to meet informally—at the luncheon table rather than around the conference table—to coordinate and expedite interdepartmental activities. And

"*Well, it takes all kinds . . . .*"

From *What's Got Your Back Up?* Copyright © 1961 by Bill Mauldin. Reprinted with the permission of Harper & Row, Publishers.

in this group we are likely to find the Under Secretary of State, the Deputy Secretary of Defense, the Under Secretary of the Treasury, and the directors of the various operating agencies: foreign aid, information, disarmament, and the Peace Corps.

The top policy officers, most of them heads of operating agencies, are generally backstopped by specialists and professional bureaucrats within their respective organizations. If we look at each of the agencies, we discover a hierarchy of decision-makers within each of the major units. Thus the official roster of the State Department lists some two dozen "principal officers," undersecretaries, assistant secretaries, the counselor, the legal adviser, and others who regularly meet with the Secretary and advise him on policy matters. All the principal officers are political appointees who serve the presidential administration. But they in turn count on the thousands of permanent career people in the Department, the foreign service and the classified civil service, to provide them with the broad range of specific intelligence which they need to advise the Secretary in particular situations.

In theory, the career service is politically neutral, willing and able to serve succeeding administrations without partisan prejudice or predilection. As a matter of fact, however, incoming political executives are liable to identify senior bureaucrats with the politics and policies of the old administration. In 1953, senior foreign service officers, many of whom had entered the service in the era of Calvin Coolidge and Herbert Hoover, were dismayed to find themselves suspect as security risks because they had risen from the ranks in the era of Franklin D. Roosevelt and Harry S. Truman. It can be said, with some exaggeration perhaps, that conspicuous success in the outgoing administration is likely to be regarded as a handicap in the next administration, and conversely that lack of recognition and failure to get ahead in the old administration may become a professional asset with the incoming administration. Bureaucrats are persons, most of them ambitious just like other people; they want to better their positions, move into more challenging and rewarding situations and they want higher pay and more prestige. Thus during the period of presidential transition many bright young bureaucrats may be observed pointedly detaching themselves from the outgoing administration as they jockey for position and status in the new administration.

If we look at the organizational charts the foreign policy machine appears to be a highly rationalized hierarchy. Each office has a particular place in the political structure and each officer performs the duties and tasks assigned to him by statute and administrative rules. If we look at the policy process, however, we perceive a community of policy-makers rather than a schematic hierarchy. Within this community, individual policy-makers play a variety of roles, depending on the times and circumstances.

To begin with, purely personal considerations cannot be discounted in the policy process. The Secretary of the Treasury was extraordinarily influential in national security decisions in the Eisenhower Administration because of President Eisenhower's implicit confidence in the opinions of George Humphrey. The Attorney General was unusually powerful in the Kennedy Administration not only because Robert Kennedy was able but because he was the President's brother. Just as personal relations between the President and his Secretary of State color their administration of foreign affairs, so also does the relationship between the Secretary of State and his principal officers shape the policy process and affect the policy output. In the Eisenhower Administration, Secretary Herter played a very different role from that of Secretary Dulles partly because Herter never enjoyed the close relationship which Dulles established with the President and partly because Herter was more inclined to seek departmental counsel than Dulles, who had remarkable confidence in his own judgment.

Though the same title remains on the door, a succession of persons in office may play very different parts in the policy process. The Special Assistant on National Security Affairs on the White House Staff has a much more influential role in the Kennedy-Johnson community of policy-makers than his predecessor held in the Eisenhower Administration. For personal as well as situational reasons, the representative to the United Nations in the Truman Administration played a much less constructive role in American foreign policy than his successors in the Eisenhower, Kennedy, and Johnson Administrations. Different people holding the same office may act quite differently, partly because the passing of time inevitably changes the situation, but also because they are different persons who operate differently and work for and with different persons.

In the community of policy-makers, personal relations involve multiple interactions. The style of an administration is determined largely by the group dynamics that exist within the President's chosen community of policy-makers. In foreign policy, the relationship between the President and the Secretary of State is important, but also important are the President's relations with the Secretary of Defense, the Director of the Budget, and the representative to the United Nations, as well as the personal relations of these men with one another and with all other members in the policy community. Hence, when an incoming President goes about selecting the principal officers of his administration, he tries to pick an all-star cast ("highly qualified"—"the best men available") but he must also be sure to assemble a company of players that can perform well together. Thus personal as well as partisan and professional considerations influence the President's selection of policy-makers.

The community of policy-makers suggests a much more personal approach to policy-making than that indicated in the *United States Government Organization Manual*. The *Manual* describes the organization and activities of each major unit in the federal government according to legal and official prescription. A casual visitor, wandering through the maze of corridors in the State Department (or the Pentagon), can observe all the *Manual* titles on the office doors. But the title on the door does not really tell who runs the office or what business actually is carried on in the office. A specific position in the departmental organization may be upgraded and given a new title to attract a particular person. One of the first requests from the Eisenhower Administration to Congress was for authorization to create a new position to signify the Administration's intention of reorganizing the State Department. The high rank was crucial in recruiting a certain businessman to take on the impossible task. An especially high-sounding title may cover up a low-grade role in foreign policy for a person representing influential interests in domestic politics—i.e., women, Negroes, and labor.

The community of policy-makers is a flexible concept. Even a conservative listing of principal officers in the major units engaged in foreign policy would include at least several hundred key positions in the executive branch. But such a large number of persons is never called together in a single group. The regular attendants at a National Security Council meeting, even during the Eisenhower Administration, which was most respectful toward the official hierarchy and most sensitive to coordinated operations, might number 30 to 50 persons—with invitations issued appropriate to the agenda under consideration.

The agenda under consideration is usually the clue to the community of policy-makers. If the agenda involves global strategy, then only the top policy officers may meet with the President. If the critical issues involve military considerations, the Chairman of the Joint Chiefs of Staff may bring with him a sizeable representation from the armed services. If the problem calls for financing, the Secretary of the Treasury and the Director of the Budget may bring in a battery of fiscal experts from their respective agencies. If, on the other hand, the issue is more narrowly focused—for example, whether the United States should shift its emphasis from military support of the Shah to economic aid for the people of Iran—then the Middle East specialists and the desk officer for Iran may join in the deliberations even though they would normally be rather far down in the hierarchy of decision-makers. In short, the community of policy-makers is a functional concept; identification of membership depends on functional roles in the policy process rather than status in the administrative hierarchy.

It is therefore not realistic to view the decision-making process in foreign policy within the strictly hierarchical pattern of the principal officers in the major executive agencies. As one old hand at the State Department put it (he should know because he was once Assistant Secretary of State, Under Secretary of State, and Secretary of State), "policy bubbles up as much as it trickles down." Ideas may move through official channels or they may be circulated through informal personal communications. In the Department of State, for example, programs are often conceived by foreign service officers in the field, or first discussed at the country desks; and high-level decisions are sometimes substantially reshaped in the programming decisions made by bureaucrats near the bottom of the totem pole.

Normally the President assumes the initiative in foreign policy, but Congress has a continuing interest and actively participates at many points in the decision-making process. Congress expects to be fully informed by the Administration and to be brought into the actual process of decision-making at an early stage. Hence, the President and his executive agencies are in constant communication with the congressional leadership and with the committees particularly charged with national defense and foreign policy. Congress may freely debate any aspect of foreign policy; although it rarely takes an adverse stand against a declared executive policy, individual members feel free to criticize and oppose. As a way of underscoring its independent role, Congress may want to take additional action to make legitimate the official policy with which it may be in full accord. On the other hand, as a means of emphasizing national unity, the President may seek a special enabling act or congressional resolution expressing approval of a specific or general course of action, even though he may be constitutionally free to act on his own. President Eisenhower, for example, sought such congressional approval for his Middle East Doctrine; President Kennedy asked for congressional endorsement in his handling of the Berlin crisis of 1961; and President Johnson asked Congress' support for any actions he might have to take if the North Vietnamese and Chinese reacted to the American air attacks against North Vietnamese PT Boats in the summer of 1964.

Not all members of Congress and not all members of a committee dealing with foreign affairs are equally interested or equally influential in matters of foreign policy. The President and his principal officers recognize and court those senators and representatives who have special knowledge and are actively interested, as well as those who hold positions of control in the congressional organization. As in the executive community of policy-makers, the measure of influence is not necessarily one of position or seniority. Senator Alexander Wiley as Chairman of the Senate Committee on Foreign Relations for the first two years of the Eisenhower Administration never attained the constructive role in foreign policy achieved by his predecessor, Senator Walter George, or his successor, Senator J. W. Fulbright.

The President himself sets the style of executive-legislative relations in foreign policy. President Eisenhower's approach to Congress was respectfully institutional; he thought it more orderly to work through the congressional leadership than through individual senators and representatives. On the other hand, Presidents Kennedy and Johnson, who arrived at the White House via Capitol Hill, retained and frequently used many of their personal contacts in Congress. Whatever his personal or partisan preference, however, the President has to deal at least formally with the power structure of Congress and on a bipartisan basis.

There are different kinds of authority and influence in the congressional organization just as there are an administrative hierarchy and a pecking order within the executive community of policy-makers. On any major policy issue, the President usually finds it politic to consult first with the top ranking *partisan leadership*—the Speaker of the House, the majority and minority floor leaders in House and Senate, and other party officers in both houses. He is also expected to consult with and fully inform the *policy leadership*—the chairmen and ranking minority members of the committees that have principal jurisdiction over foreign policy: the Senate Committee on Foreign Relations, the House Committee on Foreign Affairs, the Senate and House Committees on the Armed Services, and the Senate and House Committees on Appropriations. Other committees may share in specific foreign policy legislation, Agricultural or Banking and Currency, for example, or even the Judiciary Committees, which were very important in the long drawn-out controversy during the Eisenhower Administration over the Bricker Amendment.

Congressional relations at the operational level usually involve working directly with the *policy* specialists on the sub-committees. In terms of foreign policy, the key persons on the Appropriations Committees of House and Senate are the members of the sub-committees (especially the chairmen) charged with specific consideration of appropriations for the State Department, the Defense Department, and Foreign Operations. The sub-committees of the Senate Committee on Foreign Relations and the House Committee on Foreign Affairs, which correspond to the geographical and functional bureaus in the State Department, maintain close working relations with their counterparts in the administration. Thus the sub-committee on Europe (House or Senate) works directly with the Department's Bureau on European Affairs, and the sub-committee on International Organization works with the Bureau on International Organization. Because committee assignments carry over from one session to another, some congressmen tend to make a career of policy specialization in the legislative process, and by virtue of their specialized competence enter the community of executive-legislative policy-makers whenever their particular area of specialization happens to appear on the policy agenda.

Continuity and consistency are especially important in foreign policy, since commitments and programs involve other nations. A commitment broken or a program discontinued could have serious repercussions in international relations. Hence, an outgoing President is likely to move experienced career personnel into the administrative hierarchy as political executives turn in their resignations immediately prior to the transfer of power at the White House. Every administration finds it useful to bring some seasoned foreign service officers into the community of policy makers, men like Robert Murphy, Charles Bohlen, Llewellyn Thompson, and Alexis Johnson. For the most part, the incoming President seeks and finds his principal officers within his own party, but the bipartisan character of foreign policy makes it possible, and desirable, for him to include among his appointees qualified persons from the other party. Thus a number of distinguished names recur in the succession of administrations, John Foster Dulles, Averill Harriman, Dean Rusk, Allen Dulles, Walter Bedell Smith, Douglas Dillon, Christian Herter, Henry Cabot Lodge, and others.

In appraising the varying roles of individual policy-makers, we must first scrutinize interpersonal relations within the community of policy-makers. Even so, we must keep in mind that official duties and responsibilities within the institutional hierarchy may be more enduring in the over-all process. On November 22, 1963, President Johnson was able to count immediately on the complete loyalty of President Kennedy's official associates. Personal considerations were irrelevant in the context of national and international crisis. It was crucial not only for the nation but also for the whole world to know that the American presidency survived intact, despite the death of its great President. Word went out at once to all the embassies in Washington and to all our own diplomatic posts overseas that the succession of President Johnson would mean no change in American foreign policy. The transition from President Kennedy to President Johnson took place under tragic circumstances but in an orderly manner within the constitutional and institutional setting.

The Decisions: Strategy and Output

The development of this chapter has been based on the assumption that foreign policy in general has a rational basis and that the community of policy-makers makes a conscious effort to act rationally. (This is not to say that all governmental decisions are rational!) Within this context the totality of American foreign policy can be understood and appraised in terms of (a) the national purpose and long range goals; (b) the over-all guidelines for operations and programs which are intended to advance us toward our professed objectives; (c) the multiplicity of decisions for practical action in specific situations which often involve immediate goals.[32]

In terms of strategy, the first step in American foreign policy is to analyze our position in the external environment and to determine on a global basis as well as regionally and country by country our capacity to influence international politics. The second step is to take stock of our domestic situation, to determine where we want to go, and to set up some schedule of priorities to that end. The third step is to apprehend the plural interests within our society, and establish some criteria whereby we decide in what manner and to what extent these can and should be accommodated within the national interests. The fourth step is to fuse ideas into plans and plans into programs of action to advance our national interests in the international community. The fifth step is to organize diverse courses of action for varied situations in the external environment and at the same time to coordinate our operations abroad within guide lines that lead toward our established goals. The sixth step, and the most difficult, is to keep us moving in the direction we want to go, with firmness of purpose and faith in our goals, even though sometimes immediate steps might temporarily move us away from them. This grand strategy calls for creative imagination as well as extraordinary political perception on the part of our top policy-makers; it requires the diplomatic skills, specialized intelligence, and world-wide experience of our foreign service together with the managerial and technical competence of the bureaucrats in many agencies. But most of all it depends on the understanding and staying power of the American people. In a democratic society, the consent of the governed controls the ultimate values in the policy process.

The broad outlines of American foreign policy have not changed since the founding of the Republic. To provide for the common defense, to promote the general welfare, and to secure the blessings of liberty—these still represent the national purpose and long-range goals of the American people. But the over-all guidelines for operations and programs today must be made within the modern world. Since World War II, these guidelines have remained fairly consistent, although the impact of events at home and abroad have provoked some shifts of emphasis.

---

[32] For two recent discussions of the grand strategy of American foreign policy see Robert R. Bowie, *Shaping the Future* (New York: Columbia University Press, 1964); and Rostow, *View from the Seventh Floor*. Professor Bowie and Professor Rostow have both served as Chairman of the State Department's Policy Planning Staff.

(1) *We want to remain a democratic nation in a free world.* To this end: (a) we have tried to strengthen the political and cultural ties between us and the countries of Western Europe; (b) we have set up a North Atlantic military alliance to defend our common interests against aggression; (c) we have tried to encourage new patterns of trade and economic association among the countries of Western Europe, between them and us, and between the entire Atlantic community and the rest of the world.

(2) *We are determined to contain communism and to resist communist aggression any place in the world.* To this end: (a) we have invested in a national defense system second to none in the world, with maximum capability to deter nuclear war as well as to a full spectrum of conventional weaponry for all degrees of limited war; (b) we have entered into a series of mutual defense agreements with some 40 different countries and have established military installations in strategic places all over the world; (c) we have offered both military assistance and economic support to nations everywhere in the world who need help in strengthening their own defenses and in resisting communist aggression from without or infiltration within; (d) we have set up and supported various information, education, and propaganda programs to resist subversion of the minds of men.

(3) *We want to defend the principle of private property and the practices of private enterprise in the modern world.* To this end: (a) we have offered, in varying degrees, leadership, partnership, and assistance to speed the modernization of countries in Latin America, Africa, Asia, and the Middle East; (b) we have encouraged long-term programs of political socialization and economic development in the newly independent nations and offered them our immediate aid with capital investments and technological know-how; (c) we have tried to strengthen the Alliance for Progress between the industrial nations and the less developed nations in the western hemisphere; (d) we have tried to help create new patterns of partnership and assistance between the more advanced European powers and nations recently emerging from colonialism.

(4) *We want to build a new and peaceful international order.* To this end: (a) we have joined in the work of the United Nations and supported its many different activities; (b) we have tried to strengthen and develop regional organizations for mutual defense to supplement national devices of self-help; (c) we have continuously and patiently negotiated for international agreement on limitation, reduction, and control of armaments, especially the weapons of nuclear war.

When President Johnson delivered his 1965 State of the Union message to a joint session of Congress, he recognized that "today the State of the Union depends, in large measure, upon the state of the world." He reminded us all—for he spoke to a nation-wide audience on television as well as in person to Congress—that "Our concern and interest, compassion and vigilance, extend to every corner of a torn and troubled world. . . . We know that history is ours to make. And if there is great danger, there is now also the excitement of great expectations."

CHAPTER SIXTEEN

The American
Political System in Perspective

What should this book have done for you? Our hope may

be simply put—that this book has contributed to a greater un-

derstanding of how American politics works. When you become

more directly involved in politics, we would be horrified to think

you might complain that your college reading was "good in

theory" but "inapplicable in practice." If theories fail to explain actual practices, they are simply bad theories.

If we were to list everything we hope you have learned from this book, we would have to repeat every generalization we have offered in the preceding fifteen chapters. In considering policy outputs of the American system, we have tried to re-emphasize some of the more basic conclusions and to show how they are directly related to policy. But education is not just a matter of gaining new understandings; it is also a process of "unlearning" or getting rid of false conceptions. So we shall conclude by listing a few of the misconceptions about politics that are particularly widespread and that we trust this book has helped to clear away.

"Politics Is Dirty"

This is a persistent and puzzling myth. Since the only way people can hope to influence public policy is through the pursuit and exercise of power—that is, through *politics*—we might assume that politics would be as respected as democracy itself. Widespread suspicion of politics and politicians is even more puzzling when we remember that public officials seem, in fact, to maintain higher standards than are found in most areas of private life.

And yet the distrust persists. Apparently one reason is that politicians must make decisions of great importance to many people, and someone is always disappointed by every decision. The losers often respond to their disappointment by claiming that they got a "dirty deal." A second reason is that politics necessarily involves compromise, and it is the politicians who must make the compromises that enable people to live peaceably together. The rest of us can afford the luxury of inflexible principles and the feelings of superiority that go with them. Third, the press generally encourages an anti-political viewpoint; the occasional crooked politician receives so much publicity that he seems typical.

Finally, Americans appear to have a double standard of morals, condemning behavior in politicians that they take for granted in their own lives. Newspaper headlines indict the public official who buys a mink coat at a wholesale price, but many of the most indignant private citizens follow the same practice. We assume that the son of a business executive, even though he may be incompetent, will be given a good job in his father's organization, but we are incensed when newspaper columnists uncover a public official's attempt to do as much for his son. In business this is regarded as "family loyalty"; in politics it is labeled "nepotism." A Sherman Adams or a Bobby Baker suffers near disgrace in public life for the very "wheeling and dealing" that we applaud on the part of the enterprising businessman. True, we have a right to expect higher standards of government officials, but we should at least be aware of the sacrifices we expect of them.

"Government Is a Great, Impersonal 'It'"

All our top policy-makers in the national government are either elected by the people or appointed by the President. Even so, many citizens regard the government almost as if decisions were made by self-appointed aliens or by a set of poorly constructed "electric brains." To talk about the government as "we" would be somewhat unrealistic, but hardly more so than for students at the University of Michigan to say "we" are going to play the University of California in football. At least we elect our political representatives.

In their tendency to depersonalize government into "it," many Americans reflect their sense of alienation from government and politics. But to regard government as something alien is to introduce an irrational factor in to our political decision-making. Like any other organization, our government is made up of human beings; it differs from other organizations in that every citizen can have a part in selecting its leaders. Nevertheless, some readers find nothing strange in a newspaper editorial that urges the government to stop some activity like hydroelectric power development and "turn it back to the people." Yet this line of argument involves illogical assumptions—namely, that government officials (who are chosen by the voters) represent interests alien to those of the people, whereas private utility executives (who are not chosen by the voters) represent interests identical with those of the people. We can work out rational arguments on both sides of questions of this sort, but not in these terms. If government is not "we," the Commonwealth and Southern Electric Company is even less so.

"The National Government Is the Worst of All"

The responsible public officials who make up this ominous "it" seem to be most foreboding at the level of the national government. A nationwide organization like the United States Steel Corporation is "the industrial family that serves America" and the AFL-CIO is made up of "the nation's workers," but our national government is "the Washington bureaucracy." Many Americans seem to have this impression: All politics is dubious, but local government is best, state government is second best, and national government is the worst of all.

In this book we have been primarily concerned with national government, but in discussing federalism we gained some insight into the comparative qualities of the national and state governments. The old Jeffersonian idea that local government would be the most efficient, honest, and responsive to broad public needs seems to be an exact reversal of the facts of modern political life. The facts support a different conclusion. Inefficiency, dishonesty, and minority domination are found most often at the local level; conditions improve at the state level; and they are at their best at the national level.

The persistence of the old attitude is not easy to explain; perhaps it is simply a case of the survival, after the facts have changed, of what may once have been good theory. Whatever the situation may have been in Jefferson's time, our key problems today are national or international in scope, and the most exciting government decisions are made in Washington. As a result, able politicians find a greater challenge and opportunity there than in county offices, and the press and general public follow decisions at the national level more closely. Moreover, the constituencies of national officials are broader and therefore serve to neutralize narrow special interests. In short, the pressures of politics encourage a more statesmanlike performance from governors than from city councilmen, and from presidents than from governors.

"A Big Government with an Expanding Budget Is Ruinous"

Once a year, the American government engages in "the Spring rite of raising the national debt limit." [1] The annual ceremony always includes pronouncements of ultimate doom if the federal budget is not returned to the frugal practices of the pioneer American family.

This tendency to think of the national debt as similar to the indebtedness of a private family is highly misleading. To begin with, even the private citizen prospers by borrowing money and expanding his activities, not by saving string and staying out of debt. Even so, the average family must carefully keep its expenditures below its income if it is to remain solvent.

But business enterprises and governments are in a quite different position. In order to expand their activities, they must increase their budgets and, therefore,

---

[1] "T.R.B. from Washington," *The New Republic*, June 6, 1964.

"*We can't burden our children with deficit spending.*"

Drawing by Herblock. From *Straight Herblock* (New York: Simon & Schuster, 1964).

their debts as represented by stocks and bonds. This viewpoint is generally accepted for business corporations but not for governments. Even a leading newspaper like the *New York Herald-Tribune* occasionally denies the "supposed parallel between federal debt and corporate borrowing for investment." The *Tribune's* assumption is that corporate debts are "self-liquidating," whereas "government debts are simply a costly deferral of the payment of current bills." T. R. B., whose insights on the American scene enliven *The New Republic* every week, has engaged in a running attack on the "silly myth" that the national budget should not grow as the nation grows. "The AT&T and GM are never going to pay off their debt; not, that is, unless they go bankrupt. The Treasury is never going to pay off its debt; not, that is, unless it wants to ruin us." [2] His argument is that government investment in good roads, better schools, and TVA's is as wise as the expansion of a big corporation. Part of this investment is self-liquidating and part is not; part of it is money the government owes itself; about two-thirds of it represents actual government debt held by the public. When one stops to think in terms of the national interest, why is an expenditure of money and manpower for stronger deodorants a contribution to the national well-being while an expenditure for better schools or highways is a liability?

The alleged "burden" of the federal debt in recent years has decreased, not increased, if it is compared to the size of the population, the national income, or the Gross National Product. But while Americans admire growth in all other areas of activity, they seem peculiarly unable to recognize that an expanding nation requires expanding governmental activities.

"The Founding Fathers Were 'Above Politics'"

Some patriotic organizations seem to have the notion that schools can produce good Americans only if they present a "depoliticized" picture of our first great politicians. Perhaps a somewhat romanticized version must be presented at the secondary level, but to give students a false picture of democratic government is misguided patriotism. Countless Americans still have an image of George Washington, Thomas Jefferson, Alexander Hamilton, James Madison, Patrick Henry, and others marching forward in perfect unison, shoulder to shoulder, into the sunrise. Pictured as being above petty politics, these leaders are supposed to have been followed by all right-thinking men in adopting the Constitution (which Henry called "the most fatal possible plan for the enslavement of a free people"!) and to have launched the ship of state on calm waters without bickering over mere political differences.

In the real political world, on the other hand, different experiences and conflicting interests inevitably lead even the best-intentioned men to rational (and irrational) disagreements. Most of our Founding Fathers were great politicians. They were quite capable of expressing their disagreements in clear-cut terms and of throwing themselves into power struggles as lively as any that occur today.

---

[2] *The New Republic*, June 6, 1964. Also see the issues of January 18, 1964; February 8, 1964; November 21, 1964.

Only by understanding the special interests, the conflicting ideas, and the political strategy of the Founding Fathers can we appreciate them as real human beings—and then we can apply that understanding and appreciation to a consideration of contemporary politics.

The tragedy of the "non-political" view is that it sacrifices accuracy for the sake of patriotism, and is still a poor means of molding loyal citizens. The idea that a statesman should be "above politics" is as ridiculous as the notion that the Pope or the Archbishop of Canterbury should be "above religion." But the false image of the Foundings Fathers, coupled with the great respect they enjoy, leads to disillusionment when the citizen of today evaluates the performance of current officeholders and discovers that they are "mere politicians."

"The American Way Is the Only Democratic Way"

Any thinking person should be able to detect blind provincialism in political discussions, and to separate love of country from an irrational rejection of everything strange or new. Whether unfamiliar institutions deserve to be rejected or not, they should at least be evaluated on intellectually defensible grounds. Such practices as unitary government (instead of federalism), parliamentary supremacy (instead of separation of powers), multi-party politics (instead of the two-party system), and socialism (instead of capitalism), for example, may be "un-American" and even undesirable without being undemocratic.

The reverse side of this same coin, which pictures everything American as essential to democracy, is equally counterfeit. Our rulers are responsive enough to the desires of the ruled for our government to be classified as a democracy; so we can plausibly conclude that none of our key institutions is absolutely incompatible with democracy. But to conclude from this that every one of our institutions is *essential* to democracy is shabby logic. Separation of powers, and checks and balances, for example, were designed by men who were alarmed at the prospect of popular control over policy. And we have achieved a remarkable degree of democracy despite these barriers, not because of them. To claim that such institutions as these were designed in the interest of popular control is to misunderstand separation of powers and checks and balances, and to misinterpret the men who helped create them.

"The Individual Doesn't Count"

In a world of big business, big labor, and big government—where political analysis deals with groups like political parties, pressure groups, Congress, the administration, and the Supreme Court—the individual sometimes seems to have been dropped out of the picture. The individual's attitudes and interests are a product of the group affiliations and influences he has experienced since birth. Every one of these groups, however, is created out of the relations between individuals; take away the individuals and you have no groups—and no politics. Indeed, the welfare of individuals rather than of fatherland, class, or party holds the central place in democratic ideology. Human beings, not the groups into which they form, are the primary value of democratic politics.

An individual leader can, moreover, play a great role in shaping political events. If someone like Henry Luce, at the head of a publishing empire including *Time, Life, Sports Illustrated*, and *Fortune*, dedicates himself to a cause, his influence may be enough to tip the scales toward success or defeat. An individual politician like the great Republican progressive, George Norris of Nebraska, may wage an unrelenting campaign for a program like the Tennessee Valley Authority and see it through to victory. People of this sort work through and upon groups, but it is their individual personalities that make the indelible impression.

What of the ordinary citizen, let's say a bricklayer? How much does he count as an individual? True, he may vote, but his vote is only one among thousands or millions; he may write a letter to his congressman or his newspaper, but again it is only one among hundreds or thousands. How can he make a greater impression on politics? If he tries to cast several ballots in a single election, he may find himself in jail; if he writes too many letters, he will be written off as a "crackpot." But he need not remain a voiceless member of the "lonely crowd." If he wants to increase his influence, he can do so by working through various groups—by joining and actively participating in a union or party organization, for example. As our study of political parties suggested, local party organizations possess considerable power, and their positions of leadership are surprisingly open to ambitious citizens. Election studies have shown, in addition, that informal opinion-leaders exist at every level of society. Without commanding any official status, the politically interested and articulate citizen may not only count as an individual, but he may also assume a role of political leadership for those around him.

The bricklayer's influence may never compare with that of a Luce or a Norris, but it counts for just as much in the polling booth. And outside the polling booth, he can increase his influence through formal and informal contacts with others.

" 'Tyranny of the Majority' Is a Threat to Freedom"

This is an old and sufficiently respectable notion to be held by many college graduates. First conceived as an argument against democracy itself, the threat of majority tyranny has served as an effective weapon in opposing every extension of popular power, from universal suffrage to stronger political parties.[3] When it is examined in the light of actual experience in democracies, however, the threat disappears.

First, just what does the term mean? *Tyranny* is the imposition by rulers of severe deprivations upon those ruled, combined with the denial of any legal way (such as propaganda and election efforts) to eliminate those deprivations. When a citizen pays his taxes, is required to drive within fixed speed limits, or is forbidden to engage in specified business practices, he may feel a sense of deprivation. But we do not regard him as a victim of tyranny, because he is neither treated with capricious severity nor denied an opportunity to try to change the law.

The interests and viewpoints of Americans are extremely diverse—so diverse

---

[3] The alleged threat of tyranny is not, of course, the only argument against such extensions of popular power, as the discussion in Chapter 6 indicates.

that a majority cannot be united behind any narrowly tyrannical program. A majority coalition can be created only by a broad program representing compromises among the aims of countless minority groups. With our overlapping group memberships and with our general commitment to popular freedom, no tyrannical policy can win majority endorsement. In the United States, truly tyrannical schemes have been heard only from the "lunatic fringe."

Perhaps a better way of dispelling fears of majority tyranny is to point out that, even for moderate policies, we do not in practice find majority rule. Elections can hardly be regarded as endorsements of a specific policy. And even if they could, only about 65 per cent of the eligible voters turn out even when voting is heaviest; if the winning party gets as much as 55 per cent of the votes, it has been endorsed by only about 38 per cent of the eligible voters. In the years between elections, lack of education, leisure, and political awareness reduces interest in politics to the point where a majority of citizens can hardly be called even observers, much less active supporters, of specific proposals. Robert A. Dahl, in a keen analysis of democratic theory, concludes:

> The real world issue has not turned out to be whether a majority, much less "the" majority, will act in a tyrannical way through democratic procedures to impose its will on a (or the) minority. Instead, the more relevant question is the extent to which various minorities in a society will frustrate the ambitions of one another with the passive acquiescence or indifference of a majority of adults or voters.[4]

Democracy serves to broaden participation in politics, or to increase, as Dahl says, "the number, size, and diversity of the minorities whose preferences will influence the outcome of governmental decisions." [5] Only rarely do those actively participating make up a majority. And if we do not have *majority participation*, we need not worry about *majority tyranny*.

"Free Elections Alone Will Translate Public Opinion into Policy"

This is another idea that is older than democratic government itself. But—unlike the fear of majority tyranny—this was an assumption of those who were struggling toward democracy. In America, for example, Sam Adams dissolved his political machine after the Revolution because he saw no need for such an organization once freedom had been won. Popular suffrage seemed to promise a solution for the whole problem of making government responsible to the people. Emphasis on the vote is not misplaced, for the effectiveness of all the other means of political influence stems from the basic right to vote. When the Supreme Court's repudiation of the "white primary" gave large numbers of Negro southerners the vote in 1944, for example, they soon began to use other techniques of political pressure more effectively.

---

[4] *A Preface to Democratic Theory* (Chicago: The University of Chicago Press, 1956), p. 133.
[5] *Ibid.*

For the individual citizen to cast his vote is not enough in itself, however, because individual votes are not automatically translated into public policy. If millions of Americans voted as so many separate individuals, the results would be almost meaningless. Hundreds of candidates would receive votes, and pluralities as high as 10 per cent would be unusual; when the winners were announced, there would be no way of judging what policies had been endorsed. To give meaning to the vote, intermediary organizations—pressure groups and political parties—standing between the citizen and the government, have proved necessary in every democracy. Political parties and pressure groups serve a "middleman" function in identifying popular interests and selecting leaders. These agencies are mentioned nowhere in the written Constitution, but they are as much a part of American politics as the Congress, the President, or the Supreme Court.

"Laws Are Conceived in the Legislature"

This is a belief that is occasionally found among people unacquainted with politics, but it seldom survives even a casual study of government. In order to simplify the subject matter of politics—and to keep it noncontroversial—people some-times fail to consider the complex problems that cannot be understood by a literal reading of the Constitution. To explain the extra-constitutional role played in legislation by pressure groups, political parties, and the President, for example, is not easy. No one can deny that the Constitution says "all legislative Powers herein granted shall be vested in a Congress of the United States." So the simplest approach is to try to get across the idea that Congress legislates, the President executes, and the Supreme Court adjudicates—and let it go at that.

Even the popular press has gone beyond this simple interpretation, and any careful newspaper reader discovers that policy-making is shared by many who are not congressmen. Official action in Congress is the most important part of legisla-tion, but the policy inputs of interested groups in and out of the government help shape policy before, during, and after the congressional drama.

"Policies Are Dictated by Pressure Groups"

As an extreme reaction to their discovery of the influence of private groups on legislation, some people decide that policies are dictated by the ruthless application of pressure, with no regard for the public interest. And isolated incidents can be found to support this cynical view. *The Reporter* magazine revealed such an episode in connection with a tariff bill during the Eisenhower Administration. The "chief of the high-tariff lobby" was reported to have furnished congressmen with copies of a bill that would have made it harder to import foreign goods. The lobbyist had left blanks in one section of the bill so that each official sponsor could fill in the names of the products made in his constituency. Sixteen repre-sentatives introduced basically similar versions of the measure. The shocking revelation was that four congressmen introduced the measure exactly as it had been given to them, without even bothering to fill in the blanks.[6]

---

[6] See "Theirs Not to Reason Why," *The Reporter*, July 6, 1954, p. 2.

Sorry performances of this sort by a few congressmen who do not even read the bills they introduce lead some observers to assume that the whole congressional process is an empty show, that the public interest is always ignored, and that congressmen are simply puppets controlled by powerful lobbyists. A more balanced view, however, takes into account the checks on narrow minority control. First, political parties are based on a broad collection of interests, and the parties do exert considerable influence on their members in Congress. Second, every congressman knows that if he favors narrow minorities he may well be defeated in the next election. Third, the President, as a party leader with a national constituency, also exerts pressure on congressmen, and most presidents have a broad view of the national interest. Fourth, the solidarity of any pressure group is reduced by overlapping membership in other organizations. Finally, our widespread commitment to the basic values of the "American Creed" puts a check on any pressure group that tries to ride roughshod over the interests of others. If a pressure-group spokesman violates our concept of "fair play," legislators and administrators may be alienated rather than influenced, opposing groups may gain new adherents, members of the pressure group itself may react against their spokesmen, and new opposition organizations may be created.

"Policy Reflects Consensus"

At the other extreme, some people assume that official policy always reflects consensus or general agreement. Margaret Mead, the popular anthropologist, found that this assumption was quite accurate in the rigidly traditional Balinese civilization. She says every issue there is resolved simply by asking, "What is the place of this new proposal in our pattern of decreed and traditional behavior?" Americans, however, who become emotionally involved in public issues, find it difficult to imagine "a society in which issues as vital as migration or war are settled as formally, from the standpoint of public opinion, as is the date of Thanksgiving Day." [7] Certainly none of the policies we have discussed in preceding chapters reflected consensus. Policy in the United States represents the victory of one coalition of interests over another, with the losers protesting so loudly that no one can doubt their displeasure.

Balinese differ from Americans not in having an accepted tradition but in having a tradition that produces unquestioned answers to specific problems. Their tradition answers questions; ours provides a method for seeking answers. Any stable society requires wide acceptance of basic political procedures, and democratic government becomes impossible unless most of the losers as well as the winners are willing to accept policies determined by "consent of the governed." But this is quite different from *policy* by consensus. All Americans do not agree on even such underlying elements of our politics as the rules of Congress or the powers of the national government. What we *agree* on is, essentially, a method of governing in which policies reflect widespread interests without

---

[7] "Public Opinion Mechanisms Among Primitive Peoples," *Public Opinion Quarterly*, I (July, 1937), p. 7.

destroying the right to *disagree*. This is radically different from the idea that specific policies reflect consensus.

People often talk about "government by consensus" as if it existed, when they really mean it is an ideal they regard as desirable. Various devices that block or delay the achievement of policies that command broad support—devices like the seniority system in Congress or the filibuster in the Senate—are thus defended on the ground that they promote the ideal of government by consensus. But this is the pursuit of a will-o'-the-wisp. A device like the filibuster gives the minority a veto over policy; it does not give us consensus. When a majority of those participating in politics are prevented from enacting a policy they want, what we actually have is minority control over policy.[8]

Minority control is certainly not consensus, although many people seem to assume that it is. If the majority is prevented from enacting a new policy, these observers point out that the existence of opposition proves the lack of consensus —and the desirability of postponing the new policy. What they fail to see is that a decision to continue an old policy is just as binding—just as much an act of government—as a decision to modify that policy. If a minority keeps an old policy in effect when a majority wants to change it, the majority is forced to accept the preference of the minority. This is no less frustrating for the majority than the requirement of observing the new policy would be for the minority. The question is not how to get consensus, but who is going to be frustrated—the majority or the minority? The seniority system and the filibuster may be justified on the grounds that they give strategic minorities a negative control over policy, and that they make extra-ordinary majorities necessary to change policy; but with majorities frustrated in the first case, and with minorities frustrated in the second, this is hardly consensus.

"Ours Is a Government of Laws and Not of Men"

This idea, often heard during the American Revolution, has inspired the struggle for responsible government everywhere. It seems to be a misconception only if it is meant in a literal sense. In both Europe and America, those who fought for democratic government resented the capricious and arbitrary power of rulers, from kings to local magistrates. Like any propagandists engaged in a serious political struggle, the American revolutionists exaggerated both the evils they were trying to change—the purely personal nature of irresponsible decisions—and the improvements they could offer—the impersonality of government under law. Without eliminating personal favoritism or malice entirely, democracy has greatly reduced the exercise of personal caprice by limiting public officials to known procedures, rules, and punishments. So in a sense we have achieved what would have been regarded in the age of monarchy as something close to "a government of laws and not of men."

---

[8] As we have mentioned earlier in this chapter, and elsewhere, an absolute majority of the total adult population never participates actively in politics. When we talk about "majority control," then, it should be understood that we mean control by a majority of those actively participating.

To carry this concept to the extreme point of a literal belief in a government of laws and not of men, however, becomes both false and dangerous. Our government is made up of men, and our Constitution and laws are made, applied, and interpreted by men. This obvious truth is seldom overlooked so far as the Congress, the President, and current laws are concerned. But some people tend almost to deify the Framing Fathers and, to a lesser extent, the Supreme Court. The Framing Fathers were real, live politicians rather than so many reincarnations of Moses; they met in Philadelphia rather than on Mount Sinai; and they fought out the provisions of the document among themselves rather than waiting for divine revelation. (Franklin's suggestion that they open each session with a prayer was voted down because they had no funds to pay a parson.) Similarly, the more discerning and candid Supreme Court justices themselves have reminded us that "judges do and must legislate." Constitutions and laws are not self-enforcing. The Supreme Court offers our nearest approximation to unbiased interpretation, but it speaks not with the voice of the Constitution but with the often inharmonious voices of nine justices. If the law were self-evident, if the Court's problems were simply those of nine technical experts, we would never get five-to-four decisions.

Literal belief in a government of laws and not of men is dangerous because it leads either to blindness or to disillusionment. Anyone who thinks that judicial decisions are or should be impersonal products of "the Court," for example, must either ignore split decisions or else conclude that some of the justices have lost their reasoning powers or have become scoundrels. A realistic appraisal of the Court requires an awareness that people differ on political problems and that political decisions must be made by human beings. By giving more men a voice in making laws and establishing procedures for their enforcement and interpretation, we have gone far toward insuring "a government of laws [reflecting popular preferences] and not of [a few irresponsible] men."

"Government Is Neutral"

A final misconception entertained by a great many Americans is the idea that government is neutral. Again, this is a tendency to confuse preferences with realities. It might be nice if the government really were neutral, but the notion that government is neutral simply does not fit the facts.

A useful analytical approach is to ask of any governmental arrangement or proposal: In terms of its *effect* rather than of its declared purpose, what is its function? Then ask: Who gets—or feels—hurt by such a function, and who is—or feels—benefited? Going further, you may use your conclusions to predict the political behavior of individuals or groups in advance. Advance knowledge about what's going to happen is as much fun in politics as in horse-racing: it is less expensive when the analysis proves faulty, and more exhilarating when the analysis proves correct. Right or wrong, the habit of prediction at least gives the observer a sense of contact with the events that are shaping the future.

Let's look at a seemingly dry and neutral feature of government—the system of representation in Congress. Using the approach we have suggested, you can easily discover from your general reading that political districting in America has long been arranged to "over-represent" rural areas. This is certainly not a neutral arrangement. Among other things, it gives great weight in Congress to the needs of farmers. If you also know that congressmen from rural areas tend to be conservative, you can conclude that the present system of representation similarly functions to "over-represent" the interests of larger businesses and allied groups.

The functions of the system of representation thus automatically benefit farmers and—in a less obvious fashion—conservative business interests. In more general terms, this feature of congressional representation is sometimes decribed as protecting "the minority." But "the minority" is an even more elusive term than "the majority." There are many different and conflicting minority interests, and not all of them are benefited by the system of representation. The ones that are benefited are those that dominate under-populated political districts. Minorities within these districts, even though they are allied with majorities in "under-represented" areas, find the districting system highly "dysfunctional." Negroes, migrant workers, tenant farmers, and sharecroppers, for example, are minorities within the over-represented areas who are handicapped rather than helped by the system. They have more political interests in common with the factory workers, coal miners, and general wage-earners from under-represented urban districts than with farm or mine owners in their own districts.

If you decide to try your hand at predicting future events, you will have to keep abreast of trends too recent to have been described in your college courses. Some books still say, for example, that equal representation of the states in the Senate guarantees a majority from rural areas in that body. This was actually true for so long that many political scientists still talk about the "rural" Senate and the more nearly "urban" House. In fact, however, the national census revealed as early as 1950 that only eighteen states had rural majorities, which means that almost two-thirds of the senators were elected by predominantly urban constituencies. On the other hand, the state legislatures, which are still dominated by rural areas, draw up the districts from which members of the House are chosen, and they give more House seats to rural districts. As a result, the urban-rural relationship of the two houses has actually been reversed, and the House has become the more conservative body, checking a liberal Senate! This is exactly the opposite of what the Framing Fathers apparently intended, but new realities are not—and citizens should not be—bound by the preferences of the Framers.

In view of Supreme Court decisions requiring adherence to the "one-man—one-vote" principle in both houses of state legislatures and in the national House of Representatives, we may expect the House gradually to become less conservative. This is a prediction rather than a statement of fact. The reader might keep it in mind as one test of the validity of the analysis in this book. The facts of American politics change rapidly and constantly. Unless our analysis gives the student a way of appraising future developments, it has been of little benefit. We hope it will be of some help after the contemporary facts have drastically changed.

A Bibliographical Essay

A real study of American government may begin but it cannot end with a textbook. Without pretending to supply a complete bibliography, we shall suggest a number of books that the serious student can use to dig more deeply into American politics. Although this bibliography is selective—not even all the good books on any one problem can be included—many of the ones we do mention have fuller bibliographies on their specialized subjects. We list some classics that have stood the test of time but, since the text focuses on contemporary politics, most of the titles we suggest are fairly recent.

So many paperbound editions are now published that students can build a good personal library at low cost. Asterisks indicate volumes now available as paperbacks but, since many new titles are appearing in paperbacks every day, our listing is bound to be quickly outdated.

Part One   The Context of American Politics

Introduction to Political Science

The systematic study of government is at least as old as Aristotle's *Politics*, but political scientists still differ among themselves as to the fields, scope, and methods of political science. *American Political Science: A Profile of a Discipline* (1964), by Albert Somit and Joseph Tanenhaus, surveys current issues and trends in the profession as viewed by members of the American Political Science Association.

In *The Future of Political Science* (1963), Harold Lasswell challenges the profession to combine empirical observation with systematic analysis and offers some novel hints for significant research in political science. Carl J. Friedrich turns to the findings of psychologists, anthropologists, economists, sociologists, and historians, and tempers the traditional approach of political science with new insights and concepts in *Man and*

His Government: An Empirical Theory of Politics (1963). Karl W. Deutsch attempts to build an operational model of political systems in *The Nerves of Government: Models of Political Communication and Control* (1963).

For various approaches to the study of politics, sample some of these: Arthur F. Bentley, *The Process of Government* (1908); George E. G. Catlin, *Systematic Politics: Elementa Politica and Sociologica* (1962); Robert A. Dahl, *Modern Political Analysis* * (1963); David Easton, *The Political System: An Inquiry into the State of Political Science* (1953); Heinz Eulau, Samuel Eldersveld, and Morris Janowitz, *Political Behavior: A Reader in Theory and Research* (1956); Lewis Froman, *People and Politics* * (1962); Charles Hyneman, *The Study of Politics: The Present State of Political Science* (1959); Harold D. Lasswell and Abraham Kaplan, *Power and Society: A Framework for Political Inquiry* * (1950): Charles E. Merriam, *Systematic Politics* (1945); Austin Ranney (ed.), *Essays on the Behavioral Study of Politics* (1962); Herbert J. Storing (ed.) *Essays on the Scientific Study of Politics* (1962); Vernon Van Dyke, *Political Science: A Philosophical Analysis* (1960); T. D. Weldon, *The Vocabulary of Politics* * (1962); and Roland Young (ed.), *Approaches to the Study of Politics* * (1958).

The Cultural and Economic Context

In *The Tree of Culture* * (1955), Ralph Linton offers a good introduction to the way culture shapes politics, along with other patterns of behavior. Presentations, also available in paperback editions, of the culture concept are Ruth Benedict, *Patterns of Culture* * (1934), and Leslie A. White, *The Science of Culture* * (1949). John Dewey's *Human Nature and Conduct* (1922) is now regarded as almost a classic analysis of the impact of culture on human nature. In a different vein, stressing intimate psychological relationships rather than culture, is Charles H. Cooley, *Human Nature and the Social Order* (1902). James C. Davis has recently returned human nature to the study of political behavior with a provocative analysis, *Human Nature in Politics: The Dynamics of Political Behavior* (1963).

Explorations in Social Change (1964), edited by George K. Zollschan and Walter Hirsch, offers a variety of essays, most of them by sociologists, presenting new forms of social theory and also discussing significant changes in the American social system which condition political behavior. Gabriel Almond, *The American People and Foreign Policy* * (1950), presents a summary of many studies of the American "national character," as well as an analysis of American foreign policy in relation to that character.

General studies of the American culture by anthropologists are: Geoffrey Gorer, *The American People: A Study in National Character* * (1948); Clyde Kluckhohn, *Mirror for Man: The Relation of Anthropology to Modern Life* * (1949); and Margaret Mead, *And Keep Your Powder Dry: An Anthropologist Looks at America* (1942). Other social scientists have tackled the same problem: D. W. Brogan, *The American Character* * (1944); and David Riesman, *The Lonely Crowd: A Study of the Changing American Character* * (1953). Representatives of all the social sciences re-examine Riesman's theory in S. M. Lipset and Leo Lowenthal (eds.), *Culture and Social Character* (1961). Henry Steele Commager has collected foreign observations in *America in Perspective* * (1948). William Buchanan and Hadley Cantril discuss *How Nations See Each Other* (1953) with special emphasis on American stereotypes. Twenty foreign writers develop their "images" of America, both complimentary and critical, in *As Others See Us*, edited by Franz M. Joseph (1959). Daniel J. Boorstin discusses *The Image, or What Happened to the American Dream* (1962).

The classic study of the influence of the natural environment on American politics is Frederick Jackson Turner, *The Frontier in American History* (1920). Criticisms of the Turner thesis are presented in George Rogers Taylor (ed.), *The Turner Thesis Concerning the Role of the Frontier in American History* * (1949). Lee Benson, *Turner and Beard: American Historical Writing Reconsidered* (1960), another critical reaction, suggests new hypotheses in American history. In *The Great*

Plains (1931), W. P. Webb describes the way the unique environment of the Great Plains altered institutions brought from the eastern United States. Carl Becker, *Freedom and Responsibility in the American Way of Life* * (1955), also considers the role of the natural environment in shaping our political heritage.

Historical Statistics of the United States: Colonial Times to 1957 (1960) is the most informative single source on the characteristics of the American population. Here the Bureau of the Census presents historical data in tabular series on such various topics as consumer expenditures, social security, education, crime, armed forces, and veterans. The annual volumes of *Statistical Abstract of the United States* are a continuing source of current data on similar topics.

Oscar Handlin, *The Uprooted* * (1951) and *Race and Nationality in American Life* * (1957), are distinguished studies of the immigrant experience and the ethnic origins of the American culture. On the country's most conspicuously mistreated ethnic group, see Margaret J. Butcher, *The Negro in American Culture* * (1956), and E. Franklin Frazier, *The Negro in the U.S.* (rev., 1957). *Racial Crisis in America: Leadership in Crisis* * (1964), by Lewis Killian and Charles Grigg, reflects the experiences and research of two southern sociologists who discuss various aspects of current race relations; they conclude "there is no easy way out." M. Elaine Burgess offers us a case study of bi-racial structure in a mid-South community—"Race Relations Viewed As Power Relations"—in *Negro Leadership in a Southern City* (1962). William Brink and Louis Harris report the findings of a nation-wide survey conducted by *Newsweek* in *The Negro Revolution in America* * (1962).

Religion and Politics * (1960), edited by Peter H. Odegard, is a collection of articles on "the religious issue," especially the Roman Catholic issue in American politics. Will Herberg, *Protestant, Catholic, and Jew* * (1955), discusses the religious aspects of American society, using the sociological approach. Joseph Tussman has collected a set of significant Supreme Court decisions dealing with problems of church and state in *The Supreme Court on Church and State* * (1962). Another legal approach to the religious issue in American politics is Philip B. Kurland, *Religion and the Law: Of Church and State and the Supreme Court* (1962).

Sebastian de Grazia attempts to mirror contemporary society and offers a normative, descriptive, and highly provocative picture of the world today in *Of Time, Work, and Leisure* * (1962). The Editors of Fortune point up "urban pathology" in *The Exploding Metropolis* * (1958). Raymond Vernon reports for a team from the Graduate School of Public Administration at Harvard, investigating the economic base of the New York metropolitan region and making projections into the next generation, *Metropolis 1985* (1961).

Two general treatments with good bibliographies for pursuing class structure as a political force are Bernard Barber, *Social Stratification* (1957), and Kurt B. Mayer, *Class and Society* * (1955). Reinhard Bendix and Seymour Martin Lipset (eds.), *Class, Status and Power: A Reader in Social Stratification* (1954), offers excellent selections. Richard Centers, *The Psychology of Social Classes* (1945), focuses more directly on the impact of class on politics. Donald R. Matthews, *The Social Background of Political Decision-Makers* * (1954), includes a summary of the literature on "élite" theories as well as data on the class origins of American political leaders. C. Wright Mills has studied labor leaders, the expanding middle class, and the top decision-makers in *The New Men of Power* (1948), *White Collar* * (1951), and *The Power Elite* * (1956). Vance Packard offers a popular approach in *The Status Seekers* * (1961).

Floyd Hunter illuminates the political importance of class structure at the local level in *Community Power Structure: A Study of Decision Makers* (1953). The same author extends his interpretation of American power structure to three levels of government—community, state, and local—in *Top Leadership, U.S.A.* (1959). Robert and Helen Lynd emphasize class differences in one of the first community studies, *Middletown: A Study in Contemporary Culture* (1929). The Lynds followed up this study with *Middletown in Transition: A Study in Cultural Conflicts* (1937). Other community studies following in this tradition are: Allison Davis, Burleigh B. Gardner, and Mary R. Gardner, *Deep South: A Social Anthropological Study of Caste and Class* * (1941); John Dollard, *Cast and Class in a Southern Town* * (1949); August B. Hollingshead, *Elmtown's Youth* (1949); W. L. Warner, *et al.*, *Democracy in Jonesville* (1949); and John R. Seeley, R. A. Sim, and E. W. Loosley, *Crestwood Heights* (1956). Maurice R. Stein, *The Eclipse of Community* (1960), surveys the literature of community studies in the United States. Robert A. Dahl investigates political power in a typical American city and offers important new insights for American government and politics in *Who Governs?* * (1961). Nelson W. Polsby provides the theoretical underpinning for the same study in *Community Power and Political Theory* (1964).

L. W. Warner *et al.*, *Social Class in America* (1949), emphasizes prestige as a means of determining social position. In a light vein, Russel Lynes' *A Surfeit of Honey* (1957) appraises the newly emerging class structure. Although social scientists have tended not to analyze themselves as a subclass, Paul V. Lazarsfeld and Wagner Thielens, Jr., have done just this in *The Academic Mind: Social Scientists in a Time of Crisis* (1958).

For the extensive literature on economics and politics, a good beginning is James Madison's *Federalist* essay No. 10. In *Capitalism, Socialism, and Democracy* * (1950), Joseph Schumpeter presents a widely respected interpretation of this general problem. W. W. Rostow offers what he calls "a non-communist manifesto" in *The Stages of Economic Growth* * (1960), especially illuminating on the position of the American economy in international relations. Louis M. Hacker's *American Capitalism: Its Promise and Accomplishment* * (1957) traces the constructive role of American capitalism, while Adolph A. Berle and Gardner C. Means, in *The Modern Corporation and Private Property* (1932), discuss the political problems posed by a corporate economy. Edward S. Mason, *The Corporation in Modern Society* (1960), is a more recent treatment of the emergence of America's corporate economy. Eugene V. Rostow appraises the public law of American capitalism in *Planning for Freedom* (1960).

John Kenneth Galbraith discusses the paradox of private opulence and public poverty in *The Affluent Society* * (1958). Two critical appraisals of the American economy, both including proposals for reform, are Gunnar Myrdal, *Challenge to Affluence* (1963) and Michael Reagan, *The Managed Economy* (1963). A controversial book, and one influential in official thinking about national policy, is Michael Harrington's *The Other America* * (1964), which focuses on poverty in this country. Gabriel Kolko, *Wealth and Power in America* (1962), and J. Frederick Dewhurst and Associates, *America's Needs and Resources*, provide valuable data on the problems of rich and poor in the United States.

The Context of Ideas

Many books have been written about democracy and democratic government, but no official creed has ever been established. Leslie Lipson appraises the democratic record from the classical tradition to current variations in *The Democratic Civilization* (1964). Henry B. Mayo offers us *An Introduction to Democratic Theory* * (1960); "the method chosen is to set up a consistent and coherent theory of democracy . . . in both operational and normative terms, to explain the system and to justify it." Neal Reimer considers *The Revival of Democratic Theory* * (1962); Charles Frankel discusses *The Democratic Prospect* * (1962); and Thomas L. Thorson analyzes *The Logic of Democracy* * (1962). Gabriel Almond and Sidney Verba undertake a systematic investigation of *The Civic Culture: Political Attitudes and Democracy in Five Nations* * (1963). Robert A. Dahl's *A Preface to Democratic Theory* * (1956) is a rigorous analysis of Madisonian, populistic, and polyarchal theories of democracy.

The nature of democracy, the threats to democratic government, and defenses of democracy against alternative forms of government are found in Daniel J. Boorstin,

The Genius of American Politics * (1953); Carl J. Friedrich, *The New Image of the Common Man* (1950); Ferdinand A. Hermens, *The Representative Republic* (1958); A. D. Lindsay, *The Modern Democratic State* * (1947); and J. R. Pennock, *Liberal Democracy: Its Merits and Prospects* (1950). *Political Man* * (1959), by Seymour Lipset, is concerned with problems of cleavage and consensus in Western democratic society. Robert Lane's depth interviews with fifteen "common men" in "Eastport" is the basis of a penetrating analysis, *Political Ideology: Why the American Common Man Believes What He Does* (1962).

Among the countless works on competing ideologies, a few are Zbigniew Brzezinski, *Ideology and Power in Soviet Politics* (1962); Henry B. Mayo, *Introduction to Marxist Theory* * (1960); Herbert Marcuse, *Soviet Marxism: A Critical Analysis* (1958); Robert C. Tucker, *Philosophy and Myth in Karl Marx* * (1961); and Adam Ulam, *The Unfinished Revolution* * (1960). Notice that variations on the democratic theme are accompanied by differing versions of communism in the world today. See Alexander A. Dallin, *Diversity in International Communism* (1963).

For empirical studies of totalitarian appeals in America and Europe, see Gabriel Almond, *The Appeals of Communism* (1954), and Hadley Cantril, *The Politics of Despair* (1958). Erich Fromm discusses the burdens of independence and the psychological appeal of authoritarian movements in *Escape from Freedom* (1941). On right-wing authoritarianism in America, see T. W. Adorno *et al.*, *The Authoritarian Personality* (1950); also Daniel Bell, *The Radical Right* * (1963), and Harry Overstreet and Bonaro Overstreet, *The Strange Tactics of Extremism* (1964). A reminder of the central importance of non-authoritarian conservatism in America is found in Clinton Rossiter, *Conservatism in America* (1955).

Vernon L. Parrington's monumental work, *Main Currents in American Thought* * (1930, 3 vols.), is no doubt the most widely read history of political ideas in the United States. Parrington's own convictions were so deeply held and so eloquently expressed that his work has become important as the source of his ideas no less than a history of the ideas of others. Alpheus T. Mason's *Free Government in the Making* * (1956) is valuable both for the readings he selects and for his introductory essays. Also excellent are: Merle Curti, *The Growth of American Thought* (1943); Ralph H. Gabriel, *The Course of American Democratic Thought* (1956); Louis Hartz, *The Liberal Tradition in America* (1955); and Richard Hofstadter, *The American Political Tradition* * (1948). Four notable studies of American democracy by foreign commentators are Alexis de Tocqueville, *Democracy in America* * (2 vols., 1954); James Bryce, *The American Commonwealth* * (2 vols., 1888); Harold J. Laski, *The American Democracy* (1948); and D. W. Brogan, *Politics in America* * (1954).

Works describing the ideas of particular periods are useful for tracing the gradual victory of the idea of democracy and the continuing struggle over how far it should be extended. These include: Clinton Rossiter, *Seedtime of the Republic* (1952); Carl Becker, *The Declaration of Independence* * (rev., 1942); Merrill D. Peterson, *The Jefferson Image in the American Mind* (1962); Arthur Schlesinger, Jr., *The Age of Jackson* * (1947); Robert Green McCloskey, *American Conservatism in the Age of Enterprise* * (1951); Richard Hofstadter, *The Age of Reform: From Bryan to F.D.R.* (1956); Henry Steele Commager, *The American Mind* * (1950); James W. Prothro, *The Dollar Decade: Business Ideas in the 1920's* (1954); Frederick Lewis Allen, *Only Yesterday* * (1956), and *The Big Change* (1952); William E. Leuchtenburg, *The Perils of Prosperity, 1914–32* (1958); and Eric F. Goldman, *Rendezvous with Destiny* * (1952), and *The Crucial Decade: America 1945–1955* * (1956). Arthur Schlesinger, Jr.'s three volumes, *The Crisis of the Old Order* * (1957), *The Coming of the New Deal* (1959), and *The Politics of Upheaval* (1961), give us an exciting and authentic account of "the age of Roosevelt." Daniel Aaron traces the off-center movement of American progressivism from mid-nineteenth century to mid-twentieth century in *Men of Good Hope* * (1961).

Throughout this text we have emphasized the pluralism of America. Different sections of the country react differently to current political issues. James McBride Dabbs explains southern reactions as "the product of history" in *Who Speaks for the South?* (1964); Ralph McGill, intrepid editor of the *Atlanta Constitution*, writes from a contemporary vantage in *The South and the Southerner* * (1963); Harvard professor of philosophy Perry Miller looks at New England in *Errand Into Wilderness* (1956); and Henry Nash Smith discusses *Virgin Land: The American West as Symbol and Myth* (1957).

Many fictional works offer insights into government, and a countless number have relevance for the broad context of politics. Sinclair Lewis' *Main Street* (1921) and John Dos Passos' *The Big Money* (1936), for example, attempt to capture the dominant values of our culture for the preceding generation. Cameron Hawley, in *Executive Suite* * (1952), and Arthur Miller, in the hit play, *Death of a Salesman* (1949), dramatize similar material values in a more contemporary setting. Carl Sandburg's *Complete Poems* (1950) reflect a deep appreciation of the milieu of democratic politics (especially in "The People, Yes," pp. 439–617).

For typical "problem pieces," Richard Wright's *Native Son* * (1940) deals with the difficulties of Negroes as an ethnic minority group; Laura Z. Hobson's *Gentleman's Agreement* (1947) portrays the more subtle forms of discrimination experienced by a religious minority in America. John Hersey's *White Lotus* (1965) is a gripping and timeless story of the issues of race against race. In *Point of No Return* (1949), John P. Marquand depicts the impact of social class on the hero's life and personality; George Bernard Shaw's *Pygmalion* * (1941) is a delightful play about speech as an index of class status. Just as Hawley's *Executive Suite* deals with the problems of affluence in the current generation, John Steinbeck's *The Grapes of Wrath* * (1939) treats of the more pressing problems of poverty in the last generation.

On the provincial threat to democracy, see James G. Thurber and Elliott Nugent, *The Male Animal* (1940), a play about a college professor who withstands pressures toward conformity at the risk of losing his job. Arthur Koestler depicts communism's more overpowering pressure toward conformity in *Darkness at Noon* * (1941). The effects of enforced conformity in the seventeenth-century setting are presented—with relevance for the twentieth century—in Marian Starkey, *The Devil in Massachusetts* (1950).

The Constitutional Background and Federalism

No complete or accurate record of the Constitutional Convention of 1787 exists. Max Farrand has brought together the most comprehensive collection of debates in the Convention, including some timely correspondence of the Convention members, in *The Records of the Federal Convention of 1787* (1911, 1937), 4 vols. Jonathan Elliot has collected the primary materials on the fight for ratification: *The Debates in the Several State Conventions on the Adoption of the Federal Constitution* (1835–46), 5 vols.

The Federalist, * by Alexander Hamilton, James Madison, and John Jay, has come to be regarded as authoritative on "the intentions of the Framers," since two of the three authors were active in the Convention. A contemporary commentary, it was written as a series of partisan letters to the public in 1787 explaining and advocating the proposed Constitution. Paul Ford has gathered together considerable propaganda of the period for and against ratification in *Essays on the Constitution . . . 1787–1788* (1892).

From the legal standpoint, *The Constitution of the United States*, edited by Edward S. Corwin and prepared by the Legislative Reference Service (1953), is probably the most useful single reference volume on the "flexible Constitution." A phrase-by-phrase analysis of the Constitution, it is fully annotated with Supreme Court decisions from 1789 through 1952. The never-ending debates of Congress on the meaning of the Constitution and the nature of federalism may be traced from the first session to the present: the *Annals of Congress* (1789–1824); the *Register of Debates* (1824–27); the *Congressional Globe* (1833–1873); the *Congressional Record* (1873 to date).

In *The American Revolution* * (1957), Charles H. McIlwain offers a constitutional interpretation that is both original and provocative. A brilliant analysis of the Declaration of Independence and its philosophic import is Carl Becker, *The Declaration of Independence* * (1922, 1942). Edward Dumbauld has also made a detailed interpretation of the document in *The Declaration of Independence and What It Means Today* (1950). On the Articles of Confederation, see especially Merril M. Jensen, *The Articles of Confederation* (1950) and *The New Nation: A History of the United States During the Confederation* (1950); and Andrew C. McLaughlin, *The Confederation and the Constitution* * (1905). Seymour Martin Lipset writes about *The First New Nation: The United States in Historical and Comparative Perspective* (1963).

There are many differing interpretations of what the Framing Fathers hoped to found. Charles A. Beard, *An Economic Interpretation of the Constitution of the United States* * (1913), was highly controversial in its day and is still influential in political science. Robert E. Brown, *Charles Beard and the Constitution* (1956), and Forest McDonald, *We the People*, reappraise and attempt to break down the Beard thesis. Jackson Turner Main's study of *The Antifederalists: Critics of the Constitution, 1781–1788* * (1961) unearths evidence that supports the Beard point of view more than that of his critics. William W. Crosskey, *Politics and the Constitution* (1953), challenges some traditional concepts of constitutional law with convincing documentation.

Alfred H. Kelley and Winfred A. Harbison, *The American Constitution* (rev., 1955), presents a general picture of the growth of the American constitutional system. Andrew C. McLaughlin, *A Constitutional History of the United States* (1935), gives us another general treatment of constitutional development, somewhat bent on refuting Beard. Charles Warren, *The Making of the Constitution* (1937), also takes issue with the Beard interpretation in an almost day-to-day account of the Convention proceedings. Broadus Mitchell and Louise Mitchell trace the development of the Constitution, emphasizing the social background and the court decisions that have affected the meaning of the document over the years, in *A Biography of the Constitution of the United States* (1964).

Since history is "man writ large," biographies of Framing Fathers shed light on the genesis of our constitutional government. See, for example, biographies of John Adams, Alexander Hamilton, Thomas Jefferson, James Madison, John Marshall, George Washington, James Wilson, and others. The following books also emphasize personal influence in "the critical period": Max Farrand, *The Framing of the Constitution* (1913); Hastings Lyon, *The Constitution and the Men Who Made It* (1936); Fred Rodell, *Fifty Five Men* (1936); and Carl C. Van Doren, *The Great Rehearsal* (1948).

As to "what the Constitution really means," there is no end to controversial literature. Up to 1955, Edward S. Corwin had brought out eleven editions of *The Constitution and What It Means Today*. For varied approaches to our "flexible Constitution," see: Henry S. Commager, *The American Mind* * (1950); Louis Hartz, *The Liberal Tradition in America* (1955); Arthur N. Holcombe, *Our More Perfect Union* (1950); William B. Munro, *The Makers of the Unwritten Constitution* (1930); Charles E. Merriam, *The Written Constitution and the Unwritten Attitude* (1931); Howard L. McBain, *The Living Constitution* (1927, 1942); and Carl B. Swisher, *American Constitutional Development* (1954). Max Lerner's *America as a Civilization* * (1957), while only partly concerned with government and constitutionalism, is packed with engrossing information, discerning observations, and exciting points of view on the

American political scene. Herbert Wechsler's *Principles, Politics and Fundamental Law* (1961), propounding "neutral principles" in constitutional law, has stirred much controversy among lawyers and political scientists concerned with judicial review. Charles Black considers the Constitution as a "matter of purest politics, a structure of power" in *The Making of Constitutional Law* * (1963).

The role of the states in the more perfect union, and the relation of the states with one another, have always been the subject of political controversy. The Commission on Intergovernmental Relations in 1955 made *A Report to the President for Transmittal to Congress* covering many current problems of nation-state relations, with emphasis on financial relations. It also published fifteen *Reports of Study Committees* (1955), which together constitute a rather complete survey of problems in "the new federalism." The Senate Sub-committee on Intergovernmental Relations, established in 1962 under the Committee on Intergovernmental Operations, has held extensive hearings on intergovernmental issues. A similar Committee in the House has also been holding hearings. The published reports of these congressional committees cover a full spectrum of federal-state relationships.

Although New Deal reforms of the 1930's evoked considerable commentary on the theory of federalism, surprisingly little research has appeared on this subject, perhaps because of the general acceptance of a prominent role for the national government. Two early studies of the "new federalism" are: Jane Perry Clark, *The Rise of a New Federalism* (1938), and V. O. Key, Jr., *The Administration of Federal Grants to States* (1937). The English scholar, Kenneth C. Wheare offers us a theoretical analysis of federalism in a comparative frame of reference, *Federal Government* * (4th ed., 1964).

Recent studies of American federalism include: Vincent V. Thursby, *Interstate Cooperation* (1953); Arthur W. MacMahon (ed.), *Federalism Mature and Emergent* (1955); Redding S. Sugg Jr. and George H. Jones, *The Southern Education Board: The Years of Regional Cooperation in Higher Education* (1960); and Daniel J. Elazar, *The American Partnership* (1962). *The Federal Government and Metropolitan Areas* (1960), by Robert Connery and Richard H. Leach, reads like a staff policy paper on what "should" be the pattern of the new federalism. *Intergovernmental Relations in Review* (1960), by William Anderson, a distinguished senior political scientist, synthesizes three decades of exploration and findings on this complex subject. Another seasoned scholar of state governments provides a comprehensive text in *American Intergovernmental Relations: Their Origins, Historical Development, and Current Status* (1964), by W. B. Graves.

Part Two   Inputs of the Political System: Demands, Supports, and Apathy

Political Opinions and Voting Behavior

Two periodicals largely devoted to studies of political opinions and voting behavior are the *Public Opinion Quarterly* and the *International Journal of Opinion and Attitude Research*. Comprehensive annotated bibliographies may be found in: Bruce L. Smith, Harold D. Lasswell, and Ralph D. Casey, *Propaganda, Communication, and Public Opinion* (1946), and Bruce L. Smith and Chitra M. Smith, *International Communication and Political Opinion* (1956).

A. Lawrence Lowell, *Public Opinion and Popular Government* (1913), and Walter Lippmann, *Public Opinion* * (1922), are two early studies of public opinion. More recent coverage of the field is found in: William Albig, *Modern Public Opinion* (1956); Bernard Berelson and Morris Janowitz (eds.), *Reader in Public Opinion and Communication* (1950); Daniel Katz *et al.* (eds.), *Public Opinion and Propaganda:*

A Book of Readings (1954). Mildred Parten's *Surveys, Polls, and Samples* (1950) is an explanation of polling procedures. Hadley Cantril (ed.), *Public Opinion* (1951), is a collection of survey data from 1935 to 1946. In this textbook we have found most helpful *Public Opinion and American Democracy* (1961), in which V. O. Key, Jr. brings together much of the newer knowledge of public opinion and places it within an organized political context. For a brief yet over-all consideration of the ways people arrive at political opinions and the tools that political scientists use in analyzing public opinion, we highly recommend Robert E. Lane and David O. Sears, *Public Opinion* * (1964).

Various facets of psychology and politics are explored in: Graham Wallas, *Human Nature in Politics* (1909); Harold D. Lasswell, *Psychopathology and Politics* (1930) and *Power and Personality* (1948); Alexander H. Leighton, *The Governing of Men* (1946); T. W. Adorno *et al.*, *The Authoritarian Personality* (1950); and H. J. Eysenck, *The Psychology of Politics* (1954). On the last two references, see the commentary in Richard Christie and Marie Jahoda, *Studies in the Scope and Method of "The Authoritarian Personality"* (1954), and the exchange of comments between Richard Christie and H. J. Eysenck in the *Psychological Bulletin* (1956). For a thoughtful distinction between the dogmatic and single-minded individual who focuses his whole attention on a particular doctrine and the concerned citizen who has a general interest in the many facets of politics, read Eric Hoffer, *The True Believer* (1958). M. Brewster Smith, Jerome S. Bruner, and Robert W. White analyze the functions of opinions for personality in *Opinions and Personality* (1956). Herbert McClosky's articles on conservatism and personality represent a systematic examination of this problem by a contemporary political scientist. Also pertinent are: Robert Lane, *Political Life: Why People Get Involved in Politics* (1959), and Heinz Eulau, *The Behavioral Persuasion in Politics* * (1963).

A wide range of empirical studies represent the development of interdisciplinary research on various aspects of political socialization, especially in mass communication. Karl W. Deutsch *et al.*, present a set of models to analyze quantitative and qualitative data on national and local patterns of political relationships in *The Integration of Political Communities* * (1964). A pioneering study is Herbert Hyman's *Political Socialization* (1959). Fred Greenstein's forthcoming book on children's political views suggests an interesting new approach to understanding the early stages of political socialization.

Mass communication is a crucial tool of modern government. Two studies, one by a professional journalist, the other by a political scientist, report on the interaction of politics and the press in the communications process: Douglass Cater, *The Fourth Branch of Government* * (1959), and Dan D. Nimmo, *Newsgathering in Washington: A Study in Political Communication* (1962).

For a comprehensive summary of findings on voting behavior and for a more complete bibliography on the subject, see Seymour M. Lipset *et al.*, "The Psychology of Voting: An Analysis of Political Behavior," in Gardner Lindzey (ed.), *Handbook of Social Psychology*, II (1954). A series of election surveys begun in 1940 supplies much of our insight into voting behavior: Paul F. Lazarsfeld, Bernard Berelson, and Hazel Gaudet, *The People's Choice* (1948), and Bernard Berelson, Paul F. Lazarsfeld, and William McPhee, *Voting* (1954). Eugene Burdick and Arthur J. Brodbeck have collected, in *American Voting Behavior* (1959), a series of articles re-examining the findings of the major election studies.

The Michigan Survey Research Center, which has been doing research on voting behavior since 1948, continues to furnish us with new data as well as analysis, interpretation, and projection. See Angus Campbell, Gerald Gurin, and Warren E. Miller, *The Voter Decides* (1954); Angus Campbell and Homer C. Cooper, *Group Differences in Attitudes and Votes* (1956); and Angus Campbell, P. Converse, W. Miller, and D. Stokes, *The American Voter* (1960). Their work represents a successful attempt to put politics back into the study of political behavior by considering the influence on voting of political no less than social and economic factors. Much of the data on the 1964 elections used in this textbook was obtained in advance of publication from the Center.

At a more popular level, Samuel Lubell has written about *The Future of American Politics* * (1952) and *Revolt of the Moderates* (1956). Louis H. Bean, *How to Predict Elections* (1948), and *Influences in the 1954 Mid-Term Elections* (pamphlet, 1954), use statistical analysis of voting "cycles" in interpreting voting behavior. In *Is There a Republican Majority?* (1954), Louis Harris appraises voting patterns in the Eisenhower era. Special aspects of voting behavior are considered in: Harry M. Bain and Donald S. Hecock, *Ballot Position and Voter's Choice* * (1957); Lawrence H. Fuchs, *The Political Behavior of American Jews* (1956); Seymour M. Lipset, *Agrarian Socialism* (1950); Henry Lee Moon, *Balance of Power: The Negro Vote* (1948); Donald S. Strong, *Urban Republicanism in the South* * (1960); and Ruth G. Silva, *Rum, Religion and Votes: 1928 Re-Examined* (1962).

Party Politics and Political Leadership

Maurice Duverger, *Political Parties* (1955), is an enlightening comparative treatment; Sigmund Neumann (ed.), *Modern Political Parties* (1956), while not really a comparative analysis, offers good essays on parties in different countries. V. O. Key, Jr., *Politics, Parties, and Pressure Groups* (5th ed., 1964), and Avery Leiserson, *Parties and Politics: An Institutional and Behavioral Approach* (1958), provide excellent treatments of American political parties. Samuel J. Eldersveld, *Political Parties: A Behavioral Analysis* (1964), is both an empirical and theoretical contribution to the functions of parties. Robert Alford examines the importance of class and party in political loyalties in four countries in *Party and Society: The Anglo-American Democracies* (1963). A number of brief and refreshing accounts of American political parties have recently appeared in paperback editions: Hugh A. Bone and Austin Ranney, *Politics and Voters* * (1963); Robert A. Goldwin (ed.), *Political Parties, U.S.A.* * (1964); Fred I. Greenstein, *The American Party System and the American People* * (1963); Clinton Rossiter, *Parties and Politics in America* * (1960); and Frank Sorauf, *Political Parties in the American System* * (1964).

Readings in Political Parties and Pressure Groups * (1964), edited by Frank Munger and Douglas Price, present a variety of traditional and behavioral, substantive and methodological essays by well-known scholars. William Nisbet Chambers examines the beginnings of the party system in the United States in *Political Parties in a New Nation: The American Experience, 1776–1809* (1963), and Wilfred Binkley gives a history of shifting party doctrines and persisting bases of support in *American Political Parties* (1943).

In *The Doctrine of Responsible Party Government* (1962), Austin Ranney explores a concept that some regard as offering a model for the functioning of democratic political parties and that others regard as inappropriate or dangerous for American democracy. Pendleton Herring's *The Politics of Democracy* (1940) emphasizes the advantages of our present system of undisciplined, decentralized parties. E. E. Schattschneider champions disciplined, centralized parties in *Party Government* (1942), as does the Committee on Political Parties of the American Political Science Association (chaired by Professor Schattschneider) in *Toward a More Responsible Two-Party System* (1950). Frank J. Sorauf offers a stimulating and provocative discussion of interaction between party and constituency in the process of representation in *Party and Representation* (1963).

The student may compare the platforms of the parties for himself by consulting T. H. McKee (ed.), *National Conventions and Platforms of All Political Parties, 1789–1904* (1904), and K. H. Porter and D. B. Johnson, *National Party Platforms, 1840–1956* (1956). The *Congressional Quarterly*, which breaks down the votes in both houses of Congress in party terms, is a great aid in comparing the congressional record of the parties. On parties and political leaders in different sections, see: V. O. Key, Jr., *Southern Politics in State and Nation* (1949); Alexander Heard, *A Two-Party South?* (1952); Duane Lockard, *New England State Politics* (1959); and Alfred de Grazia, *The Western Republic, 1952 and Beyond* (1954). Two recent studies of third parties are: Irving Howe and Lewis Coser, *The American Communist Party: A Critical History* (1958); and Karl M. Schmidt's painstaking review of the ill-fated Progressive Party of 1948, *Henry A. Wallace: Quixotic Crusade* (1960). See also Elmo R. Richardson, *The Politics of Conservation: Crusades and Controversies* (1962).

For the study of party leadership, the works on psychology and politics cited in the previous section should prove helpful. Robert Michel's *Political Parties*, first published in English in 1915, is a pioneering study of the psychology of power and the sociology of leadership by a distinguished French political scientist. Alvin W. Gouldner's *Studies in Leadership* (1950) and Dwaine Marvick's *Political Decision Makers* (1961) are good collections of readings on the subject. Leaders at different levels are considered in: Charles E. Merriam, *Four American Party Leaders* (1926); H. F. Gosnell, *Machine Politics: Chicago Model* (1937); Sonya Forthal, *Cogwheels of Democracy, A Study of the Precinct Captain* (1946); Hugh A. Bone, *Grass Roots Party Leadership* (1952); and Rexford G. Tugwell, *The Art of Politics, As Practiced by Three Great Americans* (1958). Hugh A. Bone gives us a detailed description of the eight national party committees in *Party Committees and National Politics* (1958).

Biographies and autobiographies sometimes illuminate the personal tactics of persuasion in politics. Stimson Bullitt describes what it means *To Be A Politician* (1959). Richard M. Nixon gives his version of what happened to him in *Six Crises* (1962). Two recent biographies tell very different stories about senatorial party politics: A. Wigfall Green, *The Man Bilbo* (1963), and Erwin L. Levine, *Theodore Francis Green: The Rhode Island Years, 1906–1936* (1963).

Occasionally a novel captures the spirit of a political situation or leader and grippingly depicts some phase of politics—Robert Penn Warren's *All the King's Men* * (1946) is an outstanding example. Many similar stories of southern demagogues, such as John Dos Passos, *Number One* (1943), and Adria Langley, *A Lion in the Streets* (1945), are entertaining but not quite so insightful. Edwin O'Connor, *The Last Hurrah* (1956), is such a well-conceived portrayal of an old Irish boss that it sustains interest without the least reliance on a "sex angle." Eugene Burdick's *The Ninth Wave* *(1956) is a political scientist's fictionalized picture of the machinations of a western political boss who has an awesome grasp of modern campaign techniques. An amusing play about a rich former junk-man and his mistress, Garson Kanin's *Born Yesterday*, in John Gassner (ed.), *Best Plays of the Modern Theatre* (1947), is the story of an unusual lobbying team.

Pressure Politics, Interest Groups, and Public Relations

David B. Truman's *The Governmental Process* (1951) is valuable for an understanding of politics as a struggle among competing interests, and is particularly illuminating on the role of pressure groups. Other helpful general studies are: Donald C. Blaisdell, *American Democracy Under Pressure* (1957); E. Pendleton Herring, *Group Representation Before Congress* (1929), and *Public Administration and the Public Interest* (1936); Harold Lasswell, *Politics: Who Gets What, When, How* * (1936); Charles E. Merriam, *Public and Private Government* (1944); Harmon Ziegler, *Interest Groups in American Society* (1964); and Lester W. Milbrath, *The Washington Lobbyists* (1963).

Many studies have been made of particular pressure groups. For the role of labor, portrayed in case studies from the 1950 elections, see Fay Caulkins, *The CIO and the Democratic Party* (1952). An insightful study of the veterans' lobby is Mary R. Dearing, *Veterans in Politics* (1952). One example of a business lobby's tactics may be found in the Federal Trade Commission's *Summary Report . . . on Efforts by Associations and Agencies of Electric and Gas Utilities to Influence Public Opinion*, Sen. Doc. No. 92, 70th Cong., 1st Sess. (1934); a highly critical study is Robert A. Brady, *Business as a System of Power* (1943). John W. Hurst, *Law and Economic Growth: The Legal History of the Lumber Industry in Wisconsin* (1964), is a thorough-going piece of scholarship in a much broader political context than the title suggests.

Oliver Garceau's study, *The Political Life of the American Medical Association* (1941), examines one of the most powerful pressure groups. On farm organizations and the influence of business groups on farm policy, see Wesley McCune, *The Farm Bloc* (1943), and *Who's Behind Our Farm Policy?* (1956). Peter Odegard, *Pressure Politics, The Story of the Antisaloon League* (1928), and E. E. Schattschneider, *Politics, Pressures, and the Tariff* (1935), are earlier studies of two pressure-group campaigns. Phillip O. Foss does a realistic case study of the pressure politics behind our national grazing policies, *Politics and Grass* (1960); and Robert Engler shows how "the private government that controls most of the petroleum resources of the world" affects American political life, *The Politics of Oil* (1961). Clement E. Vose examines the role of interest groups in the judicial process in *Caucasians Only: The Supreme Court, the NAACP and the Restrictive Covenant Cases* (1959). Other special studies include: Clifton Brock, *Americans for Democratic Action* (1962); Abraham Holtzman, *The Townsend Movement: A Political Study* (1963); and James H. Timberlake, *Prohibition and the Progressive Movement 1900–1920* (1963).

A broadly conceived history of advertising, written in a friendly tone, is James P. Wood, *The Story of Advertising* (1958). Otis Pease's *The Responsibility of American Advertising* (1958) is more critical. The first specific study of the application of modern public-relations techniques to politics is Stanley Kelley, *Professional Public Relations and Political Power* (1956). Edward L. Bernays, a leading practitioner of the art and science of "engineering consent," has written *Propaganda* (1928), *The Engineering of Consent* (1955), and *Crystallizing Public Opinion* (1961). Vance Packard's popular-level treatment of public-relations techniques, *The Hidden Persuaders* * (1957), emphasizes the tremendous power of the public-relations fraternity. As applied to politically oriented "institutional" advertising, however, William H. Whyte, Jr., asks *Is Anybody Listening?* (1952) and suggests that such campaigns have little influence.

Three studies from the Brookings Institution deal in part with campaign propaganda, the impact of polls and mass media, and the influence of professional public relations: Stanley Kelley, Jr., *Political Campaigning* (1960); Paul T. David, Ralph M. Goldman, and Richard C. Bain, *The Politics of National Party Conventions* (1960, revised and updated in a paper back edition, 1964); and Paul T. David (ed.), *The Presidential Election and Transition, 1960–61* (1961). Theodore H. White dramatizes the influence of the mass media, especially television, in *The Making of the President, 1960* * (1961).

Frederic Wakeman's *The Hucksters* (1946) was an early fictionalized protest about the abuses of modern advertising. Frederik Pohl and C. M. Kornbluth, *The Space Merchants* * (1952), is about a future in which the advertising agencies are in complete control of society. John G. Schneider, *The Golden Kazoo* (1956), is the story of a future presidential campaign, again with the public-relations men in complete control. John Steinbeck's description of *The Short Reign of Pippin IV* (1957) transfers the same theme to the future of France.

Elections

For laws on voting and elections, consult the most recent edition of *The Book of the States*. See K. H. Porter, *A History of Suffrage in the United States* (1918), for the story of the extension of the franchise. Six volumes by Elizabeth C. Stanton and other suffragettes, *History of Woman Suffrage* (1881–1922), tell in detail how women won the right to vote. Richard Scammon has given us three volumes of basic reference materials and statistics on elections since 1946, *America Votes* (1956, 1958, 1960). Specialized studies of American elections are: Cortez A. M. Ewing, *Congressional Elections, 1896–1944* (1947), and *Primary Elections in the South* (1953); Paul T. David *et al.*, *Presidential Nominating Politics in 1952* (5 vols., 1954); and Malcolm Moos, *Politics, Presidents, and Coattails* (1952). Lucius Wilmerding, Jr., provides us with an excellent historical description of *The Electoral College* * (1958). Alexander Heard appraises *The Costs of Democracy* * (1960) with a thorough piece of research on how nominations and elections are financed in the United States.

Paul David, Ralph M. Goldman, and Richard C. Bain have done a systematic analysis of the presidential nominating process (an outgrowth of the five-volume study of the 1952 elections sponsored by the American Political Science Association), *The Politics of National Party Conventions* (1960). New research on presidential nominations may be found in Gerald Pomper, *Nominating the President* (1963); see also Paul Tillett, *Inside Politics: The National Conventions* * (1962).

An important new book on presidential elections, which examines the nominating process and the campaign within "the strategic environment," is *Presidential Elections: Strategies of American Electoral Politics,** by Nelson W. Polsby and Aaron B. Wildavsky (1964). Anthony Downs' *An Economic Theory of Democracy* (1957) proposes a thought-provoking model for an understanding of the general function of elections in a democratic system. The materials cited under "Political Opinions and Voting Behavior" are also useful in understanding the electoral system.

Part Three   *Decision-Making Agencies and Activities*

Government Documents

Government documents constitute a readily available source of important primary materials on the official agencies of government. Laurence F. Schmeckebier and Roy B. Eastin furnish a valuable guide, *Government Publications and Their Use* (rev., 1961).

The official text of all laws passed by Congress since the beginning may be found in the *Statutes at Large*, now published annually. The United States *Code* contains all the general laws currently in force, consolidated and codified under fifty titles. The most recent edition was in 1958, but the *Code* is kept up to date with annual cumulative supplements. Congressional debates are reported in the *Congressional Record* (1873 to date), *Congressional Globe* (1833–73), *Register of Debates* (1824–1837), and *Annals of Congress* (1789–1824). The bound volumes of congressional debates are usually verbatim reports, although remarks made on the floor may be expunged and many speeches never given are inserted in the *Appendix* under the privilege of "leave to print." The *Hearings* of congressional committees, with transcripts of testimony, cover the whole gamut of national politics. Congressional committees also constitute a gold mine of information, especially on matters of policy, through published staff studies, reports of congressional "study missions," and committee reports to Congress. The *Congressional Directory*, published currently, gives personnel data on Congress and other branches of the government. Each house also publishes its own *Manual*, containing its rules, orders, laws, and resolutions.

Presidential addresses and messages to Congress are currently printed in the *Congressional Record*. An excellent historical source is James D. Richardson's *Compilation of the Messages and Papers of the Presidents, 1789–1897*. Presidential proclamations appear in the *Statutes at Large*, and *The New York Times* regularly prints the texts of all important presidential addresses. Since 1935, all executive orders, and all administrative rules and regulations, are published daily in the *Federal Register*.

The *Code of Federal Regulations* codifies the vast volume of administrative rulings; first published in 1938, it is kept up to date with cumulative supplements.

The *United States Government Organization Manual,* published annually, is the official handbook of the federal government. It contains a brief description of the principal governmental agencies, including their statutory authority, organizational outline, and functions. For more specialized departmental materials, consult the *Monthly Catalogue of United States Public Documents,* which lists all titles of government publications and tells where and how they may be obtained.

Since 1875, the Government Printing Office has published the decisions of the United States Supreme Court as *United States Reports,* beginning with Vol. 91. The first ninety volumes are cited by the name of the private court reporters who compiled them: Dallas, 1–4 (1790–1800); Cranch, 1–9 (1801–1815); Wheaton, 1–12(1816–1827); Peters, 1–16 (1828–1842); Howard, 1–24 (1843–1860); Black, 1–2 (1861–1862); Wallace, 1–23 (1863–1874). *The Lawyers Edition of the U.S. Supreme Court Reports* (Lawyers' Cooperative Publishing Co., Rochester, N. Y.) and *The Supreme Court Reporter* (West Publishing Co., St. Paul, Minn.) are private editions, both including head notes and annotations.

The West Publishing Company publishes the rulings of the lower federal courts. *Federal Cases,* a series of thirty volumes, contains all the lower federal court decisions from 1789 to 1880, arranged alphabetically rather than chronologically. The *Federal Reporter,* a series of 300 volumes, reports chronologically all the cases from 1880 to 1924. From 1924, the *Federal Reporter* (2nd Series) contains the decisions of the Court of Appeals, the *Federal Supplement* the rulings of the district courts.

Congress

Many commentators have offered useful insights into the general character, the organization, and the operation of Congress. Woodrow Wilson's *Congressional Government* * (1885) remains a classic. Alfred de Grazia's *Public and Republic* (1951) examines the theory and practice of representative government, with emphasis on the historical background. Recent studies with varying points of view include: Stephen K. Bailey and Howard D. Samuel, *Congress at Work* (1952); George Galloway, *The Legislative Process in Congress* (1953); Ernest S. Griffith, *Congress, Its Contemporary Role* (rev., 1956); Bertrand M. Gross, *The Legislative Struggle: A Study in Social Combat* (1953).

Charles S. Clapp, on the staff at the Brookings Institution, organized a Round Table Conference to give a group of congressmen a chance to discuss all facets of their work. *The Congressman: His Work As He Sees It* * (1963) reports the results. John C. Wahlke and Heinz Eulau have edited a collection of essays, both behavioral and institutional analyses, in *Legislative Behavior: A Reader in Theory and Research* (1959). Roland Young examines the decision-making process of Congress and sets up a "research guide" for more exhaustive inquiries in *The American Congress* (1958). For keeping tabs on the voting record of congressmen, the *Congressional Quarterly* is almost indispensable; this privately published weekly gives the roll-call vote on all important measures, analyzes pending bills, and generally scrutinizes current congressional activities.

Stephen K. Bailey presents a case study of the Employment Act of 1946 in *Congress Makes a Law* * (1950); another case study is by Daniel A. Berman, *A Bill Becomes a Law: The Civil Rights Act of 1960* (1962). A number of recent studies focus on the interaction of party and constituency in congressional politics: Julius Turner, *Party and Constituency* (1952); David B. Truman, *The Congressional Party* (1959); and Lewis A. Froman, *Congressmen and Their Constituencies* * (1963). Kenneth Kofmehl examines the *Professional Staffs of Congress* (1962).

Robert L. Peabody and Nelson W. Polsby present *New Perspectives on the House* of *Representatives* (1964), a collection of excellent articles that demonstrate real progress in the study of legislative behavior. George B. Galloway offers us a *History of the House of Representatives* (1962). Among the many special studies of the Senate, G. H. Haynes' *The Senate of the United States* (1938) is still the standard reference, though now quite dated. Donald R. Matthews analyzes the behavior of senators as influenced by their career experiences and the environment in which they work in *U.S. Senators and Their World* * (1962). J. P. Harris, *The Advice and Consent of the Senate* (1953), is a study of the Senate role in appointments. William S. White offers an experienced Senate reporter's view of the "greatest deliberative body" in *The Citadel: The Story of the United States Senate* (1957). Senator Joseph S. Clark gives us an inside view of *The Senate Establishment* (1963). Allen Drury has written a popular novel that has also been made into a first-rate play, all about politics, especially congressmen, *Advice and Consent* (1959).

For studies of the Senate and House Committees see: David N. Farnsworth, *The Senate Committee on Foreign Relations* (1961); Herbert N. Caroll, *The House of Representatives and Foreign Affairs* (1958); and Robert K. Carr, *The House Un-American Activities Committee* (1952). Carl Beck has made a useful compilation of prosecutions for contempt of Congress, focusing primarily on the busy calendar of the House Committee on Un-American Activities, *Contempt of Congress* (1959). Much has been written on congressional investigations, including Alan Barth, *Government by Investigation* (1955), and Telford Taylor, *Grand Inquest* (1955).

The constitutional "separation of powers" complicates the over-all political process. J. Leiper Freeman, *The Political Process: Executive Bureau-Legislative Committee Relations* * (1955) examines executive-legislative relations at the working level. *The Deadlock of Democracy: Four Party Politics in America* (1963), by James MacGregor Burns, launches a full-scale attack on the existing political situation vis-à-vis the two congressional parties and the two presidential parties. *Continuing Crisis in American Politics* * (1963), Marian D. Irish (ed.), includes a number of essays on this problem. Roland Egger and Joseph Harris briefly discuss the issues between *The President and Congress* * (1963), and Walter Murphy writes on *Congress and the Court: A Case Study in the American Political Process* (1962).

Since laws are made by men, biographies of congressmen often prove illuminating on personal by-play in the legislative process. Some good examples are: L. S. Bushey, *Uncle Joe Cannon* (1927); George Norris, *Fighting Liberal* (1945); W. A. Robinson, *Thomas B. Reed* (1930); and H. Jerry Voorhis, *Confessions of a Congressman* (1948). *Profiles in Courage* * (1958) is an entertaining, albeit hero-worshiping, study of certain United States Senators, written by President Kennedy when he was still Senator Kennedy.

The President

The literature on the presidency includes an endless succession of biographies and autobiographies. Some profess to be scholarly studies of "the life and times"; some are merely debunking, written to shock and sell; some are simply campaign materials. From the point of view of political science, we suggest: Douglas Southall Freemen, *George Washington: A Biography* (6 vols., 1948–54), which was completed by J. A. Carroll and M. W. Ashworth (Vol. VII, 1957); Irving Brant, *James Madison* (1950–1960), 6 vols.; Arthur Schlesinger, Jr., *The Age of Jackson* (1945); Carl Sandburg, *Abraham Lincoln, The Prairie Years* (1926), 2 vols., and *The War Years* (1934), 4 vols.; Allan Nevins, *Grover Cleveland* (1932); Henry F. Pringle, *Theodore Roosevelt* (1931); Ray Stannard Baker, *Woodrow Wilson: Life and Letters* (1939), 8 vols.; August Heckscher (ed.), *The Politics of Woodrow Wilson* (1926); James MacGregor Burns, *Roosevelt: The Lion and the Fox* (1956); Robert E. Sherwood, *Roosevelt and Hopkins* * (1948).

To appraise first-hand accounts of recent presidencies is difficult, since the principals have still not settled their accounts with history. But we recommend as illuminating and controversial: Harry S. Truman, *Memoirs* (1956) and *Truman Speaks* (1960); Dwight D. Eisenhower, *Mandate for Change 1953–56* (1963); Marquis Childs, *Eisenhower: The Captive Hero* (1958); Robert Donovan, *The Inside Story* (1956); Sherman Adams, *First Hand Account* * (1961); and Emmet John Hughes, *The Ordeal of Power* * (1963). For a dramatic study of presidential responsibility—a novel that became a successful movie—read Fletcher Knebel and Charles W. Bailey, *Seven Days in May* (1962).

John Kennedy: A Political Profile (1960), by James MacGregor Burns, appeared as a campaign biography, but it is a more discerning study than the usual campaign material. Theodore Sorensen, who was Special Counsel to President Kennedy, gives us an inside look at *Decision-Making in the White House* (1963). A number of biographical studies by members of the White House staff who were close to President Kennedy are forthcoming.

Among general studies of the presidency, the most comprehensive is Edward S. Corwin, *The President: Office and Powers*, revised for the fourth time in 1957. More popular in treatment are: Edward S. Corwin and Louis W. Koenig, *The Presidency Today* (1956); Sidney Hyman, *The American President* (1954); and Clinton Rossiter, *The American Presidency* * (1956). James Hart examines the presidency in its formative years in *The American Presidency in Action, 1789* (1948). Harold Laski discusses *The American Presidency* * (1940) from the British point of view. *Presidential Power* * (1960), by Richard Neustadt, is concerned with "the politics of leadership," the personal power of the man in office. *The Chief Executive* (1964), by Louis W. Koenig, expertly analyzes the power and weakness of the American presidency from George Washington to Lyndon B. Johnson.

Dondale Bruce Johnson and Jack L. Walker have assembled an enterprising collection of essays by well-known authorities in *The Dynamics of the American Presidency* (1964). The institutionalization of the presidency has provoked numerous studies on the executive office. Rexford G. Tugwell provides an excellent historical survey of the American presidency since 1787, *The Enlargement of the Presidency* (1960). Edward Hobbes describes the organization man, *Behind the President* (1954). Richard Fenno examines *The President's Cabinet* * (1959), especially its development since the Wilson Administration. Corinne Silverman does a case-study on *The President's Economic Advisers* * (1959). *The Presidency: Crisis and Regeneration* (1960), by Herman Finer, is a perceptive analysis of the institution, including some highly controversial recommendations.

The rise of the vice-presidency to some degree of political stature has produced a number of studies, including: Edgar W. Waugh, *Second Consul* (1956); Irving G. Williams, *The American Vice-Presidency: New Look* (1954), and *The Rise of the Vice-Presidency* (1956). For different interpretations of the Cabinet at work, skim through some of the "memoirs" of Cabinet officers: James Byrnes, *Speaking Frankly* (1947), and *All In One Lifetime* (1958); *The Secret Diary of Harold Ickes: The First Thousand Days* (1953); and Frances Perkins, *The Roosevelt I Knew* (1946). *The Invisible Presidency* (1960), by Louis W. Koenig, goes beyond rumor and folklore in its account of White House favorites and personal confidantes.

Many political scientists are concerned with the theory and the practice of separation of powers. Wilfred E. Binkley takes a historical approach to the subject in *President and Congress* (1947). W. Y. Elliott (ed.) treats of the problem of executive-legislative relations more particularly in *United States Foreign Policy* (1952). Pendleton Herring discusses the same problem more generally in *Presidential Leadership* (1940). On the independent regulatory commissions, which are in effect a practical denial of separation of powers, see Marver H. Bernstein, *Regulating Business by Independent Commissions* (1955).

Leonard D. White has performed a herculean task in his historical but lively consideration of our early bureaucrats: *The Federalists* (1948); *The Jeffersonians* (1951); *The Jacksonians* (1954); and *The Republican Era* (1957). White also wrote *Introduction to the Study of Public Administration*, the first textbook in public administration, in 1926; its fourth edition appeared in 1955. Other early writings in public administration include: W. F. Willoughby, *Principles of Public Administration* (1927); Luther Gulick and L. Urwick, *Papers on the Science of Administration* (1937, rev., 1947); and John M. Gaus, *Reflections on Public Administration* (1947).

"Older" approaches to the study of public administration were generally reform oriented and tended to emphasize "principles" of public administration and practical problems in organization, personnel administration, and fiscal administration. Dwight Waldo, *The Administrative State* (1948) questioned the validity of principles of administration, especially those derived from scientific management in business. *Issues and Ideals in Public Administration* (1953), edited by Waldo, pursues this theme. A turning point in the study of public administration was Herbert Simon's *Administrative Behavior* (1947, rev., 1957) which focused on *behavior* in government organization, especially in decision-making. Harold Stein developed the casebook approach in *Public Administration and Policy Development* (1952).

In 1947, Talcott Parsons translated (with A. M. Henderson) and edited *The Theory of Social and Economic Organization*, a pioneer work in the systematic theory of bureaucratic organization by the German sociologist, Max Weber. This seminal study has generated various "new" approaches to the study of public administration. Recent contributions to the growing body of literature on systematic administrative theory include: Peter Blau, *The Dynamics of Bureaucracy* (2nd. ed., 1963); William J. Gore, *Administrative Decision-making: A Heuristic Model* (1964); Bertram M. Gross, *The Managing of Organizations: the Administrative Struggle* (1964); Sidney Mailick and Edward H. Van Ness (eds.), *Concepts and Issues in Administrative Behavior* (1962); Robert Presthus, *The Organizational Society* (1962); Victor A. Thompson, *Modern Organization* (1961); and Peter Woll, *American Bureaucracy* * (1963).

John J. Corson and Joseph P. Harris provide a brief introduction to the study of *Public Administration in Modern Society* * (1963). Edwin A. Bock (ed.), James W. Fesler, Harold Stein, and Dwight Waldo discuss the tools of the trade in public administration research in *Essays on the Case Method in Public Administration* (1962). Northcote Parkinson has written an amusing but thought-provoking essay on "the rising pyramid" of governmental bureaucracy in *Parkinson's Law* (1957). For a personal approach by one who spent years in the public service, read Louis Brownlow's two volumes, *A Passion for Politics* (1955) and *A Passion for Anonymity* (1958).

Paul Van Riper gives us a *History of the United States Civil Service* (1958). A symposium by the American Assembly, edited by Wallace S. Sayre, is an historical and critical account of federal personnel management: *The Federal Government Service: Its Character, Prestige and Problems* (1955). Marver H. Bernstein, *The Job of the Federal Executive* (1958), and Paul T. David and Ross Pollock, *Executives for Government* (1957), are concerned with the role of "top management," the career and political executives, in the federal service. Warner W. Lloyd, Paul Van Riper, Norman H. Martin, and Orvis F. Collins, *The American Federal Executives* (1964) present "a study of the social and personal characteristics of the civilian and military leaders of the United States government." Franklin P. Kilpatrick, Milton C. Cummings, Jr., and M. Kent Jennings report on an extensive survey by the Brookings Institution to discover what people in various categories think about the federal service, *The Image of the Federal Service* (1964); a *Source Book* presents the detailed data on which the authors base their conclusions.

The take-off point for almost any academic discussion of justice is Plato's *Republic*.*
For the views of some modern scholars, see Carl J. Friedrich and John W. Chapman
(eds.), *Nomos VI; Justice* (1964). But in this text we have been more concerned with
the role of law and the administration of justice in American government rather than
with philosophical abstractions.

As we have indicated in the text, law has many meanings. For varying views
on the role of lawyers and judges in the modern community, see: Benjamin Cardozo,
The Nature of the Judicial Process * (1921), and *Law and Literature* (1931); Edmund
Cahn, *The Sense of Injustice* (1951), and *The Moral Decision* (1955); Jerome Frank,
Law and the Modern Mind * (1930); Roscoe Pound, *Introduction to the Philosophy
of Law* * (rev., 1954); Victor G. Rosenblum, *Law as a Political Instrument* * (1955);
Arthur E. Sutherland, *The Law and One Man Among Many* (1956) and Carl J.
Friedrich, *The Philosophy of Law in Historical Perspective* * (2nd. ed., 1963). A de-
lightfully discursive approach to many facets of the law, justice, and life in general
is provided by the letters of Mr. Justice Holmes to his contemporary, Sir Frederick
Pollock, and to his long-time friend, Harold Laski: *Holmes-Pollock Letters* (1941)
2 vols., and *Holmes-Laski Letters* * (1953).

On the organization and functioning of the federal judiciary, we suggest: Henry
M. Hart and Herbert Wechsler, *The Federal Courts and the Federal System* (1953);
Lewis Mayer, *The American Legal System* (rev., 1964); Jack W. Peltason, *Federal
Courts in the Political Process* * (1955); and Walter F. Murphy and C. Herman
Pritchett, *Courts, Judges, and Politics* (1961). For a realistic appraisal of "courthouse
government," see Jerome Frank's *Courts on Trial* * (1949) and *If Men Were Angels*
(1942). James W. Hurst, in *The Growth of American Law* (1950), discusses the role
of lawyers, legislators, judges, and bureaucrats in the making of American law. Heinz
Eulau and John D. Sprague confront some of the conventional wisdom about the role
of lawyers with new empirical data in *Lawyers in Politics* * (1964). Jack Peltason
follows up the 1955 Supreme Court decision with a study of *Fifty-eight Lonely Men:
Southern Federal Judges and School Desegregation* (1961).

Good treatments of the historical development of constitutional law include:
Alfred H. Kelley and Winfred A. Harbison, *The American Constitution* (rev., 1955);
and Carl Swisher, *American Constitutional Development* (2nd ed., 1954). *Selected
Essays on Constitutional Law* (1938), 4 vols., published under the auspices of the Association of American Law Societies, is a monumental collection of classic essays in
constitutional law. Robert G. McCloskey (ed.), offers a more recent selective and
stimulating collection in *Essays in Constitutional Law* * (1957). Alan Westin has
drawn "a documentary portrait of one constitutional law case," *Youngstown Sheet
and Tube Co.* v. *Sawyer*, covering its full course from a bargaining dispute in the steel
industry to its final disposition in the Supreme Court of the United States: *The
Anatomy of a Constitutional Law Case* (1958). Sixteen historians dramatize sixteen
landmark decisions of the Supreme Court in *Quarrels That Have Shaped The
Constitution* (edited by John A. Garraty, 1964). A journalist, James E. Clayton, highlights the work of the Supreme Court in the October term of 1962, *The Making Of
Justice: The Supreme Court in Action* (1964).

The Supreme Court, as a policy-making body at the highest level of American
government, has been the focus of many critical studies. The standard, conservative,
and generally sympathetic work is Charles Warren, *The Supreme Court in United
States History* (rev., 1928). The battle between the President and the Court in the
1930's aroused public opinion to a peak of emotional intensity and provoked the
legal profession and the political scientists into writing numerous argumentative
monographs. Robert Jackson, in *The Struggle for Judicial Supremacy* (1941), details
the "court-packing plan" of President Roosevelt and its political repercussions. Ed-

ward S. Corwin becomes over-excited in *Twilight of the Supreme Court* (1934); and Robert K. Carr is not entirely calm or dispassionate in *The Supreme Court and Judicial Review* (1942). C. Herman Pritchett's *The Roosevelt Court* (1943) attempts to analyze the political behavior of the Roosevelt Court, with emphasis on the statistical approach; he does much the same for a later Court in *Civil Liberties and the Vinson Court* (1954). The standard work on judicial review is Charles G. Haines, *The American Doctrine of Judicial Supremacy* (rev., 1932), but better attuned to the new jurisprudence and legal realism is *Judicial Legislation* (1952), by Fred V. Cahill, Jr.

Because the Supreme Court in recent years has frequently been in the center of political controversy, it has evoked many new studies. Among these are: Edmond Cahn, *Supreme Court and Supreme Law* (1954); Bernard Schwartz, *The Supreme Court: Constitutional Revolution in Retrospect* (1957); Paul Freund, *On Understanding the Supreme Court* (1949); Robert Jackson, *The Supreme Court in the American System of Government* * (1955); Thomas Reed Powell, *Vagaries and Varieties in Constitutional Interpretation* (1955); and Alexander M. Bickel, *The Least Dangerous Branch* * (1962). John P. Frank, in *Marble Palace* (1958), discusses the role of the Supreme Court today in terms of "the practicalities of power" rather than of legal theory. Alpheus T. Mason writes a shrewd and skillful analysis of the personal and political factors that have colored the judicial process in *The Supreme Court from Taft to Warren* * (1958). Carl Swisher traces the more significant recent cases in constitutional law, particularly those dealing with "clear and present danger" and racial conflict, in *The Supreme Court in Modern Role* (1958). Charles Black popularizes the "legitimating" function of judicial review in *The People and the Court* (1960). Robert McCloskey puts *The American Supreme Court* * (1960) in the sweep of history and finds that the Court has been most successful when it has operated nearer the margins rather than in the center of controversy.

Walter T. Murphy examines the Supreme Court as a decision-maker in the political system in the *Elements of Judicial Strategy* (1964). Whatever Charles S. Hyneman writes is bound to be scholarly, thought-provoking, and controversial; see *The Supreme Court on Trial* (1963). Henry J. Abraham offers a traditional and comparative approach to *The Judicial Process* * (1962) as an introduction to a basic understanding of how the courts operate within the discipline of law. A brief treatment, highly useful to the beginning student in constitutional law, is Loren P. Beth, *Politics, the Constitution, and the Supreme Court* * (1962).

Students of the judicial process have recently tended to substitute quantitative methods for the traditional tools of analysis. See Glendon A. Schubert's *Constitutional Politics: The Political Behavior of Supreme Court Justices and the Constitutional Policies That They Make* (1960), *Quantitative Analysis of Judicial Behavior* (1960), and *Judicial Decision-Making* (1963). *Judicial Behavior* (1964), edited by Schubert, is a "reader in theory and research" that brings within one volume an impressive collection of essays representing an interdisciplinary and behavioral approach to the study of judicial decision-making. John Schmidhauser spotlights problems of selection and internal operation in *The Supreme Court: Its Politics, Personalities and Procedures* * (1960); see also his *Constitutional Law in the Political Process* (1963). *The Supreme Court: Views from Inside* * (1961), edited by Alan Westin, gives us the diverse views of nine justices on the nature of the judicial process, including a sophisticated debate on judicial activism versus judicial self-restraint.

When a judge puts on his judicial robes, he does not discard his own personality. Biographies of the justices are thus illuminating on the nature of the judicial process. Among many, see: Albert J. Beveridge, *Life of John Marshall* (1919), 4 vols.; Carl B. Swisher, *Roger B. Taney* (1935); Charles Fairman, *Mr. Justice Miller and the Supreme Court, 1862–1890* (1939); Willard L. King, *Melville Weston Fuller* (1950); Felix Frankfurter, *Mr. Justice Holmes and the Supreme Court* * (1938); Alpheus T. Mason,

Brandeis—A Free Man's Life (1946); Max Lerner, *The Mind and Faith of Mr. Justice Holmes* (1943); Merle J. Pusey, *Charles Evans Hughes* (1951), 2 vols.; J. Francis Paschal, *Mr. Justice Sutherland* (1951); Samuel J. Konefsky (ed.), *The Constitutional World of Mr. Justice Frankfurter* (1949); John P. Frank, *Mr. Justice Black* (1940); and Alpheus T. Mason, *Harlan Fiske Stone* (1956). Allison Dunham and Philip B. Kurland have edited "nine short essays in legal biography" dealing with Marshall, Taney, Hughes, Stone, Bradley, Holmes, Brandeis, Sutherland, and Rutledge: *Mr. Justice* (1956). Wallace Mendelson's study of *Justices Black and Frankfurter* (1961) focuses on the debate between judicial activism and judicial restraint as exemplified in the work of these two great justices on the Court.

Part Four Outputs of the Political Process: Rewards and Deprivations

Periodical Literature

Public policy changes so rapidly that anyone who wants to keep up will find current periodicals an essential source. In addition to a local newspaper, most people who want a full coverage of the news rely on *The New York Times;* unlike most slogans, this newspaper's claim of offering "All the News That's Fit to Print" is fairly accurate. In addition to comprehensive news reports, the *Times* prints the full text of important speeches, laws, and court decisions.

Weekly news magazines devote much of their space to political news and offer more interpretative treatments of important events. "The News of the Week in Review" section of the Sunday *New York Times* is probably the most impartial of these weekly surveys; its news articles follow the newspaper tradition of highly factual reporting, and its "opinion pieces" are all signed columns clearly distinguished from the news. The mass-circulation weeklies are all somewhat conservative in tone. *Time* is perhaps the most conservative of all, and its bright, authoritative tone is highly popular. *United States News and World Report* is less brash but almost equally conservative; its feature of interviews with prominent figures commands interest and sometimes "makes" news itself. *Newsweek* is perhaps the least opinionated of the three mass-circulation weeklies.

As weekly journals of opinion, *The Nation, The New Leader,* and *The New Republic* interpret events with an openly liberal bias. Although their circulation is much smaller than that of the mass-circulation weeklies, they may have a greater influence than their circulation would suggest. *The Reporter,* a fortnightly, also has a liberal editorial policy; it deals less with the news of each two-week period than with interpretation and comment on more enduring problems. *The National Review* takes the conservative approach.

The *Congressional Quarterly Weekly Report* is not sold to individuals, but it is available in libraries. Since reading the daily *Congressional Record* is extremely time-consuming, the *Congressional Quarterly's* summary of debates and report of votes are an invaluable aid to the student of politics.

The "quality" monthly magazines, notably *The Atlantic Monthly* and *Harper's,* are not devoted exclusively to public affairs, but they do offer many penetrating articles on politics. These articles represent a variety of ideological positions.

Members of the American Political Science Association were recently questioned about their publication preferences in the professional journals. Those most frequently mentioned as enhancing "professional prestige" were: *American Political Science Review, Journal of Politics, World Politics, Political Science Quarterly, Administrative Science Quarterly, Western Political Science Quarterly, Public Administration Review, Public Opinion Quarterly, Midwest Journal of Politics,* and *American Behavioral Sci-*

entist. All these journals publish research findings that are concerned with basic political problems rather than with "news." The list, however, is by no means exclusive. Other prestige journals focus on special interests. For example, many law schools publish law reviews which constitute a gold mine of discussion on legal problems involved in public policies. Scholarly writing often has an incidental topical interest, and it frequently clarifies the underlying processes that produce the news. The *Bulletin of the Public Affairs Information Service* and the *Reader's Guide to Periodical Literature* are indexes for use in locating information on current affairs in a wide variety of publications. Every issue of the *American Political Science Review* includes a listing of selected articles and documents on American government and politics which will keep you abreast of current research.

Civil Rights and Civil Liberties

Fortunately, the literature on civil rights and personal liberties seems to be endless. Allen Rutland writes about *The Birth of the Bill of Rights, 1776–1791* (1955). On the First Amendment, the classic discussion is Zechariah Chafee, Jr.'s *Free Speech in the United States* (1941). Glenn Abernathy emphasizes another guarantee of the First Amendment in *The Right of Assembly and Association* (1961). David Fellman explains what rights Americans are guaranteed when they are accused of crime in *The Defendant's Rights* (1958). In *The Rationing of Justice* (1964), Arnold S. Treback gives us a pretty grim report on *how* rights are violated and *how often* in the process of criminal justice, from arrest through conviction and appeal. The Dean of the Harvard Law School, Erwin N. Griswold, treats the Fifth Amendment as a time-honored symbol of individual liberty in the Anglo-American tradition, *The Fifth Amendment Today* * (1955). Sidney Hook, professor of philosophy at New York University, takes an opposing viewpoint in *Common Sense and the Fifth Amendment* * (1963).

Horace Flack examines the intent of the Framers in *The Adoption of the Fourteenth Amendment* (1908). *The Quest for Equality* (1960), by Robert J. Harris, is a witty and profound discussion of the Fourteenth Amendment as it was written and as it has been interpreted by the courts. John P. Roche, in *Courts and Rights* * (1961), offers us a pocket-size introduction to the American judiciary in action with emphasis on the rights of citizens in the democratic process. Robert E. Cushman, *Civil Liberties in the United States* * (1956), Osmond K. Fraenkel, *The Supreme Court and Civil Liberties* (2nd ed., 1964), and George W. Spicer, *The Supreme Court and Fundamental Freedoms* * (1959), also emphasize court cases on civil rights.

That modern government can be a safeguard rather than a threat to liberty is evident in such official reports as: *To Secure These Rights* (1947), by the President's Committee on Civil Rights; *Whom Shall We Welcome?* (1953), by the President's Commission on Immigration and Naturalization; and *Equal Protection of the Laws in Public Higher Education* (1960), by the United States Commission on Civil Rights. The *Annual Reports of the American Civil Liberties Union* are a continuing source of information on the actual as well as the legal status of civil rights in the country. The Sub-committee on Constitutional Rights of the Senate Committee on the Judiciary is an invaluable source of primary materials—hearings, staff studies, committee reports—which illustrate how the many facets of civil rights and liberties enter into the political process and emerge as public policies.

Henry Steele Commager strongly defends the majority-rule aspect of democracy, and insists that it poses no threat to minority rights, in *Majority Rule and Minority Rights* (1943). In *Communism, Conformity and Civil Liberties* (1955), Samuel A. Stouffer reports on American attitudes toward nonconformists during the "McCarthy" era. Gunnar Myrdal's *An American Dilemma: The Negro Problem and Modern Democracy* * (1944, 1964) is a monumental study of American democracy, with special emphasis on the problems of Negroes. Felix E. Oppenheim analyzes behavioral concepts of freedom, unfreedom, control, and power in *Dimensions of Freedom* (1961).

The Great Rights (1963), edited by Edmond Cahn, is a collection of essays by justices of the Supreme Court discussing various aspects of the Bill of Rights.

The rights of minority groups, as a matter of public policy, is one of the most controversial issues of our times. Henry A. Myers puts the question bluntly, *Are Men Equal?* * (1945). Wallace Mendelson provides a résumé of a five-volume report of the United States Commission on Civil Rights: *Discrimination* * (1962). Joseph Tussman has edited a collection of judicial decisions, *The Supreme Court on Racial Discrimination* * (1963). For very different viewpoints on this most disturbing problem of racism in America see: C. Vann Woodward, *The Strange Career of Jim Crow* (1955); Charles Morgan, *A Time To Speak* (1964); Lewis Killian and Charles Grigg, *Racial Crisis in America: Leadership in Crisis* * (1964); and Benjamin Muse, *Virginia's Massive Resistance* (1961). The *Race Relations Reporter*, published quarterly by the Vanderbilt University School of Law, is an excellent source for documentary materials on the race problem. Current development may also be followed in *Southern School News*.

Recent decisions of the Supreme Court interpreting the "establishment clause" and the "free exercise" of religion have created considerable excitement. *The Wall Between Church and State* * (1963), edited by Dallin H. Oaks, covers the problem from various angles. Joseph Tussman has collected the leading judicial opinions in *The Supreme Court on Church and State* * (1962). Every President from Truman to Johnson has urged change in our immigration policies. Marion T. Bennett discusses some of the issues in *American Immigration Policies* (1963). *A Nation of Immigrants,* * by President John F. Kennedy, published posthumously in 1964, was intended to back up his proposed policies to open the gates on a more rational basis than the "national origins" system.

Individual liberties versus national security is a continuing issue in American politics. For opposing views on problems of national security, see the Subcommittee on Constitutional Rights of the Senate Judiciary Committee, *Hearings, Security and Constitutional Rights* (84th Cong., 2nd Sess., 1955). For a comprehensive treatment of the legal side of the issue, see Walter Gelhorn, *Individual Freedom and Government Restraints* (1956). Harry Howe Ransome examines the agencies and institutions created for national security since World War II, *Can American Democracy Survive Cold War?* * (1963). For reactions in the era of "McCarthyism," look at Alan Barth, *The Loyalty of Free Men* * (1951); Elmer H. Davis, *But We Were Born Free* * (1954); and Owen Lattimore, *Ordeal by Slander* * (1950).

General Welfare and Common Defense

There is no end to the literature on policies to promote the general welfare and provide for the common defense. Many of the titles listed in Part One, "Cultural and Economic Context," will be useful in understanding how policy both reflects and affects the contemporary environment. Policy is goal-oriented, but the goals, like lodestars, keep moving ahead of us. President Eisenhower in 1960 appointed a Commission on National Goals; its *Report,* * with supporting essays, offered new directions for the 1960's, but already we view the future from a different perspective. In 1958, John K. Galbraith captured the mood of the time in *The Affluent Society* *; Michael Harrington focuses on a different aspect in *The Other America* * (1962); Hubert H. Humphrey, *War on Poverty* * (1964), though a piece of campaign literature, does prefigure official policies. For President Johnson's hopes and plans for "the Great Society" see his 1965 Inaugural Address, State of the Union message, budget message, and long series of special messages.

For a scholarly approach to the processes and relationships by which scarce resources are translated into public policy, see Robert A. Dahl and Charles E. Lindblom, *Politics, Economics and Welfare* (1953). Also see Eugene V. Rostow, *Planning for Freedom: The Public Law of American Capitalism* (1960), and Adolf Berle, *The*

American Economic Republic (1963). John R. Bunting discusses the relations of government and the economic order from the point of view of a forward-looking businessman in *The Hidden Face of Free Enterprise* (1964). Thurman Arnold in *The Folklore of Capitalism* * (1938) conveys some of the intellectually exciting ideas that fired the New Deal. In *The New American Political Economy: A Synthesis of Politics and Economics* (1962), Marshall E. Dimock attempts to join the process of current politics with the principles of modern economics.

The American economic system today is very much a part of the world economy. Raymond A. Bauer, Ithiel De Sola Pool, and Lewis Anthony Dexter have done an excellent study of foreign trade legislation in the broad context of the political process, *American Business and Public Policy: The Politics of Foreign Trade* (1963). Other books that may be helpful in understanding America's role in international economics include: Gunnar Myrdal, *Beyond the Welfare State* * (1960); Max F. Millikan and Donald L. M. Blackmer (eds.), *The Emerging Nations* * (1961); W. W. Rostow, *The Stages of Economic Growth, A Non-Communist Manifesto* * (1960); and John Kenneth Galbraith, *Economic Development* (1964).

Jack W. Peltason and James M. Burns (eds.), provide a good supplementary text for this volume, *Functions and Policies of American Government* (rev., 1962). Many people are skeptical about the economics that underlie the concept of "the Great Society." Two books that furnish considerable data on American economic resources and financial capabilities are: Gabriel Kolko, *Wealth and Power in America* * (1962), and James N. Morgan *et al.*, *Income and Welfare in the United States* (1962). The basic instrument for all policy-planning is the budget; see Aaron Wildavsky, *The Politics of the Budgetary Process* * (1964).

Many social scientists have examined particular aspects of public policy in the general area of economics and welfare. Among these, we mention: Walton H. Hamilton, *The Politics of Industry* (1957); Eveline M. Burns, *Social Security and Public Policy* (1956); Herman M. Somers and Anne R. Somers, *Doctors, Patients, and Health Insurance* (1961); Reo M. Christenson, *The Brannan Plan: Farm Politics and Policy* (1959); Robert C. Wood, *Suburbia: Its People and Their Politics* (1958); and Douglas Knight (ed.), *The Federal Government and Higher Education* * (1960).

The dominating issue in American national policies of the 1960's is the common defense and national survival. But this is by no means a wholly military problem; as we have indicated in the text, the military-industrial-scientific complex pervades the American economy. *Organizing for Defense* (1961) by Paul Y. Hammond traces the development of the American military establishment in the twentieth century, concentrating more on the politics of organization than on strategic policy matters. Charles J. Hitch and Roland N. McKean stress the economic choices involved in military preparedness, *The Economics of Defense in the Nuclear Age* (1960). The American Assembly, in 1961, discussed *Arms Control: Issues for the Public.** Jack Raymond, a highly knowledgeable journalist, appraises *Power at the Pentagon* (1964). Floyd Matson assesses the impact of science on our twentieth century society in *Man, Science and Society* (1964). *Scientists and National Policy-Making* (1964), edited by Robert Gilpin and Christopher Wright, examines the role of the scientific establishment in national politics and public policies.

Unlike the utopian novels of earlier generations, today's fictional views of future prospects are predominantly "futopian" in character, emphasizing the futility of man's efforts to control his destiny. Whereas Edward Bellamy's *Looking Backward* * (1889) depicted the advantages of a rationally ordered society, today's critics portray the cramping effect on individuality that a highly efficient "rationality" might bring. See, for example, Ray Bradbury, *Fahrenheit 451* * (1953); Aldous Huxley, *Brave New World* * (1932) and *Brave New World Revisited* (1958); George Orwell, *1984* * (1949); and B. F. Skinner, *Walden Two* (1948).

Foreign Policy and National Security

Foreign policy is always a highly charged issue, not only in the public forum but also in the official agencies. *The Liberal Papers* * (1962), with an introduction by Representative James Roosevelt, comprises a dozen essays, "reflective, critical, and constructive," by well-known social scientists, designed to publicize the foreign policy views of the "liberal group" in Congress. The *Conservative Papers* * (1964), with an introduction by Representative Melvin R. Laird, brings together another group of essays, by a different but equally distinguished group of scholars, to counterpose the domestic and foreign policy views of the "conservative group" in Congress.

Among a number of excellent over-all studies of foreign policy—how it is made and how it is implemented—see: Cecil V. Crabb, Jr., *American Foreign Policy in the Nuclear Age* (1965); Charles O. Lerche, *Foreign Policy of the American People* (2nd ed., 1961); James L. McCamy, *Conduct of the New Diplomacy* (1964); Paul Seabury, *Power, Freedom, and Diplomacy* (1963); and Bradford Westerfield, *The Instruments of America's Foreign Policy* (1963). *World Pressures on American Foreign Policy* * (1964), edited by Marian D. Irish, is a collection of essays by well-known political scientists who examine the pressure of external events and forces on American policy decisions. William G. Carleton offers a highly readable and realistic background for understanding *The Revolution in American Foreign Policy* * (1964), covering the period since World War II. *The Policy Machine* (1960), by Robert Ellsworth, catches the Department of State in action at the end of the Eisenhower Administration.

Many official decision-makers have published their views on foreign policy, some critical, some defensive, some after leaving office, some while still in office. Among these are Dean Acheson, *Power and Diplomacy* (1958); Thomas K. Finletter, *Foreign Policy: The Next Phase* * (1960); Charles Burton Marshall, *The Limits of Foreign Policy* (1954); Robert R. Bowie, *Shaping The Future* (1964); W. W. Rostow, *View from the Seventh Floor* (1964); and Senator J. W. Fulbright, *Old Myths and New Realities* * (1964), and *Prospects for the West* (1963).

Congressional hearings, staff studies, reports of study missions, and committee reports cover the whole range of American foreign policy. See especially the publications of the Senate Committee on Foreign Relations and the House Committee on Foreign Affairs. The annual congressional hearings on appropriations, requested by the various agencies concerned with foreign policy and national security, provide practical insights into the policy process as well as useful information on the programs and operations that constitute the substance of policies.

The role of Congress in foreign policy has recently attracted the attention of many political scientists. General works include: Robert Dahl, *Congress and Foreign Policy* * (1950), and James A. Robinson, *Congress and Foreign Policy-Making: A Study in Legislative Influence and Initiative* (1962). David N. Farnsworth has written an excellent monograph on *The Senate Committee on Foreign Relations* (1961), and Holbert S. Carroll on *The House of Representatives and Foreign Affairs* (1958).

Students of foreign policy are gratefully indebted to the Council of Foreign Relations. Its quarterly, *Foreign Affairs*, provides a forum for authoritative and scholarly articles and offers an annotated bibliography of recent books and source materials on international relations in every issue. How extensive this service is we discover in the *Foreign Affairs Bibliography 1952-62* (1964), which comprises some 8,500 listings of important books annotated by Henry L. Roberts (which explains why our selective list seems so inadequate to us!). The Council also publishes, in addition to many monographs, *Documents on American Foreign Relations* and *The United States in World Affairs*, both annual publications which are most convenient references for all students of American foreign policy. The American Assembly publishes reports of its annual meetings, many of which focus on problems of foreign policy; see, for example, *The Representation of the United States Abroad* * (1956); *The Secretary of State* * (1960); and *Cultural Affairs and Foreign Relations* * (1963).

Perhaps the publications of the Subcommittee on National Security of the Senate Committee on Government Operations are the most illuminating source of official and unofficial views on problems relating to national security. The literature on national security is limitless, and it is difficult for the lay reader to make qualitative judgments. Henry A. Kissinger argues the feasibility of "limited nuclear war" in *Nuclear Weapons and Foreign Policy* * (1957) and suggests *The Necessity for Choice* * (1961). Neville Brown presents the case for *Strategic Mobility* (1964). Frederick Gareau offers a book of readings on *The Balance of Power and Nuclear Deterrence* * (1962). *The Dispersion of Nuclear Weapons* (1964), edited by Richard Rosecrance, discusses the spread of nuclear weapons among the nations of the world.

On military policy, see Samuel P. Huntington, *The Soldier and the State: The Theory and Politics of Civil-Military Relations* (1957), and Edgar S. Furniss, Jr., *American Military Policy* (1957). Harry Howe Ransome throws light on an important but little understood aspect of security policy in *Central Intelligence and National Security* (1958). In *Strategic Intelligence* (1961), William M. McGovern describes the processes of gathering intelligence and then sets forth his ideas of what should be done in terms of national policy to meet "the shape of tomorrow." William W. Kaufmann explains (mostly in the words of the Secretary of Defense) *The McNamara Strategy* (1964), the development of a new method of decision-making in the Pentagon. Robert Murphy, a long-time career officer in the State Department, gives us a fascinating first-hand account of many crises in American diplomacy, especially in World War I and the years immediately following, in *Diplomat Among Warriors* (1964).

Less concerned with the substance of policy, more interested in developing a systematic theory of foreign policy, a number of political scientists have recently reported on their research and findings: George Modelsky, *A Theory of Foreign Policy* (1962); Richard C. Snyder, H. S. Bruck, and Burton Sapin (eds.), *Foreign Policy Decision-Making: An Approach to the Study of International Politics* (1962); Bernard C. Cohen, *The Influence of Non-governmental Groups on Foreign Policy-Making* (1959) and *The Press and Foreign Policy* * (1963); and James N. Rosenau, *Public Opinion and Foreign Policy* (1961) and (as editor) *International Politics and Foreign Policy: A Reader in Theory and Research* (1963).

Among the novels dealing with foreign policy, James Aldridge's *The Diplomat* (1950) centers on Western and Soviet diplomats in the Near East. Pat Frank builds *Affairs of State* * (1948) around a Foreign Service officer; William J. Lederer and Eugene Burdick attack American diplomatic bungling in *The Ugly American* * (1958); and Nevil Shute describes world destruction by atomic war in *On the Beach* * (1957).

The Declaration of Independence

(As it reads in the parchment copy)

The Unanimous Declaration of the Thirteen United States of America

When in the Course of human events, it becomes necessary for one people to dissolve the political bands, which have connected them with another, and to assume among the powers of the earth, the separate and equal station to which the Laws of Nature and of Nature's God entitle them, a decent respect to the opinions of mankind requires that they should declare the causes which impel them to the separation. — We hold these truths to be self-evident, that all men are created equal, that they are endowed by their Creator with certain unalienable Rights, that among these are Life, Liberty and the pursuit of Happiness. — That to secure these rights, Governments are instituted among Men, deriving their just powers from the consent of the governed, — That whenever any Form of Government becomes destructive of these ends, it is the Right of the People to alter or to abolish it, and to institute new Government, laying its foundation on such principles and organizing its powers in such form, as to them shall seem most likely to effect their Safety and Happiness. Prudence, indeed, will dictate that Governments long established should not be changed for light and transient causes; and accordingly all experience hath shewn, that mankind are more disposed to suffer, while evils are sufferable, than to right themselves by abolishing the forms to which they are accustomed. But when a long train of abuses and usurpations, pursuing invariably the same Object evinces a design to reduce them under absolute Despotism, it is their right, it is their duty, to throw off such Government, and to provide new Guards for their future security. — Such

has been the patient sufferance of these Colonies; and such is now the necessity which constrains them to alter their former Systems of Government. The history of the present King of Great Britain is a history of repeated injuries and usurpations, all having in direct object the establishment of an absolute Tyranny over these States. To prove this, let Facts be submitted to a candid world. — He has refused his Assent to Laws, the most wholesome and necessary for the public good. — He has forbidden his Governors to pass Laws of immediate and pressing importance, unless suspended in their operation till his Assent should be obtained; and when so suspended, he has utterly neglected to attend to them. — He has refused to pass other Laws for the accommodation of large districts of people, unless those people would relinquish the right of Representation in the Legislature, a right inestimable to them and formidable to tyrants only. — He has called together legislative bodies at places unusual, uncomfortable, and distant from the depository of their public Records, for the sole purpose of fatiguing them into compliance with his measures. — He has dissolved Representative Houses repeatedly, for opposing with manly firmness his invasions on the rights of the people. — He has refused for a long time, after such dissolutions, to cause others to be elected; whereby the Legislative powers, incapable of Annihilation, have returned to the People at large for their exercise; the State remaining in the meantime exposed to all the dangers of invasion from without, and convulsions within. — He has endeavoured to prevent the population of these States; for that purpose obstructing the Laws for Naturalization of Foreigners; refusing to pass others to encourage their migrations hither, and raising the conditions of new Appropriations of Lands. — He has obstructed the Administration of Justice, by refusing his Assent to Laws for establishing Judiciary powers. — He has made Judges dependent on his Will alone, for the tenure of their offices, and the amount and payment of their salaries. — He has erected a multitude of New Offices, and sent hither swarms of Officers to harrass our people, and eat out their substance. — He has kept among us, in times of peace, Standing Armies without the Consent of our legislatures. — He has affected to render the Military independent of and superior to the Civil power. — He has combined with others to subject us to a jurisdiction foreign to our constitution, and unacknowledged by our laws; giving his Assent to their Acts of pretended Legislation. — For quartering large bodies of armed troops among us: — For protecting them, by a mock Trial, from punishment for any Murders which they should commit on the Inhabitants of these States: — For cutting off our Trade with all parts of the world: — For imposing Taxes on us without our Consent: — For depriving us in many cases, of the benefits of Trial by Jury: — For transporting us beyond Seas to be tried for pretended offenses: — For abolishing the free System of English Laws in a neighboring Province, establishing therein an Arbitrary government, and enlarging its Boundaries so as to render it at once an example and fit instrument for introducing the same absolute rule into these Colonies: — For taking away our Charters, abolishing our most valuable Laws, and altering fundamentally the Forms of our Governments: — For suspending our own Legislatures, and declaring themselves invested with power to legislate for us in all cases whatsoever. — He has abdicated Government here, by declaring us out of his Protection and waging War against us. — He has plundered our seas, ravaged our Coasts, burnt our towns, and destroyed the lives of our people. — He is at this time transporting large Armies of foreign Mercenaries to compleat the works of death, desolation and tyranny, already begun with circumstances of Cruelty & perfidy, scarcely parallel'd in the most barbarous ages, and totally unworthy the Head of a civilized nation. — He

has constrained our fellow Citizens taken Captive on the high Seas to bear Arms against their Country, to become the executioners of their friends and Brethren, or to fall themselves by their hands. — He has excited domestic insurrections amongst us, and has endeavoured to bring on the inhabitants of our frontiers, the merciless Indian Savages, whose known rule of warfare, is an undistinguished destruction of all ages, sexes and conditions. In every stage of these Oppressions We have Petitioned for Redress in the most humble terms: Our repeated Petitions have been answered only by repeated injury. A Prince whose character is thus marked by every act which may define a Tyrant, is unfit to be the ruler of a free people. Nor have We been wanting in attentions to our Brittish brethren. We have warned them from time to time of attempts by their legislature to extend an unwarrantable jurisdiction over us. We have reminded them of the circumstances of our emigration and settlement here. We have appealed to their native justice and magnanimity, and we have conjured them by the ties of our common kindred to disavow these usurpations, which would inevitably interrupt our connections and correspondence. They too have been deaf to the voice of justice and of consanguinity. We must, therefore, acquiesce in the necessity, which denounces our Separation, and hold them, as we hold the rest of mankind, Enemies in War, in Peace Friends. —

We, therefore, the Representatives of the united States of America, in General Congress, Assembled, appealing to the Supreme Judge of the world for the rectitude of our intentions do, in the Name, and by the Authority of the good People of these Colonies, solemnly publish and declare, That these United Colonies are, and of Right ought to be Free and Independent States; that they are Absolved from all Allegiance to the British Crown, and that all political connection between them and the State of Great Britain, is and ought to be totally dissolved; and that as Free and Independent States, they have full Power to levy War, conclude Peace, contract Alliances, establish Commerce, and to do all other Acts and Things which Independent States may of right do. — And for the support of this Declaration, with a firm reliance on the protection of divine Providence, we mutually pledge to each other our Lives, our Fortunes and our sacred Honor.

The Constitution
of the United States of America

We the People of the United States, in Order to form a more perfect Union, establish Justice, insure domestic Tranquility, provide for the common defence, promote the general Welfare, and secure the Blessings of Liberty to ourselves and our Posterity, do ordain and establish this Constitution for the United States of America.

Article I

Section. 1. All legislative Powers herein granted shall be vested in a Congress of the United States, which shall consist of a Senate and House of Representatives.

Section. 2. The House of Representatives shall be composed of Members chosen every second Year by the People of the several States, and the Electors in each State shall have the Qualifications requisite for Electors of the most numerous Branch of the State Legislature.

No Person shall be a Representative who shall not have attained to the age of twenty five Years, and been seven Years a Citizen of the United States, and who shall not, when elected, be an Inhabitant of that State in which he shall be chosen.

Representatives and direct Taxes shall be apportioned among the several States which may be included within this Union, according to their respective Numbers, *which shall be determined by adding to the whole Number of free Persons, including those bound to Service for a Term of Years, and excluding Indians not taxed, three fifths of all other persons.*[1] The actual Enumeration shall be made within three Years after the first Meeting of the Congress of the United States, and within every subsequent Term of ten Years, in such Manner as they shall by Law direct. The Number of Representatives shall not exceed one for every thirty Thousand, but each State shall have at Least one Representative; and until such enumeration shall be made, the State of New Hampshire shall be entitled to chuse three, Massachusetts eight, Rhode-Island and Providence Plantations one, Connecticut five, New-York six, New Jersey four, Pennsylvania eight, Delaware one, Maryland six, Virginia ten, North Carolina five, South Carolina five, and Georgia three.

When vacancies happen in the Representation from any State, the Executive Authority thereof shall issue Writs of Election to fill such Vacancies.

The House of Representatives shall chuse their Speaker and other Officers; and shall have the sole Power of Impeachment.

Section. 3. The Senate of the United States shall be composed of two Senators from each State, *chosen by the Legislature thereof,*[2] for six Years; and each Senator shall have one Vote.

Immediately after they shall be assembled in Consequence of the first Election, they shall be divided as equally as may be into

[1] Throughout, italics are used to indicate passages altered by subsequent amendments. In this instance, for example, see 14th Amendment.

[2] See 17th Amendment.

three Classes. The Seats of the Senators of the first Class shall be vacated at the Expiration of the second Year, of the second Class at the Expiration of the fourth Year, and of the third Class at the Expiration of the sixth Year, so that one third may be chosen every second Year; *and if Vacancies happen by Resignation, or otherwise, during the Recess of the Legislature of any State, the Executive thereof may make temporary Appointments until the next Meeting of the Legislature, which shall then fill such Vacancies.*[3]

No Person shall be a Senator who shall not have attained to the Age of thirty Years, and been nine Years a Citizen of the United States, and who shall not, when elected, be an Inhabitant of that State for which he shall be chosen.

The Vice President of the United States shall be President of the Senate, but shall have no Vote, unless they be equally divided.

The Senate shall chuse their other Officers, and also a President pro tempore, in the Absence of the Vice President, or when he shall exercise the Office of President of the United States.

The Senate shall have the sole Power to try all Impeachments. When sitting for that Purpose, they shall be on Oath or Affirmation. When the President of the United States is tried, the Chief Justice shall preside: And no Person shall be convicted without the Concurrence of two thirds of the Members present.

Judgment in Cases of Impeachment shall not extend further than to removal from Office, and disqualification to hold and enjoy any Office of honor, Trust or Profit under the United States: but the Party convicted shall nevertheless be liable and subject to Indictment, Trial, Judgment and Punishment, according to Law.

Section. 4. The Times, Places and Manner of holding Elections for Senators and Representatives, shall be prescribed in each State by the Legislature thereof; but the Congress may at any time by Law make or alter such Regulations, except as to the Places of chusing Senators.

The Congress shall assemble at least once in every Year, and such Meeting shall be on the first Monday in December, unless they shall by Law appoint a different Day.[4]

Section. 5. Each House shall be the Judge of the Elections, Returns and Qualifications of its own Members, and a Majority of each shall constitute a Quorum to do Business;

but a smaller Number may adjourn from day to day, and may be authorized to compel the Attendance of absent Members, in such Manner, and under such Penalties as each House may provide.

Each House may determine the Rules of its Proceedings, punish its Members for disorderly Behaviour, and, with the Concurrence of two thirds, expel a Member.

Each House shall keep a Journal of its Proceedings, and from time to time publish the same, excepting such Parts as may in their Judgment require Secrecy; and the Yeas and Nays of the Members of either House on any question shall, at the Desire of one fifth of those Present, be entered on the Journal.

Neither House, during the Session of Congress, shall, without the Consent of the other, adjourn for more than three days, nor to any other Place than that in which the two Houses shall be sitting.

Section. 6. The Senators and Representatives shall receive a Compensation for their Services, to be ascertained by Law, and paid out of the Treasury of the United States. They shall in all Cases, except Treason, Felony and Breach of the Peace, be privileged from Arrest during their Attendance at the Session of their respective Houses, and in going to and returning from the same; and for any Speech or Debate in either House, they shall not be questioned in any other Place.

No Senator or Representative shall, during the Time for which he was elected, be appointed to any civil Office under the Authority of the United States, which shall have been created, or the Emoluments whereof shall have been encreased during such time; and no Person holding any Office under the United States, shall be a Member of either House during his Continuance in Office.

Section. 7. All Bills for raising Revenue shall originate in the House of Representatives; but the Senate may propose or concur with Amendments as on other Bills.

Every Bill which shall have passed the House of Representatives and the Senate, shall, before it become a Law, be presented to the President of the United States; if he approve he shall sign it, but if not he shall return it, with his Objections to that House in which it shall have originated, who shall enter the Objections at large on their Journal, and proceed to reconsider it. If after such Reconsideration two thirds of that House shall agree to pass the Bill, it shall be sent, together with the Objections,

[3] *Ibid.*
[4] See 20th Amendment.

to the other House, by which it shall likewise be reconsidered, and if approved by two thirds of that House, it shall become a Law. But in all such Cases the Votes of both Houses shall be determined by Yeas and Nays, and the Names of the Persons voting for and against the Bill shall be entered on the Journal of each House respectively. If any Bill shall not be returned by the President within ten Days (Sundays excepted) after it shall have been presented to him, the Same shall be a Law, in like Manner as if he had signed it, unless Congress by their Adjournment prevent its Return, in which Case it shall not be a Law.

Every Order, Resolution, or Vote to which the Concurrence of the Senate and House of Representatives may be necessary (except on a question of Adjournment) shall be presented to the President of the United States; and before the Same shall take Effect, shall be approved by him, or being disapproved by him, shall be repassed by two thirds of the Senate and House of Representatives, according to the Rules and Limitations prescribed in the Case of a Bill.

Section. 8. The Congress shall have Power To lay and collect Taxes, Duties, Imposts and Excises, to pay the Debts and provide for the common Defence and general Welfare of the United States; but all Duties, Imposts and Excises shall be uniform throughout the United States;

To borrow Money on the credit of the United States;

To regulate Commerce with foreign Nations, and among the several States, and with the Indian Tribes;

To establish an uniform Rule of Naturalization, and uniform Laws on the subject of Bankruptcies throughout the United States;

To coin Money, regulate the Value thereof, and of foreign Coin, and fix the Standard of Weights and Measures;

To provide for the Punishment of counterfeiting the Securities and current Coin of the United States;

To establish Post Offices and post Roads;

To promote the Progress of Science and useful Arts, by securing for limited Times to Authors and Inventors the exclusive Right to their respective Writings and Discoveries;

To constitute Tribunals inferior to the Supreme Court;

To define and punish Piracies and Felonies committed on the high Seas, and Offences against the Law of Nations;

To declare War, grant Letters of Marque and Reprisal, and make Rules concerning Captures on Land and Water;

To raise and support Armies, but no Appropriation of Money to that Use shall be for a longer Term than two Years;

To provide and maintain a Navy;

To make Rules for the Government and Regulation of the land and naval Forces;

To provide for calling forth the Militia to execute the Laws of the Union, suppress Insurrections and repel Invasions;

To provide for organizing, arming, and disciplining, the Militia, and for governing such Part of them as may be employed in the Service of the United States, reserving to the States respectively, the Appointment of the Officers, and the Authority of training the Militia according to the discipline prescribed by Congress;

To exercise exclusive Legislation in all Cases whatsoever, over such District (not exceeding ten Miles square) as may, by Cession of particular States, and the Acceptance of Congress, become the Seat of the Government of the United States, and to exercise like Authority over all Places purchased by the Consent of the Legislature of the State in which the Same shall be, for the Erection of Forts, Magazines, Arsenals, dock-Yards, and other needful Buildings;—And

To make all Laws which shall be necessary and proper for carrying into Execution the foregoing Powers, and all other Powers vested by this Constitution in the Government of the United States, or in any Department or Officer thereof.

Section. 9. The Migration or Importation of such Persons as any of the States now existing shall think proper to admit, shall not be prohibited by the Congress prior to the Year one thousand eight hundred and eight, but a Tax or duty may be imposed on such Importation, not exceeding ten dollars for each Person.

The Privilege of the Writ of Habeas Corpus shall not be suspended, unless when in Cases of Rebellion or Invasion the public Safety may require it.

No Bill of Attainder or ex post facto Law shall be passed.

No Capitation, or other direct, Tax shall be laid, unless in Proportion to the Census or Enumeration herein before directed to be taken.

No Tax or Duty shall be laid on Articles exported from any State.

No Preference shall be given by any Regulation of Commerce or Revenue to the

Ports of one State over those of another: nor shall Vessels bound to, or from, one State, be obliged to enter, clear, or pay Duties in another.

No Money shall be drawn from the Treasury, but in Consequence of Appropriations made by Law; and a regular Statement and Account of the Receipts and Expenditures of all public Money shall be published from time to time.

No title of Nobility shall be granted by the United States: And no Person holding any Office of Profit or Trust under them, shall, without the Consent of the Congress, accept of any present, Emolument, Office, or Title, of any kind whatever, from any King, Prince, or foreign State.

Section. 10. No State shall enter into any Treaty, Alliance, or Confederation; grant Letters of Marque and Reprisal; coin Money; emit Bills of Credit; make any Thing but gold and silver Coin a Tender in Payment of Debts; pass any Bill of Attainder, ex post facto Law, or Law impairing the Obligation of Contracts, or Grant any Title of Nobility.

No State shall, without the Consent of the Congress, lay any Imposts or Duties on Imports or Exports, except what may be absolutely necessary for executing its inspection Laws: and the net Produce of all Duties and Imposts, laid by any State on Imports or Exports, shall be for the Use of the Treasury of the United States; and all such Laws shall be subject to the Revision and Controul of the Congress.

No State shall, without the Consent of Congress, lay any Duty of Tonnage, keep Troops, or Ships of War in time of Peace, enter into any Agreement or Compact with another State, or with a foreign Power, or engage in War, unless actually invaded, or in such imminent Danger as will not admit of delay.

Article II

Section. 1. The executive Power shall be vested in a President of the United States of America. He shall hold his Office during the Term of four Years, and, together with the Vice President, chosen for the same Term be elected as follows:

Each State shall appoint, in such Manner as the Legislature thereof may direct, a Number of Electors, equal to the whole Number of Senators and Representatives to which the State may be entitled in the Congress: but no Senator or Representative, or Person holding an Office of Trust or Profit under the United States, shall be appointed an Elector.

The Electors shall meet in their respective States, and vote by Ballot for two Persons, of whom one at least shall not be an Inhabitant of the same State with themselves. And they shall make a List of all the Persons voted for, and of the Number of Votes for each; which List they shall sign and certify, and transmit sealed to the Seat of the Government of the United States, directed to the President of the Senate. The President of the Senate shall, in the Presence of the Senate and House of Representatives, open all the Certificates, and the Votes shall then be counted. The Person having the greatest Number of Votes shall be the President, if such Number be a Majority of the whole Number of Electors appointed; and if there be more than one who have such Majority, and have an equal Number of Votes, then the House of Representatives shall immediately chuse by Ballot one of them for President; and if no Person have a Majority, then from the five highest on the List the said House shall in like Manner chuse the President. But in chusing the President, the Votes shall be taken by States, the Representation from each State having one Vote; A quorum for this purpose shall consist of a Member or Members from two thirds of the States, and a Majority of all the States shall be necessary to a Choice. In every Case, after the Choice of the President, the Person having the greatest Number of Votes of the Electors shall be the Vice President. But if there should remain two or more who have equal Votes, the Senate shall chuse from them by Ballot the Vice President.[5]

The Congress may determine the Time of chusing the Electors, and the Day on which they shall give their Votes; which Day shall be the same throughout the United States.

No Person except a natural born Citizen, or a Citizen of the United States, at the time of the Adoption of this Constitution, shall be eligible to the Office of President; neither shall any Person be eligible to that Office who shall not have attained to the Age of thirty five Years, and been fourteen Years a Resident within the United States.

In Case of the Removal of the President from Office, or of his Death, Resignation, or Inability to discharge the Powers and Duties of the said Office, the Same shall devolve on the Vice President, and the Congress may by Law provide for the Case of

[5] Superseded by the 12th Amendment.

Removal, Death, Resignation or Inability, both of the President and Vice President, declaring what Officer shall then act as President, and such Officer shall act accordingly, until the Disability be removed, or a President shall be elected.

The President shall, at stated Times, receive for his Services, a Compensation which shall neither be encreased nor diminished during the Period for which he shall have been elected, and he shall not receive within that Period any other Emolument from the United States, or any of them.

Before he enter on the Execution of his Office, he shall take the following Oath or Affirmation:—"I do solemnly swear (or affirm) that I will faithfully execute the Office of President of the United States, and will to the best of my Ability, preserve, protect, and defend the Constitution of the United States."

Section. 2. The President shall be Commander in Chief of the Army and Navy of the United States, and of the Militia of the several States, when called into the actual service of the United States; he may require the Opinion, in writing, of the principal Officer in each of the executive Departments, upon any Subject relating to the Duties of their respective Offices, and he shall have Power to grant Reprieves and Pardons for Offences against the United States, except in Cases of Impeachment.

He shall have Power, by and with the Advice and Consent of the Senate, to make Treaties, provided two thirds of the Senators present concur; and he shall nominate, and by and with the Advice and Consent of the Senate, shall appoint Ambassadors, and other public Ministers and Consuls, Judges of the supreme Court, and all other Officers of the United States, whose Appointments are not herein otherwise provided for, and which shall be established by Law: but the Congress may by Law vest the Appointment of such inferior Officers, as they think proper, in the President alone, in the Courts of Law, or in the Heads of Departments.

The President shall have Power to fill up all Vacancies that may happen during the Recess of the Senate, by granting Commissions which shall expire at the End of their next Session.

Section. 3. He shall from time to time give to the Congress Information of the State of the Union, and recommend to their Consideration such Measures as he shall judge necessary and expedient; he may, on extraordinary Occasions, convene both Houses, or either of them, and in Case of Disagreement between them, with Respect to the Time of Adjournment, he may adjourn them to such Time as he shall think proper; he shall receive Ambassadors and other public Ministers, he shall take Care that the Laws be faithfully executed, and shall Commission all the Officers of the United States.

Section. 4. The President, Vice President, and all civil Officers of the United States, shall be removed from Office on Impeachment for, and Conviction of, Treason, Bribery, or other high Crimes and Misdemeanors.

Article III

Section. 1. The judicial Power of the United States, shall be vested in one supreme Court and in such inferior Courts as the Congress may from time to time ordain and establish. The Judges, both of the supreme and inferior Courts, shall hold their Offices during good Behavior, and shall, at stated Times, receive for their Services, a Compensation, which shall not be diminished during their Continuance in Office.

Section. 2. The judicial Power shall extend to all Cases, in Law and Equity, arising under this Constitution, the Laws of the United States, and Treaties made, or which shall be made, under their Authority;—to all Cases affecting Ambassadors, other public Ministers and Consuls;—to all Cases of admiralty and maritime Jurisdiction;—to Controversies to which the United States shall be a Party;—to Controversies between two or more States;—*between a State and Citizens of another State;*[6]—between Citizens of different States;—between Citizens of the same State claiming Lands under Grants of different States, *and between a State, or the Citizens thereof, and foreign States, Citizens, or Subjects.*[7]

In all cases affecting Ambassadors, other public Ministers and Consuls, and those in which a State shall be Party, the supreme Court shall have original Jurisdiction. In all the other Cases before mentioned, the supreme Court shall have appellate Jurisdiction, both as to Law and Fact, with such Exceptions, and under such Regulations as the Congress shall make.

The Trial of all Crimes, except in Cases of Impeachment, shall be by Jury; and such Trial shall be held in the State where the said Crimes shall have been committed; but

[6] See the 11th Amendment.
[7] *Ibid.*

when not committed within any State, the Trial shall be at such Place or Places as the Congress may by Law have directed.

Section. 3. Treason against the United States, shall consist only in levying War against them, or in adhering to their Enemies, giving them Aid and Comfort. No Person shall be convicted of Treason unless on the Testimony of two Witnesses to the same overt Act, or on Confession in open Court.

The Congress shall have Power to declare the Punishment of Treason, but no Attainder of Treason shall work Corruption of Blood, or Forfeiture except during the Life of the Person attainted.

Article IV

Section. 1. Full Faith and Credit shall be given in each State to the public Acts, Records, and judicial Proceedings of every other State. And the Congress may by general Laws prescribe the Manner in which such Acts, Records, and Proceedings shall be proved, and the Effect thereof.

Section. 2. The Citizens of each State shall be entitled to all Privileges and Immunities of Citizens in the several States.

A Person charged in any State with Treason, Felony, or other Crime, who shall flee from Justice, and be found in another State, shall on Demand of the executive Authority of the State from which he fled, be delivered up, to be removed to the State having Jurisdiction of the Crime.

No Person held to Service or Labour in one State, under the Laws thereof, escaping into another, shall, in Consequence of any Law or Regulation therein, be discharged from such Service or Labour, but shall be delivered up on Claim of the Party to whom such Service or Labour may be due.[8]

Section. 3. New States may be admitted by the Congress into this Union; but no new State shall be formed or erected within the Jurisdiction of any other State; nor any State be formed by the Junction of two or more States, or Parts of States, without the Consent of the Legislatures of the States concerned as well as of the Congress.

The Congress shall have Power to dispose of and make all needful Rules and Regulations respecting the Territory or other Property belonging to the United States; and nothing in this Constitution shall be so construed as to Prejudice any claims of the United States, or of any particular State.

[8] See 13th Amendment.

Section. 4. The United States shall guarantee to every State in this Union a Republican Form of Government, and shall protect each of them against Invasion; and on Application of the Legislature, or of the Executive (when the Legislature cannot be convened) against domestic Violence.

Article V

The Congress, whenever two thirds of both Houses shall deem it necessary, shall propose Amendments to this Constitution, or, on the Application of the Legislatures of two thirds of the several States, shall call a Convention for proposing Amendments, which, in either Case, shall be valid to all Intents and Purposes, as Part of this Constitution, when ratified by the Legislatures of three fourths of the several States, or by Conventions in three fourths thereof, as the one or the other Mode of Ratification may be proposed by the Congress; Provided that no Amendment which may be made prior to the Year One thousand eight hundred and eight shall in any Manner affect the first and fourth Clauses in the Ninth Section of the first Article; and that no State, without its Consent, shall be deprived of its equal Suffrage in the Senate.

Article VI

All Debts contracted and Engagements entered into, before the Adoption of this Constitution, shall be as valid against the United States under this Constitution, as under the Confederation.

This Constitution, and the Laws of the United States which shall be made in Pursuance thereof; and all Treaties made, or which shall be made, under the Authority of the United States, shall be the supreme Law of the Land; and the Judges in every State shall be bound thereby, any Thing in the Constitution or Laws of any State to the Contrary notwithstanding.

The Senators and Representatives before mentioned, and the Members of the several State Legislatures, and all executive and judicial Officers, both of the United States and of the several States, shall be bound by Oath or Affirmation, to support this Constitution; but no religious Test shall ever be required as a Qualification to any Office or public Trust under the United States.

Article VII

The Ratification of the Conventions of nine States, shall be sufficient for the Establishment of this Constitution between the States so ratifying the Same.

Done in Convention by the Unanimous Consent of the States present the Seventeenth Day of September in the Year of our Lord one thousand seven hundred and eighty seven and of the Independence of the United States of America the twelfth. In witness whereof We have hereunto subscribed our Names.

. . .

ARTICLES IN ADDITION TO, AND AMENDMENT OF, THE CONSTITUTION OF THE UNITED STATES OF AMERICA, PROPOSED BY CONGRESS, AND RATIFIED BY THE SEVERAL STATES, PURSUANT TO THE FIFTH ARTICLE OF THE ORIGINAL CONSTITUTION.

Amendment I

[Ratification of the first ten amendments was completed December 15, 1791]

Congress shall make no law respecting an establishment of religion, or prohibiting the free exercise thereof; or abridging the freedom of speech, or of the press; or the right of the people peaceably to assemble, and to petition the Government for a redress of grievances.

Amendment II

A well regulated Militia, being necessary to the security of a free State, the right of the people to keep and bear Arms, shall not be infringed.

Amendment III

No Soldier shall, in time of peace be quartered in any house, without the consent of the Owner, nor in time of war, but in a manner to be prescribed by law.

Amendment IV

The right of the people to be secure in their persons, houses, papers, and effects, against unreasonable searches and seizures, shall not be violated, and no Warrants shall issue, but upon probable cause, supported by Oath or affirmation, and particularly describing the place to be searched, and the persons or things to be seized.

Amendment V

No person shall be held to answer for a capital, or otherwise infamous crime, unless on a presentment or indictment of a Grand Jury, except in cases arising in the land or naval forces, or in the Militia, when in actual service in time of War or public danger; nor shall any person be subject for the same offence to be twice put in jeopardy of life or limb; nor shall be compelled in any criminal case to be a witness against himself, nor be deprived of life, liberty, or property, without due process of law; nor shall private property be taken for public use, without just compensation.

Amendment VI

In all criminal prosecutions, the accused shall enjoy the right to a speedy and public trial, by an impartial jury of the State and district wherein the crime shall have been committed, which district shall have been previously ascertained by law, and to be informed of the nature and cause of the accusation; to be confronted with the witness against him; to have compulsory process for obtaining witness in his favor, and to have the Assistance of Counsel for his defence.

Amendment VII

In Suits at common law, where the value in controversy shall exceed twenty dollars, the right of trial by jury shall be preserved, and no fact tried by a jury, shall be otherwise re-examined in any Court of the United States, than according to the rules of the common law.

Amendment VIII

Excessive bail shall not be required, nor excessive fines imposed, nor cruel and unusual punishments inflicted.

Amendment IX

The enumeration in the Constitution, of certain rights, shall not be construed to deny or disparage others retained by the people.

Amendment X

The powers not delegated to the United States by the Constitution, nor prohibited by it to the States, are reserved to the States respectively, or to the people.

Amendment XI

[January 8, 1798]

The Judicial power of the United States shall not be construed to extend to any suit in law or equity, commenced or prosecuted against one of the United States by Citizens of another State, or by Citizens or Subjects of any Foreign State.

Amendment XII

[September 25, 1804]

The Electors shall meet in their respective states and vote by ballot for President and Vice President, one of whom, at least, shall not be an inhabitant of the same state with themselves; they shall name in their ballots the person voted for as President, and in distinct ballots the person voted for as Vice President, and they shall make distinct lists of all persons voted for as President, and of all persons voted for as Vice President, and of the number of votes for each, which lists they shall sign and certify, and transmit sealed to the seat of the government of the United States, directed to the President of the Senate;—The President of the Senate shall, in the presence of Senate and House of Representatives, open all the certificates and the votes shall then be counted;—The person having the greatest number of votes for President, shall be the President, if such number be a majority of the whole number of Electors appointed; and if no person have such majority, then from the persons having the highest numbers not exceeding three on the list of those voted for as President, the House of Representatives shall choose immediately, by ballot, the President. But in choosing the President, the votes shall be taken by states, the representation from each state having one vote; a quorum for this purpose shall consist of a member or members from two thirds of the states, and a majority of all the states shall be necessary to a choice. And if the House of Representatives shall not choose a President whenever the right of choice shall devolve upon them, *before the fourth day of March next following,*[9] then the Vice President shall act as President, as in the case of the death or other constitutional disability of the President.—The person having the greatest number of votes as Vice President, shall be the Vice President, if such number be a majority of the whole number of Electors appointed, and if no person have a majority, then from the two highest numbers on the list, the Senate shall choose the Vice President; a quorum for the purpose shall consist of two-thirds of the whole number of Senators, and a majority of the whole number shall be necessary to a choice. But no person constitutionally ineligible to the office of President shall be eligible to that of Vice President of the United States.

Amendment XIII
[December 18, 1865]

Section 1. Neither slavery nor involuntary servitude, except as a punishment for crime whereof the party shall have been duly convicted, shall exist within the United States, or any place subject to their jurisdiction.

[9] Altered by the 20th Amendment.

Section 2. Congress shall have power to enforce this article by appropriate legislation.

Amendment XIV
[July 28, 1868]

Section 1. All persons born or naturalized in the United States, and subject to the jurisdiction thereof, are citizens of the United States and of the State wherein they reside. No State shall make or enforce any law which shall abridge the privileges or immunities of citizens of the United States; nor shall any state deprive any person of life, liberty, or property, without due process of law; nor deny to any person within its jurisdiction the equal protection of the laws.

Section 2. Representatives shall be apportioned among the several States according to their respective numbers, counting the whole number of persons in each State, excluding Indians not taxed. But when the right to vote at any election for the choice of electors for President and Vice President of the United States, Representatives in Congress, the Executive and Judicial officers of a State, or the members of the Legislature thereof, is denied to any of the male inhabitants of such State, being twenty one years of age, and citizens of the United States, or in any way abridged, except for participation in rebellion, or other crime, the basis of representation therein shall be reduced in the proportion which the number of such male citizens shall bear to the whole number of male citizens twenty one years of age in such State.

Section 3. No person shall be a Senator or Representative in Congress, or elector of President and Vice President, or hold any office, civil or military, under the United States, or under any State, who, having previously taken an oath, as a member of Congress, or as an officer of the United States, or as a member of any State legislature, or as an executive or judicial officer of any State, to support the Constitution of the United States, shall have engaged in insurrection or rebellion against the same, or given aid or comfort to the enemies thereof. But Congress may by a vote of two thirds of each House, remove such disability.

Section 4. The validity of the public debt of the United States, authorized by law, including debts incurred for payment of pensions and bounties for services in suppressing insurrection or rebellion, shall not be questioned. But neither the United States nor any State shall assume or pay any debt or obligation incurred in aid of insurrection or rebellion against the United States, or any claim for the loss or emancipation of any slave; but all such debts, obligations, and claims shall be held illegal and void.

Section 5. The Congress shall have power to enforce, by appropriate legislation, the provisions of this article.

Amendment XV

[March 30, 1870]

Section 1. The right of citizens of the United States to vote shall not be denied or abridged by the United States or by any State on account of race, color, or previous condition of servitude.

Section 2. The Congress shall have power to enforce this article by appropriate legislation.

Amendment XVI

[February 25, 1913]

The Congress shall have power to lay and collect taxes on incomes, from whatever source derived, without apportionment among the several States, and without regard to any census or enumeration.

Amendment XVII

[May 31, 1913]

The Senate of the United States shall be composed of two Senators from each State, elected by the people thereof, for six years; and each Senator shall have one vote. The electors in each State shall have the qualifications requisite for electors of the most numerous branch of the State legislatures.

When vacancies happen in the representation of any State in the Senate, the executive authority of such State shall issue writs of election to fill such vacancies: *Provided,* That the legislature of any State may empower the executive thereof to make temporary appointments until the people fill the vacancies by election as the legislature may direct.

This amendment shall not be so construed as to affect the election or term of any Senator chosen before it becomes valid as part of the Constitution.

Amendment XVIII

[January 29, 1919]

Section 1. *After one year from the ratification of this article the manufacture, sale, or transportation of intoxicating liquors within, the importation thereof into, or the exportation thereof from the United States and all territory subject to the jurisdiction thereof for beverage purposes is hereby prohibited.*

Section 2. *The Congress and the several States shall have concurrent power to enforce this article by appropriate legislation.*

Section 3. *This article shall be inoperative unless it shall have been ratified as an amendment to the Constitution by the legislatures of the several States, as provided in the Constitution, within seven years from the date of the submission hereof to the States by the Congress.*[10]

Amendment XIX

[August 26, 1920]

The right of citizens of the United States to vote shall not be denied or abridged by the United States or by any State on account of sex.

Congress shall have power to enforce this article by appropriate legislation.

Amendment XX

[February 6, 1933]

Section 1. The terms of the President and Vice President shall end at noon on the 20th day of January, and the terms of Senators and Representatives at noon on the 3rd day of January, of the years in which such terms would have ended if this article had not been ratified; and the terms of their successors shall then begin.

Section 2. The Congress shall assemble at least once in every year, and such meeting shall begin at noon on the 3rd day of January, unless they shall by law appoint a different day.

Section 3. If, at the time fixed for the beginning of the term of the President, the President elect shall have died, the Vice President elect shall become President. If a President shall not have been chosen before the time fixed for the beginning of his term, or if the President elect shall have failed to qualify, then the Vice President elect shall act as President until a President shall have qualified; and the Congress may by law provide for the case wherein neither a President elect nor a Vice President elect shall have qualified, declaring who shall then act as President, or the manner in which one who is to act shall be selected, and such person shall act accordingly until a Presi-

[10] Repealed by the 21st Amendment.

dent or Vice President shall have qualified.

Section 4. The Congress may by law provide for the case of the death of any of the persons from whom the House of Representatives may choose a President whenever the right of choice shall have devolved upon them, and for the case of the death of any of the persons from whom the Senate may choose a Vice President whenever the right of choice shall have devolved upon them.

Section 5. Sections 1 and 2 shall take effect on the 15th day of October following the ratification of this article.

Section 6. This article shall be inoperative unless it shall have been ratified as an amendment to the Constitution by the legislatures of three fourths of the several States within seven years from the date of its submission.

Amendment XXI

[December 5, 1933]

Section 1. The eighteenth article of amendment to the Constitution of the United States is hereby repealed.

Section 2. The transportation or importation into any State, Territory, or possession of the United States for delivery or use therein of intoxicating liquors, in violation of the laws thereof, is hereby prohibited.

Section 3. This article shall be inoperative unless it shall have been ratified as an amendment to the Constitution by conventions in the several States, as provided in the Constitution, within seven years from the date of the submission hereof to the States by the Congress.

Amendment XXII

[February 26, 1951]

Section 1. No person shall be elected to the office of the President more than twice, and no person who has held the office of President, or acted as President, for more than two years of a term to which some other person was elected President shall be elected to the office of President more than once. But this Article shall not apply to any person holding the office of President when this Article was proposed by the Congress, and

shall not prevent any person who may be holding the office of President, or acting as President, during the term within which this Article becomes operative from holding the office of President or acting as President during the remainder of such term.

Section 2. This article shall be inoperative unless it shall have been ratified as an amendment to the Constitution by the legislatures of three fourths of the several States within seven years from the date of its submission to the States by the Congress.

Amendment XXIII

[March 29, 1961]

Section 1. The District constituting the seat of Government of the United States shall appoint in such manner as the Congress may direct:

A number of electors of President and Vice President equal to the whole number of Senators and Representatives in Congress to which the District would be entitled if it were a State, but in no event more than the least populous State; they shall be in addition to those appointed by the States, but they shall be considered, for the purposes of the election of President and Vice President, to be electors appointed by a State; and they shall meet in the District and perform such duties as provided by the twelfth article of amendment.

Section 2. The Congress shall have power to enforce this article by appropriate legislation.

Amendment XXIV

[January 23, 1964]

Section 1. The right of citizens of the United States to vote in any primary or other election for President or Vice President, for electors for President or Vice President, or for Senator or Representative in Congress, shall not be denied or abridged by the United States or any state by reason of failure to pay any poll tax or other tax.

Section 2. The Congress shall have the power to enforce this article by appropriate legislation.

Index

A

Academic freedom, 533-536
Adams, James Truslow, 41*n*
Adams, Sherman, 397*n*
Adkins v. *Children's Hospital,* 578, 579, 585*n*
Adler v. *Board of Education,* 534*n*
Administrative Procedures Act of 1946, 423
Adorno, T. W., 76*n*
Advisory opinions, 497
Areopagitica, 507, 535
Affluent Society, The, 46
Agency for International Development, 420
Agricultural Adjustment Act, 586
Alexander, Herbert E., 295*n*
Alien and Sedition Acts of *1798,* 522
Alien Registration Act of *1940,* 557
Aliens (*see also* Citizenship):
  status of, 555-557
  and voting, 560
Allen, Frederick Lewis, 46*n*
Allinsmith, Beverly, 180*n*
Allinsmith, Wesley, 180*n*
Almond, Gabriel A., 6*n*, 8*n*, 16*n*, 18*n*, 75*n*, 76*n*, 78*n*, 639
Amendments to Constitution (*see also* Bills of Rights and Individual amendments):
  procedure, 113
  restrictions, 113-114
American Bar Association:
  and selection of federal judges, 482
American Commonwealth, 363
American Communications Association, C. I. O. v. *Douds,* 524*n*
American Creed (*see also* Democracy, Democratic political theory):
  consensus on, 67
  in Declaration of Independence, 63
  detractors of, 61-77
  and law of nature, 63
  as norm, 62
  and political leaders, 66, 69, 214

American Dilemma, An, 458
American economy, modern (*see also Economics*) 44-46
American Partnership, The, 129
American political character (*see also* National character):
  characteristics of, 27
  political attitudes of, 24-26
  regional variation, 27
American political system (*see* Political system)
American political thought, 61
American politics (*see* Political system, Politics)
American Revolution:
  and aristocracy, 101
  and British Colonialism, 83
  colonial communication, 89-90
  crises of nation-building, 88-92
  decision-makers, 92-93
American social character (*see also* American political character, National character, American creed):
  attributes of, 22-23
  Marxist view, 22
  material conditions, 22
  Protestant ethic, 22
  social values, 22
American Voter, The, 166
Amici curiae, 459, 492
Anderson, William, 108*n*
Annapolis Conference, 91
Anti-trust action, 582-583
Apathy (*see also* Political system, Supports):
  and democracy, 68
  and general welfare, 587-598
  and political system, 12
  and Supreme Court, 489-492
Application of rules (*see also* Outputs, Political system), 15
Aptheker v. *Secretary of State,* 524*n*, 525*n*
Aristocracy and the Constitution, 101
Armed forces personnel (*see also* Military), rights of, 515-517
Articles of Confederation:
  adoption, 86-87
  amendment procedure, 110

Articles of Confederation (*cont.*):
  and community awareness, 126
  Congress under, 87
  and economic development, 91
  executive under, 87
  and foreign commerce, 91
  and "full faith and credit," 141
  and interstate compacts, 141
  moves to amend, 91
  and national development, 126
  national identity under, 89
  and "privileges and immunities," 141
  provisions of, 86-87
  ratification of, 110
  rivalry under, 91
  and unitary government, 126
  weakness of, 89
Asch, S. E., 186*n*
Ascoli, Max, 549*n*
Attitudes (*see* Political opinion, Public opinion)
Austinians, school of law, 463
Authoritative decisions (*see* Decision-makers, Outputs, Policy-making, Political system)

B

Bailey, Stephan K., 353, 354*n*
Bailey v. *Richardson,* 453*n*
Bain, Richard C., 282*n*
Baker v. *Carr,* 33*n*, 136*n*, 137*n*, 220*n*, 330, 332, 492*n*
Balance of power, in foreign policy, 621-625
Balloting (*see also* Elections, Electoral system), mechanics of, 297-300
Barker, Ernest, 367
Barnes, William, 614*n*
Barrett, George, 35*n*
Barron v. *Baltimore,* 116, 510
Barton, Allen H., 191*n*
Beard, Charles A., 41, 94, 95, 212*n*
Becker, Carl L., 26, 63*n*
Beloff, Max, 106*n*
Benedict, Ruth, 20
Berding, Andrew, 643*n*

G